3
Auditing and Attestation

by Vincent W. Lambers, MBA, CPA
and
Richard DelGaudio, MBA, CPA

Published by

Lambers

CPA REVIEW

2004

Chapter Subjects of Volume 3—AUDITING & ATTESTATION

ACKNOWLEDGMENTS

It would be impossible to write a CPA examination book of any kind without the assistance of the American Institute of Certified Public Accountants, and their various operating divisions, in granting permission to use various materials. We respectfully acknowledge and thank those persons in the American Institute who promptly answered our inquiries.

Those areas of the set for which we received permission to use copyrighted material from the American Institute are:
- CPA Examination Questions, Problems and Solutions
- Opinions of the Financial Accounting Standards Board and Predecessor Bodies
- Adaptations, Quotations, Case Examples and Tables from *"An Auditor's Approach to Statistical Sampling"*
- *Statements on Auditing Standards* issued by AICPA
- *Statements on Standards for Accounting Review Services* issued by AICPA
- *Statements on Standards for Attestation Engagements* issued by AICPA

Richard DelGaudio, CPA
North Andover, Massachusetts
January 2004

Welcome to the New CPA Exam!

If you have taken the CPA exam before, you are now facing a *new* exam format, including some new material. However, you should know that overall the exam content has not changed very much, probably less than 20%. If you have not taken the exam before, the changes and new format mean little because you have to start from scratch anyway.

The CPA Examination

The exam is a **computer-based test (CBT).** There are four sections: Auditing & Attestation, Financial Accounting & Reporting, Regulation, and Business Environment & Concepts. Each section will include sets of multiple-choice questions **(testlets).** In addition, all sections, except the newest section added, BEC *(Business Environment & Concepts),* will contain a new case study component called **"simulations."** Simulations will provide a set of facts and require candidates to complete related tasks and access authoritative literature.

Signing up and taking the exam:

Candidates will have significant flexibility in where and when they take the CPA examination. The exam location will be Prometric Test Centers. There are some 300 test centers throughout the United States; however, not all will offer CPA exam testing. Candidates will be able to take the exam five days a week during any testing window. Weekday hours are 9am to 6pm. Many locations will have extended hours, and some test centers will offer weekend testing. International candidates will continue to be required to test within the fifty-four jurisdictions that currently administer the CPA Examination.

The first date for the new examination is April 5, 2004, which occurs in the first of four testing windows (April-May 2004). The next testing windows will be July-August and October-November. In 2005, the first testing window will be January-February.

In most jurisdictions, candidates will be able to take any or all sections of the exam during any testing window; the candidate will not be allowed, however, to take the same section more than once during any testing window.

Candidates will take different, equivalent exams consisting of items from a pool of test questions according to defined specifications. The specifications will ensure that the results are comparable. The test package delivered to the test centers will contain the test items, and also the rules for administering the tests. All items will be classified according to content and statistical properties before they are administered in an operational test. The testing software will ensure that each candidate's test contains appropriate content coverage and difficulty.

To sign up for the exam and for a list of test center locations, call 1-800-CPA EXAM or contact NASBA at www.nasba.org. Also, Prometric (www.prometric.com) will add a CPA exam page to their web site early in 2004 showing test locations.

To sign up for the exam:
Call 1-800-CPA-Exam and ask for your state representative

It is anticipated that State Boards of Accountancy will permit candidates to **take each exam section individually, and in any order, or all at one time. Once you pass a section(s) of the exam, you will likely be allowed a maximum of 18 months to pass all remaining sections in order to retain credit on the passed section(s).**

Requirements to take the examination vary from state to state, so candidates should contact the state board in their jurisdiction. After the candidate has been determined by a state board to be eligible to take the examination, the candidate will receive a Notice to Schedule (NTS). The candidate can then make an appointment on the Prometric web site, www.prometric.com, by phone or in person at a Prometric test center. Candidates are encouraged to schedule at least 45 days in advance. No candidate will be scheduled fewer than five days before testing.

EXAMINATION SECTIONS

New Section	Length Hours	Old exam counterpart
Auditing and Attestation	4.5	Auditing
Regulation (1)	3.0	Law & Professional Responsibility
Financial Accounting and Reporting (2)	4.0	Same – See note below
Business Environment & Concepts (3)	2.5	Managerial and Cost Accounting
The entire CPA examination length is 14 hours.		

(1) Includes Federal Income Tax 60%, Law and Professional Responsibility 40%
(2) Includes Fund Accounting and Not-for-Profit Organizations 20%
(3) Includes several new subjects, such as economic concepts and information technology, and traditional exam subjects, but in greater depth.
(See Content Specifications at the end of this section.)

RECOGNITION OF PARTIAL CREDIT UNDER OLD EXAM FORMAT

For those who have conditioning credit after the last paper and pencil exam in November 2003, credit is recognized for the new exam as follows:

Credit on Paper-based Exam	*Will earn CBT credit*
Auditing AUD	Auditing & Attestation
Law and Professional Responsibility LPR	Business Environment & Concepts
Accounting & Reporting ARE	Regulation
Financial Accounting & Reporting FARE	Financial Accounting & Reporting

RELEASE OF GRADES

Distribution of grades is the responsibility of state boards of accountancy. Advisory grades and diagnostic information will be provided to state boards at the end of the third month of each testing cycle or testing window. For example, grades should be available to state boards for the April-May testing period at the end of June. The passing standard for the computer-based version of the Uniform CPA Examination will be set at a scaled score of 75, as is the case today.

AICPA EXAM TUTORIAL

A CPA examination tutorial prepared and tested by the CBT exam Steering Group is available at www.cpa-exam.org. The tutorial covers the revised exam's look, feel, and functionality, as well as offers both guided and self-directed instructions. **The tutorial does not replace practice materials according to the CBT Steering Group of the AICPA**. Candidates are strongly advised to review the tutorial before taking the computer-based CPA examination.

TYPES OF QUESTIONS ON THE CPA EXAMINATION (CBT)

MULTIPLE-CHOICE QUESTIONS AND SIMULATIONS

I. The majority of the computer-based CPA examination (70-80 percent) is made up of **multiple-choice questions**. Each section of the exam will consist of "*testlets*" which are the multiple-choice questions, and two "*simulations*."

Part Four, Business Environment and Concepts (BEC), will have no simulations, only multiple-choice questions. BEC simulations will be added later.

According to the AICPA web site:

"The multiple-choice portion of the examination will appear as sequential testlets. Testlets are groups of questions that are constructed to appear together. Each exam section will include approximately three multiple-choice testlets. Each testlet will contain approximately 25 operational items (questions)."

The testlets will be "tracked" in that the second and third testlet will be adjusted by the computer to an easier or harder version. This will be based on the candidate's performance on the first testlet. The candidate won't know what version is on his/her computer screen. The third testlet may or may not be adjusted up or down. The system is equitable because the grading is also adjusted according to the track of the questions; if the student has a hard track, fewer questions need to be answered correctly; likewise, an easy track requires that more answers be correct.

The 2004 CPA Exam consists of the following number of multiple-choice questions:

AUDITING & ATTESTATION (90)
REGULATION (72)
FINANCIAL ACCOUNTING & REPORTING (90)
BUSINESS ENVIRONMENT & CONCEPTS (90)

During the exam, within each testlet, you may review and change any of your answers. **Once you have exited the testlet**, you will not be able to access your answers to any of the questions. The **same is true for the simulations** portion of the exam. Note that the time clock on the screen is "cumulative" and indicates the time left for the entire exam, not just a portion.

II. While the majority of the test is multiple-choice questions, a key part of the exam is the **"simulation"** question. According to the AICPA web site, *simulations "are condensed case studies that will test candidates' knowledge and skills using real life work-related situations."* The CPA exam candidate can expect two simulations to appear in each section with the exception of Part Four-Business Environment and Concepts. The simulations will take an estimated 35-45 minutes to complete, and will require the following:

"CPA candidates are expected to know how to use common spreadsheet and word processing functions, including writing formulae for spreadsheets. They must also have the ability to use a four-function calculator or a spreadsheet to perform standard financial calculations. In addition, candidates will be asked to use online authoritative literature. Many of the question types used in the simulations are based on familiar computer interface controls (e.g., text entry, mouse clicks, highlighting, copy and pasting). In order to become familiar with the electronic tools provided for research questions, further practice may be required."[1]

Available resources during the test will depend on the simulation that the candidate receives.

Incorporated into the simulation portion of the revised exam will be an assessment of written communication skills. The exam will test typical communications an entry-level CPA would write on the job, such as memoranda, client letters, etc.

To become familiar with navigating the computerized exam screen, it is strongly advised that the candidate visit the AICPA web site tutorial.

AICPA web site on simulations: Visit this site to become familiar with the computer format of simulated problems on the new CPA exam:

http://www.cpa-exam.org/lrc/exam_tutorial.html

---

[1] AICPA web site

Entry-level CPA skills to be measured:

1. **Analysis**: The ability to organize, process, and interpret data to develop options for decision making.
2. **Judgment**: The ability to evaluate options for decision-making and provide an appropriate conclusion.
3. **Communication**: The ability to effectively elicit and/or express information through written or oral means.
4. **Research**: The ability to locate and extract relevant information from available resource materials.
5. **Understanding**: The ability to recognize and comprehend the meaning and application of a particular matter.

Writing skills to be graded:

1. **Coherent Organization**. Candidates should organize responses so ideas are arranged logically and the flow of thought is easy to follow. Generally, short paragraphs composed of short sentences, with each paragraph limited to the development of one principal idea, can best emphasize the main points in the answer. Each principal idea should be placed in the first sentence of the paragraph, followed by supporting concepts and examples.

2. **Conciseness**. Candidates should present complete thoughts in the fewest possible words while ensuring important points are covered adequately. Short sentences and simple wording also contribute to concise writing.

3. **Clarity**. A clearly written response prevents uncertainty about the candidate's meaning or reasoning. Clarity involves using words with specific meanings, including proper technical terminology. Well-constructed sentences also contribute to clarity.

4. **Use of Standard English**. Responses should be written using Standard English. Standard English is used to carry on the daily business of the nation. It is the language of business, industry, government, education, and the professions. Standard English is characterized by exacting standards of punctuation and capitalization, by accurate spelling, by exact diction, by an expressive vocabulary, and by knowledgeable choices.

5. **Responsiveness to the Requirements of the Question**. Answers should address the requirements of the question directly and demonstrate the candidate's awareness of the purpose of the writing task. Responses should not be broad expositions on the general subject matter.

6. **Appropriateness for the Reader**. Writing appropriate for the reader takes into account the reader's background, knowledge of the subject, interests and concerns. Some questions may ask candidates to prepare a document for a certain reader, such as an engagement memorandum for a CPA's client.

MENTAL AND TECHNICAL PREREQUISITES FOR SUCCESS ON THE CPA EXAM

The exam is a test of your overall technical competency, a test to measure judgment and intelligence in the application of accounting principles, auditing standards, and procedures to practical problems, and to evaluate professional ethics. You are being tested on a basic level of knowledge in a broad spectrum of areas.

Your preparation should be geared to obtaining three things:

- **A Basic Technical Knowledge in All Areas**. The emphasis here is on basics. You don't need to know all the intricacies involved in any particular subject. What you do need to know are the major issues involved and you need to have a solid understanding of the underlying principles and concepts so you can respond to different types of questions and unfamiliar fact patterns.

- **Exam-Taking Skills.** You need weapons. You need exam-taking skills and techniques for each subject area. These will allow you to win the maximum amount of points in the shortest amount of time. The only way you can develop your skill is to PRACTICE by working hundreds of exam questions in each topic area so that answering them correctly becomes second nature. Also, don't forget to demonstrate good writing skills on all essay responses.

- **Confidence.** When you walk into that exam, you must be confident. This confidence will come as a by-product of the above two elements. To quote a former successful Lambers student, *"Study the material,......solve as many multiple-choice questions as your schedule permits. Although this is a very difficult exam, do not get discouraged. If you are prepared....you will pass this exam."*

Strategies for Answering Objective Questions

1.) <u>Cover (or do not look) at the answers</u>. They are sometimes misleading and may confuse you before you have worked the question. Covering the answers keeps you from turning one simple question into four true or false questions. Also, in many cases, two or more choices may look plausible (and in fact, both may be technically correct), but you are asked to pick the best answer. For these reasons, it is critical that you cover the answers so you can think and formulate your own response first.

2.) <u>Read the last sentence first</u>. Generally, this will tell you the requirements.

3.) <u>Decide on your answer</u> or perform the appropriate calculations if a numerical response is required--still not looking at the answers.

Read the alternatives. If one agrees with yours, select it and move on. If your answer is close, see if it is due to a procedural error. If your answer is totally out of line, reread the requirements and body to see what was missed. If all else fails, try to eliminate any answer choices and make your best guess.

General Comments and Pitfalls to Avoid

1.) **Work individual questions in order**. Make sure that you flag the ones you skip, so you can go back and answer them later. Remember, there is no penalty for guessing. Make sure you answer everything.

2.) **Watch for wrong-choice indicators**; words like, "always," "never," "only," "under no circumstances," "identical," etc. These words are usually there for a reason … and that's to indicate the **incorrect** answer.

3.) **Watch for negatively stated questions**. For example, "Which of the following is **not** a characteristic of effective internal control?"

Goal Setting: Your goal is to become a CPA, a professional. That will mean financial security, the opportunity for more fulfilling positions, possibly the opportunity to start your own firm. Keep your ultimate goals in mind as you begin. You must stay focused throughout your preparation period, and work every day to make that goal a reality.

Visualize your Goal: In the flux of daily life, it's easy to lose sight of your goals. As the saying goes, "When you're knee-high in alligators, it's easy to forget your objective was to drain the swamp." You need to visualize your goals on a daily basis. Picture yourself sitting in a plush office as the CFO of a major company, or imagine yourself owning your own firm. Expect to achieve your goal; keep a positive attitude.

Organization and Focus: Focus on your objective; do not let minor things distract you. Organize your life to accommodate the time you need to devote to preparation.

Discipline: This means studying when you feel like it *and when you don't*. Passing the CPA exam is earned day in and day out. You cannot neglect studying and cram for the exam. One more helpful hint.....do you really want to go through the whole process over again if you don't stick with it and do it right the first time?

Make the commitment, and good luck with your studies!

Benefits of Becoming a CPA

First, a little background on the Certified Public Accountant (CPA) designation. The first CPA examination was offered in the state of New York in 1896* and shortly thereafter other states offered an examination for candidates aspiring to be CPA's. Now all states and territories offer examinations for those wishing to become CPA's. Unlike many other professional designations, CPA's are licensed by the state(s) to practice the "attest to" function. This allows the CPA to attest, in the form of an opinion, as to the condition of the financial statements provided by management. The CPA's opinion may vary from outright refusal to be associated with the statements to acceptance of the statements as fairly representing the financial condition of the enterprise. In carrying out the attest function and other work, the CPA must adhere to certain auditing standards of performance including, but not limited to, independence and designated audit procedures.

The attest function carries with it a heavy responsibility because the CPA's opinion is heavily relied upon by leaders, investors and others who have an interest in the condition of a particular enterprise. Besides the attest function, the CPA's association with other work, such as tax work, carries with it a presumption of excellence because of the standards that are required of CPA's.

Individuals who are CPA's are looked up to in the world of finance and industry especially where accountability is a factor, which is almost always the case. Whether the CPA is in public practice or in an executive position, the designation is recognized as a standard of excellence. Naturally, enterprises in general are willing to pay for the presumption of excellence that the CPA demonstrates, which for the individual results in increased income.

Using the world-famous cliché, the "bottom line" is that the CPA enjoys prestige, higher income, financial security and independence to a much greater extent than the same person without it.

Vincent W. Lambers
President, Lambers CPA Review

*An excerpt from the New York State Certified Public Accountant Examination, December 1896, a Theory of Accounts question with full answer:

I. State the essential principles of double entry bookkeeping and show wherein it differs from single entry bookkeeping.

The essential principles of double entry bookkeeping are, (1) The record of every transaction involving the transfer of money or its equivalent must appear on both the debit and credit side of the ledger, thus maintaining it in balance. (2) Provision must be made for the constant differentiation under properly classified accounts of capital and revenue income and expenditure. (3) As resulting therefrom, the profit or loss determined from the collection of the preponderance of the balance of the revenue accounts must be proved by the excess of the assets over the liabilities as exhibited in the balance sheet.

The fundamental difference between single and double entry bookkeeping is this: In single entry the income and expenditure accounts are not kept, and the profit or loss for any given period is determinable solely from a comparison of the assets with the liabilities—the excess of the one over the other showing the profit or loss; the proof of the accuracy of same, though the same result being arrived at through the profit and loss account being entirely wanting.

Of minor importance also is the fact that the mathematical accuracy of the posting is in single entry bookkeeping undemonstrable in trial balance form, as in double entry.

AUDITING & ATTESTATION CONTENT SPECIFICATION OUTLINE

I. PLAN THE ENGAGEMENT, EVALUATE THE PROSPECTIVE CLIENT AND ENGAGEMENT, DECIDE WHETHER TO ACCEPT OR CONTINUE THE CLIENT AND THE ENGAGEMENT, AND ENTER INTO AN AGREEMENT WITH THE CLIENT (22%-28%)

A. Determine nature and scope of engagement
1. Auditing standards generally accepted in the United States of America (GAAS)
2. Standards for accounting and review services
3. Standards for attestation engagements
4. Compliance auditing applicable to governmental entities and other recipients of governmental financial assistance
5. Other assurance services
6. Appropriateness of engagement to meet client's needs
B. Assess engagement risk and the CPA firm's ability to perform the engagement
1. Engagement responsibilities
2. Staffing and supervision requirements
3. Quality control considerations
4. Management integrity
5. Researching information sources for planning and performing the engagement
C. Communicate with the predecessor accountant or auditor
D. Decide whether to accept or continue the client and engagement
E. Enter into an agreement with the client about the terms of the engagement
F. Obtain an understanding of the client's operations, business, and industry
G. Perform analytical procedures
H. Consider preliminary engagement materiality
I. Assess inherent risk and risk of misstatements from errors, fraud, and illegal acts by clients
J. Consider other planning matters
1. Using the work of other independent auditors
2. Using the work of a specialist
3. Internal audit function
4. Related parties and related party transactions
5. Electronic evidence
6. Risks of auditing around the computer
K. Identify financial statement assertions and formulate audit objectives
1. Significant financial statement balances, classes of transactions, and disclosures
2. Accounting estimates
L. Determine and prepare the work program defining the nature, timing, and extent of the procedures to be applied.

II. CONSIDER INTERNAL CONTROL IN BOTH MANUAL AND COMPUTERIZED ENVIRONMENTS (12%-18%)

A. Obtain an understanding of business processes and information flows
B. Identify controls that might be effective in preventing or detecting misstatements
C. Document an understanding of internal control
D. Consider limitations of internal control
E. Consider the effects of service organizations on internal control
F. Perform tests of controls
G. Assess control risk

III. OBTAIN AND DOCUMENT INFORMATION TO FORM A BASIS FOR CONCLUSIONS (32%-38%)

A. Perform planned procedures
1. Applications of audit sampling
2. Analytical procedures
3. Confirmation of balances and/or transactions with third parties
4. Physical examination of inventories and other assets
5. Other tests of details
6. Computer-assisted audit techniques, including data interrogation, extraction and analysis
7. Substantive tests before the balance sheet date
8. Tests of unusual year-end transactions
B. Evaluate contingencies

C. Obtain and evaluate lawyers' letters
D. Review subsequent events
E. Obtain representations from management
F. Identify reportable conditions and other control deficiencies
G. Identify matters for communication with audit committees
H. Perform procedures for accounting and review services engagements
I. Perform procedures for attestation engagements

IV. REVIEW THE ENGAGEMENT TO PROVIDE REASONABLE ASSURANCE THAT OBJECTIVES ARE ACHIEVED AND EVALUATE INFORMATION OBTAINED TO REACH AND TO DOCUMENT ENGAGEMENT CONCLUSIONS 8%-12%)
A. Perform analytical procedures
B. Evaluate the sufficiency and competence of audit evidence and document engagement conclusions
C. Evaluate whether financial statements are free of material misstatements
D. Consider whether substantial doubt about an entity's ability to continue as a going concern exists
E. Consider other information in documents containing audited financial statements
F. Review the work performed to provide reasonable assurance that objectives are achieved

V. PREPARE COMMUNICATIONS TO SATISFY ENGAGEMENT OBJECTIVES (12%-18%)
A. Reports
    1. Reports on audited financial statements
    2. Reports on reviewed and compiled financial statements
    3. Reports required by Government Auditing Standards
    4. Reports on compliance with laws and regulations
    5. Reports on internal control
    6. Reports on prospective financial information
    7. Reports on agreed-upon procedures
    8. Reports on the processing of transactions by service organizations
    9. Reports on supplementary financial information
    10. Special reports
    11. Reports on other assurance services
    12. Reissuance of reports
B. Other required communications
    1. Errors and fraud
    2. Illegal acts
    3. Communications with audit committees
    4. Other reporting considerations covered by statements on auditing standards and statements on standards for attestation engagements
C. Other matters
    1. Subsequent discovery of facts existing at the date of the auditor's report
    2. Consideration after the report date of omitted procedures

FINANCIAL ACCOUNTING & REPORTING CONTENT SPECIFICATION OUTLINE

I. CONCEPTS AND STANDARDS FOR FINANCIAL STATEMENTS (17%-23%)
   A. Financial accounting concepts
      1. Process by which standards are set and roles of standard-setting bodies
      2. Conceptual basis for accounting standards
   B. Financial accounting standards for presentation and disclosure in general-purpose financial statements
      1. Consolidated and combined financial statements
      2. Balance sheet
      3. Statement(s) of income, comprehensive income and changes in equity accounts
      4. Statement of cash flows
      5. Accounting policies and other notes to financial statements
   C. Other presentations of financial data (financial statements prepared in conformity with comprehensive bases of accounting other than GAAP)
   D. Financial statement analysis

II. TYPICAL ITEMS: RECOGNITION, MEASUREMENT, VALUATION, AND PRESENTATION IN FINANCIAL STATEMENTS IN CONFORMITY WITH GAAP (27%-33%)
   A. Cash, cash equivalents and marketable securities
   B. Receivables
   C. Inventories
   D. Property, plant, and equipment
   E. Investments
   F. Intangibles and other assets
   G. Payables and accruals
   H. Deferred revenues
   I. Notes and bonds payable
   J. Other liabilities
   K. Equity accounts
   L. Revenues, cost, and expense accounts

III. SPECIFIC TYPES OF TRANSACTIONS AND EVENTS: RECOGNITION, MEASUREMENT, VALUATION, AND PRESENTATION IN FINANCIAL STATEMENTS IN CONFORMITY WITH GAAP (27%-33%)
   A. Accounting changes and corrections of errors
   B. Business combinations
   C. Contingent liabilities and commitments
   D. Discontinued operations
   E. Earnings per share
   F. Employee benefits, including stock options
   G. Extraordinary items
   H. Financial instruments, including derivatives
   I. Foreign currency transactions and translation
   J. Income taxes
   K. Interest costs
   L. Interim financial reporting
   M. Leases
   N. Non-monetary transactions
   O. Related parties
   P. Research and development costs
   Q. Segment reporting
   R. Subsequent events

IV. ACCOUNTING AND REPORTING FOR GOVERNMENTAL ENTITIES (8%-12%)
   A. Governmental accounting concepts
      1. Measurement focus and basis of accounting
      2. Fund accounting concepts and application
      3. Budgetary process

B. Format and content of governmental financial statements
    1. Government-wide financial statements
    2. Governmental funds financial statements
    3. Conversion from fund to government-wide financial statements
    4. Proprietary fund financial statements
    5. Fiduciary fund financial statements
    6. Notes to financial statements
    7. Required supplementary information, including management's discussion and analysis
    8. Comprehensive annual financial report (CAFR)
C. Financial reporting entity including blended and discrete component units
D. Typical items and specific types of transactions and events: recognition, measurement, valuation and presentation in governmental entity financial statements in conformity with GAAP
    1. Net assets
    2. Capital assets and infrastructure
    3. Transfers
    4. Other financing sources and uses
    5. Fund balance
    6. Non-exchange revenues
    7. Expenditures
    8. Special items
    9. Encumbrances
E. Accounting and financial reporting for governmental not-for-profit organizations

V. ACCOUNTING AND REPORTING FOR NONGOVERNMENTAL NOT-FOR-PROFIT ORGANIZATIONS (8%-12%)
    A. Objectives, elements and formats of financial statements
        1. Statement of financial position
        2. Statement of activities
        3. Statement of cash flows
        4. Statement of functional expenses
    B. Typical items and specific types of transactions and events: recognition, measurement, valuation and presentation in the financial statements of not-for-profit organizations in conformity with GAAP
        1. Revenues and contributions
        2. Restrictions on resources
        3. Expenses, including depreciation and functional expenses
        4. Investments

I. ETHICS AND PROFESSIONAL AND LEGAL RESPONSIBILITIES (15%-20%)
A. Code of Professional Conduct
B. Proficiency, independence, and due care
C. Ethics and responsibilities in tax practice
D. Licensing and disciplinary systems imposed by the profession and state regulatory bodies
E. Legal responsibilities and liabilities
    1. Common law liability to clients and third parties
    2. Federal statutory liability
F. Privileged communications and confidentiality

II. BUSINESS LAW (20%-25%)
A. Agency
    1. Formation and termination
    2. Duties and authority of agents and principals
    3. Liabilities and authority of agents and principals
B. Contracts
    1. Formation
    2. Performance
    3. Third-party assignments
    4. Discharge, breach, and remedies
C. Debtor-creditor relationships
    1. Rights, duties, and liabilities of debtors, creditors, and guarantors
    2. Bankruptcy
D. Government regulation of business
    1. Federal securities acts
    2. Other government regulation (antitrust, pension and retirement plans, union and employee relations, and legal liability for payroll and social security taxes)
E. Uniform commercial code
    1. Negotiable instruments and letters of credit
    2. Sales
    3. Secured transactions
    4. Documents of title and title transfer
F. Real property, including insurance

III. FEDERAL TAX PROCEDURES AND ACCOUNTING ISSUES (8%-12%)
A. Federal tax procedures
B. Accounting periods
C. Accounting methods including cash, accrual, percentage of completion, completed contract, and installment sales
D. Inventory methods, including uniform capitalization rules

IV. FEDERAL TAXATION OF PROPERTY TRANSACTIONS (8%-12%)
A. Types of assets
B. Basis of assets
C. Depreciation and amortization
D. Taxable and nontaxable sales and exchanges
E. Income, deductions, capital gains and capital losses, including sales and exchanges of business property and depreciation recapture

V. FEDERAL TAXATION – INDIVIDUALS (12%-18%)
A. Gross income—inclusions and exclusions
B. Reporting of items from pass-through entities, including passive activity losses
C. Adjustments and deductions to arrive at taxable income
D. Filing status and exemptions
E. Tax computations, credits, and penalties
F. Alternative minimum tax
G. Retirement plans
H. Estate and gift taxation, including transfers subject to the gift tax, annual exclusion, and items includible and deductible from gross estate

VI. FEDERAL TAXATION—ENTITIES (22%-28%)

A. Similarities and distinctions in tax reporting among such entities as sole proprietorships, general and limited partnerships, Subchapter C corporations, Subchapter S corporations, limited liability companies, and limited liability partnerships

B. Subchapter C corporations
1. Determination of taxable income and loss, and reconciliation of book income to taxable income
2. Tax computations, credits, and penalties, including alternative minimum tax
3. Net operating losses
4. Consolidated returns
5. Entity/owner transactions, including contributions and distributions

C. Subchapter S corporations
1. Eligibility and election
2. Determination of ordinary income, separately stated items, and reconciliation of book income to taxable income
3. Basis of shareholder's interest
4. Entity/owner transactions, including contributions and liquidating and nonliquidating distributions
5. Built-in gains tax

D. Partnerships
1. Determination of ordinary income, separately stated items, and reconciliation of book income to taxable income
2. Basis of partner's interest and basis of assets contributed to the partnership
3. Partnership and partner elections
4. Partner dealing with own partnership
5. Treatment of partnership liabilities
6. Distribution of partnership assets
7. Ownership changes and liquidation and termination of partnership

E. Trusts
1. Types of trusts
2. Income and deductions
3. Determination of beneficiary's share of taxable income

BUSINESS ENVIRONMENT & CONCEPTS CONTENT SPECIFICATION OUTLINE

I. BUSINESS STRUCTURE (17%-23%)

A. Advantages, implications, and constraints of legal structures for business
1. Sole proprietorships and general and limited partnerships
2. Limited liability companies (LLC), limited liability partnerships (LLP), and joint ventures
3. Subchapter C and subchapter S corporations

B. Formation, operation, and termination of businesses

C. Financial structure, capitalization, profit and loss allocation, and distributions

D. Rights, duties, legal obligations, and authority of owners and management (directors, officers, stockholders, partners, and other owners)

II. ECONOMIC CONCEPTS ESSENTIAL TO OBTAINING AN UNDERSTANDING OF AN ENTITY'S BUSINESS AND INDUSTRY (8%-12%)

A. Business cycles and reasons for business fluctuations

B. Economic measures and reasons for changes in the economy, such as inflation, deflation and interest rate changes

C. Market influences on business strategies, including selling, supply chain, and customer management strategies

D. Implications to business of dealings in foreign currencies, hedging and exchange rate fluctuations

III. FINANCIAL MANAGEMENT (17%-23%)
    A. Financial modeling, including factors such as financial indexes, taxes and opportunity costs, and models such as economic value added, cash flow, net present value, discounted payback, and internal rate of return
        1. Objectives
        2. Techniques
        3. Limitations
    B. Strategies for short-term and long-term financing options, including cost of capital and derivatives
    C. Financial statement and business implications of liquid asset management
        1. Management of cash and cash equivalents, accounts receivable, accounts payable, and inventories.
        2. Characteristics and financial statement and business implications of loan rates (fixed vs. variable) and loan covenants

IV. INFORMATION TECHNOLOGY (IT) IMPLICATIONS IN THE BUSINESS ENVIRONMENT (22%-28%)
    A. Role of business information systems
        1. Reporting concepts and systems
        2. Transaction processing systems
        3. Management reporting systems
        4. Risks
    B. Roles and responsibilities within the IT function
        1. Roles and responsibilities of database/network/Web administrators, computer operators, librarians, systems programmers and applications programmers
        2. Appropriate segregation of duties
    C. IT fundamentals
        1. Hardware and software, networks, and data structure, analysis, and application, including operating systems, security, file organization, types of data files, and database management systems
        2. Systems operation, including transaction processing modes, such as batch, on-line, real-time, and distributed processing, and application processing phases, such as data capture, edit routines, master file maintenance; reporting, accounting, control, and management; query, audit trail, and ad hoc reports; and transaction flow
    D. Disaster recovery and business continuity, including data backup and data recovery procedures, alternate processing facilities (hot sites), and threats and risk management
    E. Financial statement and business implications of electronic commerce, including electronic fund transfers, point of sale transactions, internet-based transactions and electronic data interchange

V. PLANNING AND MEASUREMENT (22%-28%)
    A. Planning and budgeting
        1. Planning techniques, including strategic and operational planning
        2. Forecasting and projection techniques
        3. Budgeting and budget variance analysis
    B. Performance measures
        1. Organizational performance measures, including financial and nonfinancial scorecards
        2. Benchmarking, including quality control principles, best practices, and benchmarking techniques
    C. Cost measurement
        1. Cost measurement concepts (standard, joint product, and by-product costing)
        2. Accumulating and assigning costs (job order, process, and activity-based costing)
        3. Factors affecting production costs

Chapter One
Introduction, General and Field Standards

INTRODUCTION

DECISION TO ACCEPT A CLIENT

DOCUMENT ENGAGEMENT UNDERSTANDING

PLANNING THE ENGAGEMENT

REVIEW AND EVALUATION OF THE INTERNAL
CONTROL STRUCTURE (SAS No. 55 as amended)

CONSIDERATION OF FRAUD IN A FINANCIAL STATEMENT AUDIT (SAS No. 99)

ILLEGAL ACTS BY CLIENTS (SAS No. 54)

THE AUDITOR'S CONSIDERATION OF THE INTERNAL AUDIT FUNCTION IN AN AUDIT OF FINANCIAL STATEMENTS (SAS No. 65)

Chapter One
Introduction, General and Field Standards

INTRODUCTION

OBJECTIVE OF THE ORDINARY EXAMINATION OF FINANCIAL STATEMENTS

To express an opinion on reliability and fairness of management prepared financial statements by means of the auditor's report.

STANDARD SHORT-FORM AUDITOR'S REPORT—UNQUALIFIED

(Note: Audit reports are covered in detail in Chapter 3. Discussion here is for quick reference purposes only.)

The form of the standard report on financial statements covering a single year is as follows:

Independent Auditor's Report

Board of Directors
X Corporation

We have audited the accompanying balance sheet of X Company as of December 31, 20XX, and the related statements of income, retained earnings, and cash flows for the year then ended. *These financial statements are the responsibility of the Company's management. Our responsibility is to express an opinion on these financial statements based on our audit.*

We conducted our audit in accordance with auditing standards generally accepted in the United States of America. Those standards require that we plan and perform the audit to obtain reasonable assurance about whether the financial statements are free of material misstatement. An audit includes examining, on a test basis, evidence supporting the amounts and disclosures in the financial statements. An audit also includes assessing the accounting principles used and significant estimates made by management, as well as evaluating the overall financial statement presentation. We believe that our audit provides a reasonable basis for our opinion.

In our opinion, the financial statements referred to above present fairly, in all material respects, the financial position of X Company as of (at) December 31, 20XX, and the results of its operations and its cash flows for the year then ended *in conformity with accounting principles generally accepted in the United States of America.*

(Date of completion of audit)
(Firm Name and Signature)   *(Italics added for emphasis)*

Briefly, the auditors standard report may be modified and take one of the following forms:

Qualified Report—Usually issued when the auditor takes exception to a material item or items in the financial statements because of departures from GAAP. A qualified opinion may also be issued when the auditor's examination is restricted with respect to an item on the financial statements. This type of report communicates to the reader of the financial statements that management's financial reports are fairly presented "except for" a departure from GAAP, which is material enough to mention but not pervasive enough to render the financial statements misleading when taken as a whole.

Adverse Report—Issued when the auditor feels that the departures from GAAP are serious enough to render the statements misleading. In this case, the CPA was able to apply auditing procedures, but discovered material and pervasive departures from GAAP that the client refused to correct. Thus, the dividing line between "except for" (qualified) opinion and an adverse opinion is one of materiality and pervasiveness of the departure from GAAP.

Disclaimer Report—Issued when the auditor's examination was incomplete (scope restricted because of nature of examination or other audit restrictions) to the point where he was unable to express an opinion on the financial statements or where the uncertainties have a pervasive and material effect on the financial statements. Thus, a disclaimer can result from inadequate auditing procedures or material uncertainties.

A complete discussion of the auditor's reporting function is in Chapter 3.

DISTINCTION BETWEEN RESPONSIBILITIES OF AUDITOR AND MANAGEMENT

1. Fairness of the representations contained in financial statements is part of *management's responsibility*.
2. *Management* is responsible for development of adequate controls, safeguarding of assets, sound accounting policies that will produce proper statements (i.e., internal control).
3. *Auditor's responsibility* is confined to the expression of an opinion, and the adequacy of auditing procedures.
4. Purpose of the ordinary examination is not primarily the detection of fraud. Auditor is aware that fraud may exist and as such may affect the financial statements. The auditor must assess the risk that fraud may have affected the financial statements, and as such, the auditor would appropriately modify the audit procedures. (See S.A.S. No. 82 for a complete discussion of the auditor's responsibility to detect fraud.)

GENERALLY ACCEPTED AUDITING STANDARDS

Auditing "standards" differ from auditing "procedures" in that procedures relate to acts to be performed, whereas standards deal with measures of the quality of the performance of those acts and the objectives to be attained by the use of the procedures undertaken. The generally accepted auditing standards, which are interdependent and interrelated, are represented by the general standards, field standards, and reporting standards from the time the Auditing Standards Board of the AICPA will issue interpretations of the standards in publications known as Statements on Auditing Standards (SAS's).

General Standards

1. The examination is to be performed by a person or persons having *adequate technical training and proficiency* as an auditor.
2. In all matters relating to the assignment an *independence* in mental attitude is to be maintained by the auditor or auditors.
3. *Due professional care* is to be exercised in the performance of the examination and the preparation of the report.

Standards of Field Work

1. *The work is to be adequately planned*, and assistants, if any, are to be properly supervised.
2. The auditor should obtain a sufficient *understanding of the internal control structure* to plan the audit and to determine the nature, timing, and extent of tests to be performed.
3. Sufficient competent *evidential* matter is to be obtained through inspection, observation, inquiries, and confirmations to afford a reasonable basis for an opinion regarding the financial statements under examination.

Standards of Reporting

1. The report shall state whether the financial statements are presented in accordance with *generally accepted principles of accounting.*
2. The report shall identify those circumstances in which such principles have not been *consistently* observed in the current period in relation to the preceding period.
3. *Informative disclosures* in the financial statements are to be regarded as reasonably adequate unless otherwise stated in the report.
4. The report shall either contain an *expression of opinion* regarding the financial statements, taken as a whole, or an assertion to the effect that an opinion cannot be expressed. When an overall opinion cannot be expressed, the reasons therefor should be stated. In all cases where an auditor's name is associated with financial statements the report should contain a clear-cut indication of the character of the auditor's examination, if any, and the degree of responsibility he is taking.

OVERVIEW OF THE AUDIT PROCESS

A.   <u>**Decision to**</u>
<u>**Accept Client**</u>

<u>**Decision Criteria**</u>
1.   Independence
     Rule 101 Code
     of Ethics
     GAAS
2.   Competency
     Rule 201 Code
     Of Ethics
     GAAS
3.   Predecessor Auditor

B.

<u>**Document Engagement Understanding**</u>
(Engagement Letter)

C.   <u>**Plan Audit**</u>
1.   Obtain Information on:
     a.   Management
     b.   Industry
     c.   Regulation
     d.   Economy
     e.   Outside pressure

<u>**Decision on Audit Risk**</u>
   a. Potential for Errors
   b. Potential for Illegal Acts
   c. Potential for Fraud

2.   Perform Analytical Review
3.   Initial Understanding of Internal Control
4.   Audit Program
        1)   Preliminary based upon
            1-3 and planned level of reliance on
            Internal Controls
        2)   Detail nature, timing and extent
            of Tests

D.   <u>**Consider Internal Controls**</u>

Outcomes

Plan level	Confirms
of Reliance	Planned
needs to	level of
be modified	reliance

Update Planned	Go with
Audit Program	original plan
Developed in	as developed
C4 above	in C4 above

E.

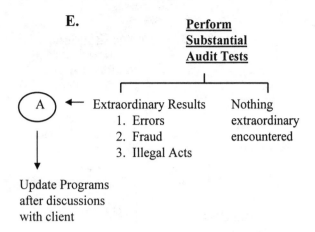

**Perform
Substantial
Audit Tests**

Extraordinary Results
1. Errors
2. Fraud
3. Illegal Acts

Nothing
extraordinary
encountered

Ⓐ

Update Programs
after discussions
with client

F.

**Obtain
Representation
Letter**

G.

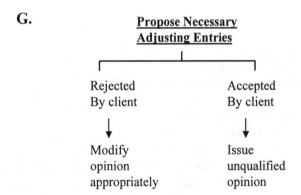

**Propose Necessary
Adjusting Entries**

Rejected
By client

Accepted
By client

Modify
opinion
appropriately

Issue
unqualified
opinion

DECISION TO ACCEPT A CLIENT

The decision to accept an engagement is made by reference to the General Standards of G.A.A.S. and by consultation with the predecessor auditor, if applicable.

GENERAL STANDARDS

The general standards are concerned with the professional training and conduct of the auditor. Specifically, there are three general standards:

1. The examination is to be performed by a person or persons having adequate **technical training** and **proficiency** in auditing.
   (This is normally interpreted to mean that the auditor has adequate formal training and a knowledge of the accounting principles used by the client.)

2. In all matters relating to the assignment, an **independence** in mental attitude is to be maintained by the auditor or auditors.
   (Since the auditor is attesting to the fairness of the financial statements, it is important that he have no bias towards the client. If the CPA is not independent of his client he must disclaim an opinion.)

3. Due professional care is to be exercised in the performance of the examination and the preparation of the report.

COMMUNICATIONS BETWEEN PREDECESSOR AND SUCCESSOR AUDITORS
(SAS NO. 84)

The purpose of the communication between predecessor and successor auditors when a change of auditors is in process is to help the successor auditor in deciding to accept the client. The term **"predecessor auditor"** refers to an auditor who has resigned or who has been notified that his services have been terminated. The term **"successor auditor"** refers to an auditor who has accepted an engagement or an auditor who has been invited to make a proposal for an engagement. This statement applies whenever an independent auditor has been retained, or is to be retained, to make an examination of financial statements in accordance with generally accepted auditing standards.

The initiative in communicating rests with the successor auditor. The communication may be either **written or oral**. Both the predecessor and successor auditors should hold in confidence information obtained from each other. This obligation applies whether or not the successor accepts the engagement.

Communications Before Successor Accepts Engagement

Inquiry of the predecessor auditor is a necessary procedure because the predecessor may be able to provide the successor with information that will assist him in determining whether to accept the engagement. **The successor should bear in mind that, among other things, the predecessor and the client may have disagreed about accounting principles, auditing procedures, or similarly significant matters.**

Request for Permission of Client to Authorize Disclosure

The successor auditor should explain to his prospective client the need to make an inquiry of the predecessor and should request permission to do so. Except as permitted by the Rules of Conduct, an auditor is precluded from disclosing confidential information obtained in the course of an audit engagement unless the client consents. **The successor auditor should ask the prospective client to authorize the predecessor to respond fully to the successor's inquiries.** If a prospective client refuses to permit the predecessor to respond or limits the response, the successor auditor should inquire as to the reasons and **consider the implications of that refusal in deciding whether to accept the engagement.**

The successor auditor should make specific and reasonable inquiries of the predecessor regarding matters that the successor believes will assist him in determining whether to accept the engagement. His inquiries should include specific questions regarding, among other things, facts that might bear on the **integrity of management**, on **disagreements with management as to accounting principles, auditing procedures,** or other **similarly significant matters**, and on the predecessor's understanding as to the reasons for the change of auditors.

The **predecessor should respond promptly** and fully, on the basis of facts known to him, to the successor's reasonable inquiries. However, **should he decide, due to unusual circumstances such as impending litigation, not to respond fully to the inquiries, he should indicate that his response is limited**. If the successor auditor receives a limited response, he should **consider its implications in deciding whether to accept the engagement.**

Other Communications

When one auditor succeeds another, the successor auditor must obtain sufficient competent evidential matter to afford a reasonable basis for expressing his opinion on the financial statements he has been engaged to examine as well as on the consistency of the application of accounting principles in the current year as compared with the preceding year. This may be done by applying appropriate auditing procedures to the account balances at the beginning of the period under examination and in some cases to transactions in prior periods. The successor auditor's examination may be facilitated by (a) making specific inquiries of the predecessor regarding matters that the successor believes may affect the conduct of his examination, such as audit areas that have required an inordinate amount of time or audit problems that arose from the condition of the accounting system and records, and (b) reviewing the predecessor auditor's working papers. In reporting on his examination, **however, the successor auditor should not make reference to the report or work of the predecessor auditor as the basis, in part, for his own opinion.**

The successor auditor should request the client to authorize the predecessor to allow a review of the predecessor's working papers. It is customary in such circumstances for the predecessor auditor to make himself available to the successor auditor for consultation and to make available for review certain of his working papers.

The predecessor and successor auditors should agree on those working papers that are to be made available for review and those that may be copied. Ordinarily, the predecessor should permit the successor to review working papers relating to matters of continuing accounting significance, such as the working paper analysis of balance sheet accounts, both current and noncurrent, and those relating to contingencies. *Valid business reasons, however, may lead the predecessor auditor to decide not to allow a review of his working papers.* When more than one successor auditor is considering acceptance of an engagement, the predecessor auditor should not be expected to make himself or his working papers available until the successor has accepted the engagement.

Financial Statements Reported On by Predecessor

If, during his examination, the successor auditor becomes aware of information that leads him to believe that financial statements reported on by the predecessor auditor may require revision, he should request his client to arrange a meeting among the three parties to discuss this information and attempt to resolve the matter. If the client refuses or if the successor is not satisfied with the result, the successor auditor may be well advised to consult with his attorney in determining an appropriate course of further action.

DOCUMENT ENGAGEMENT UNDERSTANDING

I. S.A.S. No. 83 requires that the auditor establish an understanding with the client regarding the services to be performed for each engagement.
    A. The purpose of the communication is to reduce the risk of misunderstanding.
    B. The understanding should include the objectives of the engagement, management's responsibilities, the auditor's responsibilities, and the limitations of the engagement.
    C. The understanding should also include the fact that management is responsible for adjusting the financial statements to correct material misstatements detected during the course of the audit.

II. The understanding should be documented in the working papers, preferably in a written communication with the client (i.e. engagement letter).
    A. The understanding should generally include the following matters:
        - The objective of the audit is the expression of an opinion on the financial statements.
        - Management is responsible for the entity's financial statements.
        - Management is responsible for establishing and maintaining effective internal control over financial reporting.
        - Management is responsible for identifying and ensuring that the entity complies with the laws and regulations applicable to its activities.
        - Management is responsible for making all financial records and related information available to the auditor.
        - Management is responsible for adjusting the financial statements to correct material misstatements and for affirming to the auditor in the representation letter that the effects of any uncorrected misstatements aggregated by the auditor are immaterial, both individual and in the aggregate, to the financial statements taken as a whole.
        - At the conclusion of the engagement, management will provide the auditor with a letter that confirms certain representations made during the audit.
        - The auditor is responsible for conducting the audit in accordance with generally accepted auditing standards. Those standards require that the auditor obtain reasonable rather than absolute assurance about whether the financial statements are free of material misstatement, whether caused by error or fraud. Accordingly, a material misstatement may remain undetected. Also, an audit is not designed to detect error or fraud that is immaterial to the financial statements. If, for any reason, the auditor is unable to complete the audit or is unable to form or has not formed an opinion, he or she may decline to express an opinion or decline to issue a report as a result of the engagement.
        - An audit includes obtaining an understanding of internal control sufficient to plan the audit and to determine the nature, timing, and extent of audit procedures to be performed. An audit is not designed to provide assurance on internal control or to identify reportable conditions. However, the auditor is responsible for ensuring that the audit committee or others with equivalent authority or responsibility are aware of any reportable conditions which come to his or her attention.

B. An understanding with the client also may include other matters, such as the following:
- Arrangements regarding the conduct of the engagement (for example, timing, client assistance regarding the preparation of schedules, and the availability of documents).
- Arrangements concerning involvement of specialists or internal auditors, if applicable.
- Arrangements involving a predecessor auditor.
- Arrangements regarding fees and billing.
- Any limitation of or other arrangements regarding the liability of the auditor or the client, such as indemnification to the auditor for liability arising from knowing misrepresentations to the auditor by management. (Regulators, including the Securities and Exchange Commission, may restrict or prohibit such liability limitation arrangements.)
- Conditions under which access to the auditor's working papers may be granted to others.
- Additional services to be provided relating to regulatory requirements.
- Arrangements regarding other services to be provided in connection with the engagement.

SAMPLE ENGAGEMENT LETTER

BETTER & BEST CPAs

Lambers CPA Review

This letter will confirm our understanding of the terms and objectives of our engagement and the nature and limitations of the services we will provide.

- We will audit the statement of financial condition of Lambers CPA Review as of December 31, 2010, and the related statements of Income, Retained Earnings and Cash Flows for the year then ended for the purpose of expressing an opinion on them. The financial statements are the responsibility of the management of Lambers CPA Review. Encompassed in that responsibility is the creation and maintenance of proper accounting records, the selection of appropriate accounting principles, the safeguarding of assets, and compliance with relevant laws and regulations. Our responsibility is to express an opinion on the financial statements based on our audit, and is limited to the period covered by our audit. If circumstances preclude us from issuing an unqualified opinion, we will discuss the reasons with you in advance. A report will not be issued for this engagement if we are unable to finish the audit.

- We will conduct our audit in accordance with generally accepted accounting standards. Those standards require that we plan and perform the audit to obtain reasonable assurance about whether the financial statements are free of material misstatement. An audit includes examining, on a test basis, evidence supporting the amounts and disclosures included in the financial statements. Accordingly, the areas and number of transactions selected for testing will involve judgment. It also includes assessing the accounting principles used and significant estimates made by Lambers CPA Review, as well as evaluating the overall financial statement presentation.

- Our audit is designed to provide reasonable assurance of detecting misstatements that, in our judgment, could have a material effect on the financial statements taken as a whole. Consequently, our audit will not necessarily detect all misstatements that might exist due to error, fraudulent financial reporting, or misappropriation of assets. Lambers CPA Review is responsible for establishing and maintaining a sound system of internal control, which is the best means of preventing or detecting errors, fraudulent financial reporting, and misappropriation of assets. We will inform you of all matters of fraud and material errors, and all illegal acts, unless they are clearly inconsequential, that come to our attention.

- Management is responsible for adjusting the financial statements to correct material misstatements and for affirming to the auditor in a representation letter that the effects of any uncorrected misstatements aggregated by the auditor during the current engagement and pertaining to the latest period presented are immaterial, both individually and in the aggregate to the financial statements taken as a whole.

- Our report on the financial statements is presently expected to read as follows:

  [Standard Audit Report]   Refer to page 3-1 for text

- As part of our engagement for the year ending December 31, 2010, we also will prepare the federal and state income tax returns for Lambers CPA Review.

- If you intend to publish or otherwise reproduce the financial statements and make reference to our firm, you agree to provide us with printers' proofs or masters for our review and approval before printing. You also agree to provide us with a copy of the final reproduced material for our approval before it is distributed.

- Our fees will be billed as work progresses and are based on the amount of time required plus out-of-pocket expenses. Invoices are payable upon presentation. Our initial fee estimate assumes no unexpected circumstances will be encountered. We will notify you immediately of any circumstances we encounter that could significantly affect our initial estimate of total fees, which will range from $50,000 to $75,000.

If this letter correctly expresses your understanding, please sign the enclosed copy where indicated and return it to us.

We appreciate the opportunity to serve you and trust that our association will be a long and pleasant one.

Sincerely,

John Better CPA
_____
[Engagement Partner's Signature]

Accepted and agreed to:

Vincent Lambers
_____
[Client Representative's Signature]

President
_____
[Title]

November 20, 2009
_____
[Date]

PLANNING THE ENGAGEMENT

The First Standard of Field Work
The work is to be adequately planned, and assistants, if any, are to be properly supervised.

Planning
1. *Audit planning involves developing an overall strategy* for the expected conduct and scope of the examination. The nature, extent, and timing of planning vary with the size and complexity of the entity, experience with the entity, and knowledge of the entity's business.

2. In planning his examination, the auditor should consider the nature, extent, and timing of work to be performed and *should prepare a written audit program* (or a set of written audit programs). An audit program aids in instructing assistants in the work to be done. It should set forth in reasonable detail the audit procedures that the auditor believes are necessary to accomplish the objectives of the examination.

3. In addition, planning is concerned with the following:
   a. The assignment of staff to the engagement (number and level of experience)
   b. The due dates for any financial statements, reports, tax returns, etc.
   c. Developing an understanding of the client's business and control structure.
   d. Considering the potential for complex audit areas (i.e., leases, pensions, etc.)
   e. Reviewing permanent files
   f. Reviewing prior years workpapers, if any
   g. Set tentative materiality levels based on initial review of the financial statements
   h. Determining the potential for errors or irregularities.

4. The auditor should also gain a sufficient understanding of the client's internal controls to plan the audit and to determine the nature, timing and extent of audit tests.

Supervision

1. *Supervision involves directing the efforts of assistants* who are involved in accomplishing the objectives of the examination and determining whether those objectives were accomplished. Elements of supervision include instructing assistants, keeping informed of significant problems encountered, reviewing the work performed, and dealing with differences of opinion among firm personnel.

2. Assistants should be informed of their responsibilities and the objectives of the procedures that they are to perform. They should be informed of matters that may affect the nature, extent, and timing of procedures they are to perform, such as the nature of the entity's business as it relates to their assignments and possible accounting and auditing problems.

3. The work performed by each assistant should be reviewed to determine whether it was adequately performed and to evaluate whether the results are consistent with the conclusions to be presented in the auditor's report.

4. The auditor with final responsibility for the examination and assistants should be aware of the procedures to be followed when differences of opinion concerning accounting and auditing issues exist among firm personnel involved in the examination.

REVIEW AND EVALUATION OF THE
INTERNAL CONTROL STRUCTURE (SAS No. 55 as amended)

The Second Standard of Field Work

A sufficient understanding of internal control is to be obtained to plan the audit and to determine the nature, timing, and extent of tests to be performed.

I. **Definition of Internal Control and Components**
    A. Internal control is a process - effected by an entity's board of directors, management, and other personnel - designed to provide reasonable assurance regarding the achievement of objectives in the following categories: (a) reliability of financial reporting, (b) effectiveness and efficiency of operations, and (c) compliance with applicable laws and regulations.

    B. Internal control consists of the following five interrelated components.
        1. **Control environment** sets the tone of an organization, influencing the control consciousness of its people. It is the foundation for all other components of internal control, providing discipline and structure.
        2. **Risk assessment** is the entity's identification and analysis of relevant risks to achievement of its objectives, forming a basis for determining how the risks should be managed.
        3. **Control activities** are the policies and procedures that help ensure that management directives are carried out.

4. **Information and communication** are the identification, capture, and exchange of information in a form and time frame that enable people to carry out their responsibilities.
5. **Monitoring** is a process that assesses the quality of internal control performance over time.

C. There is a direct relationship between objectives, which are what an entity seeks to achieve, and components, which represent what is needed to achieve the objectives.

D. Internal control is related to the entire entity although not all controls and objectives are relevant to an audit of the entity's financial statements.

II. Objectives of Internal Control

A. Three objectives:
1. Financial Reporting Objectives - controls that are relevant to an audit pertain to an entity's objective of preparing financial statements for external purposes that are fairly presented in conformity with generally accepted accounting principles or a comprehensive basis of accounting other than GAAP.
2. Operational Objectives - controls that relate to the effectiveness and efficiency of operations.
3. Compliance Objectives - controls that relate to entity's compliance with applicable laws and regulations.

B. During a financial statement audit the auditor is generally more concerned with financial statement controls as opposed to operational and compliance controls. However, there may be circumstances where the auditor would be concerned with operational and compliance controls because they have a bearing on the audit process. For example, controls pertaining to nonfinancial data the auditor uses in analytical procedures, such as production statistics, or pertaining to detecting noncompliance with laws or regulations having a direct and material effect on the financial statements, such as compliance with income tax laws.

III. Limitations of an Entity's Internal Control

A. **Management's responsibility** - controls are influenced and designed by management and as such will only be as effective as management desires.

B. **Reasonable assurance** - the cost of internal control should not exceed the benefits to be derived by the structure (cost-benefit relationship).

C. **Inherent limitations** - all control structures have the following inherent limitations:
1. Controls can be circumvented by collusion of employees.
2. Management can override any system of controls.
3. No system can prevent errors arising from fatigue, lack of knowledge or human error.
4. Because of the inherent limitations, control risk can never by reduced to zero in an audit. There is always some control risk, even in the "perfect" system.

D. **The control concepts apply equally to all types of information processing (manual and EDP).**

IV. Consideration of Internal Control in Planning an Audit - Auditor's Responsibility

A. **In all audits**, the auditor should obtain an **understanding** of each of the five components of internal control sufficient to plan the audit by performing procedures to understand the **design of controls** relevant to an audit of financial statements, and whether they have been **placed in operation**.

B. In planning the audit, knowledge obtained in (A) above would be used to:
1. Identify the types of potential misstatements that occur (errors, frauds, illegal acts).
2. Consider factors that affect the risk of material misstatements.
3. Make a preliminary evaluation of control risk and decide upon an initial audit approach.

C. The nature, timing, and extent of procedures the auditor chooses to obtain an **understanding** will vary depending on the size and complexity of the entity, previous experience with the entity, the nature of controls, and the extent of client documentation.

1. The auditor normally employs the following procedures to gain an **understanding**.
   - Inquiry
   - Observation
   - Examination
   - Reperformance (Testing Transactions)

D. Placed in Operation vs. Operating Effectiveness
1. Placed in operation is concerned whether an entity is **using** a particular control.
2. Operating effectiveness is concerned with how the control was **applied**, its **consistency** of use, and **by whom** it was applied.
3. **The auditor is not required to obtain knowledge about operating effectiveness as part of understanding internal control. However, if the auditor plans to assess control risk at less than the maximum, operating effectiveness must be tested.**

E. Understanding Control Components
1. **Control Environment**
   - The auditor should obtain sufficient knowledge of the control environment to understand management's and the board of directors' attitude, awareness, and actions concerning the control environment **considering both the substance of controls and the collective effect.**
   - The auditor is more concerned with the substance of the controls rather than their form because controls may be established but **not** acted upon.
   - The control environment sets the tone of an organization, influencing the control consciousness of its people. It is the foundation for all other components of internal control, providing discipline and structure. Control environment factors include the following:
     a. Integrity and ethical values.
     b. Commitment to competence.
     c. Board of directors or audit committee participation.
     d. Management's philosophy and operating style.
     e. Organizational structure.
     f. Assignment of authority and responsibility.
     g. Human resource policies and practices.

2. **Risk Assessment**
   - An entity's risk assessment for financial reporting purposes is its identification, analysis, and management of risks relevant to the preparation of financial statements that are fairly presented in conformity with generally accepted accounting principles. For example, risk assessment may address how the entity considers the possibility of unrecorded transactions or identifies and analyzes significant estimates recorded in the financial statements. Risks relevant to reliable financial reporting also relate to specific events or transactions.
   - Risks relevant to financial reporting include external and internal events and circumstances that may occur and adversely affect an entity's ability to record, process, summarize, and report financial data consistent with the assertions of management in the financial statements. Risks can arise or change due to circumstances such as:
     a. Changes in operating environment.
     b. New personnel.
     c. New or revamped information systems.
     d. Rapid growth.
     e. New technology.
     f. New lines, products, or activities.
     g. Corporate restructurings.
     h. Foreign operations.
     i. Accounting pronouncements.

- The auditor should obtain sufficient knowledge of the entity's risk assessment process to understand how management considers risks relevant to financial reporting objectives and decides about actions to address those risks.
- An entity's risk assessment differs from the auditor's consideration of audit risk in a financial statement audit. The purpose of an entity's risk assessment is to identify, analyze, and manage risks that affect all the entity objectives. In a financial statement audit, the auditor assesses inherent and control risks to evaluate the likelihood that material misstatements could occur in the financial statements.

3. **Control Activities**

Control activities are the policies and procedures that help ensure that management directives are carried out. They help ensure that necessary actions are taken to address risks to achievement of the entity's objectives. Control activities have various objectives and are applied at various organizational and functional levels. Generally, control activities that may be relevant to an audit may be categorized as policies and procedures that pertain to the following:

- Performance reviews - actual performance vs. budgets, forecasts, etc.
- Information processing - controls to check the accuracy, completeness and authorization of transactions.
- Physical controls - physical security, authorization for access to computer programs and data files, periodic counting and comparison of physical amount to control records.
- Segregation of duties - assignment of different people the responsibility of authorizing, recording transactions and maintaining custody of assets.
- Typical control activities include:
  - Capable personnel.
  - Segregation of functional responsibilities of authorization, custody, and record keeping.
  - Segregation of duties in the accounting function.
  - Periodic reconciliations.
  - Limit access to records, assets, and computer equipment and programs.
  - Prenumbered documents.
  - Specific written authorization procedures.
  - Independent checks on performance.
  - Controls over the execution of transactions.
  - Accounting entries need adequate documentation.
  - Input, process and output controls over computer processing.

- The auditor should obtain an understanding of those control activities relevant to planning the audit. **However, audit planning does not require an understanding of all control activities related to the financial statements.** Generally, as an auditor obtains an understanding of other control components knowledge of control activities is obtained. The auditor should consider the knowledge about the presence or absence of control activities obtained from the understanding of other components in determining whether it is necessary to devote additional attention to obtaining an understanding of the control activities to plan the audit.

4. **Information and Communication**

The information system relevant to financial reporting objectives, which includes the accounting system, consists of the methods and records established to record, process, summarize, and report entity transactions (as well as events and conditions) and to maintain accountability for the related assets, liabilities, and equity. The quality of system-generated information affects management's ability to make appropriate decisions in controlling the entity's activities and to prepare reliable financial reports.

The auditor should obtain sufficient knowledge of the **information system relevant to financial reporting** to understand:

- The classes of transactions in the entity's operations that are significant to the financial statements.
- How those transactions are initiated.
- The accounting records, supporting information, and specific accounts in the financial statements involved in the processing and reporting of transactions.
- The accounting processing involved from the initiation of a transaction to its inclusion in the financial statements, including **electronic means (such as computers and electronic data interchange) used to transmit, process, maintain, and access information.**
- The financial reporting process used to prepare the entity's financial statements, including significant accounting estimates and disclosures.

5. **Monitoring**

An important management responsibility is to establish and maintain internal control. Management monitors controls to consider whether they are operating as intended and that they are modified as appropriate for changes in conditions.

Monitoring is a process that assesses the quality of internal control performance over time. It involves assessing the design and operation of controls on a timely basis and taking necessary corrective actions. This process is accomplished through ongoing activities, separate evaluations, or by various combinations of the two. In many entities, internal auditors or personnel performing similar functions contribute to the monitoring of an entity's activities. Monitoring activities may include using information from communications from external parties such as customer complaints and regulator comments that may indicate problems or highlight areas in need of improvement.

The auditor should obtain sufficient knowledge of the major types of activities the entity uses to monitor internal control over financial reporting, including how those activities are used to initiate corrective action (e.g., Internal Auditors).

V. Auditor's Responsibility -- Documentation of Understanding of Controls
A. An independent auditor **must** document his/her understanding of the internal control components. Reasons:
1. Show compliance with GAAS in workpapers.

2. Serve as a point of reference for current and future audits and engagements.

B. Methods of Documentation
1. Form and extent is a matter of professional judgment based upon size and complexity of the client and size of CPA firm (more people working on audit would probably mean more extensive documentation).

2. Common forms of documentation
   a. Internal Control Questionnaire (ICQ) - a series of questions designed to elicit a "yes" or "no" answer. A "yes" answer is considered a positive attribute of the system. Conversely, a "no" answer is a weakness or deficiency in the system.

   b. Narrative (written) - memoranda describing system

   c. Flow Chart - a symbolic representation of the auditor's understanding of the system.

   d. Checklists.

   e. It is common for most CPA firms to use a combination of "a" through "d" rather than rely on one documentation style only.

VI. Auditor's Responsibility - Assessing Control Risk

A. Control Risk - the risk that the client's internal control policy and procedures are **not** effective in preventing or detecting material misstatements in the financial statements.

B. Control Risk - Assessment outcome possibilities
   1. Control Risk at the maximum
      * Conclusion based upon the auditor's judgment that the client's internal control policies and procedures do **not** reduce to a low level the potential that the financial statements are free of material errors and/or irregularities.
      * After reaching this assessment, the auditor would only be required to document in his/her workpapers the fact that control risk is at the maximum, and **not** the basis for reaching this conclusion.
      * The auditor may decide control risk is at the maximum based upon cost/benefit decisions described below (see 2b and 2c).

   2. Control Risk at less than the maximum
      a. Based upon his/her initial understanding of the internal control components, the auditor may conclude that **control risk may be less than the maximum.**

      b. The auditor in this situation must evaluate the cost/benefit of extending his/her understanding of internal controls to make a final decision concerning control risk.

      c. The cost/benefit decision is based upon the audit time involved in extending the auditor's understanding of internal controls, including tests of control, versus the time that may be saved with the possible reduction of substantive audit tests.
         * Tests of Controls - audit tests designed to determine whether specific control procedures that the auditor plans to rely on are actually in place and operating effectively in the entity under audit.
         * Substantive Tests - audit tests designed to substantiate one or more financial statement assertions.
         * Should the auditor decide not to extend his/her understanding of internal controls because of cost/benefit considerations, control risk would then be assessed at the maximum for all financial statement assertions.

      d. Should the auditor conclude that his/her understanding should be extended the following procedures would be completed:
         * Extended the understanding of control activities in order to determine what control activities are prescribed by the client, by whom are those activities (procedures) performed, **and are those procedures likely to be effective in reducing control risk**.
         * Document the understanding of those control activities in the same manner as discussed in VB2 above.
         * Perform tests of controls.
         * Assess control risk based upon the auditor's extended understanding and the results of tests of controls.

      e. If the auditor concludes that control risk is less than the maximum and the auditor plans to design substantive tests based upon that fact, the basis for assessing control risk at less than the maximum **must** be documented in the workpapers.

FLOWCHART OF AUDITOR'S
CONSIDERATION OF INTERNAL CONTROL

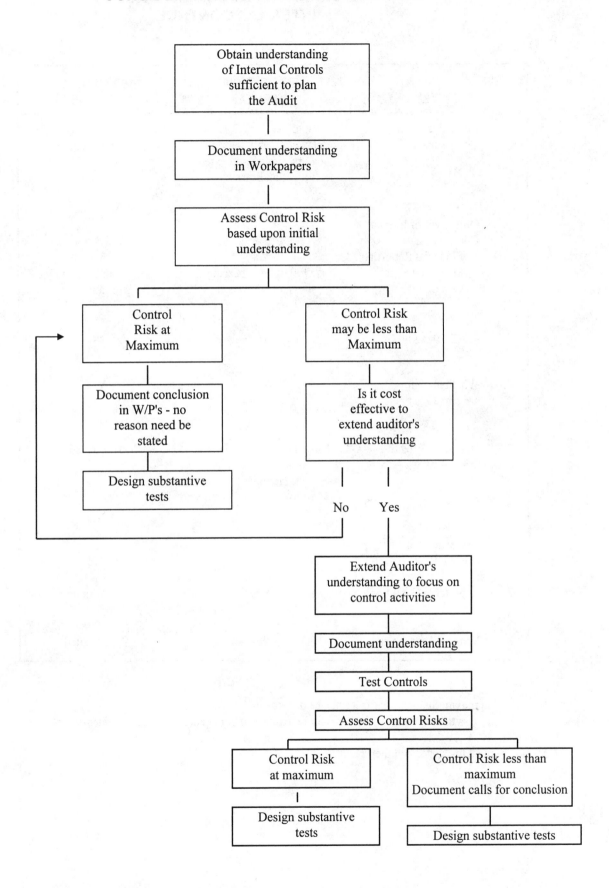

SUMMARY OF AUDITOR'S
WORKPAPER DOCUMENTATION
INTERNAL CONTROL

	Item(s)	Understanding Required	Documentation Requirement
1.	Internal Control Components	Yes, to extent necessary to plan audit and determine nature, timing and extent of audit tests	Yes, type and extent auditor's judgment
2.	Objectives of Internal Control		
	Financial Reporting	Yes	Yes
	Operational Compliance	Only if have bearing on audit process	Only if understanding obtained
3.	Design of Controls	Yes	Yes
4.	Whether Controls are placed in operation	Yes	Yes
5.	Operating Effectiveness of Controls	Only if control risk is to be assessed at less than maximum. Must use Test of Controls.	Yes, if tested**
6.	Assessment of Control Risk	Yes	Yes*
7.	Reportable Conditions	Yes	Yes, if noted
8.	Material Weaknesses	Yes	Yes, if noted

* If assessed at maximum, only that fact must be documented.
   If assessed at less than maximum, the basis for reaching that conclusion must be documented.

** Must document tests used and their results.

VII. Transaction Cycles and Internal Control Components

  A. In order to audit an entity, the auditor must become familiar with the major types of transactions engaged in by the entity and the processing of those transactions.

    1. The auditor is concerned with
- What those transactions are.
- How those transactions are initiated.
- The authorization procedures surrounding those transactions.
- The accounting records generated from those transactions.
- The manner in which those transactions are processed.
- How those transactions are reflected on the financial statements.

    2. The needed information is obtained by gaining sufficient understanding of the "Information and Processing" and "Control Activities" components of internal control.
- Auditors usually take a "transaction cycle" approach when understanding the above internal control components.
- **Transaction Cycle** refers to the policies and the sequence of procedures for processing a particular type of transaction.

  B. A transaction cycle can be represented by the following:

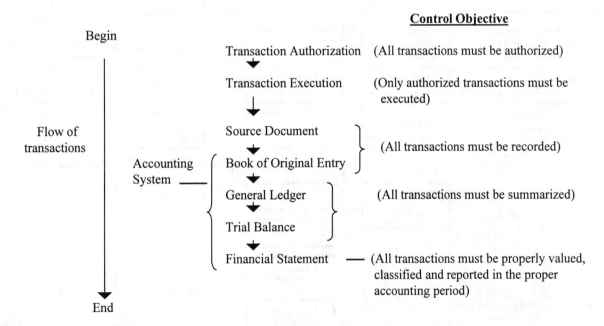

  C. Specific transaction cycles are
    1. Sales and Accounts Receivable.
    2. Cash Receipts.
    3. Purchasing and Accounts Payable.
    4. Cash Disbursements.
    5. Payroll.

The CPA Candidate must have a detailed understanding of the control activities involved in the various transaction cycles. Following is a summary of the typical control activities that should be present in an ideal system of internal control for a medium-sized manufacturing company. Questions on the CPA exam, whether objective type or essay, focus on control activities of a medium-sized manufacturing company.

D. TYPICAL ORGANIZATIONAL CHART FOR A MEDIUM-SIZED MANUFACTURING COMPANY

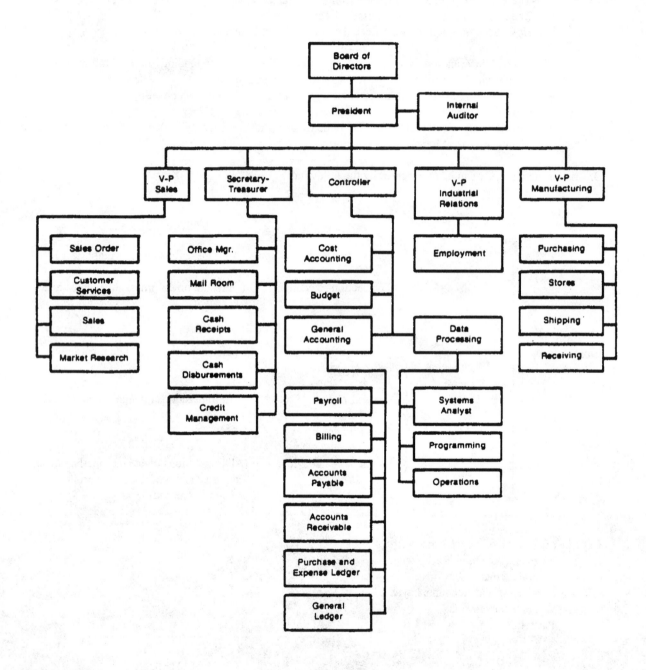

SALES AND ACCOUNTS RECEIVABLE

Control Activity	Responsibility of:	How Performed or Communicated
Credit limits are clearly defined.	Senior management	Written document
Credit limits are clearly communicated.	Senior management	Written document
The credit of prospective customers is investigated before it is extended to them.	Credit manager	Credit reports
Credit limits are periodically reviewed.	Senior management	Reviewed
The people who perform the credit function are independent of -- Sales. Billing. Collection. Accounting.	Senior management	Organization chart
Credit limits and changes in credit limits are communicated to persons responsible for approving sales orders on a timely basis.	Senior management	Written document
The company has clearly defined policies and procedures for acceptance and approval of sales orders.	Senior management	Written document
Prenumbered sales orders are used and accounted for.	N/A	N/A
Prenumbered shipping documents are used to record shipments.	N/A	N/A
Shipping document information is verified prior to shipment.	Shipping personnel	Review
The people who perform the shipping function are independent of -- Sales. Billing. Collection. Accounting.	Senior management	Organization chart
All shipping documents are accounted for.	Billing clerk	Review
Prenumbered credit memos are used to document sales returns.	N/A	N/A
All credit memos are approved and accounted for.	Credit manager	Signed

Control Activity	Responsibility of:	How Performed or Communicated
Credit memos are matched with receiving reports for returned goods.	Accounts Receivable Clerk	Reviewed
Cash sales are controlled by cash registers or prenumbered cash receipts forms.	N/A	N/A
Someone other than the cashier has custody to the cash register tape compartment.	N/A	N/A
Someone other than the cashier takes periodic readings of the cash register and balances the cash on hand.	Management	Written document
Information necessary to prepare invoices (e.g., prices, discount policies) is clearly communicated to billing personnel on a timely basis.	Management	Price lists
Prenumbered invoices are prepared promptly after goods are shipped.	Billing Clerk	--------
Quantities on the invoices are compared to shipping documents.	Billing Clerk	Review
The people who perform the billing function are independent of -- Sales. Credit. Collection. Accounting for receivables	Senior management	Organization chart
Invoices are posted to the subsidiary ledger on a timely basis.	Billing	Prepares Sales Journal
Invoices are posted to the sales and accounts receivable subsidiary ledgers or journals on a timely basis.	Accounts Receivable Clerk	Updates Records
The sales and accounts receivable balances shown in the general ledger are reconciled to the sales and accounts receivable subsidiary ledgers on a regular basis.	Personnel independent of sales and collection	Written documentation
Monthly statements are mailed to customers.	Accounts Receivable Clerk	-----
Exceptions to monthly statements are investigated and resolved.	Collection Clerk	Documented
Past due accounts are periodically reviewed for collectibility.	Senior management	Documented

CASH RECEIPTS

	Responsibility of:	How Performed or Communicated
The entity maintains records of payments on accounts by customer.	Accounts Receivable Clerk	Subsidiary ledgers
Someone other than the person responsible for maintaining accounts receivable opens the mail and lists the cash receipts.	Mail Room	Cash receipts listing
Cash receipts are deposited intact.	Cash Receipts Clerk	-----
People who handle cash receipts are adequately bonded.	Senior management	-----
Cash receipts are posted to the cash receipts journal on a timely basis.	Cash Receipts Clerk	Journal
Cash receipts are posted to the accounts receivable subsidiary ledger on a timely basis.	Accounts Receivable Clerk	From cash receipts listing
The people who enter cash receipts to the accounting system are independent of the physical handling of collections.	Senior management	Organization chart
Timely bank reconciliations are prepared or reviewed by someone independent of the cash receipts function.	Senior management	Written document

PURCHASING AND ACCOUNTS PAYABLE

	Responsibility of:	How Performed or Communicated
All purchases over a predetermined amount are approved by management.	Senior management	Sign purchase order
Non-routine purchases (for example, services, fixed assets, or investments) are approved by management.	Senior management	Sign
A purchase order system is used, prenumbered purchase orders are accounted for, and physical access to purchase orders is controlled.	Management	-----
Open purchase orders are periodically reviewed.	Purchasing agent	Review

	Responsibility of:	How Performed or Communicated

The purchasing function is independent of --

    Receiving.
    Invoice processing.   ——   Senior management   Organization chart
    Cash disbursements.

Blind copy of purchase order is forwarded to receiving personnel (no quantities or price indicated).   Purchasing agent   -----

All goods are inspected and counted when received.   Receiving Clerk   -----

Prenumbered receiving reports, or a log, are used to record the receipt of goods.   Receiving Clerk   -----

The receiving reports or log indicate the date the items were received.   Receiving Clerk   -----

The receiving function is independent of --

    Purchasing.
    Invoice processing.   ——   Senior management   Organization chart
    Cash disbursements.

Invoices from vendors are matched with applicable receiving reports and purchase orders.   Accounts Payable Clerk   Review

Invoices are reviewed for proper quantity and prices, and mathematical accuracy.   Accounts Payable Clerk   Recompute Sign

Invoices from vendors are posted to the Purchases Journal on a timely basis.   Accounts Payable Clerk   -----

The invoice processing function is independent of --

    Purchasing.
    Receiving.   ——   Senior management   Organization chart
    Cash disbursements.

CASH DISBURSEMENT

	Responsibility of:	How Documented or Communicated
All disbursements except those from petty cash are made by check.	Senior management	Policy manual
All vendor invoices are paid on a timely basis to take advantage of discounts.	Accounts Payable Clerk	File Invoices by Due Date
Supporting documentation such as invoices and receiving reports are reviewed before the checks are signed.	Treasurer	Review Sign
Supporting documents are canceled to avoid duplicate payment.	Treasurer	Cancel documents
Checks are mailed by signer.	Treasurer	Policy manual
Cash disbursements are posted to the cash disbursements journal on a timely basis.	Cash disbursements clerk	-----
Timely bank reconciliations are prepared or reviewed by the owner or manager or someone independent of the cash receipts or disbursements function.	Senior management	Review and Sign

PAYROLL

	Responsibility of:	How Performed or Communicated
Wages and salaries are approved by management.	Senior management	Written document
Salaries of senior management are based on written authorization of the board of directors.	Board of Directors	Written document
Maintenance of personnel files is under the control of the personnel department.	Senior management	Written document
Proper authorization is obtained for all payroll deductions.	Employee/Personnel Dept.	Signs documents
Access to personnel files is limited to those who are independent of the payroll or cash functions.	Personnel department	Written document
Wage and salary rates and payroll deductions are reported promptly to employees who perform the payroll processing function.	Personnel department	Written document

	Responsibility of:	How Performed or Communicated
Periodic governmental reports are filed on a timely basis.	Payroll department	Complete forms
Adequate time records are maintained for employees paid by the hour.	Time Clock	-----
Time records for hourly employees are approved by a supervisor.	Department manager	Signs time card
Payroll is calculated using authorized pay rates, payroll deductions, and time records.	Payroll accounting department	-----
Payroll registers are reviewed for accuracy.	Check signer	Reviews, Signs
Payroll cost distributions are reconciled to gross pay.	Payroll accounting department	Written document
Net pay is distributed by persons who are independent of personnel, payroll preparation, time-keeping, and check preparation functions.	Treasurer	-----
The responsibility for custody and follow-up of unclaimed wages is assigned to someone who is independent of personnel, payroll processing, and cash disbursement functions.	Treasurer	-----

Diagrammed View of Transaction Cycles

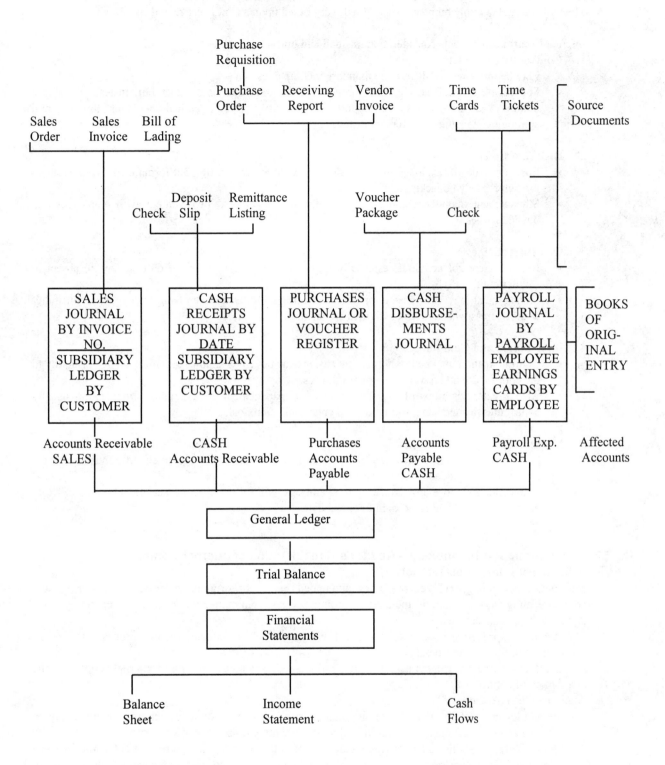

VIII. Application of Internal Control Concepts to Small and Mid-sized Entities

  A. The way internal control components apply will vary based upon an entity's size and complexity.

  B. Internal Control components consideration in small and mid-sized entities

    1. **Control Environment**
- May be implemented differently than larger companies.
- For example, small entities may not have a written code of conduct but, instead, develop a culture that emphasizes the importance of integrity and ethical behavior through oral communication and management example.

    2. **Risk Assessment**
- Basic concepts of risk assessment should be present in every entity, but formalized risk assessment procedures may be lacking.
- Management may learn about risks through direct personal involvement with employees and outside parties.

    3. **Control Activities**
- Extensive control activities, especially those involving segregation of duties, may be absent in smaller entities.
- Management may compensate for lack of control activities by exercising oversight responsibility in those areas where control activities are lacking.

    4. **Information and Communication**
- Communication may be less formal but easier to achieve in a smaller organization due primarily to the entity's size and fewer levels of employees.
- Also greater visibility of and availability of management in a smaller organization usually contributes to adequate information and communication goals.

    5. **Monitoring**
- Ongoing management activities in small and mid-sized entities are likely to contribute to the achievement of adequate monitoring procedures.
- Management's close involvement in operations will often identify significant variance from expectations and inaccuracies in financial data.

IX. Effect of Information Technology – Auditor's Consideration of Internal Control

  A. **Definition of Information Technology**

    Information technology (IT) encompasses automated means of originating, processing, storing, and communicating information, and includes recording devices, communication systems, computer systems, and other electronic devices.

  B. The auditor is primarily interested in the entity's use of IT to initiate, record, process, and report transactions or other financial data.

  C. IT can affect internal control, evidential matter, and the auditor's understanding of internal control and the assessment of control risk.

  D. Auditor's Considerations of IT

    1. The auditor may determine that assessing control risk below maximum for certain assertions may be effective and more efficient than performing only substantive tests.

    2. Alternatively, the auditor may determine that it is not practical or possible to restrict detection risk to an acceptable level by performing only substantive tests for one or more financial statement assertions. In such circumstances, the auditor should obtain evidential matter about the effectiveness of both the design and operation of controls to reduce the assessed level of control risk. Such evidential matter may be obtained from several sources including:

- o Testing the controls planned and performed concurrent with or subsequent to obtaining the understanding.
- o Performing procedures that were not specifically planned as tests of controls but that provide evidential matter about the effectiveness of the design and operation of the controls.
- o For certain assertions, the auditor may desire to further reduce the assessed level of control risk. In such cases, the auditor considers whether evidential matter sufficient to support a further reduction is likely to be available and whether performing additional tests of controls to obtain such evidential matter would be efficient.

3. The auditor may assess control risk at the maximum level because he or she believes controls are unlikely to pertain to an assertion, or are unlikely to be effective, or because evaluating the effectiveness of controls would be inefficient.

- o *However, the auditor needs to be satisfied that performing only substantive tests would be effective in restricting detection risk to an acceptable level. When evidence of an entity's initiation, recording, or processing of financial data exists only in electronic form, the ability of the auditor to obtain the desired assurance only from substantive tests would significantly diminish.*
- o The auditor uses the understanding of internal control and the assessed level of control risk to determine the nature, timing and extent of substantive tests to be performed.

X. Communication of Internal Control Related Matters Noted in an Audit (S.A.S. No. 60)

A. During the course of an audit of an entity's financial statement, the auditor may become aware of matters related to internal control that may be of interest to the audit committee of the Board of Directors or others of equivalent authority. These items are referred to as "reportable conditions" (specifically, a reportable condition relates to significant deficiencies in the design or operation of internal control).

B. Examples of reportable conditions:

Deficiencies in internal control design
- Inadequate overall internal control design
- Absence of appropriate segregation of duties consistent with appropriate control objectives
- Absence of appropriate reviews and approvals of transactions, accounting entries, or systems output
- Inadequate procedures for appropriately assessing and applying accounting principles
- Inadequate provisions for the safeguarding of assets
- Absence of other control techniques considered appropriate for the type and level of transaction activity
- Evidence that a system fails to provide complete and accurate output that is consistent with objectives and current needs because of design flaws

Failures in the operation of internal control
- Evidence of failure of identified controls in preventing or detecting misstatements of accounting information
- Evidence that a system fails to provide complete and accurate output consistent with the entity's control objectives because of the misapplication of control procedures
- Evidence of failure to safeguard assets from loss, damage or misappropriation
- Evidence of intentional override of the internal control structure by those in authority to the detriment of the overall objectives of the system
- Evidence of failure to perform tasks that are part of the internal control structure, such as reconciliations not prepared or not timely prepared
- Evidence of willful wrongdoing by employees or management
- Evidence of manipulation, falsification, or alteration of accounting records or supporting documents
- Evidence of intentional misapplication of accounting principles
- Evidence of misrepresentation by client personnel to the auditor

C. Reporting—Form and Content
1. Conditions noted by the auditor that are considered reportable or that are the result of agreement with the client should be reported, preferably in writing.
2. If information is communicated orally, the auditor should document the communication by appropriate memoranda or notations in the working papers.
3. The report should state that the communication is intended solely for the information and the use of the audit committee, management, and others within the organization. When there are requirements established by governmental authorities to furnish such reports, specific reference to such regulatory authorities may be made.
4. Any report issued on reportable conditions should:
   a. Indicate that the purpose of the audit was to report on the financial statements and not to provide assurance on the internal control structure.
   b. Include the definition of reportable conditions.
   c. Include the restriction on distribution.
5. The following is an illustration of the report encompassing the above requirements:

> In planning and performing our audit of the financial statements of the ABC Corporation for the year ended December 31, 19XX, we considered its internal control in order to determine our auditing procedures for the purpose of expressing our opinion on the financial statements and not to provide assurance on the internal control structure. However, we noted certain matters involving internal control and its operation that we consider to be reportable conditions under standards established by the American Institute of Certified Public Accountants. Reportable conditions involve matters coming to our attention relating to significant deficiencies in the design or operation of internal control that, in our judgment, could adversely affect the organization's ability to record, process, summarize, and report financial data consistent with the assertions of management in the financial statements.
>
> *(Include paragraphs to describe the reportable conditions noted.)*
>
> This report is intended solely for the information and use of the audit committee (board of directors, board of trustees, or owners in owner-managed enterprises), management, and others within the organization (or specified regulatory agency or other specified third party).

6. Because of the potential for misrepresentation of the limited degree of assurance associated with the auditor issuing a written report representing that no reportable conditions were noted during an audit, the auditor should not issue such representations.

CONSIDERATION OF FRAUD IN A FINANCIAL STATEMENT AUDIT (SAS NO. 99)

I. **Description and Characteristics of Fraud**
   A. The primary factor that distinguishes fraud from error is whether the underlying action that results in the misstatement of the financial statements is intentional (fraud) or unintentional (error).

   B. Two types of misstatements are relevant to the auditor's consideration of fraud—misstatements arising from fraudulent financial reporting and misstatements arising from misappropriation of assets.
   1. Fraudulent financial reporting may be accomplished by the following:
      - Manipulation, falsification, or alteration of accounting records or supporting documents from which financial statements are prepared.
      - Misrepresentation in or intentional omission from the financial statements of events, transactions, or other significant information.
      - Intentional misapplication of accounting principles relating to amounts, classification, manner of presentation, or disclosure.

2. Misstatements arising from misappropriation of assets involve the theft of an entity's assets. Misappropriation of assets can be accomplished in various ways, including embezzling receipts, stealing assets, or causing an entity to pay for goods or services that have not been received.

C. Three conditions generally are present when fraud occurs:
   1. Management or other employees have an *incentive* or are under *pressure,* which provides a reason to commit fraud.
   2. Circumstances exist that provide an *opportunity* for a fraud to be perpetrated.
   3. Those involved are able to *rationalize* a fraudulent act as being consistent with their personal code of ethics.

D. Management and employees engaged in fraud will take steps to conceal the fraud from the auditors and others within and outside the organization. Fraud may be concealed by withholding evidence or misrepresenting information in response to inquiries or by falsifying documentation.

E. Fraud may also be concealed through collusion among management employees, or third parties.

F. Management has a unique ability to perpetrate fraud because it frequently is in a position to directly or indirectly manipulate accounting records and present fraudulent financial information.

G. The presence of certain conditions may suggest to the auditor the possibility that fraud may exist.
   1. An important contract may be missing
   2. A subsidiary ledger may not be satisfactorily reconciled to its control account, or
   3. The results of an analytical procedure performed during the audit may not be consistent with expectations.

II. Discussion Among Engagement Personnel Regarding the Risks of Material Misstatement Due to Fraud

A. In planning the audit, members of the audit team should discuss the potential for material misstatement due to fraud.

B. The discussion should include:
   1. A sharing of the insights of the more experienced audit team members, including the auditor (usually partner) with final responsibility for the audit, based on their knowledge of the entity's business and the industry in which it operates.
   2. Emphasizing the importance of maintaining the proper state of mind throughout the audit regarding the potential for material misstatement due to fraud (professional skepticism).

III. Obtaining the Information Needed to Identify the Risks of Material Misstatement Due to Fraud

The auditor should perform the following procedures to obtain information that is used to identify the risks of material misstatement due to fraud:

A. Make inquiries of management and others within the entity to obtain their views about the risks of fraud and how they are addressed.
   - Whether management has knowledge of any fraud that has been perpetrated or any alleged or suspected fraud
   - Whether management is aware of allegations of fraud, for example, because of communications from employees, former employees, analysts, short sellers, or other investors
   - Management's understanding about the risks of fraud in the entity, including any specific fraud risks the entity has identified or account balances or classes of transactions for which a risk of fraud may be likely to exist
   - Programs and controls the entity has established to mitigate specific fraud risks the entity has identified, or that otherwise help to prevent, deter, and detect fraud, and how management monitors those programs and controls
   - For an entity with multiple locations, *(a)* the nature and extent of monitoring of operating locations or business segments, and *(b)* whether there are particular operating locations or business segments for which a risk of fraud may be more likely to exist
   - Whether and how management communicates to employees its views on business practices and ethical behavior

B. Consider any unusual or unexpected relationships that have been identified in performing analytical procedures in planning the audit.

C. Perform analytical procedures specifically designed to determine fraud risk in the revenue/receivable cycle.

D. Consider whether one or more fraud risk factors exist.

1. **Risk factors relating to misstatements arising from fraudulent financial reporting.**

   Incentives/Pressures:
   a. Financial stability or profitability is threatened by economic, industry, or entity operating conditions, such as (or as indicated by):
      — High degree of competition or market saturation, accompanied by declining margins
      — High vulnerability to rapid changes, such as changes in technology, product obsolescence, or interest rates
      — Significant declines in customer demand and increasing business failures in either the industry or overall economy
      — Operating losses making the threat of bankruptcy, foreclosure, or hostile takeover imminent
      — Recurring negative cash flows from operations or an inability to generate cash flows from operations while reporting earnings and earnings growth
      — Rapid growth or unusual profitability, especially compared to that of other companies in the same industry
      — New accounting, statutory, or regulatory requirements
   b. Excessive pressure exists for management to meet the requirements or expectations of third parties due to the following:
      — Profitability or trend level expectations of investment analysts, institutional investors, significant creditors, or other external parties (particularly expectations that are unduly aggressive or unrealistic), including expectations created by management in, for example, overly optimistic press releases or annual report messages.
      — Need to obtain additional debt or equity financing to stay competitive including financing of major research and development or capital expenditures
      — Marginal ability to meet debt repayment or other debt covenant requirements
      — Perceived or real adverse effects of reporting poor financial results on significant pending transactions, such as business combinations or contract awards
   c. Management or the board of directors' personal net worth is threatened by the entity's financial performance arising from the following:
      — Heavy concentrations of their personal net worth in the entity
      — Significant portions of their compensation (for example, bonuses, stock options, and earn-out arrangements) being contingent upon achieving aggressive targets for stock price, operating results, financial position, or cash flow
      — Personal guarantees of debts of the entity that are significant to their personal net worth
   d. There is excessive pressure on management or operating personnel to meet financial targets set up by the board of directors or management, including sales or profitability incentive goals.

   Opportunities:
   a. The nature of the industry or the entity's operations provides opportunities to engage in fraudulent financial reporting that can arise from the following:
      — Significant related-party transactions not in the ordinary course of business or with related entities not audited or audited by another firm
      — Assets, liabilities, revenues, or expenses based on significant estimates that involve subjective judgments or uncertainties that are difficult to corroborate
      — Significant, unusual, or highly complex transactions, especially those close to year end that pose difficult "substance over form" questions
      — Significant operations located or conducted across international borders in jurisdictions where differing business environments and cultures exist

     — Significant bank accounts or subsidiary or branch operations in tax-haven jurisdictions for which there appears to be no clear business justification

b. There is ineffective monitoring of management as a result of the following:
     — Domination of management by a single person or small group (in a non-owner managed business) without compensating controls
     — Ineffective board of directors or audit committee oversight over the financial reporting process and internal control

c. There is a complex or unstable organizational structure as evidenced by the following:
     — Difficulty in determining the organization or individuals that have controlling interest in the entity
     — Overly complex organizational structure involving unusual legal entities or managerial lines of authority
     — High turnover of senior management, counsel, or board members

d. Internal control components are deficient as a result of the following:
     — Inadequate monitoring of controls, including automated controls and controls over interim financial reporting (where external reporting is required)
     — High turnover rates or employment of ineffective accounting, internal audit, or information technology staff
     — Ineffective accounting and information systems including situations involving reportable conditions

Attitudes/Rationalizations:

a. Ineffective communication and support of the entity's values or ethical standards by management or the communication of inappropriate values or ethical standards

b. Non-financial management's excessive participation in or preoccupation with the selection of accounting principles or the determination of significant estimates

2. **Risk factors relating to misappropriation of assets.**

Incentives/Pressures:

a. Personal financial obligations may create pressure on management or employees with access to cash or other assets susceptible to theft to misappropriate those assets.

b. Adverse relationships between the entity and employees with access to cash or other assets susceptible to theft may motivate those employees to misappropriate those assets. For example, adverse relationships may be created by the following:
     — Known or anticipated future employee layoffs
     — Promotions, compensation, expectations or other rewards inconsistent with expectations.

Opportunities:

a. Certain characteristics or circumstances may increase the susceptibility of assets to misappropriation. For example, opportunities to misappropriate assets increase when there are the following:
     — Large amounts of cash on hand or processed
     — Inventory items that are small in size, of high value, or in high demand
     — Easily convertible assets, such as bearer bonds, diamonds, or computer chips
     — Fixed assets that are small in size, marketable, or lacking observable identification of ownership

b. Inadequate internal control over assets may increase the susceptibility of misappropriation of those assets. For example, misappropriation of assets may occur because there is the following:
     — Inadequate segregation of duties or independent checks
     — Inadequate management oversight of employees responsible for assets; for example, inadequate supervision or monitoring of remote locations
     — Inadequate job applicant screening of employees with access to assets
     — Inadequate record keeping with respect to assets
     — Inadequate system of authorization and approval of transactions (for example, in purchasing)
     — Inadequate physical safeguards over cash, investments, inventory, or fixed assets

- Lack of timely and appropriate documentation of transactions; for example, credits for merchandise returns
- Lack of mandatory vacations for employees performing key control functions
- Inadequate management understanding of information technology, which enables information technology employees to perpetrate a misappropriation
- Inadequate access controls over automated records

Attitudes/Rationalizations:

Risk factors reflective of employee attitudes/rationalizations, that allow them to justify misappropriations of assets, are generally not susceptible to observation by the auditor. Nevertheless, the auditor who becomes aware of the existence of such information should consider it in identifying the risks of material misstatement arising from misappropriation of assets. For example, auditors may become aware of the following attitudes or behavior of employees who have access to assets susceptible to misappropriation:

- Disregard for the need for monitoring or reducing risks related to misappropriations of assets
- Disregard for internal control over misappropriation of assets by overriding existing controls or by failing to correct known internal control deficiencies
- Behavior indicating displeasure or dissatisfaction with the company or its treatment of the employee
- Changes in behavior or lifestyle that may indicate assets have been misappropriated

IV. Identifying Risks That May Result in a Material Misstatement Due to Fraud

A. The auditor should use the information obtained from the procedures described in **III.** to determine material misstatement due to fraud. The identification process involves the application of professional judgment and includes consideration of a number of factors, including:

1. The *type* of risk that may exist; that is, whether it involves fraudulent financial reporting or misappropriation of assets.
2. The *significance* of the risk; that is, whether it is of a magnitude that could result in a possible material misstatement of the financial statements.
3. The *likelihood* of the risk; that is, the likelihood that it will result in a material misstatement in the financial statements.
4. The *pervasiveness* of the risk; that is, whether the potential risk is pervasive to the financial statements as a whole or specifically related to a particular assertion, account, or class of transactions.

V. Responding to the Results of the Assessment

A. The auditor responds to risks of material misstatement due to fraud in the following three ways:

1. A response to identified risks that has an overall effect on how the audit is conducted—that is, a response involving more general considerations apart from the specific procedures otherwise planned.
2. A response to identified risks involving the nature, timing, and extent of the auditing procedures to be performed.
3. A response involving the performance of certain procedures to further address the risk of material misstatement due to fraud involving management override of controls, given the unpredictable ways in which such override could occur.

VI. Evaluating Audit Test Results

A. Conditions may be identified during fieldwork that change or support a judgment regarding the assessment of the risks, such as the following:

1. Discrepancies in the accounting records, including:
   - Transactions that are not recorded in a complete or timely manner or are improperly recorded as to amount, accounting period, classification, or entity policy
   - Unsupported or unauthorized balances or transactions
   - Last-minute adjustments that significantly affect financial results
   - Evidence of employees' access to systems and records inconsistent with that necessary to perform their authorized duties

2. Conflicting or missing evidential matter, including:
   — Missing documents
   — Unavailability of other than photocopied or electronically transmitted documents when documents in original form are expected to exist.
   — Significant unexplained items on reconciliations
   — Inconsistent, vague, or implausible responses from management or employees arising from inquiries or analytical procedures
   — Unusual discrepancies between the entity's records and confirmation replies
   — Missing inventory or physical assets of significant magnitude.
   — Unavailable or missing electronic evidence, inconsistent with the entity's record retention practices or policies
   — Inability to produce evidence of key systems development and program change testing and implementation activities for current-year system changes and deployments
3. Problematic or unusual relationships between the auditor and client, including:
   — Denial of access to records, facilities, certain employees, customers, vendors, or others from whom audit evidence might be sought
   — Undue time pressures imposed by management to resolve complex or contentious issues
   — Complaints by management about the conduct of the audit or management intimidation of audit team members, particularly in connection with the auditor's critical assessment of audit evidence or in the resolution of potential disagreements with management
   — Unusual delays by the entity in providing requested information
   — Tips or complaints to the auditor about alleged fraud
   — Unwillingness to facilitate auditor access to key electronic files for testing through the use of computer-assisted audit techniques
   — Denial of access to key IT operations staff and facilities, including security, operations, and systems development personnel

B. Responding to misstatements that may be the result of fraud:
   1. If the auditor believes that the misstatement is or may be the result of fraud, and either has determined that the effect could be material to the financial statements or has been unable to evaluate whether the effect is material, the auditor should:
      a. Consider the implications for other aspects of the audit.
      b. Discuss the matter and the approach for further investigation with an appropriate level of management that is at least one level above those involved, and with senior management and the audit committee.
      c. Attempt to obtain additional evidential matter to determine whether material fraud has occurred or is likely to have occurred, and, if so, its effect on the financial statements and the auditor's report thereon.
      d. Consider the need for and timing of discussions with the audit committee or board of directors.
      e. If appropriate, suggest that the client consult with legal counsel.
   2. The auditor's consideration of the risks of material misstatement and the results of audit tests may indicate such a significant risk of material misstatement due to fraud that the auditor should consider withdrawing from the engagement and communicating the reasons for withdrawal to the audit committee or others with equivalent authority and responsibility.

VII. Communicating About Possible Fraud to Management, the Audit Committee, and Others

A. Whenever the auditor has determined that there is evidence that fraud may exist, that matter should be brought to the attention of an appropriate level of management. This is appropriate even if the matter might be considered inconsequential, such as a minor defalcation by an employee at a low level in the entity's organization. Fraud involving senior management and fraud (whether caused by senior management or other employees) that causes a material misstatement of the financial statements should be reported directly to the audit committee. In addition, the auditor should reach an understanding with the audit committee regarding the nature and extent of communications about misappropriations perpetrated by lower-level employees.

B. If the auditor, as a result of the assessment of the risks of material misstatement, has identified risks of material misstatement due to fraud that have continuing control implications (whether or not transactions or adjustments that could be the result of fraud have been detected), the auditor should consider whether these risks represent reportable conditions relating to the entity's internal control that should be communicated to senior management and the audit committee.

C. The disclosure of possible fraud to parties other than the client's senior management and its audit committee ordinarily is not part of the auditor's responsibility and ordinarily would be precluded by the auditor's ethical or legal obligations of confidentiality unless the matter is reflected in the auditor's report. The auditor should recognize, however, that in the following circumstances a duty to disclose to parties outside the entity may exist:
   1. To comply with certain legal and regulatory requirements
   2. To a successor auditor when the successor makes inquiries in accordance with SAS No. 84, *Communications Between Predecessor and Successor Auditors*
   3. In response to a subpoena
   4. To a funding agency or other specified agency in accordance with requirements for the audits of entities that receive governmental financial assistance

VIII. Documenting the Auditor's Consideration of Fraud
A. The auditor should document the following:
   1. The discussion among engagement personnel in planning the audit regarding the susceptibility of the entity's financial statements to material misstatement due to fraud, including how and when the discussion occurred, the audit team members who participated, and the subject matter discussed
   2. The procedures performed to obtain information necessary to identify and assess the risks of material misstatement due to fraud
   3. Specific risks of material misstatement due to fraud that were identified, and a description of the auditor's response to those risks
   4. If the auditor concludes that the performance of some or all of the additional procedures to further address the risk of management override of controls was unnecessary in a particular circumstance, the reasons supporting the auditor's conclusion
   5. Other conditions that caused the auditor to believe that additional auditing procedures or other responses were required, and any further responses the auditor concluded were appropriate, to address such risks or other conditions
   6. The nature of the communications about fraud made to management, the audit committee, and others

ILLEGAL ACTS BY CLIENTS (SAS NO. 54)

I. Definition of Illegal Acts
A. Refers to *violations of laws or governmental regulations*.
B. May be entered into on behalf of the entity being audited by management or employees.

II. Relation of Illegal Acts to the Financial Statements
A. Two types of illegal acts:
   1. Acts having a direct material effect on the financial statements. Examples include: tax laws affecting accrual of taxes, government regulations affecting the profit to be earned on government contracts.
      a) The auditor is more apt to discover this type of illegal act since they are usually related to the audit of specific amounts on the financial statements.
   2. Acts having an indirect effect on the financial statements. Examples include laws relating to occupational safety and health, environmental protection, etc.
      a) The auditor may not become aware of these acts unless he is informed by the client of the existence of the illegal act or of a governmental investigation.

B. Specific audit procedures may bring possible illegal acts to the auditor's attention. These include:
   1. Reading minutes
   2. Inquiry of client's legal counsel
   3. Inquiries of management and employees

C. Specific information gathered during the audit that may be indicative of an illegal act:
- Unauthorized transactions, improperly recorded transactions, or transactions not recorded in a complete or timely manner in order to maintain accountability for assets
- Investigation by a governmental agency, an enforcement proceeding, or payment of unusual fines or penalties
- Violations of laws or regulations cited in reports of examinations by regulatory agencies that have been made available to the auditor
- Large payments for unspecified services to consultants, affiliates, or employees
- Sales commissions or agents' fees that appear excessive in relation to those normally paid by the client or to the services actually received
- Unusually large payments in cash, purchases of bank cashiers' checks in large amounts payable to bearer, transfers to numbered bank accounts, or similar transactions
- Unexplained payments made to government officials or employees
- Failure to file tax returns or pay government duties or similar fees that are common to the entity's industry or the nature of its business.

D. Communications concerning illegal acts

After it has been determined that an illegal act has occurred, the auditor should report the circumstances to personnel within the client's organization at a high enough level of authority so that appropriate action can be taken by the client with respect to:

a. Consideration of remedial actions.
b. Adjustments or disclosures that may be necessary in the financial statements.
c. Disclosures that may be required in other documents (such as a proxy statement).

In some circumstances, the only persons in the organization of a sufficiently high level of authority to take necessary action may be the audit committee or the board of directors. The auditor should also consider the implications of an illegal act in relation to the intended degree of reliance to be placed on internal accounting control and the representations of management.

III. Effects On the Auditor's Report

The auditor may not be able to determine the amounts associated with certain events, taken alone or with similar events, of which he becomes aware, or whether an act is, in fact, illegal because of inability to obtain sufficient competent evidential matter. In those circumstances, the auditor should consider the need to qualify his opinion or disclaim an opinion because of the scope limitation.

If the auditor concludes that the effect of an event, taken alone or with similar events, is material in amount and that the event has not been properly accounted for or disclosed in the financial statements, he should qualify his opinion or express an adverse opinion because of the departure from generally accepted accounting principles.

The auditor may conclude that an illegal act's effects on the financial statements are not susceptible of reasonable estimation. When such an uncertainty exists, the auditor should consider the need to modify his report.

If the client informs the auditor that it will refuse to accept an auditor's report that has been modified for the reasons cited above, the auditor should withdraw from the current engagement, indicating the reasons for his withdrawal in writing to the board of directors. In such circumstances, the auditor may wish to consult with his legal counsel.

THE AUDITOR'S CONSIDERATION OF THE INTERNAL AUDIT FUNCTION IN AN AUDIT OF FINANCIAL STATEMENTS (SAS NO. 65)

The work of internal auditors cannot be substituted for the work of the independent auditor; however, the independent auditor should consider the procedures, if any, performed by internal auditors in determining the nature, timing, and extent of his own auditing procedures.

Internal auditors often perform a number of services for management, including, but not limited to, studying and evaluating internal accounting control, reviewing operating practices to promote increased efficiency and economy, and making special inquiries at management's direction.

The independent auditor should acquire an understanding of the internal audit function as it relates to the expression of an opinion on the financial statements.

Requirements

A. As part of obtaining an understanding of the internal control structure, the auditor should obtain an understanding of the internal audit function sufficient to identify those internal audit activities that are relevant to planning the audit.
   1. *Relevant activities* are those that provide evidence about the design and effectiveness of policies and procedures that pertain to the entity's ability to record, process, summarize, and report financial data. (An example of internal audit activities that are not relevant is procedures to test the efficiency of management decision-making processes.)
   2. The extent of procedures necessary to obtain the understanding varies based on the circumstances.

B. If, after obtaining an understanding of the internal audit function, the auditor concludes that the internal auditors' activities are not relevant to the financial statement audit, the auditor does not have to give further consideration to the function.
   1. Even if some internal audit activities are relevant to the audit, the auditor is still permitted to conclude that it would not be an efficient audit approach to consider the work of the internal auditors further.
   2. Additional consideration of how the internal auditors' work might affect the nature, timing and extent of audit procedures may be an efficient approach, for example, if the internal auditors have already performed procedures that the auditor would have to reperform.

C. If the auditor decides further consideration is efficient, the auditor should assess the competence and objectivity of the internal audit function in light of the intended effect of the internal auditors' work on the audit. The auditor should perform procedures to evaluate the quality and effectiveness of the internal auditors' work that significantly affects the nature, timing and extent of the auditor's procedures.

D. In addition, the auditor may request direct assistance from the internal auditors in performing the audit. When direct assistance is provided, the auditor should
   1. consider the internal auditors' competence and objectivity and
   2. supervise, review, evaluate, and test their work.

Reviewing the Competence and Objectivity of Internal Auditors

When considering the competence of internal auditors, the independent auditor should inquire about the **qualifications of the internal audit staff**, including, for example, consideration of the client's practices for hiring, training, and supervising the internal audit staff.

When considering the **objectivity** of internal auditors, **the independent auditor should consider the organizational level to which internal auditors report the results of their work and the organizational level to which they report administratively**. This frequently is an indication of the extent of their ability to act independently of the individuals responsible for the functions being audited. **One method for judging internal auditors' objectivity is to review the recommendations made in their reports.**

Evaluating the Work of Internal Auditors

In evaluating the work of internal auditors, **the independent auditor should examine, on a test basis, documentary evidence of the work performed by internal auditors** and should consider such factors as whether the scope of the work is appropriate, audit programs are adequate, working papers adequately document work performed, conclusions reached are appropriate in the circumstances, and any reports prepared are consistent with the results of the work performed. **The independent auditor should also perform tests of some of the work of internal auditors.** The extent of these tests will vary depending on the circumstances, including the type of transactions and their materiality. These tests may be accomplished by either (a) examining some of the transactions or balances that internal auditors examined, or (b) examining similar transactions or balances but not those actually examined by internal auditors. The independent auditor should compare the results of his tests with the results of the internal auditors' work in reaching conclusions on that work.

Arrangements With Internal Auditors

When the work of internal auditors is expected to be significant to the independent auditor's study and evaluation of internal accounting control, the independent auditor should, at the outset of the engagement, inform internal auditors of the reports and working papers he will need. He should also consult with internal auditors concerning work they are performing, since work not yet completed may also have a bearing on his examination. Also, work done by internal auditors will frequently be more useful to the independent auditor if plans for the work are discussed in advance.

Using Internal Auditors to Provide Direct Assistance to the Independent Auditor

The independent auditor may make use of internal auditors to provide direct assistance in performing an examination in accordance with generally accepted auditing standards. Internal auditors may assist in performing substantive tests or tests of compliance. When the independent auditor makes such use of internal auditors, he should consider their competence and objectivity and supervise and test their work to the extent appropriate in the circumstances.

Judgments on Audit Matters

When the independent auditor considers the work of internal auditors in determining the nature, timing, and extent of his own audit procedures, or when internal auditors provide direct assistance in the performance of his work, judgments as to the effectiveness of internal accounting control, sufficiency of tests performed, materiality of transactions, and other matters affecting his report on the financial statements, must be those of the independent auditor.

Chapter One – Questions
Introduction, General and Field Standards

1. Tests of controls are performed in order to determine whether or not
a. Controls are functioning as designed.
b. Necessary controls are absent.
c. Incompatible functions exist.
d. Material dollar errors exist.

2. For good internal accounting control, which of the following functions should **not** be the responsibility of the treasurer's department?
a. Data processing.
b. Handling of cash.
c. Custody of securities.
d. Establishing credit policies.

3. During an audit an internal auditor may provide direct assistance to an independent CPA in

	Obtaining an understanding of the internal control structure	Performing tests of controls	Performing substantive tests
a.	No	No	No
b.	Yes	No	No
c.	Yes	Yes	No
d.	Yes	Yes	Yes

4. Which of the following statements regarding auditor documentation of the client's system of internal control is correct?
a. Documentation must include flow charts.
b. Documentation must include procedural writeups.
c. No documentation is necessary although it is desirable.
d. No one particular form of documentation is necessary, and the extent of documentation may vary.

5. It would be appropriate for the payroll accounting department to be responsible for which of the following functions?
a. Approval of employee time records.
b. Maintenance of records of employment, discharges, and pay increases.
c. Preparation of periodic governmental reports as to employees' earnings and withholding taxes.
d. Distribution of pay checks to employees.

6. Operating control over the check signature plate normally should be the responsibility of the
a. Secretary.
b. Chief accountant.
c. Vice president of finance.
d. Treasurer.

7. Internal control over cash receipts is weakened when an employee who receives customer mail receipts also
a. Prepares initial cash receipts records.
b. Records credits to individual accounts receivable.
c. Prepares bank deposit slips for all mail receipts.
d. Maintains a petty cash fund.

8. Which of the following **best** describes proper internal control over payroll?
a. The preparation of the payroll must be under the control of the personnel department.
b. The confidentiality of employee payroll data should be carefully protected to prevent fraud.
c. The duties of hiring, payroll computation, and payment to employees should be segregated.
d. The payment of cash to employees should be replaced with payment by checks.

9. Transaction authorization within an organization may be either specific or general. An example of specific transaction authorization is the
a. Establishment of requirements to be met in determining a customer's credit limits.
b. Setting of automatic reorder points for material or merchandise.
c. Approval of a detailed construction budget for a warehouse.
d. Establishment of sales prices for products to be sold to any customer.

10. Effective internal control over purchases generally can be achieved in a well-planned organizational structure with a separate purchasing department that has
a. The ability to prepare payment vouchers based on the information on a vendor's invoice.
b. The responsibility of reviewing purchase orders issued by user departments.
c. The authority to make purchases of requisitioned materials and services.
d. A direct reporting responsibility to the controller of the organization.

11. An example of an internal control weakness is to assign to a department supervisor the responsibility for
a. Reviewing and approving time reports for subordinate employees.
b. Initiating requests for salary adjustments for subordinate employees.
c. Authorizing payroll checks for terminated employees.
d. Distributing payroll checks to subordinate employees.

12. The independent auditor should acquire an understanding of a client's internal audit function to determine whether the work of internal auditors will be a factor in determining the nature, timing, and extent of the independent auditor's procedures. The work performed by internal auditors might be such a factor when the internal auditor's work includes
a. Verification of the mathematical accuracy of invoices.
b. Review of administrative practices to improve efficiency and achieve management objectives.
c. Study and evaluation of internal accounting control.
d. Preparation of internal financial reports for management purposes.

13. It is important for the CPA to consider the competence of the audit clients' employees because their competence bears directly and importantly upon the
a. Cost/benefit relationship of the system of internal control.
b. Achievement of the objectives of the system of internal control.
c. Comparison of recorded accountability with assets.
d. Timing of the tests to be performed.

14. Which of the following would be **least** likely to be included in an auditor's tests of controls?
a. Inspection.
b. Observation.
c. Inquiry.
d. Confirmation.

15. Tests of controls are concerned primarily with each of the following questions **except**
a. How were the procedures performed?
b. Why were the procedures performed?
c. Were the necessary procedures performed?
d. By whom were the procedures performed?

16. Which of the following is a primary function of the purchasing department?
a. Authorizing the acquisition of goods.
b. Ensuring the acquisition of goods of a specified quality.
c. Verifying the propriety of goods acquired.
d. Reducing expenditures for goods acquired.

17. An auditor uses the knowledge provided by the understanding of internal control and the final assessed level of control risk primarily to determine the nature, timing, and extent of the
a. Attribute tests.
b. Compliance tests.
c. Tests of controls.
d. Substantive tests.

18. When control risk is assessed at the maximum level for all financial statement assertions, an auditor should document the auditor's

	Understanding of the entity's internal control components	*Conclusion that control risk is at the maximum level*	*Basis for concluding that control risk is at the maximum level*
a.	Yes	No	No
b.	Yes	Yes	No
c.	No	Yes	Yes
d.	Yes	Yes	Yes

19. Which of the following controls would be most effective in assuring that recorded purchases are free of material errors?
a. The receiving department compares the quantity ordered on purchase orders with the quantity received on receiving reports.
b. Vendors' invoices are compared with purchase orders by an employee who is independent of the receiving department.
c. Receiving reports require the signature of the individual who authorized the purchase.
d. Purchase orders, receiving reports, and vendors' invoices are independently matched in preparing vouchers.

20. Which of the following statements concerning material weaknesses and reportable conditions is correct?
a. An auditor should identify and communicate material weaknesses separately from reportable conditions.
b. All material weaknesses are reportable conditions.
c. An auditor should report immediately material weaknesses and reportable conditions discovered during an audit.
d. All reportable conditions are material weaknesses.

21. The auditor may observe the distribution of paychecks to ascertain whether
a. Payrate authorization is properly separated from the operating function.
b. Deductions from gross pay are calculated correctly and are properly authorized.
c. Employees of record actually exist and are employed by the client.
d. Paychecks agree with the payroll register and the time cards.

22. A flowchart is most frequently used by an auditor in connection with the
a. Preparation of generalized computer audit programs.
b. Documentation of the client's internal control procedures.
c. Use of statistical sampling in performing an audit.
d. Performance of analytical review procedures of account balances.

23. An auditor's purpose for performing tests of controls is to provide reasonable assurance that
a. The controls on which the auditor plans to rely are being applied as perceived during the preliminary evaluation.
b. The risk that the auditor may unknowingly fail to modify the opinion on the financial statements is minimized.
c. Transactions are executed in accordance with management's authorization and access to assets is limited by a segregation of functions.
d. Transactions are recorded as necessary to permit the preparation of the financial statements in conformity with generally accepted accounting principles.

24. An auditor would consider internal control over a client's payroll procedures to be ineffective if the payroll department supervisor is responsible for
a. Hiring subordinate payroll department employees.
b. Having custody over unclaimed paychecks.
c. Updating employee earnings records.
d. Applying pay rates to time tickets.

25. Which of the following departments should have the responsibility for authorizing payroll rate changes?
a. Personnel.
b. Payroll.
c. Treasurer.
d. Timekeeping.

26. When considering the objectivity of internal auditors, an independent auditor should
a. Evaluate the quality control program in effect for the internal auditors.
b. Examine documentary evidence of the work performed by the internal auditors.
c. Test a sample of the transactions and balances that the internal auditors examined.
d. Determine the organizational level to which the internal auditors report.

27. Internal control procedures are strengthened when the quantity of merchandise ordered is omitted from the copy of the purchase order sent to the
a. Department that initiated the requisition.
b. Receiving department.
c. Purchasing agent.
d. Accounts payable department.

28. An effective system of control procedures over the payroll function would include
a. Verification of agreement of job time tickets with employee clock card hours by a payroll department employee.
b. Reconciliation of totals on job time tickets with job reports by employees responsible for those specific jobs.
c. Custody of rate authorization records by the supervisor of the payroll department.
d. Preparation of payroll transaction journal entries by an employee who reports to the supervisor of the personnel department.

29. Which of the following procedures in the cash disbursements cycle should **not** be performed by the accounts payable department?
a. Comparing the vendor's invoice with the receiving report.
b. Canceling supporting documentation after payment.
c. Verifying the mathematical accuracy of the vendor's invoice.
d. Signing the voucher for payment by an authorized person.

30. Which of the following is not a reason an auditor should obtain an understanding of the components of an entity's internal control in planning an audit?
a. Identify the types of potential misstatements that can occur.
b. Design substantive tests.
c. Consider the operating effectiveness of the internal control structure.
d. Consider factors that affect the risk of material misstatements.

31. Which of the following is not a component of an entity's internal control?
a. Control risk.
b. Control procedures.
c. Information and communication.
d. The control environment.

32. When goods are received, the receiving clerk should match the goods with the
a. Purchase order and the requisition form.
b. Vendor's invoice and the receiving report.
c. Vendor's shipping document and the purchase order.
d. Receiving report and the vendor's shipping document.

33. The mailing of disbursement checks and remittance advices should be controlled by the employee who
a. Signed the checks last.
b. Approved the vouchers for payment.
c. Matched the receiving reports, purchase orders, and vendors' invoices.
d. Verified the mathematical accuracy of the vouchers and remittance advices.

34. Which of the following statements is correct concerning an auditor's communication of internal control structure related matters (reportable conditions) noted in an audit?
a. The auditor may issue a written report to the audit committee representing that no reportable conditions were noted during the audit.
b. Reportable conditions should be recommunicated each year even if the audit committee has acknowledged its understanding of such efficiencies.
c. Reportable conditions may not be communicated in a document that contains suggestions regarding activities that concern other topics such as business strategies or administrative efficiencies.
d. The auditor may choose to communicate significant internal control structure related matters either during the course of the audit or after the audit is concluded.

35. An auditor uses the knowledge provided by the understanding of internal control and the assessed level of control risk primarily to
a. Determine whether procedures and records concerning the safeguarding of assets are reliable.
b. Ascertain whether the opportunities to allow any person to both perpetrate and conceal irregularities are minimized.
c. Modify the initial assessments of inherent risk and preliminary judgments about materiality levels.
d. Determine the nature, timing, and extent of substantive tests for financial statement assertions.

36. An auditor's flowchart of a client's accounting system is a diagrammatic representation that depicts the auditor's
a. Program for tests of controls.
b. Understanding of the system.
c. Understanding of the types of irregularities that are probable, given the present system.
d. Documentation of the study and evaluation of the system.

37. After obtaining an understanding of an entity's internal control and assessing control risk, an auditor may next

a. Perform tests of controls to verify management's assertions that are embodied in the financial statements.
b. Consider whether evidential matter is available to support a further reduction in the assessed level of control risk.
c. Apply analytical procedures as substantive tests to validate the assessed level of control risk.
d. Evaluate whether the internal control structure policies and procedures detected material misstatements in the financial statements.

38. An internal control narrative indicates that an approved voucher is required to support every check request for payment of merchandise. Which of the following procedures provides the greatest assurance that this control is operating effectively?

a. Select and examine vouchers and ascertain that the related canceled checks are dated no later than the vouchers.
b. Select and examine vouchers and ascertain that the related canceled checks are dated no earlier than the vouchers.
c. Select and examine canceled checks and ascertain that the related vouchers are dated no earlier than the checks.
d. Select and examine canceled checks and ascertain that the related vouchers are dated no later than the checks.

39. For effective internal control purposes, the vouchers payable department generally should

a. Stamp, perforate, or otherwise cancel supporting documentation after payment is mailed.
b. Ascertain that each requisition is approved as to price, quantity, and quality by an authorized employee.
c. Obliterate the quantity ordered on the receiving department copy of the purchase order.
d. Establish the agreement of the vendor's invoice with the receiving report and purchase order.

40. A weakness in internal control over recording retirements of equipment may cause an auditor to

a. Trace additions to the "other assets" account to search for equipment that is still on hand but no longer being used.
b. Select certain items of equipment from the accounting records and locate them in the plant.
c. Inspect certain items of equipment in the plant and trace those items to the accounting records.
d. Review the subsidiary ledger to ascertain whether depreciation was taken on each item of equipment during the year.

41. Reportable conditions are matters that come to an auditor's attention, which should be communicated to an entity's audit committee because they represent

a. Material irregularities or illegal acts perpetrated by high-level management.
b. Significant deficiencies in the design or operation of the internal control structure.
c. Flagrant violations of the entity's documented conflict-of-interest policies.
d. Intentional attempts by client personnel to limit the scope of the auditor's field work.

42. Which of the following components of an entity's internal control includes the development of personnel manuals documenting employee promotion and training policies?

a. Control procedures.
b. Control environment.
c. Accounting system.
d. Quality control system.

43. After obtaining an understanding of an entity's internal control structure, an auditor may assess control risk at the maximum level for some assertions because the auditor

a. Believes the internal control policies and procedures are unlikely to be effective.
b. Determines that the pertinent internal control structure elements are not well documented.
c. Performs tests of controls to restrict detection risk to an acceptable level.
d. Identifies internal control policies and procedures that are likely to prevent material misstatements.

44. Which of the following control activities is not usually performed in the vouchers payable department?

a. Determining the mathematical accuracy of the vendor's invoice.
b. Having an authorized person approve the voucher.
c. Controlling the mailing of the check and remittance advice.
d. Matching the receiving report with the purchase order.

45. The primary objective of procedures performed to obtain an understanding of internal control is to provide an auditor with

a. Evidential matter to use in reducing detection risk.
b. Knowledge necessary to plan the audit.
c. A basis from which to modify tests of controls.
d. Information necessary to prepare flowcharts.

46. When assessing an internal auditor's objectivity, an independent auditor should

a. Evaluate the adequacy of the internal auditor's audit programs.
b. Inquire about the internal auditor's educational background and professional certification.
c. Consider the organizational level to which the internal auditor reports.
d. Review the internal auditor's working papers.

47. When considering internal control, an auditor should be aware of the concept of reasonable assurance, which recognizes that

a. Procedures requiring segregation of duties may be circumvented by employee collusion and management override.
b. Establishing and maintaining the internal control structure is an important responsibility of management.
c. The cost of an entity's internal control structure should **not** exceed the benefits expected to be derived.
d. Adequate safeguards over access to assets and records should permit an entity to maintain proper accountability.

48. Proper authorization procedures in the revenue cycle usually provide for the approval of bad debt write-offs by an employee in which of the following departments?

a. Treasurer.
b. Sales.
c. Billing.
d. Accounts receivable.

49. An auditor assesses control risk because it

a. Indicates where inherent risk may be the greatest.
b. Affects the level of detection risk the auditor may accept.
c. Determines whether sampling risk is sufficiently low.
d. Includes the aspects of nonsampling risk that are controllable.

50. When considering the objectivity of internal auditors, an independent auditor should

a. Test a sample of the transactions and balances that the internal auditors examined.
b. Determine the organizational level to which the internal auditors report.
c. Evaluate the quality control program in effect for the internal auditors.
d. Examine documentary evidence of the work performed by the internal auditors.

51. In an audit of financial statements in accordance with generally accepted auditing standards, an auditor is required to

a. Identify specific internal control procedures relevant to management's financial statement assertions.
b. Perform tests of controls to evaluate the effectiveness of the entity's accounting system.
c. Determine whether procedures are suitably designed to prevent or detect material misstatements.
d. Document the auditor's understanding of the entity's internal control.

52. The acceptable level of detection risk is inversely related to the

a. Assurance provided by substantive tests.
b. Risk of misapplying auditing procedures.
c. Preliminary judgment about materiality levels.
d. Risk of failing to discover material misstatements.

53. When an auditor becomes aware of a possible client illegal act, the auditor should obtain an understanding of the nature of the act to

a. Increase the assessed level of control risk.
b. Recommend remedial actions to the audit committee.
c. Evaluate the effect on the financial statements.
d. Determine the reliability of management's representations.

54. As the acceptable level of detection risk decreases, the assurance directly provided from

a. Substantive tests should increase.
b. Substantive tests should decrease.
c. Tests of controls should increase.
d. Tests of controls should decrease.

55. Mailing disbursement checks and remittance advices should be controlled by the employee who
a. Approves the vouchers for payment.
b. Matches the receiving reports, purchase orders, and vendors' invoices.
c. Maintains possession of the mechanical check-signing device.
d. Signs the checks last.

56. Immediately upon receipt of cash, a responsible employee should
a. Record the amount in the cash receipts journal.
b. Prepare a remittance listing.
c. Update the subsidiary accounts receivable records.
d. Prepare a deposit slip in triplicate.

57. What is the meaning of the generally accepted auditing standard which requires that the auditor be independent?
a. The auditor must be without bias with respect to the client under audit.
b. The auditor must adopt a critical attitude during the audit.
c. The auditor's sole obligation is to third parties.
d. The auditor may have a direct ownership interest in his client's business if it is not material.

58. What is the general character of the three generally accepted auditing standards classified as general standards?
a. Criteria for competence, independence, and professional care of individuals performing the audit.
b. Criteria for the content of the financial statements and related footnote disclosures.
c. Criteria for the content of the auditor's report on financial statements and related footnote disclosures.
d. The requirements for the planning of the audit and supervision of assistants, if any.

59. The accuracy of information included in footnotes that accompany the audited financial statements of a company whose shares are traded on a stock exchange is the primary responsibility of
a. The stock exchange officials.
b. The independent auditor.
c. The company's management.
d. The Securities and Exchange Commission.

60. A CPA is most likely to refer to one or more of the three general auditing standards in determining
a. The nature of the CPA's report qualification.
b. The scope of the CPA's auditing procedures.
c. Requirements for the review of internal control.
d. Whether the CPA should undertake an audit engagement.

61. Which of the following criteria is unique to the auditor's attest function?
a. General competence.
b. Familiarity with the particular industry of which his client is a part.
c. Due professional care.
d. Independence.

62. The auditor's report may be addressed to the company whose financial statements are being examined or to that company's
a. Chief operating officer.
b. President.
c. Board of Directors.
d. Chief financial officer.

63. When a CPA is approached to perform an audit for the first time, the CPA should make inquiries of the predecessor auditor. This is a necessary procedure because the predecessor may be able to provide the successor with information that will assist the successor in determining
a. Whether the predecessor's work should be utilized.
b. Whether the company follows the policy of rotating its auditors.
c. Whether in the predecessor's opinion internal control of the company has been satisfactory.
d. Whether the engagement should be accepted.

64. Preliminary arrangements agreed to by the auditor and the client should be reduced to writing by the auditor. The **best** place to set forth these arrangements is in
a. A memorandum to be placed in the permanent section of the auditing working papers.
b. An engagement letter.
c. A client representation letter.
d. A confirmation letter attached to the constructive services letter.

65. The element of the audit planning process most likely to be agreed upon with the client before implementation of the audit strategy is the determination of the

a. Methods of statistical sampling to be used in confirming accounts receivable.
b. Pending legal matters to be included in the inquiry of the client's attorney.
c. Evidence to be gathered to provide a sufficient basis for the auditor's opinion.
d. Schedules and analyses to be prepared by the client's staff.

66. Which of the following standards requires a critical review of the work done and the judgment exercised by those assisting in an audit at every level of supervision?

a. Proficiency.
b. Audit risk.
c. Inspection.
d. Due care.

67. Which of the following procedures would an auditor most likely perform in planning a financial statement audit?

a. Reviewing investment transactions of the audit period to determine whether related parties were created.
b. Performing analytical procedures to identify areas that may represent specific risks.
c. Reading the minutes of stockholder and director meetings to discover whether any unusual transactions have occurred.
d. Obtaining a written representation letter from the client to emphasize management's responsibilities.

68. Before accepting an audit engagement, a successor auditor should make specific inquiries of the predecessor auditor regarding

a. Disagreements the predecessor had with the client concerning auditing procedures and accounting principles.
b. The predecessor's evaluation of matters of continuing accounting significance.
c. The degree of cooperation the predecessor received concerning the inquiry of the client's lawyer.
d. The predecessor's assessments of inherent risk and judgments about materiality.

69. To exercise due professional care an auditor should

a. Attain the proper balance of professional experience and formal education.
b. Design the audit to detect all instances of illegal acts.
c. Critically review the judgment exercised by those assisting in the audit.
d. Examine all available corroborating evidence supporting management's assertions.

70. When an auditor becomes aware of a possible illegal act by a client, the auditor should obtain an understanding of the nature of the act to

a. Evaluate the effect on the financial statements.
b. Determine the reliability of management's representations.
c. Consider whether other similar acts may have occurred.
d. Recommend remedial actions to the audit committee.

71. The ultimate purpose of assessing control risk is to contribute to the auditor's evaluation of the risk that

a. Specified controls requiring segregation of duties may be circumvented by collusion.
b. Entity policies may be overridden by senior management.
c. Tests of controls may fail to identify procedures relevant to assertions.
d. Material misstatements may exist in the financial statements.

72. An auditor's primary consideration regarding an entity's internal control policies and procedures is whether the policies and procedures

a. Affect the financial statement assertions.
b. Prevent management override.
c. Relate to the control environment.
d. Reflect management's philosophy and operating style.

73. Which of the following controls most likely would help ensure that all credit sales transactions of an entity are recorded?

a. The billing department supervisor sends copies of approved sales orders to the credit department for comparison to authorized credit limits and current customer account balances.
b. The accounting department supervisor independently reconciles the accounts receivable subsidiary ledger to the accounts receivable control account monthly.
c. The accounting department supervisor controls the mailing of monthly statements to customers and investigates any differences reported by customers.
d. The billing department supervisor matches prenumbered shipping documents with entries in the sales journal.

74. An entity with a large volume of customer remittances by mail could most likely reduce the risk of employee misappropriation of cash by using

a. Employee fidelity bonds.
b. Independently prepared mailroom prelists.
c. Daily check summaries.
d. A bank lockbox system.

75. For effective internal control, the accounts payable department generally should

a. Obliterate the quantity ordered on the receiving department copy of the purchase order.
b. Establish the agreement of the vendor's invoice with the receiving report and purchase order.
c. Stamp, perforate, or otherwise cancel supporting documentation after payment is mailed.
d. Ascertain that each requisition is approved as to price, quantity, and quality by an authorized employee.

76. When the shipping department returns nonconforming goods to a vendor, the purchasing department should send to the accounting department the

a. Unpaid voucher.
b. Debit memo.
c. Vendor invoice.
d. Credit memo.

77. An entity's internal control requires for every check request that there be an approved voucher, supported by a prenumbered purchase order and a prenumbered receiving report. To determine whether checks are being issued for unauthorized expenditures, an auditor most likely would select items for testing from the population of all

a. Purchase orders.
b. Canceled checks.
c. Receiving reports.
d. Approved vouchers.

78. When there are numerous property and equipment transactions during the year, an auditor who plans to assess control risk at a low level usually performs.

a. Analytical procedures for property and equipment balances at the end of the year.
b. Tests of controls and extensive tests of property and equipment balances at the end of the year.
c. Analytical procedures for current year property and equipment transactions.
d. Tests of controls and limited tests of current year property and equipment transactions.

79. In obtaining an understanding of a manufacturing entity's internal control concerning inventory balances, an auditor most likely would

a. Review the entity's descriptions of inventory policies and procedures.
b. Perform test counts of inventory during the entity's physical count.
c. Analyze inventory turnover statistics to identify slow-moving and obsolete items.
d. Analyze monthly production reports to identify variances and unusual transactions.

80. Which of the following procedures most likely would be considered a weakness in an entity's internal controls over payroll?

a. A voucher for the amount of the payroll is prepared in the general accounting department based on the payroll department's payroll summary.
b. Payroll checks are prepared by the payroll department and signed by the treasurer.
c. The employee who distributes payroll checks returns unclaimed payroll checks to the payroll department.
d. The personnel department sends employees' termination notices to the payroll department.

81. Which of the following controls would an entity most likely use in safeguarding against the loss of marketable securities?
a. An independent trust company that has **no** direct contact with the employees who have record keeping responsibilities has possession of the securities.
b. The internal auditor verifies the marketable securities in the entity's safe each year on the balance sheet date.
c. The independent auditor traces all purchases and sales of marketable securities through the subsidiary ledgers to the general ledger.
d. A designated member of the board of directors controls the securities in a bank safe-deposit box.

82. Which of the following representations should **not** be included in a report on internal control related matters noted in an audit?
a. Reportable conditions related to the internal control structure design exist, but **none** is deemed to be a material weakness.
b. There are **no** significant deficiencies in the design or operation of the internal control structure.
c. Corrective follow-up action is recommended due to the relative significance of material weaknesses discovered during the audit.
d. The auditor's consideration of the internal control structure would **not** necessarily disclose all reportable conditions that exist.

83. Before accepting an audit engagement, a successor auditor should make specific inquiries of the predecessor auditor regarding the predecessor's
a. Opinion of any subsequent events occurring since the predecessor's audit report was issued.
b. Understanding as to the reasons for the change of auditors.
c. Awareness of the consistency in the application of GAAP between periods.
d. Evaluation of all matters of continuing accounting significance.

84. Which of the following factors most likely would cause an auditor not to accept a new audit engagement?
a. An inadequate understanding of the entity's internal control structure.
b. The close proximity to the end of the entity's fiscal year.

c. Concluding that the entity's management probably lacks integrity.
d. An inability to perform preliminary analytical procedures before assessing control risk.

85. The audit work performed by each assistant should be reviewed to determine whether it was adequately performed and to evaluate whether the
a. Auditor's system of quality control has been maintained at a high level.
b. Results are consistent with the conclusions to be presented in the auditor's report.
c. Audit procedures performed are approved in the professional standards.
d. Audit has been performed by persons having adequate technical training and proficiency as auditors.

86. An auditor obtains knowledge about a new client's business and its industry to
a. Make constructive suggestions concerning improvements to the client's internal control structure.
b. Develop an attitude of professional skepticism concerning management's financial statement assertions.
c. Evaluate whether the aggregation of known misstatements causes the financial statements taken as a whole to be materially misstated.
d. Understand the events and transactions that may have an effect on the client's financial statements.

87. Jones, CPA, is auditing the financial statements of XYZ Retailing, Inc. What assurance does Jones provide that direct effect illegal acts that are material to XYZ's financial statements, and illegal acts that have a material, but indirect effect on the financial statements will be detected?

	Direct effect illegal acts	Indirect effect illegal acts
a.	Reasonable	None
b.	Reasonable	Reasonable
c.	Limited	None
d.	Limited	Reasonable

88. An auditor concludes that a client has committed an illegal act that has not been properly accounted for or disclosed. The auditor should withdraw from the engagement if the
a. Auditor is precluded from obtaining sufficient competent evidence about the illegal act.
b. Illegal act has an effect on the financial statements that is both material and direct.
c. Auditor cannot reasonably estimate the effect of the illegal act on the financial statements.
d. Client refuses to accept the auditor's report as modified for the illegal act.

89. Because of the risk of material misstatement, an audit of financial statements in accordance with generally accepted auditing standards should be planned and performed with an attitude of
a. Objective judgment.
b. Independent integrity.
c. Professional skepticism.
d. Impartial conservatism.

90. An auditor's flowchart of a client's accounting system is a diagrammatic representation that depicts the auditor's
a. Assessment of control risk.
b. Identification of weaknesses in the system.
c. Assessment of the control environment's effectiveness.
d. Understanding of the system.

91. Management's attitude toward aggressive financial reporting and its emphasis on meeting projected profit goals most likely would significantly influence an entity's control environment when
a. The audit committee is active in overseeing the entity's financial reporting policies.
b. External policies established by parties outside the entity affect its accounting practices.
c. Management is dominated by one individual who is also a shareholder.
d. Internal auditors have direct access to the board of directors and entity management.

92. An auditor should obtain sufficient knowledge of an entity's accounting system to understand the
a. Safeguards used to limit access to computer facilities.
b. Process used to prepare significant accounting estimates.
c. Procedures used to assure proper authorization of transactions.
d. Policies used to detect the concealment of irregularities.

93. When obtaining an understanding of an entity's internal control procedures, an auditor should concentrate on the substance of the procedures rather than their form because
a. The procedures may be operating effectively but may not be documented.
b. Management may establish appropriate procedures but not enforce compliance with them.
c. The procedures may be so inappropriate that no reliance is contemplated by the auditor.
d. Management may implement procedures whose costs exceed their benefits.

94. Which of the following most likely would not be considered an inherent limitation of the potential effectiveness of an entity's internal control?
a. Incompatible duties.
b. Management override.
c. Mistakes in judgment.
d. Collusion among employees.

95. After obtaining an understanding of internal control and assessing control risk, an auditor decided not to perform additional tests of controls. The auditor most likely concluded that the
a. Additional evidence to support a further reduction in control risk was not cost beneficial to obtain.
b. Assessed level of inherent risk exceeded the assessed level of control risk.
c. Internal control structure was properly designed and justifiably may be relied on.
d. Evidence obtainable through tests of controls would not support an increased level of control risk.

96. Which of the following audit procedures would an auditor most likely perform to test controls relating to management's assertion concerning the completeness of sales transactions?

a. Verify that extensions and footings on the entity's sales invoices and monthly customer statements have been recomputed.
b. Inspect the entity's reports of prenumbered shipping documents that have not been recorded in the sales journal.
c. Compare the invoiced prices on prenumbered sales invoices to the entity's authorized price list.
d. Inquire about the entity's credit granting policies and the consistent application of credit checks.

97. Which of the following internal control procedures most likely would assure that all billed sales are correctly posted to the accounts receivable ledger?

a. Daily sales summaries are compared to daily postings to the accounts receivable ledger.
b. Each sales invoice is supported by a prenumbered shipping document.
c. The accounts receivable ledger is reconciled daily to the control account in the general ledger.
d. Each shipment on credit is supported by a prenumbered sales invoice.

98. An auditor most likely would assess control risk at the maximum if the payroll department supervisor is responsible for

a. Examining authorization forms for new employees.
b. Comparing payroll registers with original batch transmittal data.
c. Authorizing payroll rate changes for all employees.
d. Hiring all subordinate payroll department employees.

99. In a properly designed internal control system, the same employee most likely would match vendors' invoices with receiving reports and also

a. Post the detailed accounts payable records.
b. Recompute the calculations on vendors' invoices.
c. Reconcile the accounts payable ledger.
d. Cancel vendors' invoices after payment.

100. Which of the following internal control activities most likely would prevent direct labor hours from being charged to manufacturing overhead?

a. Periodic independent counts of work in process for comparison to recorded amounts.
b. Comparison of daily journal entries with approved production orders.
c. Use of time tickets to record actual labor worked on production orders.
d. Reconciliation of work-in-process inventory with periodic cost budgets.

101. Which of the following internal control procedures most likely would be used to maintain accurate inventory records?

a. Perpetual inventory records are periodically compared with the current cost of individual inventory items.
b. A just-in-time inventory ordering system keeps inventory levels to a desired minimum.
c. Requisitions, receiving reports, and purchase orders are independently matched before payment is approved.
d. Periodic inventory counts are used to adjust the perpetual inventory records.

102. An auditor tests an entity's policy of obtaining credit approval before shipping goods to customers in support of management's financial statement assertion of

a. Valuation or allocation.
b. Completeness.
c. Existence or occurrence.
d. Rights and obligations.

103. Which of the following procedures would an auditor most likely include in the initial planning of a financial statement audit?

a. Obtaining a written representation letter from the client's management.
b. Examining documents to detect illegal acts having a material effect on the financial statements.
c. Considering whether the client's accounting estimates are reasonable in the circumstances.
d. Determining the extent of involvement of the client's internal auditors.

104. Which of the following factors most likely would influence an auditor's determination of the auditability of an entity's financial statements?

a. The complexity of the accounting system.
b. The existence of related party transactions.
c. The adequacy of the accounting records.
d. The operating effectiveness of control procedures.

105. Hill, CPA, has been retained to audit the financial statements of Monday Co. Monday's predecessor auditor was Post, CPA, who has been notified by Monday that Post's services have been terminated. Under these circumstances, which party should initiate the communications between Hill and Post?

a. Hill, the successor auditor.
b. Post, the predecessor auditor.
c. Monday's controller or CFO.
d. The chairman of Monday's board of directors.

106. The senior auditor responsible for coordinating the field work usually schedules a pre-audit conference with the audit team primarily to

a. Give guidance to the staff regarding both technical and personnel aspects of the audit.
b. Discuss staff suggestions concerning the establishment and maintenance of time budgets.
c. Establish the need for using the work of specialists and internal auditors.
d. Provide an opportunity to document staff disagreements regarding technical issues.

107. To obtain an understanding of a continuing client's business in planning an audit, an auditor most likely would

a. Perform tests of details of transactions and balances.
b. Review prior-year working papers and the permanent file for the client.
c. Read specialized industry journals.
d. Reevaluate the client's internal control environment.

108. In planning an audit of a new client, an auditor most likely would consider the methods used to process accounting information because such methods

a. Influence the design of internal control.
b. Affect the auditor's preliminary judgment about materiality levels.
c. Assist in evaluating the planned audit objectives.
d. Determine the auditor's acceptable level of audit risk.

109. Which of the following statements is not correct about materiality?

a. The concept of materiality recognizes that some matters are important for fair presentation of financial statements in conformity with GAAP, while other matters are not important.
b. An auditor considers materiality for planning purposes in terms of the largest aggregate level of misstatements that could be material to any one of the financial statements.
c. Materiality judgments are made in light of surrounding circumstances and necessarily involve both quantitative and qualitative judgments.
d. An auditor's consideration of materiality is influenced by the auditor's perception of the needs of a reasonable person who will rely on the financial statements.

110. Which of the following circumstances most likely would cause an auditor to consider whether material misstatements exist in an entity's financial statements?

a. Management places little emphasis on meeting earnings projections.
b. The board of directors makes all major financing decisions.
c. Reportable conditions previously communicated to management are not corrected.
d. Transactions selected for testing are not supported by proper documentation.

111. When assessing the internal auditors' competence, the independent CPA should obtain information about the

a. Organizational level to which the internal auditors report.
b. Educational background and professional certification of the internal auditors.
c. Policies prohibiting the internal auditors from auditing areas where relatives are employed.
d. Internal auditors' access to records and information that is considered sensitive.

112. Proper segregation of duties reduces the opportunities to allow persons to be in positions to both

a. Journalize entries and prepare financial statements.
b. Record cash receipts and cash disbursements.
c. Establish internal controls and authorize transactions.
d. Perpetuate and conceal errors and irregularities.

113. In an audit of financial statements, an auditor's primary consideration regarding an internal control policy or procedure is whether the policy or procedure

a. Reflects management's philosophy and operating style.
b. Affects management's financial statement assertions.
c. Provides adequate safeguards over access to assets.
d. Enhances management's decision-making processes.

114. Which of the following are considered control environment factors?

	Detection risk	Personnel policies and practices
a.	Yes	Yes
b.	Yes	No
c.	No	Yes
d.	No	No

115. The ultimate purpose of assessing control risk is to contribute to the auditor's evaluation of the risk that

a. Tests of controls may fail to identify procedures relevant to assertions.
b. Material misstatements may exist in the financial statements.
c. Specified controls requiring segregation of duties may be circumvented by collusion.
d. Entity policies may be overridden by senior management.

116. To obtain evidential matter about control risk, an auditor selects tests from a variety of techniques including

a. Inquiry.
b. Analytical procedures.
c. Calculation.
d. Confirmation.

117. Which of the following is a step in an auditor's decision to assess control risk at below the maximum?

a. Apply analytical procedures to both financial data and nonfinancial information to detect conditions that may indicate weak controls.

b. Perform tests of details of transactions and account balances to identify potential errors and irregularities.
c. Identify specific internal control policies and procedures that are likely to detect or prevent material misstatements.
d. Document that the additional audit effort to perform tests of controls exceeds the potential reduction in substantive testing.

118. The likelihood of assessing control risk too high is the risk that the sample selected to test controls

a. Does not support the auditor's planned assessed level of control risk when the true operating effectiveness of the control structure justifies such an assessment.
b. Contains misstatements that could be material to the financial statements when aggregated with misstatements in other account balances or transactions classes.
c. Contains proportionately fewer monetary errors or deviations from prescribed internal control structure policies or procedures than exist in the balance or class as a whole.
d. Does not support the tolerable error for some or all of management's assertions.

119. Upon receipt of customers' checks in the mailroom, a responsible employee should prepare a remittance listing that is forwarded to the cashier. A copy of the listing should be sent to the

a. Internal auditor to investigate the listing for unusual transactions.
b. Treasurer to compare the listing with the monthly bank statement.
c. Accounts receivable bookkeeper to update the subsidiary accounts receivable records.
d. Entity's bank to compare the listing with the cashier's deposit slip.

120. Proper authorization of write-offs of uncollectible accounts should be approved in which of the following departments?

a. Accounts receivable.
b. Credit.
c. Accounts payable.
d. Treasurer.

121. Which of the following procedures most likely would not be an internal control procedure designed to reduce the risk of errors in the billing process?
a. Comparing control totals for shipping documents with corresponding totals for sales invoices.
b. Using computer programmed controls on the pricing and mathematical accuracy of sales invoices.
c. Matching shipping documents with approved sales orders before invoice preparation.
d. Reconciling the control totals for sales invoices with the accounts receivable subsidiary ledger.

122. In assessing control risk for purchases, an auditor vouches a sample of entries in the voucher register to the supporting documents. Which assertion would this test of controls most likely support?
a. Completeness.
b. Existence or occurrence.
c. Valuation or allocation.
d. Rights and obligations.

123. Which of the following internal control procedures is not usually performed in the vouchers payable department?
a. Matching the vendor's invoice with the related receiving report.
b. Approving vouchers for payment by having an authorized employee sign the vouchers.
c. Indicating the asset and expense accounts to be debited.
d. Accounting for unused prenumbered purchase orders and receiving reports.

124. Which of the following questions would an auditor least likely include on an internal control questionnaire concerning the initiation and execution of equipment transactions?
a. Are requests for major repairs approved at a higher level than the department initiating the request?
b. Are prenumbered purchase orders used for equipment and periodically accounted for?
c. Are requests for purchases of equipment reviewed for consideration of soliciting competitive bids?
d. Are procedures in place to monitor and properly restrict access to equipment?

125. The objective of tests of details of transactions performed as tests of controls is to
a. Monitor the design and use of entity documents such as prenumbered shipping forms.
b. Determine whether internal control structure policies and procedures have been placed in operation.
c. Detect material misstatements in the account balances of the financial statements.
d. Evaluate whether internal control structure procedures operated effectively.

126. Which of the following tests of controls most likely would help assure an auditor that goods shipped are properly billed?
a. Scan the sales journal for sequential and unusual entries.
b. Examine shipping documents for matching sales invoices.
c. Compare the accounts receivable ledger to daily sales summaries.
d. Inspect unused sales invoices for consecutive prenumbering.

127. Reportable conditions are matters that come to an auditor's attention that should be communicated to an entity's audit committee because they represent
a. Disclosures of information that significantly contradict the auditor's going concern assumption.
b. Material irregularities or illegal acts perpetrated by high-level management.
c. Significant deficiencies in the design or operation of the internal control structure.
d. Manipulation or falsification of accounting records or documents from which financial statements are prepared.

128. Which of the following statements is correct concerning an auditor's required communication of reportable conditions?
a. A reportable condition previously communicated during the prior year's audit that remains uncorrected causes a scope limitation.
b. An auditor should perform tests of controls on reportable conditions before communicating them to the client.
c. An auditor's report on reportable conditions should include a restriction on the distribution of the report.
d. An auditor should communicate reportable conditions after tests of controls, but before commencing substantive tests.

129. In assessing the competence and objectivity of an entity's internal auditor, an independent auditor least likely would consider information obtained from
a. Discussions with management personnel.
b. External quality reviews of the internal auditor's activities.
c. Previous experience with the internal auditor.
d. The results of analytical procedures.

130. The element of the audit planning process most likely to be agreed upon with the client before implementation of the audit strategy is the determination of the
a. Evidence to be gathered to provide a sufficient basis for the auditor's opinion.
b. Procedures to be undertaken to discover litigation, claims, and assessments.
c. Pending legal matters to be included in the inquiry of the client's attorney.
d. Timing of inventory observation procedures to be performed.

131. A successor auditor most likely would make specific inquiries of the predecessor auditor regarding
a. Specialized accounting principles of the client's industry.
b. The competency of the client's internal audit staff.
c. The uncertainty inherent in applying sampling procedures.
d. Disagreements with management as to auditing procedures.

132. Which of the following statements would **least** likely appear in an auditor's engagement letter?
a. Fees for our services are based on our regular per diem rates, plus travel and other out-of-pocket expenses.
b. During the course of our audit we may observe opportunities for economy in, or improved controls over, your operations.
c. Our engagement is subject to the risk that material errors or irregularities, including fraud and defalcations, if they exist, will **not** be detected.
d. After performing our preliminary analytical procedures we will discuss with you the other procedures we consider necessary to complete the engagement.

133. Which of the following procedures would an auditor most likely perform in planning a financial statement audit?
a. Inquiring of the client's legal counsel concerning pending litigation.
b. Comparing the financial statements to anticipated results.
c. Examining computer generated exception reports to verify the effectiveness of internal controls.
d. Searching for unauthorized transactions that may aid in detecting unrecorded liabilities.

134. The in-charge auditor most likely would have a supervisory responsibility to explain to the staff assistants
a. That immaterial irregularities are **not** to be reported to the client's audit committee.
b. How the results of various auditing procedures performed by the assistants should be evaluated.
c. What benefits may be attained by the assistants' adherence to established time budgets.
d. Why certain documents are being transferred from the current file to the permanent file.

135. Which of the following would an auditor most likely use in determining the auditor's preliminary judgment about materiality?
a. The anticipated sample size of the planned substantive tests.
b. The entity's annualized interim financial statements.
c. The results of the internal control questionnaire.
d. The contents of the management representation letter.

136. As the acceptable level of detection risk decreases, an auditor may
a. Reduce substantive testing by relying on the assessments of inherent risk and control risk.
b. Postpone the planned timing of substantive tests from interim dates to the year end.
c. Eliminate the assessed level of inherent risk from consideration as a planning factor.
d. Lower the assessed level of control risk from the maximum level to below the maximum.

137. Which of the following characteristics most likely would heighten an auditor's concern about the risk of intentional manipulation of financial statements?
a. Turnover of senior accounting personnel is low.
b. Insiders recently purchased additional shares of the entity's stock.
c. Management places substantial emphasis on meeting earnings projections.
d. The rate of change in the entity's industry is slow.

138. The third general standard states that due care is to be exercised in the performance of an audit. This standard is ordinarily interpreted to require
a. Thorough review of the existing safeguards over access to assets and records.
b. Limited review of the indications of employee fraud and illegal acts.
c. Objective review of the adequacy of the technical training and proficiency of firm personnel.
d. Critical review of the judgment exercised at every level of supervision.

139. The primary objective of procedures performed to obtain an understanding of the internal control structure is to provide an auditor with
a. Knowledge necessary for audit planning.
b. Evidential matter to use in assessing inherent risk.
c. A basis for modifying tests of controls.
d. An evaluation of the consistency of application of management's policies.

140. The overall attitude and awareness of an entity's board of directors concerning the importance of the internal control structure usually is reflected in its
a. Computer-based controls.
b. System of segregation of duties.
c. Control environment.
d. Safeguards over access to assets.

141. When considering the internal control structure, an auditor should be aware of the concept of reasonable assurance, which recognizes that
a. Internal control policies and procedures may be ineffective due to mistakes in judgment and personal carelessness.
b. Adequate safeguards over access to assets and records should permit an entity to maintain proper accountability.

c. Establishing and maintaining the internal control structure is an important responsibility of management.
d. The cost of an entity's internal control structure should **not** exceed the benefits expected to be derived.

142. Control risk should be assessed in terms of
a. Specific control procedures.
b. Types of potential irregularities.
c. Financial statement assertions.
d. Control environment factors.

143. When an auditor assesses control risk at the maximum level, the auditor is required to document the auditor's

	Understanding of the entity's accounting system	Basis for concluding that control risk is at the maximum level
a.	No	No
b.	No	Yes
c.	Yes	No
d.	Yes	Yes

144. Sound internal control procedures dictate that immediately upon receiving checks from customers by mail, a responsible employee should
a. Add the checks to the daily cash summary.
b. Verify that each check is supported by a prenumbered sales invoice.
c. Prepare a duplicate listing of checks received.
d. Record the checks in the cash receipts journal.

145. An auditor generally tests the segregation of duties related to inventory by
a. Personal inquiry and observation.
b. Test counts and cutoff procedures.
c. Analytical procedures and invoice recomputation.
d. Document inspection and reconciliation.

146. After obtaining an understanding of the internal control structure and assessing control risk, an auditor decided to perform tests of controls. The auditor most likely decided that

a. It would be efficient to perform tests of controls that would result in a reduction in planned substantive tests.
b. Additional evidence to support a further reduction in control risk is **not** available.
c. An increase in the assessed level of control risk is justified for certain financial statement assertions.
d. There were many internal control structure weaknesses that could allow errors to enter the accounting system.

147. To provide assurance that each voucher is submitted and paid only once, an auditor most likely would examine a sample of paid vouchers and determine whether each voucher is

a. Supported by a vendor's invoice.
b. Stamped "paid" by the check signer.
c. Prenumbered and accounted for.
d. Approved for authorized purchases.

148. Which of the following statements is correct concerning reportable conditions in an audit?

a. An auditor is required to search for reportable conditions during an audit.
b. All reportable conditions are also considered to be material weaknesses.
c. An auditor may communicate reportable conditions during an audit or after the audit's completion.
d. An auditor may report that **no** reportable conditions were noted during an audit.

149. An internal auditor's work would most likely affect the nature, timing, and extent of an independent CPA's auditing procedures when the internal auditor's work relates to assertions about the

a. Existence of contingencies.
b. Valuation of intangible assets.
c. Existence of fixed asset additions.
d. Valuation of related party transactions.

150. In assessing the objectivity of internal auditors, an independent auditor should

a. Evaluate the quality control program in effect for the internal auditors.
b. Examine documentary evidence of the work performed by the internal auditors.
c. Test a sample of the transactions and balances that the internal auditors examined.

d. Determine the organizational level to which the internal auditors report.

151. In planning an audit, the auditor's knowledge about the design of relevant internal control policies and procedures should be used to

a. Identify the types of potential misstatements that could occur.
b. Assess the operational efficiency of the internal control structure.
c. Determine whether controls have been circumvented by collusion.
d. Document the assessed level of control risk.

152. Which of the following auditor concerns most likely could be so serious that the auditor concludes that a financial statement audit **cannot** be conducted?

a. The entity has **no** formal written code of conduct.
b. The integrity of the entity's management is suspect.
c. Procedures requiring segregation of duties are subject to management override.
d. Management fails to modify prescribed controls for changes in conditions.

153. Management philosophy and operating style most likely would have a significant influence on an entity's control environment when

a. The internal auditor reports directly to management.
b. Management is dominated by one individual.
c. Accurate management job descriptions delineate specific duties.
d. The audit committee actively oversees the financial reporting process.

154. Which of the following is a management control method that most likely could improve management's ability to supervise company activities effectively?

a. Monitoring compliance with internal control requirements imposed by regulatory bodies.
b. Limiting direct access to assets by physical segregation and protective devices.
c. Establishing budgets and forecasts to identify variances from expectations.
d. Supporting employees with the resources necessary to discharge their responsibilities.

155. In an audit of financial statements in accordance with generally accepted auditing standards, an auditor is required to
a. Document the auditor's understanding of the entity's internal control structure.
b. Search for significant deficiencies in the operation of the internal control structure.
c. Perform tests of controls to evaluate the effectiveness of the entity's accounting system.
d. Determine whether control procedures are suitably designed to prevent or detect material misstatements.

156. Which of the following internal controls most likely would reduce the risk of diversion of customer receipts by an entity's employees?
a. A bank lockbox system.
b. Prenumbered remittance advices.
c. Monthly bank reconciliations.
d. Daily deposit of cash receipts.

157. In obtaining an understanding of an entity's internal control structure policies and procedures that are relevant to audit planning, an auditor is required to obtain knowledge about the
a. Design of the policies and procedures pertaining to the internal control structure elements.
b. Effectiveness of the policies and procedures that have been placed in operation.
c. Consistency with which the policies and procedures are currently being applied.
d. Control procedures related to each principal transaction class and account balance.

158. Which of the following is a control procedure that most likely could help prevent employee payroll fraud?
a. The personnel department promptly sends employee termination notices to the payroll supervisor.
b. Employees who distribute payroll checks forward unclaimed payroll checks to the absent employees' supervisors.
c. Salary rates resulting from new hires are approved by the payroll supervisor.
d. Total hours used for determination of gross pay are calculated by the payroll supervisor.

159. Which of the following controls would a company most likely use to safeguard marketable securities when an independent trust agent is **not** employed?
a. The investment committee of the board of directors periodically reviews the investment decisions delegated to the treasurer.
b. Two company officials have joint control of marketable securities, which are kept in a bank safe-deposit box.
c. The internal auditor and the controller independently trace all purchases and sales of marketable securities from the subsidiary ledgers to the general ledger.
d. The chairman of the board verifies the marketable securities, which are kept in a bank safe-deposit box, each year on the balance sheet date.

160. In assessing control risk, an auditor ordinarily selects from a variety of techniques, including
a. Inquiry and analytical procedures.
b. Reperformance and observation.
c. Comparison and confirmation.
d. Inspection and verification.

161. Which of the following statements is correct concerning an auditor's assessment of control risk?
a. Assessing control risk may be performed concurrently during an audit with obtaining an understanding of the entity's internal control structure.
b. Evidence about the operation of control procedures in prior audits may **not** be considered during the current year's assessment of control risk.
c. The basis for an auditor's conclusions about the assessed level of control risk need **not** be documented unless control risk is assessed at the maximum level.
d. The lower the assessed level of control risk, the less assurance the evidence must provide that the control procedures are operating effectively.

162. An auditor assesses control risk because it
a. Is relevant to the auditor's understanding of the control environment.
b. Provides assurance that the auditor's materiality levels are appropriate.
c. Indicates to the auditor where inherent risk may be the greatest.
d. Affects the level of detection risk that the auditor may accept.

163. Assessing control risk at below the maximum level most likely would involve
a. Performing more extensive substantive tests with larger sample sizes than originally planned.
b. Reducing inherent risk for most of the assertions relevant to significant account balances.
c. Changing the timing of substantive tests by omitting interim-date testing and performing the tests at year end.
d. Identifying specific internal control structure policies and procedures relevant to specific assertions.

164. After assessing control risk at below the maximum level, an auditor desires to seek a further reduction in the assessed level of control risk. At this time, the auditor would consider whether
a. It would be efficient to obtain an understanding of the entity's accounting system.
b. The entity's internal control structure policies and procedures have been placed in operation.
c. The entity's internal control structure policies and procedures pertain to any financial statement assertions.
d. Additional evidential matter sufficient to support a further reduction is likely to be available.

165. When assessing control risk below the maximum level, an auditor is required to document the auditor's

	Understanding of the entity's control environment	Basis for concluding that control risk is below the maximum level
a.	Yes	No
b.	No	Yes
c.	Yes	Yes
d.	No	No

166. When there are numerous property and equipment transactions during the year, an auditor who plans to assess control risk at a low level usually performs
a. Tests of controls and extensive tests of property and equipment balances at the end of the year.
b. Analytical procedures for current year property and equipment transactions.
c. Tests of controls and limited tests of current year property and equipment transactions.
d. Analytical procedures for property and equipment balances at the end of the year.

167. An auditor suspects that a client's cashier is misappropriating cash receipts for personal use by lapping customer checks received in the mail. In attempting to uncover this embezzlement scheme, the auditor most likely would compare the
a. Dates checks are deposited per bank statements with the dates remittance credits are recorded.
b. Daily cash summaries with the sums of the cash receipts journal entries.
c. Individual bank deposit slips with the details of the monthly bank statements.
d. Dates uncollectible accounts are authorized to be written off with the dates the write-offs are actually recorded.

168. In testing controls over cash disbursements, an auditor most likely would determine that the person who signs checks also
a. Reviews the monthly bank reconciliation.
b. Returns the checks to accounts payable.
c. Is denied access to the supporting documents.
d. Is responsible for mailing the checks.

169. For effective internal control, the accounts payable department generally should
a. Stamp, perforate, or otherwise cancel supporting documentation after payment is mailed.
b. Ascertain that each requisition is approved as to price, quantity, and quality by an authorized employee.
c. Obliterate the quantity ordered on the receiving department copy of the purchase order.
d. Establish the agreement of the vendor's invoice with the receiving report and purchase order.

170. In determining the effectiveness of an entity's policies and procedures relating to the existence or occurrence assertion for payroll transactions, an auditor most likely would inquire about and
a. Observe the segregation of duties concerning personnel responsibilities and payroll disbursement.
b. Inspect evidence of accounting for prenumbered payroll checks.
c. Recompute the payroll deductions for employee fringe benefits.
d. Verify the preparation of the monthly payroll account bank reconciliation.

171. In obtaining an understanding of a manufacturing entity's internal control structure concerning inventory balances, an auditor most likely would

a. Analyze the liquidity and turnover ratios of the inventory.
b. Perform analytical procedures designed to identify cost variances.
c. Review the entity's descriptions of inventory policies and procedures.
d. Perform test counts of inventory during the entity's physical count.

172. An auditor's letter issued on reportable conditions relating to an entity's internal control structure observed during a financial statement audit should

a. Include a brief description of the tests of controls performed in searching for reportable conditions and material weaknesses.
b. Indicate that the reportable conditions should be disclosed in the annual report to the entity's shareholders.
c. Include a paragraph describing management's assertion concerning the effectiveness of the internal control structure.
d. Indicate that the audit's purpose was to report on the financial statements and **not** to provide assurance on the internal control structure.

173. The work of internal auditors may affect the independent auditor's

I. Procedures performed in obtaining an understanding of the internal control structure.
II. Procedures performed in assessing the risk of material misstatement.
III. Substantive procedures performed in gathering direct evidence.

a. I and II only.
b. I and III only.
c. II and III only.
d. I, II, and III.

174. During the initial planning phase of an audit, a CPA most likely would

a. Identify specific internal control activities that are likely to prevent fraud.
b. Evaluate the reasonableness of the client's accounting estimates.
c. Discuss the timing of the audit procedures with the client's management.
d. Inquire of the client's attorney as to whether any unrecorded claims are probable of assertion.

175. In creating lead schedules for an audit engagement, a CPA often uses automated workpaper software. What client information is needed to begin this process?

a. Interim financial information such as third quarter sales, net income, and inventory and receivables balances.
b. Specialized journal information such as the invoice and purchase order numbers of the last few sales and purchases of the year.
c. General ledger information such as account numbers, prior-year account balances, and current-year unadjusted information.
d. Adjusting entry information such as deferrals and accruals, and reclassification journal entries.

176. To reduce the risks associated with accepting e-mail responses to requests for confirmation of accounts receivable, an auditor most likely would

a. Request the senders to mail the original forms to the auditor.
b. Examine subsequent cash receipts for the accounts in question.
c. Consider the e-mail responses to the confirmations to be exceptions.
d. Mail second requests to the e-mail respondents.

Chapter One - Problems
Introduction, General and Field Standards

NUMBER 1

The flowchart on the following page depicts the activities relating to the purchasing, receiving, and accounts payable departments of Model Company, Inc.

Required:
Based only on the flowchart, describe the internal control procedures (strengths) that most likely would provide reasonable assurance that specific internal control objectives for the financial statement assertions regarding purchases and accounts payable will be achieved. Do **not** describe weaknesses in the internal control structure.

NUMBER 2

An auditor's working papers include the narrative description below of the cash receipts and billing portions of the internal control structure of Rural Building Supplies, Inc. Rural is a single-store retailer that sells a variety of tools, garden supplies, lumber, small appliances, and electrical fixtures to the public, although about half of Rural's sales are to construction contractors on account. Rural employs 12 salaried sales associates, a credit manager, three full-time clerical workers, and several part-time cash register clerks and assistant bookkeepers. The full-time clerical workers perform such tasks as cash receipts, billing, and accounting and are adequately bonded. They are referred to in the narrative as "accounts receivable supervisor," "cashier," and "bookkeeper."

NARRATIVE

Retail customers pay for merchandise by cash or credit card at cash registers when merchandise is purchased. A contractor may purchase merchandise on account if approved by the credit manager based only on the manager's familiarity with the contractor's reputation. After credit is approved, the sales associate files a prenumbered charge form with the accounts receivable (A/R) supervisor to set up the receivable.

The A/R supervisor independently verifies the pricing and other details on the charge form by reference to a management-authorized price list, corrects any errors, prepares the invoice, and supervises a part-time employee who mails the invoice to the contractor. The A/R supervisor electronically posts the details of the invoice in the A/R subsidiary ledger; simultaneously, the transaction's details are transmitted to the bookkeeper. The A/R supervisor also prepares a monthly computer-generated A/R subsidiary ledger without a reconciliation with the A/R control account and a monthly report of overdue accounts.

The cash receipts functions are performed by the cashier who also supervises the cash register clerks. The cashier opens the mail, compares each check with the enclosed remittance advice, stamps each check "for deposit only," and lists checks for deposit. The cashier then gives the remittance advices to the bookkeeper for recording. The cashier deposits the checks daily separate from the daily deposit of cash register receipts. The cashier retains the verified deposit slips to assist in reconciling the monthly bank statements, but forwards to the bookkeeper a copy of the daily cash register summary. The cashier does not have access to the journals or ledgers.

The bookkeeper receives the details of transactions from the A/R supervisor and the cashier for journalizing and posting to the general ledger. After recording the remittance advices received from the cashier, the bookkeeper electronically transmits the remittance information to the A/R supervisor for subsidiary ledger updating. The bookkeeper sends monthly statements to contractors with unpaid balances upon receipt of the monthly report of overdue balances from the A/R supervisor. The bookkeeper authorizes the A/R supervisor to write off accounts as

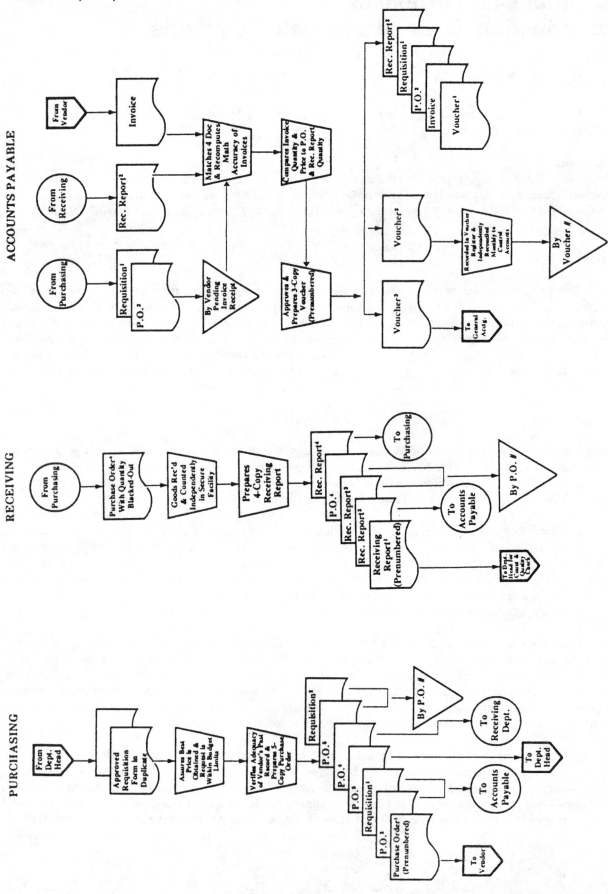

uncollectible when six months have passed since the initial overdue notice was sent. At this time, the credit manager is notified by the bookkeeper not to grant additional credit to that contractor.

Required:
Based only on the information in the narrative, describe the internal control weaknesses in Rural's internal control structure concerning the cash receipts and billing functions. Organize the weaknesses by employee job function: Credit manager, A/R supervisor, Cashier, and Bookkeeper. Do **not** describe how to correct the weaknesses.

NUMBER 3

A partially-completed charge sales systems flowchart follows on the next page. The flowchart depicts the charge sales activities of the Bottom Manufacturing Corporation.

A customer's purchase order is received and a six-part sales order is prepared, therefrom. The six copies are initially distributed as follows:

> Copy No. 1: Billing copy--to billing department.
> Copy No. 2: Shipping copy--to shipping department.
> Copy No. 3: Credit copy--to credit department.
> Copy No. 4: Stock request copy--to credit department.
> Copy No. 5: Customer copy--to customer.
> Copy No. 6: Sales order copy--file in sales order department.

When each copy of the sales order reaches the applicable department or destination, it calls for specific internal control procedures and related documents. Some of the procedures and related documents are indicated on the flowchart. Other procedures and documents are labeled letters a to r.

Required: List the procedures or the internal documents that are labeled letters c to r in the flowchart of Bottom Manufacturing Corporation's charge sales system.

Organize your answer as follows (note that an explanation of the letters a and b which appear in the flowchart are entered as examples): (See Flowchart Symbols, Chapter 7.)

Flowchart Symbol Letter	*Procedures or Internal Document*
a.	Prepare six-part sales order.
b.	File by order number.

BOTTOM MANUFACTURING CORPORATION
Flowchart of Credit Sales Activities

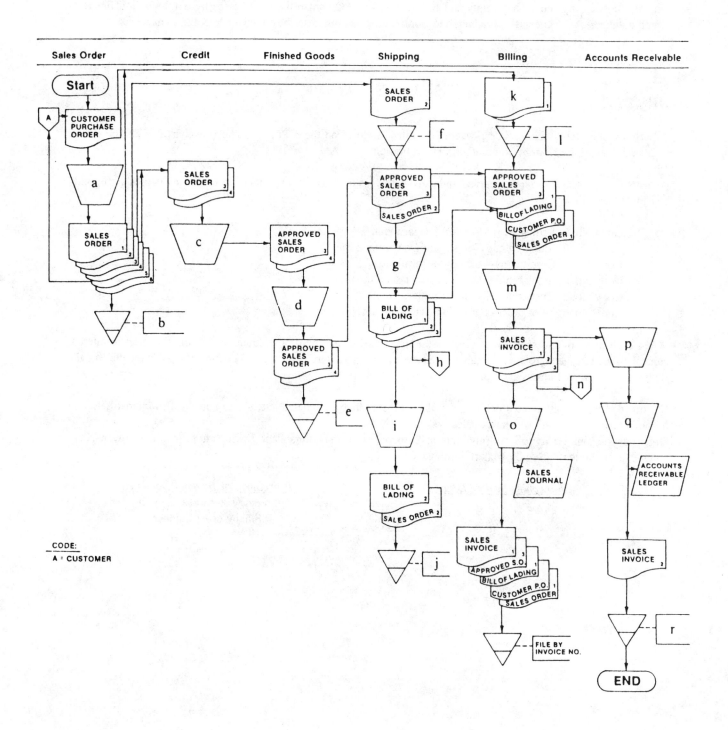

NUMBER 4

Dodd, CPA, audited Adams Company's financial statements for the year ended December 31, 1989. On November 1, 1990, Adams notified Dodd that it was changing auditors and that Dodd's services were being terminated. On November 5, 1990, Adams invited Hall, CPA, to make a proposal for an engagement to audit its financial statements for the year ended December 31, 1990.

Required:
a.   What procedures concerning Dodd should Hall perform before accepting the engagement?
b.   What additional procedures should Hall consider performing during the planning phase of this audit (after acceptance of the engagement) that would **not** be performed during the audit of a continuing client?

NUMBER 5

An auditor is required to obtain a sufficient understanding of each of the elements of an entity's internal control structure. This is necessary to plan the audit of the entity's financial statements and to assess control risk.

Required:
a.   For what purposes should an auditor's understanding of the internal control structure elements be used in planning an audit?
b.   What is required for an auditor to assess control risk at below the maximum level?
c.   What should an auditor consider when seeking a further reduction in the planned assessed level of control risk?
d.   What are an auditor's documentation requirements concerning an entity's internal control structure and the assessed level of control risk?

NUMBER 6

The following illustrates a **MANUAL SYSTEM FOR EXECUTING PURCHASES AND CASH DISBURSEMENTS TRANSACTIONS.**

Required:
Indicate what each of the letters (A) through (L) represent. Do not discuss adequacies or inadequacies in the system of internal control.

(Number 6 continued on next page.)

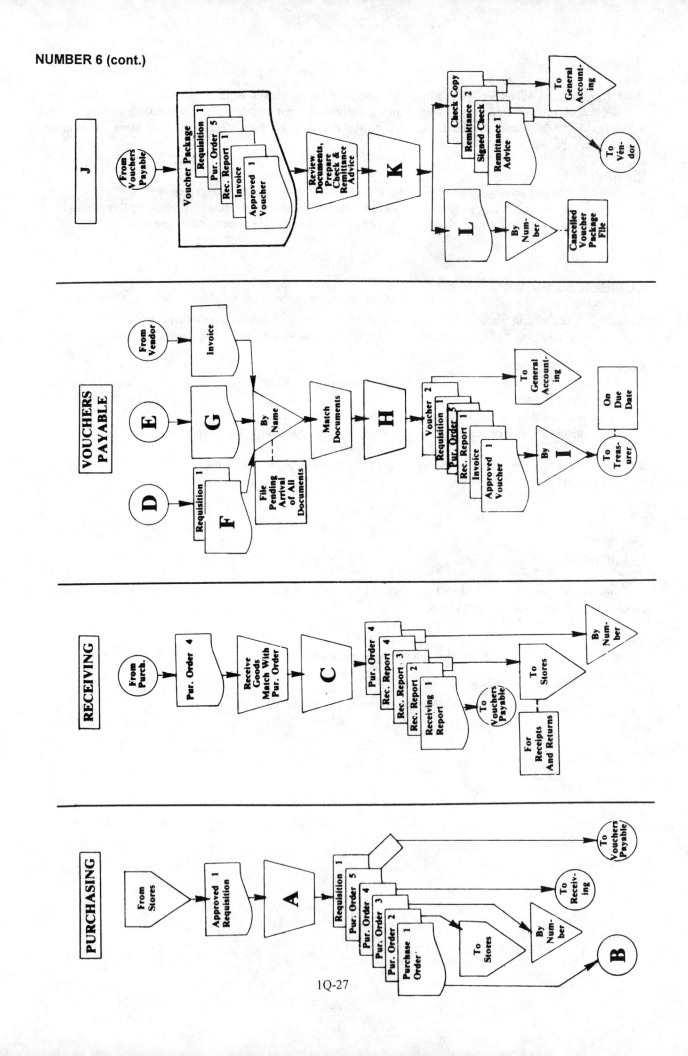

NUMBER 7

Number 7 consists of 13 items. Select the **best** answer for each item. Answer all items.

Required:
The flowchart on the next page depicts part of a client's revenue cycle. Some of the flowchart symbols are labeled to indicate control procedures and records. For each symbol numbered 61 through 73, select one response from the answer lists below. Each response in the lists may be selected once or **not** at all.

Answer Lists

Operations and control procedures

A.   Enter shipping data
B.   Verify agreement of sales order and shipping document
C.   Write off accounts receivable
D.   To warehouse and shipping department
E.   Authorize account receivable write-off
F.   Prepare aged trial balance
G.   To sales department
H.   Release goods for shipment
I.   To accounts receivable department
J.   Enter price data
K.   Determine that customer exists
L.   Match customer purchase order with sales order
M.   Perform customer credit check
N.   Prepare sales journal
O.   Prepare sales invoice

Documents, journals, ledgers, and files

P.   Shipping document
Q.   General ledger master file
R.   General journal
S.   Master price file
T.   Sales journal
U.   Sales invoice
V.   Cash receipts journal
W.   Uncollectible accounts file
X.   Shipping file
Y.   Aged trial balance
Z.   Open order file

NUMBER 8

During the course of an audit made in accordance with generally accepted auditing standards, an auditor may become aware of matters relating to the client's internal control structure that may be of interest to the client's audit committee or to individuals with an equivalent level of authority and responsibility, such as the board of directors, the board of trustees, or the owner in an owner-managed enterprise.

Required:
a.   What are meant by the terms, "reportable conditions" and "material weaknesses"?
b.   What are an auditor's responsibilities in identifying and reporting these matters?

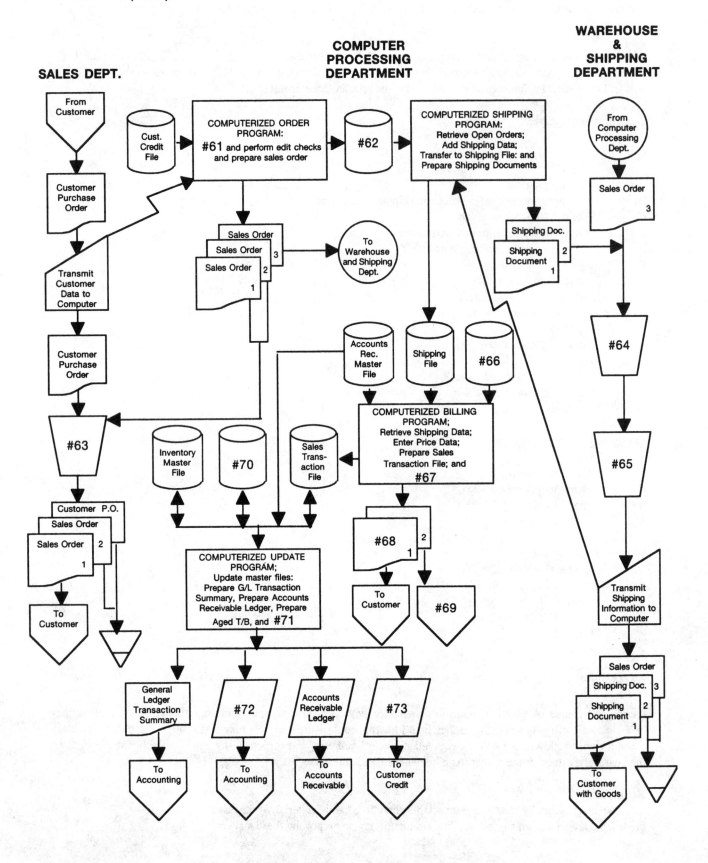

NUMBER 9

Number 9 consists of 15 items pertaining to an auditor's risk analysis of an entity. Select the best answer for each item.

Bond, CPA, is considering audit risk at the financial statement level in planning the audit of Toxic Waste Disposal (TWD) Company's financial statements for the year ended December 31, 1993. TWD is a privately-owned entity that contracts with municipal governments to remove environmental wastes. Audit risk at the financial statement level is influenced by the risk of material misstatements, which may be indicated by a combination of factors related to management, the industry, and the entity.

Required:
Based only on the information below, indicate whether each of the following factors (**Items 106 through 120**) would most likely increase audit risk (I), decrease audit risk (D), or have **no** effect on audit risk (N).

Items to be Answered:

Company Profile

106. This was the first year TWD operated at a profit since 1989 because the municipalities received increased federal and state funding for environmental purposes.

107. TWD's Board of Directors is controlled by Mead, the majority stockholder, who also acts as the chief executive officer.

108. The internal auditor reports to the controller and the controller reports to Mead.

109. The accounting department has experienced a high rate of turnover of key personnel.

110. TWD's bank has a loan officer who meets regularly with TWD's CEO and controller to monitor TWD's financial performance.

111. TWD's employees are paid biweekly.

112. Bond has audited TWD for five years.

Recent Developments

113. During 1993, TWD changed its method of preparing its financial statements from the cash basis to generally accepted accounting principles.

114. During 1993, TWD sold one half of its controlling interest in United Equipment Leasing (UEL) Co. TWD retained significant interest in UEL.

115. During 1993, litigation filed against TWD in 1988 alleging that TWD discharged pollutants into state waterways was dropped by the state. Loss contingency disclosures that TWD included in prior years' financial statements are being removed for the 1993 financial statements.

116. During December 1993, TWD signed a contract to lease disposal equipment from an entity owned by Mead's parents. This related party transaction is not disclosed in TWD's notes to its 1993 financial statements.

117. During December 1993, TWD completed a barter transaction with a municipality. TWD removed waste from a municipally-owned site and acquired title to another contaminated site at below market price. TWD intends to service this new site in 1994.

118. During December 1993, TWD increased its casualty insurance coverage on several pieces of sophisticated machinery from historical cost to replacement cost.

119. Inquiries about the substantial increase in revenue TWD recorded in the fourth quarter of 1993 disclosed a new policy. TWD guaranteed to several municipalities that it would refund the federal and state funding paid to TWD if any municipality fails federal or state site clean-up inspection in 1994.

120. An initial public offering of TWD's stock is planned for late 1994.

NUMBER 10

Number 10 consists of 15 items. Select the best answer for each item.

Field, CPA, is auditing the financial statements of Miller Mailorder, Inc. (MMI) for the year ended January 31, 1995. Field has compiled a list of possible errors and fraud that may result in the misstatement of MMI's financial statements, and a corresponding list of internal control activities that, if properly designed and implemented, could assist MMI in preventing or detecting the errors and fraud.

Required:
For each possible error and fraud numbered **106 through 120**, select one internal control activity from the answer list that, if properly designed and implemented, most likely could assist MMI in preventing or detecting the errors and fraud. Each response in the list of internal control activities may be selected once, more than once, or not at all.

Possible Errors and Fraud
106. Invoices for goods sold are posted to incorrect customer accounts.

107. Goods ordered by customers are shipped, but are **not** billed to anyone.

108. Invoices are sent for shipped goods, but are **not** recorded in the sales journal.

109. Invoices are sent for shipped goods and are recorded in the sales journal, but are **not** posted to any customer account.

110. Credit sales are made to individuals with unsatisfactory credit ratings.

111. Goods are removed from inventory for unauthorized orders.

112. Goods shipped to customers do **not** agree with goods ordered by customers.

113. Invoices are sent to allies in a fraudulent scheme and sales are recorded for fictitious transactions.

114. Customers' checks are received for less than the customers' full account balances, but the customers' full account balances are credited.

115. Customers' checks are misappropriated before being forwarded to the cashier for deposit.

116. Customers' checks are credited to incorrect customer accounts.

117. Different customer accounts are each credited for the same cash receipt.

118. Customers' checks are properly credited to customer accounts and are properly deposited, but errors are made in recording receipts in the cash receipts journal.

119. Customers' checks are misappropriated after being forwarded to the cashier for deposit.

120. Invalid transactions granting credit for sales returns are recorded.

Internal Control Activities

A. Shipping clerks compare goods received from the warehouse with the details on the shipping documents.

B. Approved sales orders are required for goods to be released from the warehouse.

C. Monthly statements are mailed to all customers with outstanding balances.

D. Shipping clerks compare goods received from the warehouse with approved sales orders.

E. Customer orders are compared with the inventory master file to determine whether items ordered are in stock.

F. Daily sales summaries are compared with control totals of invoices.

G. Shipping documents are compared with sales invoices when goods are shipped.

H. Sales invoices are compared with the master price file.

I. Customer orders are compared with an approved customer list.

J. Sales orders are prepared for each customer order.

K. Control amounts posted to the accounts receivable ledger are compared with control totals of invoices.

L. Sales invoices are compared with shipping documents and approved customer orders before invoices are mailed.

M. Prenumbered credit memos are used for granting credit for goods returned.

N. Goods returned for credit are approved by the supervisor of the sales department.

O. Remittance advices are separated from the checks in the mailroom and forwarded to the accounting department.

P. Total amounts posted to the accounts receivable ledger from remittance advices are compared with the validated bank deposit slip.

Q. The cashier examines each check for proper endorsement.

R. Validated deposit slips are compared with the cashier's daily cash summaries.

S. An employee, other than the bookkeeper, periodically prepares a bank reconciliation.

T. Sales returns are approved by the same employee who issues receiving reports evidencing actual return of goods.

NUMBER 11

Green, CPA, is considering audit risk at the financial statement level in planning the audit of National Federal Bank (NFB) Company's financial statements for the year ended December 31, 1990. Audit risk at the financial statement level is influenced by the risk of material misstatements, which may be indicated by a combination of factors related to management, the industry, and the entity. In assessing such factors Green has gathered the following information concerning NFB's environment.

Company profile:
NFB is a federally-insured bank that has been consistently more profitable than the industry average by marketing mortgages on properties in a prosperous rural area, which has experienced considerable growth in recent years. NFB packages its mortgages and sells them to large mortgage investment trusts. Despite recent volatility of interest rates, NFB has been able to continue selling its mortgages as a source of new lendable funds.

NFB's board of directors is controlled by Smith, the majority stockholder, who also acts as the chief executive officer. Management at the bank's branch offices has authority for directing and controlling NFB's operations and is compensated based on branch profitability. The internal auditor reports directly to Harris, a minority shareholder, who also acts as chairman of the board's audit committee.

The accounting department has experienced little turnover in personnel during the five years Green has audited NFB. NFB's formula consistently underestimates the allowance for loan losses, but its controller has always been receptive to Green's suggestions to increase the allowance during each engagement.

Recent developments:
During 1990, NFB opened a branch office in a suburban town thirty miles from its principal place of business. Although this branch is not yet profitable due to competition from several well-established regional banks, management believes that the branch will be profitable by 1992.

Also, during 1990, NFB increased the efficiency of its accounting operations by installing a new, sophisticated computer system.

Required:
Based only on the information above, describe the factors that most likely would have an effect on the risk of material misstatements. Indicate whether each factor increases or decreases the risk. Use the format illustrated below.

Environmental factor	*Effect on risk of material misstatements*
Branch management has authority for directing and controlling operations.	Increase

NUMBER 12

Butler, CPA, has been engaged to audit the financial statement of Young Computer Outlets, Inc., a new client. Young is a privately-owned chain of retail stores that sells a variety of computer software and video products. Young uses an in-house payroll department at its corporate headquarters to compute payroll data, and to prepare and distribute payroll checks to its 300 salaried employees.

Butler is preparing an internal control questionnaire to assist in obtaining an understanding of Young's internal control and in assessing control risk.

Required:
Prepare a "Payroll" segment of Butler's internal control questionnaire that would assist in obtaining an understanding of Young's internal control and in assessing control risk.

Do **not** prepare questions relating to cash payrolls, EDP applications, payments based on hourly rates, piece-work, commissions, employee benefits (pensions, health care, vacations, etc.), or payroll tax accruals other than withholdings.

Use the format in the following example:

| *Question* | *Yes* | *No* |
| Are paychecks prenumbered and accounted for? | | |

NUMBER 13

Kent, CPA, is the engagement partner on the financial statement audit of Super Computer Services Co. (SCS) for the year ended April 30, 1998. On May 6, 1998, Smith, the senior auditor assigned to the engagement, had the following conversation with Kent concerning the planning phase of the audit:

Kent: Do you have all the audit programs updated yet for the SCS engagement?

Smith: Mostly, I still have work to do on the fraud risk assessment.

Kent: Why? Our "errors and irregularities" program from last year is still OK. It's passed peer review several times. Besides, we don't have specific duties regarding fraud. If we find it, we'll deal with it then.

Smith: I don't think so. That new CEO, Mint, has almost no salary, mostly bonuses and stock options. Doesn't that concern you?

Kent: No. Mint's employment contract was approved by the Board of Directors just three months ago. It was passed unanimously.

Smith: I guess so, but Mint told those stock analysts that SCS's earnings would increase 30% next year. Can Mint deliver numbers like that?

Kent: Who knows? We're auditing the '98 financial statements, not '99. Mint will probably amend that forecast every month between now and next May.

Smith: Sure, but all this may change our other audit programs.

Kent: No, it won't. The programs are fine as is. If you find fraud in any of your tests, just let me know. Maybe we'll have to extend the tests. Or maybe we'll just report it to the audit committee.

Smith: What would they do? Green is the audit committee's chair, and remember, Green hired Mint. They've been best friends for years. Besides, Mint is calling all the shots now. Brown, the old CEO, is still on the Board, but Brown's never around. Brown's even been skipping the Board meetings. Nobody in management or on the Board would stand up to Mint.

Kent: That's nothing new. Brown was like that years ago. Brown caused frequent disputes with Jones, CPA, the predecessor auditor. Three years ago, Jones told Brown how ineffective the internal audit department was then. Next thing you know, Jones is out and I'm in. Why bother? I'm just as happy that those understaffed internal auditors don't get in our way. Just remember, the bottom line is . . . are the financial statements fairly presented? And they always have been. We don't provide any assurance about fraud. That's management's job.

Smith: But what about the lack of segregation of duties in the cash disbursements department? That clerk could write a check for anything.

Kent: That's a reportable condition every year and probably will be again this year. But we're talking cost-effectiveness here, not fraud. We just have to do lots of testing on cash disbursements and report it again.

Smith: What about the big layoffs coming up next month? It's more than a rumor. Even the employees know it's going to happen, and they're real uptight about it.

Kent: I know, it's the worst kept secret at SCS, but we don't have to consider that now. Even if it happens, it will only improve next year's financial results. Brown should have let these people go years ago. Let's face it, how else can Mint even come close to the 30% earnings increase next year?

Required:
Begin the answer to each requirement (i.e., A, B, and C) on the top of a new page.

a.   Describe the fraud risk factors that are indicated in the dialogue above.

b.   Describe Kent's misconceptions regarding the consideration of fraud in the audit of SCS's financial statements that are contained in the dialogue above **and** explain why each is a misconception.

c.   Describe an auditor's working paper documentation requirements regarding the assessment of the risk of material misstatement due to fraud.

NUMBER 14

A number of procedures are performed by the auditor in the assessment of control risk.

Procedures:

1. The auditor tests the effectiveness of the controls.

2. The auditor prepares flowcharts, narratives, questionnaires, or other material.

3. The auditor considers the factors affecting the risk of material misstatement.

4. The auditor documents the reasons for assessing control risk at the maximum.

5. The auditor designs substantive tests.

6. The auditor collects evidence on the operating effectiveness of the procedures.

7. The auditor records the basis for determining that the controls are working as designed.

8. The auditor considers whether the evidence supports a lower assessed level of control risk.

9. The auditor applies limited substantive tests to determine whether a control is operational.

10. The auditor identifies the types of potential misstatement.

Required:

Match the statement that most closely relates to the procedures that an auditor may perform in this process. A statement may be used more than once or not at all.

Statements:

A. Describes a reason for the auditor to obtain an understanding of internal control.

B. Describes what is required for an auditor to assess control risk below the maximum.

C. Describes the documentation requirements for the understanding of internal control and assessment of control risk.

D. Describes a procedure that would not be performed.

AUDITING SIMULATION

During the course of an audit of an entity's financial statement, the auditor may become aware of matters related to internal control that may be of interest to the audit committee of the Board of Directors or others of equivalent authority.

Deficiencies in internal control design
- Inadequate overall internal control design
- Absence of appropriate segregation of duties consistent with appropriate control objectives
- Absence of appropriate reviews and approvals of transactions, accounting entries, or systems output
- Inadequate procedures for appropriately assessing and applying accounting principles
- Inadequate provisions for the safeguarding of assets
- Absence of other control techniques considered appropriate for the type and level of transaction activity
- Evidence that a system fails to provide complete and accurate output that is consistent with objectives and current needs because of design flaws

Failures in the operation of internal control
- Evidence of failure of identified controls in preventing or detecting misstatements of accounting information
- Evidence that a system fails to provide complete and accurate output consistent with the entity's control objectives because of the misapplication of control procedures
- Evidence of failure to safeguard assets from loss, damage or misappropriation
- Evidence of intentional override of the internal control structure by those in authority to the detriment of the overall objectives of the system
- Evidence of failure to perform tasks that are part of the internal control structure, such as reconciliations not prepared or not timely prepared
- Evidence of willful wrongdoing by employees or management
- Evidence of manipulation, falsification, or alteration of accounting records or supporting documents
- Evidence of intentional misapplication of accounting principles
- Evidence of misrepresentation by client personnel to the auditor

Required: Compose an internal control letter for the ABC Corporation for the year ended December 31, 20XX. Select at least three internal control deficiencies and/or failures that you would communicate to the client.

Chapter One - Solutions to Questions
Introduction, General and Field Standards

1. (a) Tests of controls are designed to determine whether the control procedures prescribed by the client are actually functioning. An example of a test of controls would be to examine purchase orders for proper authorization.

2. (a) Data processing is a recording function and thus should be under the direction of the controller. Answers (b), (c) and (d) are functions of the treasurer's department since they are "custodial" in nature.

3. (d) In performing an audit, the CPA may request direct assistance from internal auditors. For example, internal auditors may assist the independent CPA in obtaining an understanding of the internal control structure or in performing tests of controls or substantive tests.

4. (d) The auditor is required to assess the internal control structure as part of the audit process. The documentation provides evidence that the auditor has complied with the second standard of field work. The extent and type of documentation is left to the auditor's judgment.

5. (c) This department has access to the records necessary to prepare payroll tax reports.

6. (d) Treasurer is responsible for cash disbursements.

7. (b) There is a control weakness because the employee has both custody of an asset (cash) and the accounting record (accounts receivable subsidiary ledgers).

8. (c) The authorization of transactions, record keeping, and custodial functions should be segregated.

9. (c) Special authorization refers to a certain item. General authorization refers to classes of items.

10. (c) Purchasing agent has authority to purchase, not authority to initiate purchases.

11. (d) Department supervisor authorizes payroll and should not be responsible for distribution (custodial function—custody of checks).

12. (c) The work of internal auditors is a part of, but not a substitute for, the independent auditor's evaluation of internal control. Answer (a) is work not necessarily performed by internal auditors. Answers (b) and (d) do not directly affect internal accounting control.

13. (b) One of the basic elements of an adequate system of internal control is competent personnel with clear lines of authority and responsibility.

14. (d) Inquiry is the first step in determining the client's control system. The system is then tested by applying the procedures detailed in answers (a) and (b). Answer (d) is used to verify balances, not test controls.

15. (b) The question deals with the primary questions asked in testing controls. The auditor is least concerned with why. He performs the procedures because he is concerned with control which centers primarily on how, where and who, as opposed to why (this is answered in the understanding of the system).

16. (b) The purchasing department's function is solely to purchase previously authorized goods and services at the desired quality and best price. They have no function in authorization for purchase receiving or payment.

17. (d) Substantive tests are audit tests performed to substantiate the fairness of presentation of each account on the financial statements. The nature, timing, and extent of substantive tests is determined by the creditor's assessment of control risk. Answers (a), (b) and (c) are synonymous terms, and these tests are used to determine whether internal control procedures are actually in place in the client's operation.

18. (b) GAAS requires that the auditor understand the entity's control structure elements and to document the assessed level of control risk. If control risk is assessed at the maximum, no reasons need to be stated. However, if control risk is assessed at less than the maximum, the reasons for assessing it at less than the maximum must be documented.

19. (d) In order to prevent material errors in recording purchases, an employee who is independent of the purchasing or receiving function should compare the quantity purchased with the quantity received and the quantity billed by the vendor. This is the function of the accounts payable clerk.

20. (b) A material weakness is a condition where control procedures are not suitably designed or operating effectively to prevent or detect an error or irregularity in the normal course of business by employees performing their assigned duties. Therefore, accounting records and financial statements may be incorrect. A reportable condition is a situation in the control structure that may be designed ineffectively or not operating properly, but the deficiency has no effect on the timely recording and summarizing accounting transactions. According to GAAS, both situations a material weakness and a reportable condition are reportable conditions, but a reportable condition may not be a material weakness.

21. (c) Answers (a), (b) and (d) are incorrect because the auditor can ascertain that these controls are in place by other means through records available within the company. However, in order to determine whether a given employee actually exists, the auditor must observe the actual distribution of checks and would usually include the employee providing some form of personal identification.

22. (b) The auditor may document his understanding of the client's internal control through the use of a narrative, internal control questionnaire or flowchart or any other appropriate means. Therefore, answer (b) is the correct answer.

23. (a) The purpose of tests of controls is to provide reasonable assurance that internal controls are being applied as determined by the auditor during the review of the internal control structure.

24. (b) The payroll accounting department has a recording responsibility and as such it should not have custody of unclaimed payroll checks (custody of an asset). If the payroll accounting department had custody of payroll checks, its employees could add a fictitious employee to the payroll and subsequently obtain the check.

25. (a) In an organizational structure, the personnel department is delegated the authorization power over pay rates.

26. (d) In order to evaluate the objectivity of internal auditors, it is necessary for the independent CPA to determine the organizational level to which the internal auditor reports. If, for example, the internal auditor reports to the controller, it would be impossible for the internal auditor to be objective.

27. (b) The receiving department copy of the purchase order should be "blind" (i.e., quantities omitted). This ensures that the receiving department personnel count the incoming merchandise. Thus the company will end up paying only for what was received, which may not be what was billed by the vendor.

28. (a) Control procedures over the payroll function include the reconciliation of job time tickets to employee clock card hours. Answer (b) is incorrect because the reconciliation should be done by the payroll department, not the individual employee responsible for those jobs.

29. (b) The supporting documentation should be canceled by the check signer (usually the treasurer) and not the accounts payable department.

30. (c) An auditor should obtain an understanding of the internal control structure to plan the audit and to determine the nature, timing, and extent of substantive tests to be performed. The auditor's understanding will help identify types of potential misstatements that can occur [answer (a)] and factors that affect the risk of material misstatements [answer (d)]. These answers affect the nature, timing, and extent of tests. Answer (c) deals with the effect of the internal control structure on the client's operations, not its effect on the nature, timing and extent of the auditor's tests.

31. (a) An entity's internal control structure consists of three elements: the control environment, the accounting system, and control procedures.

32. (c) When goods are received, they should be examined for quantity to determine agreement with the amount ordered (purchase order) and the amount the vendor claims to have shipped (vendor's shipping document). The receiving clerk prepares a receiving report which indicates the quantity received. Agreement of quantity on receiving report with quantity on vendor's invoice is usually determined before payment, not at time of receipt of the goods.

33. (a) Before checks are prepared, employees approve the vouchers for payment, match documents and verify mathematical accuracy. Checks are prepared and then signed by an individual with proper authority who also controls the mailing of the checks. Keeping the control of mailing with the employee who signed the checks, instead of sending them back to an employee who performed an earlier procedure in the disbursements process, prevents alterations of check amounts and payees.

34. (d) Because timely communication may be important, the auditor may choose to communicate significant matters during the course of the audit rather than after the audit is completed. The decision on whether interim communication should be issued would be influenced by the relative significance of the matters noted and the urgency of corrective follow-up action. Answer (a) is incorrect because of the potential for misinterpretation of the limited degree of assurance associated with the auditor issuing a written report representing that no reportable conditions were noted. Answer (b) is incorrect because the auditor may decide the matter does not have to be reported if the audit committee has acknowledged its understanding and consideration of deficiencies in the internal control structure and the related risks. Answer (c) is a situation which is specifically allowed.

35. (d) The second standard of field work states that, "The auditor should obtain a sufficient understanding of the internal control structure to plan the audit and to determine the nature, timing and extent of tests to be performed." These tests are the substantive tests for financial statement assertions. The auditor does not use the knowledge provided by the understanding of the internal control structure and the assessed level of control risk to determine the reliability of procedures to safeguard assets [answer (a)] and opportunities to perpetrate and conceal irregularities [answer (b)]; instead, the safeguarding of assets and minimization of irregularities affect the understanding of the control structure and assessment of control risk. Answer (c) is unrelated to internal control structure. Inherent risk, which is the susceptibility of a balance or transaction to an error, and materiality judgments are not directly affected by the control structure.

36. (b) There are three common methods the auditor uses to document his understanding of the internal control structure (control environment, accounting system, control procedures) in the audit workpapers—narrative, flowchart, and internal control questionnaire. Answer (a) refers to an audit program, which takes the form of a series of procedures, not a flowchart. Answer (c) is part of what the auditor does in obtaining an understanding of the accounting system but is not something that would typically be presented diagrammatically in a flowchart. Also, a flowchart is not used to document the auditor's evaluation of an accounting system [answer (d)].

37. (b) After the auditor assesses control risk, he may desire a further reduction in the assessed level of control risk for some assertions. He would then decide if it is likely that additional evidential matter could be obtained to support a lower assessed level of control risk for these assertions. If yes, and it is likely to be efficient to obtain such evidential matter, the auditor would then perform additional tests of controls. Next, whether the auditor performed additional tests of controls or not, the auditor would document the basis for conclusions about the assessed level of control risk and design substantive tests. Answer (a) incorrectly refers to tests of controls, instead of substantive tests, as tests of financial statement assertions. Analytical procedures, used as substantive tests [answer (c)], would

not typically be performed immediately after assessing control risk, but rather after designing substantive tests. Answer (d) might be part of tests of controls or obtaining an understanding of the control structure, neither of which occurs immediately after assessing control risk.

38. (d) The auditor wants to determine if checks are only written after a voucher, which would be dated no later than the check, has been approved. This is a test of validity which involves going back in a system. Answers (a) and (b) are testing completeness by going forward in the system from vouchers to checks. Answer (c) is looking for vouchers approved after the check is written, which is a departure from the control procedure.

39. (d) The vouchers payable department approves vendors' invoices for payment. Before approval, the invoice should be compared with supporting documents. The other answers are desirable internal control procedures, but they are typically performed by other departments—cash disbursements [answer (a)] and purchasing [answers (b) and (c)].

40. (b) A weakness in controls over recording equipment retirements increases the risk that equipment which is removed from the plant is not removed from the accounting records. When the auditor selects items in the accounting records and tries to locate them in the plant, he may discover retired equipment that is still in the accounting records. Answer (a) is testing the correctness of the "other assets" account, which should include equipment that is on hand but not in use. Answer (c) is a test to determine that equipment on hand, not retired equipment, is included in the accounting records. Answer (d) tests accuracy and completeness of depreciation expense.

41. (b) Reportable conditions are defined as matters the auditors believe should be communicated to the client's audit committee because they represent significant deficiencies in the design or operation of the internal control structure.

42. (b) The entity's internal control structure consists of the control procedures, the control environment and the accounting system. The control environment consists of management's and the board of directors' philosophy, operating style, attitude to work controls, the entity's organizational structure, and personnel policies and procedures. The accounting system consists of the methods and records used to identify, assemble, classify, and record transactions. The control procedures are the policies and procedures established to provide reasonable assurance that specific control objectives are met and include segregation of duties, authorization methods and independent checks on performance. The organization's personnel manuals would be part of the control environment.

43. (a) Control risk is the risk that the client's internal control structure will not be effective in preventing, detecting, and correcting errors and irregularities in the normal course of business. Thus, if the auditor assesses control risk at the maximum, the auditor has determined that risk of errors and irregularities being present in account balances is very likely.

44. (c) The check signer is responsible for the mailing of the check and remittance advice. The check would not be returned to the vouchers payable department for mailing because it could be altered as to payee and/or amount. Answers (a), (b) and (d) are valid procedures that are performed by the vouchers payable department.

45. (b) The second standard of field work states, "The auditor should obtain a sufficient understanding of the Internal Control Structure to plan the audit and to determine the nature, timing, and extent of tests to be performed."

46. (c) Objectivity refers to the potential bias of the internal auditor. Objectivity is enhanced by having the internal auditor report to a level of management sufficiently removed from the accounting function (preferably the board of directors). Answers (a), (b), and (d) relate to the competency of internal auditors rather than their objectivity.

47. (c) Because of the inherent limitations of any internal control structure it may be impossible to provide absolute assurance that the objectives of internal control are satisfied. Reasonable assurance, which recognizes that the cost of an entity's internal control structure should not exceed the benefits that are expected to be derived, may be enough. Answer (a) is an example of an inherent limitation of an entity's internal control structure.

48. (a) Authorization for write-off of bad debts rests with the credit manager. The credit manager, organizationally, reports to the treasurer.

49. (b) Detection risk is the risk that the auditor's procedures are not sufficiently extensive to discover an error or an irregularity should one exist in an account. Detection risk is minimized by selecting a large sample size. Control risk is the risk that the client's internal controls are not sufficient to prevent, detect, and correct errors and irregularities in the normal course of business. Thus, when control risk is high, the auditor would choose a large sample size in order to minimize detection risk.

50. (b) Objectivity refers to the potential biasness of the internal auditor. Objectivity is enhanced by having the internal auditor report to a level of management sufficiently removed from the accounting function (preferably the board of directors). Answers (a), (c) and (d) relate to the quality of the internal auditor's work rather than the objectivity of the internal auditors.

51. (d) If the auditor does not plan to reduce the audit sample size based upon an assessment of control risk (the auditor, for example, may consider control risk to be at the maximum), all the auditor is required to do is to document the client's internal control structure. Answers (a), (b) and (c) imply that the auditor is planning to reduce the audit sample size based upon an assessment of control risk which is below the maximum.

52. (a) Detection risk is the risk that the auditor's procedures will not detect an error in an account when in fact one exists. As the auditor's assurance that there are no errors in an account balance by applying substantive procedures is increased, the auditor's detection risk by definition may decrease.

53. (c) Illegal acts have financial statement implications in that the client may be faced with fines or penalties as a result of the illegal acts. Such contingencies should be recognized in the financial statements. Thus, the auditor must obtain an understanding of the illegal acts in order to consider its potential financial statement effect.

54. (a) When detection risk decreases, the auditor will accept a smaller chance of not detecting an error; therefore, the auditor would test more transactions. That is, the auditor would increase the scope of substantive testing.

55. (d) Once the checks have been signed, they should not be returned to any employee involved in the disbursement cycle of the entity. Answers (a), (b) and (c) represent tasks performed by individuals in the disbursement cycle. Therefore, these individuals should not be responsible for mailing the disbursement checks.

56. (b) The initial task in the cash receipts cycle is to establish immediate control over incoming cash receipts. This control is achieved by listing incoming cash receipts. The task is performed by the employee responsible for opening the mail.

57. (a) Since the auditor is working in an "attest" function, he can have no interest in the client operations or else his objective judgment would be biased.

58. (a) The general standards concern the auditor as an individual and describe his audit competence, need for independence, and require due professional care.

59. (c) The auditor is responsible for his report only; management is responsible for the statements and disclosures.

60. (d) General standards refer to the training and proficiency of the auditor.

61. (d) Without independence the auditor cannot objectively issue an opinion.

62. (c) The independent auditor's report should be addressed to the client, the board of directors, or the stockholders, depending on the circumstances.

63. (d) This is a major consideration for the successor CPA to determine whether to accept the engagement. "The successor auditor should make specific and reasonable inquiries of the predecessor regarding matters that the successor believes will assist him in determining whether to accept the engagement."

64. (b) Engagement letters are used each time the CPA is associated with the financial statements. Their purpose is to clarify the nature of the engagement and have management agree to this (evidenced by signing the engagement letter).

65. (d) Answers (a), (b) and (c) involve judgment by the auditor only and as such the decision process only involves the auditor. Answer (d), however, would necessarily have to involve the client since the client will be preparing the schedules.

66. (d) The third general standard of GAAS states in part that "due professional care" is to be exercised in the conduct of the audit. The implicit meaning of this standard is that each level of personnel within a CPA firm be adequately supervised. The purpose of the review is to critically review the work done and the judgment exercised by all staff levels.

67. (b) Generally accepted audit standards require that in a financial statement audit, the CPA is required to perform analytical procedures in the planning stage and final review stage of the audit.

68. (a) Before accepting an audit engagement, a successor auditor should make inquiries of the predecessor auditor in order to assist the successor auditor in deciding whether to accept the client. Answer (a) is correct because disagreements concerning audit procedures could affect the scope of the audit and the final expression of an opinion.

69. (c) The third general standard is: Due professional care is to be exercised in the performance of the audit and the preparation of the report. Exercise of due care requires critical review at every level of supervision of the work done and the judgment exercised by those assisting in the audit. Answer (a) relates to the first general standard. Answers (b) and (d) incorrectly include the word "all." Auditors are not expected to examine all the evidence and detect all illegal acts.

70. (a) The objective of an audit of financial statements is the expression of an opinion on the fairness with which they present financial position, results of operations, and cash flows in conformity with generally accepted accounting principles. When the auditor becomes aware of information concerning a possible illegal act, the auditor should obtain sufficient information to evaluate the effect on the financial statements. Answers (b) and (c) are implications for other aspects of the audit. The audit committee should be informed, but it is not the auditor's responsibility to recommend remedial actions, as indicated in answer (d).

71. (d) Control risk is defined as the risk that a material misstatement that could occur in an assertion will not be prevented or detected on a timely basis by an entity's internal control structure policies or procedures. The auditor assesses control risk as part of his overall evaluation of the risk that material misstatements may exist in the financial statements.

72. (a) Internal control structure policies and procedures relevant to an audit are those that pertain to an entity's ability to record, process, summarize, and report financial data consistent with management's assertions. The auditor's primary concern is the affect those policies and procedures have on the financial statement assertions. Management override, answer (b), is an inherent limitation of internal control structures. Answer (c) is one element of the internal control structure. Answer (d) is a factor comprising the control environment element of the internal control structure.

73. (d) A sale typically occurs and should be recorded when goods are shipped. Matching prenumbered shipping documents with sales journal entries is a good control to ensure that all sales are recorded. All the shipping documents should be accounted for as either resulting in a journal entry or having been voided.

74. (d) When a bank lockbox system is used, customers send their remittances directly to the bank, thus eliminating the possibility of employees misappropriating those cash receipts. Answers (b) and (c) do provide some control but involve employees. Answer (a) provides protection if a theft of cash occurs, rather than preventing the misappropriation.

75. (b) To avoid paying incorrect or duplicate amounts to vendors, the accounts payable department should compare the quantities and prices on the vendor's invoice to the quantities noted on the receiving report and to what was requested on the purchase order. Answers (a), (c) and (d) are good controls, but do not involve the accounts payable department. The control in answer (a) involves the receiving department. The control in answer (c) is performed by the treasurer or cash disbursements clerk. The control in answer (d) involves the requisitioning and purchasing departments.

76. (b) The accounting department is responsible for recording amounts due to vendors. If goods are returned to a vendor, a debit memo should be prepared indicating that the buyer is debiting the vendor's payable account. The purchasing department may prepare the debit memo, but the accounting department needs the debit memo to record the reduction in the account payable account.

77. (b) The objective is to determine whether checks have been issued for unauthorized expenditures that are not supported with an approved voucher, a purchase order, and a receiving report. The direction of testing would be from the cash disbursement back through to the beginning of the transaction. If any of the necessary documents is missing, the expenditure may not have been authorized. Testing from the other documents forward will not reveal unauthorized transactions because those documents provide the authorization for expenditures.

78. (d) An auditor assesses control risk to determine the acceptable detection risk and extent of substantive tests to perform. When an auditor plans to assess control risk at a low level, he must identify specific policies and procedures that are likely to prevent or detect material misstatements, and he must perform tests of controls to evaluate the effectiveness of such policies and procedures. If, based on the tests of controls, the control risk is assessed at a low level, the auditor may limit the extent of substantive testing. Answers (a) and (c) do not include references to tests of controls, which would be required. Answer (b) includes extensive substantive tests, which is incorrect.

79. (a) An auditor is required to obtain an understanding of a client's internal control structure. Reviewing policies and procedures manuals that describe a client system such as inventory and the related controls is a standard audit step in obtaining that understanding. The procedures presented in answers (b), (c), and (d) are designed to test dollar amounts in the financial statements, not to understand the internal control structure.

80. (c) Documents should not flow back through a system. If checks are returned to a record keeping department, such as the payroll department as in this case, they may be misallocated or may represent unauthorized or invalid payments, such as payments to fictitious or terminated employees in this case. The other choices are examples of internal control strengths.

81. (a) A basic control procedure is to separate custody of assets from the record keeping for those assets. Using an independent trust company to hold securities is a very common procedure. Answer (d), which assigns custody of the securities to one individual in the organization, is not very practical for marketable securities, nor is it a common control procedure. Answer (b) provides assurance at one point in time only; however, losses could occur during the year. Answer (c) does not go beyond ledger accounts, providing no safeguard against theft of the physical securities.

82. (b) During an audit, if the auditor discovers "reportable conditions", which are significant deficiencies in the design or operation of the internal control structure, he should communicate them to the audit committee. If no significant deficiencies are found, the auditor should not issue a written report representing that no reportable conditions were noted because of the potential for misinterpretation. Answers (c) and (d) are typical inclusions in the report. Answer (a) is acceptable since a reportable condition may or may not be of such a magnitude as to be considered a "material weakness".

83. (b) Inquiry of the predecessor auditor before accepting an audit engagement is a necessary procedure because the predecessor auditor may be able to provide the successor auditor with information that will assist him or her in determining whether to accept the engagement. The inquiries should include specific questions regarding the predecessor's understanding as to the reason for the change of auditors. Answers (a), (c) and (d) are unrelated to the question of client acceptance and would have no significance for the predecessor auditor unless they led the successor to believe that financial statements reported on by the predecessor may require revision.

84. (c) CPA firms should have quality control systems that include policies and procedures for deciding whether to accept or continue a client in order to minimize the likelihood of association with a client whose management lacks integrity. Accordingly, if a new client's management probably lacks integrity, an auditor would likely not accept the new audit engagement. Answer (b) may be a factor affecting client acceptance but, although early appointment is preferable, an auditor may accept an engagement near or after the close of the fiscal year. The situations presented in answers (a) and (d) would typically not arise until after the new engagement was accepted.

85. (b) The first standard of field work requires supervision of assistants, if any. Supervision involves directing the efforts of assistants who are involved in accomplishing the objectives of the audit and determining whether those objectives were accomplished. An element of supervision is reviewing the work performed by each assistant to determine whether it was adequately performed and to evaluate whether the results are consistent with the conclusions to be presented in the auditor's report. Answer (a) refers to quality control standards that are CPA-firm based and distinct from the responsibility of individuals to adequately supervise each assistant on a particular engagement. Answer (c) refers to audit procedures, which would be approved as part of the planning process, not as part of the review process. Answer (d) relates to the first general standard which requires that the audit be performed by person(s) with adequate training and proficiency, rather that to the review of assistant's work, which is the supervision requirement of the first field work standard.

86. (d) An auditor obtains knowledge about a new client's business and its industry as part of audit planning. The auditor should obtain a level of knowledge of the entity's business that will enable him or her to plan and perform the audit in accordance with generally accepted auditing standards. That level of knowledge should enable him or her to obtain an understanding of the events, transactions, and practices that may have a significant effect on the financial statements. Knowledge of a client's business and industry can help an auditor provide constructive suggestions, answer (a), and evaluate misstatements, answer (c), but the reason to obtain such knowledge is to plan the audit engagement. All audits should be planned and performed with an attitude of professional skepticism, answer (b). This skepticism is not developed by obtaining knowledge about a client's business and industry.

87. (a) The auditor's responsibility in regard to illegal acts having a direct and material affect on the financial statements is the same as that for errors and irregularities; that is, to design the audit to provide reasonable assurance of detecting such illegal acts. An audit provides no assurance that illegal acts that have an indirect effect on the financial statements will be detected because the auditor, who is proficient in accounting and auditing, does not have sufficient basis for recognizing all possible violations of laws and regulations and may not become aware of these illegal acts unless informed by the client.

88. (d) If the auditor concludes that an illegal act has a material effect on the financial statements, and the act has not been properly accounted for or disclosed, the auditor should express a qualified or adverse opinion. If the client refuses to accept the auditor's report, the auditor should withdraw from the engagement and indicate the reasons for withdrawal in writing to the audit committee or board of directors. Answer (a) would cause the auditor to disclaim an opinion on the financial statements, which would not result in withdrawing from the engagement unless the client refused to accept the disclaimer. Answer (b) would not result in withdrawal if the client properly accounts for the illegal act. Answer (c) would not result in withdrawal if the client properly discloses the contingency and/or the auditor includes the uncertainty in the auditor's report.

89. (c) An audit of financial statements in accordance with generally accepted auditing standards should be planned and performed with an attitude of professional skepticism, which means that the auditor neither assumes that management is dishonest nor assumes unquestioned honesty. The auditor attributes of objectivity, independence, integrity, impartiality, and conservatism presented in answers (a), (b) and (d) are desirable, but not specifically required in planning and performing an audit.

90. (d) The auditor must document the understanding of a client's internal control structure. Such documentation may include flowcharts, questionnaires, decision tables, or memorandum. Flowcharts, which are diagrams that show a sequence of operations or processes, would not typically be used to describe or depict other work done by the auditor in meeting the second standard of field work regarding internal control structure. Thus, although the auditor would perform the activities listed in answers (a), (b) and (c), he or she would probably use means other than flowcharts to document the work that was done.

91. (c) The control environment represents the collective effort of various factors on enhancing or mitigating the effectiveness of specific control procedures and policies. Management's philosophy and operating style is a factor that has a significant influence on the control environment, particularly when management is dominated by one or a few individuals. Characteristics of management philosophy and style include management's approach to taking and monitoring business risks; management's attitudes and actions toward financial reporting; and management's emphasis on meeting budget, profit, and other financial and operating goals. Audit committees, answer (a), external influences, answer (b), and an internal audit function, answer (d), are also control environment factors. However, domination of management by one individual who is also a shareholder is a control environment factor that could have significantly more influence on the effectiveness of control procedures and policies - especially in a negative way.

92. (b) The auditor should obtain sufficient knowledge of the accounting system to understand the classes of transactions in the entity's operations that are significant to the financial statements; how those transactions are initiated; the accounting records, supporting documents, and specific accounts involved in processing and reporting transactions; the accounting processes involved from the initiation of a transaction to its inclusion in the financial statements, including how the computer is used; and the financial reporting process used to prepare financial statements, including significant estimates and disclosures. The process to prepare significant estimates is thus part of the accounting system, which consists of the methods and records established to identify, assemble, analyze, classify, record, and report an entity's transactions and to maintain accountability for the related assets and liabilities. Answers (a), (c) and (d) are examples of control procedures and do not fall under the accounting system definition.

93. (b) The auditor should concentrate on the substance of management's policies, procedures, and related actions rather than their form because management may establish appropriate policies and procedures but not act on them. Answer (a) is incorrect because the lack of documentation is a form issue whereas operating effectiveness relates to substance, which is what interests the auditor. Answer (c) is incorrect because if the auditor does not plan to rely, the difference between form and substance is irrelevant. Answer (d) is not related to the question in that it deals with management's cost/benefit evaluation of implementing controls, not substance v. form.

94. (a) Segregating incompatible duties is a typical control procedure. Thus, the existence of incompatible duties is a weakness in control procedures, not an inherent limitation of the internal control structure. Even if control policies and procedures are placed in operation, the potential effectiveness of an entity's internal control structure is subject to inherent limitations. Mistakes in the application of policies and procedures may arise from such causes as mistakes in judgment, which is answer (c), as well as personal carelessness, fatigue, and distraction. Also, policies and procedures that require segregation of duties can be circumvented by management override or collusion among internal or external parties, which are answers (b) and (d).

95. (a) After obtaining an understanding of the internal control structure and assessing control risk, the auditor may desire a further reduction in the assessed level of control risk for certain assertions. In such cases, the auditor considers whether additional evidential matter sufficient to support a further reduction is likely to be available, and whether it would be cost efficient to perform tests of controls to obtain that evidential matter. If the auditor decides not to perform additional tests it is likely that the auditor concluded that additional evidence to support a further reduction in control risk was not likely to be available or was not cost beneficial to obtain, which is the answer in this case. Answer (b) is incorrect because inherent risk has no direct bearing on the assessment of control risk. Answer (c) is incorrect because the design of the internal control structure has to be tested for effectiveness in order to rely on the controls. The word "increase" makes answer (d) incorrect.

96. (b) If the auditor is concerned with completeness, he or she would test the client's controls that are designed to determine that all sales that occur are recorded. These controls could include the entity accounting for all prenumbered shipping documents, which provide the basis for recording sales, to determine that none have been omitted. Answer (a) deals with mathematical accuracy, not completeness. Answers (c) and (d) deal with authorization of prices and credit, not with completeness.

97. (a) If an entity wants to be sure that all billed sales are correctly posted to the accounts receivable subsidiary ledger, an internal control procedure that compares invoices or billings to the subsidiary ledger entries should be designed. Thus, comparing daily summaries of billed sales to daily postings to the receivables ledger will provide the necessary assurance. Answers (b) and (d), which compare invoices and shipments, do not include any comparisons with postings to the accounts receivable ledger. Answer (c), which compares general and subsidiary ledgers, does not include comparisons to billings or invoices.

98. (c) Authorization and recording are incompatible functions that should be assigned to different individuals. In this case, authorization of payroll changes, which is typically the responsibility of the human resources department, should be segregated from recording payroll, which is the responsibility of the payroll department. If the payroll department supervisor is responsible for these two functions, the entity's internal control structure may be inadequate to prevent or detect material misstatements in the payroll area. Thus, the auditor would assess control risk at the maximum. Answers (a) and (b) are activities that the payroll department supervisor may want to perform to verify the accuracy of the payroll and are compatible with the payroll department's responsibility. Answer (d) is compatible with payroll department activities. Although it might be preferable for the human resources or personnel department to be responsible for the formal hiring of employees, departments such as payroll must get involved in the hiring process when it involves their department employees.

99. (b) The accounts payable, or vouchers payable, department has the responsibility to prepare vouchers for payment. As part of that process, an employee in that department should check vendors' invoices for mathematical accuracy by recomputing calculations and extensions, and should match the vendors' invoices with receiving reports and purchase orders for quantities, prices, and terms. Answers (a) and (c) are posting and reconciling activities that should be performed by accounting department employees who are not involved in preparing vouchers for payment. Answer (d) is incorrect because an employee in the treasurer's department should cancel invoices after they are paid.

100. (c) Time tickets should be designed to keep track of hours worked, by whom, and on what production orders. After approval by a production supervisor, time tickets provide the information on number of hours worked directly on specific production orders. If time tickets are properly used to record actual hours worked on orders, approval and/or review of these cards should prevent direct labor hours from being incorrectly charged to manufacturing overhead. Answer (a) is incorrect because counts of work in process will not provide breakdowns between direct and indirect costs and therefore would not prevent direct labor hours from being incorrectly charged to overhead. Answer (b) is incorrect because errors may be made on the production orders. In order to prevent and/or detect errors regarding direct labor hours, the production orders would have to be compared to time tickets. Answer (d) is incorrect because work-in-process inventory is a total which combines direct labor and manufacturing overhead. Even if this total is correct, direct labor could have been incorrectly charged to manufacturing overhead.

101. (d) Accurate inventory records would reflect actual quantities in existence. If a company periodically counts inventory and adjusts the perpetual inventory records accordingly, those inventory records are likely to be accurate. Answer (a) is incorrect because current cost may not be the basis used to value inventory; a company may be using last-in-first-out, standard costs, lower of cost or market, etc. Answer (b) addresses management's concern about excessive inventory levels, not the accuracy of inventory records. Answer (c) is a procedure that relates to the accuracy of amounts paid to vendors.

102. (a) The valuation or allocation assertion concerns collectibility of receivables. That is, accounts receivable should be valued at estimated net realizable value, after deducting an allowance for uncollectible accounts. If an entity has credit approval policies, the gross and net amounts presented for receivables on the balance sheet are more likely to be fairly stated. The completeness assertion in answer (b) is concerned with whether or not all sales that have occurred are recorded, not whether or not those sales will generate collectible receivables. The existence or occurrence assertion in answer (c) is concerned with whether or not recorded sales and receivables are valid and

not fictitious, rather than the amount collectible. The rights and obligations assertion in answer (d) is concerned with whether or not the entity owns the receivable, not the amount collectible.

103. (d) AU 311 states that the procedures that an auditor may consider in planning the audit usually involve a review of his records relating to the entity and discussion with other firm personnel and personnel of the entity. An example of those procedures is to determine the extent of involvement, if any, of consultants, specialists, and internal auditors. Choice (a) is incorrect because a written representation letter is required, but is not a part of the planning process (it is obtained the last day of field work). Choice (b) is incorrect because an auditor must consider illegal acts that might have a material effect on the financial statements, but that is not part of the planning process. Choice (c) is incorrect because determining the reasonableness of accounting estimates is accomplished by gathering evidence that support the estimations in the field work phase and not in the planning stage.

104. (c) AU 319 states that the auditor's understanding of the internal control structure may sometimes raise doubts about the auditability of an entity's financial statements. Concerns about the integrity of the entity's management may be so serious as to cause the auditor to conclude that the risk of management misrepresentations in the financial statements is such that an audit cannot be conducted. Concerns about the nature and extent of an entity's records may cause the auditor to conclude that it is unlikely that sufficient competent evidential matter will be available to support an opinion on the financial statements. Choice (a) is incorrect because the complexity of the accounting system would not influence the auditor negatively. Choice (b) is incorrect because related party transactions would be closely scrutinized by the auditor but would not influence the auditor negatively. Choice (d) is incorrect because the operating effectiveness of the control procedure would influence the level of risk the auditor is willing to assume but not the auditability of the financial statements.

105. (a) AU 315 states that the initiative in communicating rests with the successor auditor. The communication may be either written or oral. Both the predecessor and successor auditors should hold in confidence information obtained from each other. This obligation applies whether or not the successor accepts the engagement. Before contacting the predecessor, the successor auditor must have the permission from the client to do so.

106. (a) AU 311 states that a pre-engagement audit conference is a meeting between the senior auditor and the other members of the audit team to discuss the time and review the general plan of the audit. Specific personnel are assigned to specific areas at that time and each member of the team is evaluated to determine that each member is independent of the client. A list of related parties is distributed to enable staff members to recognize related party transactions when they encounter them. Choices (b) and (c) *could be part* of the discussion, but they are not the primary reasons for the meeting. Furthermore, the initial time budget is the responsibility of the partner and the senior in charge and the decision to rely on specialists and internal auditors is not made by the audit staff. Choice (d) is incorrect because disagreements regarding technical issues are discussed and resolved after field work has started.

107. (b) AU 311 states that knowledge of an entity's business is ordinarily obtained through experience with the entity or its industry and inquiry of personnel of the entity. Working papers from prior years may contain useful information about the nature of the business, organizational structure, operating characteristics, and transactions that may require special consideration. Other sources may be audit guides, industry publications, financial statements of other entities in the industry, textbooks, periodicals, and individuals knowledgeable about the industry. Choice (a) is incorrect because tests of transactions and balances will not provide the auditor with an overall understanding of the client's business. Choice (c) might be correct for a new client, but the question states that this is a continuing client. The firm has obtained an understanding of the client's business in prior years and documented that understanding in the working papers. Choice (d) is incorrect because evaluating the internal control environment will not provide the auditor with an overall understanding of the client's business.

108. (a) AU 311 states that the auditor should consider the methods the entity uses to process accounting information because such methods influence the design of the internal control structure. The extent to which computer processing is used in accounting applications, as well as the complexity of that processing, may also influence the nature, timing, and extent of audit procedures. Choices (b), (c), and (d) are incorrect because materiality, audit objectives, and acceptable level of audit risk are not based on the methods used to process accounting information.

109. (b) AU 312 states that, in planning the audit, the auditor should use judgment as to the appropriately low level of audit risk and the preliminary judgment about materiality levels in a manner that can be expected to provide, within the inherent limitations of the auditing process, sufficient evidential matter to obtain reasonable assurance about whether the financial statements are free of material misstatement. Materiality levels include an overall level for each statement; however, because the statements are interrelated, and for reasons of efficiency, the auditor ordinarily considers materiality for planning purposes in terms of the smallest aggregate level of misstatements that could be considered material to any one of the financial statements. For example, if misstatements aggregating approximately $100,000 would have a material effect on income but such misstatements would have to aggregate approximately to $200,000 to materially affect financial position, it would not be appropriate to design auditing procedures that would be expected to detect misstatements of approximately $200,000. The lower amount is normally used. Choice (a) is incorrect because the concept of materiality recognizes that some matters are important, while other matters are not, for fair presentation of financial statements in conformity with GAAP. Choices (c) and (d) are incorrect because the auditor's consideration of materiality is a matter of professional judgment and is influenced by a perception of the needs of a reasonable person who will rely on the financial statements. Materiality is "the magnitude of an omission or misstatement of accounting information that, in the light of surrounding circumstances, makes it probable that the judgment of a reasonable person relying on the information would have been changed or influenced by the omission."

110. (d) AU 316 states that if a condition or circumstance differs adversely from the auditor's expectation, the auditor needs to consider the reason for such a difference. For example:

- Analytical procedures disclose significant differences from expectations.
- Significant unreconciled differences between reconciliations of a control account and subsidiary records.
- Confirmation requests disclose significant differences or yield fewer responses than expected.
- Transactions selected for testing are not supported by proper documentation.
- Supporting records or files that should be readily available are not promptly produced when requested.
- Audit tests detect errors that apparently were known to client personnel, but were not voluntarily disclosed.

When such conditions exist, the planned scope of audit procedures should be reconsidered. As the differences from expectations increase, the auditor should consider whether the assessment of the risk of material misstatement of the financial statements made in the planning stage of the engagement is still appropriate. Choices (a) and (b) are encouraging factors that management is not willing to circumvent the rules just to meet earnings projections and that the board of directors makes all financial decisions. Choice (c) is incorrect because uncorrected conditions do not necessarily mean that material misstatements exist.

111. (b) AU 322 states that when assessing the internal auditors' competence, the auditor should obtain or update information from prior years about such factors as:

- Educational level and professional experience of internal auditors.
- Professional certification and continuing education.
- Audit policies, programs, and procedures.
- Practices regarding assignment of internal auditors.
- Supervision and review of internal auditors' activities.
- Quality of working-paper documentation, reports, and recommendations.
- Evaluation of internal auditors' performance.

Choices (a), (c), and (d) are not among the factors listed above.

112. (d) AU 319 states that control procedures are those policies and procedures, in addition to the control environment and accounting system, that management has established to provide reasonable assurance that specific entity objectives will be achieved. Control procedures have various objectives and are applied at various organizational and data processing levels. They may also be integrated into specific components of the control environment and the accounting system. Generally, they may be categorized as procedures that pertain to:

- Proper authorization of transactions and activities.
- Segregation of duties that reduce the opportunities to both perpetrate and conceal irregularities, assigning different people the responsibilities of authorizing transactions, recording transactions, and maintaining custody of assets.
- Design and use of adequate documents and records to help ensure the proper recording of transactions and events, such as monitoring the use of prenumbered shipping documents.

113. (b) The reason that the auditor evaluates control risk (i.e., internal control) is to determine the risk that the financial statements may contain an error or be affected by fraud. Since the financial statements are considered to be assertions made by management, answer (b) is correct because it refers to management's assertion.

114. (c) AU 319 states that detection risk is the risk that an error or irregularity won't be detected by the audit. It is unrelated to the client's control environmental factors. The control environment represents the collective effect of various factors on establishing, enhancing, and mitigating the effectiveness of specific policies and procedures such as:

- Management's philosophy and operating style.
- The entity's organizational structure.
- The functioning of the board of directors and its committees, particularly the audit committee.
- Methods of assigning authority and responsibility.
- Management's control methods for monitoring and following up on performance, including internal auditing.
- Personnel policies and practices.
- Various external influences that affect an entity's operations and practices.

115. (b) AU 319 states that the ultimate purpose of assessing control risk is to contribute to the auditor's evaluation of the risk that material misstatements exist in the financial statements. The process of assessing control risk (together with assessing inherent risk) provides evidential matter about the risk that such misstatements may exist in the financial statements. The auditor uses this evidential matter as part of the reasonable basis for an opinion. Choice (a) is incorrect because failure to identify procedures relevant to assertions is not the ultimate purpose of assessing risk. Choices (c) and (d) are incorrect because collusion or management that override policies are inherent risks that the auditor cannot totally eliminate and therefore cannot be the ultimate purpose of assessing control.

116. (a) AU 319 states that when the auditor assesses control risk at below the maximum level, he should obtain sufficient evidential matter to support that assessed level. The type of evidential matter, its source, its timeliness, and the existence of other evidential matter related to the conclusion to which it leads, all bear on the degree of assurance evidential matter provides. These characteristics influence the nature, timing, and extent of the tests of controls that the auditor applies to obtain evidential matter about control risk. The auditor selects such tests from a variety of techniques such as inquiry, observation, inspection, and reperformance of a policy or procedure that pertains to an assertion. No one specific test of controls is always necessary, applicable, or equally effective in every circumstance. Choices (b), (c), and (d) are incorrect because they are direct tests of financial statement balances (substantive tests), and not tests of controls which provide evidence about control risk.

117. (c) AU 319 states that the auditor may make a preliminary assessment of control risk at less than a high level only when the auditor:

- is able to identify policies and procedures of the accounting and internal control systems relevant to specific assertions which are likely to prevent or detect material misstatements in the financial statements; and
- plans to perform tests of control to support the assessment.

Choice (a) is incorrect because analytical procedures or tests of reasonableness test amounts of financial data. Choice (b) is incorrect because tests of details are performed as a substantive test to determine material mistakes in the financial statements. Choice (d) is incorrect because, if the audit effort of performing tests of controls exceeds the potential reduction in substantive testing, tests of controls will not be performed because doing so would reduce audit efficiency.

118. (a) AU 350 states that the risk of incorrect rejection and the risk of assessing control risk too high relate to the efficiency of the audit. If the auditor's evaluation of a sample leads him to unnecessarily assess control risk too high for an assertion, he would ordinarily increase the scope of substantive tests to compensate for the perceived ineffectiveness of the internal control structure policy or procedure. Although the audit may be less efficient in these circumstances, the audit is, nevertheless, effective. Choice (b) is incorrect because tests of controls are not designed to directly detect misstatements. Tests of controls directed toward the operating effectiveness of an internal control policy and procedure are concerned with how the policy is applied, and how consistent and by whom it was applied. Choice (d) is incorrect because tolerable errors are related to substantive tests of details.

119. (c) A copy of the remittance listing is sent to the accounts receivable clerk and posted to the subsidiary records. Accounting for assets is a function that should be separated from the custody of those assets. The accounts receivable bookkeeper maintains records of the balance owed by each customer, while the cashier has custody of the cash. The cashier does not have an opportunity to cover a shortage of cash by using checks received on account because the AR ledger would indicate a different balance than that owed. There is no need to send copies to the internal auditor, the treasurer, or the bank, because the goal is to establish accountability for the asset.

120. (d) The treasurer has responsibility for custody of assets; therefore, authorizing the write-off of a receivable (an asset) is the responsibility of the treasurer. Choice (a) is incorrect because A/R is an accounting function that should be separated from the custody of the asset. Choice (b) is incorrect because the credit department authorized credit to customers and they should not be in the position of writing-off what they authorized. Choice (c) is incorrect because the accounts payable department has nothing to do with receivables.

121. (d) The reconciliation provides evidence that sales which have been invoiced are recorded in the accounts receivable subsidiary ledger but does not reduce the risk of errors in billing. Choice (a) is incorrect because it reduces the risk of errors in the billing process by providing evidence that all items shipped were included in the sales invoices. Choice (b) is incorrect because it reduces the risk of errors in the billing process by controlling the mathematical accuracy of the computations on the sales invoices. Choice (c) is incorrect because matching shipping documents with sales orders reduces the risk of errors in the billing process by providing evidence that approved sales orders were shipped before being invoiced.

122. (b) AU 326 states that assertions about existence or occurrence deal with whether assets or liabilities of the entity exist at a given date and whether recorded transactions have occurred during a given period. For example, management asserts that finished goods inventories in the balance sheet are available for sale, or management asserts that sales in the income statement represent the exchange of goods or services with customers for cash or other consideration. Choice (a) is incorrect because tracing supports completeness. Choices (c) and (d) are incorrect because valuation and rights would not be tested from the voucher register to the supporting documents.

123. (d) The unused forms should be accounted for by the department in which the forms are prepared - purchase orders in the purchasing department and receiving reports in the receiving department. Choice (a) is incorrect because the reconciliation of vouchers payable with the receiving report is done before the authorization of payment of the invoice. Choice (b) is incorrect because vouchers payable should approve vouchers for payment by having an authorized employee sign the voucher. Choice (c) is incorrect because vouchers payable should indicate on the voucher the accounts to be debited when the voucher is authorized for payment.

124. (d) An internal control questionnaire concerning the initiation and execution of equipment transactions would not be concerned with equipment that is owned and in place because it is not part of the current transactions. Choice (a) is incorrect because requests for major repairs should be authorized at a higher level to control the use of the assets. Choice (b) is incorrect because prenumbered purchase orders should be used for the purchases. Choice (c) is incorrect because requests for purchases of equipment should be reviewed for consideration of soliciting bids.

125. (d) AU 319 states that the substantive tests that the auditor performs consist of tests of details of transactions and balances and analytical procedures. In assessing control risk, the auditor also may use tests of details of transactions as tests of controls. The objective of tests of details of transactions performed as substantive tests is to detect material misstatements in the financial statements. The objective of tests of details of transactions performed as tests of controls is to evaluate whether an internal control structure policy or procedure operated effectively.

Although these objectives are different, both may be accomplished concurrently through performance of a test of details on the same transaction. The auditor should recognize, however, that careful consideration should be given to the design and evaluation of such tests to ensure that both objectives will be accomplished. Choices (a), (b), and (c) are incorrect because tests of details would not be used to monitor the design of the documents, nor the internal control policy, nor to detect material misstatements.

126. (b) The auditor is looking for evidence to prove that goods shipped are properly billed. To accomplish the completeness of the billing process for all goods shipped, it is necessary to sample from a population that includes all goods shipped by examining a sample of shipping documents and tracing them to matching sales invoices.

127. (c) AU 325 states that during the course of an audit, the auditor may become aware of matters relating to the internal control structure that may be of interest to the audit committee. The matters that this section requires for reporting to the audit committee are referred to as reportable conditions. Specifically, these are matters coming to the auditor's attention that should be communicated to the audit committee because they represent significant deficiencies in the design or operation of the internal control structure, which could adversely affect the organization's ability to record, process, summarize, and report financial data consistent with the assertions of management in the financial statements. Choice (a) is incorrect because information that greatly contradicts the auditor's going concern assumption is not considered reportable conditions. Choices (b) and (d) are incorrect because material irregularities and significant deficiencies are not considered reportable conditions.

128. (c) AU 325 states that the report should state that the communication is intended solely for the information and the use of the audit committee, management, and others within the organization. When there are requirements established to furnish such reports, specific reference to such regulatory authorities may be made. Any report on reportable conditions should:

- Indicate that the purpose of the audit was to report on the financial statements and not to provide assurance on the internal control structure.
- Include the definition of reportable conditions.
- Include the restriction on distribution.

Choice (a) is incorrect because reportable conditions may represent a conscious decision by management to accept that degree of risk because of cost or other considerations. The auditor can elect to use a preliminary substantive approach to test balances so internal control deficiencies do not necessarily constitute scope limitation. Choice (b) is incorrect because no requirement to perform tests of controls exists. Reportable conditions may be identified through the consideration of the internal control structure applications of audit procedures to balances or transactions during the course of an audit. Choice (d) is incorrect because they can be reported at any time.

129. (d) AU 322 states that in assessing competence and objectivity, the auditor usually considers information obtained from previous experience with the internal audit function, from discussions with management personnel, and from a recent external quality review, if performed, of the internal audit function's activities. The auditor may also use professional internal auditing standards as criteria in making the assessment. If the auditor determines that the internal auditors are sufficiently competent and objective, the auditor should then consider how the internal auditors' work may affect the audit. The other choices are all considered by the auditor as per above and therefore incorrect.

130. (d) The client is responsible for counting inventory and the auditor is responsible for observing the client's count. Since the timing of the observation depends on the timing of the count, there must be agreement between the auditor and client regarding the inventory observation procedures before the auditor finalizes an audit strategy for inventory. Answers (a), (b) and (c) are evidence-gathering issues that are decided by the auditor without specific regard to timing and other client concerns. Independently of the client, the auditor determines the extent of evidence needed in the audit, the nature of procedures to follow in the audit, and the scope of issues to be addressed in a legal letter.

131. (d) A successor auditor is required to make inquiries of the predecessor auditor regarding matters that the successor believes will assist him in determining whether he should accept a new audit engagement. The inquiries, which focus on the integrity of management and the reasons for the change in auditors, should include specific questions regarding disagreements with management as to accounting principles, auditing procedures, or other similarly significant matters. Answers (a) and (b) are issues which may surface when the successor communicates with the predecessor auditor, but are not directly related to the client acceptance decision. Answer (c) is unrelated to the successor/predecessor interaction.

132. (d) An engagement letter sets forth the terms of the engagement and the level of responsibility the auditor is assuming in the engagement. Typical points covered include the type of service to be performed, dates covered, professional standards to be followed, description of procedures to be employed, limited responsibility for detection of fraud, report on control deficiencies, other work to be performed, client assistance, and fees. The engagement letter does not typically include statements regarding future discussions about audit procedures after analytical procedures are performed. Answers (a), (b) and (c) are examples of points that are usually included in an engagement letter.

133. (b) As part of planning, an auditor is required to use analytical procedures to enhance the auditor's understanding of the client's business and to identify areas that may represent specific risks relevant to the audit. Analytical procedures involve comparisons of financial statement amounts to expectations developed by the auditor. Anticipated results, such as budgets and forecasts, is one source for developing such expectations. Other sources include prior period information, current period relationships within the financial statements, industry information, and relevant nonfinancial information. Answers (a) and (d) are procedures that are typically performed at the end of the audit, not during the planning stage. Answer (c) is a test of controls, not a planning procedure.

134. (b) Supervision involves directing the efforts of assistants who are involved in accomplishing the objectives of the audit and determining whether those objectives were accomplished. The in-charge auditor, as part of his supervisory responsibility, should review the work of each assistant to determine whether it was adequately performed and to evaluate whether the results are consistent with the conclusions to be presented in the auditor's report. This review and evaluative process should be explained to staff assistants by the in-charge auditor. Answers (a), (c) and (d) are issues that the in-charge may discuss with assistants but they are related more to staff development than to the in-charge's supervisory responsibility.

135. (b) In planning the audit, the auditor should consider his preliminary judgment about materiality levels. In some situations, this is done before the financial statements under audit have been prepared. In such a situation, the auditor's preliminary judgment about materiality might be based on the entity's annualized interim statements, or financial statements of one or more prior annual periods. Answers (a), (c) and (d) are incorrect because the auditor's preliminary judgment about materiality levels is considered in planning the audit, before sample sizes and substantive test are planned, and before internal control questionnaires and management representation letters are prepared.

136. (b) Detection risk is the risk that the auditor will not detect a material misstatement that exists in an assertion. As the acceptable level of detection risk decreases, the assurance provided from substantive tests should increase. Since applying substantive tests as of an interim date rather than as of the year-end potentially increases the risk that misstatements that may exist will not be detected, if the auditor wants to decrease detection risk, he may decide to perform substantive tests at year-end rather than at an interim date. Answer (a) is incorrect because substantive tests should be increased when allowable detection risk decreases. Answer (c) is incorrect because inherent risk cannot be ignored. Answer (d) is incorrect because control risk cannot be lowered without additional testing of controls.

137. (c) Material misstatements, including intentional manipulation of financial statements, are more likely to occur when management places undue emphasis on meeting earnings projections, especially if compensation is affected by meeting earnings targets. Another management characteristic that increases the risk of intentional manipulation is high turnover of senior accounting personnel, not the low turnover indicated in answer (a). Similarly, a rapid rate of change in an entity's industry would heighten an auditor's concern rather than a slow rate of change, as presented in answer (d). The auditor may be more concerned if insiders are selling stock, rather than purchasing stock, as presented in answer (b).

138. (d) The third general standard requires the independent auditor to perform his work with due care. Exercise of due care requires critical review at every level of supervision of the work done and the judgment exercised by those assisting in the audit. Answer (a) is incorrect because it is related to the second standard of field work, not the third general standard, and because the auditor may not thoroughly review all controls in all engagements. Answer (b) is incorrect because the auditor would thoroughly review indications of fraud and illegal acts, rather than limit his review. Answer (c) is incorrect because it is related to the first general standard, not the third, and because the adequacy of training and proficiency is not something the auditor objectively reviews.

139. (a) The second standard of field work requires the auditor to obtain an understanding of the internal control structure to plan the audit. The primary objective, therefore, of performing procedures to obtain that understanding is to provide the auditor with the knowledge necessary for audit planning. Answer (b) deals with inherent risk, which is assessed independent of the internal control structure. Answer (c) refers to tests of controls, modification of which would be based on information obtained after initially designing those tests. Evaluating consistent application of management policies, answer (d), may be of interest to the auditor but it is not the primary objective of performing procedures to understand the internal control structure.

140. (c) An entity's internal control structure consists of three elements: the control environment, the accounting system, and control procedures. The control environment reflects the overall attitude, awareness, and actions of the board of directors, management, owners, and others concerning the importance of control and its emphasis in the entity. Answers (a), (b) and (d) are examples of control procedures.

141. (d) Because of the inherent limitations of any internal control structure, it may be impossible to provide absolute assurance that the objectives of internal control are satisfied. Reasonable assurance, which recognizes that the cost of an entity's internal control structure should not exceed the benefits that are expected to be derived, may be enough. Answers (a) and (c) are correct statements about the internal control structure, but they are unrelated to the concept of reasonable assurance. Answer (b), which is also unrelated to the concept of reasonable assurance, is incorrect because adequate safeguards over access to assets and records would not be enough to maintain proper accountability; additional controls would be necessary.

142. (c) Assessing control risk is the process of evaluating the effectiveness of an entity's internal control structure in preventing or detecting material misstatements in financial statement assertions. Thus, control risk should be assessed in terms of those financial statement assertions. Answers (a) and (d) refer to control procedures and control environment factors, which, as elements of the internal control structure, provide input for assessing control risk. Answer (b) is incorrect because control risk assessment is concerned not only with potential irregularities, which are intentional misstatements, but also with unintentional errors.

143. (c) The auditor is required by the second standard of field work to obtain an understanding of the client's internal control structure, which includes the control environment, the accounting system, and control procedures. The auditor is also required to document his understanding of the internal control structure and his conclusions about the assessed level of control risk. If the auditor decides to assess control risk at the maximum, the basis for that conclusion does not have to be stated. If, however, control risk is assessed at less than the maximum, the basis for that conclusion must be documented.

144. (c) The initial task in the cash receipts cycle is to establish immediate control over incoming cash receipts. This control is achieved by having the employee who is responsible for opening the mail prepare listings of checks received. Answers (a) and (d) are procedures that should be performed later in the processing of cash receipts as checks are deposited and recorded. Answer (b) is not a control procedure that is typically found in the cash receipts cycle.

145. (a) Some internal control procedures, such as the segregation of duties, may not generate an audit trail of documents that the auditor can inspect. The auditor can test this type of control procedure by making inquiries of client personnel and observing who performs what duties. Answers (b) and (c) are procedures that relate more to substantive tests of financial statement amounts, rather than to tests of controls. Answer (d) is incorrect because

segregation of duties related to inventory is a control that is not evidenced by documents that the auditor can inspect.

146. (a) If the controls appear to be effective, the auditor would test the controls and if they were found to be effective the auditor would assess control risk below the maximum and reduce the extent of substantive testing. These tests of controls should only be performed when it is efficient to do so. It would be efficient if less time and effort would be spent testing controls than could be saved in substantive tests due to the lower control risk assessment. Answer (b) is incorrect because if the auditor does not expect to find evidence to support a reduction in his control risk assessment, he will not perform additional tests of controls. Answers (c) and (d) are incorrect because tests of controls are performed when control risk assessments are decreasing and there are internal control strengths, not when control risk is increasing and there are weaknesses in controls.

147. (b) In order to avoid duplicate payments, an entity's check signer should cancel the documents supporting the payment and stamp the voucher as "paid." If the auditor wants assurance that vouchers are not paid more than once, the auditor would select a sample of paid vouchers and determine if they have been stamped "paid." Answers (a) and (d) are incorrect because the auditor would determine if each voucher is supported by a vendor's invoice and is approved for authorized purchases if the auditor wanted assurance that the payment was for a valid authorized purchase, not to determine that vouchers have been paid only once. Answer (c) is incorrect because the auditor would determine that vouchers are prenumbered and accounted for if the auditor wanted assurance that no vouchers were lost or omitted.

148. (c) Reportable conditions are matters coming to the auditor's attention that, in his judgment, should be communicated to the audit committee because they represent significant deficiencies in the design or operation of the internal control structure. Because timely communication may be important, the auditor may choose to communicate such matters during the course of the audit rather than after the audit is completed. An auditor is not required to search for reportable conditions, as stated in answer (a), and should not, therefore, issue a written report representing that no reportable conditions were noted during the audit, as stated in answer (d). Answer (b) is incorrect because only some reportable conditions are of such a magnitude as to be considered a material weakness, which is defined as a reportable condition in which the design or operation of internal control structure elements does not reduce to a relatively low level the risk that material errors or irregularities may occur and not be detected by employees in the normal course of performing their assigned functions.

149. (c) In making judgments about the extent of the effect of an internal auditor's work on the CPA's auditing procedures, the CPA should consider the materiality of financial statement amounts, the risk of material misstatement, and the degree of subjectivity involved in the evaluation of the audit evidence gathered in support of the assertions. Work done by internal auditors related to assertions about fixed asset additions, because such assertions involve a low degree of subjectivity and may have a lower risk of material misstatement, will likely affect the CPA's auditing procedures. Answers (a), (b) and (d) deal with contingencies, valuation, and related-party transactions, which are examples of assertions that might have high risk or involve a high degree of subjectivity.

150. (d) If the independent auditor decides that it would be efficient to consider how the internal auditors' work might affect the audit, the independent auditor should assess the competence and objectivity of the internal audit function. When assessing objectivity, the auditor should determine the organizational status of the internal auditor, including the level to which the internal auditor reports. Answers (a), (b) and (c) are procedures that the independent auditor would perform to assess the internal auditors' competence, not objectivity.

151. (a) The auditor should obtain an understanding of a client's internal control structure, including knowledge about the design of relevant policies, procedures and records and whether they have been placed in operation by the entity. In planning the audit, such knowledge should be used to identify types of material misstatements, consider factors that affect the risk of material misstatements, and design substantive tests. Answer (b), which refers to operational efficiency, is a management concern rather than a planning objective of the auditor. Answer (c) is incorrect because the potential for collusion is an inherent limitation of an entity's internal control structure. Accordingly, based only on the auditor's knowledge of the design of control policies and procedures, the auditor cannot determine if controls have been circumvented by collusion. Answer (d) is incorrect because the auditor, after

obtaining knowledge about the design of control policies and procedures, must also evaluate the internal control structure before documenting the assessed level of control risk in the workpapers.

152. (b) The auditor's understanding of an entity and its internal control structure may raise doubts about the auditability of that entity's financial statements. For example, concerns may arise about the integrity of the entity's management. These concerns may be so serious as to cause the auditor to conclude that the risk of management misrepresentations in the financial statements is such that an audit cannot be conducted. Answers (a) and (d) may be concerns for the auditor, but since codes of conduct are not required business practice and changes in controls are often dictated by cost-benefit considerations, these concerns are not so serious as to render financial statements unauditable. Answer (c) is incorrect because management override of controls is an inherent limitation of any internal control structure.

153. (b) Management philosophy and operating style, which is one of the various factors that have an effect on the control environment, encompass a broad range of characteristics. Such characteristics may include management's approach to taking and monitoring risks, management's attitudes and actions toward financial reporting, and management's emphasis on meeting financial and operating goals. These characteristics have a significant influence on the control environment, particularly when management is dominated by one or a few individuals. Answer (a), which refers to the internal audit function, answer (c) which refers to a method of assigning authority and responsibility, and answer (d), which refers to audit committees, are incorrect because they are not part of management philosophy and operating style, but rather are part of other control environment factors.

154. (c) Management control methods is a control environment factor that affects management's ability to effectively supervise overall company activities. These methods include establishing systems that set forth management's plans and the results of actual performance, establishing methods that identify variances from budgets and forecasts, and using methods to investigate variances. Answer (a) refers to external influences, which is a separate control environment factor that includes monitoring and compliance requirements imposed by regulatory bodies. Answer (b) is a control procedure, rather than a part of management controls or the control environment. Answer (d) refers to personnel policies and practices, which is a separate control environment factor that includes giving employees the necessary resources to discharge their responsibilities.

155. (a) The auditor is required to document the auditor's understanding of the entity's internal control structure. The form and extent of documentation may be influenced by the size and complexity of the entity, but in all audits this understanding must be documented. Answer (b) is incorrect because searching for deficiencies in the internal control structure is not required when performing a financial statement audit in accordance with GAAS. Answer (c) is incorrect because the auditor only performs tests of controls when the auditor plans to assess control risk below the maximum. Answer (d) is incorrect because if the auditor assesses control risk at the maximum, he or she does not have to determine whether control procedures are suitably designed.

156. (a) When a bank lockbox system is used, customers, in effect, send their remittances directly to the bank, thus eliminating the possibility of employees misappropriating those cash receipts. The other answers are internal control procedures that involve employees. Answer (b) is incorrect because in addition to using prenumbered remittance advices, an employee would have to account for their sequence to determine if any have been returned, but the accompanying cash not properly recorded. Answer (c) is incorrect because a reconciliation of cash per bank and cash per books will not detect cash receipts that have not been properly recorded and not deposited in the bank. Answer (d) is incorrect because depositing cash receipts daily will not, by itself, reduce the risk of misappropriated cash receipts.

157. (a) The auditor should obtain an understanding of each of the internal control structure elements to plan the audit. The understanding should include knowledge about the design of relevant policies, procedures, and records and whether they have been placed in operation by the entity. Answer (b) is incorrect because the auditor, although he or she may be concerned with effectiveness of policies and procedures when control risk is assessed below the maximum, is not required to obtain knowledge about operating effectiveness as part of the understanding of the internal control structure. Answer (c) is incorrect because consistency in applying policies or procedures is related to operating effectiveness. Answer (d) is incorrect because audit planning does not require an understanding of the

control procedures related to each account balance, transaction class, and disclosure component in the financial statements.

158. (a) Payroll fraud could involve fictitious employees and/or fictitious salary rates. In order to prevent these frauds, new hires, terminations of employees, and salary rates should be approved by the personnel department, which in turn should keep the payroll department and employee supervisors informed on a timely basis. Answer (b) is incorrect because an unclaimed payroll check, which may have been written for a fictitious or recently terminated employee, should be returned to the treasurer. Answer (c) is incorrect because the personnel department is responsible for approving salary rates, whereas the payroll supervisor is responsible for accounting for the payroll. Answer (d) is incorrect because employee supervisors calculate the total hours used by the payroll department in determining gross pay.

159. (b) Keeping marketable securities in a bank safe-deposit box and assigning joint control to two officials should reduce the likelihood of those securities being misappropriated. These physical security and access controls are likely to be used to safeguard marketable securities when an independent trust agent is not employed. Answers (a), (c) and (d) are incorrect because the listed controls will not physically safeguard and prevent the misuse of marketable securities. Reviewing investment decisions will not determine if securities have been misappropriated. Comparing subsidiary and general ledgers will not necessarily prevent securities from being stolen, nor detect transactions that have not entered the accounting system. Annual physical verification by the chairman of the board is not a timely control and has limited effectiveness.

160. (b) In assessing control risk, the auditor may perform tests of controls directed toward the effectiveness of the design or operation of an internal control structure policy or procedure. These tests include inquiries, inspection of documents and reports, observation, and reperformance of the application of the policy or procedure by the auditor. Answers (a), (c) and (d) are incorrect because analytical procedures, comparison and confirmation, and verification are examples of substantive tests, not tests of controls used to assess control risk.

161. (a) The objective of procedures performed to understand the internal control structure is to provide the auditor with knowledge necessary for audit planning. The objective of tests of controls is to provide the auditor with evidence to use in assessing control risk. Because procedures performed to achieve one of these objectives may also pertain to the other objective, understanding the internal control structure and assessing control risk may be performed concurrently in an audit. Answer (b) is incorrect because findings from prior audits are considered in the current year's control risk assessment. Answer (c) is incorrect because when the auditor assesses control risk at the maximum, the auditor should document his or her conclusion that control risk is at the maximum, but need not document the basis for that conclusion. Answer (d) is incorrect because the auditor needs additional evidence for lower levels of assessed control risk.

162. (d) Using the audit risk model (audit risk = inherent risk x control risk x detection risk), acceptable detection risk can be calculated as a function of allowable audit risk, inherent risk, and control risk. In order to determine his or her acceptable level of detection risk, the auditor must therefore assess control risk. Answer (a) is incorrect because the auditor obtains an understanding of the internal control structure before assessing control risk. Answer (b) is incorrect because materiality levels are based on factors other than assessed control risk. Answer (c) is incorrect because inherent risk assessment is independent from control risk assessment.

163. (d) Assessing control risk at below the maximum involves identifying specific internal control structure policies and procedures relevant to specific assertions that are likely to prevent or detect material misstatements in those assertions, and performing tests of controls to evaluate the effectiveness of such policies and procedures. Answers (a) and (c) are incorrect because if control risk is assessed below the maximum the auditor would perform fewer substantive tests, perhaps at an earlier or interim date, since less assurance is needed from substantive tests. Answer (d) is incorrect because inherent risk is independent from control risk.

164. (d) After obtaining the understanding of the internal control structure and assessing control risk, the auditor may desire to seek a further reduction in the assessed level of control risk for certain assertions. In such cases, the auditor considers whether additional evidential matter sufficient to support a further reduction is likely to be available, and whether it would be efficient to perform tests of controls to obtain that evidential matter. Answers (a)

and (b) are incorrect because the auditor obtains an understanding of the accounting system and considers whether policies and procedures have been placed in operation as part of the auditor's understanding of the internal control structure. Answer (c) is incorrect because the auditor identifies internal control structure policies and procedures relevant to financial statement assertions as part of the auditor's assessment of control risk at below the maximum.

165. (c) The auditor is required to document the auditor's understanding of the entity's internal control structure, which includes the control environment, regardless of the assessed level of control risk. If the auditor assesses control risk at the maximum level, the auditor should document his or her conclusion that control risk is at the maximum level but need not document the basis for that conclusion. If the auditor assesses control risk below the maximum, the auditor should document his or her conclusion and the basis for that conclusion.

166. (c) An auditor assesses control risk to determine acceptable detection risk and the nature, extent and timing of substantive tests to perform. When an auditor plans to assess control risk at a low level, the auditor must identify specific policies and procedures that are likely to prevent or detect material misstatements, and he or she must perform tests of controls to evaluate the effectiveness of such policies and procedures. If, based on tests of controls, the control risk is assessed at a low level, the auditor may limit the extent of substantive testing. Answer (a) includes extensive substantive tests, which would not be done when control risk is assessed at a low level. Answers (b) and (d) refer only to analytical procedures, which are substantive tests, and do not include tests of controls, which are necessary in order to assess control risk at a low level.

167. (a) Lapping can occur when cash/check that is received from a customer is misappropriated and a subsequent cash receipt is credited to that customer's account. If the auditor suspects lapping of cash receipts, the auditor should compare the dates checks are listed on bank statements to the dates customer credits are recorded in customer receivable accounts. This would help find credits given to customers on dates that differ from the date the deposit was made. Answers (b) and (c) will not detect lapping because they deal with totals, rather than specific customer accounts. If the total on a cash summary equals the total recorded in the cash receipts journal, or if the total for a given deposit is the same on a bank deposit slip as on the bank statement, postings to individual customer accounts may still be incorrect. Answer (d) has nothing to do with dates cash/checks are received.

168. (d) The individual who signs checks should also mail the checks to reduce the likelihood of others accessing and misusing checks. Answer (a) is incorrect because the individual with custody of an asset, such as access to blank checks, should not be responsible for reconciling or comparing assets and records. Answer (b) is incorrect because if checks are returned to accounts payable, amounts or payees can be altered or the checks otherwise misappropriated. Answer (c) is incorrect because the person who signs the checks should review the supporting documents for agreement with the checks and then cancel those documents to avoid reuse.

169. (d) In order to avoid paying incorrect or duplicate amounts to vendors, the accounts payable department should clerically check the quantities, prices and mathematical calculations on the vendor's invoice and compare the invoice to the receiving report and purchase order. Answer (a) is a control procedure that should be performed by the treasurer or cash disbursements clerk. Answer (b) is a control procedure that involves the requisitioning and purchasing departments. Answer (c) is a control procedure that involves the purchasing and receiving departments.

170. (a) Assertions about existence or occurrence deal with whether assets or liabilities of the entity exist at a given date and whether recorded transactions occurred during a given period. Segregating payroll-related duties such as authorizing new hires and wage rates, as is done by a personnel department, and disbursing payroll checks, as is done by the treasurer, reduces the likelihood that fictitious payroll transactions that did not occur will get recorded. The auditor, therefore, inquires about and observes the segregation of payroll-related duties. Answer (b), which is concerned with omitted checks, relates to the completeness assertion. Answer (c), which is concerned with appropriate amounts, relates to the valuation assertion. Answer (d) relates more to completeness and valuation than to existence or occurrence.

171. (c) An auditor is required to obtain an understanding of the internal control structure. In obtaining that understanding, the auditor makes inquiries of management, inspects documents and records, and observes entity activities and operations. Reviewing descriptions of inventory policies and procedures, such as might be found in policies and procedures manuals, would be an example of a procedure performed by the auditor to obtain an understanding of the inventory internal control structure. Answers (a), (b) and (d) are substantive tests that are designed to tests dollar amounts in the financial statements, not to understand the internal control structure.

172. (d) Reportable conditions are matters coming to the auditor's attention that represent significant deficiencies in the design or operation of an entity's internal control structure. In a financial statement audit, the auditor is not obligated to search for reportable conditions nor to provide assurance on the internal control structure. If reportable conditions are discovered, they should be communicated to the entity's audit committee. In order to avoid misunderstandings regarding the auditor's responsibility, any report issued on reportable conditions should indicate that the purpose of the audit was to report on the financial statements and not to provide assurance on the internal control structure. Answer (a) is incorrect because it incorrectly states that the auditor is searching for reportable conditions. Answer (b) is incorrect because the audit committee does not have to inform others of the reportable conditions. Answer (c) is incorrect because a financial statement audit does not include auditing management assertions about effectiveness of the internal control structure.

173. (d) The internal auditors' work may affect the nature, timing, and extent of the audit, including procedures the auditor performs when obtaining an understanding of the entity's internal control structure, procedures the auditor performs when assessing risk, and substantive procedures the auditor performs. Answers (a), (b) and (c) are incorrect because the work of internal auditors affects all three of the procedures listed.

174. (c) The planning phase of the audit involves making preliminary judgements about materiality, audit risk and timing of procedures. Answers (a), (b) and (d) are procedures that would be completed during the evidence gathering phase rather than the planning phase.

175. (c) Lead schedules are audit workpapers that contain unadjusted general ledger amounts for all accounts. In order to prepare these schedules, the names, account numbers, and unadjusted general ledger amounts must be determined. A typical lead schedule would appear as follows:

Client Name
Account Name and Number
Audit Date

Prior Year Balance	Current Year Balance	Adjustments Dr Cr	Audited Balance
XXXX	YYY	ZZZ	YYYZZZ

176. (a) The problem with e-mail responses to audit confirmation requests is that the origin of the e-mail is not secure. That means that someone other than the recipient of the confirmation request may respond. By requesting a "hard copy" of the confirmation, the auditor may place greater reliance on the communication.

Chapter One - Solutions to Problems
Introduction, General and Field Standards

NUMBER 1

The internal control procedures that most likely would provide reasonable assurance that specific control objectives for the financial statement assertions regarding purchases and accounts payable will be achieved are
1. Proper authorization of requisitions by department head is required before purchase orders are prepared.
2. Purchasing department assures that requisitions are within budget limits before purchase orders are prepared.
3. The adequacy of each vendor's past record as a supplier is verified.
4. Secure facilities limit access to the goods during the receiving activity.
5. Receiving department makes a blind count of the goods received, independently of any other department.
6. The requisitioning department head independently verifies the quantity and quality of the goods received.
7. Requisitions, purchase orders, and receiving reports are matched with vendor invoices as to quantity and price.
8. Accounts payable department recomputes the mathematical accuracy of each invoice.
9. The voucher register is independently reconciled to the control accounts monthly.
10. All supporting documentation is required for payment and is made available to the treasurer.
11. The purchasing, receiving, and accounts payable functions are segregated.

NUMBER 2

Credit Manager

1. The credit manager approves credit for purchases on account from customers based on familiarity.
2. Bad credit can be extended to these customers increasing risk for the company.
3. A copy of the customer order form is not maintained by the credit manager.
4. A copy of the order form is not sent to shipping to generate a packing slip.
5. The credit manager does not prepare a monthly report about the collectibility of all past due accounts.

Accounts Receivable Supervisor

1. The accounts receivable supervisor should not be authorizing price changes because they are incompatible duties.
2. Sales and A/R should not be recorded until confirmation has been received that the goods have been shipped.
3. The A/R supervisor should not reconcile the A/R ledger with the control account.
4. The A/R supervisor should not receive the sales order form and record A/R.
5. The A/R supervisor does not account for the numerical sequence of customer sales orders.
6. The subsidiary A/R ledger is not reconciled to the general ledger.
7. Access to assets is not limited and controlled.

Cashier

1. The cashier should not supervise the cash register clerks.
2. The cashier should not be responsible for opening the mail.
3. Someone else in the mailroom should receive and prepare the check control listing.
4. One copy of the listing should be sent to the cashier.
5. The remittance advice and a copy of the control listing should be sent to the A/R supervisor.
6. Remittance advice should not be sent to the bookkeeper.
7. The cashier should not reconcile the bank account.

Bookkeeper

1. The bookkeeper should not receive A/R details from the accounts receivable supervisor.
2. The bookkeeper does not need remittance advice from the cashier to journalize and post to the general ledger.
3. The cashier provides a copy of the daily cash register summary for that purpose.
4. The bookkeeper should not mail monthly statements to customers.
5. An employee who does not handle cash receipts should mail monthly statements to customers.
6. The credit manager, not the bookkeeper, should authorize the write-off of uncollectible accounts.
7. The credit manager, not the bookkeeper, should decide whether to grant more credit to customers.

NUMBER 3

Flowchart Symbol Letter	Internal Control Procedure or Internal Document
c.	Approve customer credit and terms.
d.	Release merchandise to shipping department.
e.	File by sales order number.
f.	File pending receipt of merchandise.
g.	Prepare bill of lading.
h.	Copy of bill of lading to customer.
i.	Ship merchandise to customer.
j.	File by sales order number.
k.	Customer purchase order and sales order.
l.	File pending notice of shipment.
m.	Prepare three-part sales invoice.
n.	Copy of invoice to customer.
o.	Post to (or enter in) sales journal.
p.	Account for numerical sequence.
q.	Post to customer accounts.
r.	File by (payment due) date.

NUMBER 4

a. The procedures Hall should perform before accepting the engagement include the following:
1. Hall should explain to Adams the need to make an inquiry of Dodd and should request permission to do so.
2. Hall should ask Adams to authorize Dodd to respond fully to Hall's inquiries.
3. If Adams refuses to permit Dodd to respond or limits Dodd's response, Hall should inquire as to the reasons and consider the implications in deciding whether to accept the engagement.
4. Hall should make specific and reasonable inquiries of Dodd regarding matters Hall believes will assist in determining whether to accept the engagement, including specific questions regarding:
   - Facts that might bear on the integrity of management;
   - Disagreements with management as to accounting principles, auditing procedures, or other similarly significant matters;
   - Dodd's understanding as to the reasons for the change of auditors.
5. If Hall receives a limited response, Hall should consider its implications in deciding whether to accept the engagement.

b. The additional procedures Hall should consider performing during the planning phase of this audit that would not be performed during the audit of a continuing client may include the following:

1. Hall may apply appropriate auditing procedures to the account balances at the beginning of the audit period and, possibly, to transactions in prior periods.
2. Hall may make specific inquiries of Dodd regarding matters Hall believes may affect the conduct of the audit, such as
   - Audit areas that have required an inordinate amount of time;
   - Audit problems that arose from the condition of the accounting system and records.
3. Hall may request Adams to authorize Dodd to allow a review of Dodd's working papers.
4. Hall should document compliance with firm policy regarding acceptance of a new client.
5. Hall should start obtaining the documentation needed to create a permanent working paper file.

NUMBER 5

a. In planning an audit, an auditor's understanding of the internal control structure elements should be used to identify the types of potential misstatements that could occur, to consider the factors affecting the risk of material misstatement, and to influence the design of substantive tests.

b. An auditor obtains an understanding of the design of relevant internal control structure policies and procedures and whether they have been placed in operation. Assessing control risk at below the maximum level further involves identifying specific policies and procedures relevant to specific assertions that are likely to prevent or detect material misstatements in those assertions. It also involves performing tests of controls to evaluate the operating design and effectiveness of such policies and procedures.

c. When seeking a further reduction in the assessed level of control risk, an auditor should consider whether additional evidential matter sufficient to support a further reduction is likely to be available, and whether it would be efficient to perform tests of controls to obtain that evidential matter.

d. An auditor should document the understanding of an entity's internal control structure elements obtained to plan the audit. The auditor also should document the basis for the auditor's conclusion about the assessed level of control risk. If control risk is assessed at the maximum level, the auditor should document that conclusion, but is not required to document the basis for that conclusion. However, if the assessed level of control risk is below the maximum level, the auditor should document the basis for the conclusion that the effectiveness of the design and operation of internal control structure policies and procedures supports that assessed level.

NUMBER 6

A. Prepare purchase order
B. To vendor
C. Prepare receiving report
D. From purchasing
E. From receiving
F. Purchase order no. 5
G. Receiving report no. 1
H. Prepare and approve voucher
I. Unpaid voucher file, filed by due date
J. Treasurer
K. Sign checks and cancel voucher package documents
L. Canceled voucher package

NUMBER 7

61.   M
62.   Z
63.   L
64.   B
65.   H
66.   S
67.   O
68.   U
69.   I
70.   Q
71.   N
72.   T
73.   Y

NUMBER 8

a.   Reportable conditions are matters that come to an auditor's attention, which, in the auditor's judgment, should be communicated to the client's audit committee or its equivalent because they represent significant deficiencies in the design or operation of the internal control structure, which could adversely affect the organization's ability to record, process, summarize, and report financial data consistent with the assertions of management in the financial statements.

Material weaknesses are reportable conditions in which the design or operation of specific internal control structure elements do not reduce, to a relatively low level, the risk that errors or irregularities in amounts that would be material in relation to the financial statements being audited may occur and not be detected within a timely period by employees in the normal course of performing their assigned functions.

b.   An auditor is required to identify reportable conditions that come to the auditor's attention in the normal course of an audit, but is not obligated to search for reportable conditions. The auditor uses judgment as to which matters are reportable conditions. Provided the audit committee has acknowledged its understanding and consideration of such deficiencies and the associated risks, the auditor may decide certain matters do not need to be reported unless, because of changes in management or the audit committee, or because of the passage of time, it is appropriate to do so.

Conditions noted by the auditor that are considered reportable should be reported, preferably in writing. If information is communicated orally, the auditor should document the communication. The report should state that the communication is intended solely for the information and use of the audit committee, management, and others within the organization.

The auditor may identify and communicate separately those reportable conditions the auditor considers to be material weaknesses, but may not state that no reportable conditions were noted during the audit. Reportable conditions may be communicated during the course of the audit rather than after the audit is concluded, depending on the relative significance of the matters noted and the urgency of corrective follow-up action.

NUMBER 9

106.	D	Decrease
107.	I	Increase
108.	I	Increase
109.	I	Increase
110.	D	Decrease
111.	N	No effect
112.	D	Decrease
113.	I	Increase
114.	I	Increase
115.	D	Decrease
116.	I	Increase
117.	I	Increase
118.	N	No effect
119.	I	Increase
120.	I	Increase

NUMBER 10

106.	C.
107.	G.
108.	F.
109.	K.
110.	I.
111.	B.
112.	D.
113.	L.
114.	P.
115.	C.
116.	C.
117.	P.
118.	S.
119.	P.
120.	N.

NUMBER 11

The factors most likely to have an effect on the risk of material misstatements and their resulting effect include the following:

Environmental factor	Effect on risk of material misstatements
Government regulation over the banking industry is extensive.	Decrease
NFB operates profitably in a growing prosperous area.	Decrease
Overall demand for the industry's product is high.	Decrease
Interest rates have been volatile recently.	Increase
The availability of funds for additional mortgages is promising.	Decrease
The principal shareholder is also the chief executive officer and controls the board of directors.	Increase
Branch management is compensated based on branch profitability.	Increase
The internal auditor reports directly to the chairman of the board's audit committee, a minority shareholder.	Decrease
The accounting department has experienced little turnover in personnel recently.	Decrease
NFB is a continuing audit client.	Decrease
Management fails to establish proper procedures to provide reasonable assurance of reliable accounting estimates.	Increase
Management has been receptive to Green's suggestions relating to accounting adjustments.	Decrease
NFB recently opened a new branch office that is not yet profitable.	Increase
NFB recently installed a new sophisticated computer system.	Increase

NUMBER 12

Young Computer Outlets, Inc.
Payroll
Internal Control Questionnaire

Question	Yes	No
1. Are payroll changes (hires, separations, salary changes, overtime, bonuses, promotions, etc.) properly authorized and approved?		
2. Are discretionary payroll deductions and withholdings authorized in writing by employees?		

3. Are the employees who perform each of the following payroll functions independent of the other five functions?

- personnel and approval of payroll changes
- preparation of payroll data
- approval of payroll
- signing of paychecks
- distribution of paychecks
- reconciliation of payroll account

4. Are changes in standard data on which payroll is based (hires, separations, salary changes, promotions, deduction and withholding changes, etc.) promptly input to the system to process the payroll?

5. Is gross pay determined by using authorized salary rates and time and attendance records?

6. Is there a suitable chart of accounts and/or established guidelines for determining salary account distribution and for recording payroll withholding liabilities?

7. Are clerical operations in payroll preparation verified?

8. Is payroll preparation and recording reviewed by supervisors or internal audit personnel?

9. Are payrolls approved by a responsible official before payroll checks are issued?

10. Are payrolls disbursed through an imprest account?

11. Is the payroll bank account reconciled monthly to the general ledger?

12. Are payroll bank reconciliations properly approved and differences promptly followed up?

13. Is the custody and follow-up of unclaimed salary checks assigned to a responsible official?

14. Are differences reported by employees followed up on a timely basis by persons not involved in payroll preparation?

15. Are there procedures (e.g., tickler files) to assure proper and timely payment of withholdings to appropriate bodies and to file required information returns?

16. Are employee compensation records reconciled to control accounts?

17. Is access to personnel and payroll records, checks, forms, signature plates, etc. limited?

NUMBER 13

a. There are many fraud risk factors that are indicated in the dialogue. Among the fraud risk factors are the following:

- A significant portion of Mint's compensation is represented by bonuses and stock options. Although this arrangement has been approved by SCS's Board of Directors, this may be a motivation for Mint, the new CEO, to engage in fraudulent financial reporting.

- Mint's statement to the stock analysts that SCS's earning would increase 30% next year may be both an unduly aggressive and unrealistic forecast. That forecast may tempt Mint to intentionally misstate certain ending balances this year that would increase the profitability of the next year.

- SCS's Audit committee may not be sufficiently objective because Green, the chair of the audit committee, hired Mint, the new CEO, and they have been best friends for years.

- One individual, Mint, appears to dominate management without any compensating controls. Mint seems to be making all the important decisions without any apparent input from other members of management or resistance from the Board of Directors.

- There were frequent disputes between Brown, the prior CEO, who like Mint apparently dominated management and the Board of Directors, and Jones, the predecessor auditor. This fact may indicate that an environment exists in which management will be reluctant to make any changes that Kent suggests.

- Management seems to be satisfied with an understaffed and ineffective internal audit department. This situation displays an inappropriate attitude regarding the internal control environment.

- Management has failed to properly monitor and correct a significant deficiency in its internal control – the lack of segregation of duties in cash disbursements. This disregard for the control environment is also a risk factor.

- Information about anticipated future layoffs has spread among the employees. This information may cause an increase in the risk of material misstatement arising from the misappropriation of assets by dissatisfied employees.

b. Kent has many misconceptions regarding the consideration of fraud in the audit of SCS's financial statements that are contained in the dialogue. Among Kent's misconceptions are the following:

- Kent states that an auditor does not have specific duties regarding fraud. In fact, an auditor has a responsibility to specifically assess the risk of material misstatement due to fraud and to consider that assessment in designing the audit procedures to be performed.

- Kent is not concerned about Mint's employment contract. Kent should be concerned about a CEO's contract that is based primarily on bonuses and stock options because such an arrangement may indicate a motivation for management to engage in fraudulent financial reporting.

- Kent does not think that Mint's forecast for 1999 has an effect on the financial statement audit for 1998. However, Kent should consider the possibility that Mint may intentionally misstate the 1998 ending balances to increase the reported profit in 1999.

- Kent believes that the audit programs are fine as is. Actually, Kent should modify the audit programs because of the many risk factors that are present in the SCS audit.

- Kent is not concerned that the internal audit department is ineffective and understaffed. In fact, Kent should be concerned that SCS has permitted this situation to continue because it represents a risk factor relating to misstatements arising from fraudulent financial reporting and/or misappropriation of assets.
- Kent states that an auditor provides no assurances about fraud because that's management's job. In fact, an auditor has a responsibility to plan and perform an audit to obtain reasonable assurance about whether the financial statements are free of material misstatement, whether caused by error or fraud.
- Kent is not concerned that the prior year's reportable condition has not been corrected. However, Kent should be concerned that the lack of segregation of duties in the cash disbursements department represents a risk factor relating to misstatements arising from the misappropriation of assets.
- Kent does not believe that the rumors about big layoffs in the next month have an effect on audit planning. In planning the audit, Kent should consider this risk factor because it may cause an increase in the risk of material misstatement arising from the misappropriation of assets by dissatisfied employees.

c. In planning a financial statement audit, the auditor should document in the working papers evidence of the performance of the assessment of the risk of material misstatement due to fraud. Where risk factors are identified, the documentation should include those risk factors identified and the auditor's response to those risk factors, individually or in combination. In addition, during the performance of the audit, the auditor may identify fraud risk factors or other conditions that cause the auditor to believe that an additional response is required. The auditor should document such risk factors or other conditions, and any further response that an auditor concludes is appropriate.

NUMBER 14:   1B,   2C,   3A,   4D,   5A,   6B,   7C,   8B,   9D,   10A

SOLUTION TO AUDITING SIMULATION

ABC Corporation
123 Main Street
New York, NY

Board of Directors:

In planning and performing our audit of the financial statements of the ABC Corporation for the year ended December 31, 20XX, we considered its internal control in order to determine our auditing procedures for the purpose of expressing our opinion on the financial statements and not to provide assurance on the internal control structure. However, we noted certain matters involving internal control and its operation that we consider to be reportable conditions under standards established by the American Institute of Certified Public Accountants. Reportable conditions involve matters coming to our attention relating to significant deficiencies in the design or operation of internal control that, in our judgment, could adversely affect the organization's ability to record, process, summarize, and report financial data consistent with the assertions of management in the financial statements.

During the prior audit, internal control deficiencies were suggested and agreement made that these deficiencies would be corrected. Our review disclosed that several important items were either not implemented or are not functioning properly.

We have noted a lack of appropriate reviews and approval of transactions in several important areas. Such reviews were not made, or review and approval actions not documented.

Two instances were noted where important assets were not properly safeguarded from loss, damage or misappropriation. In one instance, insurance was found to be inadequate and in the other, assets were not inventoried periodically as required and asset responsibility was not documented.

Details of these items are included in Exhibit A.

This report is intended solely for the information and use of the board of directors, the audit committee, and management.

Signature and Date

Chapter Two
The Third Standard of Field Work—Evidence

EVIDENTIAL MATTER (SAS No. 31 As Amended)

AUDIT TESTS

SPECIAL AUDIT PROCEDURES AND PROBLEMS

Chapter Two
The Third Standard of Field Work—Evidence

Sufficient competent evidential matter is to be obtained through inspection, observation, inquiries, and confirmation, to afford a reasonable basis for an opinion regarding the financial statements under examination.

EVIDENTIAL MATTER (SAS No. 31 As Amended)

Most of the independent auditor's work in forming an opinion on financial statements consists of obtaining and evaluating evidential matter concerning *management assertions in the form of financial statements.* The measure of the validity of such evidence for audit purposes lies in the judgment of the auditor.

1. NATURE OF ASSERTIONS

Assertions are representations by management that are embodied in financial statement components. They can be either explicit or implicit and can be classified according to the following broad categories:

a. *Existence or occurrence*—deal with whether assets or liabilities of the entity exist at a given date and whether recorded transactions have occurred during a given period (i.e., all transactions are valid).

b. *Completeness*—deal with whether all transactions and accounts that should be presented in the financial statements are so included (i.e., no omitted transactions).

c. *Rights and obligations*—deal with whether assets are the rights of the entity (i.e., ownership) and liabilities are the obligations of the entity at a given date.

d. *Valuation or allocation*—deal with whether asset, liability, revenue, and expense components have been included in the financial statements at appropriate amounts (proper dollar values and proper time period).

e. *Presentation and disclosure*—deal with whether particular components of the financial statements are properly classified, described, and disclosed.

2. USE OF ASSERTIONS IN DEVELOPING AUDIT OBJECTIVES AND DESIGNING SUBSTANTIVE TESTS

In obtaining evidential matter in support of financial statement assertions, the auditor develops specific audit objectives in the light of those assertions. In developing the audit objectives of a particular engagement, the auditor should consider the specific circumstances of the entity, including the nature of its economic activity and the accounting practices unique to its industry.

There is not necessarily a one-to-one relationship between audit objectives and procedures. Some auditing procedures may relate to more than one objective. On the other hand, a combination of auditing procedures may be needed to achieve a single objective.

In selecting particular substantive tests to achieve the audit objectives that have been developed, an auditor considers, among other things, the extent of reliance, if any, to be placed on internal accounting control, the relative risk of errors or irregularities that would be material to financial statements, and the expected effectiveness and efficiency of such tests.

The nature, timing, and extent of the procedures to be applied on a particular engagement are a matter of professional judgment to be determined by the auditor, based on the specific circumstances.

In entities where significant information is transmitted, processed, or accessed electronically, the auditor may determine that it is not practical or possible to reduce detection risk to an acceptable level by performing only substantive tests for one or more financial statement assertions. For example, the potential for improper initiation or alteration of information to occur and not be detected may be greater if information is produced, maintained, or accessed only in electronic form. In such circumstances, the auditor should perform tests of controls to gather evidential matter to use in assessing control risk, or consider the effect on his or her report.

3. NATURE OF EVIDENTIAL MATTER

Evidential matter supporting the financial statements consists of the underlying accounting data and all corroborating information available to the auditor.

By itself, accounting data cannot be considered sufficient support for financial statements.

Corroborating evidential matter includes documentary material such as checks, invoices, contracts, and minutes of meetings; confirmations and other written representations by knowledgeable people; information obtained by the auditor from inquiry, observation, inspection, and physical examination.

The auditor tests underlying accounting data by analysis and review, by retracing the procedural steps followed in the accounting process and in developing the work sheets and allocations involved, by recalculation, and by reconciling related types and applications of the same information.

In certain entities, some of the accounting data and corroborating evidential matter are available only in electronic form. Source documents such as purchase orders, bills of lading, invoices, and checks are replaced with electronic messages. For example, entities may use Electronic Data Interchange (EDI) or image processing systems. In EDI, the entity and its customers or suppliers use communication links to transact business electronically. Purchase, shipping, billing, cash receipt, and cash disbursement transactions are often consummated entirely by the exchange of electronic messages between the parties. In image processing systems, documents are scanned and converted into electronic images to facilitate storage and reference, and the source documents may not be retained after conversion. Certain electronic evidence may exist at a certain point in time. However, such evidence may not be retrievable after a specified period of time if files are changed and if backup files do not exist. Therefore, the auditor should consider the time during which information exists or is available in determining the nature, timing, and extent of his or her substantive tests, and, if applicable, tests of controls.

4. COMPETENCE OF EVIDENTIAL MATTER

To be competent, evidence must be both **valid** and **relevant**. The validity of evidential matter is so dependent on the circumstances under which it is obtained that generalizations about the reliability of various types of evidence are subject to important exceptions. If the possibility of important exceptions is recognized, however, the following presumptions, which are not mutually exclusive, about the validity of evidential matter in auditing have some usefulness:

a.   When evidential matter can be obtained from independent sources outside an entity, it provides greater assurance of reliability for the purposes of an independent audit than that secured solely within the entity.
b.   When accounting data and financial statements are developed under satisfactory conditions of internal accounting control, there is more assurance about their reliability than when they are developed under unsatisfactory conditions of internal accounting control.
c.   The independent auditor's direct personal knowledge, obtained through physical examination, observation, computation, and inspection, is more persuasive than information obtained indirectly.

5. SUFFICIENCY OF EVIDENTIAL MATTER

The independent auditor's objective is to obtain sufficient competent evidential matter to provide him with a reasonable basis for forming an opinion. In the great majority of cases, *the auditor finds it necessary to rely on evidence that is **persuasive** rather than **convincing***.

As a guiding rule, there should be a rational relationship between the cost of obtaining evidence and the usefulness of the information obtained.

6. EVALUATION OF EVIDENTIAL MATTER

In evaluating evidential matter, the auditor considers whether specific audit objectives have been achieved. In developing his opinion, the auditor should give consideration to relevant evidential matter regardless of whether it appears to corroborate or to contradict the assertions in the financial statements.

AUDIT TESTS

I. AUDIT TESTS

Audit tests are procedures that an auditor adopts to obtain evidence concerning a particular facet of the entity being audited or the financial statements under audit.

II. PURPOSE OF TESTS

A. Tests to evaluate the effectiveness of the design and operation of internal controls -- called **Tests of Controls.**

B. Tests to detect material misstatements in financial statement assertions -- called **Substantive Tests.**

III. TYPES OF AUDIT TESTS

A. Analytical Procedures (SAS No. 56)

1. Basic premise is that plausible relationships exist among data and that these relationships may reasonably be expected to exist and continue in the absence of known conditions to the contrary.

2. The use of analytical procedures requires judgment by the auditor and can be used:
   a. To assist the auditor in planning the nature, timing, and extent of other auditing procedures (required in an audit).
   b. As a substantive test to obtain evidence concerning account balances (elective in an audit).
   c. As an overall review of financial data in the final review stages of the audit (required in an audit).

3. Analytical procedures involve comparisons of recorded amounts, or ratios developed from recorded amounts, to expectations developed by the auditor. The following represent sources of information the auditor may use for developing expectations:
   a. Financial information for comparable prior period(s) giving consideration to known changes
   b. Anticipated results—for example, budgets, or forecasts including extrapolations from interim or annual data
   c. Relationships among elements of financial information within the period
   d. Information regarding the industry in which the client operates—for example, gross margin information
   e. Relationships of financial information with relevant nonfinancial information.

4. Plausibility versus Predictability of Relationships
   a. As higher levels of assurance are desired from analytical relationships, more predictable relationships are required to develop the expectation.
   b. Relationships in a stable environment are usually more predictable than relationships in a dynamic or unstable environment.
   c. Relationships involving balance sheet accounts are less predictable than income statement amounts because balance sheet accounts are as of a point in time whereas income statement amounts cover a period of time.
   d. Relationships involving transactions subject to management discretion are usually less predictable than those that are not. Management can exercise discretion in the timing of events, thus affecting the predictability of the results.

B. Inquiry and Observation
  1. Uses:
      a. As a **test of controls** when no audit trail of documentary evidence exists. For example, the auditor may ask different individuals about how a particular task is accomplished, then the auditor would observe if in fact the operation is being performed as stated. Inquiry, in and of itself, is not sufficient evidence of effective operation of controls.
      b. As a **substantive test**. For example, such as observation of a fixed asset or inventory is a substantive test relating to the existence assertion. Likewise, inquiry of management or reading loan documents provides substantive evidence about the terms of loan agreements.

C. Transaction Testing
  1. Tests of transactions consist of the examination of the documents and accounting records involved in the processing of specific transactions.
  2. Uses:
      a. As a **test of controls** when the auditor examines documentation to determine if controls have been applied as prescribed.
          • Called an *inspection test* when the auditor examines a document for a particular characteristic such as signatures on checks.
          • Called a *reperformance test* when the auditor repeats controls performed by the client. For example, a control may require employees to match vendors' invoices with purchase orders and receiving reports. The auditor tests the controls by repeating the client procedures.
      b. As a **substantive test** when an auditor examines transaction documentation to determine if dollar value errors exist in a balance. For example, if the auditor examines documentation supporting individual debit entries to an equipment account to determine if the balance is fairly stated.

D. Tests of Balances (Details)
  1. Tests of balances are procedures applied to **individual items** that compose an account balance (i.e. accounts receivable).
  2. Tests of balances are substantive tests only because they are designed to detect misstatements by direct testing of the items that make up the ending balance of an account.
  3. Involves the following types of audit procedures:
       Confirmation
       Inquiry
       Observation
       Inspection
       Documentation (vouching)

EXAMPLES OF AUDIT
TESTS AND THEIR CLASSIFICATION

		Purpose of Test	
		Substantive Test	Tests of Controls
Type of Test	Analytical Procedures	Yes Example A	No, only used as Substantive Tests
	Inquiry and Observation	Yes Example H	Yes Examples B, C, I
	Tests of Transactions	Yes Example D	Yes Examples E, F
	Tests of Balances (Details)	Yes Examples G, H	No, only used as Substantive Tests

Examples:

A. Comparison of this year's expenses with last year's expenses.

B. Observation by auditor that cash is deposited daily by a specific clerk.

C. Inquiry by auditor about who deposits cash and how often.

D. Examination of invoices to support additions (specific transactions) to fixed assets account during year.

E. Examine sales invoices to see if initials of credit manager are there to indicate a credit file and credit approval (Inspection Test).

F. Vouch from sales invoices to credit files to see if customer has a credit file and has been approved for credit (Reperformance Test).

G. Confirmation of year-end balances in accounts receivable.

H. Observation of the existence of a building.

I. Extended walk-through of an application.

SEQUENCE OF IDENTIFYING SPECIFIC AUDIT PROCEDURES
GENERALIZED AUDIT APPROACH

(NOTE: The letters A, B, C, D, E refer to specific sections of this chapter which follow.)

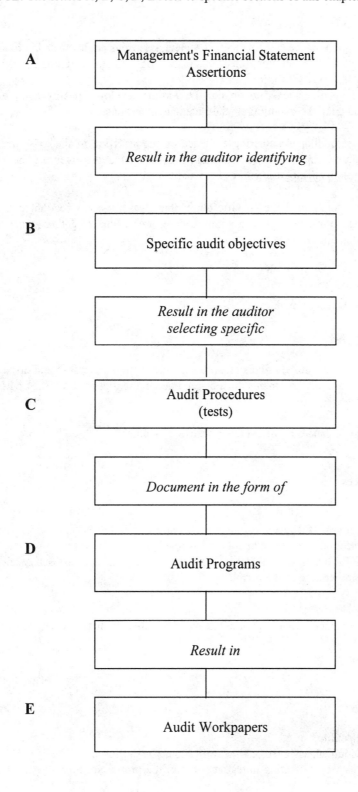

A — Management's Financial Statement Assertions

Result in the auditor identifying

B — Specific audit objectives

Result in the auditor selecting specific

C — Audit Procedures (tests)

Document in the form of

D — Audit Programs

Result in

E — Audit Workpapers

A. MANAGEMENT ASSERTIONS IN FINANCIAL STATEMENTS
a) Existence or occurrence
b) Completeness
c) Rights and obligations
d) Valuation or allocation (cut off)
e) Presentation (classification) and disclosure

B. SPECIFIC AUDIT OBJECTIVES

1. A misrepresentation of any of the five financial statement assertions could cause the financial statements to be materially misstated (the auditor must exercise judgment in determining what is a material misstatement).

2. To determine what type of evidence to obtain, the auditor develops specific audit objectives for each account balance based upon the overall financial statement assertions.

   For example: If the auditor is gathering evidence on the assertion of the **existence** of inventory, the auditor's objective would be to gather evidence that the inventory included on the balance sheet **physically** existed as of the audit date.

3. Once the auditor has determined the specific audit objectives for each account balance, based on the financial statement assertions, appropriate audit procedures are selected to gather evidence.

4. Following are audit objectives for various account balances:

Cash
1. Existence—Verification of cash balances.
   a. On hand
   b. In banks
   c. In transit
2. Classification—Restricted or committed funds must be segregated from other cash and disclosed.
3. Allocation—Cash receipts and disbursements must be recorded in the proper accounting period.

Accounts Receivable
1. Existence—Verify that the balances represent amounts owed by others.
2. Classification:
   a. Trade
   b. Officers and employees
   c. Other
   d. Current or noncurrent
3. Value—The allowance for doubtful accounts must be adequate so that A/R is stated at net realizable value.
4. Disclosure—Pledged, discounted, assigned or sold receivables must be disclosed.
5. Allocation—Sales and sales transactions that result in accounts receivable, and cash receipts that affect A/R must be recorded in the proper accounting period.

Notes Receivable
1. Existence—Verify that the balances represent amounts owed by others including **accrued interest**.
2. Classification:
   a. Trade
   b. Officers and employees
   c. Other (nontrade)
   d. Current or noncurrent
   e. Due from affiliates
3. Value—Are the notes collectible?
4. Disclosure—Pledged, discounted, assigned or sold notes should be disclosed.
5. Allocation—Are the transactions affecting notes recorded in the proper accounting period including accrued interest?

Inventories

1. Existence—Verify physical existence of products, material, work-in-process, supplies, in transit and consignments.
2. Value—That the inventory has been priced according to GAAP consistently applied.
3. Inventory tabulations are accurate by verification of footings, extensions and summaries. Obsolete, slow-moving and nonsalable items are reduced to NRV. Classification—That inventories are classified by type such as finished goods, work-in-process, raw material and manufacturing supplies.
4. Disclosure—The method of valuation such as FIFO, LIFO, average, etc., is required to be disclosed (APB 22). Inventories pledged should be disclosed.
5. Allocation—Verify that sales and purchases have been recorded in the correct accounting period.

Fixed Assets

1. Existence—Verify the physical existence of fixed assets as carryovers from prior years or additions of the current year.
2. Valuation—Verify that the cost of retired and abandoned assets along with related depreciation has been removed from the accounts. Verify that current depreciation charges are adequate under the company's depreciation policy consistently applied.
3. Classification—That carrying value and classification are according to GAAP.
4. Disclosure—Depreciation accounting policies are disclosed and all significant liens or encumbrances on fixed assets.

Investments

1. Existence—Establish the physical existence of stocks, bonds, notes, mortgages, venture agreements and insurance policies by physical inspection or confirmation.
2. Value—Verify that the underlying assets will support the carrying value and whether a permanent decline in value has occurred.
3. Classification and Method of Accounting—Verify according to GAAP as:
   a. Current
   b. Noncurrent
   c. Cost
   d. Equity method
   e. Consolidation
   f. Intercompany eliminations

   Income—Verify that income from investments has been reported according to GAAP.
   a. Interest
   b. Dividends
   c. Equity method pickup
   d. Consolidated NI
   e. Gains or losses
4. Disclosure—Significant accounting policies, affiliation with related entities and significant transactions. Disclose encumbrances and liens.

Prepayments, Deferred Charges and Intangibles

1. Existence:
   a. Prepayments—Verify that such items represent benefits assignable to future periods according to GAAP.
   b. Deferred Charges—Differ from prepayments in that they are assignable over longer periods (bond discount). Verify as in (a). R&D as defined in FASB No. 2 should be expensed.
   c. Intangibles—Verify that carrying value is assignable to future periods as a benefit. Must be amortized over a maximum of 40 years.
2. Classification—Properly classified:
   a. Current (prepayments)
   b. Noncurrent
3. Valuation—Amortization policies are according to GAAP and reasonable.
4. Disclosure—Significant accounting policies have been disclosed.

Liabilities

1. Existence—Verify that recorded liabilities exist and that there are no unrecorded liabilities:
    a. Accounts payable
    b. Notes payable
    c. Bonds
    d. Product warranties
    e. Pensions
    f. Leases
    g. Contingencies (adjustment type)
    h. Lawsuits
    i. Income taxes
    j. Contracts

2. Valuation—Verify that the carrying value of liabilities is according to GAAP and is reasonable. Problem areas—warranties, pensions, contingencies, lawsuits, income taxes, contracts.

3. Classification—Verify according to current and noncurrent.

4. Disclosure—Verify that disclosure is according to GAAP. Principal areas of disclosure, liabilities and others are:
    a. Foreign currency translation
    b. Business combinations
    c. Contracts
    d. Leases and lease commitments
    e. Deferred income taxes
    f. Pension plans
    g. Contingencies
    h. Contracts
    i. Early extinguishment of debt
    j. Accounting changes
    k. Nonmonetary translations
    l. Stock options
    m. Restrictive covenants

5. Allocation—Verify that liabilities have been recorded in the right period according to GAAP.

6. Completeness— Verify that the entity has complied with all applicable laws, rules and regulations which could materially result in liabilities, direct or indirect.

Stockholders' Equity

1. Classification—Verify that the amounts included are properly classified according to GAAP:
    a. Capital stock
        1) Common and preferred
    b. Capital contributed by source
        1) Paid-in surplus
    c. Retained earnings
        1) Appropriated and unappropriated
2. Valuation—That the amounts included in S.E. since inception of the company and during the audit period are according to GAAP.
3. Disclosure—Verify that disclosure has been made of dividend restrictions, stock subscription rights, stock options, stock repurchase plans, preferred dividends in arrears, liquidation preferences and restrictive covenants.

Revenues, Costs and Expenses

1. Allocation—Verify that such items are in the proper accounting period.
2. Verify that costs, expenses have been matched with revenue.
3. Nonoperating income or loss has been identified and properly classified.
4. The income presents on a consistent basis the results of operations.
5. Disclosure—Accounting policies affecting net income have been disclosed.

SPECIAL NOTE ON THE COMPLETENESS ASSERTION:

The audit of financial statements in accordance with GAAS must also verify that the financial statements are complete. That is, all transactions that should be recorded in the financial statements are in fact recorded (no transactions are omitted). Procedures to verify this question include all the specific procedures to verify the other financial statement assertions plus the use of analytical procedures.

Below is a summary of specific audit procedures that address the completeness assertion:

a. Sales-and-purchases cutoff procedures that include tracing shipping and receiving documents processed after the audit period to accounting records for the proper period.*

b. Analytical procedures in which the auditor investigates relationships among data that indicate a financial statement account or balance may be understated. For example, the auditor may obtain evidence that all interest-bearing debt is recorded by examining the relationship between recorded interest expense and the average balance of interest-bearing debt outstanding for the period. Disproportionate relationships based on the auditor's knowledge of interest rates should be investigated. Other examples include: a comparison of investment income to average investments for the period to test whether income earned on investments is recorded; the relationship of average pay times number of employees to payroll expense to substantiate that salaries are recorded; and the relationship of membership fee revenue to the number of members of an organization.

c. Confirmations of balances or transactions designed to identify unrecorded amounts, such as accounts payable confirmations that request the creditor to specify the amount of the client's obligation.

d. Tests of bank reconciliations, including examination of checks clearing the bank after the audit period to identify cash disbursements processed but not recorded or inappropriately recorded in the subsequent period.

e. Reading the minutes of the meetings (of the) board of directors and stockholders and tracing transactions authorized in the minutes to amounts recorded in the accounting records.

f. Overall reconciliations using financial and nonfinancial data, such as "proofs" of cash and sales.

* Cutoff tests are specific audit tests that are performed to ensure that transactions have been recorded in the proper accounting period (Financial Statement assertions of valuation and allocation and completeness).

Specific procedures to conduct:

1. *Sales Cutoff test:*
   Select a sampling of shipping documents (i.e. Bills of Lading) for a period of time before and after the audit date (for example, 3 days prior to and after the audit date). For the shipping documents selected, obtain the matching customer invoices. Determine that the date on the invoice corresponds to the date on the shipping document. For example, an item shipped before year end should be billed to the customer before year end.

2. *Purchase Cutoff test:*
   Select a sample of receiving reports for a period of time before year end and after year end. For the receiving documents selected, determine that purchases and accounts payable are recorded in the same period as the item was received by examining entries in the purchases journal and inspecting vendor invoices.

Testing for under- and over- statement

- To test for understatement of account balances, begin with source documents and trace to recordings in the accounting records.

  Example:
  To test for unrecorded sales, select a sample of shipping documents. Determine for each shipping document selected that:
  1) a customer invoice was prepared
  2) an entry was recorded in the sales journal, and
  3) the customer's subsidiary accounts receivable balance was up to date.

- To test for overstatement, select a sample of items that have been recorded in the accounting records and determine that source documents exist for the transaction.

  Example:
  To test for overstated sales, select a sample of items recorded in the sales journal. Determine that:
  1) A customer invoice exists for the item.
  2) That evidence of shipment exists (i.e. Bill of Lading).
  3) That a customer purchase order exists.

C.   AUDIT PROCEDURES

Procedure	Description	Examples	Related Assertions
Physical examination	Identification of an item's quantity and at times quality.	Test counts of inventory, cash count, securities count.	Primary: Existence. Secondary: Valuation or allocation, and rights and obligations.
Confirmation	Direct inquiry of independent parties outside the client organization.	Confirming accounts receivable, bank confirmations, notes payable.	Primary: Existence, rights and obligations, completeness. Secondary: Valuation or allocation.
Vouching	Review of source documents that support recorded transactions or amounts. (Test for overstatement.)	Checking recorded sales transactions for agreement with sales invoices and shipping documents.	Primary: Existence, rights and obligations, valuation or allocation, and presentation and disclosure. Does not relate to completeness.
Tracing	Tracing source documents to the amounts in the accounting records. (Testing for understatement.) Also verifying one accounting record with another.	Tracing shipping documents to recorded sales in the accounting records.	Primary: Completeness. Secondary: Valuation or allocation, presentation.
Reperformance	Auditor repetition of client bookkeeping functions such as posting.	Determining that journal entries have been posted to the proper accounts, recomputing client depreciation calculations.	Primary: Valuation or allocation. Secondary: Existence, completeness.

Scanning	Visual review of accounting records, reports and schedules to detect unusual items.	Scanning the charges to the repairs expense account for large items that may be capital additions.	All assertions.
Inquiry	Questioning management and employees. Reading client minutes of meetings such as Board of Directors or stockholders.	Asking if contingencies exist, obtaining a client representation letter.	All assertions. This technique provides limited reliability.
Inspection	Looking at documents in other than vouching or tracing procedures.	Inspection of notes, contracts, insurance policies, leases, and minutes.	All assertions.
Analytical procedures		Comparing gross margin percentages over time, relationship of bad debt write-offs to the accounts receivable balance.	All assertions.
Observation	Visually viewing client activities or locations.	Observation of bookkeeping routines, receiving or shipping activities.	All assertions.

SUMMARY OF AUDIT PROCEDURES EMPLOYED TO TEST MANAGEMENT ASSERTIONS

ASSERTION	TYPICAL AUDIT PROCEDURES
Presentation and Disclosure	1. Inquiry of management. 2. Reviewing contracts, agreements, and minutes of meetings.
Existence or Occurrence	1. Confirmation 2. Inspection 3. Vouching and documentation.
Rights and obligations	1. Review cutoff through examination of documents 2. Inquiry
Completeness	1. Analytical procedures 2. Vouching 3. Confirmation 4. Cutoff tests
Valuation	1. Confirmation 2. Vouching and documentation 3. Recalculation

D. AUDIT PROGRAMS—GENERAL AUDIT PROCEDURES

1. Audit programs are required to be prepared in all audits conducted in accordance with GAAS. The purpose of audit programs is two-fold:
   a) To show evidence in the workpapers that the audit was adequately planned, and
   b) To serve as a step-by-step guide for the audit of a particular account.
2. The following audit programs are typical procedures that are normally performed during an audit:

Planning

1. Obtain a client engagement letter or document understanding in workpapers.
2. Obtain from client any special reporting requirements regarding loan or debenture agreement or S.E.C. requirements.
3. Review client's internal control structure.
4. Prepare a budget.

Cash

1. Review internal control before year end.
2. Confirm all accounts with bank with which company transacted business during year as of _____ .
3. Arrange to receive cutoff bank statements, and canceled checks and bank advices for the period up to 2 weeks after year end.
4. Verify the propriety of the bank reconciliation and all reconciled items. Trace any unreturned O/S check amounts to supporting documents.
5. For bank cutoff statement:
   a. Verify the deposits in transit into the bank reconciliation.
   b. Make sure that all the checks dated at year end or prior are listed as O/S on the bank reconciliation.
   c. Review source documents for items not clearing in the bank's cutoff statement (i.e., purchase order, invoice or bank deposit receipt).
6. Perform interbank transfer test to determine if transfers between corporate accounts have been properly recorded.
7. Count petty cash, reconcile with vouchers to balance sheet date. (NOTE: This should be done during inventory observation.)
8. If cash disbursement test reveals that internal control over cash is weak, do a proof of cash for an interim month. Month chosen _____
   a. For that month, test foot books of original entry (i.e., cash receipts and cash disbursements) and trace to general ledger; and reconcile to bank deposits and withdrawals.
   b. Clear all outstanding items.
9. Note for financial statement presentation of any cash restrictions (i.e., 90-day notice accounts, certificate of deposit, etc.).
10. Conclude as to audit objectives.

Accounts Receivable

1. Review internal control before year end.
2. Obtain A/R aging, as of date of interim work or year end as applicable.
   a. Select A/R balances for positive confirmation, and confirm a representative sample of total dollar value and number of accounts.
   b. Agree the aged listing to the G/L control account.
3. Send second requests two weeks after original request.
4. Obtain explanations for all differences.
5. For nonreplies, perform alternate verification procedures. Trace all entries on customer A/R card to subsequent cash receipts, proof of delivery, or authorized credit issuance.
6. Summarize confirmation results, and conclude as to adequacy.

If interim audit work was performed, do step 7; otherwise omit.

7. Obtain year-end A/R aging:
   a. Reconcile the interim to year-end balance by tracing to sales register, C/R register, and any adjustments, and summarize on a work paper.
   b. Foot the aged T/B.
   c. Agree total to G/L.
   d. Compare the individual customer balances for interim versus year end and investigate unusual differences.
   e. Review for any large credit balances; consider reclassifying as accounts payable.
8. Obtain an analysis of allowance for bad debts.
   a. One showing beginning balance, expense additions, deductions (write-offs) and ending balance.
   b. A second schedule showing composition of ending balance (i.e., those accounts deemed uncollectible).
   c. Determine reasonableness of allowance for bad debts by reference to aged A/R T/B and discussions with credit department.
9. Review sales cutoff before and after year-end tracing from sales register to shipping documents, and relating the test to documents (bills of lading) obtained at the year-end inventory.
10. Review credit memos for authenticity and proper approval.
11. Conclude on propriety of A/R, bad debt expense, and allowance for uncollectible accounts.

Inventory

1. Review internal control prior to year end.
2. Send confirmations to any locations outside the factory where the client's inventory is held.
3. Physical inventory observation:
   a. Prior to inventory date, determine that proper instructions have been issued to client personnel. Review procedures with company controller.
   b. If tags are used, obtain tag control of those issued and those used.
   c. Tour premises and determine that inventory is not moving and that no shipping or receiving is going on.
   d. Determine that slow-moving obsolete inventory and customer inventory are prominently marked and are not being counted. Make a note of these items to insure that they have not been included in the priced inventory listing.
   e. Determine that the tags are being filled out in accordance with instructions.
   f. Make test counts, recording a few from all areas and all classes (RM, W/P and FG) of inventory for subsequent tie-in to priced inventory.
   g. Obtain shipping and receiving cutoff documents.
   h. **Obtain carbon copy of all tags prior to end of physical inventory and check into tag listing.**
   i. If perpetual system is in use, select a sample from perpetual records and trace to inventory count to the floor and count some items on the floor and trace to the perpetual records.
   j. If inventory tags are not used (i.e., if the inventory is listed on count sheets), test that all items are being counted by reference to audit procedures in (i). In addition, count the number of inventory sheets and note the last item on each sheet in order that we may test to see if we received a complete priced inventory.
4. **Inventory Valuation**
   a. Obtain a complete listing of the priced inventory.
   b. **Quantities**:
      1. Trace all test counts obtained at the time of the physical to final inventory.
      2. Trace listing of obsolete items to priced inventory in order to verify their exclusion.
   c. Prices:
      1. **Raw Materials**
         a) Select a representative sample and trace to the vendor invoice or cost card to determine that the correct prices were used.
      2. **W.I.P. and Finished Goods**
         a) Select a sample and trace to cost records.
         b) Do an overhead cost calculation to determine if overhead application is correct.
         c) Select a sample and test if cost buildup procedure for material, labor and overhead is adequate to yield reasonable pricing.

5. **Inventory Summarization**
   a. Test extensions of final inventory.
   b. Foot the summarization, and agree the total to the G/L control total.
   c. Compare list with prior years and investigate any large differences and compare for obsolete items or item written off in prior year and included this year.
6. **Cutoff**
   a. Review cutoff with reference to shipping and receiving documents from the physical and incorporate the work with that done in A/R and A/P.
7. **Lower of Cost or Market Test**
   a. For a reasonable sample, compare inventory value with recent sales invoices. Examine gross profits by product line if possible.
8. **Slow Moving or Obsolete Inventory**
   a. Review purchase records and/or perpetual records and compare inventory lists and any available activity reports for slow moving or obsolete inventory. Evaluate what reserve should be applied, if any.
9. If applicable, review perpetual cards for large fluctuations of quantity and investigate.
10. Conclude on inventory valuation and cutoff.

Prepaids and Other Assets

1. Review internal control prior to year end.
2. Prepaid insurance
   a. Obtain schedule from client.
   b. Test calculation of prepaid and expense amounts
   c. Review major insurance policies.
   d. Review audits regarding W/C and product liability.
   e. Vouch premium payment to invoice.
   f. Review adequacy of insurance coverage.
   g. Confirm any policies with cash value.
3. Other prepaid and deferred charges
   a. Obtain schedule from client.
   b. Review schedule for propriety by checking calculations to supporting documents.
   c. Review amortization rates of intangibles if appropriate.
4. Conclusion.

Fixed Assets

1. Review internal control prior to year end.
2. Obtain a summary schedule of fixed assets and related accumulated depreciation; check beginning balances to permanent file.
3. Obtain detailed schedule of additions and disposals and trace to schedule in item 2.
   a. For significant purchases review invoice. Scope _____
   b. Inspect major asset additions.
4. Review analysis of repair accounts and reclassify material amounts if necessary.
5. Test depreciation calculation and reconcile expense to addition to accumulated depreciation accounts and expense accounts.
6. Obtain schedule of sales or disposals.
   a. Review supporting documents and determine proper gain or loss or adjustment to basis of like asset acquired.
   b. Vouch proceeds to documents.
   c. Check that the proper amounts of cost and accumulated depreciation have been removed from books.
7. Obtain necessary items to compute investment credit.
8. Note any liens on fixed assets for footnote disclosure.
9. Conclusion.

Notes Payable and Long-Term Debt

1. Review internal control prior to year end.
2. Obtain a schedule of notes payable with interest paid, accrued, and expensed and prepaid, and classify as to current and noncurrent.
3. Confirm balances, collateral, and interest rates with payee. Determine if in default and obtain default letters if needed.
4. Vouch changes for period.
5. Obtain copy of agreement for permanent file and note if provisions are being adhered to.
6. Check interest calculations and reconcile to ledger.
7. Conclusion.

Accounts Payable

1. Review internal control prior to year end.
2. Obtain list of accounts payable and trace to source invoices for proper recording and reconcile with general ledger. Scope _____
3. Obtain vendor statements and reconcile to list (for significant vendors).
    a. Consider confirmation of significant balances, including zero balances.
    b. Reconcile returned confirms, if used.
4. Review debit balances (material amounts) and consider reclassification and confirmation.
5. Review old or disputed items and document.
6. Search for unrecorded liabilities—subsequent events.
    a. Review minutes for liabilities.
    b. For several days immediately after balance sheet date: Scope: _____
       1. Examine recorded vouchers and cash disbursements for proper period recording.
       2. Examine unentered vouchers and invoices and unmatched receiving reports for possible adjustment.
       3. Cross reference to inventory section cutoff work.
7. Conclude.

Other Liabilities and Accrued Expenses

1. Review internal control prior to year end.
2. Obtain schedules from client for:
    a. Withheld taxes.
    b. Accrued payroll, commissions, payroll taxes.
    c. Other accrued expenses.
3. Review source documents to determine propriety of accrual and test amounts.
4. Compare to prior year accruals and document differences.
5. Ascertain no material unrecorded accruals by reference to subsequent payments.
6. Conclude.

Tax Provisions

1. Obtain an analysis of federal and state provisions and expense accounts and reconcile to ledger.
2. Vouch payments made during period.
3. Examine revenue agent reports received during period and review any adjustments booked.
4. Obtain or prepare a reconciliation of income per books, per taxes.
5. Check provisions for period considering Schedule M items, investment credit, N.O.L.C., etc.
6. Review for proper allocation of timing differences, etc.
7. Conclusion.

Capital Stock

1. Obtain schedule of each class from articles of incorporation, and from minutes determine amount issued and reconcile to ledger.
2. Confirmation with:
   a. Transfer agent as to total shares authorized and issued, shares in name of client, and holders of 10% or more, unbilled fees, etc.
   b. Registrar, same as in (a).
   c. Compare (a) and (b) to pertinent schedules in permanent file.
3. Review and vouch to source documents any changes during period.
4. Obtain pertinent data on:
   a. Any options granted or exercised.
   b. Warrants granted or exercised.
   c. Rights.
   d. Conversion features of debenture issues.
   e. Treasury stock.
      1. Obtain schedule regarding number of shares, cost, etc.
      2. Review period transactions for proper accounting treatment.

Paid-in Surplus

1. Obtain schedule and reconcile to ledger and #1 above.

Retained Earnings

1. Schedule.
2. Verify dividends paid or declared and if applicable dividend status on preferred cumulative stock.
3. Vouch period's activity.

E. AUDIT DOCUMENTATION (SAS NO. 96)

The auditor should prepare and maintain working papers, the form and content of which should be designed to meet the circumstances of a particular engagement. The information contained in working papers constitutes the principal record of the work that the auditor has done and the conclusions reached concerning significant matters.

Functions and Nature of Audit Documentation

1. Audit documentation serves to
   a. provide the principal support for the auditor's opinion,
   b. aid the auditor in the conduct and supervision of the engagement.
   c. indicate the engagement team members that prepared and supervised the work.

2. Documentation includes records kept by the auditor of the procedures applied, the tests performed, the information obtained, and the pertinent conclusions reached in the engagement. Examples of working papers are audit programs, analyses, memoranda, letters of confirmation and representation, abstracts of company documents, and schedules or commentaries prepared or obtained by the auditor. Working papers also may be in the form of data stored on tapes, films, or other media.

3. Factors affecting the auditor's judgment about the quantity, type and content of the working papers for a particular engagement include
   a. The nature of the engagement
   b. The nature of the auditor's report
   c. The nature of the financial statements, schedules, or other information on which the auditor is reporting.
   d. The nature and condition of the client's records.
   e. The degree of reliance on internal accounting control.
   f. The needs in the particular circumstances for supervision and review of the work.

Content of Audit Documentation

The quantity and form of documentation will vary with the circumstances, but it should include the following:

1. That the accounting records agree or reconcile to the financial statements.

2. Abstracts or copies of significant contracts or agreements that the auditor examined in order to evaluate the accounting for significant transactions.

3. Audit documentation of tests of controls and substantive tests of balances that involve the inspection of documents or confirmation should include an identification of the items tested.
   a. When *a random sample is selected*, the documentation should include *identifying characteristics*, such as specific invoice numbers of the items selected, and *the listing*.
   b. When a *scope of items is selected* (e.g., all items over a certain amount) the documentation need describe *the scope* and *the listing*.
   c. When a *systematic sample is selected* from a population of documents, the documentation need only provide an *identification of the source documents, the starting point and the sampling interval.*

4. Documentation of audit findings or issues that the auditor considers significant, including the specific actions taken to address the issue, and the conclusions reached.

5. Documentation of the nature and effect of aggregated misstatements and the auditor's basis for a conclusion as to whether they cause the financial statements to be materially misstated.

6. When an analytical procedure is performed as the principal substantive test of a significant financial assertion (account balance) the auditor must document:
   a. The factors considered in developing the expectations for the choice of a particular analytical procedure.
   b. Whether the results of the analytical procedure are consistent with the auditor's expectation.
   c. Any additional audit procedures that the auditor adopts as a result of applying the analytical procedure.

7. With respect to going concern issues, document:
   a. The conditions or events that led him or her to believe there is substantial doubt about the entity's ability to continue as a going concern.
   b. The work performed in connection with the auditor's evaluation of management's plans.
   c. The auditor's conclusion as to whether substantial doubt remains about the entity's ability to continue as a going concern for a reasonable period of time.
   d. The consideration and effect of that conclusion on the financial statements, disclosures and the audit report.

Ownership and Custody of Working Papers

Working papers are the property of the auditor, and some states have statutes that designate the auditor as the owner of the working papers. The auditor's rights of ownership, however, are subject to ethical limitations relating to the confidential relationship with clients.

Certain of the auditor's working papers may sometimes serve as a useful reference source for his client, but the working papers should not be regarded as a part of, or substitute for, the client's accounting records.

The auditor should adopt reasonable procedures for safe custody of his working papers and should retain them for a period sufficient to meet the needs of his practice and to satisfy any pertinent legal requirements of records retention.

SPECIAL AUDIT PROCEDURES AND PROBLEMS

RELATED PARTY TRANSACTIONS (SAS No. 45)

There are specific procedures with respect to related party transactions that should be considered by the auditor when performing an examination of financial statements in accordance with generally accepted auditing standards.

Related Party Defined

The term "related parties" means the reporting entity, its **affiliates, principal owners, management** and members of their immediate **families, entities** for which investments are accounted for by the equity method, and any other party with which the reporting entity may deal when one party has the ability to significantly influence the management or operating policies of the other, to the extent that one of the transacting parties might be prevented from fully pursuing its own separate interests. Related parties also exist when another entity has the ability to **significantly influence** the management or operating policies of the transacting parties, or when another entity has an ownership interest in one of the transacting parties and the ability to significantly influence the other, to the extent that one or more of the transacting parties might be prevented from fully pursuing its own separate interests.

Examples of Related Party Transactions

Examples of related party transactions include transactions between a parent company and its subsidiaries, transactions between or among subsidiaries of a common parent, and transactions in which the reporting entity participates with other affiliated businesses, with management or with principal stockholders (or other ownership interests). Transactions between or among the foregoing parties are considered to be related party transactions even though they may not be given accounting recognition. For example, an entity may provide services to a related party without charge.

Sometimes two or more entities are under common ownership or management control, but they do not transact business between or among themselves. Mere existence of common control, however, may result in operating results or financial position significantly different from those that would have been obtained if the entities were autonomous. For example, two or more entities in the same line of business may be commonly controlled by a party with the ability to increase or decrease the volume of business done by each. Consequently, the nature of the common control should be disclosed.

An entity may be economically dependent on one or more parties with which it transacts a significant volume of business, such as a sole or major customer, supplier, franchisor, franchisee, distributor, general agent, borrower, or lender. Such parties should not be considered related parties solely by virtue of economic dependency unless one of them clearly exercises significant management or ownership influence over the other. Disclosure of economic dependency may, however, be necessary for a fair presentation of financial position, results of operations, or cash flows in conformity with generally accepted accounting principles.

Accounting Considerations

Except for the disclosure requirements of the Securities and Exchange Commission's Regulation S-X and the accounting treatment prescribed by certain Opinions of the Accounting Principles Board when related parties are involved, established accounting principles ordinarily do not require transactions with related parties to be accounted for on a basis different from that which would be appropriate if the parties were not related. Until such time as applicable accounting principles are established by appropriate authoritative bodies, the auditor should view related party transactions within the framework of existing pronouncements, placing primary emphasis on the adequacy of disclosure of the existence of such transactions and their significance in the financial statements of the reporting entity.

Generally, *financial statements should recognize the economic <u>substance</u> of transactions rather than merely their legal <u>form</u>*. Accounting Principles Board Statement No. 4, paragraph 35, states: "Although financial accounting is concerned with both the legal and economic effects of transactions and other events and many of its conventions are based on legal rules, the economic substance of transactions and other events are usually emphasized when economic substance differs from legal form."

Examples of transactions that raise questions as to their substance and that may be indicative of the existence of related parties are the following:

1. Borrowing or lending on an interest-free basis or at a rate of interest significantly above or below current market rates.
2. Selling real estate at a price that differs significantly from its appraised value.
3. Exchanging property for similar property in a nonmonetary transaction.
4. Making loans with no scheduled terms as to when or how the funds will be repaid.

Audit Procedures

During an examination made in accordance with generally accepted auditing standards, an auditor should be aware of the possible existence of **material related party transactions that could affect the financial statements**. The auditor should obtain an understanding of management responsibilities and the relationship of each component to the total entity, evaluate internal accounting controls over management activities, and consider the business purpose served by the various components of the entity. Normally, the business structure and style of operating are based on the abilities of management, tax and legal considerations, product diversification, and geographical location. Experience has shown, however, that business structure and operating style are occasionally deliberately designed to obscure related party transactions.

In the absence of evidence to the contrary, transactions with related parties should not be assumed to be outside the ordinary course of business. The auditor should, however, be aware of the possibility that transactions with related parties may have been motivated solely, or in large measure, by conditions similar to the following:

1. Lack of sufficient working capital or credit to continue the business.
2. An urgent desire for a continued favorable earnings record in the hope of supporting the price of the company's stock.
3. An overly optimistic earnings forecast.
4. Dependence on a single or relatively few products, customers, or transactions, for the ongoing success of the venture.
5. A declining industry characterized by a large number of business failures.
6. Excess capacity.
7. Significant litigation, especially litigation between stockholders and management.
8. Significant obsolescence dangers because the company is in a high-technology industry.

Determining the Existence of Related Parties

The auditor should place emphasis on auditing material transactions with parties he knows are related to the reporting entity. Certain relationships, such as parent-subsidiary or investor-investee, may be clearly evident.

Determining the existence of others requires the application of specific audit procedures which may include the following:

1. Evaluate the company's procedures for identifying and properly accounting for related party transactions.
2. Inquire of appropriate management personnel as to the names of all related parties and whether there were any transactions with these parties during the period.
3. Review filings by the reporting entity with the Securities and Exchange Commission and other regulatory agencies for the names of related parties and for other businesses in which officers and directors occupy directorship or management positions.

USING THE WORK OF A SPECIALIST (SAS No. 73)

A specialist is a person (or firm) possessing special skill or knowledge in a particular field other than accounting or auditing, such as actuaries, appraisers, attorneys, engineers, and geologists.

Decision to Use the Work of a Specialist

During his examination an auditor may encounter matters potentially material to the fair presentation of financial statements in conformity with generally accepted accounting principles that require special knowledge and that in his judgment require using the work of a specialist.

Examples of the types of matters that the auditor may decide require him to consider using the work of a specialist include, but are not limited to the following:
1. Valuation (e.g., works of art, special drugs, and restricted securities).
2. Determination of physical characteristics relating to quantity on hand or condition (e.g., mineral reserves, or materials stored in piles above ground).
3. Determination of amounts derived by using specialized techniques or methods (e.g., certain actuarial determinations).
4. Interpretation of technical requirements, regulations, or agreements (e.g., the potential significance of contracts or other legal documents, or legal title to property).

In performing an examination of financial statements in accordance with generally accepted auditing standards, the auditor may use the work of a specialist as an audit procedure to obtain competent evidential matter. The circumstances surrounding the use of a specialist differ. Although the familiarity of individual auditors with the work performed by certain types of specialists may differ, the auditing procedures necessary to comply with generally accepted auditing standards need not vary as a result of the extent of the auditor's knowledge.

Selecting a Specialist

The auditor should satisfy himself concerning the professional qualifications and reputation of the specialist by inquiry or other procedures, as appropriate. The auditor should consider the following:
1. The professional certification, license, or other recognition of the competence of the specialist in his field, as appropriate.
2. The reputation and standing of the specialist in the views of his peers and others familiar with his capability or performance.
3. The relationship, if any, of the specialist to the client.

Ordinarily, the auditor should attempt to obtain a specialist who is unrelated to the client. However, when the circumstances so warrant, work of a specialist having a relationship to the client may be acceptable. Work of a specialist unrelated to the client will usually provide the auditor with greater assurance of reliability because of the absence of a relationship that might impair objectivity.

An understanding should exist among the auditor, the client, and the specialist as to the nature of the work to be performed by the specialist. Preferably, the understanding should be documented and should cover the following:
1. The objectives and scope of the specialist's work.
2. The specialist's representations as to his relationship, if any, to the client.
3. The methods or assumptions to be used.
4. A comparison of the methods or assumptions to be used with those used in the preceding period.
5. The specialist's understanding of the auditor's corroborative use of the specialist's findings in relation to the representations in the financial statements.
6. The form and content of the specialist's report that would enable the auditor to make the evaluation.

Using the Findings of the Specialist

Although the appropriateness and reasonableness of methods or assumptions used and their application are the responsibility of the specialist, the auditor should obtain an understanding of the methods or assumptions used by the specialist to determine whether the findings are suitable for corroborating the representations in the financial statements. The auditor should consider whether the specialist's findings support the related representations in the financial statements and make appropriate tests of accounting data provided by the client to the specialist.

Ordinarily, the auditor would use the work of the specialist unless his procedures lead him to believe that the findings are unreasonable in the circumstances. **If the specialist is related to the client, the auditor should**

consider performing additional procedures with respect to some or all of the related specialist's assumptions, methods, or findings to determine that the findings are not unreasonable or engage an outside specialist for that purpose.

Effect of the Specialist's Work On the Auditor's Report

If the auditor determines that the specialist's findings support the related representations in the financial statements, he may reasonably conclude that he has obtained sufficient competent evidential matter. If there is a material difference between the specialist's findings and the representations in the financial statements, or if the auditor believes that the determinations made by the specialist are unreasonable, he should apply additional procedures. If, after applying any additional procedures that might be appropriate, he is unable to resolve the matter, the auditor should obtain the opinion of another specialist, unless it appears to the auditor that the matter cannot be resolved. A matter that has not been resolved will ordinarily cause the auditor to conclude that he should qualify his opinion or disclaim an opinion, because the inability to obtain sufficient competent evidential matter as to an assertion of material significance in the financial statements constitutes a scope limitation.

The auditor may conclude, after performing additional procedures, including possibly obtaining the opinion of another specialist, that the representations in the financial statements are not in conformity with generally accepted accounting principles. In that event, he should express a qualified or adverse opinion.

Reference to the Specialist in the Auditor's Report

When expressing an unqualified opinion, the auditor should **not** refer to the work or findings of the specialist. Such a reference in an unqualified opinion might be misunderstood to be a qualification of the auditor's opinion or a division of responsibility, neither of which is intended. Further, there may be an inference that the auditor making such reference performed a more thorough audit than an auditor not making such reference.

If the auditor decides to modify his opinion as a result of the report or findings of the specialist, reference to and identification of the specialist may be made in the auditor's report if the auditor believes such reference will facilitate an understanding of the reason for the modification.

INQUIRY OF A CLIENT'S LAWYER CONCERNING LITIGATION, CLAIMS, AND ASSESSMENTS (SAS No. 12)

In General

In forming an opinion on financial statements, evidential matter relating to litigation, claims and assessments is a significant audit concern of the auditor. Such evidential matter usually lies outside the financial records, and because of its nature it is difficult for the auditor to determine its existence, and, beyond that, the effect on the financial statements. *__Management and legal counsel__ of the entity are usually the __primary__ source of representation* and assurances as to the adequacy of financial presentation and disclosure of such matters. *__Refusal of legal counsel to furnish__* requested information where counsel has given substantive attention to the matter is a *__limitation on the scope of the examination and precludes an unqualified opinion__*.

Audit Objectives

For litigation, claims, and assessments, the independent auditor should obtain evidential matter as to:
1. The existence of a condition, situations, or set of circumstances indicating an uncertainty as to the possible loss to an entity arising from litigation, claims and assessments.
2. The period in which the underlying cause for legal action occurred.
3. The degree of probability of an unfavorable outcome.
4. The amount or range of potential loss.

Audit Procedures

1. Inquire of management as to the policies and procedures adopted for identifying, evaluating, and accounting for litigation, claims, and assessments.
2. Obtain from management a representation letter containing a **description and evaluation of litigation, claims, and assessments** that existed at the date of the balance sheet being reported on, and during the period from the balance sheet date to the date the information is furnished, with an identification of those matters **referred to**

legal counsel. Obtain **assurances from management**, ordinarily in writing, that they have disclosed all such matters required to be disclosed by FASB #5, Accounting for Contingencies.

3. Examine documents in the client's possession concerning litigation, claims, and assessments, including correspondence and invoices from lawyers.
4. Obtain assurance from management, ordinarily in **writing**, that it has disclosed all unasserted claims that the lawyer has advised them are probable of assertion and must be disclosed in accordance with FASB #5. Also, the auditor, with the client's permission, should inform the lawyer that the client has given the auditor this assurance.
5. Read minutes of meetings of stockholders, directors, and appropriate committees held during and subsequent to the period being examined.
6. Read contracts, loan agreements, leases, and correspondence from taxing or other governmental agencies, and similar documents.
7. Obtain information concerning guarantees from bank confirmation forms.
8. Inspect other documents for possible guarantees by the client.

Client's Lawyer Inquiries

A letter of audit inquiry to the client's lawyer is the auditor's primary means of obtaining corroboration of the information furnished by management concerning litigation, claims, and assessments. Evidential matter obtained from the client's inside general counsel or legal department **may** provide the auditor with the necessary corroboration, but evidential matter from inside counsel is not a substitute for information that outside counsel may refuse to furnish to the auditor.

A letter of audit inquiry should include:
1. Identification of the company, including subsidiaries, and the date of the examination.
2. A list or request for a list from counsel that describes and evaluates pending or threatened litigation, claims, and assessments with respect to which the lawyer has been engaged and to which he has devoted **substantive** attention on behalf of the company.
3. A list prepared by management that describes and evaluates unasserted claims and assessments that management considers to be probable of assertion, and that, if asserted, would have at least a **reasonable possibility of an unfavorable outcome**, with respect to which the lawyer has devoted substantive attention on behalf of the company.
4. As to each matter, a request that the lawyer either furnish the following information or comment on those matters as to which **his views may differ from those stated by management**, as appropriate:
   a. A description of the nature of the matter, the progress of the case to date, and the action the company intends to take (for example, to contest the matter vigorously or to seek an out-of-court settlement).
   b. An evaluation of the **likelihood of an unfavorable outcome** and an estimate, if one can be made, of the amount or **range of potential loss**.
   c. With respect to a list prepared by management, an identification of the omission of any pending or threatened litigation, claims, and assessments, or a statement that the list of such matters is complete.
5. A statement that, in the case of an unasserted possible claim or assessment that may call for financial statement disclosure, the lawyer, as a matter of professional responsibility to the client, should advise and consult with the client concerning the question of disclosure and the requirements of FASB #5. The lawyer should confirm this understanding in the reply.
6. The lawyer should identify the nature of and reasons for any limitation on his response. Matters that are not material should be excluded from inquiry.

In special circumstances, the auditor may obtain a response concerning matters covered by the audit inquiry letter in a conference, which offers an opportunity for a more detailed discussion and explanation than a written reply. The auditor should **appropriately document conclusions reached concerning the need for accounting for or disclosure of litigation, claims, and assessments**.

A lawyer may be required by his Code of Professional Responsibility to resign his engagement if his advice concerning these matters is disregarded by the client. When the auditor is aware that a client has changed lawyers or that a lawyer engaged by the client has resigned, the auditor should inquire as to the reasons.

Limitations On the Scope of a Lawyer's Response

A lawyer may appropriately limit his response if he has not given substantive attention to the matter. Also, a lawyer's response may be limited to matters that are considered individually or collectively material to the financial statements, provided the lawyer and auditor have reached an understanding on the limits of materiality for this purpose. **Such limitations are not limitations on the scope of the auditor's examination.**

A lawyer's refusal to furnish the information requested in an inquiry letter, either in writing or orally where the lawyer has devoted substantive attention, would be a **limitation on the scope of the auditor's examination sufficient to preclude an unqualified opinion**.

A lawyer's response to such an inquiry and the procedures set forth previously provide the auditor with sufficient evidential matter to satisfy himself concerning the accounting for and reporting of pending and threatened litigation, claims and assessments. The auditor obtains sufficient evidential matter to satisfy himself concerning reporting for those unasserted claims and assessments required to be disclosed in financial statements from the **foregoing procedures** and the **lawyer's specific acknowledgment of his responsibility to his client in respect to disclosure obligations**. This approach with respect to unasserted claims and assessments is necessitated by the public interest in protecting the confidentiality of lawyer-client communications.

Other Limitations On a Lawyer's Response

A lawyer may be unable to respond concerning the likelihood of an unfavorable outcome of litigation, claims, and assessments or the amount or range of potential loss, because of **inherent uncertainties**. Factors influencing the likelihood of an unfavorable outcome may sometimes not be within a lawyer's competence to judge; historical experience of the entity in similar litigation or the experience of other entities may not be relevant or available; and the amount of the possible loss frequently may vary widely at different stages of litigation. Consequently, a lawyer may not be able to form a conclusion with respect to such matters. **In such circumstances, the auditor ordinarily will conclude that the financial statements are affected by an uncertainty concerning the outcome of a future event which is not susceptible of reasonable estimation** (a condition for accrual under FASB #5 is that the amount of loss can be reasonably estimated). If the effect of the matter on the financial statements could be material, the auditor ordinarily will conclude that he is unable to express an unqualified opinion.

CLIENT REPRESENTATIONS (SAS No. 85)

There is a requirement that the independent auditor obtain certain written representations from management as a part of an examination made in accordance with generally accepted auditing standards and provides guidance concerning the representations to be obtained.

Reliance on Management Representations

Representations from management are part of the evidential matter the independent auditor obtains, but they are not a substitute for the application of those auditing procedures necessary to afford a reasonable basis for his opinion on the financial statements. Written representations from management ordinarily confirm oral representations given to the auditor.

The auditor obtains written representations from management relating to its knowledge or intent when he believes they are necessary to complement his other auditing procedures.

Obtaining Written Representations

The specified written representations obtained by the auditor will depend on the circumstances of the engagement and the nature and basis of presentation of the financial statements. They ordinarily include the following matters, if applicable:
1. Management's acknowledgment of its responsibility for the fair presentation in the financial statements of financial position, results of operations, and cash flows in conformity with generally accepted accounting principles or other comprehensive basis of accounting.
2. Availability of all financial records and related data.

3. Management is responsible for adjusting the financial statements to correct material misstatements and that any unrecorded misstatements aggregated by the auditor are immaterial to the financial statements of the current period. A summary of the unrecorded misstatements should be included in or attached to the representation letter.
4. Completeness and availability of all minutes of meetings of stockholders, directors, and committees of directors.
5. Absence of errors in the financial statements and unrecorded transactions.
6. Information concerning fraud involving management or employees that could have a material effect on the financial statements.
7. Information concerning related party transactions and related amounts receivable or payable.
8. Noncompliance with aspects of contractual agreements that may affect the financial statements.
9. Information concerning subsequent events.
10. Irregularities involving management or employees.
11. Communications from regulatory agencies concerning noncompliance with, or deficiencies in, financial reporting practices.
12. Plans or intentions that may affect the carrying value or classification of assets or liabilities.
13. Disclosure of compensating balance or other arrangements involving restrictions on cash balances, and disclosure of line-of-credit or similar arrangements.
14. Reduction of excess or obsolete inventories to net realizable value.
15. Losses from sales commitments.
16. Satisfactory title to assets, liens on assets, and assets pledged as collateral.
17. Agreements to repurchase assets previously sold.
18. Losses from purchase commitments for inventory quantities in excess of requirements or at prices in excess of market.
19. Violations or possible violations of laws or regulations whose effects should be considered for disclosure in the financial statements or as a basis for recording a loss contingency.
20. Other liabilities and gain or loss contingencies that are required to be accrued or disclosed by Statement of Financial Accounting Standards No. 5.
21. Unasserted claims or assessments that the client's lawyer has advised are probable of assertion and must be disclosed in accordance with FASB No. 5.
22. Capital stock repurchase options or agreements or capital stock reserved for options, warrants, conversions, or other requirements.

Management's Consideration of Unrecorded Misstatements

The representation letter obtained by the auditor must include, in addition to the items noted in the previous section, the following:

1. An acknowledgement by management that it has considered the financial statement misstatements aggregated by the auditor during the current engagement, and has concluded that any unrecorded misstatements are immaterial, both individually and in the aggregate, to the financial statements as a whole.
2. *Example:*
   "We believe that the effects of the unrecorded financial statement misstatements summarized in the attached schedule are immaterial, both individually and in the aggregate, to the financial statements."

Scope Limitations

Management's refusal to furnish a written representation that the auditor believes is essential constitutes a limitation on the scope of the auditor's examination sufficient to preclude an unqualified opinion. Further, the auditor should consider the effects of management's refusal on his ability to rely on other of their representations.

Representation letters should be prepared on the client's stationery and signed by appropriate officers and employees. In most cases the CPA will draft the representation letter, but the officer or employee must accept the statements in the letter as his own representations.

It is important that the representation letter be signed by one or more officers or responsible employees who are knowledgeable about the particular area or activity reported upon. For example (and depending on the circumstances), the company secretary might prepare the representation concerning minutes of the board of directors, the controller might affirm the fair presentation of the financial statements and recording of liabilities, and the purchasing agent might report on the purchase commitments.

All client representations should be obtained before the end of field work. If the representation letter refers to events occurring in the subsequent period, it is appropriate that the letter be signed, dated, and delivered to the auditor on the last day of field work.

Client representation letters are evidential matter supporting the auditor's opinion. Accordingly, they should be prepared for each succeeding examination of financial statements. If the auditor's report is updated, he should obtain from the client an additional representation as to events occurring subsequent to the date of his previous report.

AUDITING ACCOUNTING ESTIMATES (SAS No. 57)

An accounting estimate is the approximation of a financial statement element, item, or account. Accounting estimates are often included in historical financial statements because:

1. The measurement of some amounts or the valuation of some accounts is uncertain, pending the outcome of future events.
2. Relevant data concerning events that have already occurred cannot be accumulated on a timely, cost-effective basis.

Management is responsible for making the accounting estimates used in the financial statements. The auditor is responsible for evaluating the reasonableness of accounting estimates. Thus, the auditor should approach the audit of accounting estimates with an attitude of professional skepticism, and be aware of the fact that estimates are the result of both subjective and objective factors.

Developing Accounting Estimates

Management is responsible for establishing a process for preparing accounting estimates. Although the process may not be documented or formally applied, it normally consists of:
1. Identifying situations for which accounting estimates are required.
2. Identifying the relevant factors that may affect the accounting estimate.
3. Accumulating relevant, sufficient, and reliable data on which to base the estimate.
4. Developing assumptions that represent management's judgment of the most likely circumstances and events with respect to the relevant factors.
5. Determining the estimated amount based on the assumptions and other relevant factors.
6. Determining that the accounting estimate is presented in conformity with applicable accounting principles and that disclosure is adequate.

Internal Control Structure Related to Accounting Estimates

An entity's internal control structure may reduce the likelihood of material misstatements of accounting estimates. Specific relevant aspects of that structure include the following:
1. Management communication of the need for proper accounting estimates
2. Accumulation of relevant, sufficient, and reliable data on which to base an accounting estimate
3. Preparation of the accounting estimate by qualified personnel
4. Adequate review and approval of the accounting estimates by appropriate levels of authority, including—
   a. Review of sources of relevant factors
   b. Review of development of assumptions
   c. Review of reasonableness of assumptions and resulting estimates
   d. Consideration of the need to use the work of specialists
   e. Consideration of changes in previously established methods to arrive at accounting estimates
5. Comparison of prior accounting estimates with subsequent results to assess the reliability of the process used to develop estimates
6. Consideration by management of whether the resulting accounting estimate is consistent with the operational plans of the entity.

Evaluating Accounting Estimates

The auditor's objective when evaluating accounting estimates is to obtain sufficient competent evidential matter to provide reasonable assurance that:
1. All accounting estimates that could be material to the financial statements have been developed.
2. Those accounting estimates are reasonable in the circumstances.

Evaluating Reasonableness

1. In evaluating the reasonableness of an estimate, the auditor normally concentrates on key factors and assumptions that are:
   a. Significant to the accounting estimate.
   b. Sensitive to variations.
   c. Deviations from historical patterns.
   d. Subjective and susceptible to misstatement and bias.

   The auditor normally should consider the historical experience of the entity in making past estimates as well as the auditor's experience in the industry. However, changes in facts, circumstances, or entity's procedures may cause factors different from those considered in the past to become significant to the accounting estimate.

2. In evaluating reasonableness, the auditor should obtain an understanding of how management developed the estimate. Based on that understanding, the auditor should use one or a combination of the following approaches:
   a. Review and test the process used by management to develop the estimate.
   b. Develop an independent expectation of the estimate to corroborate the reasonableness of management's estimate.
   c. Review subsequent events or transactions occurring prior to completion of fieldwork.

3. *Review and test management's process.* In many situations, the auditor assesses the reasonableness of an accounting estimate by performing procedures to test the process used by management to make the estimate. The following are procedures the auditor may consider performing when using this approach:
   a. Identify whether there are controls over the preparation of accounting estimates and supporting data that may be useful in the evaluation.
   b. Identify the sources of data and factors that management used in forming the assumptions, and consider whether such data and factors are relevant, reliable, and sufficient for the purpose based on information gathered in other audit tests.
   c. Consider whether there are additional key factors or alternative assumptions about the factors.
   d. Evaluate whether the assumptions are consistent with each other, the supporting data, relevant historical data, and industry data.
   e. Analyze historical data used in developing the assumptions to assess whether the data is comparable and consistent with data of the period under audit, and consider whether such data is sufficiently reliable for the purpose.
   f. Consider whether changes in the business or industry may cause other factors to become significant to the assumptions.
   g. Review available documentation of the assumptions used in developing the accounting estimates and inquire about any other plans, goals, and objectives of the entity, as well as consider their relationship to the assumptions.
   h. Consider using the work of a specialist regarding certain assumptions.
   i. Test the calculations used by management to translate the assumptions and key factors into the accounting estimate.

4. *Develop an expectation.* Based on the auditor's understanding of the facts and circumstances, he may independently develop an expectation as to the estimate by using other key factors or alternative assumptions about those factors.

5. ***Review subsequent events or transactions***. Events or transactions sometimes occur subsequent to the date of the balance sheet, but prior to the completion of fieldwork, that are important in identifying and evaluating the reasonableness of accounting estimates or key factors or assumptions used in the preparation of the estimate. In such circumstances, an evaluation of the estimate or of a key factor or assumption may be minimized or unnecessary as the event or transaction can be used by the auditor in evaluating their reasonableness.

COMMUNICATION WITH AUDIT COMMITTEES (SAS No. 61)

The auditor has a requirement under GAAS to determine certain matters that relate to the conduct of an audit which are communicated to those having responsibility for oversight of the financial reporting process (usually considered to be the client's audit committee).

1. Generally the auditor must report items that relate to the scope and results of the audit process that may assist the audit committee with its oversight responsibility.

2. The auditor is not required to communicate with management but may do so if the auditor feels that management will benefit from such communications.

3. May be written or oral (must be documented in workpapers).

4. Items that must be communicated include:
   a. The auditor's responsibilities under GAAS and the objectives of an audit.
   b. Significant Accounting Policies including:
      —Management's selection of significant accounting policies.
      —Methods used to account for unusual nonrecurring transactions.
   c. The process management used in arriving at certain estimates used in financial statements and the basis for the auditor's conclusion regarding their fairness.
   d. Audit Adjustments—The uncorrected misstatements affecting the financial statements that management considered immaterial.
   e. Other matters including the use of specialists and difficulties encountered in the audit.

5. Note the items in (D) above are in addition to certain communications required by other statements on Auditing Standards (GAAS). These include:
   a. Communication of internal control structure related matters noted in an audit.
   b. The reporting of errors and irregularities.
   c. The reporting of illegal acts.

Chapter Two -- Questions
The Third Standard of Field Work -- Evidence

1. Which of the following is **not** a typical analytical review procedure?
a. Study of relationships of financial information with relevant nonfinancial information.
b. Comparison of financial information with similar information regarding the industry in which the entity operates.
c. Comparison of recorded amounts of major disbursements with appropriate invoices.
d. Comparison of recorded amounts of major disbursements with budgeted amounts.

2. Auditors may use positive and/or negative forms of confirmation requests for accounts receivable. An auditor most likely will use
a. The positive form to confirm all balances regardless of size.
b. A combination of the two forms, with the positive form used for large balances and the negative form for the small balances.
c. A combination of the two forms, with the positive form used for trade receivables and the negative form for other receivables.
d. The positive form when controls related to receivables are satisfactory, and the negative form when controls related to receivables are unsatisfactory.

3. Of the following which is the **least** persuasive type of audit evidence?
a. Documents mailed by outsiders to the auditor.
b. Correspondence between auditor and vendors.
c. Copies of sales invoices inspected by the auditor.
d. Computations made by the auditor.

4. Analytical review procedures are
a. Substantive tests designed to evaluate a system of internal control.
b. Compliance tests designed to evaluate the validity of management's representation letter.
c. Substantive tests designed to evaluate the reasonableness of financial information.
d. Compliance tests designed to evaluate the reasonableness of financial information.

5. A CPA auditing an electric utility wishes to determine whether all customers are being billed. The CPA's best direction of test is from the
a. Meter department records to the billing (sales) register.
b. Billing (sales) register to the meter department records.
c. Accounts receivable ledger to the billing (sales) register.
d. Billing (sales) register to the accounts receivable ledger.

6. Which of the following audit procedures is most effective in testing credit sales for understatement?·
a. Age accounts receivable.
b. Confirm accounts receivable.
c. Trace sample of initial sales slips through summaries to recorded general ledger sales.
d. Trace sample of recorded sales, from general ledger to initial sales slip.

7. One reason why the independent auditor makes an analytic review of the client's operations is to identify
a. Weaknesses of a material nature in the system of internal control.
b. Noncompliance with prescribed control procedures.
c. Improper separation of accounting and other financial duties.
d. Unusual transactions.

8. The auditor obtains corroborating evidential matter for accounts receivable by using positive or negative confirmation requests. Under which of the following circumstances might the negative form of the accounts receivable confirmation be useful?
a. A substantial number of accounts are in dispute.
b. Internal control over accounts receivable is ineffective.
c. Client records include a large number of relatively small balances.
d. The auditor believes that recipients of the requests are unlikely to give them consideration.

9. An auditor is testing sales transactions. One step is to trace a sample of debit entries from the accounts receivable subsidiary ledger back to the supporting sales invoices. What would the auditor intend to establish by this step?
a. All sales have been recorded.
b. Debit entries in the accounts receivable subsidiary ledger are properly supported by sales invoices.
c. All sales invoices have been properly posted to customer accounts.
d. Sales invoices represent bona fide sales.

10. Approximately 95% of returned positive account-receivable confirmations indicated that the customer owed a smaller balance than the amount confirmed. This might be explained by the fact that
a. The cash-receipts journal was held open after year end.
b. There is a large number of unrecorded liabilities.
c. The sales journal was closed prior to year end.
d. The sales journal was held open after year end.

11. An auditor should examine minutes of board of directors' meetings
a. Through the date of his report.
b. Through the date of the financial statements.
c. On a test basis.
d. Only at the beginning of the audit.

12. The return of a positive account-receivable confirmation without an exception attests to the
a. Collectibility of the receivable balance.
b. Accuracy of the receivable balance.
c. Accuracy of the aging of accounts receivable.
d. Accuracy of the allowance for bad debts.

13. During his examination of a January 19, 19X3, cut-off bank statement, an auditor noticed that the majority of checks listed as outstanding at December 31, 19X2, had not cleared the bank. This would indicate
a. A high probability of lapping.
b. A high probability of kiting.
c. That the cash-disbursements journal had been held open past December 31, 19X2.
d. That the cash-disbursements journal had been closed prior to December 31, 19X2.

14. Which one of the following procedures would **not** be appropriate for an auditor in discharging his responsibilities concerning the client's physical inventories?
a. Confirmation of goods in the hands of public warehouses.
b. Supervising the taking of the annual physical inventory.
c. Carrying out physical inventory procedures at an interim date.
d. Obtaining written representation from the client as to the existence, quality, and dollar amount of the inventory.

15. As part of an audit, a CPA must request a representation letter from his client. Which one of the following is **not** a valid purpose of such a letter?
a. To provide audit evidence.
b. To emphasize to the client his responsibility for the correctness of the financial statements.
c. To satisfy himself by means of other auditing procedures when certain customary auditing procedures are not performed.
d. To provide possible protection to the CPA against a charge of knowledge in cases where fraud is subsequently discovered to have existed in the accounts.

16. To **best** ascertain that a company has properly included merchandise that it owns in its ending inventory, the auditor should review and test the
a. Terms of the open purchase orders.
b. Purchase cut-off procedures.
c. Contractual commitments made by the purchasing department.
d. Purchase invoices received on or around year end.

17. Which of the following audit procedures would be **least** likely to lead the auditor to find unrecorded fixed asset disposals?
a. Examination of insurance policies.
b. Review of repairs and maintenance expense.
c. Review of property tax files.
d. Scanning of invoices for fixed asset additions.

18. The physical count of inventory of a retailer was higher than shown by the perpetual records. Which of the following could explain the difference?
a. Inventory items had been counted but the tags placed on the items had **not** been taken off the items and added to the inventory accumulation sheets.
b. Credit memos for several items returned by customers had **not** been prepared.
c. **No** journal entry had been made on the retailer's books for several items returned to its suppliers.
d. An item purchased "FOB shipping point" had **not** arrived at the date of the inventory count and had **not** been reflected in the perpetual records.

19. In order to efficiently establish the correctness of the accounts payable cutoff, an auditor will be **most** likely to
a. Coordinate cutoff tests with physical inventory observation.
b. Compare cutoff reports with purchase orders.
c. Compare vendors' invoices with vendors' statements.
d. Coordinate mailing of confirmations with cutoff tests.

20. As a result of analytical review procedures, the independent auditor determines that the gross profit percentage has declined from 30% in the preceding year to 20% in the current year. The auditor should
a. Express an opinion which is qualified due to inability of the client company to continue as a going concern.
b. Evaluate management's performance in causing this decline.
c. Require footnote disclosure.
d. Consider the possibility of an error in the financial statements.

21. The third standard of field work states that sufficient competent evidential matter is to be obtained through inspection, observation, inquiries, and confirmations to afford a reasonable basis for an opinion regarding the financial statements under audit. The substantive evidential matter required by this standard may be obtained, in part, through
a. Flowcharting the internal control structure.
b. Proper planning of the audit engagement.
c. Analytical procedures.
d. Auditor working papers.

22. In designing written audit programs, an auditor should establish specific audit objectives that relate primarily to the
a. Timing of audit procedures.
b. Cost-benefit of gathering evidence.
c. Selected audit techniques.
d. Financial statement assertions.

23. Which of the following presumptions does not relate to the competence of audit evidence?
a. The more effective the internal control structure, the more assurance it provides about the accounting data and financial statements.
b. An auditor's opinion, to be economically useful, is formed within reasonable time and based on evidence obtained at a reasonable cost.
c. Evidence obtained from independent sources outside the entity is more reliable than evidence secured solely within the entity.
d. The independent auditor's direct personal knowledge, obtained through observation and inspection, is more persuasive than information obtained indirectly

24. For all audits of financial statements made in accordance with generally accepted auditing standards, the use of analytical procedures is required to some extent

	In the planning stage	As a substantive test	In the review stage
a.	Yes	No	Yes
b.	No	Yes	No
c.	No	Yes	Yes
d.	Yes	No	No

25. Which of the following procedures is least likely to be performed before the balance sheet date?
a. Testing of internal control over cash.
b. Confirmation of receivables
c. Search for unrecorded liabilities.
d. Observation of inventory.

26. Which of the following procedures would an auditor ordinarily perform during the review of subsequent events?
a. Review the cut-off bank statements for the period after the year-end.
b. Inquire of the client's legal counsel concerning litigation.
c. Investigate reportable conditions previously communicated to the client.
d. Analyze related party transactions to discover possible irregularities.

27. Six months after issuing an unqualified opinion on audited financial statements, an auditor discovered that the engagement personnel failed to confirm several of the client's material accounts receivable balances. The auditor should first
a. Request the permission of the client to undertake the confirmation of accounts receivable.
b. Perform alternative procedures to provide a satisfactory basis for the unqualified opinion.
c. Assess the importance of the omitted procedures to the auditor's ability to support the previously expressed opinion.
d. Inquire whether there are persons currently relying, or likely to rely, on the unqualified opinion.

28. Which of the following circumstances is most likely to cause an auditor to consider whether a material misstatement exists?
a. Transactions selected for testing are not supported by proper documentation.
b. The turnover of senior accounting personnel is exceptionally low.
c. Management places little emphasis on meeting earnings projections.
d. Operating and financing decisions are dominated by several persons.

29. The primary objective of analytical procedures used in the final review stage of an audit is to
a. Obtain evidence from details tested to corroborate particular assertions.
b. Identify areas that represent specific risks relevant to the audit.
c. Assist the auditor in assessing the validity of the conclusions reached.
d. Satisfy doubts when questions arise about a client's ability to continue in existence.

30. To help plan the nature, timing, and extent of substantive auditing procedures, preliminary analytical procedures should focus on
a. Enhancing the auditor's understanding of the client's business and events that have occurred since the last audit date.
b. Developing plausible relationships that corroborate anticipated results with a measurable amount of precision.
c. Applying ratio analysis to externally generated data such as published industry statistics or price indices.
d. Comparing recorded financial information to the results of other tests of transactions and balances.

31. Cooper, CPA, is auditing the financial statements of a small rural municipality. The receivable balances represent residents' delinquent real estate taxes. The internal control structure at the municipality is weak. To determine the existence of the accounts receivable balances at the balance sheet date, Cooper would most likely
a. Send positive confirmation requests.
b. Send negative confirmation requests.
c. Examine evidence of subsequent cash receipts.
d. Inspect the internal records such as copies of the tax invoices that were mailed to the residents.

32. An auditor would most likely verify the interest earned on bond investments by
a. Vouching the receipt and deposit of interest checks.
b. Confirming the bond interest rate with the issuer of the bonds.
c. Recomputing the interest earned on the basis of face amount, interest rate, and period held.
d. Testing the internal controls over cash receipts.

33. Which of the following most likely would be detected by an auditor's review of a client's sales cut-off?
a. Unrecorded sales for the year.
b. Lapping of year-end accounts receivable.
c. Excessive sales discounts.
d. Unauthorized goods returned for credit.

34. Auditors should request that an audit client send a letter of inquiry to those attorneys who have been consulted concerning litigation, claims, or assessments. The primary reason for this request is to provide
a. Information concerning the progress of cases to date.
b. Corroborative evidential matter.
c. An estimate of the dollar amount of the probable loss.
d. An expert opinion as to whether a loss is possible, probable, or remote.

35. A written client representation letter most likely would be an auditor's best source of corroborative information of a client's plans to
a. Terminate an employee pension plan.
b. Make a public offering of its common stock.
c. Settle an outstanding lawsuit for an amount less than the accrued loss contingency.
d. Discontinue a line of business.

36. In an audit of contingent liabilities, which of the following procedures would be least effective?
a. Reviewing a bank confirmation letter.
b. Examining customer confirmation replies.
c. Examining invoices for professional services.
d. Reading the minutes of the board of directors.

37. An auditor searching for related party transactions should obtain an understanding of each subsidiary's relationship to the total entity because:
a. This may permit the audit of intercompany account balances to be performed as of concurrent dates.
b. Intercompany transactions may have been consummated on terms equivalent to arm's-length transactions.
c. This may reveal whether particular transactions would have taken place if the parties had not been related.
d. The business structure may be deliberately designed to obscure related party transactions.

38. An auditor concludes that the omission of a substantive procedure considered necessary at the time of the examination may impair the auditor's present ability to support the previously expressed opinion. The auditor need not apply the omitted procedure if
a. The risk of adverse publicity or litigation is low.
b. The results of other procedures that were applied tend to compensate for the procedure omitted.

c. The auditor's opinion was qualified because of a departure from generally accepted accounting principles.
d. The results of the subsequent period's tests of controls make the omitted procedure less important.

39. Each of the following might, by itself, form a valid basis for an auditor to decide to omit a test except for the
a. Difficulty and expense involved in testing a particular item.
b. Degree of reliance on the relevant internal controls.
c. Relative risk involved.
d. Relationship between the cost of obtaining evidence and its usefulness.

40. Soon after Boyd's audit report was issued, Boyd learned of certain related party transactions that occurred during the year under audit. These transactions were not disclosed in the notes to the financial statements. Boyd should
a. Plan to audit the transactions during the next engagement.
b. Recall all copies of the audited financial statements.
c. Determine whether the lack of disclosure would affect the auditor's report.
d. Ask the client to disclose the transactions in subsequent interim statements.

41. When using the work of a specialist, an auditor may refer to and identify the specialist in the auditor's report if the
a. Auditor wishes to indicate a division of responsibility.
b. Specialist's work provides the auditor greater assurance of reliability.
c. Auditor expresses an adverse opinion as a result of the specialist's findings.
d. Specialist is not independent of the client.

42. Negative confirmation of accounts receivable is less effective than positive confirmation of accounts receivable because
a. A majority of recipients usually lack the willingness to respond objectively.
b. Some recipients may report incorrect balances that require extensive follow-up.
c. The auditor can not infer that all nonrespondents have verified their account information.
d. Negative confirmations do not produce evidential matter that is statistically quantifiable.

43. An auditor's program to examine long-term debt should include steps that require
a. Examining bond trust indentures.
b. Inspecting the accounts payable subsidiary ledger.
c. Investigating credits to the bond interest income account.
d. Verifying the existence of the bondholders.

44. Which of the following documentation is required for an audit in accordance with generally accepted auditing standards?
a. An internal control questionnaire.
b. A client engagement letter.
c. A planning memorandum or checklist.
d. A client representation letter.

45. If specific information comes to an auditor's attention that implies the existence of possible illegal acts that could have a material, but indirect effect on the financial statements, the auditor should next
a. Apply audit procedures specifically directed to ascertaining whether an illegal act has occurred.
b. Seek the advice of an informed expert qualified to practice law as to possible contingent liabilities.
c. Report the matter to an appropriate level of management at least one level above those involved.
d. Discuss the evidence with the client's audit committee, or others with equivalent authority and responsibility.

46. To determine whether accounts payable are complete, an auditor performs a test to verify that all merchandise received is recorded. The population of documents for this test consists of all
a. Vendor's invoices.
b. Purchase orders.
c. Receiving reports.
d. Canceled checks.

47. Which of the following internal control procedures most likely addresses the completeness assertion for inventory?
a. Work in process account is periodically reconciled with subsidiary records.
b. Employees responsible for custody of finished goods do not perform the receiving function.
c. Receiving reports are prenumbered and periodically reconciled.
d. There is a separation of duties between payroll department and inventory accounting personnel.

48. Tracing bills of lading to sales invoices provides evidence that
a. Shipments to customers were invoiced.
b. Shipments to customers were recorded as sales.
c. Recorded sales were shipped.
d. Invoiced sales were shipped.

49. Analytical procedures used in planning an audit should focus on identifying
a. Material weaknesses in the internal control structure.
b. The predictability of financial data from individual transactions.
c. The various assertions that are embodied in the financial statements.
d. Areas that may represent specific risks relevant to the audit.

50. Which of the following audit procedures is best for identifying unrecorded trade accounts payable?
a. Examining unusual relationships between monthly accounts payable balances and recorded cash payments.
b. Reconciling vendors' statements to the file of receiving reports to identify items received just prior to the balance sheet date.
c. Reviewing cash disbursements recorded subsequent to the balance sheet date to determine whether the related payables apply to the prior period.
d. Investigating payables recorded just prior to and just subsequent to the balance sheet date to determine whether they are supported by receiving reports.

51. The negative request form of accounts receivable confirmation is useful particularly when the

	Assessed level of control risk relating to receivables is	Number of small balances is	Consideration by the recipient is
a.	Low	Many	Likely
b.	Low	Few	Unlikely
c.	High	Few	Likely
d.	High	Many	Likely

52. A basic premise underlying the application of analytical procedures is that

a. The study of financial ratios is an acceptable alternative to the investigation of unusual fluctuations.
b. Statistical tests of financial information may lead to the discovery of material errors in the financial statements.
c. Plausible relationships among data may reasonably be expected to exist and continue in the absence of known conditions to the contrary.
d. These procedures cannot replace tests of balances and transactions.

53. An auditor's purpose in reviewing the renewal of a note payable shortly after the balance sheet date most likely is to obtain evidence concerning management's assertions about

a. Existence or occurrence.
b. Presentation and disclosure.
c. Completeness.
d. Valuation or allocation.

54. An auditor's purpose in reviewing credit ratings of customers with delinquent accounts receivable most likely is to obtain evidence concerning management's assertions about

a. Presentation and disclosure.
b. Existence or occurrence.
c. Rights and obligations.
d. Valuation or allocation.

55. Which of the following statements concerning evidential matter is correct?

a. Competent evidence supporting management's assertions should be convincing rather than merely persuasive.
b. An effective internal control structure contributes little to the reliability of the evidence created within the entity.
c. The cost of obtaining evidence is not an important consideration to an auditor in deciding what evidence should be obtained.
d. A client's accounting data cannot be considered sufficient audit evidence to support the financial statements.

56. In testing the existence assertion for an asset, an auditor ordinarily works from the

a. Financial statements to the potentially unrecorded items.
b. Potentially unrecorded items to the financial statements.
c. Accounting records to the supporting evidence.
d. Supporting evidence to the accounting records.

57. In an audit of inventories, an auditor would least likely verify that

a. All inventory owned by the client is on hand at the time of the count.
b. The client has used proper inventory pricing.
c. The financial statement presentation of inventories is appropriate.
d. Damaged goods and obsolete items have been properly accounted for.

58. The scope of an audit is not restricted when an attorney's response to an auditor as a result of a client's letter of audit inquiry limits the response to

a. Matters to which the attorney has given substantive attention in the form of legal representation.
b. An evaluation of the likelihood of an unfavorable outcome of the matters disclosed by the entity.
c. The attorney's opinion of the entity's historical experience in recent similar litigation.
d. The probable outcome of asserted claims and pending or threatened litigation.

59. Two assertions for which confirmation of accounts receivable balances provides primary evidence are

a. Completeness and valuation.
b. Valuation and rights and obligations.
c. Rights and obligations and existence.
d. Existence and completeness.

60. Cutoff tests designed to detect credit sales made before the end of the year that have been recorded in the subsequent year provide assurance about management's assertion of

a. Presentation.
b. Completeness.
c. Rights.
d. Existence.

61. An auditor's analytical procedures most likely would be facilitated if the entity
a. Corrects material weaknesses in internal control before the beginning of the audit.
b. Develops its data from sources solely within the entity.
c. Segregates obsolete inventory before the physical inventory count.
d. Uses a standard cost system that produces variance reports.

62. If the objective of a test of details is to detect overstatements of sales, the auditor should trace transactions from the
a. Cash receipts journal to the sales journal.
b. Sales journal to the cash receipts journal.
c. Source documents to the accounting records.
d. Accounting records to the source documents.

63. Which of the following procedures most likely would justify the use of the negative form of accounts receivable confirmation?
a. A small number of accounts may be in dispute and the accounts receivable balance arises from sales to a few major customers.
b. A small number of accounts may be in dispute and the accounts receivable balance arises from sales to many customers with small balances.
c. A substantial number of accounts may be in dispute and the accounts receivable balance arises from sales to a few major customers.
d. A substantial number of accounts may be in dispute and the accounts receivable balance arises from sales to many customers with small balances.

64. The audit working paper that reflects the major components of an amount reported in the financial statements is the
a. Interbank transfer schedule.
b. Carryforward schedule.
c. Supporting schedule.
d. Lead schedule.

65. An auditor concluded that no excessive costs for idle plant were charged to inventory. This conclusion most likely related to the auditor's objective to obtain evidence about the financial statement assertions regarding inventory, including presentation and disclosure and
a. Valuation and allocation.
b. Completeness.

c. Existence or occurrence.
d. Rights and obligations

66. Which of the following types of audit evidence is the **least** persuasive?
a. Prenumbered purchase order forms.
b. Bank statements obtained from the client.
c. Test counts of inventory performed by the auditor.
d. Correspondence from the client's attorney about litigation.

67. Which of the following combinations of procedures would an auditor most likely perform to obtain evidence about fixed asset additions?
a. Inspecting documents and physically examining assets.
b. Recomputing calculations and obtaining written management representations.
c. Observing operating activities and comparing balances to prior period balances.
d. Confirming ownership and corroborating transactions through inquiries of client personnel.

68. An auditor most likely would inspect loan agreements under which an entity's inventories are pledged to support management's financial statement assertion of
a. Existence or occurrence.
b. Completeness.
c. Presentation and disclosure.
d. Valuation or allocation.

69. An auditor most likely would analyze inventory turnover rates to obtain evidence concerning management's assertions about
a. Existence or occurrence.
b. Rights and obligations.
c. Presentation and disclosure.
d. Valuation or allocation.

70. Which of the following procedures would an auditor most likely perform to verify management's assertion of completeness?
a. Compare a sample of shipping documents to related sales invoices.
b. Observe the client's distribution of payroll checks.
c. Confirm a sample of recorded receivables by direct communication with the debtors.
d. Review standard bank confirmations for indications of kiting.

71. An auditor's decision either to apply analytical procedures as substantive tests or to perform tests of transactions and account balances usually is determined by the
a. Availability of data aggregated at a high level.
b. Relative effectiveness and efficiency of the tests.
c. Timing of tests performed after the balance sheet date.
d. Auditor's familiarity with industry trends.

72. Analytical procedures used in the overall review stage of an audit generally include
a. Considering unusual or unexpected account balances that were **not** previously identified.
b. Performing tests of transactions to corroborate management's financial statement assertions.
c. Gathering evidence concerning account balances that have **not** changed from the prior year.
d. Retesting control procedures that appeared to be ineffective during the assessment of control risk.

73. In using the work of a specialist, an understanding should exist among the auditor, the client, and the specialist as to the nature of the specialist's work. The documentation of this understanding should cover
a. A statement that the specialist assumes **no** responsibility to update the specialist's report for future events or circumstances.
b. The conditions under which a division of responsibility may be necessary.
c. The specialist's understanding of the auditor's corroborative use of the specialist's findings.
d. The auditor's disclaimer as to whether the specialist's findings corroborate the representations in the financial statements.

74. To which of the following matters would materiality limits **not** apply when obtaining written client representations?
a. Losses from sales commitments.
b. Unasserted claims and assessments.
c. Irregularities involving management.
d. Noncompliance with contractual agreements.

75. Which of the following factors most likely would affect an auditor's judgment about the quantity, type, and content of the auditor's working papers?
a. The assessed level of control risk.
b. The likelihood of a review by a concurring (second) partner.
c. The number of personnel assigned to the audit.
d. The content of the management representation letter.

76. Which of the following most likely would indicate the existence of related parties?
a. Writing down obsolete inventory just before year end.
b. Failing to correct previously identified internal control structure deficiencies.
c. Depending on a single product for the success of the entity.
d. Borrowing money at an interest rate significantly below the market rate.

77. Which of the following procedures would an auditor most likely perform to obtain evidence about the occurrence of subsequent events?
a. Recomputing a sample of large-dollar transactions occurring after year end for arithmetic accuracy.
b. Investigating changes in stockholders' equity occurring after year end.
c. Inquiring of the entity's legal counsel concerning litigation, claims, and assessments arising after year end.
d. Confirming bank accounts established after year end.

78. Which of the following matters is an auditor required to communicate to an entity's audit committee?

I. Disagreements with management about matters significant to the entity's financial statements that have been satisfactorily resolved.
II. Initial selection of significant accounting policies in emerging areas that lack authoritative guidance.

a. I only.
b. II only.
c. Both I and II.
d. Neither I nor II.

79. Auditors try to identify predictable relationships when using analytical procedures. Relationships involving transactions from which of the following accounts most likely would yield the highest level of evidence?
a. Accounts receivable.
b. Interest expense.
c. Accounts payable.
d. Travel and entertainment expense.

80. An auditor selected items for test counts while observing a client's physical inventory. The auditor then traced the test counts to the client's inventory listing. This procedure most likely obtained evidence concerning management's assertion of
a. Rights and obligations.
b. Completeness.
c. Existence or occurrence.
d. Valuation.

81. In testing plant and equipment balances, an auditor examines new additions listed on an analysis of plant and equipment. This procedure most likely obtains evidence concerning management's assertion of
a. Completeness.
b. Existence or occurrence.
c. Presentation and disclosure.
d. Valuation or allocation.

82. In evaluating an entity's accounting estimates, one of an auditor's objectives is to determine whether the estimates are
a. Not subject to bias.
b. Consistent with industry guidelines.
c. Based on objective assumptions.
d. Reasonable in the circumstances.

83. Which of the following audit procedures is best for identifying unrecorded trade accounts payable?
a. Reviewing cash disbursements recorded subsequent to the balance sheet date to determine whether the related payables apply to the prior period.
b. Investigating payables recorded just prior to and just subsequent to the balance sheet date to determine whether they are supported by receiving reports.
c. Examining unusual relationships between monthly accounts payable balances and recorded cash payments.
d. Reconciling vendors' statements to the file of receiving reports to identify items received just prior to the balance sheet date.

84. In testing for unrecorded retirements of equipment, an auditor most likely would
a. Select items of equipment from the accounting records and then locate them during the plant tour.
b. Compare depreciation journal entries with similar prior-year entries in search of fully depreciated equipment.

c. Inspect items of equipment observed during the plant tour and then trace them to the equipment subsidiary ledger.
d. Scan the general journal for unusual equipment additions and excessive debits to repairs and maintenance expense.

85. An auditor most likely would extend substantive tests of payroll when
a. Payroll is extensively audited by the state government.
b. Payroll expense is substantially higher than in the prior year.
c. Overpayments are discovered in performing tests of details.
d. Employees complain to management about too much overtime.

86. A client has a large and active investment portfolio that is kept in a bank safe deposit box. If the auditor is unable to count the securities at the balance sheet date, the auditor most likely will
a. Request the bank to confirm to the auditor the contents of the safe deposit box at the balance sheet date.
b. Examine supporting evidence for transactions occurring during the year.
c. Count the securities at a subsequent date and confirm with the bank whether securities were added or removed since the balance sheet date.
d. Request the client to have the bank seal the safe deposit box until the auditor can count the securities at a subsequent date.

87. Which of the following is required documentation in an audit in accordance with generally accepted auditing standards?
a. A flowchart or narrative of the accounting system describing the recording and classification of transactions for financial reporting.
b. An audit program setting forth in detail the procedures necessary to accomplish the engagement's objectives.
c. A planning memorandum establishing the timing of the audit procedures and coordinating the assistance of entity personnel.
d. An internal control questionnaire identifying policies and procedures that assure specific objectives will be achieved.

88. In using the work of a specialist, an auditor referred to the specialist's findings in the auditor's report. This would be an appropriate reporting practice if the

a. Client is **not** familiar with the professional certification, personal reputation, or particular competence of the specialist.

b. Auditor, as a result of the specialist's findings, adds an explanatory paragraph emphasizing a matter regarding the financial statements.

c. Client understands the auditor's corroborative use of the specialist's findings in relation to the representations in the financial statements.

d. Auditor, as a result of the specialist's findings, decides to indicate a division of responsibility with the specialist.

89. Zero Corp. suffered a loss that would have a material effect on its financial statements on an uncollectible trade account receivable due to a customer's bankruptcy. This occurred suddenly due to a natural disaster ten days after Zero's balance sheet date, but one month before the issuance of the financial statements and the auditor's report. Under these circumstances,

	The financial statements should be adjusted	The event requires financial statement disclosure, but no adjustment	The auditor's report should be modified for a lack of consistency
a.	Yes	No	No
b.	Yes	No	Yes
c.	No	Yes	Yes
d.	No	Yes	No

90. Which of the following statements ordinarily is included among the written client representations obtained by the auditor?

a. Compensating balances and other arrangements involving restrictions on cash balances have been disclosed.

b. Management acknowledges responsibility for illegal actions committed by employees.

c. Sufficient evidential matter has been made available to permit the issuance of an unqualified opinion.

d. Management acknowledges that there are no material weaknesses in the internal control.

91. Which of the following auditing procedures most likely would assist an auditor in identifying related party transactions?

a. Retesting ineffective internal control procedures previously reported to the audit committee.

b. Sending second requests for unanswered positive confirmations of accounts receivable.

c. Reviewing accounting records for nonrecurring transactions recognized near the balance sheet date.

d. Inspecting communications with law firms for evidence of unreported contingent liabilities.

92. Before applying principal substantive tests to the details of accounts at an interim date prior to the balance sheet date, an auditor should

a. Assess control risk at below the maximum for the assertions embodied in the accounts selected for interim testing.

b. Determine that the accounts selected for interim testing are not material to the financial statements taken as a whole.

c. Consider whether the amounts of the year-end balances selected for interim testing are reasonably predictable.

d. Obtain written representations from management that all financial records and related data will be made available.

93. After field work audit procedures are completed, a partner of the CPA firm who has not been involved in the audit performs a second or wrap-up working paper review. This second review usually focuses on

a. The fair presentation of the financial statements in conformity with GAAP.

b. Irregularities involving the client's management and its employees.

c. The materiality of the adjusting entries proposed by the audit staff.

d. The communication of internal control weaknesses to the client's audit committee.

94. On the basis of audit evidence gathered and evaluated, an auditor decides to increase the assessed level of control risk from that originally planned. To achieve an overall audit risk level that is substantially the same as the planned audit risk level, the auditor would

a. Decrease substantive testing.

b. Decrease detection risk.

c. Increase inherent risk.

d. Increase materiality levels.

95. During the annual audit of Ajax Corp., a publicly held company, Jones, CPA, a continuing auditor, determined that illegal political contributions had been made during each of the past seven years, including the year under audit. Jones notified the board of directors about the illegal contributions, but they refused to take any action because the amounts involved were immaterial to the financial statements.

Jones should reconsider the intended degree of reliance to be placed on the
a. Letter of audit inquiry to the client's attorney.
b. Prior years' audit programs.
c. Management representation letter.
d. Preliminary judgment about materiality levels.

96. An entity's income statements were misstated due to the recording of journal entries that involved debits and credits to an unusual combination of expense and revenue accounts. The auditor most likely could have detected this irregularity by
a. Tracing a sample of journal entries to the general ledger.
b. Evaluating the effectiveness of the internal control structure policies and procedures.
c. Investigating the reconciliations between controlling accounts and subsidiary records.
d. Performing analytical procedures designed to disclose differences from expectations.

97. Which of the following documentation is not required for an audit in accordance with generally accepted auditing standards?
a. A written audit program setting forth the procedures necessary to accomplish the audit's objectives.
b. An indication that the accounting records agree or reconcile with the financial statements.
c. A client engagement letter that summarizes the timing and details of the auditor's planned field work.
d. The basis for the auditor's conclusions when the assessed level of control risk is below the maximum level.

98. Audit programs should be designed so that
a. Most of the required procedures can be performed as interim work.
b. Inherent risk is assessed at a sufficiently low level.

c. The auditor can make constructive suggestions to management.
d. The audit evidence gathered supports the auditor's conclusions.

99. The permanent file of an auditor's working papers generally would not include
a. Bond indenture agreements.
b. Lease agreements.
c. Working trial balance.
d. Flowchart of the internal control structure.

100. Which of the following presumptions is correct about the reliability of evidential matter?
a. Information obtained indirectly from outside sources is the most reliable evidential matter.
b. To be reliable, evidential matter should be convincing rather than persuasive.
c. Reliability of evidential matter refers to the amount of corroborative evidence obtained.
d. An effective internal control structure provides more assurance about the reliability of evidential matter.

101. Which of the following auditing procedures most likely would provide assurance about a manufacturing entity's inventory valuation?
a. Testing the entity's computation of standard overhead rates.
b. Obtaining confirmation of inventories pledged under loan agreements.
c. Reviewing shipping and receiving cutoff procedures for inventories.
d. Tracing test counts to the entity's inventory listing.

102. In establishing the existence and ownership of a long-term investment in the form of publicly-traded stock, an auditor should inspect the securities or
a. Correspond with the investee company to verify the number of shares owned.
b. Inspect the audited financial statements of the investee company.
c. Confirm the number of shares owned that are held by an independent custodian.
d. Determine that the investment is carried at the lower of cost or market.

103. An auditor's purpose in reviewing credit ratings of customers with delinquent accounts receivable most likely is to obtain evidence concerning management's assertions about

a. Valuation or allocation.
b. Presentation and disclosure.
c. Existence or occurrence.
d. Rights and obligations.

104. Determining that proper amounts of depreciation are expensed provides assurance about management's assertions of valuation or allocation and

a. Presentation and disclosure.
b. Completeness.
c. Rights and obligations.
d. Existence or occurrence.

105. In auditing accounts receivable the negative form of confirmation request most likely would be used when

a. Recipients are likely to return positive confirmation requests without verifying the accuracy of the information.
b. The combined assessed level of inherent and control risk relative to accounts receivable is low.
c. A small number of accounts receivable are involved but a relatively large number of errors are expected.
d. The auditor performs a dual purpose test that assesses control risk and obtains substantive evidence.

106. When using confirmations to provide evidence about the completeness assertion for accounts payable, the appropriate population most likely would be

a. Vendors with whom the entity has previously done business.
b. Amounts recorded in the accounts payable subsidiary ledger.
c. Payees of checks drawn in the month after the year end.
d. Invoices filed in the entity's open invoice file.

107. In evaluating the reasonableness of an accounting estimate, an auditor most likely would concentrate on key factors and assumptions that are

a. Consistent with prior periods.
b. Similar to industry guidelines.
c. Objective and not susceptible to bias.
d. Deviations from historical patterns.

108. In auditing payroll, an auditor most likely would

a. Verify that checks representing unclaimed wages are mailed.
b. Trace individual employee deductions to entity journal entries.
c. Observe entity employees during a payroll distribution.
d. Compare payroll costs with entity standards or budgets.

109. In auditing long-term bonds payable, an auditor most likely would

a. Perform analytical procedures on the bond premium and discount accounts.
b. Examine documentation of assets purchased with bond proceeds for liens.
c. Compare interest expense with the bond payable amount for reasonableness.
d. Confirm the existence of individual bond-holders at year end.

110. In performing tests concerning the granting of stock options, an auditor should

a. Confirm the transaction with the Secretary of State in the state of incorporation.
b. Verify the existence of option holders in the entity's payroll records or stock ledgers.
c. Determine that sufficient treasury stock is available to cover any new stock issued.
d. Trace the authorization for the transaction to a vote of the board of directors.

111. An auditor analyzes repairs and maintenance accounts primarily to obtain evidence in support of the audit assertion that all

a. Noncapitalizable expenditures for repairs and maintenance have been recorded in the proper period.
b. Expenditures for property and equipment have been recorded in the proper period.
c. Noncapitalizable expenditures for repairs and maintenance have been properly charged to expense.
d. Expenditures for property and equipment have not been charged to expense.

112. Before applying substantive tests to the details of asset accounts at an interim date, an auditor should assess
a. Control risk at below the maximum level.
b. Inherent risk at the maximum level.
c. The difficulty in controlling the incremental audit risk.
d. Materiality for the accounts tested as insignificant.

113. "There are no violations or possible violations of laws or regulations whose effects should be considered for disclosure in the financial statements or as a basis for recording a loss contingency." The foregoing passage most likely is from a(an)
a. Client engagement letter.
b. Report on compliance with laws and regulations.
c. Management representation letter.
d. Attestation report on an internal control structure.

114. Which of the following statements is correct about the auditor's use of the work of a specialist?
a. The specialist should not have an understanding of the auditor's corroborative use of the specialist's findings.
b. The auditor is required to perform substantive procedures to verify the specialist's assumptions and findings.
c. The client should not have an understanding of the nature of the work to be performed by the specialist.
d. The auditor should obtain an understanding of the methods and assumptions used by the specialist.

115. The primary reason an auditor requests letters of inquiry be sent to a client's attorneys is to provide the auditor with
a. The probable outcome of asserted claims and pending or threatened litigation.
b. Corroboration of the information furnished by management about litigation, claims, and assessments.
c. The attorneys' opinions of the client's historical experiences in recent similar litigation.
d. A description and evaluation of litigation, claims, and assessments that existed at the balance sheet date.

116. After determining that a related party transaction has, in fact, occurred, an auditor should
a. Add a separate paragraph to the auditor's standard report to explain the transaction.
b. Perform analytical procedures to verify whether similar transactions occurred, but were not recorded.

c. Obtain an understanding of the business purpose of the transaction.
d. Substantiate that the transaction was consummated on terms equivalent to an arm's-length transaction.

117. An auditor ordinarily uses a working trial balance resembling the financial statements without footnotes, but containing columns for
a. Cash flow increases and decreases.
b. Audit objectives and assertions.
c. Reclassifications and adjustments.
d. Reconciliations and tickmarks.

118. Which of the following factors would **least** likely affect the quantity and content of an auditor's working papers?
a. The condition of the client's records.
b. The assessed level of control risk.
c. The nature of the auditor's report.
d. The content of the representation letter.

119. Which of the following matters is an auditor required to communicate to an entity's audit committee?
a. The basis for assessing control risk below the maximum.
b. The process used by management in formulating sensitive accounting estimates.
c. The auditor's preliminary judgments about materiality levels.
d. The justification for performing substantive procedures at interim dates.

120. Which of the following relatively small misstatements most likely could have a material effect on an entity's financial statements?
a. An illegal payment to a foreign official that was **not** recorded.
b. A piece of obsolete office equipment that was **not** retired.
c. A petty cash fund disbursement that was **not** properly authorized.
d. An uncollectible account receivable that was **not** written off.

121. An auditor should design the written audit program so that
a. All material transactions will be selected for substantive testing.
b. Substantive tests prior to the balance sheet date will be minimized.
c. The audit procedures selected will achieve specific audit objectives.
d. Each account balance will be tested under either tests of controls or tests of transactions.

122. The audit program usually **cannot** be finalized until the
a. Consideration of the entity's internal control structure has been completed.
b. Engagement letter has been signed by the auditor and the client.
c. Reportable conditions have been communicated to the audit committee of the board of directors.
d. Search for unrecorded liabilities has been performed and documented.

123. An auditor would **least** likely initiate a discussion with a client's audit committee concerning
a. The methods used to account for significant unusual transactions.
b. The maximum dollar amount of misstatements that could exist without causing the financial statements to be materially misstated.
c. Indications of fraud and illegal acts committed by a corporate officer that were discovered by the auditor.
d. Disagreements with management as to accounting principles that were resolved during the current year's audit.

124. Tracing shipping documents to prenumbered sales invoices provides evidence that
a. No duplicate shipments or billings occurred.
b. Shipments to customers were properly invoiced.
c. All goods ordered by customers were shipped.
d. All prenumbered sales invoices were accounted for.

125. An auditor vouched data for a sample of employees in a payroll register to approved clock card data to provide assurance that
a. Payments to employees are computed at authorized rates.
b. Employees work the number of hours for which they are paid.
c. Segregation of duties exist between the preparation and distribution of the payroll.
d. Internal controls relating to unclaimed payroll checks are operating effectively.

126. Which of the following types of audit evidence is the most persuasive?
a. Prenumbered client purchase order forms.
b. Client work sheets supporting cost allocations.
c. Bank statements obtained from the client.
d. Client representation letter.

127. An auditor most likely would inspect loan agreements under which an entity's inventories are pledged to support management's financial statement assertion of
a. Presentation and disclosure.
b. Valuation or allocation.
c. Existence or occurrence.
d. Completeness.

128. In auditing intangible assets, an auditor most likely would review or recompute amortization and determine whether the amortization period is reasonable in support of management's financial statement assertion of
a. Valuation or allocation.
b. Existence or occurrence.
c. Completeness.
d. Rights and obligations.

129. Cutoff tests designed to detect purchases made before the end of the year that have been recorded in the subsequent year most likely would provide assurance about management's assertion of
a. Valuation or allocation.
b. Existence or occurrence.
c. Completeness.
d. Presentation and disclosure.

130. An auditor most likely would make inquiries of production and sales personnel concerning possible obsolete or slow-moving inventory to support management's financial statement assertion of
a. Valuation or allocation.
b. Rights and obligations.
c. Existence or occurrence.
d. Presentation and disclosure.

131. In confirming with an outside agent, such as a financial institution, that the agent is holding investment securities in the client's name, an auditor most likely gathers evidence in support of management's financial statement assertions of existence or occurrence and
a. Valuation or allocation.
b. Rights and obligations.
c. Completeness.
d. Presentation and disclosure.

132. Which of the following statements is correct concerning the use of negative confirmation requests?
a. Unreturned negative confirmation requests rarely provide significant explicit evidence.
b. Negative confirmation requests are effective when detection risk is low.
c. Unreturned negative confirmation requests indicate that alternative procedures are necessary.
d. Negative confirmation requests are effective when understatements of account balances are suspected.

133. When an auditor does **not** receive replies to positive requests for year-end accounts receivable confirmations, the auditor most likely would
a. Inspect the allowance account to verify whether the accounts were subsequently written off.
b. Increase the assessed level of detection risk for the valuation and completeness assertions.
c. Ask the client to contact the customers to request that the confirmations be returned.
d. Increase the assessed level of inherent risk for the revenue cycle.

134. Analytical procedures used in the overall review stage of an audit generally include
a. Gathering evidence concerning account balances that have **not** changed from the prior year.
b. Retesting control procedures that appeared to be ineffective during the assessment of control risk.
c. Considering unusual or unexpected account balances that were **not** previously identified.
d. Performing tests of transactions to corroborate management's financial statement assertions.

135. Which of the following would **not** be considered an analytical procedure?
a. Estimating payroll expense by multiplying the number of employees by the average hourly wage rate and the total hours worked.
b. Projecting an error rate by comparing the results of a statistical sample with the actual population characteristics.
c. Computing accounts receivable turnover by dividing credit sales by the average net receivables.
d. Developing the expected current-year sales based on the sales trend of the prior five years.

136. While observing a client's annual physical inventory, an auditor recorded test counts for several items and noticed that certain test counts were higher than the recorded quantities in the client's perpetual records. This situation could be the result of the client's failure to record
a. Purchase discounts.
b. Purchase returns.
c. Sales.
d. Sales returns.

137. To gain assurance that all inventory items in a client's inventory listing schedule are valid, an auditor most likely would trace
a. Inventory tags noted during the auditor's observation to items listed in the inventory listing schedule.
b. Inventory tags noted during the auditor's observation to items listed in receiving reports and vendors' invoices.
c. Items listed in the inventory listing schedule to inventory tags and the auditor's recorded count sheets.
d. Items listed in receiving reports and vendors' invoices to the inventory listing schedule.

138. When control risk is assessed as low for assertions related to payroll, substantive tests of payroll balances most likely would be limited to applying analytical procedures and
a. Observing the distribution of paychecks.
b. Footing and crossfooting the payroll register.
c. Inspecting payroll tax returns.
d. Recalculating payroll accruals.

139. In performing a search for unrecorded retirements of fixed assets, an auditor most likely would
a. Inspect the property ledger and the insurance and tax records, and then tour the client's facilities.
b. Tour the client's facilities, and then inspect the property ledger and the insurance and tax records.
c. Analyze the repair and maintenance account, and then tour the client's facilities.
d. Tour the client's facilities, and then analyze the repair and maintenance account.

140. Which of the following procedures would an auditor most likely perform in auditing the statement of cash flows?
a. Compare the amounts included in the statement of cash flows to similar amounts in the prior year's statement of cash flows.
b. Reconcile the cutoff bank statements to verify the accuracy of the year-end bank balances.
c. Vouch all bank transfers for the last week of the year and first week of the subsequent year.
d. Reconcile the amounts included in the statement of cash flows to the other financial statements' balances and amounts.

141. In determining whether transactions have been recorded, the direction of the audit testing should be from the
a. General ledger balances.
b. Adjusted trial balance.
c. Original source documents.
d. General journal entries.

142. Which of the following statements is correct concerning an auditor's use of the work of a specialist?
a. The work of a specialist who is related to the client may be acceptable under certain circumstances.
b. If an auditor believes that the determinations made by a specialist are unreasonable, only a qualified opinion may be issued.
c. If there is a material difference between a specialist's findings and the assertions in the financial statements, only an adverse opinion may be issued.
d. An auditor may **not** use a specialist in the determination of physical characteristics relating to inventories.

143. In using the work of a specialist, an auditor may refer to the specialist in the auditor's report if, as a result of the specialist's findings, the auditor

a. Becomes aware of conditions causing substantial doubt about the entity's ability to continue as a going concern.
b. Desires to disclose the specialist's findings, which imply that a more thorough audit was performed.
c. Is able to corroborate another specialist's earlier findings that were consistent with management's representations.
d. Discovers significant deficiencies in the design of the entity's internal control structure that management does **not** correct.

144. The refusal of a client's attorney to provide information requested in an inquiry letter generally is considered
a. Grounds for an adverse opinion.
b. A limitation on the scope of the audit.
c. Reason to withdraw from the engagement.
d. Equivalent to a reportable condition.

145. Which of the following procedures would an auditor most likely perform in obtaining evidence about subsequent events?
a. Determine that changes in employee pay rates after year end were properly authorized.
b. Recompute depreciation charges for plant assets sold after year end.
c. Inquire about payroll checks that were recorded before year end but cashed after year end.
d. Investigate changes in long-term debt occurring after year end.

146. To which of the following matters would materiality limits **not** apply in obtaining written management representations?
a. The availability of minutes of stockholders' and directors' meetings.
b. Losses from purchase commitments at prices in excess of market value.
c. The disclosure of compensating balance arrangements involving related parties.
d. Reductions of obsolete inventory to net realizable value.

147. The date of the management representation letter should coincide with the date of the
a. Balance sheet.
b. Latest interim financial information.
c. Auditor's report.
d. Latest related party transaction.

148. When auditing related party transactions, an auditor places primary emphasis on
a. Ascertaining the rights and obligations of the related parties.
b. Confirming the existence of the related parties.
c. Verifying the valuation of the related party transactions.
d. Evaluating the disclosure of the related party transactions.

149. Which of the following procedures would an auditor ordinarily perform first in evaluating management's accounting estimates for reasonableness?
a. Develop independent expectations of management's estimates.
b. Consider the appropriateness of the key factors or assumptions used in preparing the estimates.
c. Test the calculations used by management in developing the estimates.
d. Obtain an understanding of how management developed its estimates.

150. Which of the following pairs of accounts would an auditor most likely analyze on the same working paper?
a. Notes receivable and interest income.
b. Accrued interest receivable and accrued interest payable.
c. Notes payable and notes receivable.
d. Interest income and interest expense.

151. An auditor's working papers serve mainly to
a. Provide the principal support for the auditor's report.
b. Satisfy the auditor's responsibilities concerning the Code of Professional Conduct.
c. Monitor the effectiveness of the CPA firm's quality control procedures.
d. Document the level of independence maintained by the auditor.

152. Which of the following procedures would an auditor **least** likely perform before the balance sheet date?
a. Confirmation of accounts payable.
b. Observation of merchandise inventory.
c. Assessment of control risk.
d. Identification of related parties.

153. What type of analytical procedure would an auditor most likely use in developing relationships among balance sheet accounts when reviewing the financial statements of a nonpublic entity?
a. Trend analysis.
b. Regression analysis.
c. Ratio analysis.
d. Risk analysis.

154. An auditor is considering whether the omission of a substantive procedure considered necessary at the time of an audit may impair the auditor's present ability to support the previously expressed opinion. The auditor need **not** apply the omitted procedure if the
a. Financial statements and auditor's report were **not** distributed beyond management and the board of directors.
b. Auditor's previously expressed opinion was qualified because of a departure from GAAP.
c. Results of other procedures that were applied tend to compensate for the procedure omitted.
d. Omission is due to unreasonable delays by client personnel in providing data on a timely basis.

155. Which of the following statements is correct concerning an auditor's required communication with an entity's audit committee?
a. This communication is required to occur before the auditor's report on the financial statements is issued.
b. This communication should include management changes in the application of significant accounting policies.
c. Any significant matter communicated to the audit committee also should be communicated to management.
d. Significant audit adjustments proposed by the auditor and recorded by management need **not** be communicated to the audit committee.

156. An auditor may achieve audit objectives related to particular assertions by
a. Performing analytical procedures.
b. Adhering to a system of quality control.
c. Preparing auditor working papers.
d. Increasing the level of detection risk.

157. The confirmation of customers' accounts receivable rarely provides reliable evidence about the completeness assertion because
a. Many customers merely sign and return the confirmation without verifying its details.
b. Recipients usually respond only if they disagree with the information on the request.
c. Customers may **not** be inclined to report understatement errors in their accounts.
d. Auditors typically select many accounts with low recorded balances to be confirmed.

158. Which of the following sets of information does an auditor usually confirm on one form?
a. Accounts payable and purchase commitments.
b. Cash in bank and collateral for loans.
c. Inventory on consignment and contingent liabilities.
d. Accounts receivable and accrued interest receivable.

159. An auditor's analytical procedures most likely would be facilitated if the entity
a. Segregates obsolete inventory before the physical inventory count.
b. Uses a standard cost system that produces variance reports.
c. Corrects material weaknesses in internal control before the beginning of the audit.
d. Develops its data from sources solely within the entity.

160. To measure how effectively an entity employs its resources, an auditor calculates inventory turnover by dividing average inventory into
a. Net sales.
b. Cost of goods sold.
c. Operating income.
d. Gross sales.

161. The usefulness of the standard bank confirmation request may be limited because the bank employee who completes the form may
a. Not believe that the bank is obligated to verify confidential information to a third party.
b. Sign and return the form without inspecting the accuracy of the client's bank reconciliation.
c. Not have access to the client's cutoff bank statement.
d. Be unaware of all the financial relationships that the bank has with the client.

162. An auditor most likely would limit substantive audit tests of sales transactions when control risk is assessed as low for the existence or occurrence assertion concerning sales transactions and the auditor has already gathered evidence supporting
a. Opening and closing inventory balances.
b. Cash receipts and accounts receivable.
c. Shipping and receiving activities.
d. Cutoffs of sales and purchases.

163. Which of the following procedures would an auditor most likely perform in searching for unrecorded liabilities?
a. Trace a sample of accounts payable entries recorded just before year end to the unmatched receiving report file.
b. Compare a sample of purchase orders issued just after year end with the year-end accounts payable trial balance.
c. Vouch a sample of cash disbursements recorded just after year end to receiving reports and vendor invoices.
d. Scan the cash disbursements entries recorded just before year end for indications of unusual transactions.

164. An auditor traced a sample of purchase orders and the related receiving reports to the purchases journal and the cash disbursements journal. The purpose of this substantive audit procedure most likely was to
a. Identify unusually large purchases that should be investigated further.
b. Verify that cash disbursements were for goods actually received.
c. Determine that purchases were properly recorded.
d. Test whether payments were for goods actually ordered.

165. Which of the following explanations most likely would satisfy an auditor who questions management about significant debits to the accumulated depreciation accounts?
a. The estimated remaining useful lives of plant assets were revised upward.
b. Plant assets were retired during the year.
c. The prior year's depreciation expense was erroneously understated.
d. Overhead allocations were revised at year end.

166. Which of the following circumstances most likely would cause an auditor to suspect an employee payroll fraud scheme?
a. There are significant unexplained variances between standard and actual labor cost.
b. Payroll checks are disbursed by the same employee each payday.
c. Employee time cards are approved by individual departmental supervisors.
d. A separate payroll bank account is maintained on an imprest basis.

167. The objective of tests of details of transactions performed as substantive tests is to
a. Comply with generally accepted auditing standards.
b. Attain assurance about the reliability of the accounting system.
c. Detect material misstatements in the financial statements.
d. Evaluate whether management's policies and procedures operated effectively.

168. Which of the following statements is correct concerning an auditor's use of the work of a specialist?
a. The auditor need **not** obtain an understanding of the methods and assumptions used by the specialist.
b. The auditor may **not** use the work of a specialist in matters material to the fair presentation of the financial statements.
c. The reasonableness of the specialist's assumptions and their applications are strictly the auditor's responsibility.
d. The work of a specialist who has a contractual relationship with the client may be acceptable under certain circumstances.

169. Which of the following is an audit procedure that an auditor most likely would perform concerning litigation, claims, and assessments?
a. Request the client's lawyer to evaluate whether the client's pending litigation, claims, and assessments indicate a going concern problem.
b. Examine the legal documents in the client's lawyer's possession concerning litigation, claims, and assessments to which the lawyer has devoted substantive attention.
c. Discuss with management its policies and procedures adopted for evaluating and accounting for litigation, claims, and assessments.
d. Confirm directly with the client's lawyer that all litigation, claims, and assessments have been recorded or disclosed in the financial statements.

170. Which of the following procedures would an auditor most likely perform to obtain evidence about the occurrence of subsequent events?
a. Confirming a sample of material accounts receivable established after year end.
b. Comparing the financial statements being reported on with those of the prior period.
c. Investigating personnel changes in the accounting department occurring after year end.
d. Inquiring as to whether any unusual adjustments were made after year end.

171. Which of the following matters would an auditor most likely include in a management representation letter?
a. Communications with the audit committee concerning weaknesses in the internal control structure.
b. The completeness and availability of minutes of stockholders' and directors' meetings.
c. Plans to acquire or merge with other entities in the subsequent year.
d. Management's acknowledgment of its responsibility for the detection of employee fraud.

172. Which of the following auditing procedures most likely would assist an auditor in identifying related party transactions?
a. Inspecting correspondence with lawyers for evidence of unreported contingent liabilities.
b. Vouching accounting records for recurring transactions recorded just after the balance sheet date.
c. Reviewing confirmations of loans receivable and payable for indications of guarantees.
d. Performing analytical procedures for indications of possible financial difficulties.

173. The permanent (continuing) file of an auditor's working papers most likely would include copies of the
a. Lead schedules.
b. Attorney's letters.
c. Bank statements.
d. Debt agreements.

174. Which of the following statements is correct about an auditor's required communication with an entity's audit committee?

a. Any matters communicated to the entity's audit committee also are required to be communicated to the entity's management.

b. The auditor is required to inform the entity's audit committee about significant errors discovered by the auditor and subsequently corrected by management.

c. Disagreements with management about the application of accounting principles are required to be communicated in writing to the entity's audit committee.

d. Weaknesses in the internal control structure previously reported to the entity's audit committee are required to be communicated to the audit committee after each subsequent audit until the weaknesses are corrected.

175. Which of the following events occurring after the issuance of an auditor's report most likely would cause the auditor to make further inquiries about the previously issued financial statements?

a. An uninsured natural disaster occurs that may affect the entity's ability to continue as a going concern.

b. A contingency is resolved that had been disclosed in the audited financial statements.

c. New information is discovered concerning undisclosed lease transactions of the audited period.

d. A subsidiary is sold that accounts for 25% of the entity's consolidated net income.

Chapter Two – Problems
The Third Standard of Field Work—Evidence

NUMBER 1

Green, CPA, is auditing the financial statements of Taylor Corporation for the year ended December 31, 1989. Green plans to complete the field work and sign the auditor's report about May 10, 1990. Green is concerned about events and transactions occurring after December 31, 1989, that may affect the 1989 financial statements.

Required:
a. What are the general types of subsequent events that require Green's consideration and evaluation?
b. What are the auditing procedures Green should consider performing to gather evidence concerning subsequent events?

NUMBER 2

Kent, CPA, is engaged in the audit of Davidson Corp.'s financial statements for the year ended December 31, 1989. Kent is about to commence auditing Davidson's employee pension expense, but Kent's preliminary inquiries concerning Davidson's defined benefit pension plan lead Kent to believe that some of the actuarial computations and assumptions are so complex that they are beyond the competence ordinarily required of an auditor. Kent is considering engaging Park, an actuary, to assist with this portion of the audit.

Required:
a. What are the factors Kent should consider in the process of selecting Park?
b. What are the matters that should be understood among Kent, Park, and Davidson's management as to the nature of the work to be performed by Park?
c. May Kent refer to Park in the auditor's report if Kent decides to issue an unqualified opinion? Why?
d. May Kent refer to Park in the auditor's report if Kent decides to issue other than an unqualified opinion as a result of Park's findings? Why?

NUMBER 3

Larkin, CPA, has been engaged to audit the financial statements of Vernon Distributors, Inc., a continuing audit client, for the year ended September 30, 1991. After obtaining an understanding of Vernon's internal control structure, Larkin assessed control risk at the maximum level for all financial statement assertions concerning investments. Larkin determined that Vernon is unable to exercise significant influence over any investee and none are related parties.

Larkin obtained from Vernon detailed analyses of its investments in domestic securities showing:

*   The classification between current and noncurrent portfolios;
*   A description of each security, including the interest rate and maturity date of bonds and par value and dividend rate on stocks;
*   A notation of the location of each security, either in the Treasurer's safe or held by an independent custodian;
*   The number of shares of stock or face amount of bonds held at the beginning and end of the year;
*   The beginning and ending balances at cost and at market, and the unamortized premium or discount on bonds;
*   Additions to and sales from the portfolios for the year, including date, number of shares, face amount of bonds, cost, proceeds, and realized gain or loss;
*   Valuation allowances at the beginning and end of the year and changes therein;
*   Accrued investment income for each investment at the beginning and end of the year, and income earned and collected during the year.

Larkin then prepared the following partial audit program of substantive auditing procedures:

1. Foot and crossfoot the analyses.
2. Trace the ending totals to the general ledger and financial statements.
3. Trace the beginning balances to the prior year's working papers.
4. Obtain positive confirmation as of the balance sheet date of the investments held by any independent custodian.
5. Determine that income from investments has been properly recorded as accrued or collected by reference to published sources, by computation, and by tracing to recorded amounts.
6. For investments in nonpublic entities, compare carrying value to information in the most recently available audited financial statements.
7. Determine that all transfers between the current and noncurrent portfolios have been properly authorized and recorded.
8. Determine that any other-than-temporary decline in the price of an investment has been properly recorded.

Required:

a. Identify the primary financial statement assertion relative to investments that would be addressed by each of the procedures #4 through #8 and describe the primary audit objective of performing that procedure. Use the format illustrated below.

Primary Assertion	Objective

b. Describe three additional substantive auditing procedures Larkin should consider in auditing Vernon's investments.

NUMBER 4

The purpose of all auditing procedures is to gather sufficient competent evidence for an auditor to form an opinion regarding the financial statements taken as a whole.

Required:

a. In addition to the example below, identify and describe five means or techniques of gathering audit evidence used to evaluate a client's inventory balance.

Technique	Description
Observation	An auditor watches the performance of some function, such as a client's annual inventory count.

b. Identify the five general assertions regarding a client's inventory balance and describe one **different** substantive auditing procedure for each assertion. Use the format illustrated below.

Assertion	Substantive Auditing Procedure

NUMBER 5

Kane, CPA, is auditing Star Wholesaling Company's financial statements and is about to perform substantive audit procedures on Star's trade accounts payable balances. After obtaining an understanding of Star's internal control structure for accounts payable, Kane assessed control risk at near the maximum. Kane requested and received from Star a schedule of the trade accounts payable prepared using the trade accounts payable subsidiary ledger (voucher register).

Required:

Describe the substantive audit procedures Kane should apply to Star's trade accounts payable balances. Do **not** include procedures that would be applied only in the audit of related party payables, amounts withheld from employees, and accrued expenses such as pensions and interest.

NUMBER 6

Cook, CPA, has been engaged to audit the financial statements of General Department Stores, Inc., a continuing audit client, which is a chain of medium-sized retail stores. General's fiscal year will end on June 30, 1993, and General's management has asked Cook to issue the auditor's report by August 1, 1993. Cook will not have sufficient time to perform all of the necessary field work in July 1993, but will have time to perform most of the field work as of an interim date, April 30, 1993.

For the accounts to be tested at the interim date, Cook will also perform substantive tests covering the transactions of the final two months of the year. This will be necessary to extend Cook's conclusions to the balance sheet date.

Required:

a. Describe the factors Cook should consider before applying principal substantive tests to General's balance sheet accounts at April 30, 1993.

b. For accounts tested at April 30, 1993, describe how Cook should design the substantive tests covering the balances as of June 30, 1993, and the transactions of the final two months of the year.

NUMBER 7

Question Number 7 consists of 9 items. Select the **best** answer for each item. **Answer all items.**

To support financial statement assertions, an auditor develops specific audit objectives. The auditor then designs substantive tests to satisfy or accomplish each objective.

Required:

Items 1 through 9 represent audit objectives for the investments, accounts receivable, and property and equipment accounts. To the right of each set of audit objectives is a listing of possible audit procedures for that account. For each audit objective, select the audit procedure that would primarily respond to the objective. Select only one procedure for each audit objective. A procedure may be selected only once, or not at all.

Items to be Answered:

Audit Objectives for Investments	*Audit Procedures for Investments*
1. Investments are properly described and classified in the financial statements.	A. Trace opening balances in the subsidiary ledger to prior year's audit working papers.
2. Recorded investments represent investments actually owned at the balance sheet date.	B. Determine that employees who are authorized to sell investments do not have access to cash.
	C. Examine supporting documents for a sample of investment transactions to verify that prenumbered documents are used.
	D. Determine that any impairments in the price of investments have been properly recorded.
	E. Verify that transfers from the current to the noncurrent investment portfolio have been properly recorded.
	F. Obtain positive confirmations as of the balance sheet date of investments held by independent custodians.
	G. Trace investment transactions to minutes of the Board of Directors meetings to determine that transactions were properly authorized.

NUMBER 7 (cont.)

Audit Objectives for Accounts Receivable

3. Accounts receivable represent all amounts owed to the entity at the balance sheet date.

4. The entity has legal right to all accounts receivable at the balance sheet date.

5. Accounts receivable are stated at net realizable value.

6. Accounts receivable are properly described and presented in the financial statements.

Audit Procedures for Accounts Receivable

A. Analyze the relationship of accounts receivable and sales and compare it with relationships for preceding periods.

B. Perform sales cut-off tests to obtain assurance that sales transactions and corresponding entries for inventories and cost of goods sold are recorded in the same and proper period.

C. Review the aged trial balance for significant past due accounts.

D. Obtain an understanding of the business purpose of transactions that resulted in accounts receivable balances.

E. Review loan agreements for indications of whether accounts receivable have been factored or pledged.

F. Review the accounts receivable trial balance for amounts due from officers and employees.

G. Analyze unusual relationships between monthly accounts receivable balances and monthly accounts payable balances.

Audit Objectives for Property & Equipment

7. The entity has legal right to property and equipment acquired during the year.

8. Recorded property and equipment represent assets that actually exist at the balance sheet date.

9. Net property and equipment are properly valued at the balance sheet date.

Audit Procedures for Property & Equipment

A. Trace opening balances in the summary schedules to the prior year's audit working papers.

B. Review the provision for depreciation expense and determine that depreciable lives and methods used in the current year are consistent with those used in the prior year.

C. Determine that the responsibility for maintaining the property and equipment records is segregated from the responsibility for custody of property and equipment.

D. Examine deeds and title insurance certificates.

E. Perform cut-off tests to verify that property and equipment additions are recorded in the proper period.

F. Determine that property and equipment is adequately insured.

G. Physically examine all major property and equipment additions.

NUMBER 8

Number 8 consists of 6 items. Select the best answers for each item. Answer all items. Your grade will be based on the total number of correct answers.

Required:

Items 99 through 104 represent the items that an auditor ordinarily would find on a client-prepared bank reconciliation. The accompanying **List of Auditing Procedures** represents substantive auditing procedures. For each item, select one or more procedures, as indicated, that the auditor most likely would perform to gather evidence in support of that item. The procedures on the **List** may be selected once, more than once, or not at all.

Assume:

- The client prepared the bank reconciliation on 10/2/94.

- The bank reconciliation is mathematically accurate.

- The auditor received a cutoff bank statement dated 10/7/94 directly from the bank on 10/11/94.

- The 9/30/94 deposit in transit, outstanding checks #1281, #1285, #1289, and #1292, and the correction of the error regarding check #1282 appeared on the cutoff bank statement.

- The auditor assessed control risk concerning the financial statement assertions related to cash at the maximum.

General Company
Bank Reconciliation
1st National Bank of U.S. Bank Account
September 30, 1994

99. Select 2 Procedures - <u>Balance per bank</u>				$28,375
100. Select 5 Procedures - <u>Deposits in transit</u>				
	9/29/94		$4,500	
	9/30/94		1,525	6,025
				34,400
101. Select 5 Procedures - <u>Outstanding checks</u>				
	# 988	8/31/94	2,200	
	#1281	9/26/94	675	
	#1285	9/27/94	850	
	#1289	9/29/94	2,500	
	#1292	9/30/94	7,225	(13,450)
				20,950
102. Select 1 Procedure - <u>Customer note collected by bank</u>				(3,000)
103. Select 2 Procedures - <u>Error: Check #1282, written on 9/26/94</u>				
	for $270 was erroneously charged by bank			
	as $720; bank was notified on 10/2/94			450
104. Select 1 Procedure - <u>Balance per books</u>				$18,400

List of Auditing Procedures

A. Trace to cash receipts journal.

B. Trace to cash disbursements journal.

C. Compare to 9/30/94 general ledger.

D. Confirm directly with bank.

E. Inspect bank credit memo.

F. Inspect bank debit memo.

G. Ascertain reason for unusual delay.

H. Inspect supporting documents for reconciling item **not** appearing on cutoff statement.

I. Trace items on the bank reconciliation to cut-off statement.

J. Trace items on the cutoff statement to bank reconciliation.

NUMBER 9

Analytical procedures are an important part of the audit process and consist of evaluations of financial information made by the study of plausible relationships among both financial and non-financial data. Analytical procedures are used to assist in planning other auditing procedures, as substantive tests in obtaining evidential matter, and as an overall review of the financial information.

Required:

a. Describe the objectives and the characteristics of analytical procedures used in planning an audit.

b. Describe the factors that influence an auditor's decision to select analytical procedures as substantive tests, including the factors that affect their effectiveness and efficiency.

c. Describe an auditor's objectives in applying analytical procedures in the overall review stage of an audit and which analytical procedures generally would be included in the overall review stage.

NUMBER 10

Required:

Items 1 through 12 represent possible errors and irregularities that an auditor suspects are present. The accompanying *List of Auditing Procedures* represents procedures that the auditor would consider performing to gather evidence concerning possible errors and irregularities. For each item, select one or two procedures, as indicated, that the auditor most likely would perform to gather evidence in support of that item. The procedures on the list may be selected once, more than once, or not at all.

Possible Errors and Irregularities

1. The auditor suspects that a kiting scheme exists because an accounting department employee who can issue and record checks seems to be leading an unusually luxurious lifestyle. **(Select only 1 procedure)**

2. The auditor suspects that the controller wrote several checks and recorded the cash disbursements just before the year end but did not mail the checks until after the first week of the subsequent year. **(Select only 1 procedure)**

3. The entity borrowed funds from a financial institution. Although the transaction was properly recorded, the auditor suspects that the loan created a lien on the entity's real estate that is not disclosed in its financial statements. **(Select only 1 procedure)**

4. The auditor discovered an unusually large receivable from one of the entity's new customers. The auditor suspects that the receivable may be fictitious because the auditor has never heard of the customer and because the auditor's initial attempt to confirm the receivable has been ignored by the customer. **(Select only 2 procedures)**

5. The auditor suspects that fictitious employees have been placed on the payroll by the entity's payroll supervisor, who has access to payroll records and to the paychecks. **(Select only 1 procedure)**

6. The auditor suspects that selected employees of the entity received unauthorized raises from the entity's payroll supervisor, who has access to payroll records. **(Select only 1 procedure)**

7. The entity's cash receipts of the first few days of the subsequent year were properly deposited in its general operating account after the year end. However, the auditor suspects that the entity recorded the cash receipts in its books during the last week of the year under audit. **(Select only 1 procedure)**

8. The auditor suspects that vouchers were prepared and processed by an accounting department employee for merchandise that was neither ordered nor received by the entity. **(Select only 1 procedure)**

9. The details of invoices for equipment repairs were not clearly identified or explained to the accounting department employees. The auditor suspects that the bookkeeper incorrectly recorded the repairs as fixed assets. **(Select only 1 procedure)**

10. The auditor suspects that a lapping scheme exists because an accounting department employee who has access to cash receipts also maintains the accounts receivable ledger and refuses to take any vacation or sick days. **(Select only 2 procedures)**

11. The auditor suspects that the entity is inappropriately increasing the cash reported on its balance sheet by drawing a check on one account and not recording it as an outstanding check on that account, and simultaneously recording it as a deposit in a second account. **(Select only 1 procedure)**

12. The auditor suspects that the entity's controller has overstated sales and accounts receivable by recording fictitious sales to regular customers in the entity's books. **(Select only 2 procedures)**

List of Auditing Procedures

A. Compare the details of the cash receipts journal entries with the details of the corresponding daily deposit slips.

B. Scan the debits to the fixed asset accounts and vouch selected amounts to vendors' invoices and management's authorization.

C. Perform analytical procedures that compare documented authorized pay rates to the entity's budget and forecast.

D. Obtain the cutoff bank statement and compare the cleared checks to the year-end bank reconciliation.

E. Prepare a bank transfer schedule.

F. Inspect the entity's deeds to its real estate.

G. Make inquiries of the entity's attorney concerning the details of real estate transactions.

H. Confirm the terms of borrowing arrangements with the lender.

I. Examine selected equipment repair orders and supporting documentation to determine the propriety of the charges.

J. Send requests to confirm the entity's accounts receivable on a surprise basis at an interim date.

K. Send a second request for confirmation of the receivable to the customer and make inquiries of a reputable credit agency concerning the customer's creditworthiness.

L. Examine the entity's shipping documents to verify that the merchandise that produced the receivable was actually sent to the customer.

M. Inspect the entity's correspondence files for indications of customer disputes or for evidence that certain shipments were on consignment.

N. Perform edit checks of data on the payroll transaction tapes.

O. Inspect payroll check endorsements for similar handwriting.

P. Observe payroll check distribution on a surprise basis.

Q. Vouch data in the payroll register to documented authorized pay rates in the human resources department's files.

R. Reconcile the payroll checking account and determine if there were unusual time lags between the issuance and payment of payroll checks.

S. Inspect the file of prenumbered vouchers for consecutive numbering and proper approval by an appropriate employee.

T. Determine that the details of selected prenumbered vouchers match the related vendors' invoices.

U. Examine the supporting purchase orders and receiving reports for selected paid vouchers.

NUMBER 11

Most of an auditor's work in forming an opinion on financial statements consists of obtaining and evaluating evidential matter concerning the financial statement assertions.

Required:
a.   What is the definition of "financial statement assertion?"
     Do not list the assertions.

b.   What is the relationship between audit objectives and financial statement assertions?

c.   What should an auditor consider in developing the audit objectives of a particular engagement?

d.   What is the relationship between audit objectives and audit procedures?

e.   What are an auditor's primary considerations when selecting particular substantive tests to achieve audit objectives?

NUMBER 12

Miller, CPA, is engaged to audit the financial statements of Superior Wholesaling for the year ended December 31, 1996. Miller obtained and documented an understanding of superior's internal control relating to accounts receivable and assessed control risk relating to accounts receivable at the maximum level. Miller requested and obtained from Superior an aged accounts receivable schedule listing the total amount owed by each customer as of December 31, 1996, and sent positive confirmation requests to a sample of the customers. Subsequently, Miller tested the accuracy of the aged accounts receivable schedule. Miller has asked Adler, the staff assistant assigned to the engagement, to follow up on the eight returned confirmations that follow. Assume that each confirmation is material if the potential misstatement is projected to the population.

Required:
a.   Describe the procedure(s), if any, that Adler should perform to resolve each of the eight confirmations that were returned. Assume that Superior will record any necessary adjusting entries and that Adler will verify that they are appropriate.

b.   Assume that Miller sent second requests for accounts receivable balances initially selected for confirmation for which no responses were received. Describe the alternative substantive procedures that Miller should consider applying to the accounts receivable selected for confirmation for which no responses were received to Miller's second requests. Assume that these accounts receivable in the aggregate, when projected as misstatements to the population, would affect Miller's decision about whether the financial statements are materially misstated.

c.   In addition to performing the confirmation procedures and alternative procedures described in requirements **(a)** and **(b)** and the procedures described in the first paragraph above, what additional substantive procedures should Miller consider performing to complete the audit of Superior's accounts receivable and related allowances? Assume that all accounts receivable are trade receivables.

Superior Wholesaling, Inc.
123 Commercial Blvd.
Anytown, USA

January 15, 1997

Atom Co.
362 Main Street   **Confirm #11**
Anytown, USA

Dear **C. L. Adams:**

Our auditor, Miller, CPA, is currently auditing our financial statements. To facilitate this audit, please confirm the balance due us as of December 31, 1996, which is shown on our records as **$15,000**. Indicate in the space below whether this is in agreement with your records. If there are exceptions, please provide any information that will assist the auditor in reconciling the difference.

Please mail your reply directly to Miller, CPA. A stamped, self-addressed envelope is enclosed for your convenience.

Sincerely,
J. Blake
J. Blake, Controller
Superior Wholesaling, Inc.

To Miller, CPA:
The amount shown above is correct as of December 31, 1996, except as follows:

Yes, we ordered $15,000 worth of merchandise from Superior in November. However, we mailed Superior a check for $15,000 on 12/18/96.

Name **C.L. Adams** Position **Acctg. Mgr.**
Date **1/22/97**

Note to files: Blake indicates that the check was received and deposited on 12/28/96, but posted to the wrong customer's account.
                                                                    C. Miller

---

Superior Wholesaling, Inc.
123 Commercial Blvd.
Anytown, USA

January 15, 1997

Baker Co.
18 Lakeview Drive   **Confirm #28**
Central City, USA

Dear **S. Brown:**

Our auditor, Miller, CPA, is currently auditing our financial statements. To facilitate this audit, please confirm the balance due us as of December 31, 1996, which is shown on our records as **$25,000**. Indicate in the space below whether this is in agreement with your records. If there are exceptions, please provide any information that will assist the auditor in reconciling the difference.

Please mail your reply directly to Miller, CPA. A stamped, self-addressed envelope is enclosed for your convenience.

Sincerely,
J. Blake
J. Blake, Controller
Superior Wholesaling, Inc.

To Miller, CPA:
The amount shown above is correct as of December 31, 1996, except as follows:

Sure we ordered $25,000 of merchandise on Oct. 10, 1996, but Superior was out-of-stock until recently. They back-ordered the goods and we finally received them on Jan. 6, 1997.

Name **S. Brown** Position **A/P Supervisor**
Date **Jan. 18, 1997**

Superior Wholesaling, Inc.
123 Commercial Blvd.
Anytown, USA

January 15, 1997

Clark Retailing
35 Lincoln Avenue   **Confirm #34**
Jackson, USA

Dear **J. P. Cummings:**

Our auditor, Miller, CPA, is currently auditing our financial statements. To facilitate this audit, please confirm the balance due us as of December 31, 1996, which is shown on our records as **$32,000**. Indicate in the space below whether this is in agreement with your records. If there are exceptions, please provide any information that will assist the auditor in reconciling the difference.

Please mail your reply directly to Miller, CPA. A stamped, self-addressed envelope is enclosed for your convenience.

Sincerely,
J. Blake
J. Blake, Controller
Superior Wholesaling, Inc.

To Miller, CPA:
The amount shown above is correct as of December 31, 1996, except as follows:

We received $24,000 of goods on consignment from Superior on 12/10/96, but they're not sold yet!

Name **J. Cummings**   Position **President**
Date **1/19/97**

Superior Wholesaling, Inc.
123 Commercial Blvd.
Anytown, USA

January 15, 1997

Delta Outlet Stores, Inc.
Sunshine Mall   **Confirm #41**
River City, USA

Dear **R. Dunn:**

Our auditor, Miller, CPA, is currently auditing our financial statements. To facilitate this audit, please confirm the balance due us as of December 31, 1996, which is shown on our records as **$45,000**. Indicate in the space below whether this is in agreement with your records. If there are exceptions, please provide any information that will assist the auditor in reconciling the difference.

Please mail your reply directly to Miller, CPA. A stamped, self-addressed envelope is enclosed for your convenience.

Sincerely,
J. Blake
J. Blake, Controller
Superior Wholesaling, Inc.

To Miller, CPA:
The amount shown above is correct as of December 31, 1996, except as follows:

No way! Superior promised these goods in 10 days on Dec. 2nd. When we didn't receive them, I canceled the order on Dec. 12th. General Wholesaling shipped us similar goods overnight!

Name **R. Dunn** Position **General Manager**
Date **Jan. 18th**

Superior Wholesaling, Inc.
123 Commercial Blvd.
Anytown, USA

January 15, 1997

Eagle Distributors
2700 Ocean Shore Blvd. **Confirm #58**
Ocean City, USA

Dear **T. Engle:**

Our auditor, Miller, CPA, is currently auditing our financial statements. To facilitate this audit, please confirm the balance due us as of December 31, 1996, which is shown on our records as **$59,000**. Indicate in the space below whether this is in agreement with your records. If there are exceptions, please provide any information that will assist the auditor in reconciling the difference.

Please mail your reply directly to Miller, CPA. A stamped, self-addressed envelope is enclosed for your convenience.

Sincerely,
J. Blake
J. Blake, Controller
Superior Wholesaling, Inc.

To Miller, CPA:
The amount shown above is correct as of December 31, 1996, except as follows:

I use an accounts payable voucher system by individual invoice. I can't verify $59,000, but Superior is one of my regular suppliers. I am sure I probably owe them something.

_____

Name T. Engle   Position Acctg. Mgr   Date 1-20-97

Superior Wholesaling, Inc.
123 Commercial Blvd.
Anytown, USA

January 15, 1997

Franklin Co.
17 United Street   **Confirm #67**
Industry City, USA

Dear **S. Brown:**

Our auditor, Miller, CPA, is currently auditing our financial statements. To facilitate this audit, please confirm the balance due us as of December 31, 1996, which is shown on our records as **$65,000**. Indicate in the space below whether this is in agreement with your records. If there are exceptions, please provide any information that will assist the auditor in reconciling the difference.

Please mail your reply directly to Miller, CPA. A stamped, self-addressed envelope is enclosed for your convenience.

Sincerely,
J. Blake
J. Blake, Controller
Superior Wholesaling, Inc.

To Miller, CPA:
The amount shown above is correct as of December 31, 1996, except as follows:

_____
_____
_____

Name   Position   Date

Note to files: This confirmation was returned by the postal service as "return to sender -- no such addressee at this location."

C. Miller

Superior Wholesaling, Inc.
123 Commercial Blvd.
Anytown, USA

January 15, 1997

Grove Retailing
3838 Curtis Blvd.   **Confirm #71**
Union Center, USA

Dear **H. Gates:**

Our auditor, Miller, CPA, is currently auditing our financial statements. To facilitate this audit, please confirm the balance due us as of December 31, 1996, which is shown on our records as **$75,000.** Indicate in the space below whether this is in agreement with your records. If there are exceptions, please provide any information that will assist the auditor in reconciling the difference.

Please mail your reply directly to Miller, CPA. A stamped, self-addressed envelope is enclosed for your convenience.

Sincerely,
J. Blake
J. Blake, Controller
Superior Wholesaling, Inc.

To Miller, CPA:
The amount shown above is correct as of December 31, 1996, except as follows:

Our records show that a check for $75,000 was mailed on 12/27/96.

Name **H. Gates** Position **Controller**
Date **1/22/97**

Superior Wholesaling, Inc.
123 Commercial Blvd.
Anytown, USA

January 15, 1997

Hall Enterprises, Inc.
55 Green Street   **Confirm #86**
Grant City, USA

Dear **K. Hines:**

Our auditor, Miller, CPA, is currently auditing our financial statements. To facilitate this audit, please confirm the balance due us as of December 31, 1996, which is shown on our records as **$80,000.** Indicate in the space below whether this is in agreement with your records. If there are exceptions, please provide any information that will assist the auditor in reconciling the difference.

Please mail your reply directly to Miller, CPA. A stamped, self-addressed envelope is enclosed for your convenience.

Sincerely,
J. Blake
J. Blake, Controller
Superior Wholesaling, Inc.

To Miller, CPA:
The amount shown above is correct as of December 31, 1996, except as follows:

Mailed that check for full amount on 1-3-97: merchandise was only received on 12-23-96.

Name **K. Hines** Position **Accountant**
Date **1-18-97**

NUMBER 13

Cook, CPA, is auditing the financial statements of DollarMart, a local retailer of clothes, appliances, sporting goods, and electronics. During prior years' audits of DollarMart, Cook noticed that management was less concerned about the timely recording of expenses and liabilities than revenues and assets. As a result, very little of DollarMart's internal control resources were expended in assuring an accurate and timely recording of accounts payable. Cook also believes that DollarMart's management may be motivated to delay recording its liabilities at year end, so Cook is approaching the search for unrecorded liabilities with caution.

Required:

a. What substantive auditing procedures would Cook most likely consider performing in searching for DollarMart's unrecorded liabilities?

b. How would the nature, timing, and extent of Cook's substantive auditing procedures most likely be affected by DollarMart's deficient control environment?

NUMBER 14

Smith, CPA, is the supervising partner of the financial statement audit of Digit Sales Co., a publicly-held entity that files reports with the SEC. Hall, the senior auditor assigned to the engagement, had the following conversation with Smith at the end of the field work:

Smith: Don't you think that Digit's board of directors would be surprised with those huge inventory adjustments that we had Digit book last week?

Hall: I guess so, but what about that new assistant controller, Green? What incompetence!

Smith: Well, I suppose Green has a bit to learn about GAAP, but I was really upset when Dodd, the controller, contacted that other CPA firm about the contingent liability I wanted booked.

Hall: Which one was that?

Smith: You know, the employment discrimination suit filed by the union.

Hall: Oh, now I remember. Digit's going to lose that one big time.

Smith: Right! You know it. I know it. The lawyer knows it. Even Dodd knows it. But it wasn't booked until the other CPAs agreed with me.

Hall: Well, the important thing is that they did book it. I was more upset about their two-week delay in having the financial statements completed on time.

Smith: I know it cost us a lot of time, but Dodd was never late on that before. Maybe I should change the dates on next year's engagement letter rather than complain to the board.

Hall: How about that large receivable?

Smith: What a joke! Dodd wouldn't write that overdue account off and Digit doesn't even sell that model anymore. At least Green was on our side.

Hall: They never did collect a penny on that account.

Smith: I heard that the customer finally filed for bankruptcy last month.

Hall: At least Dodd finally booked the write-off after that poorly-timed vacation.

Smith: I suppose so, but I still can't believe that Dodd took two weeks off near the end of our field work.

Hall: Actually, that was great. With Dodd gone, Green booked that inventory adjustment without much of a battle.

Smith: Sure, but we couldn't finish the field work until Dodd signed the rep letter and booked that receivable write-off. The report was late and it caused me grief with our managing partner.

Hall: But that's not fair. It wasn't our fault. The bottom line is they got a clean opinion and this job is history.

Smith: Not really. We haven't communicated with the audit committee yet.

Hall: What do we have to tell them? They got an unqualified opinion . . . and remember, there were only a few reportable conditions. I'm out of here.

Required:

a.   From the discussion above, what specific matters is Smith **required** to communicate to Digit's audit committee? Do **not** include matters that are **not required** to be communicated under GAAS.

b.   What other matters (omitted from the discussion above) is Smith **required** to communicate to Digit's audit committee under GAAS?

NUMBER 15

The following Accounts Receivable—Confirmation Statistics working paper (indexed B-3) was prepared by an audit assistant during the calendar year 1991 audit of Lewis County Water Co., Inc., a continuing audit client. The engagement supervisor is reviewing the working papers.

Lewis County Water Co., Inc.
ACCOUNTS RECEIVABLE—CONFIRMATION STATISTICS
12/31/91

	Index	B-3

	Accounts		Dollars	
	Number	Percent	Amount	Percent
Confirmation Requests				
Positives	54	2.7%	$ 260,000	13.0%
Negatives	140	7.0%	20,000	10.0%
Total sent	194	9.7%	280,000	23.0%
Accounts selected/client asked us not to confirm	6	0.3%		
Total selected for testing	200	10.0%		
Total accounts receivable at 12/31/91, confirm date	2,000	100.0%	$2,000,000√*	100.0%
RESULTS				
Replies received through 2/25/92				
Positives -- no exception	44 C	2.2%	180,000	9.0%
Negatives -- did not reply or replied "no exception"	120 C	6.0%	16,000	.8%
Total confirmed without exception	164	8.2%	196,000	9.8%
Differences reported and resolved, no adjustment				
Positives	6 ∅	.3%	30,000	1.5%
Negatives	12	.6%	2,000	.1%
Total	18 ‡	.9%	32,000	1.6%
Differences found to be potential adjustments				
Positives	2 CX	.1%	10,000	.5%
Negatives	8 CX	.4%	2,000	.1%
Total -- .6% adjustment, immaterial	10	.5%	12,000	.6%
Accounts selected/client asked us not to confirm	6	.3%		

Tickmark Legend
√   Agreed to accounts receivable subsidiary ledger
*   Agreed to general ledger and lead schedule
∅   Includes one related party transaction
C   Confirmed without exception, W/P B-4
CX   Confirmed with exception, W/P B-5

Overall conclusion -- The potential adjustment of $12,000 or .6% is below materiality threshold; therefore, the accounts receivable balance is fairly stated.

Required: Describe the deficiencies in the working paper that the engagement supervisor should discover. Assume that the accounts were selected for confirmation on the basis of a sample that was properly planned and documented on working paper B-2.

NUMBER 16

Temple, CPA, is auditing the financial statements of Ford Lumber Yards, Inc., a privately held corporation with 300 employees and five shareholders, three of whom are active in management. Ford has been in business for many years but has never had its financial statements audited. Temple suspects that the substance of some of Ford's business transactions differs from their form because of the pervasiveness of related party relationships and transactions in the local building supplies industry.

Required:

The audit procedures Temple should apply to identify Ford's related party relationships and transactions include some of the following procedures. For each of the following procedures, indicate (Y) for "Yes" if the procedure is one that Temple would likely apply and (N) for "No" if the procedure is one that Temple would not likely apply.

1. Evaluate the company's procedures for identifying and properly reporting related party relationships and transactions.

2. Request from management the names of all related parties and inquire whether there were any related party transactions.

3. Review confirmations of accounts receivable, particularly for the small balances.

4. Review tax returns and filings with other regulatory agencies for the names of related parties.

5. Review cash receipts for a few days prior to and after year-end, particularly for significant amounts of currency.

6. Review the stock certificate book to identify the shareholders.

7. Review the minutes of board of directors' meetings.

8. Review conflict-of-interest statements obtained by the company from its management.

9. Review the extent and nature of business transacted with major customers, suppliers, borrowers, and lenders.

10. Request from the client's competitors the names of known related parties.

11. Review all investment transactions to determine whether the investment created related party relationships.

12. Review accounting records for large, unusual, or nonrecurring transactions or balances, paying particular attention to transactions recognized at or near the end of the reporting period.

13. Review invoices from law firms that have performed services for the company for indications of the existence of related party relationships or transactions.

14. Review accounting records for consistently recurring transactions that, in the aggregate, are considered immaterial.

NUMBER 17

The purpose of all auditing procedures is to gather sufficient competent evidence for an auditor to form an opinion regarding the financial statements taken as a whole.

Required:

Seven procedures for gathering audit evidence to evaluate a client's inventory balance are listed below. Match the description that follows with the appropriate procedure. Not all descriptions are used.

Procedure:

1. Observation

2. Analysis

3. Comparison

4. Inquiry

5. Confirmation

6. Inspection

7. Calculation

Description:

A. An auditor combines amounts in meaningful ways to allow the application of audit judgment, such as the determination of whether a proper inventory cutoff was performed.

B. An auditor examines documents relating to transactions and balances, such as shipping and receiving records to establish ownership of inventory.

C. An auditor reads the footnote disclosures for adequacy of disclosure.

D. An auditor obtains acknowledgements in writing from third parties of transactions or balances, such as inventory in public warehouses or on consignment.

E. An auditor recomputes certain amounts, such as the multiplication of quantity times price to determine inventory amounts.

F. An auditor questions client personnel about events and conditions, such as obsolete inventory.

G. An auditor relates two or more amounts, such as inventory cost in perpetual inventory records to costs as shown on vendor invoices as part of the evaluation of whether inventory is priced at the lower of cost or market.

H. An auditor watches the performance of some function, such as a client's annual inventory count.

Chapter Two -- Solutions to Questions
The Third Standard of Field Work -- Evidence

1. (c) Analytical review procedures are designed to discover unusual relationships. Answers (a), (b) and (d) are examples of analytical review procedures.

2. (b) Positive confirmation requests ask for a reply whether or not the balance is correct. A negative request asks for a reply only if the balance is incorrect. With a large number of accounts, positive requests are used with large balances and negative requests are used for small balances.

3. (c) The competency (reliability) of evidence depends upon the degree of control exercised over the evidence by the client. The client does not have any control in answers (a), (b) and (d). The client does have control over sales invoices and, thus, it is the least competent.

4. (c) Analytical review procedures are substantive tests. Answer (a) is incorrect because substantive tests do not evaluate a system of internal control, the auditor does. Answers (b) and (d) are incorrect because analytical review procedures are not compliance tests.

5. (a) Trace from source documents to records to ensure all items have been billed.

6. (c) Source document to accounting records.

7. (d) Comparison, trend and ratios are analytical tools used by the auditor to detect unusual transactions.

8. (c) In this case, no one account has a material effect on the balance; thus, negative confirms are in order.

9. (b) The client is not inflating sales or accounts receivable by making fictitious entries.

10. (d) Shipments made after year end were included in customers' year end accounts receivable balances. Consequently, customers' accounts payable balances at year end were smaller than confirmed.

11. (a) The review of corporate minutes is a standard part of work done in the subsequent period.

12. (b) Verification from an independent third party as to the validity of an account balance.

13. (c) Normally, the auditor would expect most checks to clear during the period from year end to the date of his cut-off bank statement.

14. (b) It is not the auditor's responsibility to supervise the inventory taking, but rather to observe the physical inventory.

15. (c) Client representations in any form (written or oral) must be supported by other audit evidence.

16. (b) Purchase cutoff procedures are designed to determine that items actually received in inventory have been included in the proper period.

17. (b) The question deals with fixed asset disposals. The auditor examines repairs and maintenance accounts to find unrecorded fixed asset additions.

18. (b) The physical inventory was higher than the perpetual record which indicates that inventory was not booked as received or that returns to suppliers were not recorded. Answer (b) meets the criteria for the answer.

19. (a) Cutoff tests are used to determine whether items have been recorded in the proper period. By coordinating cutoff tests with the physical inventory, auditors can determine if the items are physically present.

20. (d) Analytical review procedures are designed to detect unusual fluctuations in financial statement account balances. They are not conclusive evidence in the same respect as confirmation or documentation. The results of these analytical procedures should be investigated, however, if unusual relationships are revealed.

21. (c) Substantive audit procedures include test of balances and analytical procedures. The objectives of analytical procedures is to gather evidence concerning the completeness of the items included in the financial statements, and to indicate unusual fluctuations in account balances that may require more detailed substantive audit procedures.

22. (d) In planning an audit, an auditor is required to prepare written audit programs. These programs should set forth in reasonable detail the audit procedures that the auditor believes are necessary to accomplish the objectives of the audit. Those objectives are to determine whether or not the financial statements are fairly presented in accordance with GAAP. That is, whether or not the financial statement assertions embodied in the financial statement components are fairly stated, in all material respects. The timing and cost-benefit issues presented in answers (a) and (b) have a bearing on audit procedures and audit programs but are not related to establishing audit objectives. Answer (c) is incorrect because audit techniques are selected to meet auditor objectives, not to establish those objectives.

23. (b) There should be a rational relationship between the cost of obtaining evidence and the usefulness of the information obtained. However, when considering competency of evidence, time and cost are not relevant. The three presumptions made about the competency of evidence are presented in answers (a), (c) and (d). (a) The more effective the internal control structure, the more assurance it provides about the reliability of accounting data and financial statements. (c) When evidential matter can be obtained from independent sources outside the entity, it is more competent than evidential matter secured solely within the entity. (d) The independent auditor's direct personal knowledge, obtained through examination, observation, computation, and inspection, is more persuasive than information obtained indirectly.

24. (a) Analytical procedures are required by GAAS in the planning and review stages of an audit. Analytical procedures are substantive audit tests, but as a substantive test they are used to plan the audit and in the final review.

25. (c) The auditor is concerned with unrecorded liabilities as of the balance sheet date (completeness assertion), thus audit procedures performed to identify unrecorded liabilities before the balance sheet date would be meaningless. Accounts receivable may be confirmed prior to the balance sheet date if the auditor concludes internal controls surrounding accounts receivable are effective [answer (b)]. Inventory counts may be observed prior to year if the client maintains perpetual inventory records and the controls surrounding those records are effective [answer (d)].

26. (b) GAAS requires that the auditor must obtain an attorney's letter date as of the last day of field work (audit report date). Information received from the client's attorney may be the basis for an adjustment of the financial statement as of year end or the basis for financial statement disclosures of events occurring during the subsequent period.

27. (c) Before undertaking any audit procedures, the auditor would determine whether omitted procedures constitute the ability to issue an opinion. If the omitted procedures were deemed to be necessary to support the opinion issued, the auditor would attempt to perform such procedures.

28. (a) If transactions are not supported by proper documentation, it may indicate that the transactions are fictitious. IF so, the financial statements would be materially misstated.

29. (c) The objective of analytical procedures used in the overall review stage of the audit is to assist the auditor in assessing the conclusions reached and in the evaluation of the overall financial statement presentation. Answer (a) refers to substantive tests of details, not analytical procedures. Answer (b) is an objective of analytical procedures used in planning the audit. Answer (d) involves the auditor obtaining information about management's plans and assessing the likelihood that such plans can be implemented; these are not analytical procedures.

30. (a) The purpose of applying analytical procedures in planning the audit is to assist in planning the nature, timing, and extent of auditing procedures that will be used to obtain evidential matter for specific account balances or classes of transactions. To accomplish this, the analytical procedures used in planning the audit should focus on enhancing the auditor's understanding of the client's business and the transactions and events that have occurred since the last audit date, and identifying areas that may represent specific risks relevant to the audit. Answer (b) refers to analytical procedures used as substantive tests.

31. (a) Confirmation of receivables is a generally accepted auditing procedure. The use of positive confirmation requests is preferable when individual account balances are relatively large or when there is reason to believe that there may be a substantial number of accounts in dispute or with inaccuracies or irregularities. The negative form is useful when internal control surrounding accounts receivable is considered to be effective. In this case, although the individual accounts may not be relatively large, the internal control structure is weak and the balances, since they are delinquent, may be in dispute. Answer (c) would be an appropriate procedure but these balances are delinquent, suggesting that there will be limited receipts subsequent to year end. Answer (d) is incorrect because internal evidence is not as competent as external evidence.

32. (c) The amount of interest earned is based on face amount, interest rate, and time period. Since this is a bond investment, the auditor can examine the actual bond instrument and recompute the interest earned. Such evidence, obtained directly by the auditor's recalculation, is very competent. Answers (a) and (d) relate to cash received, not interest earned. Answer (b) would only provide evidence about the interest rate, not the face amount and time period.

33. (a) An auditor reviews a client's sales cut-off to determine if year-end sales are being recorded in the correct period. Sales records are compared with shipping documents. If, assuming title passes at time of shipment, goods were shipped before year end and no sale was recorded as of year end, the auditor will have detected unrecorded sales. Similarly, if a sale was recorded as of year end, but goods were not shipped until the following year, sales would be overstated.

34. (b) A letter of audit inquiry to the client's lawyer is the auditor's primary means of obtaining corroboration of the information furnished by management concerning litigation, claims, and assessments. The matters included in answers (a), (c) and (d) could be covered in a letter of audit inquiry but the primary reason for the request is to provide corroborative evidential matter.

35. (d) In some cases, the corroborating information that can be obtained by the application of auditing procedures other than inquiry is limited. When a client plans to discontinue a line of business, for example, the auditor may not be able to obtain information through other auditing procedures to corroborate the plan or intent. Accordingly, the auditor should obtain a written representation to provide confirmation of management's intent. The client's plans included in the other answers, in comparison to the plans to discontinue a line of business, could be more readily corroborated by other evidence.

36. (b) A primary objective when auditing liabilities is to determine that they are all properly included. Accordingly, the auditor has to search for liabilities that exist as of balance sheet date. In searching for contingent liabilities, the auditor will typically review bank confirmation letters for any indication of direct or contingent liabilities, examine invoices for professional services especially from attorneys who may be working on pending litigation, and read minutes of the board of directors for indications of lawsuits or other contingencies. Answer (b) refers to customer confirmations which are typically used to provide evidence about recorded amounts, not to search for unrecorded items.

37. (d) In determining the scope of work to be performed with respect to possible transactions with related parties, the auditor should obtain an understanding of management responsibilities and the relationship of each component to the total entity. Normally, the business structure is based on the abilities of management, tax and legal considerations, product diversification, and geographical location. Experience has shown, however, that business structure may be deliberately designed to obscure related party transactions. Therefore, when searching for related party transactions the auditor should obtain an understanding of each subsidiary's relationship to the total entity.

38. (b) When an auditor concludes that an auditing procedure considered necessary at the time of the examination was omitted from his examination of financial statements, he should assess the importance of the omitted procedure to his present ability to support his previously expressed opinion. A review of his working papers, discussion of the circumstances, and a reevaluation of the overall scope of the examination may be helpful in making this assessment. For example, the results of other procedures that were applied may tend to compensate for the one omitted or make its omission less important. Also, subsequent examinations may provide audit evidence in support of the previously expressed opinion. This last comment is not the same as answer (d) which refers to tests of controls in subsequent periods, not audit evidence.

39. (a) The auditor's objective is to obtain sufficient competent evidential matter to provide him with a reasonable basis for forming an opinion. There should be a rational relationship between the cost of obtaining that evidence and the usefulness of the information obtained. In determining the usefulness of evidence, relative risk may properly be given consideration. Also, the auditor's understanding and evaluation of the internal control structure affects the nature, timing, and extent of testing. The matter of difficulty and expense involved in testing a particular item is not in itself a valid basis for omitting the test.

40. (c) If the auditor becomes aware of facts that existed at the report date, he should determine whether the facts would have affected the audit report. If they would have affected his report and people are currently relying on the report, the auditor should advise the client to make appropriate disclosures of the facts and their impact. Answer (a) does not address what the auditor should do regarding the current year's audit. Answers (b) and (d) would be considered only after the auditor determined that the lack of footnote disclosure affected his report.

41. (c) If the auditor decides to give an adverse opinion as a result of the report or findings of a specialist, reference to and identification of the specialist may be made if it will facilitate an understanding of the reason for the modified opinion. When expressing an unqualified opinion, the auditor should not refer to the work or findings of a specialist—regardless of whether or not the specialist's work provided reliable evidence [answer (b)] or the specialist is independent of the client [answer (d)]. Such a reference might be misunderstood to be a qualification of the auditor's opinion or a division of responsibility [answer (a)], neither of which is intended.

42. (c) A negative confirmation requests a response only if the debtor disagrees with the information given; thus, the auditor infers from a nonresponse that the balance is correct. The auditor cannot, however, infer that all nonrespondents have verified their account information. This is not a verification by the debtor because many debtors simply do not respond for reasons other than agreeing with the balance. A positive confirmation requests a response whether or not the debtor is in agreement with the client. The balance is verified only when the debtor responds or the auditor is satisfied by performing other audit procedures. Answers (a) and (b) could apply to positive or negative confirmations. Answer (d) is incorrect because the auditor can statistically quantify the result of either confirmation approach.

43. (a) When auditing notes payable and long-term debt, the auditor should obtain copies of agreements and determine if provisions are being adhered to. If the debt is in the form of bonds, the agreement is the bond trust indenture. Answer (b) does not relate to long-term debt, but short-term payables. Answer (c) refers to interest income, rather than interest expense. Answer (d) deals with existence of bondholders; the auditor is concerned with existence of the debt.

44. (d) There is a requirement that the independent auditor obtain certain written representations from management as a part of an examination made in accordance with generally accepted auditing standards. The documentation listed in the other answers is not required by auditing standards. An internal control questionnaire is one of several approaches to documenting the auditor's understanding of the internal control structure. Auditors are encouraged to obtain an engagement letter to eliminate misunderstandings. An audit program is required, a planning memorandum is not.

45. (a) When the auditor becomes aware of information concerning a possible illegal act, the auditor should obtain an understanding of the nature of the act, related circumstances, and sufficient other information to ascertain whether an illegal act has occurred. In doing so, the auditor should **inquire** of management at a level above those involved, if possible. If management does not provide satisfactory information that there has been no illegal act, the auditor would consider the activities presented in answers (b), (c) and (d). Answer (c), **reporting** the matter to a higher level of management, would not be appropriate until the auditor determines that an illegal act has occurred.

46. (c) The question is concerned with the completeness of the accounts payable balance, i.e., whether everything that should be recorded as a payable is in fact included in the balance. To test the completeness of an item in the financial statements, the auditor would draw a sample from the population that represents the source documents. In this case the source document is the receiving report which indicates the **date** the company received the merchandise and thus, depending on the shipping terms, when the title passes and a liability recognized.

47. (c) The completeness assertion made by management in the form of financial statements means that no transactions that should be recorded on the books of the entity has been omitted. Answer (a) is incorrect because it deals with items already recorded. Answer (b) is incorrect because it does not deal with the accounting records at all. Answer (d) is incorrect because again it does not deal with accounting records. Answer (c) is correct because by having the receiving reports prenumbered, the reconciliation process will include determining the status of each receiving report as being matched with a vendor invoice and recorded, awaiting matching, voided, or unmatched and thus unrecorded.

48. (a) By tracing bills of lading to sales invoices, the auditor will confirm that all shipments have been invoiced, that is, that each shipment resulted in a sales invoice being prepared. Answer (b) is incorrect because the auditor would have to trace sales invoices to the sales journal to prove that all shipments were recorded as sales. Answers (c) and (d) are incorrect because the direction of the test will not prove that recorded sales were shipped or that invoiced sales were shipped because the auditor's starting point is what has been shipped, not with what has been recorded.

49. (d) Analytical procedures are substantive audit tests that are used in the planning phase of the audit to identify unusual fluctuations or relationships among financial data. The discovery of unusual fluctuations or relationships may indicate the presence of an error in the particular account so tested. The indication that an account may contain an error will cause the auditor to modify subsequent substantive tests because of the risk that an account contains a possible error.

50. (c) The question concerns unrecorded accounts payable at the balance date. Answer (a) is not valid because other items in addition to accounts payable affect cash disbursements (payroll, for example). Answer (b) is incorrect because receiving reports are matched with vendor invoices, not vendor statements. Answer (d) is incorrect because the auditor would be testing accounts payable that have been recorded, not unrecorded. Such a test should start with receiving reports, not accounts payable. Answer (c) is correct because in reviewing subsequent cash disbursements the auditor would review whether an invoice paid in the current period actually was received in the prior period.

51. (a) Negative accounts receivable requests elicit a reply only if the confirmed amount is incorrect. The validity of this form of confirmation request is less than if positive confirmations (elicit a reply whether or not the item is correct) are used. For that reason negative confirmations are used when control risk is low (risk of error is small), the number of small balances are many (auditor attempts to get wide coverage), and the likelihood of reply by the recipient is high (willing to reply if account is incorrect).

52. (c) The application of analytical procedures to financial statements is based upon the presumption that plausible relationships exist among data (for example, that a company consistently marks up its products to earn a 30% gross profit). An auditor applying analytical procedures would then expect the gross profit percentage to be approximately 30%.

53. (b) The presentation and disclosure assertion relates to the fact that the financial statements should reflect all pertinent information necessary to reach an informed decision concerning the company. By reviewing the renewal of a note payable after year end the auditor will be able to determine whether the year-end financial statements include all pertinent information such as due date, interest rate and collateral, if any.

54. (d) The auditor's review of credit ratings of customers with delinquent accounts is normally accomplished during an audit in order to test the adequacy of the allowance for doubtful accounts. The auditor is trying to validate the proper dollar balance in the account. The valuation assertion is concerned with proper dollar valuation.

55. (d) A client's accounting data would include the books of original entry, the general ledger and the trial balance. This source of evidence cannot be considered sufficient because entries could be made into the client's records without sufficient documents. Thus recorded transactions must be traced to supporting documentation in order to corroborate its validity.

56. (c) The existence assertion is concerned that all items recorded in the accounting records are valid (not fictitious). Therefore, the auditor is testing what has been recorded and the direction of the test is from the accounting records to the supporting documentation.

57. (a) The question asks what the auditor would be **least** likely to be concerned with in the audit of inventories. The auditor would be least concerned about whether all inventory owed by the client is on hand at the time of the inventory count. Why? Inventory may be stored at a public warehouse, or out on consignment, or in transit from a vendor with freight terms of F.O.B. shipping point. In all the foregoing cases, these amounts should be included in inventory even though they are not physically on hand.

58. (a) During the audit of financial statements, the auditor is required to send a letter of audit inquiry to the client's legal counsel concerning claims, litigation and assessments. It is reasonable to assume that an attorney would be responsible to respond concerning only those items that he has given substantive attention. He would not be able to respond to items he has not given substantive attention (the attorney has no knowledge). Therefore, such a limited response on the part of an attorney would not be considered a scope limitation.

59. (c) The existence assertion refers to the validity of the item. In other words, has a real transaction taken place or is the accounts receivable real. The rights and obligations assertion refers to the ownership of assets or liabilities. It answers the question, "Does the entity have a legal right to the asset?" When a customer replies to a confirmation request obviously the customer must exist and the client must have legal title to the receivable. If either of these were not correct the customer would take exception to the confirmation and/or it would be retained as undeliverable by the post office.

60. (b) The completeness assertion means that nothing has been omitted from the financial statements that should be recorded during a particular period. By performing a cutoff test the auditor is searching for items that have been omitted from the financial statements of the current period.

61. (d) The purpose of analytical procedures is to identify unusual fluctuations in data. A variance report indicates fluctuations from *expected* results, and thus would be helpful as an analytical procedure.

62. (d) The objective is to test whether recorded sales are valid (not overstated). The auditor is answering the question, "Is this recorded sale a valid transaction?" In order to answer that question, the auditor would start with the recorded sales and look for documentation corroborating its validity.

63. (b) Negative confirmation requests ask the respondent to reply only if the stated receivable information is *incorrect.* The presumption is that a non-reply to a confirmation request is evidence that the account balance is correct. Thus, negative confirmation procedures would not be used when there is a likelihood that accounts are in dispute. They would be used where a small number of accounts are in dispute.

64. (d) The question is a definition of the answer.

65. (a) Assertions about valuation or allocation deal with whether asset, liability, revenue, and expense components have been included in the financial statements at appropriate amounts. If the auditor is concluding that no excessive costs were charged to inventory, he or she has gathered evidence regarding valuation of amounts in the inventory account. Proper costing of inventory does not relate to the assertions presented in the other answers. The completeness assertion in answer (b) deals with whether all accounts and transactions, such as those related to inventory, that should be presented in the financial statements are so included. The existence or occurrence assertion in answer (c) deals with whether assets of the entity, such as inventory, exist at a given date and whether recorded transactions, such as those related to inventory, have occurred during a given period. The rights and obligations assertion in answer (d) deals with whether assets, such as inventory, are the rights of the entity.

66. (a) Internal evidence, consisting of documents such as purchase orders that are produced within the client's system, is generally considered low in competence and therefore the least persuasive. Answer (b), which is an example of external-internal evidence, is considered more competent. Answer (c), which is evidence obtained directly from an external source, is better than evidence that goes through the client before reaching the auditor. Answer (d) is an example of the most persuasive evidence because it is obtained directly by the auditor through physical observation.

67. (a) The auditor wants to determine that the addition exists, is properly valued and is owned by the client. Physical examination by the auditor provides competent evidence of existence. Inspection of purchase and title documents by the auditor provides evidence regarding amounts and ownership. Answers (b) and (d) involve evidence-gathering procedures that rely on client claims, which are not very persuasive types of evidence. Answer (c) is an analytical procedure that would be performed to determine the reasonableness of balances; it is only suggestive of accuracy.

68. (c) Assertions about presentation and disclosure deal with whether particular components of the financial statements are properly classified, described, and disclosed. An auditor would inspect loan agreements regarding pledged inventories to determine that management has adequately disclosed the security arrangements.

69. (d) Assertions about valuation or allocation deal with whether asset, liability, revenue, and expense components have been included in the financial statements at appropriate amounts. An auditor would look at inventory turnover rates to determine if the inventory amount on the balance sheet and the cost of goods sold amount on the income statement are reasonable, in relation to each other.

70. (a) Assertions about completeness deal with whether all transactions and accounts that should be presented in the financial statements are so included. To test management's assertion that all sales are included on the income statement, the auditor would compare shipping documents, which typically provide evidence that a sale has occurred and should be recorded, to related sales invoices, which provide the basis for recording the sales transactions. Answers (b), (c) and (d) are tests that are designed to determine existence of transactions or balances. The concern of the auditor in (b), (c) and (d) is with fictitious or overstated amounts, not omitted or incomplete amounts.

71. (b) Substantive tests, which are comprised of analytical procedures and tests of details (transactions and account balances), must be performed to substantiate the financial statement assertions. The decision about which procedures to use to achieve a particular audit objective is based on the auditor's judgment on the expected effectiveness and efficiency of the available procedures.

72. (a) The overall review would generally include reading the financial statements and notes and considering the adequacy of evidence gathered in response to unusual or unexpected balances identified in planning the audit or in the course of the audit, and unusual or unexpected balances or relationships that were not previously identified. Answer (b), which is a substantive test of transactions, and answer (d), which is a test of controls, are not analytical procedures. Answer (c) could include analytical procedures, but would typically be done in the course of the audit not at the overall review stage.

73. (c) The understanding among the auditor, the client, and the specialist should be documented and should cover: the specialist's understanding of the auditor's corroborative use of the specialist's findings, the objectives and scope of the specialist's work, the specialist's relationship to the client, the methods or assumptions to be used, a comparison of the methods and assumptions to those used in the preceding period, and the form and content of the specialist's report.

74. (c) Irregularities are intentional misstatements or omissions of amounts or disclosures in financial statements. A typical client representation letter states that there have been no irregularities involving management or employees who have significant roles in the internal control structure. Materiality could apply to irregularities involving other employees as well as the matters listed in answers (b) and (d). Material losses are usually associated with purchase commitments, not the sales commitments indicated in answer (a).

75. (a) Factors affecting the auditor's judgment about the quantity, type, and content of the working papers for a particular engagement include; the nature of the engagement, the nature of the auditor's report, the nature of the financial statements on which the auditor is reporting, the nature and condition of the client's records, the assessed level of control risk, and the needs in the particular circumstances for supervision and review of the work. Although answers (b) and (c) could be related to supervision and review, answer (a) is the best choice because it is specifically included above as a factor. The content of the letter referred to in answer (d) is determined by the auditor; it does not affect the auditor's judgment about working papers.

76. (d) Borrowing or lending on an interest-free basis or at a rate of interest significantly above or below market rates prevailing at the time of the transaction would be an example of a transaction which, because of its very nature, may be indicative of the existence of related parties. A borrowing between unrelated parties should be at or near the market rate of interest.

77. (c) The auditor should inquire of the entity's legal counsel regarding any events occurring after year end as part of the auditor's search for subsequent events, which are events or transactions that occur subsequent to the balance sheet date but prior to the issuance of the auditor's report that have a material effect on the financial statements and therefore require adjustment or disclosure in the statements. Answer (b) is a good choice since the auditor would inquire of officers as to whether there was any change in capital stock. The reference to "investigating" in answer (b), however, results in answer (c) being the better choice. An auditor would also review large-dollar transaction after year-end to determine if they are recorded in the proper period, not for arithmetic accuracy as noted in answer (a). Answer (d) has no direct impact on the current financial statements.

78. (c) An auditor is required to ensure that the audit committee receives information regarding the scope and results of the audit. Included in the matters to be communicated are disagreements with management about significant matters (whether or not resolved) and the initial selection of and changes in significant accounting policies.

79. (b) When using analytical procedures to identify predictable relationships, higher levels of evidence will be obtained when those relationships are most predictable. Relationships involving income statement accounts, such as interest expense, tend to be more predictable than relationships involving only balance sheet accounts, such as those listed in answers (a) and (c), because income statement accounts represent transactions over a period of time rather than a point in time. Also, interest expense, which can be related to debt, is more predictable than the travel and entertainment expense listed in answer (d), which is more subject to management discretion.

80. (b) Assertions about completeness deal with whether all accounts and transactions that should be presented in the financial statements are so included. If an auditor test counts selected items while observing a client's physical inventory and then traces those counts to the client's inventory listing, the auditor is obtaining evidence that all inventory items that should be included in the listing, which becomes the basis for the financial statement amounts, are so included. The assertions presented in answers (a), (c) and (d) are not tested by this procedure. If an inventory item is test counted and on the listing, the client may not have the rights to that item. In order to test existence, the auditor would compare the listing to the actual items on hand instead of comparing the test counts to the listing. Valuation of inventory includes tests of lower of cost and market, not just quantities obtained during test counts.

81. (b) Management's assertion of existence or occurrence deals with whether assets of the entity, such as plant and equipment, exist at a given date and whether recorded transactions, such as plant and equipment additions, have occurred during a given period. If the auditor physically examines new additions listed on an analysis of plant and equipment, the auditor is obtaining evidence about the existence or occurrence assertion. The assertions presented in answers (a), (c) and (d) are not tested by this procedure. The auditor would test in the opposite direction for completeness. That is, the auditor would select items of plant and equipment or transactions involving plant and equipment and determine if they have been properly included in the plant and equipment balance rather than working from the account balance back to the physical item or transaction documentation. The presentation and disclosure assertion deals with whether particular components of the financial statements are properly classified, described and disclosed, not whether additions to an account exist or occurred. Valuation and allocation of plant and equipment deal with whether plant and equipment has been included in the financial statements at appropriate amounts. The auditor would test initial valuation at cost and the allocation of that cost to periods benefited, through depreciation.

82. (d) The auditor's objective when evaluating accounting estimates is to obtain sufficient competent evidential matter to provide reasonable assurance that all accounting estimates that could be material to the financial statements have been developed; those accounting estimates are reasonable in the circumstances; and the accounting estimates are presented in conformity with applicable accounting principles and are properly disclosed. Answers (a) and (c) are incorrect because estimates are based on subjective as well as objective factors and may involve biased judgments made by management. Answer (b) presents a procedure the auditor would perform to determine whether the estimates are reasonable. In addition to consistency with industry data, the auditor would evaluate consistency with other supporting and relevant historical data.

83. (a) The auditor reviews cash disbursements recorded in the period subsequent to the balance sheet date to determine if they represent payments for goods and/or services received during the period ending on the balance sheet date. If so, the auditor would then determine whether or not they have been properly recorded in the period prior to the balance sheet date. This review of subsequent payments is designed to identify unrecorded trade accounts payable and other unrecorded liabilities. Answer (b) would not detect unrecorded liabilities because it is testing recorded payables, not potentially unrecorded payables. Answer (c) is incorrect because cash payments are made for many items, not just for accounts payable. Therefore, the relationship between cash payments and accounts payable balances may fluctuate based on other activity. Answer (d) is incorrect because reconciling vendor statements to receiving reports would not disclose unrecorded liabilities unless comparisons were also made with recorded payables and cash payments.

84. (a) The auditor can test for unrecorded retirements of equipment by selecting items of equipment listed in the accounting records and trying to physically locate them. If the item of equipment has been retired, it will not exist in the client's plant and the auditor will not be able to locate it. Answer (b) deals with fully depreciated equipment that, if still in use, may not have been retired. Answer (c) tests whether or not equipment in use is included in the accounting records, not whether assets not in use due to retirement are included in the accounting records. Answer (d) focuses on additions of equipment rather than retirements, especially additions that may have been incorrectly recorded as repairs and maintenance. This scanning of the general journal would not provide evidence about unrecorded retirements except possibly for a retirement that was part of a trade-in.

85. (c) If overpayments are discovered by the auditor, this suggests that errors and/or irregularities exist. Accordingly, the auditor would extend substantive tests of payroll. Answer (a) presents a situation that may lead the auditor to decrease substantive testing. Answer (b) is a trend that the auditor would evaluate as part of analytical procedures work. If the increase in payroll expense is explained by plausible relationships with other financial and other nonfinancial data, substantive testing would not be extended. Answer (d) is incorrect because overtime concerns of employees do not suggest that the accounting for overtime is incorrect.

86. (d) Physically counting securities is a common audit procedure designed to test existence of an investment portfolio at balance sheet date and to assure the auditor that the securities are not used to cover cash shortages. If the auditor is unable to count securities that are kept in a bank safe deposit box on the balance sheet date, the auditor would want the bank to secure the box until such time as the auditor could perform the count. Answer (a) is not an option because a bank cannot typically access a safe deposit box without the depositor. Answer (b) is a procedure that the auditor would perform during the year to test transactions; however, to test existence and to decrease the likelihood that securities are used to cover shortages at balance sheet date, the auditor should count the securities. Answer (c) is incorrect because the bank would not be able to confirm whether securities were added or removed; it could only confirm whether or not the safe deposit box was accessed, as indicated by a broken seal.

87. (b) In planning the audit, the auditor should consider the nature, extent and timing of work to be done and should prepare a written audit program. This program, or set of programs, should present in reasonable detail the audit procedures considered necessary to accomplish the objectives of the audit. Answers (a) and (d) refer to flowcharts and internal control questionnaires, which are optional methods used to document the auditor's understanding of the client's internal control structure. Since there are alternatives available to the auditor, flowcharts and questionnaires are not required documentation. Answer (c) refers to a planning memorandum, which may be helpful in an audit but is not required by generally accepted auditing standards.

88. (b) When expressing an unqualified opinion, the auditor should not refer to the work of a specialist because such a reference may be misunderstood. However, if as a result of the specialist's work, the auditor decides to depart from an unqualified opinion or to add a paragraph describing an uncertainty, a going concern issue, or an emphasis of a matter, the auditor may refer to the specialist in the auditor's report. Answers (a) and (c) would have no effect on the auditor's report. The auditor, not the client, should consider the specialist's certification, reputation and competency before using the specialist's work. Also, an understanding should exist among the auditor, client and specialist regarding the work to be performed by the specialist. Answer (d) is incorrect because the auditor is responsible for the audit opinion and the evidence-gathering procedures followed in the audit. The auditor can not share responsibility with a specialist.

89. (d) An event or transaction that occurs after the balance sheet date but before the issuance of the financial statements is referred to as a subsequent event, of which there are two types. The first type provides evidence about conditions that existed at the balance sheet date and affect the estimates inherent in the process of preparing financial statements. The financial statements should be adjusted for any changes in estimates resulting from this first type of subsequent event. The second type of subsequent event consists of events that provide evidence with respect to conditions that did not exist as of the balance sheet date. These events should not result in an adjustment but may require disclosure if material. The situation presented in this question is an example of the second type of subsequent event that would not result in financial statement adjustment but should be disclosed. Reporting on consistency is not affected by subsequent events.

90. (a) The auditor is required to obtain written representations from management. The specific written representations ordinarily confirm oral representations given to the auditor and relate to management knowledge and intent. They ordinarily include disclosure of compensating balance or other arrangements involving restrictions on cash balances, and disclosure of line-of-credit or similar arrangements. Answers (b) and (d) are not included in the client representation letter. Management cannot acknowledge responsibility for illegal acts committed by employees and cannot acknowledge that there are no material weaknesses in internal control. Answer (c) is incorrect because the client does not determine the sufficiency of evidential matter necessary for an unqualified opinion; the auditor does this.

91. (c) The auditor should test material transactions with parties related to the entity being audited to determine that the financial statements adequately disclose these related party transactions. Among the procedures an auditor would follow to identify these transactions is to review accounting records for large, unusual, or nonrecurring transactions or balances, paying particular attention to transactions recognized at or near the end of the reporting period. Answer (a) is incorrect because retesting the effectiveness of control procedures will not help the auditor identify related-party transactions. Answer (b) is a procedure that is followed when customers do not respond to confirmation requests, which is less likely to be the case if the customer is a related party. Answer (d) is incorrect because inquiry of lawyers may provide information about litigation, claims and assessments, not about related party transactions.

92. (c) One of the factors the auditor should consider before performing substantive tests at an interim date prior to the balance sheet date is whether or not the year-end balances of the accounts selected for interim examination are reasonably predictable. The auditor should also consider whether there are changing conditions that might predispose management to misstate financial statements in the remaining period and whether it is cost-effective to perform interim tests. Answer (a) is incorrect because assessing control risk below the maximum is not required in order to have a reasonable basis for extending audit conclusions from an interim date to the balance sheet date. Answer (b) is incorrect because immaterial accounts are less likely to be tested at interim or at year end. Answer (d) is incorrect because written representations from management about the availability of records and data are always obtained, whether or not the auditor performs interim testing.

93. (a) QC 10-1.19 states that the purpose of a financial statement audit is to express an opinion regarding the statements and if they are **"presented fairly, in all material respects, in conformity with generally accepted accounting principles."** All the other choices are items that would be considered by the reviewing partner, but the emphasis is on whether the financial statements support the opinion paragraph of the audit report.

94. (b) AU 312 states that detection risk should bear an inverse relationship to inherent and control risk. The less the inherent and control risk the auditor believes exists, the greater the acceptable level of detection risk. Conversely, when the inherent and control risk increases, the auditor must decrease the detection risk. These components of audit risk may be assessed in quantitative terms such as percentages or in non-quantitative terms that range, for example, from a minimum to a maximum.

95. (c) AU 317 states that the auditor may conclude that withdrawal is necessary when the client does not take the remedial action that the auditor considers necessary in the circumstances, *even when* the illegal act is not material to the financial statements. Factors that should affect the auditor's conclusion include the implications of the failure to take remedial action, which may affect the auditor's *ability to rely on management representations*, and the effects of continuing association with the client.

96. (d) AU 329 states that analytical procedures used in planning the audit generally use data aggregated at a high level. An unusual combination of expense and revenue accounts in a journal entry might result in unusual aggregate information. Choice (a) is incorrect because tracing proves completeness and would not detect unusual relationships between the numbers. Choices (b) and (c) are incorrect because evaluating the effectiveness of the system of internal control or reconciling controlling accounts to the subsidiary ledger would not detect unusual relationships between the numbers.

97. (c) AU 311 states that an engagement letter is normally required by GAAS. However, it would be foolish these days to operate without one. It focuses on the overall goals of the engagement, records to be provided by the client, and the type of report, the scope of the engagement, the timing of the field work, a fraud disclaimer, and the set fee. Choice (a) is incorrect because in planning the audit, the auditor should consider the nature, extent, and timing of work to be performed and should prepare a written audit program. An audit program aids in instructing assistants in the work to be done. It should set forth in reasonable detail the audit procedures that the auditor believes are necessary to accomplish the objectives of the audit. Choice (b) is incorrect because the content of working papers should be sufficient to show that the accounting records agree or reconcile with the financial statements or other information reported on and that the applicable standards of field work have been observed. Choice (d) is incorrect because the auditor should document his conclusion for assessing control risk below the max. However, for those

assertions where control risk is assessed at the maximum level, the auditor should document that control risk is at the maximum level but need not document the basis for that conclusion.

98. (d) AU 339 states that the purpose of a financial statement audit is to express an opinion regarding the presentation of the statements. The quantity, type, and content of working papers vary with the circumstances, but they should be sufficient to show that the accounting records agree or reconcile with the financial statements or other information reported on and that the applicable standards of field work have been observed. Working papers ordinarily should include documentation showing that:

- The work has been adequately planned and supervised, indicating observance of the first standard of field work.
- A sufficient understanding of the internal control structure has been obtained to plan the audit and to determine the nature, timing, and extent of tests to be performed.
- The audit evidence obtained, the auditing procedures applied, and the testing performed have provided *sufficient competent evidential matter* to afford a reasonable basis for an opinion.

99. (c) The permanent file would include information of continuing accounting significance, so that the auditor could refer to it year after year. This information could include a schedule of accumulated depreciation, an analysis of contingencies, bond and lease agreements which will be in effect in future years, and a flowchart of the internal control structure. The trial balance is for a particular period and part of the current year working papers.

100. (d) AU 326 states that to be competent, evidence must be both valid and relevant. The more effective the internal control structure, the more assurance it provides about the reliability of accounting data and financial statements. The validity of evidential matter is so dependent on the circumstances under which it is obtained that generalizations about the reliability of various types of evidence are subject to important exceptions. If the possibility of important exceptions is recognized, however, the following presumptions, which are not mutually exclusive, about the validity of evidential matter in auditing have some usefulness:

- When evidential matter can be obtained from independent sources outside an entity, it provides greater assurance of reliability for the purposes of an independent audit than that secured solely within the entity.
- The more effective the internal control structure, the more assurance it provides about the reliability of the accounting data and financial statements.
- The independent auditor's direct personal knowledge, obtained through physical examination, observation, computation, and inspection, is more persuasive than information obtained indirectly.

Choice (a) is incorrect because information obtained **directly** is most reliable. Choice (b) is incorrect because evidence should be persuasive not convincing. Choice (c) is incorrect because corroborating evidence provides assurance about the sufficiency and not the reliability of the data.

101. (a) AU 326 states that evidence about the valuation assertion that inventories are properly stated at cost (except when market is lower) is provided by:

- Examining paid vendors' invoices.
- Reviewing direct labor rates.
- Testing the computation of standard overhead rates.
- Examining analyses of purchasing and manufacturing variances.

Choice (b) is incorrect because obtaining confirmation of inventories pledged under loan agreements provides assurance about presentation and disclosures. Choice (c) is incorrect because reviewing shipping and cutoff procedures for inventory provides assurance of clients' completeness of accounting records. Choice (d) is incorrect because tracing test counts to the entity's inventory listing provides assurance about completeness.

102. (c) AU 332 states that evidential matter about the existence, ownership, and cost of long-term investments includes accounting records and documents of the investor relating to acquisition. In the case of investments in the form of securities (such as stocks, bonds, and notes), this evidential matter should be corroborated by inspection of the securities, or in appropriate circumstances, by written confirmation from an independent custodian of securities on deposit, pledged, or in safekeeping. Choice (a) is incorrect because the investee company may not have timely and up-to-date information regarding ownership of stock. Choices (b) and (d) are incorrect because they support valuation of the investment and not inspection of the securities.

103. (a) AU 326 states that assertions about valuation or allocation deal with whether asset, liability, revenue, and expense components have been included in the financial statements at appropriate amounts. For example, management asserts that property is recorded at historical cost and that such cost is allocated to the appropriate accounting periods. Management asserts that AR included in the balance sheet are stated at net realizable value.

104. (a) AU 326 states that assertions about valuation or allocation deal with whether asset, liability, revenue, and expense components have been included in the financial statements at appropriate amounts. For example, management asserts that property is recorded at historical cost and that such cost is systematically allocated to appropriate accounting periods. Similarly, management asserts that trade A/R included in the balance sheet are stated at net realizable value. Determining that proper amounts of depreciation are expensed provides assurance about the assertions of valuation or allocation amounts and presentation such as an expense on the I/S. The other assertions relate to balance sheet items rights and obligations or to transactions about completeness or existence.

105. (b) AU 330 states that the negative confirmation form requests the recipient to respond only if he or she disagrees with the information stated on the request. Negative confirmation requests may be used to reduce audit risk to an acceptable level when:

- the combined assessed level of inherent and control risk is low,
- a large number of small balances is involved, and
- the auditor has no reason to believe that the recipients of the requests are unlikely to give them consideration.

106. (a) AU 330 states that confirmation requests can be designed to elicit evidence that addresses the completeness assertion: that is, if properly designed, confirmations may provide evidence to aid in assessing whether all transactions and accounts that should be included in the financial statements are included. Their effectiveness in addressing the completeness assertion depends in part on whether the auditor selects from an appropriate population for testing. For example, when using confirmations to provide evidence about the completeness assertion for accounts payable, the appropriate population might be a list of vendors rather than the amounts recorded in the accounts payable subsidiary ledger. Choice (b) is incorrect because confirming amounts recorded would be existence and not completeness. Choice (c) is incorrect because while these checks are investigated by the auditor, the amount is not confirmed. Choice (d) is incorrect because some invoices could be excluded from the file, impairing completeness.

107. (d) AU 342 states that the auditor should consider the historical experience of the entity in making past estimates as well as the auditor's experience in the industry. However, changes in facts, circumstances, or the entity's procedures may cause factors different from those in the past to become significant to the accounting estimate. In evaluating the reasonableness of an estimate, the auditor concentrates on key factors that are:

- Significant to the accounting estimate.
- Sensitive to variations.
- Deviations from historical patterns.
- Subjective and susceptible to misstatement and bias.

108. (d) AU 8012 states that auditors commonly use analytical procedures to provide evidence concerning payroll when control risk is low. Analytical procedures include comparison of financial information with:

- comparable information for a prior period or periods,
- anticipated results, such as budgets or forecasts, and
- similar industry information, such as a comparison of the entity's ratio of sales to accounts receivable with industry averages or with other entities of comparable size in the same industry.
- study relationships among elements of financial information that would be expected to conform to a predictable pattern based on the entity's experience, such as a study of gross margin percentage.
- study relationships between financial information and relevant non-financial information, such as a study of payroll costs to number of employees.

Choice (a) is incorrect because to verify that checks are mailed does not prevent mailing the checks to nonexistent personnel. Choice (b) is incorrect because tracing does not include observing payroll. Choice (c) is incorrect because observing payroll distribution would be effective to prevent checks from being distributed to non-employees, but the auditor is only satisfying that particular procedure. The question asked is of a general nature.

109. (c) AU 8502 states that auditors commonly use inquiries and analytical procedures to provide evidence concerning loans when control risk is low. These procedures would include:

- Obtain from management a schedule of loans payable and determine if the total agrees with the trial balance.
- Inquire whether there are any loans where management has not complied with provisions of the loan agreement and inquire as to management's actions and if appropriate adjustments have been made in the F/S.
- Consider the reasonableness of interest expense in relation to loan balances.
- Inquire whether loans payable are secured.
- Inquire whether loans payable have been classified between noncurrent and current.

Choice (a) is incorrect because the auditor would recalculate the premium and discount rather than performing an analytical procedure. Choice (b) is incorrect because the auditor would analyze the instrument rather than the assets purchased document to check for liens. Choice (d) is incorrect because the auditor would confirm the balance, not the existence of bondholders.

110. (d) The auditor would normally determine that a stock option was authorized by tracing the authorization to the minutes of the board of directors. Choice (a) is incorrect because the Secretary of State would have no knowledge of a stock option granted by a corporation. Choice (b) is incorrect because options might be issued to people or other entities that do not currently own stock in the corporation and who do not work for the corporation. Choice (c) is incorrect because stock options may be distributed from authorized common stock instead of using treasury shares to fulfill the options.

111. (d) AU 326 states that an auditor who is analyzing the repairs and maintenance accounts is testing transactions that have been recorded in the accounts. Sampling from transactions that have been recorded provides evidence in support of the presentation and disclosure assertion. Assertions about presentation and disclosure deal with whether particular components of the financial statements are properly classified, described, and disclosed. For example, management asserts that obligations classified as long-term liabilities in the balance sheet will not mature within one year. Or management asserts that amounts presented as extraordinary items in the income statement are properly classified and described. The auditor is obtaining evidence that transactions recorded in repairs and maintenance accounts do represent expenditures properly charged to expense, not assets which should be capitalized. The cost of capitalized assets is allocated to the periods benefited in a systematic and rational manner, depreciated, depleted, or amortized, not expensed in the period incurred. The other choices would not constitute the primary purpose because the auditor should be selecting from expenditures that did occur, not from the expenditures that were recorded in the repairs and maintenance accounts.

112. (c) AU 313 states that before applying principal substantive tests to the details of asset or liability accounts at an interim date, the auditor should assess the difficulty in controlling the incremental audit risk. In addition, the auditor should consider the cost of the substantive tests that are necessary to cover the remaining period in a way that will provide the appropriate audit assurance at the balance-sheet date. Applying principal substantive tests to the details of asset and liability accounts at an interim date may not be cost-effective if substantive tests to cover the remaining period cannot be restricted due to the assessed level of control risk. Choice (a) is incorrect because assessing control risk at below a maximum is not required in order to have a reasonable basis for extending an auditing conclusion from interim to the balance sheet date. Choices (b) and (d) are incorrect because inherent risk or materiality of the accounts are generally not a factor in the decision to apply substantive tests at an interim date.

113. (c) AU 317 states that the auditor ordinarily obtains written representations from management concerning the absence of violations or possible violations of laws or regulations whose effects should be considered for disclosure in the financial statements or as a basis for recording a loss contingency.

114. (d) AU 336 states that an understanding should exist among the auditor, the client, and the specialist as to the nature of the work to be performed by the specialist. Preferably, the understanding should be documented and should cover the following:

- The objectives and scope of the specialist's work.
- The specialist's representations as to his relationship, if any, to the client.
- The methods or assumptions to be used.
- A comparison of the methods or assumptions to be used with those used in the preceding period.
- The specialist's understanding of the auditor's corroborative use of the specialist's findings in relation to the representations in the financial statements.

Although the appropriateness and reasonableness of methods or assumptions used and their application are the responsibility of the specialist, the auditor should obtain an understanding of the methods or assumptions used by the specialist to determine whether the findings are suitable for corroborating the representations in the financial statements. The auditor should consider whether the specialist's findings support the related representations in the financial statements and make appropriate tests of accounting data provided by the client to the specialist. Choices (a) and (c) are incorrect because an understanding should exist between the auditor, the client, and the specialist as per above. Choice (b) is incorrect because the auditor should consider performing substantive procedures to verify the specialist findings only if the specialist is related to the client.

115. (b) AU 337 states that a letter of audit inquiry to the client's lawyer is the auditor's primary means of obtaining corroboration of the information furnished by management concerning litigation, claims, and assessments. Choice (a) is incorrect because the primary source of this information is management. Choice (c) is incorrect because the attorney's opinion is secondary. Choice (d) is incorrect because the attorney is asked to comment on management's description and evaluate litigation claims that exist at the balance sheet date.

116. (c) AU 334 states that after identifying related party transactions, the auditor should apply the procedures necessary to obtain satisfaction concerning the purpose, nature, and extent of these transactions and their effect on the financial statements. The procedures should be directed toward obtaining and evaluating sufficient competent evidential matter and should extend beyond inquiry of management. Procedures that should be considered include:

- Obtain an understanding of the business purpose of the transaction.
- Examine invoices, executed copies of agreements, contracts, and other pertinent documents, such as receiving reports and shipping documents.
- Determine whether the transaction has been approved by the board of directors or other appropriate officials.
- Test for reasonableness the compilation of amounts to be disclosed, or considered for disclosure, in the financial statements.

Choice (a) is incorrect because while an extra paragraph is added, related party transactions are generally disclosed in the footnotes. Choice (b) is incorrect because analytical procedures are not effective to identify related party transactions. Choice (d) is incorrect because it is difficult to validate that the transactions were consummated on terms equivalent to other arm's-length transactions.

117. (c) AU 329 states that the auditor's working trial balance includes the balances in the client's accounts which will become the final financial statement balances. To produce those final figures, the initial figures are reclassified to the correct accounts and adjusted to the correct balances required by generally accepted accounting principles. This is done with reclassification and adjustment columns in the working trial balance.

118. (d) AU 339 states that the factors affecting the auditor's judgment about the quantity, type, and content of the working papers for a particular engagement include:

- the nature of the engagement,
- the nature of the auditor's report,
- the nature of the financial statements, schedules, or other information on which the auditor is reporting,
- the nature and condition of the client's records,
- the assessed level of control risk, and
- the needs in the particular circumstances for supervision and review of the work.

119. (b) AU 380 states that accounting estimates are an integral part of the financial statements prepared by management and are based upon management's current judgments. Those judgments are normally based on knowledge and experience about past and current events and assumptions about future events. Certain accounting estimates are particularly sensitive because of their significance to the financial statements and because of the possibility that future events affecting them may differ markedly from management's current judgments. The auditor should determine that the audit committee is informed about the process used by management in formulating particularly sensitive accounting estimates and about the basis for the auditor's conclusions regarding the reasonableness of those estimates. Choices (a), (c), and (d) are incorrect because they deal with the auditor's judgment and no explanation is needed to the committee.

120. (a) An illegal payment that is not recorded will directly misstate the financial statements by the amount omitted. In addition, there is the potential for a material contingent liability for the fines and/or penalties that may arise from the illegal activity. Answers (b), (c) and (d) present examples of misstatements that only affect the financial statements by the amount of the misstatement, which if small will not have a material effect on the financial statements.

121. (c) An auditor should prepare written audit programs, which aid in instructing assistants in the work to be done. Although the form and extent of detail will vary, the audit program should set forth the audit procedures that the auditor believes are necessary to accomplish the objectives of the audit. Answer (a) is incorrect because substantive tests, which include tests of balances as well as tests of transactions, do not have to be designed to test every material transaction, if the auditor can be satisfied by other procedures. Answer (b) is incorrect because for some audit engagements it may be more efficient to perform selected substantive tests before year end. Answer (d) is incorrect because the auditor does not test all transactions and balances.

122. (a) An audit program sets forth the audit procedures the auditor believes are necessary to accomplish the objectives of the audit. Audit procedures consist of tests of controls and substantive tests. The audit program cannot be finalized until the auditor completes his review of the internal control structure because substantive tests are designed using the knowledge obtained from understanding the internal control structure. Answers (b), (c) and (d) are incorrect because finalization of the audit program does not depend on signing an engagement letter, which typically occurs at the very beginning of the audit; or communicating reportable conditions, which can occur during or at the end of the audit; or searching for unrecorded liabilities, which is one of the last audit procedures performed by the auditor.

123. (b) The auditor is required to communicate certain matters to those having responsibility for oversight of the financial reporting process, which is typically the audit committee. Generally the auditor must report items that relate to the scope and results of the audit process that may assist the audit committee with its oversight responsibility. Because materiality judgments made by the auditor do not directly affect the audit committee's responsibility, they are not typically communicated to that committee. Answers (a), (c) and (d) are items that are usually communicated because unusual transactions, indications of fraud, and disagreements with management do affect the audit committee's responsibility.

124. (b) By tracing shipping documents to sales invoices, the auditor will obtain evidence that all shipments have been invoiced; that is, that each shipment resulted in a sales invoice being prepared. Answer (a) is incorrect because tracing shipping documents to invoices will not detect duplicate shipments if both a shipping document and invoice were prepared for the duplicate shipment. Answer (c) is incorrect because the auditor would have to trace customer orders to shipping documents to determine if all orders have been shipped. Answer (d) is incorrect because if the auditor wants to account for all invoices, he should start his test with invoices, not shipping documents.

125. (b) An auditor examines approved clock card data to determine the number of hours an employee worked. Comparing the payroll register to clock data provides assurance that the number of hours used to compute the payroll is the number of hours worked. Answers (a), (c) and (d) are incorrect because looking at clock card data will not provide information regarding pay rates, segregation of duties, or controls over unclaimed payroll checks.

126. (c) Evidence generated by external parties, such as a bank, is more competent, and therefore more persuasive, than evidence generated internally by the client. A bank statement, even if obtained from the client rather than directly from the bank, is more persuasive than internally-generated evidence. Answers (a), (b) and (d) are examples of internally-generated documents, worksheets and letters, which are less persuasive than a bank statement.

127. (a) Assertions about presentation and disclosure deal with whether particular components of the financial statements are properly classified, described, and disclosed. An auditor would inspect loan agreements regarding pledged inventories to determine that management has adequately disclosed the security arrangements.

128. (a) Assertions about valuation or allocation deal with whether asset, liability, revenue, and expense components have been included in the financial statements at appropriate amounts. An auditor would review and recompute amortization and determine if the amortization period is reasonable to support management's assertion that amounts shown in the financial statements for intangible assets and amortization expense are appropriate.

129. (c) Assertions about completeness deal with whether all transactions and amounts that should be presented in the financial statements are so included. Cutoff tests provide assurance that all purchases made before the end of the year, which should therefore be included in that year's financial statements, are so included.

130. (a) Assertions about valuation or allocation deal with whether asset, liability, revenue, and expense components have been included in the financial statements at appropriate amounts. Inquiries and other tests designed to determine if inventory is obsolete or slow-moving will help provide assurance that inventory, which should be adjusted to lower of cost or market, is properly valued on the financial statements.

131. (b) Assertions about rights and obligations deal with whether assets are the rights of the entity and liabilities are the obligations of the entity at a given date. Assertions about existence or occurrence deal with whether assets or liabilities of the entity exist at a given date and whether recorded transactions have occurred during a given period. Confirming that an outside agent is holding investment securities in the client's name provides evidence that the securities exist at a given date and that they are owned by the client on that date.

132. (a) The negative form of confirmation requests the recipient to respond only if he or she disagrees with the information stated on the request. If negative confirmation requests are not returned, the auditor infers that there were no disagreements when, in fact, the intended third parties may not have received the confirmation requests and/or may not have verified that the information contained on them is correct. Answer (b) is incorrect because negative confirmation requests should only be used when the control risk and inherent risk are low, thus allowing for a higher detection risk, not a low detection risk. Answer (c) is incorrect because an unreturned negative

confirmation request requires no additional follow up. Answer (d) is incorrect because negative confirmations provide some assurance about existence of accounts; that is, account balances are not overstated.

133. (c) When the auditor has not received replies to positive accounts receivable confirmation requests, he or she should apply alternative procedures such as examining subsequent cash receipts. Before applying alternative procedures, the auditor would typically mail a second request and ask the client to encourage the customer to respond. Answer (a) is incorrect because the auditor, through confirmations, is testing the existence of the receivable at year-end. Writing off an account after year-end provides no evidence that it was a valid asset. Answer (b) is incorrect because the auditor must obtain sufficient evidence regarding the existence assertion and cannot trade off one assertion with others. Answer (d) is incorrect because inherent risk would not be reassessed due to lack of response to confirmation requests.

134. (c) The objective of analytical procedures in the final overall review stage of the audit is to assist the auditor in assessing the conclusions reached and in the evaluation of the overall financial statement presentation. The overall review would generally include considering unusual or unexpected balances or relationships that were not previously identified. Answers (a) and (d) relate to substantive tests that are performed during the audit, not analytical procedures used in the final stage of the audit. Answer (b) relates to tests of controls, which would not be performed if control procedures appeared to be ineffective.

135. (b) Analytical procedures consist of evaluations of financial information made by a study of plausible relationships among both financial and nonfinancial data, and involve comparisons of recorded amounts, or ratios developed from recorded amounts, to expectations developed by the auditor. Projecting error rates based on sample results relates more to tests of controls, rather than to analytical procedures. Answer (a), which involves developing an expectation or estimate using financial and nonfinancial information, is an analytical procedure. Answer (c), which involves computing ratios, and answer (d), which involves developing expectations based on prior year trends, are also examples of analytical procedures.

136. (d) If physical inventory is higher than the perpetual record, as indicated by the test counts, then the client either failed to record an addition to inventory or recorded a decrease in inventory that did not occur. Failing to record sales returns, which increase the physical inventory, would explain why the perpetual record was understated. Answers (a), (b) and (c) are incorrect because purchase discounts, purchase returns, and sales all decrease the perpetual record of inventory, and if not recorded would overstate the perpetual record, rather than understate it.

137. (c) In order to determine that items on an inventory listing are valid and in fact exist at physical inventory date, the auditor would select items on that listing and trace them to inventory tags and count sheets that were prepared during the physical inventory count. Answers (a) and (d) are tests that may provide some assurance regarding completeness of the inventory listing rather than its validity, as the direction of testing is from supporting documents, such as tags and invoices, to the inventory listing rather than from the listing to supporting documents. Answer (b) is incorrect because comparing inventory tags to receiving reports and vendor invoices does not involve any tracing to or from the inventory listing.

138. (d) When the auditor determines that the internal control structure is effective and thus the control risk is assessed as low, the auditor may alter the nature, timing, and extent of substantive tests performed. In the case of assertions related to payroll, the auditor may decide to limit substantive tests to performing analytical procedures, which would evaluate the reasonableness of payroll-related amounts for the year, and recalculating payroll accruals, which would provide some assurance that the year-end adjustments are proper. Answer (a) is typically a test of controls, rather than a substantive test. Answers (b) and (c) are incomplete tests in that the payroll register and payroll tax returns would have to be compared to other payroll records in order to provide any assurance that payroll balances were fairly stated.

139. (a) In searching for unrecorded retirements of fixed assets the auditor would select items included in the property ledger and other records and then, by touring the client's facilities, look to see if they are on hand. A fixed asset that is not on hand but is included in the records may indicate that a retirement was not recorded. Answer (b) would not detect unrecorded retirements because the auditor, in touring the client facilities first, will note assets that are on hand, rather than those which have been retired or otherwise disposed of. Answers (c) and (d) are incorrect because the auditor analyzes the repair and maintenance account to find unrecorded fixed asset additions, not retirements.

140. (d) The statement of cash flows presents amounts for financing and investing activities, which come from changes in balance sheet accounts, and operating activities, which come from income statement accounts. Therefore, the auditor, in auditing the statement of cash flows, would reconcile the amounts shown in that statement to the other financial statements. Answer (a) is incorrect because cash flow activities typically vary from year to year and do not follow predictable patterns. Answers (b) and (c) are procedures that are performed to audit the year-end balance in the cash account, not cash flow activity.

141. (c) When testing to determine that transactions have been recorded, which relates to the completeness assertion, the auditor would select original source documents, such as sales invoices, and trace them to the records, such as the sales journal. Answers (a), (b) or (d) could be the starting point if the auditor wanted to determine that all recorded transactions were valid, which is the existence assertion. To test existence or occurrence, the auditor would start with ledger balances, an adjusted trial balance, or journal entries and vouch them back to source documents.

142. (a) Ordinarily, the auditor should attempt to obtain a specialist who is unrelated to the client. However, when the circumstances so warrant, work of a specialist who has a relationship with the client may be acceptable. Answers (b) and (d) are incorrect because the auditor would apply additional procedures if the specialist's determinations are unreasonable or if the specialist's findings do not support the financial statement assertions, and, depending on the results of those additional procedures, the auditor would issue the appropriate report. Answer (d) is incorrect because a specialist, which is a person or firm that possesses skills in fields other than accounting and auditing, can be used to evaluate inventory characteristics that fall outside the auditor's expertise.

143. (a) If the auditor, as a result of the report or findings of a specialist, decides to add explanatory language to the auditor's report regarding a going concern issue, he or she may refer to and identify the specialist in that auditor's report. Answers (b), (c) and (d) are incorrect because the auditor should only refer to the specialist if, as a result of the specialist's work, the auditor decides to add explanatory language to his or her report or depart from an unqualified opinion. Otherwise, such a reference may be misunderstood to be a qualification of the auditor's opinion or a division of responsibility, neither of which is intended. Further, there may be an inference that the auditor making such reference performed a more thorough audit than an auditor not making such a reference.

144. (b) A lawyer's refusal to furnish the information requested in an inquiry letter would be a limitation on the scope of the audit. Such an inability to obtain sufficient competent evidence may require the auditor to qualify the opinion or disclaim an opinion. An adverse opinion, answer (a), is issued when the financial statements are not fairly stated, not when there is inadequate evidence. An auditor does not typically withdraw from an engagement, answer (c), unless the client refuses to accept an auditor's report. A reportable condition, answer (d), is a deficiency in the internal control structure, which is unrelated to legal letters.

145. (d) The auditor is concerned with subsequent events, which occur subsequent to the balance-sheet date but prior to the issuance of the auditors's report, that may have a material affect on the financial statements and therefore require adjustment or disclosure in the statements. Because changes in long-term debt occurring after year end may require disclosure to keep the financial statements from being misleading, the auditor should investigate such changes. The procedures described in answers (a), (b) and (c) would not likely reveal events that could have a material affect on the current financial statements.

146. (a) A typical management representation letter refers to the completeness and availability of all minutes of meetings of stockholders, directors and committees of directors. Materiality does not apply to these minutes of meetings. The management representation letter typically also refers to the matters listed in answers (b), (c) and (d), but materiality limits could apply to losses from purchase commitments, related party disclosures, and inventory reductions.

147. (c) Because the auditor is concerned with events occurring through the date of the auditor's report that may require adjustment to or disclosure in the financial statements, the representations included in the management representation letter should be dated as of the date of the auditor's report. The dates listed in answers (a), (b) and (d) are incorrect.

148. (d) Established accounting principles ordinarily do not require transactions with related parties to be accounted for on a basis different from that which would be appropriate if the parties were not related. Therefore, the auditor should view related party transactions within the framework of existing pronouncements, placing primary emphasis on the adequacy of disclosure of such transactions. Because transactions with related parties are more likely to raise questions as to their economic substance, the auditor is more concerned with evaluating the disclosure of those transactions than with determining the rights of related parties, answer (a), confirming the existence of related parties, answer (b), or verifying the valuation of related party transactions, answer (c).

149. (d) The auditor is responsible for evaluating the reasonableness of accounting estimates made by management and, as a first step, should obtain an understanding of how management developed its estimates. Based on that understanding, the auditor should develop an independent expectation of the estimates, as indicated in answer (a), and/or review and test the process used by management to develop the estimates, as reflected in answers (b) and (c), and/or review subsequent events or transactions occurring prior to the completion of fieldwork.

150. (a) The interest income account should reflect interest earned during the period under audit. In analyzing interest income, the auditor would also analyze accounts, such as notes receivable, that affect the balance in the interest income account. Answers (b), (c) and (d) list accounts that are independent of each other; that is, activity in the first account listed has no affect on the second account listed.

151. (a) Working papers are records kept by the auditor of the procedures applied, the tests performed, the information obtained, and the pertinent conclusions reached in an engagement. Working papers serve mainly to provide the principal support for the auditor's report and to aid the auditor in the conduct and supervision of the engagement. Because workpapers are prepared for individual engagements, they do not address all of the broader issues raised by answers (b), (c) and (d). For example, working papers do not address contingent fees, which are dealt with in the Code of Conduct; hiring practices, which are part of CPA firm quality controls; and spousal ownership of client stock, which is an independence issue.

152. (a) Confirming accounts payable is the least likely procedure, of those listed, that the auditor would perform prior to the balance sheet date. The auditor would prefer to perform payables confirmation work as of year end because, when auditing payables, the auditor is most concerned with the completeness of payables at the year end balance sheet date. Answer (b) is incorrect because inventory observation is often done at an interim date, partly because of practical business reasons such as the time needed to compile the physical inventory results. Answers (c) and (d) are procedures that are typically performed at the earliest stages of the audit as they affect the planning of other audit procedures.

153. (c) Analytical procedures involve comparisons of recorded amounts, or ratios developed from recorded amounts, to expectations developed by the auditor. If the auditor wants to develop relationships among balance sheet accounts, he or she would calculate and evaluate financial statement ratios such as the current ratio and debt to equity ratio. Answers (a) and (b) are incorrect because they do not focus on relationships among accounts. Trend analysis looks at relationships over time. Regression analysis measures the rate at which a dependent variable changes in relation to an independent variable. Answer (d) is incorrect because risk analysis is a very broad term that is not directly related to analytical procedures.

154. (c) When the auditor concludes that an auditing procedure considered necessary at the time of the audit was omitted, he should assess the importance of the omitted procedure to his present ability to support the previously issued opinion. A review of his working papers and discussions with engagement personnel may be helpful in making this assessment. He may decide not to apply the omitted procedure, for example, if the results of other procedures that were applied compensate for the one omitted. Answers (a), (b) and (d) are incorrect because the extent of reliance on the auditor's opinion, the type of opinion given, and the reasons for the omitted procedure should not affect the auditor's decision to perform the omitted procedure.

155. (b) Among the matters to be communicated to the audit committee is information about the initial selection of and changes in significant accounting policies and their application. Answer (a) is incorrect because the communication must occur on a timely basis, which can be before or after the auditor's report is issued. Answer (c) is incorrect because the auditor is not required to communicate with management regarding audit committee concerns, although the auditor is not precluded from doing so. Answer (d) is incorrect because significant audit adjustments, whether or not recorded, must be communicated to the audit committee.

156. (a) In obtaining evidential matter in support of financial statement assertions, the auditor develops specific objectives in the light of those assertions. In order to achieve the audit objectives developed by the auditor, he or she performs substantive tests. Since analytical procedures are a type of substantive test, they can be performed to achieve audit objectives related to particular assertions. Answers (b), (c) and (d) are incorrect because they are not audit procedures. Quality control systems are concerned with how CPA firms are organized. Working papers document the work done by the auditor and the auditor's conclusions. The level of allowable detection risk depends on audit risk, inherent risk and control risk.

157. (c) Accounts receivable confirmations are likely to be more effective for the existence assertion than for the completeness assertion. Customers of a client are more likely to report a balance that is nonexistent or overstated, rather than a balance that is incomplete or understated. Answer (a) is an incorrect statement because if customers do not verify the details of a confirmation, evidence is not being gathered about any assertion, not just the completeness assertion. Answer (b) is not true for positive confirmations and disagreements that would be reported by customers would likely be related to overstatements, not understatements. Answer (d) in incorrect because when confirming receivables, auditors focus on larger, material balances.

158. (b) The standard bank confirmation form is used to obtain bank confirmation of deposit and loan balances. The confirmation of loan balances includes a request for due dates, interest rates, and collateral descriptions. Answer (a) is incorrect because an accounts payable confirmation typically asks the vendor to indicate balances due; reference to purchase commitments is not standard. Answer (c) is incorrect because the party who would be able to confirm consigned inventory would not be in a position to confirm contingent liabilities. Answer (d) is incorrect because accounts receivable confirmations typically ask the customer to indicate if the balance is correct; reference to accrued interest receivable is not a standard part of that confirmation request.

159. (b) Analytical procedures involve comparisons of recorded amounts or ratios developed from recorded amounts to expectations developed by the auditor. There are various sources of information, such as anticipated results reflected in budgets, for developing these auditor expectations. Since a standard cost system that produces variance reports is based on budgets, analytical procedures would be facilitated when such a system is used. Answers (a) and (c) are unrelated to analytical procedures. Segregating obsolete inventory allows for a more accurate physical inventory count and observation. Correcting internal control weaknesses could affect the auditor's assessment of control risk. Answer (d) is incorrect because the level of assurance provided from analytical procedures is affected by the reliability of the data being analyzed, and data generated solely within the entity is not very reliable.

160. (b) Inventory turnover, which is an operations ratio that calculates how many times inventory is sold during a period of time such as a year, is calculated by dividing average inventory into cost of goods sold. Answers (a), (c) and (d) are incorrect because inventory is divided into cost of goods sold, not into net sales, operating income, or gross sales.

161. (d) The AICPA Standard Form to Confirm Account Balance Information With Financial Institutions is designed to substantiate information that is stated on the confirmation request. If the bank employee who completes the form is unaware of all financial relationships that the bank has with the client, the response may not provide information beyond that which is specifically requested. This limits the usefulness of the standard bank confirmation request. Answer (a) is incorrect because banks are typically responsive to a client's request of its bank to verify information to a third party, the auditor. Answers (b) and (c) are incorrect because the employee who completes the form does not need to inspect nor access the client's bank reconciliation and cutoff bank statement.

162. (b) If the control risk for the existence or occurrence assertion regarding sales transactions is assessed as low, there is a reduced likelihood that sales are overstated. Substantive tests of sales would be limited as a result. If, in addition, the auditor has already gathered evidence regarding cash receipts and accounts receivable, which are the debit sides of the credits to the sales account, the auditor has already obtained some evidence about sales and would therefore limit any additional testing of sales transactions. Answer (a) is incorrect because the inventory balances are not directly related to the sales account. Answers (c) and (d) are incorrect because, although shipping activities and cutoffs of sales relate to sales transactions, receiving activities and cutoffs of purchases do not.

163. (c) An auditor searches for unrecorded liabilities to determine if there are liabilities that were not recorded in the year being audited that should be recorded in that year. A procedure performed to find these unrecorded liabilities is to vouch a sample of cash disbursements recorded just after year-end to receiving reports and vendor invoices. If the payment was for goods or services received before year-end, the auditor would review the details of accounts payable and other liabilities to determine that a liability is properly recorded as of year end. Answer (a) is incorrect because the auditor is concerned about omitted, unrecorded payables. Tracing recorded payables to receiving reports is a test of recorded liabilities that will not detect unrecorded liabilities. Answer (b) is incorrect because a liability is incurred when goods or services are received, not when a purchase order is issued. Answer (d) is incorrect because cash disbursements made before year end are in payment of recorded liabilities, not unrecorded liabilities.

164. (c) The purpose of a substantive audit procedure that traces a transaction forward in an accounting system is to determine if that transaction was properly recorded for the correct amount in the correct accounting period. This procedure primarily tests the completeness assertion. Tracing purchase orders to receiving reports to purchase journals and cash disbursement journals will provide evidence that purchase transactions have been properly recorded, and not omitted. Answer (a) is incorrect because testing a sample of purchase orders may not detect unusually large purchases. Answers (b) and (d) are incorrect because the direction of testing would be from the cash disbursements journal to receiving reports and purchase orders if the purpose was to determine if disbursements were for goods received and ordered.

165. (b) When a plant asset, such as equipment, is retired, the asset account is credited and the related accumulated depreciation account is debited. Therefore, an acceptable explanation for significant debits to the accumulated depreciation accounts would be that plant assets were retired during the year. Answers (a) and (d) are incorrect because they involve changes in estimates, which are accounted for prospectively in the future. Accumulated depreciation accounts are not adjusted for changes in estimates such as changes in estimated useful lives and revisions of overhead allocations. Answer (c) is incorrect because if the prior year's depreciation was understated, the correction of this error would involve a credit to accumulated depreciation, not a debit.

166. (a) Standard labor cost is based on expectations and budgets. If actual labor cost is significantly different from standard labor cost, the resultant variances should be analyzed by the auditor. If these variances are not readily explainable, the auditor may suspect payroll fraud. Answers (b), (c) and (d) are desirable controls that reduce the likelihood of payroll fraud. Payroll checks can be distributed by the same employee each pay day, particularly if that individual is associated with the treasury or cash disbursements function. Employee time cards should be approved by supervisors. Using a separate payroll account that is reimbursed from other general bank accounts provides additional control over payroll disbursements.

167. (c) Substantive tests are defined as tests of details and analytical procedures performed to detect material misstatements in the account balance, transaction class, and disclosure components of financial statements. Answer (a) is incorrect because the objective of tests of details of transactions performed as substantive tests is to detect material misstatements, not to comply with generally accepted auditing standards (GAAS), Even though GAAS do indicate that the auditor should perform substantive tests for significant account balances and transaction classes, GAAS do not indicate that tests of details of transactions have to be performed and that the objective of such tests is to comply with GAAS. Answers (b) and (d) are incorrect because tests of controls, not substantive tests, are performed to attain assurance about the reliability of the accounting system and the effectiveness of management's policies and procedures.

168. (d) The work of a specialist who has a relationship with the client may be acceptable under certain circumstances. If the specialist has a relationship with the client, the auditor should assess the risk that the specialist's objectivity might be impaired. If the auditor believes the relationship might impair the specialist's objectivity, the auditor should perform additional procedures to determine that the specialist's findings are not unreasonable or should engage another specialist for that purpose. Answer (a) is incorrect because the auditor should obtain an understanding of the methods and assumptions used by the specialist. Answer (b) is incorrect because the auditor may use the specialist's work in material matters. Answer (c) is incorrect because the appropriateness and reasonableness of methods and assumptions used and their application are the responsibility of the specialist, not the auditor.

169. (c) Since the events or conditions that should be considered in the accounting for and reporting of litigation, claims, and assessments are matters within the direct knowledge of management of an entity, management is the primary source about such matters. Accordingly, the auditor should inquire of and discuss with management the policies and procedures adopted for identifying, evaluating, and accounting for litigation, claims, and assessments. Answer (a) is incorrect because the auditor, not the client's lawyer, has the responsibility to evaluate whether a going concern problem exists. Answer (b) is incorrect because the auditor is not responsible for examining documents in the lawyer's possession. Answer (d) is incorrect because proper recording and disclosure are accounting and auditing issues, not legal issues.

170. (d) The auditor should perform auditing procedures with respect to the period after the balance-sheet date for the purpose of ascertaining the occurrence of subsequent events that may require adjustment or disclosure. Included in those auditing procedures is inquiring of and discussing with officers and other executives having responsibility for financial and accounting matters as to whether any unusual adjustments had been made during the period from the balance-sheet date to the date of inquiry. Answer (a) is incorrect because confirmation of receivables is done before year-end. Answer (b) is incorrect because this is an analytical review procedure that is done at the beginning of the audit as part of audit planning. Answer (c) is incorrect because personnel changes in the accounting department after year-end do not typically relate to subsequent events that could affect the financial statements.

171. (b) Although the specific representations obtained by the auditor in a management representation letter will depend on the circumstances of the engagement and the nature and basis of presentation of the financial statements, they ordinarily include the completeness and availability of all minutes of meetings of stockholders, directors, and committees of directors. Answer (a) is incorrect because communications with the audit committee concerning weaknesses in controls is the auditor's responsibility, not management's. Answer (c) is incorrect because plans to acquire or merge with other entities in the future do not affect the current period's financial statements. Answer (d) is incorrect because the management representation letter, which does include reference to irregularities involving management or employees, does not indicate that management is responsible for detecting employee fraud.

172. (c) The auditor performs various procedures to identify material transactions with parties known to be related and for identifying material transactions that may be indicative of the existence of previously undetermined relationships. One such procedure is reviewing confirmations of loans receivable and payable for indications of guarantees. When guarantees are indicated, the auditor should determine their nature and the relationships, if any, of the guarantors to the reporting entity. Answers (a), (b) and (d) are incorrect because they do not focus on and may not identify related party transactions; rather, they focus on discovering contingent liabilities, evaluating subsequent events, and determining if there are going concern problems.

173. (d) The permanent file of an auditor's working papers contains information and documents of continuing interest. Examples of such items are debt agreements, the corporate charter and bylaws, contracts such as leases and royalty agreements, and continuing schedules of accounts whose balances are carried forward for several years. Answers (a), (b) and (c) relate to the current year under audit and would be included in the current file of an auditor's working papers.

174. (b) Items that are usually communicated to the audit committee include significant accounting policies, management's process involved in determining significant accounting estimates, significant audit adjustments, disagreements with management and their resolution, consultation with other accountants, and difficulties encountered in the audit. Significant errors discovered by the auditor and subsequently corrected by management would fall under the items listed above. Answer (a) is incorrect because the auditor is not required to communicate with management but may do so if the auditor feels that management will benefit from such communication. Answer (c) is incorrect because the communication with the audit committee may be written or oral. Answer (d) is incorrect because it is not necessary to repeat the communication of recurring matters each year.

175. (c) When the auditor becomes aware of information that relates to financial statements previously reported on by the auditor, but which was not known to the auditor at the date of the auditor's report and which is of such a nature that the auditor would have investigated it had it come to the auditor's attention during the course of the audit, the auditor should make further inquiries about the previously issued financial statements. New information concerning undisclosed lease transactions of the audited period would lead the auditor to make further inquiries to determine if the new information is reliable and whether the facts existed at the date of the auditor's report. Answers (a) and (d) are events that did not exist at the date of the auditor's report and would not require any additional investigation by the auditor about the previously issued financial statements. Answer (b), which resolves a contingency that had been properly accounted for, would not cause the auditor to reevaluate the previously issued financial statements.

Chapter Two - Solutions to Problems
The Third Standard of Field Work—Evidence

NUMBER 1

a. The first type of subsequent events includes those events that provide additional evidence concerning conditions that existed at the balance sheet date and affect the estimates inherent in the process of preparing financial statements. This type of subsequent events requires that the financial statements be adjusted for any changes in estimates resulting from the use of such additional evidence.

The second type of subsequent events consists of those events that provide evidence concerning conditions that did not exist at the balance sheet date but arose subsequent to that date. These events should not result in adjustment to the financial statements but may be such that disclosure is required to keep the financial statements from being misleading.

b. The auditing procedures Green should consider performing to gather evidence concerning subsequent events include the following:

- Compare the latest available interim statements with the financial statements being audited.
- Ascertain whether the interim statements were prepared on the same basis as the audited financial statements.
- Inquire whether any contingent liabilities or commitments existed at the balance sheet date or the date of inquiry.
- Inquire whether there was any significant change in the capital stock, long-term debt, or working capital to the date of inquiry.
- Inquire about the current status of items in the audited financial statements that were accounted for on the basis of tentative, preliminary, or inconclusive data.
- Inquire about any unusual adjustments made since the balance sheet date.
- Read or inquire about the minutes of meetings of stockholders or the board of directors.
- Inquire of the client's legal counsel concerning litigation claims, and assessments.
- Obtain a management representation letter, dated as of the date of Green's report, as to whether any subsequent events would require adjustment or disclosure.
- Make such additional inquiries or perform such additional procedures Green considers necessary and appropriate.

NUMBER 2

a. The factors Kent should consider in the process of selecting Park include:

- Park's professional certification, license, or other recognition of Park's competence.
- Park's reputation and standing in the views of Park's peers and others familiar with Park's capability or performance.
- Park's relationship, if any, to Davidson Corporation.

b. The understanding among Kent, Park, and Davidson's management as to the nature of the work to be performed by Park should cover:

•The objectives and scope of Park's work.
•Park's representations as to Park's relationship, if any, to Davidson.
•The methods or assumptions to be used.
•A comparison of the methods or assumptions to be used with those used in the preceding period.
•Park's understanding of Kent's corroborative use of Park's findings.
•The form and content of Park's report that would enable Kent to evaluate Park's findings.

c. Kent may not refer to Park in the auditor's report if Kent decides to issue an unqualified opinion. Such a reference might be misunderstood to be a qualification, a division of responsibility, or an inference that a more thorough audit was performed.

d. Kent may refer to Park in the auditor's report if Kent decides to issue other than an unqualified opinion as a result of Park's findings. Reference is permitted if it will facilitate an understanding of the reason for the modification.

NUMBER 3

a.

	Primary Assertion	Objective
4.	Existence or occurrence	To determine that the custodian holds the securities as identified in the confirmation.
5.	Completeness	To determine that all income and related collections from the investments are properly recorded.
6.	Valuation or allocation	To determine that the market or other value of the investments is fairly stated.
7.	Presentation and disclosure	To determine that the financial statement presentation and disclosure of investments is in conformity with generally accepted accounting principles consistently applied.
8.	Valuation or allocation	To determine that the market or other value of the investments is fairly stated and the loss is properly recognized and recorded.

b. Larkin should consider applying the following additional substantive auditing procedures in auditing Vernon's investments:

- Inspect securities on hand in the presence of the custodian.
- Examine supporting evidence (broker's advices, etc.) for transactions between the balance sheet date and the inspection date.
- Obtain confirmation from the issuers or trustees for investments in nonpublic entities.
- Examine contractual terms of debt securities and preferred stock.
- Determine that sales and purchases were properly approved by the Board of Directors or its designee.
- Examine broker's advices in support of transactions or confirm transactions with broker.
- Determine that gains and losses on dispositions have been properly computed.
- Trace payments for purchases to canceled checks, and proceeds from sales to entries in the cash receipts journal.
- Determine that the amortization of premium and discount on bonds has been properly computed.
- Determine that market value for both current and long-term portfolios has been properly computed by tracing quoted market prices to competent published or other sources.
- Compute the unrealized gains and losses on both current and long-term portfolios for marketable equity securities.
- Determine that the unrealized gains and losses on the current portfolio have been properly classified in the income statement, and the unrealized gains and losses on the noncurrent portfolio have been properly classified in the equity section of the balance sheet.
- Ascertain whether any investments are pledged as collateral or encumbered by liens, and, if so, are properly disclosed.

NUMBER 4

a. The means or techniques of gathering audit evidence, in addition to the example, are as follows:

Technique	Description
Inquiry	An auditor questions client personnel about events and conditions, such as obsolete inventory.
Confirmation	An auditor obtains acknowledgments in writing from third parties of transactions or balances, such as inventory in public warehouses or on consignment.
Calculation or Recomputation	An auditor recomputes certain amounts, such as the multiplication of quantity times price to determine inventory amounts.
Analysis	An auditor combines amounts in meaningful ways to allow the application of audit judgment, such as determination of whether a proper inventory cutoff was performed.
Inspection	An auditor examines documents relating to transactions and balances, such as shipping and receiving records to establish ownership of inventory.
Comparison	An auditor relates two or more amounts, such as inventory cost in perpetual inventory records to costs as shown on vendor invoices as part of the evaluation of whether inventory is priced at the lower of cost or market.

b. Substantive auditing procedures that would satisfy the five general assertions regarding a client's inventory balance include the following:

(one different procedure required for each assertion)

Assertion	Substantive Auditing Procedure
1. Existence or Occurrence	• Observe physical inventory counts. • Obtain confirmation of inventories at locations outside the entity. • Test inventory transactions between a preliminary physical inventory date and the balance sheet date. • Review perpetual inventory records, production records, and purchasing records for indications of current activity. • Compare inventories with a current sales catalog and subsequent sales and delivery reports. • Use the work of specialists to corroborate the nature of specialized products.
2. Completeness	• Observe physical inventory counts. • Analytically review the relationship of inventory balances to recent purchasing, production, and sales activities. • Test shipping and receiving cutoff procedures. • Obtain confirmation of inventories at locations outside the entity. • Trace test counts recorded during the physical inventory observation to the inventory listing. • Account for all inventory tags and count sheets used in recording the physical inventory counts. • Test the clerical accuracy of inventory listings. • Reconcile physical counts to perpetual records and general ledger balances and investigate significant fluctuations.
3. Rights and Obligations	• Observe physical inventory counts. • Obtain confirmation of inventories at locations outside the entity. • Examine paid vendors' invoices, consignment agreements, and contracts. • Test shipping and receiving cutoff procedures.

Assertion	Substantive Auditing Procedure
4. Valuation or Allocation	<ul><li>Examine paid vendors' invoices.</li><li>Review direct labor rates.</li><li>Test the computation of standard overhead rates.</li><li>Examine analyses of purchasing and manufacturing standard cost variances.</li><li>Examine an analysis of inventory turnover.</li><li>Review industry experience and trends.</li><li>Analytically review the relationship of inventory balances to anticipated sales volume.</li><li>Tour the plant.</li><li>Inquire of production and sales personnel concerning possible excess or obsolete inventory items.</li><li>Obtain current market value quotations.</li><li>Review current production costs.</li><li>Examine sales after year-end and open purchase order commitments.</li></ul>
5. Presentation and Disclosure	<ul><li>Review drafts of the financial statements.</li><li>Compare the disclosures made in the financial statements to the requirements of generally accepted accounting principles.</li><li>Obtain confirmation of inventories pledged under loan agreements.</li></ul>

NUMBER 5

The substantive audit procedures Kane should apply to Star's trade accounts payable balances include the following:

- Foot the schedule of the trade accounts payable.
- Agree the total of the schedule to the general ledger trial balance.
- Compare a sample of individual account balances from the schedule with the accounts payable subsidiary ledger.
- Compare a sample of individual account balances from the accounts payable subsidiary ledger with the schedule.
- Investigate and discuss with management any old or disputed payables.
- Investigate debit balances and, if significant, consider requesting positive confirmations and propose reclassification of the amounts.
- Review the minutes of board of directors' meetings and any written agreements and inquire of key employees as to whether any assets are pledged to collateralize payables.
- Performing cut-off tests.
- Performing analytical procedures.

Confirm or verify recorded accounts payable balances by:

- Reviewing the voucher register or subsidiary accounts payable ledger and consider confirming payables of a sample of vendors.
- Requesting a sample of vendors to provide statements of account balances as of the date selected.
- Investigating and reconciling differences discovered during the confirmation procedures.
- Testing a sample of unconfirmed balances by examining the related vouchers, invoices, purchase orders, and receiving reports.

Perform a search for recorded liabilities by:

- Examining files of receiving reports unmatched with vendors' invoices, searching for items received before the balance sheet date but not yet billed or on the schedule.
- Inspecting files of unprocessed invoices, purchase orders, and vendors' statements.
- Reviewing support for the cash disbursements journal, the voucher register, or canceled checks for disbursements after the balance sheet date to identify transactions that should have been recorded at the balance sheet date, but were not.
- Inquiring of key employees about additional sources of unprocessed invoices or other trade payables.

NUMBER 6

a. Before applying principal substantive tests to balance sheet accounts at April 30, 1993, the interim date, Cook should assess the difficulty in controlling incremental audit risk. Cook should consider whether

- Cook's experience with the reliability of the accounting records and management's integrity has been good;
- Rapidly changing business conditions or circumstances may predispose General's management to misstate the financial statements in the remaining period;
- The year-end balances of accounts selected for interim testing will be predictable;
- General's procedures for analyzing and adjusting its interim balances and for establishing proper accounting cutoffs will be appropriate;
- General's accounting system will provide sufficient information about year-end balances and transactions in the final two months of the year to permit investigation of unusual transactions, significant fluctuations, and changes in balance compositions that may occur between the interim and balance sheet dates;
- The cost of the substantive tests necessary to cover the final two months of the year and provide the appropriate audit assurance at year end is substantial.

Assessing control risk at below the maximum would not be required to extend the audit conclusions from the interim date to the year end; however, if Cook assesses control risk at the maximum during the final two months, Cook should consider whether the effectiveness of the substantive tests and cover that period will be impaired.

b. Cook should design the substantive tests so that the assurance from those tests and the tests to be applied as of the interim date, and any assurance provided from the assessed level of control risk, achieve the audit objectives at year end. Such tests should include the comparison of year-end information with comparable interim information to identify and investigate unusual amounts. Other analytical procedures and/or substantive tests should be performed to extend Cook's conclusions relative to the assertions tested at the interim date to the balance sheet date.

NUMBER 7

1.	E		6.	F
2.	F		7.	D
3.	B		8.	G
4.	E		9.	B
5.	C			

NUMBER 8

99.   D   Confirm directly with bank.
           I   Trace items on the bank reconciliation to cutoff statement.

The auditor would confirm the balance with the bank and trace the items to the cutoff statement.

100.   A   Trace to cash receipts journal.
          G   Ascertain reason for unusual delay.
          H   Inspect supporting documents for reconciling items not appearing on cutoff statement.
          I   Trace items on the bank reconciliation to cutoff statement.
          J   Trace items on the cutoff statement to bank reconciliation.

The auditor traces all deposits in transit to the reconciliation and to the cash receipts journal to prove completeness. If there are any items that do not appear on the cutoff statement, the auditor should investigate the delay.

101.   B   Trace to cash disbursements journal.
          G   Ascertain reason for unusual delay.
          H   Inspect supporting documents for reconciling items not appearing on cutoff statement.
          I   Trace items on the bank reconciliation to cutoff statement.
          J   Trace items on the cutoff statement to bank reconciliation.

The auditor traces the outstanding checks to the cash disbursement journal and to the bank cutoff statement. In addition, the auditor traces all checks that cleared to make sure that they were properly listed.

102.   E   Inspect bank credit memo.

The credit memo generally does not appear on the cutoff statement, nor is it confirmed with the bank.

103.   E   Inspect bank credit memo.
          I   Trace items on the bank reconciliation to cutoff statement.

The bank credited the account for $720 instead of $270. The auditor should trace the item and reconcile it.

104.   C   Compare to 9/30/94 general ledger.

The company's books and records should agree with the balance.

NUMBER 9

A. SAS No 56 (AU 329) describes analytical procedures as:

- Comparison of current year account balances to balances for one or more comparable periods.
- Comparison of the current year account balances to anticipated results found in the company's budgets.
- Evaluation of the relationships of current year account balances to other current year balances for conformity with predictable patterns based on the company's experience.
- Comparison of current year account balances and financial relationships; for example, ratios with similar information for the industry in which the company operates.
- Study of the relationships of current year account balances with relevant nonfinancial information.

Analytical procedures are performed at any of three times during an engagement. Analytical procedures are required to be performed in the *planning phase* and *during the completion phase* of the audit. However, they are often done during the testing phase.

The purpose of applying analytical procedures in planning the audit is to:

- enhance the auditor's understanding of the client's business and the transactions and events that have occurred since the last audit.
- identify areas that may represent risks relevant to the audit.

Therefore the objective of the procedures is to identify unusual transactions and events, and amounts, ratios and trends that might indicate matters that have financial statement and audit planning ramifications.

Analytical procedures used in planning the audit generally use data aggregated at a high level. Furthermore, the sophistication, extent, and timing of the procedures which are based on the auditor's judgment may vary widely depending on the size and complexity of the client. For some entities, the procedures may consist of reviewing changes in account balances, or reviewing the minutes of the meetings of the board of directors. For other entities, the procedures might involve an extensive analysis of quarterly financial statements, mathematical times series and regression analysis, ratio, and trend analysis. In both cases, the analytical procedures, combined with the auditor's knowledge of the business, serve as a basis for additional inquiries and effective planning. Although analytical procedures used in planning the audit often use only financial data, sometimes relevant nonfinancial information is considered as well, such as number of employees, square footage of selling space, volume of goods produced, and similar information which may contribute to accomplishing the purpose of the procedures.

B. The auditor's decision to select analytical procedures as substantive tests is based on the auditor's judgment on the expected effectiveness and efficiency of the available procedures. For some assertions, analytical procedures are effective in providing the appropriate level of assurance. For other assertions, however, analytical procedures may not be as effective or efficient as tests of details in providing the desired level of assurance. The expected effectiveness and efficiency of an analytical procedure depends on several factors:

- Nature of the assertion.
- Plausibility and Predictability of the Relationship.
- Availability and Reliability of the Data.
- Precision of the Expectation.

C. The objective of analytical procedures used in the overall review stage of the audit is to assist the auditor in assessing the conclusions reached and in the evaluation of the overall financial statement presentation. A wide variety of analytical procedures may be useful for this purpose. The overall review would generally include reading the financial statements and notes and considering:

- the adequacy of evidence gathered in response to unusual or unexpected balances identified in planning the audit or in the course of the audit and
- unusual or unexpected balances or relationships that were not previously identified. Results of an overall review may indicate that additional evidence may be needed.

Analytical procedures may be effective and efficient tests for assertions in which potential misstatements would not be apparent from an examination of the detailed evidence or in which detailed evidence is not readily available. For example, comparisons of aggregate salaries paid with the number of personnel may indicate unauthorized payments that may not be apparent from testing individual transactions. The auditor needs to understand the reasons that make relationships plausible because data sometimes appear to be related when they are not, which could lead the auditor to erroneous conclusions. In addition, the presence of an unexpected relationship can provide important evidence when appropriately scrutinized. The auditor obtains assurance from analytical procedures based upon the consistency of the recorded amounts with expectations developed from data derived from other sources.

NUMBER 10

1.	Select 1	E
2.	Select 1	D
3.	Select 1	H
4.	Select 2	K, L
5.	Select 1	P
6.	Select 1	Q
7.	Select 1	A
8.	Select 1	U
9.	Select 1	B
10.	Select 2	A, J
11.	Select 1	E
12.	Select 2	J, L

NUMBER 11

a. Financial statement assertions are representations by management that are embodied in financial statement components.

b. In obtaining evidential matter in support of financial statement assertions, an auditor develops specific audit objectives in the light of those assertions.

c. In developing the audit objectives of a particular engagement, an auditor should consider the specific circumstances of the entity, including the nature of its economic activity and the accounting practices unique to its industry.

d. There is not necessarily a one-to-one relationship between audit objectives and procedures. Some auditing procedures may relate to more than one objective. On the other hand, a combination of auditing procedures may be needed to achieve a single objective. The procedures adopted should be adequate to achieve the audit objectives.

e. In selecting particular substantive tests to achieve audit objectives, an auditor considers, among other things, the risk of material misstatement in the financial statements, including the assessed levels of control risk, and the expected effectiveness and efficiency of such tests. An auditor's considerations also include the nature and materiality of the items being tested, the kinds and competence of available evidential matter, and the nature of the audit objective to be achieved.

NUMBER 12

a.

Confirmation #11 -- Atom. Adler should determine that Superior received and deposited Atom's check on December 28, 1996, by examining supporting documentation, e.g., the entry in the cash receipts journal and either Superior's deposit ticket or its bank statement. Adler should also determine the account to which the check was recorded and why it was not credited to Atom's account.

Confirmation #28 -- Baker. Adler should examine the terms of the sale and the shipping documents, especially whether the sale/shipment was to be FOB shipping point or FOB destination and the date the goods were shipped to Baker, to verify when the criteria for revenue recognition were met.

Confirmation #34 -- Clark. Adler should read Superior's correspondence files for evidence concerning the terms of the shipment to Clark to determine whether the criteria for revenue recognition were met.

Confirmation #41 -- Delta. Adler should investigate whether the merchandise was ever shipped to Delta and, if so, whether the sale was ever consummated, or whether the merchandise was returned, or whether Superior expects it to be returned.

Confirmation #58 -- Eagle. Adler should send a second request to Eagle providing the individual invoice numbers and amounts or attaching copies of the individual unpaid invoices that Eagle's accounts payable voucher system can verify. In the alternative, Adler should examine shipping documents and subsequent cash receipts.

Confirmation #67 -- Franklin. Adler should determine Franklin's correct address and send a second request.

Confirmation #71 -- Grove. Adler should determine when the check was received and where it was recorded by examining Superior's cash receipts records, bank statements, and accounts receivable detail.

Confirmation #86 -- Hall. No additional procedures are necessary to resolve this confirmation request, although Adler may want to trace the cash receipt to verify that Hall's check was actually received, deposited, and credited to Hall's account in January 1997.

b. When replies to positive confirmation requests have not been received, Miller should apply alternative substantive procedures to the nonresponding accounts receivable. Miller most likely would examine subsequent cash receipts for the accounts that have been paid. This would include matching such receipts with the actual items being paid. In addition, especially for receivables that have not been paid, Miller should inspect shipping documents or other client documentation (e.g., sales invoices, customers' purchase orders, etc.) that may provide evidence for the existence assertion. Miller should also consider reading any correspondence in Superior's files that may indicate disagreements with its customers about the amounts billed or the terms of the sales. In addition, Miller may consider contacting a reputable credit agency to verify the existence of customers who are new to the client or who Miller may be unfamiliar with.

c. The additional substantive procedures that Miller should consider performing to complete the audit of Superior's accounts receivable and related allowances include the following:

- Test the cut-off of sales, cash receipts, and sales returns and allowances.
- Evaluate the reasonableness of all allowances against receivables.
- Perform analytical procedures for accounts receivable, such as sales returns and allowances to sales, bad debt expense to net credit sales, accounts receivable turnover, and days' sales in receivables.
- Determine that Superior's revenue recognition policies are appropriate, including policies for consignment sales.
- Review activity after the balance sheet date for unusual transactions, such as large sales returns.
- Determine whether any accounts receivable are pledged or factored.
- Determine that the presentation and disclosure of accounts receivable and related allowances are in conformity with general accepted accounting principles.

NUMBER 13

a. In searching for DollarMart's unrecorded liabilities, Cook most likely would review DollarMart's cash disbursements journal near the conclusion of field work for checks written after year end and examine the supporting documentation, such as receiving reports and vendors' invoices, for selected disbursements to determine that the related accounts payable were properly recorded and to verify the cutoff of DollarMart's receipt of inventory. Alternatively, Cook could review DollarMart's voucher register for selected transactions similarly recorded shortly after year end and examine the supporting detail to identify items that should have been recorded at the balance sheet date, but were not.

Cook most likely would consider examining files of receiving reports and comparing them to recorded accounts payable entries. This would assist Cook in searching for significant merchandise received before year end to verify DollarMart's schedule of merchandise received but not yet billed. Cook may also consider inspecting DollarMart's files of unprocessed vendors' invoices, vendors' statements, and outstanding purchase orders, and comparing them with the receiving records and accounts payable entries for unrecorded liabilities.

Although confirmations are usually not the best source of evidence for unrecorded accounts payable, Cook may consider confirming selected accounts payable with vendors, including regular suppliers showing small or zero balances at year end.

Cook most likely would consider performing analytical procedures such as comparing gross margin, purchases, or certain expense account balances with those of the prior year to identify any large changes that should be investigated because they may represent unrecorded liabilities.

Additionally, Cook may tailor the management representation letter to impress upon DollarMart the need to be concerned about unrecorded accounts payable.

b. Cook most likely would perform more substantive auditing procedures at year end because of DollarMart's deficient control environment. For example, Cook would be more likely to confirm DollarMart's accounts payable. Tests would most likely be performed further into the subsequent year and at a lower dollar value or materiality level than otherwise.

NUMBER 14

a. Smith should inform Digit's audit committee about the inventory adjustments arising from the audit. These adjustments probably have a significant effect on the financial statements and should be included among the required matters to be communicated to the audit committee.

Dodd's consultation with another CPA firm concerning the previously unrecorded contingent liability should also be discussed with the audit committee. Smith should make the audit committee aware of Smith's views about any significant matters that were the subject of that consultation.

Smith should also inform the audit committee of any serious difficulties encountered in dealing with management related to the performance of the audit. Specifically, the two-week delay in completing the financial statements and the unavailability of Dodd, the controller, near the end of the field work should be reported to the audit committee.

Smith's disagreement with Dodd over the write-off of the overdue account receivable, even though satisfactorily resolved, should also be discussed with the audit committee.

Finally, the reportable conditions that Smith became aware of during the audit should be communicated to the audit committee.

b. In order for Digit's audit committee to understand the nature of the assurance that an audit provides, Smith should communicate the level of responsibility assumed under generally accepted auditing standards. The audit committee should understand that an audit is designed to obtain reasonable, rather than absolute, assurance about the financial statements.

Smith should also determine that Digit's audit committee is informed about the initial selection of and changes in significant accounting policies and their application. The audit committee would be interested in the methods Digit uses to account for significant unusual transactions and accounting policies in controversial or emerging areas for which there is no authoritative guidance or consensus.

The audit committee should also be informed about the accounting estimates that are based upon management's judgments, the processes used to formulate particularly sensitive estimates, and the basis for Smith's conclusions regarding the reasonableness of those estimates.

Additionally, Smith should discuss with the audit committee Smith's responsibility for other information in documents containing audited financial statements, such as the "Management's Discussion and Analysis of Financial Condition and Results of Operations" that is presented in the annual report to shareholders. Smith should also discuss any procedures performed and the results.

Smith should also discuss with the audit committee any major issues that were discussed with management in connection with the recurring retention of Smith's CPA firm, including discussions regarding the application of accounting principles and auditing standards.

Finally, Smith should be assured that the audit committee is informed about any irregularities and illegal acts that Smith becomes aware of during the audit unless those matters are clearly inconsequential. However, if senior management is involved in an irregularity or illegal act, Smith should communicate directly with the audit committee.

NUMBER 15

The working paper contains the following deficiencies:

The working paper was not initialed and dated by the audit assistant.

Negative confirmations not returned cannot be considered to be accounts "confirmed without exception."

The two positive confirmations that were sent but were unanswered are not accounted for.

There is no documentation of alternate procedures, possible scope limitation, or other working paper reference for the six accounts selected for confirmation that the client asked the auditor not to confirm.

The dollar amount and percent of the six accounts selected for confirmation that the client asked the auditor not to confirm is omitted from the "Dollars" columns for the "Total selected for testing."

The "Dollar--Percent" for "Confirmation Requests--Negatives" is incorrectly calculated at 10%.

There is no indication of follow-up or cross-referencing of the account confirmed--related party transaction.

The tickmark "‡" is used but is not explained in the tickmark legend.

There is no explanation or proposed disposition of the 10 differences aggregating $12,000.

The overall conclusion reached is not appropriate.

There is no notation that a projection from the sample to the population was made.

There is no reference to second requests.

Cross-referencing is incomplete, such as the 18 "Differences reported and resolved, no adjustment" and "Confirmation Requests" to confirmation control schedule.

NUMBER 16

1. Y
2. Y
3. N
4. Y
5. N
6. Y
7. Y
8. Y
9. Y
10. N
11. N
12. Y
13. Y
14. N

NUMBER 17

1. H
2. A
3. G
4. F
5. D
6. B
7. E

Chapter Three
Standards of Reporting

Chapter Three
Standards of Reporting

THE AUDITOR'S REPORT—INTRODUCTION

The auditor's report is the means by which his opinion is expressed on the financial statements of an enterprise. The financial statements are those of management, including all related disclosures. While the auditor may suggest adjustments and even draft footnotes for management to append to the financial statements, it should be kept in mind that the auditor's report is the only means by which the auditor can disclose without management's acquiescence.

The wording of the auditor's short-form report is **standard** for a very important reason. The report contains precisely the meaning the auditor wants to convey to readers of financial statements. Changes or the use of substitute words could give rise to doubt as to the meaning of the report and cause confusion among users as to the auditor's responsibility.

What does the standard short-form report mean—what are its important elements? The AICPA recommended form:

Independent Auditor's Report ← _(Title Required)_

To the Board of Directors and
Stockholders of ABC Company

We have audited the accompanying balance sheet of ABC Company as of [at] December 31, 20XX, and the related statements of income, retained earnings, and cash flows for the year then ended. These financial statements are the responsibility of the Company's management. Our responsibility is to express an opinion on these financial statements based on our audit.

We conducted our audit in accordance with auditing standards generally accepted in the United States of America. Those standards require that we plan and perform the audit to obtain reasonable assurance about whether the financial statements are free of material misstatement. An audit includes examining, on a test basis, evidence supporting the amounts and disclosures in the financial statements. An audit also includes assessing the accounting principles used and significant estimates made by management, as well as evaluating the overall financial statement presentation. We believe that our audit provides a reasonable basis for our opinion.

In our opinion, the financial statements referred to above present fairly, in all material respects, the financial position of ABC Company as of [at] December 31, 20XX, and the results of its operations and its cash flows for the year then ended in conformity with accounting principles generally accepted in the United States of America.

Firm's signature
Report date (must coincide with date on client representation letter).

Note these important elements contained in the above standard short-form report:

1. The auditor's opinion normally covers four financial statements:
    *   Balance sheet
    *   Income statement
    *   Retained earnings
    *   Statement of cash flows

2. The examination was made in accordance with generally accepted auditing standards (GAAS). By this statement, the auditor states that the General Standards, the Standards of Field Work and Reporting Standards have been observed in forming an opinion. When the auditor makes this statement, the responsibility assumed encompasses the total weight of these standards as formulated by the accounting profession.

3. That the financial statements "present fairly." In this context, the term is not one of precise measurement, but conveys an exactitude of presentation in which reasonable and qualified professionals may differ, but within immaterial limits.

4. That the financial statements are in conformity with generally accepted accounting principles (GAAP). GAAP involve not only those principles that are the subject of pronouncements by the AICPA and other professional groups and regulatory authorities, but those which become acceptable through common usage by business. Issuances of the Financial Accounting Standards Board (FASB) and its predecessors prevail where a conflict exists. Obviously, if a CPA makes this statement in his report, it presumes that he knows generally accepted accounting principles and that he has determined that the management of the enterprise has followed these principles in preparing their financial statements.

5. An assertion by the auditor of a belief that the audit provides a reasonable basis for his opinion.

    Note also that the report is in three paragraphs:
    1. The first paragraph is called the *"introductory" paragraph*.
    2. The second is called the *"scope" paragraph*, including any limitations.
    3. The third is called the *"opinion" paragraph*.

The First Standard of Reporting
The report shall state whether the financial statements are presented in accordance with generally accepted accounting principles.

A. Includes not only principles and practices but also methods of applying them.

B. May require exercise of auditor's judgment as to general acceptance where no formal pronouncement has been made.

C. **THE MEANING OF "PRESENT FAIRLY IN CONFORMITY WITH GENERALLY ACCEPTED ACCOUNTING PRINCIPLES" IN THE INDEPENDENT AUDITOR'S REPORT (SAS No. 69)**

    1. **GAAP Defined**
        The first standard of reporting requires an auditor who has examined financial statements in accordance with generally accepted auditing standards to state in his report whether the statements are presented in accordance with generally accepted accounting principles. The phrase "generally accepted accounting principles" is a technical accounting term which encompasses the conventions, rules, and procedures necessary to define accepted accounting practice at a particular time. It includes not only broad guidelines of general application, but also detailed practices and procedures. Those conventions, rules, and procedures provide a standard by which to measure financial presentations.

    2. **Relationship of "Fairness" to GAAP**
        The independent auditor's judgment concerning the "fairness" of the over-all presentation of financial statements should be applied within the framework of generally accepted accounting principles. Without that framework, the auditor would have no uniform standard for judging the presentation of financial position, results of operations, and cash flows in financial statements.

The auditor's opinion that financial statements present fairly should be based on his judgment as to whether:

a. The accounting principles selected and applied have *general acceptance.*
b. The accounting principles *are appropriate* in the circumstances.
c. The financial statements, including the related notes, *are informative about matters* that may affect their use, understanding, and interpretation.
d. The information presented in the financial statements is *classified and summarized in a reasonable manner;* that is, neither too detailed nor too condensed.
e. The financial statements *reflect the underlying events and transactions* in a manner that presents the financial position, results of operations, and cash flows stated within a range of acceptable limits; that is, limits that are reasonable and practicable to attain in financial statements.

Generally accepted accounting principles are relatively objective; that is, they are sufficiently established so that independent auditors usually agree on their existence. Nevertheless, the identification of an accounting principle as generally accepted in particular circumstances requires judgment. No single source of reference exists for all established accounting principles. Rule 203 of the AICPA Code of Professional Ethics requires compliance with accounting principles promulgated by the FASB and its predecessors. Other sources of established accounting principles are AICPA accounting interpretations, AICPA industry audit guides and accounting guides, and industry accounting practices. Depending on their relevance in the circumstances, the auditor may also wish to refer to APB statements, AICPA statements of position, pronouncements of other professional associations and regulatory agencies, such as the Securities and Exchange Commission, and accounting textbooks and articles. Also, the Governmental Accounting Standards Board (GASB) is considered a source of GAAP for governmental units.

Generally accepted accounting principles recognize the importance of recording transactions in accordance with their substance. The auditor should consider whether **the substance of transactions differs materially from their form**.

The auditor should be familiar with alternative accounting principles that may be applicable to the transaction or facts under consideration and realize that an accounting principle may have only limited usage but still have general acceptance. On occasion, established accounting principles may not exist for recording and presenting a specific event or transaction because of developments such as new legislation or the evolution of a new type of business transaction.

Specifying the circumstances in which one accounting principle should be selected from among alternative principles is the function of bodies having authority to establish accounting principles. **When criteria for selection among alternative accounting principles have not been established to relate accounting methods to circumstances, the auditor may conclude that more than one accounting principle is appropriate in the circumstance.** The auditor should recognize, however, that there may be unusual circumstances in which the selection and application of specific accounting principles from among alternative principles may make the financial statements taken as a whole misleading.

D. *If the financial statements are not in accordance with GAAP, the auditor must so state in his report.* Generally, the effect would be an "except for" opinion (qualified). However, if in the auditor's judgment the departure is sufficiently material and pervasive that the statements are not presented fairly in accordance with GAAP, the auditor will issue an adverse opinion. The report must contain an additional explanatory paragraph in which the auditor would disclose the effect of the departure on income, earnings per share, retained earnings and the specific item in question. This paragraph would become the third paragraph of the report and it would directly follow the "scope" (second) paragraph of the auditor's report. The opinion paragraph would include a direct reference to the explanatory paragraph as a basis for the opinion.

EXHIBIT I
GAAP HIERARCHY SUMMARY* (SAS 69)

	Nongovernmental Entities	State and Local Governments	Federal Government
Established Accounting Principles	a. FASB Statements and Interpretations, APB Opinions, and AICPA Accounting Research Bulletins.	a. GASB Statements and Interpretations, plus AICPA and FASB pronouncements if made applicable to state and local governments by a GASB Statement or Interpretation.	a. Officially established accounting principles, consisting of Federal Accounting Standards Advisory Board (FASAB) Statements and interpretations, as well as AICPA and FASB pronouncements specifically made applicable to federal governmental entities by FASAB Statements or Interpretations. FASAB Statements and Interpretations will be periodically incorporated in a publication by the FASAB.
	b. FASB Technical Bulletins, AICPA Industry Audit and Accounting Guides, and AICPA Statements of Position.	b. GASB Technical Bulletins, and the following pronouncements if specifically made applicable to state and local governments by the AICPA: AICPA Industry Audit and Accounting Guides and AICPA Statements of Position.	b. Consists of FASAB Technical Bulletins and, if specifically made applicable to federal governmental entities by the AICPA and cleared by the FASAB, AICPA Industry Audit and Accounting Guides and AICPA Statements of Position.
	c. Consensus positions of the FASB Emerging Issues Task Force and AICPA Practice Bulletins.	c. Consensus positions of the GASB Emerging Issues Task Force and AICPA Practice Bulletins if specifically made applicable to state and local governments by the AICPA.	c. Consists of AICPA AcSEC Practice Bulletins if specifically made applicable to federal governmental entities and cleared by the FASAB, as well as Technical Releases of the Accounting and Auditing Policy Committee of the FASAB.
	d. AICPA accounting interpretations, "Qs and As" published by the FASB staff, as well as industry practices widely recognized and prevalent.	d. "Qs and As" published by the GASB staff, as well as industry practices widely recognized and prevalent.	d. Consists of implementation guides published by the FASAB staff, as well as practices that are widely recognized and prevalent in the federal government.
Other Accounting Literature**	Other accounting literature, including FASB Concepts Statements; APB Statements; AICPA Issues Papers; International Accounting Standards Committee Statements; GASB Statements, Interpretations, and Technical Bulletins; pronouncements of other professional associations or regulatory agencies; AICPA *Technical Practice Aids*; and accounting textbooks, handbooks, and articles.	Other accounting literature, including GASB Concepts Statements; pronouncements in categories (a) through (d) of the hierarchy for nongovernmental entities when not specifically made applicable to state and local governments; APB Statements; FASB Concepts Statements; AICPA Issues Papers; International Accounting Standards Committee Statements; pronouncements of other professional associations or regulatory agencies; AICPA *Technical Practice Aids*; and accounting textbooks, handbooks, and articles.	

* Paragraph references correspond to the paragraphs of this Statement that describe the categories of the GAAP hierarchy.

** In the absence of established accounting principles, the auditor may consider other accounting literature, depending on its relevance in the circumstances.

Departures from GAAP

1. Defined as a material misrepresentation in the financial statements due to intentional (fraud) or unintentional (mistake/error) departures from accounting pronouncements *(i.e., Exhibit 1).*

2. Materiality is a matter of auditor's judgment, and it is generally defined as what a "reasonable person" would consider significant.

3. Material departures from GAAP would cause the auditor to issue either:

Qualified		Adverse
"Except for"	or	Opinion
Opinion		

   The choice is a matter of auditor's judgment.

4. **Qualified "Except for" Opinion** -- on the whole, the financial statements present fairly, but there are material errors in the financial statement that the user should be concerned with.

5. **Adverse Opinion** -- the financial statements are, on the whole, misleading. Any potential user of the financial statements may therefore reach conclusions about the entity's financial position and results of operations that are inappropriate. In other words, the financial statements are not reliable and should not be used for decision making purposes.

6. Report Example -- Departure from GAAP.

   ### _Departure Material "Except for" Opinion_
   Standard introductory paragraph
   Standard Scope paragraph

   (*Explanatory paragraph*)
   "The company has excluded from property and debt in the accompanying balance sheet certain lease obligations, which, in our opinion, should be capitalized in order to conform with generally accepted accounting principles. If these lease obligations were capitalized, property would be increased by $......., long-term debt by $......., and retained earnings by $....... as of December 31, 20XX, and net income and earnings per share would be increased (decreased) by $....... and $....... respectively for the year then ended."

   (*Opinion Paragraph*)
   "In our opinion, except for the effects of not capitalizing lease obligations, as discussed in the preceding paragraph, the financial statements present fairly..."

   ### _Departure Very Material Adverse Opinion_ (Financial statements are misleading).
   Standard Introductory Paragraph
   Standard Scope Paragraph
   Explanatory Paragraph as above

   (*Opinion paragraph*)
   "In our opinion, because of the failure to capitalize lease obligations, as discussed in the preceding paragraph, the financial statements do not present fairly..."

The Second Standard of Reporting

The report shall identify those circumstances in which such principles have not been consistently observed in the current period in relation to the preceding period.

A. The objective of this standard is to assure that the comparability of financial statements between periods has not been affected by changes in accounting principles, practices, or methods of application. *Note that the audit report makes no reference to consistency unless there has been a change that would require the auditor's report to be modified.*

B. Types of accounting changes:
   1. Accounting changes—Changes in **accounting principles** or **changes in the reporting entity**.
      a. Examples of changes in accounting principles:
         - LIFO to FIFO
         - Completed Contract to Percentage of Completion
         - Changes in depreciation methods
      b. Examples of changes in the reporting entity:
         - Consolidated statements in place of combined statements
      c. ***These changes require that the auditor modify his standard report if material*** *(see Part C below):*
   2. An error in previously issued financial statements:
      a. ***Does not require modification of the auditor's report;*** however, footnote disclosure is required in the financial statements.
      b. Prior years' financial statements must be restated to reflect the error correction.
   3. Changes in classification of items in the financial statements:
      a. ***Does not require modification of the auditor's report.***
      b. Prior years' financial statements should be restated, if applicable.

C. The auditor has a responsibility to determine if there is a sound business reason for the change. There is a presumption that accounting principles, once adopted, should not be changed unless the new principle would present the results of operations and financial position of the entity more fairly than the old principle. This is a subjective decision on the part of the auditor, not the client, because the auditor is expressing the opinion on the client's financial statements.

In arriving at the decision, the auditor would consider the guidance in SAS No. 69. (Refer to SAS No. 69 reproduced earlier in this chapter.)

If the auditor concludes that the client has sufficient justification for changing an accounting principle, the auditor would be <u>required</u> to modify the audit report as follows:

AUDITOR'S REPORT—REFERENCE TO CHANGE IN GAAP

Independent Auditor's Report

To the Board of Directors and
Stockholders of ABC Company

(Same first and second paragraphs as the standard report.)

In our opinion, the financial statements referred to above present fairly, in all material respects, the financial position of X Company as of December 31, 20XX, and the results of its operations and its cash flows for the year then ended in conformity with accounting principles generally accepted in the United States of America.

As discussed in Note X to the financial statements, the Company changed its method of computing depreciation in 20XX.

Firm's signature
Date of report

Note: The above is not a qualified opinion. It is an unqualified opinion with an "emphasis of a matter" paragraph.

Should the auditor conclude that sufficient justification **has not been** demonstrated by the client, a qualified except for or adverse opinion should be issued on the financial statements. For audit report purposes, a changing GAAP without sufficient justification is considered to be a departure from GAAP. A qualified report because the auditor has concluded the client does not have reasonable justification for a GAAP change is illustrated below:

**MANAGEMENT DOES NOT HAVE REASONABLE JUSTIFICATION
FOR A CHANGE IN ACCOUNTING PRINCIPLE**

Independent Auditor's Report

To the Board of Directors and
Stockholders of ABC Company

(Same first and second paragraphs as the standard report.)

As disclosed in Note X to the financial statements, the Company adopted the first-in, first-out method of accounting for its inventories in 20XX, whereas it previously used the last-in, first-out method. Although use of the first-in, first-out method is in conformity with generally accepted accounting principles, in our opinion, the Company has not provided reasonable justification for making this change as required by generally accepted accounting principles.

In our opinion, except for the change in accounting principle discussed in the preceding paragraph, the financial statements referred to above present fairly, in all material respects, the financial position of X Company as of December 31, 20XX, and the results of its operations and its cash flows for the year then ended in conformity with accounting principles generally accepted in the United States of America.

Firm's signature
Date of report

The Third Standard of Reporting
Informative disclosures in the financial statements are to be regarded as reasonably adequate unless otherwise stated in the report.

A. No reference is made in the auditor's report with respect to disclosure unless the auditor feels that adequate disclosure has not been made.

B. GAAP requires certain disclosures to be made in the footnotes to the financial statements or on the financial statements themselves.

C. Inadequate disclosures in the financial statements are considered to be departures from GAAP and are handled in the auditor's report in a similar manner. That is, the auditor must choose between issuing a qualified except for or adverse opinion.

D. Following is an example of a qualified opinion:

QUALIFIED OPINION FOR A DISCLOSURE DEPARTURE

Independent Auditor's Report

To the Board of Directors and
Stockholders of X Company

We have audited the accompanying balance sheet of X Company as of December 31, 20XX, and the related statements of income, retained earnings, and cash flows for the year then ended. These financial statements are the responsibility of the Company's management. Our responsibility is to express an opinion on these financial statements based on our audit.

We conducted our audit in accordance with auditing standards generally accepted in the United States of America. Those standards require that we plan and perform the audit to obtain reasonable assurance about whether the financial statements are free of material misstatement. An audit includes examining, on a test basis, evidence supporting the amounts and disclosures in the financial statements. An audit also includes assessing the accounting principles used and significant estimates made by management, as well as evaluating the overall financial statement presentation. We believe that our audit provides a reasonable basis for our opinion.

The Company's financial statements do not disclose the amount of future commitments under long-term operating leases. In our opinion, disclosure of that information is required by generally accepted accounting principles.

In our opinion, except for the omission of the information discussed in the preceding paragraph, the financial statements referred to above present fairly, in all material respects, the financial position of X Company as of December 31, 20XX, and the results of its operations and its cash flows for the year then ended in conformity with accounting principles generally accepted in the United States of America.

Firm's signature
Report date

E. **Auditor's Responsibility—Disclosure of Events Subsequent to the Audit Date (Subsequent Events)**
 1. The term "subsequent events" applies to events or transactions which occur after the balance sheet date, but prior to the issuance of the financial statements and the auditor's report.

 2. **Two Types of Subsequent Events**
     a. Events that provide additional *evidence concerning conditions that existed at year-end*. These types of events require adjustment of the financial statements.

     Examples:
     - Settlement of an accrued liability in excess of its recorded amount.
     - Evidence that an account receivable is no longer collectible because of bankruptcy proceedings.

     b. Events that provide *evidence of conditions that did not exist at year-end* and **should not result in adjustment of the financial statements**. These events require disclosure if material.

     Examples:
     - Sale of a bond or capital stock issue.
     - Purchase of a business.
     - Settlement of litigation when the event giving rise to the claim took place subsequent to the balance sheet date.
     - Loss of plant or inventories as a result of fire or flood.
     - Losses on receivables resulting from conditions arising subsequent to the balance sheet date.

3. **Auditing Procedures in the Subsequent Period**
   The "subsequent period" extends from the balance sheet date to the date of the auditor's report. The auditor's report is dated at the conclusion of field work.

   While the auditor is not expected to conduct a continuing review of matters during the subsequent period, there are certain specific procedures to be applied to transactions after the balance sheet date such as:

   a. Procedures to assure that proper cut-offs have been made. Cut-offs most generally relate to audit procedures to assure that transactions have been recorded in the correct accounting period and that material items have been given consistent treatment.

      Cut-Off Examples:
      (1) Invoices are received at year-end but arrival of the goods has been delayed and the goods were not included in the ending inventory count. If the invoices are recorded as purchases, net income will be understated.
      (2) Sales orders are received at year-end, but shipment takes place at a later date. If sales are recorded and the goods are included in the ending inventory count, net income will be overstated.

   b. Consideration of data to assist the auditor in evaluating the recorded amount of assets and liabilities as of the balance sheet date. In this connection, any information which adds to the reliability of the estimates made as of year-end should be used. Examples are: collectibility of receivables, realization of investments, market value of inventory at year-end (if pertinent).
   c. Read and compare the latest interim statements, if any, with the statements being reported upon. Make inquiries as to officers and others responsible as to whether interim statements were prepared on the same basis as those under examination.
   d. Make further inquiries as to (1) any contingent liabilities or commitments, (2) significant changes in capital stock, long-term debt, or working capital, (3) update the status of items in the financial statements accounted for on a tentative basis, (4) any unusual adjustments have been made.
   e. Read the minutes of meetings, directors' and others.
   f. Obtain a lawyer's letter as to description and evaluation of litigation, claims, and contingent liabilities as of the balance sheet date and during the subsequent period.
   g. Obtain a letter of representation, dated as of the date of the auditor's report, from the chief executive officer and chief financial officer as to subsequent events that might in the officer's opinion require adjustment or disclosure of the financial statements as of year end. (Note: generally this date is considered to be the date of client representation letter.)

4. **Dating of the Auditor's Report**
   The completion of field work should be used as the date of auditor's report. The auditor has no responsibility for audit procedures as to events subsequent to the date of his report.

5. **Events Subsequent to Date of Report But Before Issuance**
   When events subsequent to the date of the report come to the auditor's attention, he should:
   - Adjust the financial statements if necessary.
   - The date of report need not be changed unless the event is disclosed.
   - If the event is disclosed, whether or not adjustment is made, the auditor should either:
     a. Date his report as of the latest date. This extends his responsibility for all subsequent events up to the new date.
     b. Use "dual dating," in which his report date is unchanged except for the specific event. This relieves the auditor of responsibility for other matters arising after the end of field work.
        - If the event results in a qualified opinion, the auditor should give the report a new date or use "dual dating."

- If for any reason the auditor reissues his report, he should use the original report date. Where a subsequent event has been brought to the auditor's attention, a reissuance of the report may not be desirable. Regardless, the auditor should use care to avoid the report dating problems outlined previously.

The Fourth Standard of Reporting

The report shall either contain an expression of opinion regarding the financial statements, taken as a whole, or an assertion to the effect that an opinion cannot be expressed; the reasons therefor should be stated. In all cases where an auditor's name is associated with financial statements, the report should contain a clear-cut indication of the character of the auditor's examination, if any, and the degree of responsibility he is taking.

The objective of this standard is to enable users of financial statements an opportunity to determine the extent to which the financial statements may be relied upon. The audit report is the only means of communication that the auditor has with the user of financial statements. The audit report is the representation of the auditor, and, as such, sets forth the scope of examination and his opinion as to the fairness, adherence to GAAP, and consistency of the financial statements and disclosures. Anytime an auditor is associated, whether in an auditing capacity or preparer of financial statements, he must indicate the scope of his engagement and the conclusion reached (opinion) if any.

OTHER REPORTING CONSIDERATIONS

Scope Limitations

A. *Definition of Scope Limitation:* The inability to gather sufficient competent evidential matter upon which to base an opinion.

B. May occur because of:
   1. Timing of audit work
   2. Inability to gather evidence
   3. Inadequate internal controls
   4. Inadequate accounting records

C. Usually, if material, results in a disclaimer of an opinion; however, a qualified "except for" opinion may be issued.

D. Typical scope limitations tested on the audit exam include:
   1. Receivable not confirmed
      a. No restrictions imposed by client and auditor performs alternate procedures—unqualified opinion.
      b. Client restricts confirmation procedures—usually results in disclaimer of opinion.

   2. Ending inventory observation omitted
      a. Auditor is able to perform. Alternate procedures available (perpetual records, past year-end count and reconcile to year-end amounts). Issue unqualified opinion.
      b. Auditor is not able to perform. Alternate procedure unavailable. Disclaim or qualify opinion based upon materiality.
      c. Client does not allow observation of inventory count —always disclaim if material.

E. Failure of the client to issue a representation letter as required by SAS No. 85 and failure of the client's attorney to respond to a confirmation request (SAS No. 12) always are considered to be material scope limitations. The auditor's report would thus have to be qualified or would contain a disclaimer of an opinion.

AUDITOR'S REPORT QUALIFIED FOR A SCOPE LIMITATION

Independent Auditor's Report

To the Board of Directors and
Stockholders of X Company

(Same first paragraph as the standard report)

Except as discussed in the following paragraph, we conducted our audit in accordance with auditing standards generally accepted in the United States of America. Those standards require that we plan and perform the audit to obtain reasonable assurance about whether the financial statements are free of material misstatement. An audit includes examining, on a test basis, evidence supporting the amounts and disclosures in the financial statements. An audit also includes assessing the accounting principles used and significant estimates made by management, as well as evaluating the overall financial statement presentation. We believe that our audits provide a reasonable basis for our opinion.

We were unable to obtain audited financial statements supporting the Company's investment in a foreign affiliate stated at $XXX at December 31, 20XX, or its equity in earnings of that affiliate of $XXX, which is included in net income for the year then ended as described in Note X to the financial statements; nor were we able to satisfy ourselves about the carrying value of the investments in the foreign affiliate or the equity in its earnings by other auditing procedures.

In our opinion, except for the effects of such adjustments, if any, as might have been determined to be necessary had we been able to examine evidence regarding the foreign affiliate investment and earnings, the financial statements referred to in the first paragraph present fairly, in all material respects, the financial position of X Company as of December 31, 20XX, and the results of its operations and its cash flows for the year then ended in conformity with accounting principles generally accepted in the United States of America.

Firm's signature
Date of report

DISCLAIMER OF OPINION FOR A SCOPE LIMITATION

Independent Auditor's Report

To the Board of Directors and
Stockholders of X Company

We were engaged to audit the accompanying balance sheet of X Company as of December 31, 20XX, and the related statements of income, retained earnings, and cash flows for the year then ended. These financial statements are the responsibility of the Company's management.

(Second paragraph of standard report should be omitted)

The Company did not make a count of its physical inventory in 20XX, stated in the accompanying financial statements at $XXX as of December 31, 20XX. Furthermore, evidence supporting the cost of property and equipment acquired prior to December 31, 20XX, is no longer available. The Company's records do not permit the application of other auditing procedures to inventories or property and equipment.

Since the Company did not take physical inventories and we were not able to apply other auditing procedures to satisfy ourselves as to inventory quantities and the cost of property and equipment, the scope of our work was not sufficient to enable us to express, and we do not express, an opinion on the accompanying financial statements.

Firm's signature
Date of report

Uncertainties

A. Definition: Matters involving future events, the outcome of which is not susceptible of reasonable estimation at the date of the auditor's report. The matter is expected to be resolved at a future date when sufficient evidence concerning its outcome will be available.

B. Examples include: lawsuits, tax claims, contracts in dispute, questions concerning going concern.

C. FASB No. 5, Accounting for Contingencies, provides guidance regarding whether an uncertainty would be reflected in the financial statements as an accrual or as a footnote disclosure only.

1. In order for a loss contingency (gain contingencies are never recognized) to be accrued, the loss must be both probable and the amount of loss must be estimable. *In this case the auditor would not need to modify his report for the uncertainty, if the client agrees to reflect the liability in the financial statements.*

2. If the loss contingency did not meet the criteria for accrual, then footnote disclosure would be made in the financial statements and *the auditor may modify his report to* **add a fourth paragraph immediately following the opinion paragraph. Such a paragraph would be considered as an emphasis of matter in the financial statements and not a qualification.**

> *Note:* *Modification of the auditor's report by adding an additional paper is not required for loss contingencies that are footnoted in the financial statements. However, the auditor may decide to emphasize the matter by including an additional paragraph to the standard report.*

> *Example*: **(If auditor decides to refer to the uncertainty)**
> Standard Introductory Paragraph
> Standard Scope Paragraph
> Standard Opinion Paragraph

EXPLANATORY PARAGRAPH
DESCRIBING AN UNCERTAINTY

As discussed in Note X to the financial statements, the Company is a defendant in a lawsuit alleging infringement of certain patent rights and claiming royalties and punitive damages. The Company has filed a counteraction, and preliminary hearings and discovery proceedings on both actions are in progress. The ultimate outcome of the litigation cannot presently be determined. Accordingly, no provision for any liability that may result upon adjudication has been made in the accompanying financial statements.

3. If the auditor is unable to obtain sufficient evidential matter to support management's assertions about the nature of a matter involving an uncertainty and its presentation in the financial statements, the auditor should consider the need to qualify or disclaim an opinion for a scope limitation.

4. If the auditor concludes that the matter involving an uncertainty is not adequately disclosed or valued correctly in the financial statements, the auditor should express a qualified "except for" or adverse opinion depending upon the materiality of the item.

The Auditor's Consideration of an Entity's Ability to Continue as a Going Concern (SAS No. 59)

Going concern relates to the entity's ability to continue to meet its obligations as they become due without substantial disposal of assets, restructuring of debt, externally forced revisions of its operations, or similar actions.

Auditing standards do not require any specific auditing procedures to be employed with respect to the going concern issue. Rather the standards state that normal auditing procedures should be sufficient in determining whether a going concern issue exists. Even though no specific procedures are required, the auditor must document his/her conclusions with respect to the going concern issue in the audit workpapers.

The Auditor's Responsibility—Going Concern

A. The auditor is not responsible for predicting future conditions or events. The fact that the entity may cease to exist as a going concern subsequent to receiving a report from the auditor that does not refer to substantial doubt, even within one year following the date of the financial statements, does not, in itself, indicate inadequate performance by the auditor.
B. The auditor has a responsibility to evaluate whether there is substantial doubt about the entity's ability to continue as a going concern for a *reasonable period of time, not to exceed one year beyond the date of the financial statements being audited.*
C. The auditor's evaluation is based on knowledge of relevant conditions and events that exist at or have occurred prior to the completion of field work.
D. Information about such conditions or events is obtained from the application of auditing procedures planned and performed to achieve audit objectives in the financial statements being audited. No special audit procedures must be implemented.

The Auditor's Consideration of Conditions and Events

A. In performing audit procedures, the auditor may identify information about certain conditions or events that, when considered in the aggregate, indicate that there could be substantial doubt. For example:
   1. Negative trends (for example, recurring operating losses).
   2. Other indications of possible financial difficulties (for example, default on loan or similar agreements).
   3. Internal matters (for example, work stoppages or other labor difficulties).
   4. External matters that have occurred (for example, legal proceedings, legislation, or similar matters that might jeopardize an entity's ability to operate.

Consideration of Management's Plans

A. If, after considering the identified conditions and events in the aggregate, the auditor believes that there is substantial doubt, he should consider management's plans for dealing with the adverse effects of the conditions and events.
B. The auditor should obtain information about the plans and consider whether it is likely that the adverse effects will be mitigated for a reasonable period of time and that such plans can be effectively implemented.
C. The auditor's considerations relating to management plans may include the following:
   1. Plans to dispose of assets.
   2. Plans to borrow money or restructure debt.
   3. Plans to reduce or delay expenditures.
   4. Plans to increase ownership equity.
D. When evaluating management's plans, the auditor should identify those elements that are particularly significant to overcoming the adverse effects of the conditions and events and should plan and perform auditing procedures to obtain evidence about them.

Consideration of Financial Statement Effects

When, after considering management's plans, the auditor concludes that there is substantial doubt, he should consider the possible effects on the financial statements and the adequacy of the related disclosures.

Consideration of the Effects on the Auditor's Report

A. If, after considering identified conditions and events and management's plans, the auditor concludes that substantial doubt remains, the audit report should include an explanatory paragraph (following the opinion paragraph) to reflect that conclusion. An example follows:

> The accompanying financial statements have been prepared assuming that Company Y will continue as a going concern. As discussed in Note X to the financial statements, Company Y has suffered recurring losses from operations and has a net capital deficiency that raises *substantial doubt** about the entity's ability to *continue as a going concern**. Management's plans in regard to these matters are also described in Note X. The financial statements do not include any adjustments that might result from the outcome of this uncertainty.
>
> _____
>
> *Must include these terms

> This additional paragraph does not constitute a qualified opinion but rather it is regarded as an emphasis paragraph.

B. If the auditor concludes that the entity's disclosures with respect to the entity's ability to continue as a going concern for a reasonable period of time are inadequate, a departure from GAAP exists. This may result in either a qualified (except for) or an adverse opinion.

USING THE WORK AND REPORTS OF OTHER AUDITORS

The auditor must decide whether he is the principal auditor. His decision is based on:
- Materiality of the portion audited by him.
- Extent of over-all knowledge of financial statements.
- Importance of components audited by him.

If the auditor decides he is the principal auditor, depending on the circumstances, he may decide to:
1. Express an opinion without reference to other auditor(s).
2. Refer to the other auditor's examination and indicate the division of responsibility in the rendering of the opinion.
3. Qualify or disclaim an opinion in that he cannot assume responsibility for the other auditor's work insofar as it relates to the principal auditor's opinion.

Principal auditor would be able to use the other auditor's report, with or without reference, if:
1. The other auditor is an associated or correspondent firm whose work is acceptable to the principal auditor, or
2. The work is performed under the principal auditor's guidance and control, or
3. The principal auditor takes steps to satisfy himself as to the other auditor's examination, or
4. The portion of the financial statements involving the other auditor is not material.

Regardless, the principal auditor should:
1. Make inquiries concerning the professional reputation and independence of the other auditor to one or more of the following:
   a. AICPA and/or state society
   b. Other practitioners
   c. Bankers and other audit grantors

2. Obtain a representation from the other auditor that he is independent under AICPA and SEC requirements.

3. Ascertain through the other auditor:
   a. That he is aware what component he is to examine and that his report will be relied on by the principal auditor.
   b. That he is familiar with GAAP and GAAS.
   c. That he knows the required statements and schedules to be filed with regulatory agencies (SEC).
   d. That a review of matters affecting elimination of intercompany transactions and uniformity of accounting practices among the components will be made.

   Note: Inquiries under 1 and 3 (b) and (c) will ordinarily not be necessary if the principal auditor already knows the professional reputation of the other auditor.

   If he decides **not** to make reference to the other auditor's report, he should also **consider** one or more of the following procedures:

   1. Visit the other auditor and discuss the procedures followed.
   2. Review the audit program and/or workpapers of the other auditor.

   If the other auditor's report is qualified, the principal auditor must decide, based on the materiality and nature of the qualification, the effect on his report. If it **is not material**, he may omit reference to the qualification in his own unqualified opinion. When the other auditor's report is presented, the principal auditor may wish to make reference to the qualification and its disposition.

USING THE WORK AND REPORTS OF OTHER AUDITORS

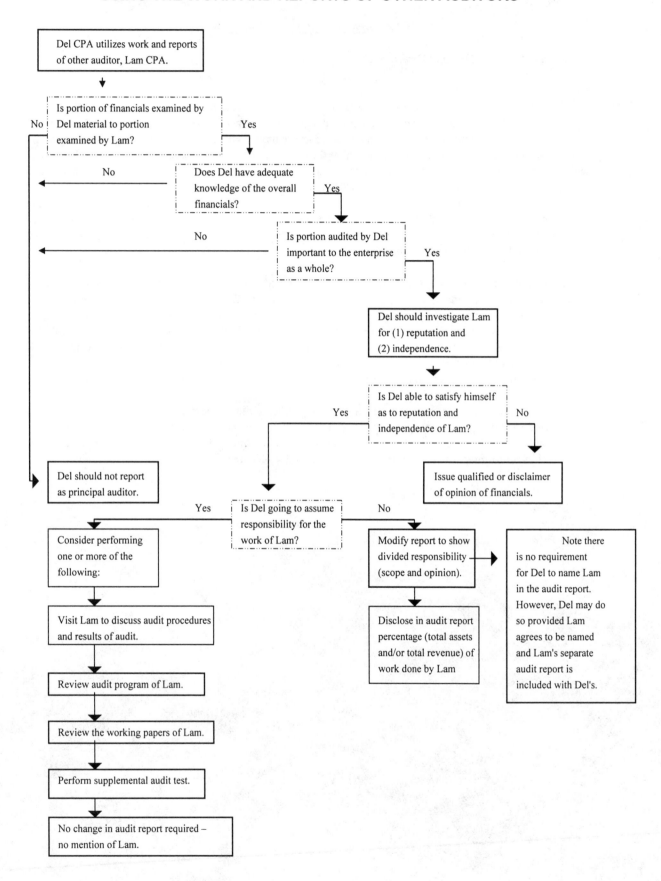

EXAMPLE OF REFERENCE TO OTHER AUDITOR

Independent Auditor's Report

Stockholders and Board of Directors
XYZ Corporation

We have audited the accompanying consolidated balance sheets of XYZ Corporation as of July 31, 20XX and 20YY, and the related consolidated statements of income, retained earnings, and cash flows for the years then ended. These financial statements are the responsibility of the Company's management. Our responsibility is to express an opinion on these financial statements based on our audits. We did not audit the financial statements of ABC Corporation, a consolidated subsidiary in which the Company had an equity interest of 84% as of July 31, 20XX, which statements reflect total assets of $2,400,000 and $2,200,000 as of July 31, 20XX and 20YY, respectively, and total revenues of $3,400,000 and $3,000,000 for the years then ended. Those statements were audited by other auditors whose report has been furnished to us, and our opinion, insofar as it relates to the amounts included for ABC Corporation, is based solely on the report of the other auditors.

We conducted our audits in accordance with auditing standards generally accepted in the United States of America. Those standards require that we plan and perform the audit to obtain reasonable assurance about whether the financial statements are free of material misstatement. An audit includes examining, on a test basis, evidence supporting the amounts and disclosures in the financial statements. An audit also includes assessing the accounting principles used and significant estimates made by management, as well as evaluating the overall financial statement presentation. We believe that our audits and the report of other auditors provide a reasonable basis for our opinion.

In our opinion, based on our audits and the report of other auditors, the consolidated financial statements referred to above present fairly, in all material respects, the financial position of XYZ Corporation as of December 31, 20XX and 20YY, and the results of its operations and its cash flows for the years then ended in conformity with accounting principles generally accepted in the United States of America.

Signature
Date

SUMMARY OF AUDITOR'S REPORTS

Circumstances	Type of Opinion			
	Unqualified	Qualified	Adverse	Disclaimer
1. Departure from GAAP		X	X	
2. Inadequate Disclosure		X	X	
3. Uncertainty				
a. Adequately disclosed or adjusted in financial statements	X			
b. Adequately disclosed but auditor unwilling to issue unqualified opinion because of **potential** adverse impact of uncertainty.				X
c. Not adequately disclosed or adjusted in financial statements*		X	X	
4. Going Concern				
a. Adequately Disclosed in financial statements.	X			
b. Not adequately disclosed*		X	X	
5. Scope Limitations		X		X
6. Auditor Lacks Independence				X
7. Change in GAAP (consistency)				
a. Newly adopted principle not GAAP*		X	X	
b. Adequate justification for change	X			
c. No adequate justification for change*		X	X	
d. Incorrect method for accounting for the change*		X	X	
8. Using the work of other auditors				
a. No reference in consolidated audit report	X			
b. Reference in consolidated audit report	X			
c. Other auditor refers to a departure from GAAP in separate report.				
1). Not material to consolidated financial statement presentation	X			
2). Material to consolidated financial statement presentation*		X	X	

* Reported on as departure from GAAP/inadequate disclosure.

SUMMARY OF MODIFICATIONS
TO STANDARD AUDITOR'S REPORT

Modifications Needed

Type of Report	Reasons for Issuance	Introductory	Scope	Explanatory Paragraph	Opinion Paragraph
1. Qualified "Except for"	1) Departure from GAAP	None	None	1) Refers to departure and effects on financial statements. Precedes opinion paragraph.	1) Refers to Explanatory paragraph. 2) Presents fairly except for.
	2) Inadequate Disclosure	None	None	1) Discloses omitted information. 2) Precedes opinion paragraph.	1) As above
	3) Scope Limitation	None	1) Add to beginning of paragraph "Except as discussed in following paragraph ...."	1) Discloses Scope Limitation. 2) Precedes opinion paragraph.	1) As above
2. Adverse	1) Departure from GAAP	None	None	1) Refers to departure from GAAP and effects on Financial Statements. Precedes opinion paragraph.	1) Refers to explanatory paragraph. 2) Do not present fairly.

SUMMARY OF MODIFICATIONS (cont.)

Modifications Needed

Type of Report	Reasons for Issuance	Introductory	Scope	Explanatory Paragraph	Opinion Paragraph
3. Disclaimer	1) Scope Limitation	Modified 1) "We were engaged to audit ...." 2) Leave out last sentence.	1) Eliminated not needed.	1) Describes Scope limitation.	1) Refers to preceding paragraph. 2) Disclaims opinion.
	2) Lack of Independence	Not needed	Not needed	Not needed	Disclaims Opinion
	3) Uncertainty	Considered Scope Limitation. Refer to 3 (Disclaimer) 1 (Scope Limitation) above.			
4. Unqualified Opinion with required additional information.	1) Justified Change in GAAP.	None	None	Refers to Footnote in Financial Statements explaining change. Paragraph placed after opinion paragraph.	None
	2) Going Concern adequately disclosed in the Financial Statements.	None	None	Refers to Footnote in the Financial Statements disclosing the uncertainty. Paragraph placed after opinion paragraph.	None

OTHER INFORMATION IN DOCUMENTS CONTAINING AUDITED FINANCIAL STATEMENTS (SAS No. 8)

An entity may publish various documents that contain "other information" in addition to audited financial statements and the independent auditor's report thereon. This statement is applicable only to other information contained in (a) annual reports to holders of securities or beneficial interests, annual reports of organizations for charitable or philanthropic purposes distributed to the public, and annual reports filed with regulatory authorities under the Securities and Exchange Act of 1934, or (b) other documents to which the auditor, at the client's request, devotes attention.

Other information in a document may be relevant to an independent auditor's examination or to the continuing propriety of his report. **The auditor's responsibility with respect to information in a document does not extend beyond the financial information identified in his report, and the auditor has no obligation to perform any procedures to corroborate other information contained in a document.** However, he should read the other information and consider whether such information, or the manner of its presentation, is materially inconsistent with information, or the manner of its presentation, appearing in the financial statements. **If the auditor concludes that there is a material inconsistency, he should determine whether the financial statements, his report, or both, require revision.** If he concludes that they do not require revision, he should request the client to revise the other information. **If the other information is not revised to eliminate the material inconsistency, he should consider other actions such as (1) revising his report to include an explanatory paragraph describing the material inconsistency, (2) withholding the use of his report in the document, or (3) withdrawing from the engagement.** The action he takes will depend on the particular circumstances and the significance of the inconsistency in the other information.

Other Material Misstatements of Fact

If the auditor becomes aware of information that he believes is a material misstatement of fact that is not a material inconsistency as previously described, he should discuss the matter with the client. In connection with this discussion, the auditor should consider that he may not have the expertise to assess the validity of the statement, that there may be no standards by which to assess its presentation, and that there may be valid differences of judgment or opinion. If the auditor concludes he has a valid basis for concern, he should propose that the client consult with some other party whose advice might be useful to the client, such as the client's legal counsel.

If, after discussing the matter, the auditor concludes that a material misstatement of fact remains, the action he takes will depend on his judgment in the particular circumstances. He should consider steps such as notifying his client in writing of his views concerning the information and consulting his legal counsel as to further appropriate action in the circumstances.

REPORTS ON COMPARATIVE FINANCIAL STATEMENTS (SAS No. 58)

Auditor's Standard Report On Comparative Financial Statements

The fourth standard of reporting requires that an auditor's report contain either an expression of opinion regarding the financial statements taken as a whole or an assertion to the effect that an opinion cannot be expressed. Reference in the fourth reporting standard to the financial statements "taken as a whole" should now be considered to apply not only to the financial statements of the current period but also to those of one or more prior periods that are presented on a comparative basis with those of the current period. Therefore, a continuing auditor should update his report on the individual financial statements of the one or more prior periods presented on a comparative basis with those of the current period.

Report With Differing Opinions

Since the auditor's report on comparative financial statements applies to the individual financial statements presented, an auditor may modify his opinion or disclaim an opinion with respect to one or more financial statements for one or more periods, while expressing an unqualified opinion on the other financial statements presented. When this situation occurs, the auditor should disclose all the substantive reasons for modifying or disclaiming an opinion in a separate explanatory paragraph(s) of his report and should include in the opinion paragraph an appropriate modification or disclaimer of opinion and a reference to the explanatory paragraph(s).

Report With an Updated Opinion Different From a Previous Opinion

If, during his current examination, an auditor becomes aware of circumstances or events that affect the financial statements of a prior period, he should consider such matters when updating his report on the financial statements of the prior period. The following circumstances or events ordinarily should cause an auditor to express an opinion different from that expressed in an earlier report on the financial statements of the prior period:

- **Subsequent restatement of prior-period financial statements**. If an auditor has previously modified his opinion on financial statements of a prior period because of a departure from generally accepted accounting principles, and the prior-period financial statements are restated in the current period to conform with generally accepted accounting principles, the auditor's updated report on the financial statements of the prior period should indicate that the statements have been restated and should express an unqualified opinion with respect to the restated financial statements.

If, in an updated report, an auditor expresses an opinion different from his previous opinion on the financial statements of a prior period, he should disclose all the substantive reasons for the different opinion in a separate explanatory paragraph(s) of his report. The explanatory paragraph(s) should disclose:
   a. The date of the auditor's previous report.
   b. The type of opinion previously expressed.
   c. The circumstances or events that caused the auditor to express a different opinion.
   d. That the auditor's updated opinion on the financial statements of the prior period is different from his previous opinion on those statements.

Report of Predecessor Auditor

A predecessor auditor ordinarily would be in a position to reissue his report on the financial statements of a prior period at the request of a former client if he is able to make satisfactory arrangements with his former client to perform this service and if he performs the procedures described.

Predecessor Auditor's Report Reissued

Before reissuing (or consenting to the reuse of) a report previously issued on the financial statements of a prior period, a predecessor auditor should consider whether his previous opinion on those statements is still appropriate.

Consequently, a predecessor auditor should:
   a. Read the financial statements of the current period.
   b. Compare the prior-period financial statements that he reported on with the financial statements to be presented for comparative purposes.
   c. Obtain a letter of representations from the successor auditor. The letter of representations should state whether the successor's examination revealed any matters that, in the successor's opinion, might have a material effect on, or require disclosure in, the financial statements reported on by the predecessor auditor.

A predecessor auditor who has agreed to reissue his report may become aware of events or transactions occurring subsequent to the date of his previous report on the financial statements of a prior period that may affect his previous opinion. In such circumstances, the predecessor auditor should make inquiries and perform other procedures that he considers necessary. He should then decide, on the basis of the evidential matter obtained, whether to revise his opinion.

A predecessor auditor's knowledge of the current affairs of his former client is obviously limited in the absence of a continuing relationship. Consequently, when reissuing his report on prior-period financial statements, a predecessor auditor should use the date of his previous report to avoid any implication that he has examined any records, transactions, or events after that date. If the predecessor auditor revises his report, or if the financial statements are restated, he should dual-date his report.

Predecessor Auditor's Report Not Presented

If the financial statements of a prior period have been examined by a predecessor auditor whose report is not presented, the successor auditor should indicate in the scope paragraph of his report:

    a.   That the financial statements of the prior period were examined by other auditors.

    b.   The date of their report.

    c.   The type of opinion expressed by the predecessor auditor.

    d.   The substantive reasons therefor, if it was other than unqualified.

ASSOCIATION WITH FINANCIAL STATEMENTS (SAS No. 26)

1.   The fourth standard of reporting is:

> The report shall either contain an expression of opinion regarding the financial statements, taken as a whole, or an assertion to the effect that an opinion cannot be expressed. When an overall opinion cannot be expressed, the reasons therefor should be stated. In all cases where an auditor's name is associated with financial statements, the report should contain a clear-cut indication of the character of the auditor's examination, if any, and the degree of responsibility he is taking.

> The objective of the fourth reporting standard is to prevent misinterpretation of the degree of responsibility the accountant assumes when his name is associated with financial statements.

2.   An accountant is associated with financial statements when he has consented to the use of his name in a report, document, or written communication containing the statements. Also, when an accountant submits to his client or others financial statements that he has prepared or assisted in preparing, he is deemed to be associated even though the accountant does not append his name to the statements.

3.   An accountant may be associated with audited or unaudited financial statements.

Disclaimer of Opinion on Unaudited Financial Statements—Public Companies
(see Chapter Five for reports on review and compilation services for <u>Nonpublic</u> Companies.)

When an accountant is associated with the financial statements of a <u>public entity</u>, but has not audited or reviewed such statements, the form of report to be issued is as follows:

> The accompanying balance sheet of X Company as of December 31, 20XX, and the related statements of income, retained earnings, and cash flows for the year then ended were not audited by us and, accordingly, we do not express an opinion on them.
>
>   (Signature and date)

When an accountant issues this form of disclaimer of opinion, he has no responsibility to apply any procedures beyond reading the financial statements for obvious material errors.

If the accountant is aware that his name is to be included in a client-prepared written communication of a public entity containing financial statements that have not been audited or reviewed, he should request (a) that his name not be included in the communication or (b) that the financial statements be marked as unaudited and that there be a notation that he does not express an opinion on them. If the client does not comply, the accountant should advise the client that he has not consented to the use of his name and should consider what other actions might be appropriate.

Disclaimer of Opinion When Not Independent

The second general standard requires that "in all matters relating to the assignment, an independence in mental attitude is to be maintained by the auditor or auditors". Whether the accountant is independent is something he must decide as a matter of professional judgment.

When an accountant is not independent, any procedures he might perform would not be in accordance with generally accepted auditing standards, and he would be precluded from expressing an opinion on such statements. Accordingly, he should disclaim an opinion with respect to the financial statements and should state specifically that he is not independent.

An example of such a report is as follows:

> We are not independent with respect to XYZ Company, and the accompanying balance sheet as of December 31, 20XX, and the related statements of income, retained earnings, and cash flows for the year then ended were not audited by us and, accordingly, we do not express an opinion on them.
>
> (Signature and date)

Circumstances Requiring a Modified Disclaimer

If the accountant concludes on the basis of facts known to him that the unaudited financial statements on which he is disclaiming an opinion are not in conformity with generally accepted accounting principles, which include adequate disclosure, he should suggest appropriate revision; failing that, he should describe the departure in his disclaimer of opinion.

When the effects of the departure on the financial statements are not reasonably determinable, the disclaimer of opinion should so state.

If the client will not agree to revision of the financial statements or will not accept the accountant's disclaimer of opinion with the description of the departure from generally accepted accounting principles, the accountant should refuse to be associated with the statements and, if necessary, withdraw from the engagement.

SUPPLEMENTARY INFORMATION REQUIRED BY THE FINANCIAL ACCOUNTING STANDARDS BOARD (SAS No. 52)

The Financial Accounting Standards Board (FASB) develops standards for financial reporting, including standards for financial statements and for certain other information supplementary to financial statements. This Statement provides the independent auditor with guidance on the nature of procedures to be applied to supplementary information required by the FASB, and it describes the circumstances that would require the auditor to report concerning such information.

Involvement with Supplementary Information Required by the FASB

The auditor should apply certain limited procedures to supplementary information required by the FASB and should report deficiencies in, or the omission of, such information.

Procedures

The auditor should consider whether supplementary information is required by the FASB in the circumstances. If supplementary information is required, the auditor should ordinarily apply the following procedures to the information.

a. Inquire of management regarding the methods of preparing the information, including (1) whether it is measured and presented within guidelines prescribed by the FASB, (2) whether methods of measurement or presentation have been changed from those used in the prior period and the reasons for any such changes, and (3) any significant assumptions or interpretations underlying the measurement or presentation.

b. Compare the information for consistency with (1) management's responses to the foregoing inquiries, (2) audited financial statements, and (3) other knowledge obtained during the examination of the financial statements.

c. Consider whether representations on supplementary information required by the FASB should be included in specific written representations obtained from management.

d. Apply additional procedures, if any, that other Statements prescribe for specific types of supplementary information required by the FASB.

e. Make additional inquiries if application of the foregoing procedures causes the auditor to believe that the information may not be measured or presented within applicable guidelines.

Circumstances Requiring Reporting on Supplementary Information Required by the FASB

Since the supplementary information is not audited and is not a required part of the basic financial statements, the auditor need not expand his report on the audited financial statements to refer to the supplementary information or to his limited procedures except in the following circumstances. The auditor's report should be expanded if:

a. the supplementary information that the FASB requires to be presented in the circumstances is omitted,

b. the auditor has concluded that the measurement or presentation of the supplementary information departs materially from guidelines prescribed by the FASB, or

c. the auditor is unable to complete the prescribed procedures.

The following are examples of additional paragraphs an auditor might use in these circumstances.

Omission of Supplementary Information Required by the FASB

The Company has not presented (describe the supplementary information required by the FASB in the circumstances) that the Financial Accounting Standards Board has determined is necessary to supplement, although not required to be part of, the basic financial statements.

Material Departures from FASB Guidelines

The (specifically identify the supplementary information) on page xx is not a required part of the basic financial statements, and we did not audit and do not express an opinion on such information. However, we have applied certain limited procedures, which consisted principally of inquiries of management regarding the methods of measurement and presentation of the supplementary information. As a result of such limited procedures, we believe that the (specifically identify the supplementary information) is not in conformity with guidelines established by the Financial Accounting Standards Board because (describe the material departure(s) from the FASB guidelines).

Prescribed Procedures Not Completed

The (specifically identify the supplementary information) on page xx is not a required part of the basic financial statements, and we did not audit and do not express an opinion on such information. Further, we were unable to apply to the information certain procedures prescribed by professional standards because (state the reasons).

Even though he is unable to complete the prescribed procedures, if, on the basis of facts known to him, the auditor concludes that the supplementary information has not been measured or presented within FASB guidelines, he should suggest appropriate revision; failing that, he should describe the nature of any material departures(s) in his report.

REPORTING ON CONDENSED FINANCIAL STATEMENTS AND SELECTED FINANCIAL DATA (SAS No. 42)

1. This SAS discusses reporting on a client-prepared document on—

a. Condensed financial statements (either for an annual or an interim period) that are derived from audited financial statements of a public entity that is required to file, at least annually, complete audited financial statements with a regulatory agency.

b. Selected financial data that are derived from audited financial statements of either a public or a nonpublic entity and that are presented in a document that includes audited financial statements (or, with respect to a public entity, that incorporates audited financial statements by reference to information filed with a regulatory agency).

Condensed Financial Statements

Condensed financial statements are presented in considerably less detail than complete financial statements. For this reason, they should be read in conjunction with the entity's most recent complete financial statements that include all the disclosures required by generally accepted accounting principles.

An auditor may be engaged to report on condensed financial statements that are derived from audited financial statements. Because condensed financial statements do not constitute a fair presentation of financial position, results of operations, and cash flows in conformity with generally accepted accounting principles, an auditor should not report on condensed financial statements in the same manner as he reported on the complete financial statements from which they are derived. To do so might lead users to assume, erroneously, that the condensed financial statements include all the disclosures necessary for complete financial statements. For the same reason, it is desirable that the condensed financial statements be so marked.

The auditor's report on condensed financial statements that are derived from financial statements that he has audited should indicate (a) that the auditor has examined and expressed an opinion on the complete financial statements, (b) the date of the auditor's report on the complete financial statements, (c) the type of opinion expressed, and (d) whether, in the auditor's opinion, the information set forth in the condensed financial statements is fairly stated in all material respects in relation to the complete financial statements from which it has been derived.

The following is an example of wording that an auditor may use in the circumstances:

> We have examined, in accordance with auditing standards generally accepted in the United States of America, the consolidated balance sheet of X Company and subsidiaries as of December 31, 20XX, and the related consolidated statements of income, retained earnings, and cash flows for the year then ended (not presented herein); and in our report dated February 15, 20X1, we expressed an unqualified opinion on those consolidated financial statements. In our opinion, the information set forth in the accompanying condensed consolidated financial statements is fairly stated in all material respects in relation to the consolidated financial statements from which it has been derived.

A client might make a statement in a client-prepared document that names the auditor and also states that condensed financial statements have been derived from audited financial statements. Such a statement does not, in itself, require the auditor to report on the condensed financial statements, provided that they are included in a document that contains audited financial statements (or that incorporates such statements by reference to information filed with a regulatory agency). However, if such a statement is made in a client-prepared document of a public entity that is required to file, at least annually, complete audited financial statements with a regulatory agency and that document does not include audited financial statements (or does not incorporate such statements by reference to information filed with a regulatory agency), the auditor should request that the client either (a) not include the auditor's name in the document or (b) include the auditor's report on the condensed financial statements. If the client will neither delete the reference to the auditor nor allow the appropriate report to be included, the auditor should advise the client that he does not consent to either the use of his name or the reference to him, and he should consider what other actions might be appropriate.

Selected Financial Data

An auditor may be engaged to report on selected financial data that are included in a client-prepared document that contains audited financial statements. The report should indicate (a) that the auditor has examined and expressed an opinion on the complete financial statements, (b) the type of opinion expressed, and (c) whether, in the auditor's opinion, the information set forth in the selected financial data is fairly stated in all material respects in relation to the complete financial statements from which it has been derived.

Chapter Three - Questions
Standards of Reporting

REPORTS ON AUDITED
FINANCIAL STATEMENTS

1. An auditor's opinion exception arising from a limitation on the scope of his examination should be explained in
a. A footnote to the financial statements.
b. The auditor's report.
c. Both a footnote to the financial statements and the auditor's report.
d. Both the financial statements (immediately after the caption of the item or items which could not be verified) and the auditor's report.

2. An auditor's report makes reference to the basic financial statements, which are customarily considered to be the balance sheet and the statements of
a. Income and cash flows.
b. Income, changes in retained earnings, and cash flows.
c. Income, retained earnings, and cash flows.
d. Income and retained earnings.

3. When a client declines to make essential disclosures in the financial statements or in the footnotes, the independent auditor should
a. Provide the necessary disclosures in the auditor's report and appropriately modify the opinion.
b. Explain to the client that an adverse opinion must be issued.
c. Issue an unqualified report and inform the stockholders of the improper disclosure in an "unaudited" footnote.
d. Issue an opinion "subject to" the client's lack of disclosure of supplementary information as explained in a middle paragraph of the report.

4. In determining the type of opinion to express, an auditor assesses the nature of the report qualifications and the materiality of their effects. Materiality will be the primary factor considered in the choice between
a. An "except for" opinion and an adverse opinion.
b. An "except for" opinion and a qualified opinion.
c. An adverse opinion and a disclaimer of opinion.
d. A qualified opinion and a piecemeal opinion.

5. Limitation on the scope of the auditor's examination may require the auditor to issue a qualified opinion or to disclaim an opinion. Which of the following would generally be a limitation on the scope of the auditor's examination?
a. The unavailability of sufficient competent evidential matter.
b. The engagement of the auditor to report on only one basic financial statement.
c. The examination of a subsidiary's financial statements by an auditor other than the one who examines and reports on the consolidated financial statements.
d. The engagement of the auditor after year end.

6. When an adverse opinion is expressed, the opinion paragraph should include a direct reference to
a. A footnote to the financial statements which discusses the basis for the opinion.
b. The scope paragraph which discusses the basis for the opinion rendered.
c. A separate paragraph which discusses the basis for the opinion rendered.
d. The consistency or lack of consistency in the application of generally accepted accounting principles.

7. A company issues audited financial statements under circumstances which require the presentation of a statement of cash flows. If the company refuses to present a statement of cash flows, the independent auditor should
a. Disclaim an opinion.
b. Prepare a statement of cash flows and note in a middle paragraph of the report that this statement is auditor-prepared.
c. Prepare a statement of cash flows and disclose in a footnote that this statement is auditor-prepared.
d. Qualify his opinion with an "except for" qualification and a description of the omission in a middle paragraph of the report.

8. An auditor is confronted with an exception considered sufficiently material as to warrant some deviation from the standard unqualified auditor's report. If the exception relates to a departure from generally accepted accounting principles, the auditor must decide between expressing a (an)
a.   Adverse opinion and a "special report".
b.   Adverse opinion and an "except for" opinion.
c.   Adverse opinion and a disclaimer of opinion.
d.   Disclaimer of opinion and a "special report".

9. When, in the auditor's judgment, the financial statements are not presented fairly in conformity with generally accepted accounting principles, the auditor will issue a(n)
a.   Qualified opinion.
b.   Special report.
c.   Disclaimer of opinion.
d.   Adverse opinion.

10. An auditor's report included an additional paragraph disclosing that there is a difference of opinion between the auditor and the client for which the auditor believed an adjustment to the financial statements should be made. The opinion paragraph of the auditor's report most likely expressed a(n)
a.   Unqualified opinion.
b.   "Except for" opinion.
c.   Modified opinion.
d.   Disclaimer of opinion.

11. An auditor refers to significant related party transactions in a middle paragraph of the report. If the ensuing opinion paragraph contains the words, "with the foregoing explanation," the auditor's report would be considered a(n)
a.   Unqualified opinion with appropriate reference to the middle paragraph.
b.   Example of inappropriate reporting.
c.   Adverse opinion.
d.   Negative assurance opinion.

12. Loeb, CPA, has completed preparation of the Bloto Company's unaudited financial statements and has prepared the following report to accompany them:

The accompanying balance sheet of the Bloto Company as of August 31, 19X5, and the related statements of income, retained earnings, and cash flows for the year then ended were not audited by us and accordingly we do not express an opinion on them.

The financial statements fail to disclose that the debentures issued on July 15, 19X2, limit the payment of cash dividends to the amount of earnings after August 31, 19X3. The company's statements of income for the years 19X4 and 19X5, both of which are unaudited, show this amount to be $18,900. Generally accepted accounting principles require disclosure of matters of this nature.

Which of the following comments **best** describes the appropriateness of this report?
a.   The report is satisfactory.
b.   The report is deficient because Loeb does not describe the scope of the review.
c.   The report is deficient because the second paragraph gives the impression that some audit work was done.
d.   The report is deficient because the explanatory comment in the second paragraph should precede the opinion paragraph.

13. Morgan, CPA, is the principal auditor for a multinational corporation. Another CPA has examined and reported on the financial statements of a significant subsidiary of the corporation. Morgan is satisfied with the independence and professional reputation of the other auditor, as well as the quality of the other auditor's examination. With respect to Morgan's report on the financial statements, taken as a whole, Morgan
a.   Must **not** refer to the examination of the auditor.
b.   Must refer to the examination of the other auditor.
c.   May refer to the examination of the other auditor.
d.   May refer to the examination of the other auditor, in which case Morgan must include in the auditor's report on the consolidated financial statements, a qualified opinion with respect to the examination of the other auditor.

14. Which of the following material events occurring subsequent to the balance sheet date would require an adjustment to the financial statements before they could be issued?
a.   Sale of long-term debt or capital stock.
b.   Loss of a plant as a result of a flood.
c.   Major purchase of a business which is expected to double the sale volume.
d.   Settlement of litigation, in excess of the recorded liability.

15. In connection with the annual audit, which of the following is **not** a "subsequent events" procedure?
a. Review available interim financial statements.
b. Read available minutes of meetings of stockholders, directors, and committees, and as to meetings for which minutes are not available, inquire about matters dealt with at such meetings.
c. Make inquiries with respect to the financial statements covered by the auditor's previously issued report if new information has become available during the current examination that might affect that report.
d. Discuss with officers the current status of items in the financial statements that were accounted for on the basis of tentative, preliminary or inconclusive data.

16. When a principal auditor decides to make reference to the examination of another auditor, the principal auditor's report should indicate clearly the division of responsibility between the portions of the financial statements covered by each auditor. In which paragraph(s) of the report should the division of responsibility be stated?
a. Only the opinion paragraph.
b. Either the scope or opinion paragraph.
c. Only the introductory paragraph.
d. The introductory, scope and opinion paragraphs.

17. When the report of a principal auditor makes reference to the examination made by another auditor, the other auditor may be named if express permission to do so is given and
a. The report of the principal auditor names the other auditor in the opinion paragraph.
b. The principal auditor accepts responsibility for the work of the other auditor.
c. The report of the other auditor is presented together with the report of the principal auditor.
d. The other auditor is **not** an associate or correspondent firm whose work is done at the request of the principal auditor.

18. An auditor performs interim work at various times throughout the year. The auditor's subsequent events work should be extended to the date of
a. A post-dated footnote.
b. The next scheduled interim visit.
c. The final billing for audit services rendered.
d. The auditor's report.

19. In connection with the examination of the consolidated financial statements of Mott Industries, Frazier, CPA, plans to refer to another CPA's examination of the financial statements of a subsidiary company. Under these circumstances Frazier's report must disclose
a. The name of the other CPA and the type of report issued by the other CPA.
b. The magnitude of the portion of the financial statements examined by the other CPA.
c. The nature of Frazier's review of the other CPA's work.
d. In a footnote the portions of the financial statements that were covered by the examinations of both auditors.

20. Jones, CPA, is the principal auditor who is auditing the consolidated financial statements of his client. Jones plans to refer to another CPA's examination of the financial statements of a subsidiary company but does **not** wish to present the other CPA's audit report. Both Jones and the other CPA's audit reports have noted no exceptions to generally accepted accounting principles. Under these circumstances the opinion paragraph of Jones' consolidated audit report should express
a. An unqualified opinion.
b. A referral report.
c. An "except for" opinion.
d. A principal opinion.

21. Which of the following will not result in modification of the auditor's report due to a scope limitation?
a. Restrictions imposed by the client.
b. Reliance placed on the report of another auditor.
c. Inability to obtain sufficient competent evidential matter.
d. Inadequacy in the accounting records.

22. An auditor's report contains the following sentences:

We did not examine the financial statements of B Company, a consolidated subsidiary, which statements reflect total assets and revenues constituting 20 percent and 22 percent, respectively, of the related consolidated totals. These statements were examined by other auditors whose report thereon has been furnished to us, and our opinion expressed herein, insofar as it relates to the amounts included for B Company, is based solely upon the report of the other auditors.

These sentences
a. Disclaim an opinion.
b. Qualify the opinion.
c. Divide responsibility.
d. Are an improper form of reporting.

23. King, CPA, was engaged to audit the financial statements of Newton Company after its fiscal year had ended. King neither observed the inventory count nor confirmed the receivables by direct communication with debtors, but was satisfied concerning both after applying alternative procedures. King's auditor's report most likely contained a(an)
a. Qualified opinion.
b. Disclaimer of opinion.
c. Unqualified opinion.
d. Unqualified opinion with an explanatory paragraph.

24. In which of the following circumstances would an auditor be most likely to express an adverse opinion?
a. Information comes to the auditor's attention that raises substantial doubt about the entity's ability to continue as a going concern.
b. The chief executive officer refuses the auditor access to minutes of board of directors' meetings.
c. Tests of controls show that the entity's internal control structure is so poor that it **cannot** be relied upon.
d. The financial statements are **not** in conformity with the FASB Statements regarding the capitalization of leases.

25. A principal auditor decides not to refer to the audit of another CPA who audited a subsidiary of the principal auditor's client. After making inquiries about the other CPA's professional reputation and independence, the principal auditor most likely would
a. Add an explanatory paragraph to the auditor's report indicating that the subsidiary's financial statements are **not** material to the consolidated financial statements.
b. Document in the engagement letter that the principal auditor assumes **no** responsibility for the other CPA's work and opinion.
c. Obtain written permission from the other CPA to omit the reference in the principal auditor's report.
d. Contact the other CPA and review the audit programs and working papers pertaining to the subsidiary.

26. When there has been a change in accounting principle that materially affects the comparability of the comparative financial statements presented and the auditor concurs with the change, the auditor should

	Concur explicitly with the change	Issue an "except for" qualified opinion	Refer to the change in an explanatory paragraph
a.	No	No	Yes
b.	Yes	No	Yes
c.	Yes	Yes	No
d.	No	Yes	No

27. Comparative financial statements include the prior year's statements that were audited by a predecessor auditor whose report is not presented. If the predecessor's report was unqualified, the successor should
a. Express an opinion on the current year's statements alone and make **no** reference to the prior year's statements.
b. Indicate in the auditor's report that the predecessor auditor expressed an unqualified opinion.
c. Obtain a letter of representations from the predecessor concerning any matters that might affect the successor's opinion.
d. Request the predecessor auditor to reissue the prior year's report.

28. A limitation on the scope of an auditor's examination sufficient to preclude an unqualified opinion will always result when management
a. Engages the auditor after the year-end physical inventory count is completed.
b. Fails to correct a material internal control weakness that had been identified during the prior year's audit.
c. Refuses to furnish a management representation letter to the auditor.
d. Prevents the auditor from reviewing the working papers of the predecessor auditor.

29. An auditor who qualifies an opinion because of an insufficiency of evidential matter should describe the limitation in an explanatory paragraph. The auditor should also refer to the limitation in the

	Scope paragraph	Opinion paragraph	Notes to the financial statements
a.	Yes	No	Yes
b.	No	Yes	No
c.	Yes	Yes	No
d.	Yes	Yes	Yes

30. An auditor concludes that there is a material inconsistency in the other information in an annual report to shareholders containing audited financial statements. If the auditor concludes that the financial statements do **not** require revision, but the client refuses to revise or eliminate the material inconsistency, the auditor may

a.　Issue an "except for" qualified opinion after discussing the matter with the client's board of directors.

b.　Consider the matter closed since the other information is **not** in the audited financial statements.

c.　Disclaim an opinion on the financial statements after explaining the material inconsistency in a separate explanatory paragraph.

d.　Revise the auditor's report to include a separate explanatory paragraph describing the material inconsistency.

31. An auditor may **not** issue a qualified opinion when

a.　A scope limitation prevents the auditor from completing an important audit procedure.

b.　The auditor's report refers to the work of a specialist.

c.　An accounting principle at variance with generally accepted accounting principles is used.

d.　The auditor lacks independence with respect to the audited entity.

32. Unaudited financial statements for the prior year presented in comparative form with audited financial statements for the current year should be clearly marked to indicate their status and

I.　The report on the prior period should be reissued to accompany the current period report.

II.　The report on the current period should include as a separate paragraph a description of the responsibility assumed for the prior period's financial statements.

a.　I only.

b.　II only.

c.　Both I and II.

d.　Either I or II.

33. When a publicly-held company refuses to include in its audited financial statements any of the segment information that the auditor believes is required, the auditor should issue a(an)

a.　Unqualified opinion with a separate explanatory paragraph emphasizing the matter.

b.　"Except for" qualified opinion because of inadequate disclosure.

c.　Adverse opinion because of the lack of conformity with generally accepted accounting principles.

d.　Disclaimer of opinion because of the significant scope limitation.

34. When a client will **not** permit inquiry of outside legal counsel, the audit report will ordinarily contain a(an)

a.　Disclaimer of opinion.

b.　"Except for" qualified opinion.

c.　Referral opinion.

d.　Unqualified opinion with a separate explanatory paragraph.

35. When there is a significant change in accounting principle, an auditor's report should refer to the lack of consistency in

a.　The scope paragraph.

b.　An explanatory paragraph between the second paragraph and the opinion paragraph.

c.　The opinion paragraph.

d.　An explanatory paragraph following the opinion paragraph.

36. How are management's responsibility and the auditor's report represented in the standard auditor's report?

	Management's responsibility	Auditor's responsibility
a.	Explicitly	Explicitly
b.	Implicitly	Implicitly
c.	Implicitly	Explicitly
d.	Explicitly	Implicitly

37. Restrictions imposed by a client prohibit the observation of physical inventories, which account for 35% of all assets. Alternative audit procedures cannot be applied, although the auditor was able to examine satisfactory evidence for all other items in the financial statements. The auditor should issue a(an)
a. "Except for" qualified opinion.
b. Disclaimer of opinion.
c. Unqualified opinion with a separate explanatory paragraph.
d. Unqualified opinion with an explanation in the scope paragraph.

38. A limitation on the scope of an auditor's examination sufficient to preclude an unqualified opinion will usually result when management
a. Presents financial statements that are prepared in accordance with the cash receipts and disbursements basis of accounting.
b. States that the financial statements are **not** intended to be presented in conformity with generally accepted accounting principles.
c. Does **not** make the minutes of the Board of Directors' meetings available to the auditor.
d. Asks the auditor to report on the balance sheet and **not** on the other basic financial statements.

39. Grant Company's financial statements adequately disclose uncertainties that concern future events, the outcome of which are **not** susceptible of reasonable estimation. The auditor's report should include a(an)
a. Unqualified opinion.
b. Special report paragraph.
c. "Except for" qualified opinion.
d. Adverse opinion.

40. An auditor should disclose the substantive reasons for expressing an adverse opinion in an explanatory paragraph
a. Preceding the scope paragraph.
b. Preceding the opinion paragraph.
c. Following the opinion paragraph.
d. Within the notes to the financial statements.

41. When management does **not** provide reasonable justification that a change in accounting principle is preferable and it presents comparative financial statements, the auditor should express a qualified opinion
a. Only in the year of the accounting principle change.
b. Each year that the financial statements initially reflecting the change are presented.
c. Each year until management changes back to the accounting principle formerly used.
d. Only if the change is to an accounting principle that is **not** generally accepted.

42. When an independent CPA is associated with the financial statements of a publicly held entity but has **not** audited or reviewed such statements, the appropriate form of report to be issued must include a(an)
a. Compilation report.
b. Disclaimer of opinion.
c. Unaudited association report.
d. Qualified opinion.

43. Which of the following audit procedures would most likely assist an auditor in identifying conditions and events that may indicate there could be substantial doubt about an entity's ability to continue as a going concern?
a. Review compliance with the terms of debt agreements.
b. Confirmation of accounts receivable from principal customers.
c. Reconciliation of interest expense with debt outstanding.
d. Confirmation of bank balances.

44. An explanatory paragraph following the opinion paragraph of an auditor's report describes an uncertainty as follows:

> As discussed in Note X to the financial statements, the Company is a defendant in a lawsuit alleging infringement of certain patent rights and claiming damages. Discovery proceedings are in progress. The ultimate outcome of the litigation cannot presently be determined. Accordingly, no provision for any liability that may result upon adjudication has been made in the accompanying financial statements.

What type of opinion should the auditor express under these circumstances?
a. Unqualified.
b. "Subject to" qualified.
c. "Except for" qualified.
d. Disclaimer.

45. When a qualified opinion results from a limitation on the scope of the audit, the situation should be described in an explanatory paragraph
a. Preceding the opinion paragraph and referred to only in the scope paragraph of the auditor's report.
b. Following the opinion paragraph and referred to in both the scope and opinion paragraphs of the auditor's report.
c. Following the opinion paragraph and referred to only in the scope paragraph of the auditor's report.
d. Preceding the opinion paragraph and referred to in both the scope and opinion paragraphs of the auditor's report.

46. Under which of the following circumstances would a disclaimer of opinion **not** be appropriate?
a. The auditor is engaged after fiscal year-end and is unable to observe physical inventories or apply alternative procedures to verify their balances.
b. The auditor is unable to determine the amounts associated with illegal acts committed by the client's management.
c. The financial statements fail to contain adequate disclosure concerning related party transactions.
d. The client refuses to permit its attorney to furnish information requested in a letter of audit inquiry.

47. In which of the following circumstances would an auditor usually choose between issuing a qualified opinion or a disclaimer of opinion?
a. Departure from generally accepted accounting principles.
b. Inadequate disclosure of accounting policies.
c. Inability to obtain sufficient competent evidential matter.
d. Unreasonable justification for a change in accounting principle.

48. Which of the following phrases should be included in the opinion paragraph when an auditor expresses a qualified opinion?

	When read in conjunction with Note X	With the foregoing explanation
a.	Yes	No
b.	No	Yes
c.	Yes	Yes
d.	No	No

49. When an auditor expresses an adverse opinion, the opinion paragraph should include
a. The principal effects of the departure from generally accepted accounting principles.
b. A direct reference to a separate paragraph disclosing the basis for the opinion.
c. The substantive reasons for the financial statements being misleading.
d. A description of the uncertainty or scope limitation that prevents an unqualified opinion.

50. Under which of the following circumstances would a disclaimer of opinion **not** be appropriate?
a. The financial statements fail to contain adequate disclosure of related party transactions.
b. The client refuses to permit its attorney to furnish information requested in a letter of audit inquiry.
c. The auditor is engaged after fiscal year-end and is unable to observe physical inventories or apply alternative procedures to verify their balances.
d. The auditor is unable to determine the amounts associated with illegal acts committed by the client's management.

51. When reporting on comparative financial statements, which of the following circumstances ordinarily should cause the auditor to change the previously issued opinion on the prior year's financial statements?
a. The prior year's financial statements are restated following a pooling of interests in the current year.
b. A departure from generally accepted accounting principles caused an adverse opinion on the prior year's financial statements and those statements have been properly restated.
c. A change in accounting principle caused the auditor to make a consistency modification in the current year's auditor's report.
d. A scope limitation caused a qualified opinion on the prior year's financial statements but the current year's opinion was properly unqualified.

52. If an auditor is satisfied that there is only a remote likelihood of a loss resulting from the resolution of a matter involving an uncertainty, the auditor normally would express a(an)
a. Unqualified opinion.
b. Unqualified opinion with a separate explanatory paragraph.
c. Qualified opinion or disclaimer of opinion, depending upon the materiality of the loss.
d. Qualified opinion or disclaimer of opinion, depending on whether the uncertainty is adequately disclosed.

53. When an auditor qualifies an opinion because of inadequate disclosure, the auditor should describe the nature of the omission in a separate explanatory paragraph and modify the

	Introductory paragraph	Scope paragraph	Opinion paragraph
a.	Yes	No	No
b.	Yes	Yes	No
c.	No	Yes	Yes
d.	No	No	Yes

54. An auditor includes a separate paragraph in an otherwise unmodified report to emphasize that the entity being reported upon had significant transactions with related parties. The inclusion of this separate paragraph

a. Is appropriate and would **not** negate the unqualified opinion.
b. Is considered an "except for" qualification of the opinion.
c. Violates generally accepted auditing standards if this information is already disclosed in footnotes to the financial statements.
d. Necessitates a revision of the opinion paragraph to include the phrase "with the foregoing explanation."

55. When an auditor concludes there is substantial doubt about an entity's ability to continue as a going concern for a reasonable period of time, the auditor's responsibility is to
a. Prepare prospective financial information to verify whether management's plans can be effectively implemented.
b. Project future conditions and events for a period of time **not** to exceed one year following the date of the financial statements.
c. Issue a qualified or adverse opinion, depending upon materiality, due to the possible effects on the financial statements.
d. Consider the adequacy of disclosure about the entity's possible inability to continue as a going concern.

56. The following explanatory paragraph was included in an auditor's report to indicate a lack of consistency:

"As discussed in note T to the financial statements, the company changed its method of computing depreciation in 1990."

How should the auditor report on this matter if the auditor concurred with the change?

	Type of opinion	Location of explanatory paragraph
a.	Unqualified	Before opinion paragraph
b.	Unqualified	After opinion paragraph
c.	Qualified	Before opinion paragraph
d.	Qualified	After opinion paragraph

57. After issuing a report, an auditor has **no** obligation to make continuing inquiries or perform other procedures concerning the audited financial statements, unless

a. Information, which existed at the report date and may affect the report, comes to the auditor's attention.
b. Management of the entity requests the auditor to reissue the auditor's report.
c. Information about an event that occurred after the end of field work comes to the auditor's attention.
d. Final determinations or resolutions are made of contingencies that had been disclosed in the financial statements.

58. How does an auditor make the following representations when issuing the standard auditor's report on comparative financial statements?

	Examination of evidence on a test basis	Consistent application of accounting principles
a.	Explicitly	Explicitly
b.	Implicitly	Implicitly
c.	Implicitly	Explicitly
d.	Explicitly	Implicitly

59. An auditor was unable to obtain sufficient competent evidential matter concerning certain transactions due to an inadequacy in the entity's accounting records. The auditor would choose between issuing a(an)

a. Qualified opinion and an unqualified opinion with an explanatory paragraph.
b. Unqualified opinion with an explanatory paragraph and an adverse opinion.
c. Adverse opinion and a disclaimer of opinion.
d. Disclaimer of opinion and a qualified opinion.

60. Green, CPA, concludes that there is substantial doubt about JKL Co.'s ability to continue as a going concern. If JKL's financial statements adequately disclose its financial difficulties, Green's auditor's report should

	Include an explanatory paragraph following the opinion paragraph	Specifically use the words "going concern"	Specifically use the words "substantial doubt"
a.	Yes	Yes	Yes
b.	Yes	Yes	No
c.	Yes	No	Yes
d.	No	Yes	Yes

61. When audited financial statements are presented in a client's document containing other information, the auditor should

a. Perform inquiry and analytical procedures to ascertain whether the other information is reasonable.
b. Add an explanatory paragraph to the auditor's report without changing the opinion on the financial statements.
c. Perform the appropriate substantive auditing procedures to corroborate the other information.
d. Read the other information to determine that it is consistent with the audited financial statements.

62. An auditor's report contains the following sentences:

We did not audit the financial statements of JK Co., a wholly-owned subsidiary, which statements reflect total assets and revenues constituting 17 percent and 19 percent, respectively, of the related consolidated totals. Those statements were audited by other auditors whose report has been furnished to us, and our opinion, insofar as it relates to the amounts included for JK Co., is based solely on the report of the other auditors.

These sentences

a. Are an improper form of reporting.
b. Divide responsibility.
c. Disclaim an opinion.
d. Qualify the opinion.

63. When an independent CPA assists in preparing the financial statements of a publicly held entity, but has **not** audited or reviewed them, the CPA should issue a disclaimer of opinion. In such situations, the CPA has **no** responsibility to apply any procedures beyond

a. Documenting that the internal control structure is **not** being relied on.
b. Reading the financial statements for obvious material misstatements.
c. Ascertaining whether the financial statements are in conformity with GAAP.
d. Determining whether management has elected to omit substantially all required disclosures.

64. When an auditor concludes there is substantial doubt about a continuing audit client's ability to continue as a going concern for a reasonable period of time, the auditor's responsibility is to

a. Issue a qualified or adverse opinion, depending upon materiality, due to the possible effects on the financial statements.
b. Consider the adequacy of disclosure about the client's possible inability to continue as a going concern.
c. Report to the client's audit committee that management's accounting estimates may need to be adjusted.
d. Reissue the prior year's auditor's report and add an explanatory paragraph that specifically refers to "substantial doubt" and "going concern."

65. Reference in a principal auditor's report to the fact that part of the audit was performed by another auditor most likely would be an indication of the

a. Divided responsibility between the auditors who conducted the audits of the components of the overall financial statements.
b. Lack of materiality of the portion of the financial statements audited by the other auditor.
c. Principal auditor's recognition of the other auditor's competence, reputation, and professional certification.
d. Different opinions the auditors are expressing on the components of the financial statements that each audited.

66. In May 1994, an auditor reissues the auditor's report on the 1992 financial statements at a continuing client's request. The 1992 financial statements are not restated and the auditor does not revise the wording of the report. The auditor should

a. Dual date the reissued report.
b. Use the release date of the reissued report.
c. Use the original report date on the reissued report.
d. Use the current-period auditor's report date on the reissued report.

67. An auditor includes a separate paragraph in an otherwise unmodified report to emphasize that the entity being reported on had significant transactions with related parties. The inclusion of this separate paragraph

a. Is considered an "except for" qualification of the opinion.
b. Violates generally accepted auditing standards if this information is already disclosed in footnotes to the financial statements.
c. Necessitates a revision of the opinion paragraph to include the phrase "with the foregoing explanation."
d. Is appropriate and would **not** negate the unqualified opinion.

68. On March 15, 1994, Kent, CPA, issued an unqualified opinion on a client's audited financial statements for the year ended December 31, 1993. On May 4, 1994, Kent's internal inspection program disclosed that engagement personnel failed to observe the client's physical inventory. Omission of this procedure impairs Kent's present ability to support the unqualified opinion. If the stockholders are currently relying on the opinion, Kent should first

a. Advise management to disclose to the stockholders that Kent's unqualified opinion should **not** be relied on.
b. Undertake to apply alternative procedures that would provide a satisfactory basis for the unqualified opinion.
c. Reissue the auditor's report and add an explanatory paragraph describing the departure from generally accepted auditing standards.
d. Compensate for the omitted procedure by performing tests of controls to reduce audit risk to a sufficiently low level.

69. For an entity that does **not** receive governmental financial assistance, an auditor's standard report on financial statements generally would **not** refer to

a. Significant estimates made by management.
b. An assessment of the entity's accounting principles.
c. Management's responsibility for the financial statements.
d. The entity's internal control structure.

70. Due to a scope limitation, an auditor disclaimed an opinion on the financial statements taken as a whole, but the auditor's report included a statement that the current asset portion of the entity's balance sheet was fairly stated. The inclusion of this statement is

a. Not appropriate because it may tend to overshadow the auditor's disclaimer of opinion.
b. Not appropriate because the auditor is prohibited from reporting on only one basic financial statement.
c. Appropriate provided the auditor's scope paragraph adequately describes the scope limitations.
d. Appropriate provided the statement is in a separate paragraph preceding the disclaimer of opinion paragraph.

71. When there has been a change in accounting principles, but the effect of the change on the comparability of the financial statements is **not** material, the auditor should

a. Refer to the change in an explanatory paragraph.
b. Explicitly concur that the change is preferred.
c. Not refer to consistency in the auditor's report.
d. Refer to the change in the opinion paragraph.

72. When single-year financial statements are presented, an auditor ordinarily would express an unqualified opinion in an unmodified report if the

a. Auditor is unable to obtain audited financial statements supporting the entity's investment in a foreign affiliate.
b. Entity declines to present a statement of cash flows with its balance sheet and related statements of income and retained earnings.
c. Auditor wishes to emphasize an accounting matter affecting the comparability of the financial statements with those of the prior year.
d. Prior year's financial statements were audited by another CPA whose report, which expressed an unqualified opinion, is **not** presented.

73. When financial statements contain a departure from GAAP because, due to unusual circumstances, the statements would otherwise be misleading, the auditor should explain the unusual circumstances in a separate paragraph and express an opinion that is

a. Unqualified.
b. Qualified.
c. Adverse.
d. Qualified or adverse, depending on materiality.

74. Park, CPA, was engaged to audit the financial statements of Tech Co., a new client, for the year ended December 31, 1993. Park obtained sufficient audit evidence for all of Tech's financial statement items except Tech's opening inventory. Due to inadequate financial records, Park could not verify Tech's January 1, 1993, inventory balances. Park's opinion on Tech's 1993 financial statements most likely will be

	Balance sheet	Income statement
a.	Disclaimer	Disclaimer
b.	Unqualified	Disclaimer
c.	Disclaimer	Adverse
d.	Unqualified	Adverse

75. Which paragraphs of an auditor's standard report on financial statements should refer to generally accepted auditing standards (GAAS) and generally accepted accounting principles (GAAP) in which paragraphs?

	GAAS	GAAP
a.	Opening	Scope
b.	Scope	Scope
c.	Scope	Opinion
d.	Opening	Opinion

76. What is an auditor's responsibility for supplementary information, such as segment information, which is outside the basic financial statements, but required by the FASB?

a. The auditor has **no** responsibility for required supplementary information as long as it is outside the basic financial statements.
b. The auditor's only responsibility for required supplementary information is to determine that such information has **not** been omitted.
c. The auditor should apply certain limited procedures to the required supplementary information, and report deficiencies in, or omissions of, such information.
d. The auditor should apply tests of details of transactions and balances to the required supplementary information, and report any material misstatements in such information.

77. In auditing the financial statements of Star Corp., Land discovered information leading Land to believe that Star's prior year's financial statements, which were audited by Tell, require substantial revisions. Under these circumstances, Land should

a. Notify Star's audit committee and stockholders that the prior year's financial statements **cannot** be relied on.
b. Request Star to reissue the prior year's financial statements with the appropriate revisions.
c. Notify Tell about the information and make inquiries about the integrity of Star's management.
d. Request Star to arrange a meeting among the three parties to resolve the matter.

78. In which of the following circumstances would an auditor be most likely to express an adverse opinion?

a. The chief executive officer refuses the auditor access to minutes of board of directors' meetings.
b. Tests of controls show that the entity's internal control structure is so poor that it **cannot** be relied upon.
c. The financial statements are **not** in conformity with the FASB Statements regarding the capitalization of leases.
d. Information comes to the auditor's attention that raises substantial doubt about the entity's ability to continue as a going concern.

79. When qualifying an opinion because of an insufficiency of audit evidence, an auditor should refer to the situation in the

	Opening (introductory) paragraph	Scope paragraph
a.	No	No
b.	Yes	No
c.	Yes	Yes
d.	No	Yes

80. When unaudited financial statements of a nonpublic entity are presented in comparative form with audited financial statements in the subsequent year, the unaudited financial statements should be clearly marked to indicate their status and

I. The report on the unaudited financial statements should be released.
II. The report on the audited financial statements should include a separate paragraph describing the responsibility assumed for the unaudited financial statements.

a. I only.
b. II only.
c. Both I and II.
d. Either I or II.

81. An auditor expressed a qualified opinion on the prior year's financial statements because of a lack of adequate disclosure. These financial statements are properly restated in the current year and presented in comparative form with the current year's financial statements. The auditor's updated report on the prior year's financial statements should

a. Be accompanied by the auditor's original report on the prior year's financial statements.
b. Continue to express a qualified opinion on the prior year's financial statements.
c. Make **no** reference to the type of opinion expressed on the prior year's financial statements.
d. Express an unqualified opinion on the restated financial statements of the prior year.

82. An auditor issued an audit report that was dual dated for a subsequent event occurring after the completion of field work but before issuance of the auditor's report. The auditor's responsibility for events occurring subsequent to the completion of field work was

a. Limited to include only events occurring up to the date of the last subsequent event referenced.
b. Limited to the specific event referenced.
c. Extended to subsequent events occurring through the date of issuance of the report.
d. Extended to include all events occurring since the completion of field work.

83. Which of the following conditions or events most likely would cause an auditor to have substantial doubt about an entity's ability to continue as a going concern?

a. Cash flows from operating activities are negative.
b. Research and development projects are postponed.
c. Significant related party transactions are pervasive.
d. Stock dividends replace annual cash dividends.

84. Before reissuing the prior year's auditor's report on the financial statements of a former client, the predecessor auditor should obtain a letter of representations from the
a. Former client's management.
b. Former client's attorney.
c. Former client's board of directors.
d. Successor auditor.

85. Subsequent to the issuance of an auditor's report, the auditor became aware of facts existing at the report date that would have affected the report had the auditor then been aware of such facts. After determining that the information is reliable, the auditor should next
a. Determine whether there are persons relying or likely to rely on the financial statements who would attach importance to the information.
b. Request that management disclose the newly discovered information by issuing revised financial statements.
c. Issue revised pro forma financial statements taking into consideration the newly discovered information.
d. Give public notice that the auditor is no longer associated with financial statements.

86. An auditor concludes that a client's illegal act, which has a material effect on the financial statements, has not been properly accounted for or disclosed. Depending on the materiality of the effect on the financial statements, the auditor should express either a(an)
a. Adverse opinion or a disclaimer of opinion.
b. Qualified opinion **or** an adverse opinion.
c. Disclaimer of opinion **or** an unqualified opinion with a separate explanatory paragraph.
d. Unqualified opinion with a separate explanatory paragraph **or** a qualified opinion.

87. Cooper, CPA, believes there is substantial doubt about the ability of Zero Corp. to continue as a going concern for a reasonable period of time. In evaluating Zero's plans for dealing with the adverse effects of future conditions and events, Cooper most likely would consider, as a mitigating factor, Zero's plans to
a. Discuss with lenders the terms of all debt and loan agreements.
b. Strengthen internal controls over cash disbursements.
c. Purchase production facilities currently being leased from a related party.
d. Postpone expenditures for research and development projects.

88. Harris, CPA, has been asked to audit and report on the balance sheet of Fox Co. but not on the statements of income, retained earnings, or cash flows. Harris will have access to all information underlying the basic financial statements. Under these circumstances, Harris may
a. Not accept the engagement because it would constitute a violation of the profession's ethical standards.
b. Not accept the engagement because it would be tantamount to rendering a piecemeal opinion.
c. Accept the engagement because such engagements merely involve limited reporting objectives.
d. Accept the engagement but should disclaim an opinion because of an inability to apply the procedures considered necessary.

89. Which of the following statements is a basic element of the auditor's standard report?
a. The disclosures provide reasonable assurance that the financial statements are free of material misstatement.
b. The auditor evaluated the overall internal control structure.
c. An audit includes assessing significant estimates made by management.
d. The financial statements are consistent with those of the prior period.

90. An auditor may **not** issue a qualified opinion when
a. An accounting principle at variance with GAAP is used.
b. The auditor lacks independence with respect to the audited entity.
c. A scope limitation prevents the auditor from completing an important audit procedure.
d. The auditor's report refers to the work of a specialist.

91. An auditor would express an unqualified opinion with an explanatory paragraph added to the auditor's report for

	An unjustified accounting change	A material weakness in the internal control structure
a.	Yes	Yes
b.	Yes	No
c.	No	Yes
d.	No	No

92. Under which of the following circumstances would a disclaimer of opinion **not** be appropriate?
a. The auditor is unable to determine the amounts associated with an employee fraud scheme.
b. Management does **not** provide reasonable justification for a change in accounting principles.
c. The client refuses to permit the auditor to confirm certain accounts receivable or apply alternative procedures to verify their balances.
d. The chief executive officer is unwilling to sign the management representation letter.

93. Digit Co. uses the FIFO method of costing for its international subsidiary's inventory and LIFO for its domestic inventory. Under these circumstances, the auditor's report on Digit's financial statements should express an
a. Unqualified opinion.
b. Opinion qualified because of a lack of consistency.
c. Opinion qualified because of a departure from GAAP.
d. Adverse opinion.

94. The fourth standard of reporting requires the auditor's report to contain either an expression of opinion regarding the financial statements taken as a whole or an assertion to the effect that an opinion cannot be expressed. The objective of the fourth standard is to prevent
a. An auditor from expressing different opinions on each of the basic financial statements.
b. Restrictions on the scope of the audit, whether imposed by the client or by the inability to obtain evidence.
c. Misinterpretations regarding the degree of responsibility the auditor is assuming.
d. An auditor from reporting on one basic financial statement and **not** the others.

95. In which of the following circumstances would an auditor **not** express an unqualified opinion?
a. There has been a material change between periods in accounting principles.
b. Quarterly financial data required by the SEC has been omitted.
c. The auditor wishes to emphasize an unusually important subsequent event.
d. The auditor is unable to obtain audited financial statements of a consolidated investee.

96. An explanatory paragraph following the opinion paragraph of an auditor's report describes an uncertainty as follows:

> As discussed in Note X to the financial statements, the Company is a defendant in a lawsuit alleging infringement of certain patent rights and claiming damages. Discovery proceedings are in progress. The ultimate outcome of the litigation cannot presently be determined. Accordingly, no provision for any liability that may result upon adjudication has been made in the accompanying financial statements.

What type of opinion should the auditor express under these circumstances?
a. Adverse.
b. Qualified due to a scope limitation.
c. Qualified due to a GAAP violation.
d. Unqualified.

97. Which of the following phrases would an auditor most likely include in the auditor's report when expressing a qualified opinion because of inadequate disclosure?
a. Subject to the departure from generally accepted accounting principles, as described above.
b. With the foregoing explanation of these omitted disclosures.
c. Except for the omission of the information discussed in the preceding paragraph.
d. Does **not** present fairly in all material respects.

98. Kane, CPA, concludes that there is substantial doubt about Lima Co.'s ability to continue as a going concern for a reasonable period of time. If Lima's financial statements adequately disclose its financial difficulties, Kane's auditor's report is required to include an explanatory paragraph that specifically uses the phrase(s)

	"Possible discontinuance of operations"	"Reasonable period of time, **not** to exceed one year"
a.	Yes	Yes
b.	Yes	No
c.	No	Yes
d.	No	No

99. Mead, CPA, had substantial doubt about Tech Co.'s ability to continue as a going concern when reporting on Tech's audited financial statements for the year ended June 30, 1994. That doubt has been removed in 1995. What is Mead's reporting responsibility if Tech is presenting its financial statements for the year ended June 30, 1995, on a comparative basis with those of 1994?

a. The explanatory paragraph included in the 1994 auditor's report should **not** be repeated.
b. The explanatory paragraph included in the 1994 auditor's report should be repeated in its entirety.
c. A different explanatory paragraph describing Mead's reasons for the removal of doubt should be included.
d. A different explanatory paragraph describing Tech's plans for financial recovery should be included.

100. In the first audit of a new client, an auditor was able to extend auditing procedures to gather sufficient evidence about consistency. Under these circumstances, the auditor should

a. Not report on the client's income statement.
b. Not refer to consistency in the auditor's report.
c. State that the consistency standard does **not** apply.
d. State that the accounting principles have been applied consistently.

101. When reporting on comparative financial statements, an auditor ordinarily should change the previously issued opinion on the prior-year's financial statements if the

a. Prior year's financial statements are restated to conform with generally accepted accounting principles.
b. Auditor is a predecessor auditor who has been requested by a former client to reissue the previously issued report.
c. Prior year's opinion was unqualified and the opinion on the current year's financial statements is modified due to a lack of consistency.
d. Prior year's financial statements are restated following a pooling of interests in the current year.

102. Jewel, CPA, audited Infinite Co.'s prior-year financial statements. These statements are presented with those of the current year for comparative purposes without Jewel's auditor's report, which expressed a qualified opinion. In drafting the current year's auditor's report, Crain, CPA, the successor auditor, should

I. Not name Jewel as the predecessor auditor
II. Indicate the type of report issued by Jewel.
III. Indicate the substantive reasons for Jewel's qualification.

a. I only.
b. I and II only.
c. II and III only.
d. I, II, and III.

103. The introductory paragraph of an auditor's report contains the following sentences:

We did not audit the financial statements of EZ Inc., a wholly-owned subsidiary, which statements reflect total assets and revenues constituting 27 percent and 29 percent, respectively, of the related consolidated totals. Those statements were audited by other auditors whose report has been furnished to us, and our opinion, insofar as it relates to the amounts included for EZ Inc., is based solely on the report of the other auditors.

These sentences
a. Indicate a division of responsibility.
b. Assume responsibility for the other auditor.
c. Require a departure from an unqualified opinion.
d. Are an improper form of reporting.

104. March, CPA, is engaged by Monday Corp., a client, to audit the financial statements of Wall Corp., a company that is not March's client. Monday expects to present Wall's audited financial statements with March's auditor's report to 1st Federal Bank to obtain financing in Monday's attempt to purchase Wall. In these circumstances, March's auditor's report would usually be addressed to
a. Monday Corp., the client that engaged March.
b. Wall Corp., the entity audited by March.
c. 1st Federal Bank.
d. Both Monday Corp. and 1st Federal Bank.

105. An auditor concludes that there is substantial doubt about an entity's ability to continue as a going concern for a reasonable period of time. If the entity's financial statements adequately disclose its financial difficulties, the auditor's report is required to include an explanatory paragraph that specifically uses the phrase(s)

	"Reasonable period of time, not to exceed one year"	*"Going concern"*
a.	Yes	Yes
b.	Yes	No
c.	No	Yes
d.	No	No

106. In the first audit of a client, an auditor was not able to gather sufficient evidence about the consistent application of accounting principles between the current and the prior year, as well as the amounts of assets or liabilities at the beginning of the current year. This was due to the client's record retention policies. If the amounts in question could materially affect current operating results, the auditor would
a. Be unable to express an opinion on the current year's results of operations and cash flows.
b. Express a qualified opinion on the financial statements because of a client-imposed scope limitation.
c. Withdraw from the engagement and refuse to be associated with the financial statements.
d. Specifically state that the financial statements are **not** comparable to the prior year due to an uncertainty.

107. What is an auditor's reporting responsibility concerning information accompanying the basic financial statements in an auditor-submitted document?
a. The auditor should report on all the accompanying information included in the document.
b. The auditor should report on the accompanying information only if the auditor participated in its preparation.
c. The auditor should report on the accompanying information only if the auditor did **not** participate in its preparation.
d. The auditor should report on the accompanying information only if it contains obvious material misstatements.

Chapter Three - Problems
Standards of Reporting

NUMBER 1

The auditor's standard report consists of a statement describing the nature of the examination, and an expression of the auditor's opinion. There are circumstances where the auditor's standard report is modified by adding one or more separate explanatory paragraphs, and/or modifying the wording of the scope paragraph or opinion paragraph.

For purposes of this question, assume the auditor is independent and has previously expressed an unqualified opinion on the prior year's financial statements. For the current year, only single-year (not comparative) statements are presented.

Required: Identify the circumstances necessitating modification of the auditor's standard report. For each circumstance indicate the types of opinion that would be appropriate and describe the report modifications.

Organize the answer as indicated in the following example:

Circumstances	Type of Opinion	Report Modification
1. The financial statements are materially affected by a departure from generally accepted accounting principles.	1. The auditor should express an "except for" qualified opinion or an adverse opinion.	1. The auditor should explain the basis and effects of the departure in an explanatory paragraph and modify the opinion paragraph.

NUMBER 2

Number 2 consists of 7 items. Select the **best** answer for each item. **Answer all items.**

Required:
Items 1 through 7 present various independent factual situations an auditor might encounter in conducting an audit. List A represents the types of opinions the auditor ordinarily would issue and List B represents the report modifications (if any) that would be necessary. For each situation, select one response from List A and one item from List B. Select as the **best** answer for each item, the action the auditor normally would take. The types of opinions in List A and the report modifications in List B may be selected once, more than once, or not at all.

Assume:
- The auditor is independent.
- The auditor previously expressed an unqualified opinion on the prior year's financial statements.
- Only single-year (not comparative) statements are presented for the current year.
- The conditions for an unqualified opinion exist unless contradicted in the factual situations.
- The conditions stated in the factual situations are material.
- No report modifications are to be made except in response to the factual situation.

Items to be Answered:

1. In auditing the long-term investments account, an auditor is unable to obtain audited financial statements for an investee located in a foreign country. The auditor concludes that sufficient competent evidential matter regarding this investment cannot be obtained.

2. Due to recurring operating losses and working capital deficiencies, an auditor has substantial doubt about an entity's ability to continue as a going concern for a reasonable period of time. However, the financial statement disclosures concerning these matters are adequate.

3. A principal auditor decides to take responsibility for the work of another CPA who audited a wholly-owned subsidiary of the entity and issued an unqualified opinion. The total assets and revenues of the subsidiary represent 17% and 18%, respectively, of the total assets and revenues of the entity being audited.

4. An entity issues financial statements that present financial position and results of operations but omits the related statement of cash flows. Management discloses in the notes to the financial statements that it does not believe the statement of cash flows to be a useful financial statement.

5. An entity changes its depreciation method for production equipment from the straight-line to a units-of-production method based on hours of utilization. The auditor concurs with the change although it has a material effect on the comparability of the entity's financial statements.

6. An entity is a defendant in a lawsuit alleging infringement of certain patent rights. However, the ultimate outcome of the litigation cannot be reasonably estimated by management. The auditor believes there is a reasonable possibility of a significantly material loss, but the lawsuit is adequately disclosed in the notes to the financial statements.

7. An entity discloses in the notes to the financial statements certain lease obligations. The auditor believes that the failure to capitalize these leases is a departure from generally accepted accounting principles.

List A	List B
Types of Opinions	**Report Modifications**
A. An "except for" qualified opinion	H. Describe the circumstances in an explanatory paragraph *preceding* the opinion paragraph *without modifying* the three standard paragraphs.
B. An unqualified opinion	
C. An adverse opinion	
D. A disclaimer of opinion	I. Describe the circumstances in an explanatory paragraph *following* the opinion paragraph *without modifying* the three standard paragraphs.
E. Either an "except for" qualified opinion or an adverse opinion	
F. Either a disclaimer of opinion or an "except for" qualified opinion	J. Describe the circumstances in an explanatory paragraph *preceding* the opinion paragraph and *modify* the *opinion* paragraph.
G. Either an adverse opinion or a disclaimer of opinion	K. Describe the circumstances in an explanatory paragraph *following* the opinion paragraph and *modify* the *opinion* paragraph.
	L. Describe the circumstances in an explanatory paragraph *preceding* the opinion paragraph and *modify* the *scope* and *opinion* paragraphs.
	M. Describe the circumstances in an explanatory paragraph *following* the opinion paragraph and *modify* the *scope* and *opinion* paragraphs.
	N. Describe the circumstances within the *scope* paragraph without adding an explanatory paragraph.
	O. Describe the circumstances within the *opinion* paragraph without adding an explanatory paragraph.
	P. Describe the circumstances within the *scope* and *opinion* paragraphs without adding an explanatory paragraph.
	Q. Issue the *standard* auditor's report *without modification.*

NUMBER 3

Number 3 consists of 8 items. Select the best answers for each item. Answer all items. Your grade will be based on the total number of correct answers.

Required:
Items 91 through 98 present various independent factual situations an auditor might encounter in conducting an audit. List A represents the types of opinions the auditor ordinarily would issue and List B represents the report modifications (if any) that would be necessary. For each situation, select one response from List A and one from List B. Select as the **best** answers for each item, the action the auditor normally would take. The types of opinions in List A and the report modifications in List B may be selected once, more than once, or not at all.

Assume:
- The auditor is independent.

- The auditor previously expressed an unqualified opinion on the prior year's financial statements.

- Only single-year (not comparative) statements are presented for the current year.

- The conditions for an unqualified opinion exist unless contradicted by the facts.

- The conditions stated in the factual situations are material.

- No report modifications are to be made except in response to the factual situation.

91. An auditor hires an actuary to assist in corroborating a client's complex pension calculations concerning accrued pension liabilities that account for 35% of the client's total liabilities. The actuary's findings are reasonably close to the client's calculations and support the financial statements.

92. A client holds a note receivable consisting of principal and accrued interest payable in 1998. The note's maker recently filed a voluntary bankruptcy petition, but the client failed to reduce the recorded value of the note to its net realizable value, which is approximately 20% of the recorded amount.

93. An auditor is engaged to audit a client's financial statements after the annual physical inventory count. The accounting records are not sufficiently reliable to enable the auditor to become satisfied as to the year-end inventory balances.

94. Big City is required by GASB to present supplementary information outside the basic financial statements concerning the disclosure of pension information. Big City's auditor determines that the supplementary information, which is not required to be part of the basic financial statements, is omitted.

95. A client's financial statements do not disclose certain long-term lease obligations. The auditor determines that the omitted disclosures are required by FASB.

96. A principal auditor decides not to take responsibility for the work of another CPA who audited a wholly-owned subsidiary of the principal auditor's client. The total assets and revenues of the subsidiary represent 27% and 28%, respectively, of the related consolidated totals.

97. A client changes its method of accounting for the cost of inventories from FIFO to LIFO. The auditor concurs with the change although it has a material effect on the comparability of the financial statements.

98. Due to losses and adverse key financial ratios, an auditor has substantial doubt about a client's ability to continue as a going concern for a reasonable period of time. The client has adequately disclosed its financial difficulties in a note to its financial statements, which do not include any adjustments that might result from the outcome of this uncertainty.

List A	List B
Types of Opinions	**Report Modifications**
A. Either an "except for" qualified opinion or an adverse opinion	H. Describe the circumstances in an explanatory paragraph *without modifying* the three standard paragraphs.
B. Either a disclaimer of opinion or an "except for" qualified opinion	I. Describe the circumstances in an explanatory paragraph and *modify* the *opinion* paragraph.
C. Either an adverse opinion or a disclaimer of opinion	J. Describe the circumstances in an explanatory paragraph and *modify* the *scope* and *opinion* paragraphs.
D. An "except for" qualified opinion	K. Describe the circumstances in an explanatory paragraph and *modify* the *introductory, scope,* and *opinion* paragraphs.
E. An unqualified opinion	L. Describe the circumstances within the *scope* paragraph without adding an explanatory paragraph.
F. An adverse opinion	M. Describe the circumstances within the *opinion* paragraph without adding an explanatory paragraph.
G. A disclaimer of opinion	N. Describe the circumstances within the *scope* and *opinion* paragraphs without adding an explanatory paragraph.
	O. Describe the circumstances within the *introductory, scope,* and *opinion* paragraphs without adding an explanatory paragraph.
	P. Issue the *standard* auditor's report *without modification.*

NUMBER 4

Number 4 consists of 15 items. Select the **best** answer for each item.

Required:

Items 91 through 105 represent a series of unrelated statements, questions, excerpts, and comments taken from various parts of an auditor's working paper file. Below the items is a list of the likely sources of the statements, questions, excerpts, and comments. Select, as the best answer for each item, the most likely source. Select only one source for each item. A source may be selected once, more than once, or not at all.

Statements, Questions, Excerpts, and Comments

91. There are no material transactions that have not been properly recorded in the accounting records underlying the financial statements.

92. In connection with an audit of our financial statements, management has prepared, and furnished to our auditors, a description and evaluation of certain contingencies.

93. Provision has been made for any material loss to be sustained in the fulfillment of, or from the inability to fulfill, any sales commitments.

94. Fees for our services are based on our regular per diem rates, plus travel and other out-of-pocket expenses.

95. The objective of our audit is to express an unqualified opinion on the financial statements, although it is possible that facts or circumstances encountered may preclude us from expressing an unqualified opinion.

96. There have been no fraudulent activities involving employees that could have a material effect on the financial statements.

97. Are you aware of any facts or circumstances that may indicate a lack of integrity by any member of senior management?

98. If a difference of opinion on a practice problem existed between engagement personnel and a specialist or other consultant, was the difference resolved in accordance with firm policy and appropriately documented?

99. Although we have not conducted a comprehensive, detailed search of our records, no other deposit or loan accounts have come to our attention except as noted below.

100. At the conclusion of our audit, we will request certain written representations from you about the financial statements and related matters.

101. We have no plans or intentions that may materially affect the carrying value or classification of assets and liabilities.

102. As discussed in Note 14 to the financial statements, the Company has had numerous dealings with businesses controlled by, and people who are related to, the officers of the Company.

103. There were unreasonable delays by management in permitting the commencement of the audit and in providing needed information.

104. If this statement is not correct, please write promptly, using the enclosed envelope, and give details of any differences directly to our auditors.

105. The Company has suffered recurring losses from operations and has a net capital deficiency that raises substantial doubt about its ability to continue as a going concern.

List of Sources
A. Partner's engagement review program.

B. Communication with predecessor auditor.

C. Auditor's engagement letter.

D. Management representation letter.

E. Standard financial institution confirmation request.

F. Auditor's communication with the audit committee.

G. Auditor's report.

H. Letter for underwriters.

I. Audit inquiry letter to legal counsel.

J. Accounts receivable confirmation.

NUMBER 5

Perry & Price, CPAs, audited the consolidated financial statements of Bond Company for the year ended December 31, 1998, and expressed an adverse opinion because Bond carried its plant and equipment at appraisal values and provided for depreciation on the basis of such values.

Perry & Price also audited Bond's financial statements for the year ended December 31, 1999. These consolidated financial statements are being presented on a comparative basis with those of the prior year, and an unqualified opinion is being expressed.

Smith, the engagement supervisor, instructed Adler, an assistant on the engagement, to draft the auditor's report on May 3, 2000, the date of completion of the field work. In drafting the report, Adler considered the following:

- Bond recently changed its method of accounting for plant and equipment and restated its 1998 consolidated financial statements to conform with GAAP. Consequently, the CPA firm's present opinion on those statements is different (unqualified) from the opinion expressed on May 12, 1999.

- Larkin & Lake, CPAs, audited the financial statements of BX, Inc., a consolidated subsidiary of Bond, for the year ended December 31, 1999. The subsidiary's financial statements reflected total assets and revenues of 2% and 3%, respectively, of the consolidated totals. Larkin and Lake expressed an unqualified opinion and furnished Perry & Price with a copy of the auditor's report. Perry & Price has decided to assume responsibility for the work of Larkin & Lake insofar as it relates to the expression of an opinion on the consolidated financial statements taken as a whole.

- Bond is a defendant in a lawsuit alleging patent infringement. This is adequately disclosed in the notes to Bond's financial statements, but no provision for liability has been recorded because the ultimate outcome of the litigation cannot presently be determined.

Auditor's Report

We have audited the accompanying consolidated balance sheets of Bond Company and subsidiaries as of December 31, 1999 and 1998, and the related consolidated statements of income, retained earnings, and cash flows for the years then ended. These financial statements are the responsibility of the Company's management. Our responsibility is to express an opinion on these financial statements based on our audits.

We conducted our audits in accordance with generally accepted auditing standards. Those standards require that we plan and perform the audit to obtain reasonable assurance about whether the financial statements are free of material misstatement. An audit includes examining, on a test basis, evidence supporting the amounts and disclosures in the financial statements. An audit also includes assessing the accounting principles used, as well as evaluating the overall financial statement presentation. We believe that our audits provide a reasonable basis for our opinion.

In our previous report, we expressed an opinion that the 1998 financial statements did not fairly present financial position, results of operations, and cash flows in conformity with generally accepted accounting principles because the Company carried it plant and equipment at appraisal values and provided for depreciation on the basis of such values. As described in Note 12, the Company has changed its method of accounting for these items and restated its 1998 financial statements to conform with generally accepted accounting principles. Accordingly, our present opinion on the 1998 financial statements, as presented herein, is different from that expressed in our previous report.

In our opinion, the consolidated financial statements referred to above present fairly, in all material respects, the financial position of Bond Company and subsidiaries as of December 31, 1999 and 1998, and the results of its operations and its cash flows for the years then ended in conformity with generally accepted accounting principles except for the change in accounting principles, with which we concur, and the uncertainty, which is discussed in the following explanatory paragraph.

The Company is a defendant in a lawsuit alleging infringement of certain patent rights. The Company has filed a counteraction, and preliminary hearings and discovery proceedings are in progress. The ultimate outcome of the litigation cannot presently be determined. Accordingly, no provision for any liability that may result upon adjudication has been made in the accompanying financial statements.

Perry & Price, CPAs
May 3, 2000

Required:

Smith reviewed Adler's draft and indicated in the Supervisor's Review Notes below that were deficiencies in Adler's draft. Items 1 through 15 represent the deficiencies noted by Smith. For each deficiency, indicate whether Smith is correct (C) or incorrect (I) in the criticism of Adler's draft.

Supervisor's Review Notes

1. The report is improperly titled.

2. All the basic financial statements are not properly identified in the introductory paragraph.

3. There is no reference to the American Institute of Certified Public Accountants in the introductory paragraph.

4. Larkin & Lake are not identified in the introductory and opinion paragraphs.

5. The subsidiary, BX, Inc., is not identified, and the magnitude of BX's financial statements is not disclosed in the introductory paragraph.

6. The report does not state in the scope paragraph that generally accepted auditing standards require analytical procedures to be performed in planning an audit.

7. The report does not state in the scope paragraph that an audit includes assessing internal control.

8. The report does not state in the scope paragraph that an audit includes assessing significant estimates made by management.

9. The date of the previous report (May 12, 1999) is not disclosed in the first explanatory paragraph.

10. It is inappropriate to disclose in the first explanatory paragraph the circumstances that caused Perry & Price to express a different opinion on the 1998 financial statements.

11. The concurrence with the accounting change is inappropriate in the opinion paragraph.

12. Reference to the (litigation) uncertainty should not be made in the opinion paragraph.

13. The last explanatory paragraph describing the (litigation) uncertainty needs not to be added to the report.

14. The letter of inquiry to Bond's lawyer concerning litigation, claims, and assessments is not referred to in the scope paragraph.

15. The report is not dual dated, but it should be because of the change of opinion on the 1998 financial statements.

NUMBER 6

Number 6 consists of 13 items pertaining to possible deficiencies in an accountant's review report. Select the **best** answer for each item.

Jordan & Stone, CPAs, audited the financial statements of Tech Co., a nonpublic entity, for the year ended December 31, 1991, and expressed an unqualified opinion. For the year ended December 31, 1992, Tech issued comparative financial statements. Jordan & Stone reviewed Tech's 1992 financial statements and Kent, an assistant on the engagement, drafted the accountants' review report below. Land, the engagement supervisor, decided not to reissue the prior year's auditors' report, but instructed Kent to include a separate paragraph in the current year's review report describing the responsibility assumed for the prior year's audited financial statements. This is an appropriate reporting procedure.

Land reviewed Kent's draft and indicated in the *Supervisor's Review Notes* below that there were several deficiencies in Kent's draft.

Accountant's Review Report

We have reviewed and audited the accompanying balance sheets of Tech Co. as of December 31, 1992 and 1991, and the related statements of income, retained earnings, and cash flows for the years then ended, in accordance with Statements on Standards for Accounting and Review Services issued by the American Institute of Certified Public Accountants and generally accepted auditing standards. All information included in these financial statements is the representation of the management of Tech Co.

A review consists principally of inquiries of company personnel and analytical procedures applied to financial data. It is substantially less in scope than an audit in accordance with generally accepted auditing standards, the objective of which is the expression of an opinion regarding the financial statements taken as a whole.

Based on our review, we are not aware of any material modifications that should be made to the accompanying financial statements. Because of the inherent limitations of a review engagement, this report is intended for the information of management and should not be used for any other purpose.

The financial statements for the year ended December 31, 1991, were audited by us and our report was dated March 2, 1992. We have no responsibility for updating that report for events and circumstances occurring after that date.

Jordan and Stone, CPAs
March 1, 1993

Required:

Items 61 through 73 represent deficiencies noted by Land. For each deficiency, indicate whether Land is correct (C) or incorrect (I) in the criticism of Kent's draft.

Items to be Answered:

Supervisor's Review Notes
61. There should be **no** reference to the prior year's audited financial statements in the first (introductory) paragraph.

62. All the current-year basic financial statements are **not** properly identified in the first (introductory) paragraph.

63. There should be **no** reference to the American Institute of Certified Public Accountants in the first (introductory) paragraph.

64. The accountant's review and audit responsibilities should follow management's responsibilities in the first (introductory) paragraph.

65. There should be **no** comparison of the scope of a review to an audit in the second (scope) paragraph.

66. Negative assurance should be expressed on the current year's reviewed financial statements in the second (scope) paragraph.

67. There should be a statement that **no** opinion is expressed on the current year's financial statements in the second (scope) paragraph.

68. There should be a reference to "conformity with generally accepted accounting principles" in the third paragraph.

69. There should no restriction on the distribution of the accountant's review report in the third paragraph.

70. There should be **no** reference to "material modifications" in the third paragraph.

71. There should be an indication of the type of opinion expressed on the prior year's audited financial statements in the fourth (separate) paragraph.

72. There should be an indication that **no** auditing procedures were performed after the date of the report on the prior year's financial statements in the fourth (separate) paragraph.

73. There should be **no** reference to "updating the prior year's auditor's report for events and circumstances occurring after that date" in the fourth (separate) paragraph.

Chapter Three - Solutions to Questions
Standards of Reporting

1. (b) The auditor's scope of examination was limited in this case, and since the first paragraph of the auditor's report indicates his scope, this exception should be reported here.

2. (c) These statements are required for complete presentation under GAAP.

3. (a) Disclosure is the third standard of reporting and thus failure to disclose would result in a qualified report. Answer (b) is incorrect because a qualified report would be issued instead of an adverse opinion. The key is that this item was material to qualify, but not pervasive which would result in an adverse opinion.

4. (a) "Except for" and "adverse" opinions are concerned with departures from GAAP. The difference in which opinion to render is determined by materiality and pervasiveness.

5. (a) Limitations on the scope of the audit can come about by client restrictions, inability to obtain sufficient competent evidential matter or inadequacy of client accounting records. Answer (b) is incorrect because the auditor can report on only one basic financial statement. Answer (c) is incorrect because the use of another auditor is not a scope limitation. Answer (d) is incorrect because this would not necessarily result in a scope limitation.

6. (c) An explanatory paragraph is used when the opinion paragraph is to be modified. A reference in the opinion paragraph to middle paragraph explains the reason for the modification.

7. (d) The statement of cash flows is required by GAAP and its omission results in a qualified except for opinion. The statement of cash flows, for reporting purposes, is considered the omission of a disclosure.

8. (b) Deviations from GAAP result in either an "except for" qualification or an adverse opinion.

9. (d) The question states the auditor concludes the statements are **not** in conformity with GAAP. In order to make this statement in his report, the auditor must issue an adverse opinion. A qualification, rather than an adverse opinion, still states the financial statements present fairly, except for... An adverse opinion states the "financial statements do not present fairly..."

10. (b) An adjustment represents a departure from GAAP. Thus an "except for" opinion is in order.

11. (b) The auditor cannot use his report to explain problems with or disclosures required by the client in their financial statements. "With the foregoing explanation" implies the auditor's opinion is conditional upon the disclosure in his report, and it is not.

12. (a) The report is satisfactory because when the CPA is preparing unaudited statements, he has the responsibility to ensure that the statements are in accordance with GAAP. If they are not, the CPA must propose adjustments, and if the client refuses to book said adjustments, to so disclose in his report.

13. (c) The principal auditor may or may not refer to the other auditor's examination. If he does, he is sharing the responsibility for his opinion. If he accepts full responsibility, no reference is made to the other auditor. Choices (a) and (b) are wrong because of the word "must." Choice (d) is incorrect because it does not result in a qualified opinion.

14. (d) There are two types of subsequent events. 1) Requires disclosure of events of importance subsequent to the balance sheet date but prior to issuance of the report. The important point here is the amounts on the statements are correct as of year end. 2) Requires a change in the amount previously determined as of the balance sheet date. New information is available that sheds new light on amounts previously estimated. Answers (a), (b), (c), are type 1, and answer (d) is type 2.

15. (c) This item refers to the prior year's report. The auditor is responsible for subsequent events only through the date of his report.

16. (d) The auditor should refer to the division of responsibility in the introductory, scope and opinion paragraphs. See example in text.

17. (c) When the other auditor is named, his report must be presented.

18. (d) The auditor's subsequent events work extends through the date of his audit report.

19. (b) When referring to another auditor's work, the principal auditor must disclose the scope of the second auditor's examination in relation to the total consolidated assets of both companies.

20. (a) Part of the examination may be performed by another CPA with no effect on the principal auditor's opinion unless, of course, there is a problem that would normally require modification of the auditor's report.

21. (b) If the CPA relies on the work of another auditor, it does not constitute a scope limitation. Answers (a), (c), and (d) constitute scope limitations.

22. (c) The reference is to work performed by other auditors. This does not constitute a reporting problem, but rather divides the responsibility for the opinion between the principal auditor (the auditor signing the opinion) and another auditor who has performed part of the examination.

23. (c) Observation of the inventory count and confirmation of receivables is normally performed during an audit. However, if circumstances do not permit these procedures to be performed, the auditor may apply alternative audit procedures that may include observation of an inventory count at a later date and the verification of receivable balances by auditing subsequent cash receipts. If the auditor is able to employ alternative procedures he considers appropriate in the circumstances, no modification or qualification of the audit report is necessary.

24. (d) Adverse opinions may be issued when there is a material and pervasive departure from GAAP or substantial deficiencies in disclosures (footnotes to financial statements). Answer (d) is a departure from GAAP and could be the basis for the issuance of an adverse opinion. Answers (a) and (c) may result in a disclaimer of opinion, not an adverse opinion. Answer (b) is a scope limitation and may result in a qualified opinion or a disclaimer of an opinion.

25. (d) If an auditor decides that he or she is the principal auditor and that he or she can use the other auditor's report, because the other auditor is reputable and independent, the principal auditor must decide whether or not to make reference to the other auditor. If the principal auditor decides not to refer to the other auditor, he or she should visit the other auditor, discuss the procedures followed, and review the audit program and working papers of the other auditor. Answer (a) is incorrect because if the principal auditor decides not to refer to the other auditor, no references of any kind would be made in the report. Answer (b) would not fulfill the principal auditor's reporting responsibilities. Answer (c) is incorrect because permission would only be necessary if the principal auditor decides to refer to and name the other auditor.

26. (a) The only reporting requirement necessary when there has been an accounting change is for the auditor to add a fourth paragraph to his report. The fourth paragraph would be placed directly after the opinion paragraph and it would refer to a footnote in the financial statements that describes the nature of the change in the accounting principle.

27. (b) GAAS explicitly states that if the predecessor's report is not presented with the comparative financial statements, the current (successor) auditor's report must refer to the fact that the predecessor expressed an unqualified opinion on the prior year's financial statements. In order to do this the successor should modify the introductory paragraph of his report to include information about the prior year's audit.

28. (c) Generally accepted auditing standards require the auditor to obtain written representations from management. Management's refusal to furnish those written representations, therefore, would always constitute a limitation on the scope of the auditor's examination which in turn would preclude an unqualified opinion. Answers (a) and (d) could result in scope limitations if the auditor is unable to satisfy himself by alternative procedures.

29. (c) When a qualified opinion results from a limitation on the scope of the audit or an insufficiency of evidential matter, the situation should be described in an explanatory paragraph preceding the opinion paragraph and referred to in both the scope and opinion paragraphs of the auditor's report. It is not appropriate for the scope of the audit to be explained in a note to the financial statements, since the description of the audit scope is the responsibility of the auditor and not that of his client.

30. (d) The auditor's responsibility with respect to information in an annual report does not extend beyond the financial information identified in his report. However, he should read the other information and consider whether it is materially inconsistent with information appearing in the financial statements. If he concludes that the other information is inconsistent and the client refuses to correct the inconsistency, the auditor should either revise his report to include an explanatory paragraph describing the material inconsistency, withhold the use of his report in the annual report, or withdraw from the engagement.

31. (d) When an accountant is not independent, any procedures he might perform would not be in accordance with generally accepted auditing standards, and he would be precluded from expressing an opinion on such statements. Accordingly, he should disclaim an opinion on such statements. Accordingly, he should disclaim an opinion with respect to those financial statements. The other answers could result in qualified opinions, but lack of independence will always result in a disclaimer of opinion.

32. (d) When unaudited financial statements are presented in comparative form with audited financial statements in any document, other than in documents filed with the Securities and Exchange Commission, the financial statements that have not been audited should be clearly marked to indicate their status and either the report on the prior period should be reissued or the report on the current period should include as a separate paragraph an appropriate description of the responsibility assumed for the financial statements of the prior period.

33. (b) Segment information is one of the disclosures required by generally accepted accounting principles. If the entity refuses to include in the financial statements part or all of the segment information that the auditor believes is required to be disclosed, the auditor should modify his opinion on the financial statements because of inadequate disclosure and should describe the type of information omitted. The auditor is not required to provide the omitted segment information in his report. When the financial statements, including the accompanying notes, fail to disclose required information, the auditor should express a qualified or adverse opinion. Answer (b) refers to a qualified opinion because of inadequate disclosure. Answer (c) refers to an adverse opinion because of lack of conformity with generally accepted accounting principles, not because of inadequate disclosure.

34. (a) When restrictions that significantly limit the scope of the audit are imposed by the client, ordinarily the auditor should disclaim an opinion on the financial statements. A letter of inquiry to the client's lawyer is the primary means of obtaining corroboration of the information furnished by management concerning litigation, claims, and assessments. Accordingly, the client not permitting the auditor to inquire of outside legal counsel is a significant scope limitation that would result in a disclaimer of opinion.

35. (d) When there has been a change in accounting principles or in the method of their application, the auditor should refer to the change in an explanatory paragraph (following the opinion paragraph) which identifies the nature of the change and refers the reader to the note in the financial statements that discusses the change. The other paragraphs in the auditor's report are not affected.

36. (a) The auditor's standard report includes a statement that the financial statements are the responsibility of the Company's management and that the auditor's responsibility is to express an opinion on the financial statements based on his audit.

37. (b) Restrictions on the scope of an audit such as the timing of the work, inability to obtain sufficient competent evidential matter, or an inadequacy in the accounting records, may require an auditor to qualify his opinion or disclaim an opinion. When restrictions that significantly limit the scope of the audit are imposed by the client, ordinarily the auditor should disclaim an opinion on the financial statements.

38. (c) The auditor will typically want the client to make all minutes of meetings of stockholders, directors and committees of directors available. If management does not make these minutes available to the auditor, this would be considered a scope restriction which could result in the auditor qualifying his opinion or disclaiming an opinion. Answer (a) refers to financial statements prepared in conformity with a basis of accounting other than GAAP. The auditor can express an unqualified opinion on whether these financial statements are presented fairly in conformity with the cash basis. The auditor's report on these cash-basis financial statements would include a statement that they were prepared using a basis of accounting other than GAAP and would refer the reader to a note in the financial statements where management states that the financial statements are not intended to be presented in accordance with GAAP [answer (b)]. Answer (d) involves a situation which has limited reporting objectives; the auditor can issue an unqualified opinion on one basic financial statement and not on the others.

39. (a) An uncertainty exists when the outcome of future events that may affect the financial statements is not susceptible of reasonable estimation by management and it cannot be determined whether the financial statements should be adjusted or in what amount. Such uncertainties may require an explanatory paragraph in the auditor's report. The uncertainties would not affect the other paragraphs in the report and would not result in a qualified opinion [answer (c)] or adverse opinion [answer (d)]. Answer (b) is no longer a reporting option.

40. (b) When the auditor expresses an adverse opinion, he should disclose in a separate explanatory paragraph preceding the opinion paragraph of his report all the substantive reasons for his adverse opinion and the principal effects of the subject matter of the adverse opinion on financial position, results of operations, and cash flows, if practicable.

41. (b) If management has not provided reasonable justification for a change in accounting principle, the auditor should express a qualified opinion or, if the effect of the change is sufficiently material, express an adverse opinion on the financial statements. The auditor would express the same opinion each year those financial statements are presented. The auditor would **not** qualify the report only the year of the change [answer (a)] and would **not** qualify his opinion on financial statements covering periods subsequent to the year of change [answer (c)]. The auditor's exception relates to the accounting change and does not affect the status of the newly adopted principle. Accordingly, while expressing an exception for the year of change, the opinion regarding the subsequent years' statements need not express an exception to use of the newly adopted principle.

42. (b) When an accountant is associated with the financial statements of a public entity, but has not audited or reviewed such statements, the report to be issued is a disclaimer of opinion. Answer (a) applies only to financial statements of nonpublic entities. Answer (c) is made up. Answer (d) applies to audits of financial statements.

43. (a) Review of compliance with terms of debt and loan agreements is an audit procedure that may identify conditions and events that indicate there could be substantial doubt about an entity's ability to continue as a going concern for a reasonable period of time. Default on such agreements may indicate possible financial difficulty. The audit procedures listed in answers (b), (c) and (d) would be less likely to identify information about an entity's ability to continue as a going concern.

44. (a) The paragraph is referring to the uncertainty that the company will remain a going concern. Material uncertainties cause the auditor to modify the audit report by adding a fourth paragraph that follows the opinion paragraph. However, the type of opinion issued is unqualified.

45. (d) Since the opinion resulted from a scope limitation, reference to the explanatory paragraph needs to be made in the scope paragraph. This is done by adding the phrase, "Except as discussed in the following paragraph, we conducted ...," to the beginning of the scope paragraph. The opinion paragraph is also modified as follows: "In my opinion, except for ..., the financial statements ... ."

46. (c) Answers (a), (b) and (d) are scope limitations which, depending upon materiality, usually lead to a disclaimer of an opinion. Answer (c) refers to inadequate disclosure which is a departure from GAAP and, if material, would lead to a qualified except for opinion or an adverse opinion.

47. (c) Answers (a), (b) and (d) are all departures from GAAP and, as such, would lead to qualified or adverse opinions. Answer (c) is a description of a scope limitation which would lead to a qualified except for opinion or a disclaimer of an opinion depending on materiality.

48. (d) A qualified opinion should include the word "except" or "exception" in a phrase such as "except for" or "with the exception of." Phrases such as "subject to" and "with the foregoing explanation" are not clear or forceful enough and should not be used. Since accompanying notes are part of the financial statements, wording such as "fairly presented, in all material respects, when read in conjunction with Note X" is likely to be misunderstood and should not be used.

49. (b) When an adverse opinion is expressed, the opinion paragraph should include a direct reference to a separate paragraph preceding the opinion paragraph that discloses all the substantive reasons for the adverse opinion and the principal effects on the financial statements, if practicable. Answers (a) and (c) apply to the separate paragraph, not the opinion paragraph. Answer (d) does not refer to adverse opinions, but to uncertainties and scope limitations, which would be described in a separate paragraph, not the opinion paragraph.

50. (a) A disclaimer of opinion should not be used when the auditor believes that there are material departures from generally accepted accounting principles, including inadequate disclosure. A disclaimer is appropriate in answers (b), (c) and (d), which are situations where the auditor may be unable to express an opinion because he has not performed an audit sufficient in scope to enable him to form an opinion.

51. (b) An auditor may update an opinion on prior period financial statements. An updated opinion means that an auditor may change (update) his opinion on previously issued financial statements because of new facts coming to the auditor's attention in the current period that affect a prior period. Such a situation is described in this question. The client departed from GAAP in the prior period; however, in the current period, the client wishes to restate the prior period financial statements to be in conformity with GAAP.

52. (a) Uncertainties may cause the auditor to expand the standard unqualified opinion by adding a fourth paragraph referring to a footnote in the financial statement describing the uncertainty. However, since this uncertainty was described as remote, no footnote disclosure is necessary. Therefore, the auditor would issue a standard three-paragraph unqualified opinion.

53. (d) The explanatory paragraph would be inserted between the scope paragraph and opinion paragraph. The opinion paragraph would refer to the explanatory paragraph as a basis for the qualification. The scope and introductory paragraph would not be modified.

54. (a) The inclusion of such a paragraph is appropriate. The auditor is emphasizing a matter in the financial statements.

55. (d) The client has a responsibility to disclose in the financial statements concerns regarding the entity's ability to continue as a going concern. The auditor has a responsibility to consider whether the disclosure should be made and, if made, is it adequate. If the auditor concludes that disclosure is not adequate, then the auditor should issue a qualified except-for opinion.

56. (b) A justified change in an accounting principle results in the auditor issuing an unqualified opinion. However, the auditor must include a separate paragraph in the audit report referring to a footnote in the financial statements describing the change. This additional paragraph would follow the opinion paragraph.

57. (a) An auditor has no responsibility to perform any additional auditing procedures after the audit report is issued except in the following two situations:
1. The auditor omitted an auditing procedure that should have been performed, for example, obtaining a client representation letter, and
2. Information that comes to the auditor's attention that existed at the report date, and this information, if known, may have affected the auditor's report.

58. (d) There is a specific statement in the audit report to examining evidence on a test basis. However, there is no reference to the consistent application of GAAP. The reference is implicit because the phrase, "presents fairly in accordance with GAAP," includes the fact that GAAP has been consistently applied.

59. (d) The inability to obtain sufficient competent evidential matter is the definition of a scope limitation. A scope limitation would lead the auditor to issue a qualified except-for opinion or disclaim an opinion.

60. (a) If the auditor concludes that there is substantial doubt about an entity's ability to continue as a going concern for a reasonable time, he should express that conclusion through the use of the phrase "substantial doubt about its (the entity's) ability to continue as a going concern." That conclusion should be reflected in an explanatory paragraph following the opinion paragraph.

61. (d) The auditor's report does not extend beyond the financial information identified in the report and the auditor has no obligation to perform any procedures to corroborate other information. However, the auditor should read the other information in a client's document that includes audited financial statements and consider whether such information is materially inconsistent with information appearing in the audited financial statements.

62. (b) In a situation where a principal auditor uses the work and report of another auditor who has audited the financial statements of a subsidiary, the principal auditor may decide to take responsibility for the work and report of the other auditor and would make no reference to the other auditor. If the principal auditor decides not to assume that responsibility, his report should make reference to the audit of the other auditor and should indicate clearly the division of responsibility between himself and the other auditor. Appropriate wording is illustrated in the question.

63. (b) When a CPA is associated with the financial statements of a public entity but has not audited or reviewed such statements, the CPA should issue a disclaimer of opinion. When a CPA issues such a disclaimer, he or she has no responsibility to apply any procedures beyond reading the financial statements for obvious material errors. Answers (a) and (c) are incorrect because the CPA has a responsibility to read the financial statements, not to document the internal control structure or ascertain whether the financial statements are in conformity with GAAP. Answer (d) is incorrect because the CPA is not responsible for determining whether management elected to omit substantially all disclosures, although the CPA will likely discover this when reading the financial statements.

64. (b) When, after considering management's plans, the auditor concludes there is substantial doubt about the entity's ability to continue as a going concern for a reasonable period of time, the auditor should consider the possible effects on the financial statements and the adequacy of the related disclosure. In addition, the auditor's report should include an explanatory paragraph after the opinion paragraph to reflect the conclusion about the entity's ability to continue as a going concern. The auditor would not issue a qualified or adverse opinion, as indicated in answer (a), unless the disclosure was inadequate. Answer (c) is incorrect because the auditor's responsibility to determine that the audit committee is informed about significant accounting estimates is separate from the auditor's consideration of the going concern issue. Answer (d) is incorrect because substantial doubt about an entity's ability to continue as a going concern that arose in the current period does not imply that a basis for such doubt existed in the prior period, and, therefore should not affect the auditor's report on prior periods.

65. (a) When a principal auditor uses the work and reports of other auditors who conducted audits of components of the overall financial statements, he or she must decide whether to make reference to those other auditors. If the principal auditor decides to assume responsibility for the other auditor's work, no reference is made to the other auditor in the principal auditor's audit report. If the principal auditor decides not to assume that responsibility, the principal auditor's report will refer to the other auditor and will indicate the division of responsibility between the principal and other auditors. Answer (b) is incorrect because the principal auditor would not make reference to the other auditor if the portion audited by the other auditor were immaterial. Answer (c) is incorrect because the principal auditor would inquire as to the other auditor's competency, reputation and certification whether or not reference is made to the other auditor in the principal auditor's report. Answer (d) is incorrect because different opinions would not necessarily result in a reference in the principal auditor's report. The principal auditor does, however, consider the other auditor's opinion in arriving at the overall opinion.

66. (c) When an auditor is requested by a client to reissue a previously issued report, the auditor has no responsibility to make further investigation or inquiry as to events that may have occurred during the period between the original report date and the release of reissued reports. Accordingly, the auditor should use the original report date on the reissued report because use of the original report date removes any implication that records, transactions, or events after that date have been examined or reviewed. Answers (a), (b) and (d) are incorrect because if the auditor used dual dates, release date, or current report date, there would be an implication that the report was revised and/or additional work was done by the auditor.

67. (d) The auditor may wish to emphasize a matter regarding the client's financial statements while expressing an unqualified opinion. Examples of matters that could be emphasized include the client entity being part of a larger business enterprise, an unusual subsequent event, or significant transactions with related parties. Adding an explanatory emphasis paragraph does not qualify the opinion, as incorrectly indicated in answer (a). Answer (b) is incorrect because generally accepted auditing standards allow the auditor to emphasize information that is adequately disclosed in the financial statements. If disclosure were inadequate, the auditor would issue a qualified or adverse opinion. Answer (c) is incorrect because the opinion is not qualified because of the emphasis paragraph and therefore phrases such as "with the foregoing explanation" should not be used.

68. (b) If an auditor concludes that the omission of an auditing procedure considered necessary at the time of the audit, such as physical inventory observation, impairs his or her present ability to support the previously expressed opinion on the financial statements, and the auditor believes that there are currently people relying on the opinion, the auditor should promptly undertake to apply the omitted procedure or alternative procedures that would provide a satisfactory basis for the opinion. Answer (a) is incorrect because the auditor's unqualified opinion should be relied on if the auditor performs procedures that now provide a satisfactory basis for that unqualified opinion. Answer (c) is incorrect because if the auditor is now able to perform the omitted procedure or alternative procedures that provide a basis for the opinion, GAAS is not violated. Answer (d) is incorrect because observation of inventory is a required substantive test that cannot be replaced by tests of controls.

69. (d) The auditor obtains an understanding of the internal control structure to plan the audit and to determine the nature, extent and timing of tests to be performed, but makes no reference to the entity's internal control structure in the standard report on financial statements. In an audit of an entity that receives governmental financial assistance, the auditor's report would refer to internal control structure and compliance with laws and regulations. The estimates and accounting principles noted in answers (a) and (b) are referred to in the scope paragraph. Management's responsibility, answer (d), is included in the introductory paragraph.

70. (a) When an auditor disclaims an opinion or issues an adverse opinion on the financial statements as a whole, he or she should not then express any opinion on other identified items in the financial statements. Such piecemeal opinions would tend to overshadow or contradict a disclaimer or adverse opinion. Answer (b) is incorrect because the auditor is allowed to accept limited reporting engagements that involve reporting on one basic financial statement and not the others. Answer (c) is incorrect because describing the scope limitation, which is required, would not eliminate the prohibition on issuing a piecemeal opinion. Answer (d) is incorrect because the auditor cannot include a statement that a piece of the financial statements was correct when a disclaimer is issued on the financial statements as a whole.

71. (c) If the change in accounting principles or in the method of their application has an immaterial affect on the comparability of the financial statements, the auditor would not refer to consistency in the report. Answer (a) would be correct if the effect of the change was material. Answer (b) is incorrect because the auditor's concurrence with a change is implicit unless the auditor takes exception to the change by expressing a qualified or adverse opinion on the financial statements. Answer (d) is incorrect because a change in accounting principle, if material, is not referred to in the opinion paragraph, but in an explanatory paragraph following the opinion paragraph.

72. (d) The auditor is required to report on the financial statements presented. If single-year financial statements are presented and the prior year's financial statements are not presented, the auditor will report on the single-year only. If the auditor has performed an audit in accordance with generally accepted auditing standards and has concluded that the single-year financial statements are presented fairly in accordance with generally accepted accounting principles, he or she can express an unqualified opinion in an unmodified report. Answer (a) is incorrect because a scope limitation, such as not being able to obtain audited financial statements of a material investee, would cause the auditor to qualify or disclaim the opinion. Answer (b) is incorrect because if the statement of cash flows is omitted, the auditor will typically qualify the opinion for inadequate disclosure. Answer (c) is incorrect because if the auditor wants to emphasize an accounting matter affecting the comparability of financial statements with those of the preceding year, the auditor will modify the report by adding a separate emphasis paragraph.

73. (a) Rule 203 of the AICPA Code of Professional Conduct states that an auditor shall not express an opinion that financial statements are presented in conformity with GAAP if such statements contain a departure from promulgated accounting principles. The rule provides, however, that if the statements contain such a departure from GAAP and the auditor can demonstrate that due to unusual circumstances the financial statements would otherwise have been misleading, the auditor can express an unqualified opinion but must describe the departure, its approximate effects, if practicable, and the reasons why compliance with the principle would result in a misleading statement. This type of situation is very rare. Typically, a departure from GAAP will result in a qualified or adverse opinion, depending on materiality, as indicated in answer (d). Answers (b), (c) and (d) are incorrect in this case because an unqualified opinion would be appropriate.

74. (b) The auditor can express an unqualified opinion on the balance sheet because he or she has obtained sufficient audit evidence for the year-end inventory balance, which is the amount that appears on the year-end balance sheet. If the auditor is unable to obtain sufficient audit evidence for the opening inventory, the auditor cannot conclude that cost of goods sold for the year, which is affected by beginning inventory, is fairly stated. Accordingly, the auditor could not express an unqualified opinion on the income statement. Answers (a), (c) and (d) are incorrect because the auditor would issue an unqualified opinion on the balance sheet and a disclaimer for the income statement.

75. (c) The auditor's standard report identifies the financial statements audited in an opening introductory paragraph. The nature of an audit, which is an examination in accordance with GAAS, is described in a scope paragraph. The auditor's conclusion regarding the fairness of the financial statements in accordance with GAAP is expressed in a separate opinion paragraph. Answers (a), (b) and (d) are incorrect because GAAS is referred to in the scope paragraph and GAAP is referred to in the opinion paragraph.

76. (c) Although the auditor has no responsibility to audit information outside the basic financial statements, he or she does have some responsibility regarding such information. The extent of such responsibility varies with the nature of the information. If the supplementary information is required by the FASB or GASB, the auditor should apply certain limited procedures and should report deficiencies in, or omission of, such information. Answer (a) is incorrect because the auditor has to perform limited procedures. Answer (b) is incorrect because the auditor's responsibility extends beyond determining if the information has not been omitted. The auditor is also concerned with the measurement and presentation of required supplementary information. Answer (d) is incorrect because the auditor is required to perform limited procedures such as inquires and comparisons, not tests of details of transactions and balances.

77. (d) If during his audit the successor auditor becomes aware of information that leads him to believe that financial statements reported on by the predecessor auditor may require revision, he should request his client to arrange a meeting among the three parties to discuss the information and to resolve the matter. Answers (a) and (b) are actions that would not be taken until after discussion with the predecessor auditor. Answer (c) is incorrect because the client should participate in the initial discussions with the predecessor auditor and because making inquiries about management integrity will not help to resolve the matter.

78. (c) If financial statements are not in conformity with the FASB Statements regarding the capitalization of leases, those financial statements are not in accordance with GAAP. If such a departure from GAAP is material, the auditor would issue a qualified opinion. If the auditor believes that the financial statements as a whole are not presented fairly in accordance with GAAP as a result of this departure from FASB Statements, he or she would issue an adverse opinion. Answer (a) is incorrect because this would be a scope restriction that could result in a qualified opinion or disclaimer, not an adverse opinion. Answer (b) is incorrect because a poor internal control structure would affect control risk assessment and the design of tests, not the type of auditor's report. Answer (d) is incorrect because this would result in an explanatory paragraph describing the going concern uncertainty or a disclaimer, not an adverse opinion.

79. (d) An insufficiency of audit evidence is a scope limitation that would result in a qualified opinion or disclaimer. The restriction on the audit scope would be described in an explanatory paragraph preceding the opinion paragraph and referred to in both the scope and opinion paragraphs. Answer (a) is incorrect because reference to the scope limitation is made in the scope paragraph. Answers (b) and (c) are incorrect because no reference is made to the scope limitation in the introductory paragraph.

80. (d) When unaudited financial statements are presented in comparative form with audited financial statements, the financial statements that have not been audited should be clearly marked to indicate their status and either the report of the prior period should be reissued or the report on the current period should include as a separate paragraph an appropriate description of the responsibility assumed for the financial statements of the prior period. Answers (a), (b) and (c) are incorrect because either reissuance or reference in a separate paragraph is acceptable.

81. (d) A continuing auditor should update his or her report on the financial statements of the prior periods presented on a comparative basis with those of the current period. If the prior period financial statements have been restated to conform with GAAP, including adequate disclosure, the auditor should express an unqualified opinion with respect to the restated financial statements. The auditor should disclose all the substantive reasons for the different opinion in a separate explanatory paragraph preceding the opinion paragraph. The explanatory paragraph discloses the date of the prior report, the type of opinion expressed, the circumstances causing the auditor to express a different opinion, and that the updated opinion is different from the previous opinion. Answer (a) is incorrect because the original report on the prior period does not accompany the updated report. Answer (b) is incorrect because the updated opinion would be unqualified if the financial statements were restated to include adequate disclosure, which was the reason for originally qualifying the opinion. Answer (c) is incorrect because the explanatory paragraph in the updated report would disclose the type of opinion expressed on the prior year's financial statements.

82. (b) AU 530 states that the independent auditor has two methods available for dating the report when a subsequent event disclosed in the financial statements occurs after completion of field work but before issuance of the report. He may use "dual dating," for example, "February 16, 19??, except for Note ?, as to which the date is March 1, 19??" or he may date the report as of the later date. In the former instance, the responsibility for events occurring subsequent to the completion of field work is limited to the specific event referred to in the note or otherwise disclosed. In the latter instance, the independent auditor's responsibility for subsequent events extends to the date of the report and, accordingly, the subsequent events procedures should be extended to that date.

83. (a) AU 341 states that in performing audit procedures the auditor may identify information about certain conditions or events that, when considered in the aggregate, indicate there could be substantial doubt about the entity's ability to continue as a going concern for a reasonable period of time. The significance of such conditions and events will depend on the circumstances, and some may have significance only when viewed in conjunction with others. The following are examples of such conditions and events:

- Negative trends--for example, recurring operating losses, working capital deficiencies, negative cash flows from operating activities, adverse key financial ratios.
- Other indications of possible financial difficulties: default on loan or similar agreements, arrearages in dividends, denial of usual trade credit from suppliers, restructuring of debt, noncompliance with statutory capital requirements, need to seek new sources or methods of financing or to dispose of substantial assets.
- Internal matters: work stoppages or other labor difficulties, substantial dependence on the success of a particular project, uneconomic long-term commitments, need to significantly revise operations. External matters that have occurred-for example, legal proceedings, legislation, or similar matters that might jeopardize an entity's ability to operate; loss of a key franchise, license, or patent; loss of a principal customer or supplier; uninsured or underinsured catastrophe such as a drought, earthquake, or flood.

84. (d) AU 508 states that before reissuing (or consenting to the reuse of) a report previously issued on the financial statements of a prior period, a predecessor auditor should consider whether his previous report on those statements is still appropriate. Either the current form or manner of presentation of the financial statements of the prior period or one or more subsequent events might make a predecessor auditor's previous report inappropriate. Consequently, a predecessor auditor should:
- read the financial statements of the current period, compare the prior-period financial statements that he reported on with the financial statements to be presented for comparative purposes, and
- obtain a letter from the successor auditor. The letter of representations should state whether the successor's audit revealed any matters that in the successor's opinion might have a material effect on, or require disclosure in, the financial statements reported on by the predecessor auditor.

85. (a) AU 561 states that when subsequently discovered information is found both to be reliable and to have existed at the date of the auditor's report, the auditor should take action if the nature and effect of the matter are such that:
- the report would have been affected if the information had been known at the date of the report and had not been reflected in the financial statements and
- he believes there are persons currently relying or likely to rely on the financial statements who would attach importance to the information. Consideration should be given, among other things, to the time elapsed since the financial statements were issued.

86. (b) If a client does not properly account for or disclose an illegal act, and as a result the financial statements are materially misstated, the auditor cannot issue an unqualified opinion. Because the auditor knows that the financial statements contain material departures from GAAP, the auditor should issue a qualified or adverse opinion. Answers (a) and (c) are incorrect because in this situation the auditor knows that the financial statements are not in accordance with GAAP and therefore the auditor cannot issue a disclaimer, which is reserved for situations when the auditor cannot conclude as to whether or not the financial statements are fairly presented. Answer (d) is incorrect because an unqualified opinion can only be issued when the financial statements are fairly presented in all material respects, not when the financial statements are materially misstated.

87. (d) If the auditor believes there is substantial doubt about the ability of an entity to continue as a going concern for a reasonable period of time, the auditor should consider management's plans for dealing with the adverse effects of the conditions and events that gave rise to the substantial doubt. The auditor's considerations relating to management's plans may include plans to dispose of assets, plans to borrow money or restructure debt, plans to reduce or delay expenditures, and plans to increase ownership equity. Postponing expenditures for research and development projects would be a way of delaying expenditures, which could mitigate the effects of conditions or events that gave rise to the auditor's substantial doubt. Answer (a) involves discussion of debt terms, which are not as meaningful as plans to restructure debt. Answer (b) refers to internal controls, which are not mitigating factors that the auditor would consider. Answer (c) involves the purchase of assets, rather than plans to dispose of assets.

88. (c) The auditor may be asked to report on one basic financial statement and not on the others. Such engagements involve limited reporting objectives. If the auditor has access to information underlying the basic financial statements and if he applies all the procedures he considers necessary in the circumstances, these engagements do not involve scope limitations, and the auditor can accept them. Answer (a) is incorrect because there would be no violation of ethical standards in accepting such an engagement. Answer (b) is incorrect because an opinion on the balance sheet is not a piecemeal opinion, which is an expression of an opinion as to certain identified items in the financial statements, not a complete financial statement. Answer (d) is incorrect because a disclaimer would not be given if there are no scope limitations.

89. (c) The auditor's standard report identifies the financial statements in an opening introductory paragraph, describes the nature of an audit in a scope paragraph, and expresses the auditor's opinion in a separate opinion paragraph. A statement included in the scope paragraph is "An audit also includes assessing the accounting principles used and significant estimates made by management..." Answers (a), (b) and (d) are incorrect because they are not explicitly stated in the auditor's standard report.

90. (b) If the auditor lacks independence, the auditor should issue a disclaimer of opinion. A qualified opinion is expressed when there is a lack of sufficient competent evidential matter or there are restrictions on the scope of the audit, or when the auditor believes that the financial statements contain a material departure from GAAP. Answers (a) and (c) are reasons for issuing a qualified opinion because they refer to departures from GAAP and to restrictions on the scope of the audit. Answer (d) is incorrect because the auditor may refer to the work of a specialist when issuing a qualified opinion if the auditor believes such reference will facilitate an understanding of the reason for departing from an unqualified opinion.

91. (d) If the auditor is not satisfied that management's justification for a change in accounting principle is justified, his opinion should be qualified for a departure from GAAP. Material weaknesses in internal control must be reported to the audit committee and affect the design of substantive tests, but are not noted in the auditor's opinion. Answers (a), (b) and (c) are incorrect because an unqualified opinion would not be issued when there is a departure from GAAP, and an explanatory paragraph would not be added for internal control weaknesses.

92. (b) A disclaimer of opinion states that the auditor does not express an opinion on the financial statements. It is appropriate when the auditor has not performed an audit sufficient in scope to enable him to form an opinion on the financial statements. A disclaimer would not be appropriate when the auditor determines that the financial statements contain a departure from GAAP, such as when the client's management does not adequately justify a change in accounting principle. The other answers are incorrect because they are situations that could give rise to a disclaimer. Answers (a) and (c) illustrate lack of sufficient competent evidence about the financial statement effects of a fraud scheme and accounts receivable balances. Answer (d) is a specific departure from generally accepted auditing standards, which require the auditor to obtain written representations from management.

93. (a) An auditor can issue an unqualified opinion when segments of an entity use different accounting methods, if those methods are in accordance with GAAP, which they are in this case. Answer (b) is incorrect because lack of consistency does not give rise to a qualified opinion, and consistency from period to period in accounting methods is the issue in a consistency paragraph, not consistent use of methods across business segments. Answer (c) is incorrect because FIFO and LIFO are GAAP. Answer (d) is incorrect because an adverse opinion is issued when the financial statements as a whole are not presented fairly in accordance with GAAP, which is not the case here.

94. (c) The objective of the fourth standard of reporting is to prevent misinterpretation of the degree of responsibility the auditor is assuming when his or her name is associated with financial statements. Answer (a) is incorrect because the auditor may express an unqualified opinion on one of the financial statements and express a qualified or adverse opinion or disclaim an opinion on another. Answer (b) is incorrect because scope restrictions are not addressed by reporting standards. Answer (d) is incorrect because the auditor is not prohibited from reporting on one financial statement and not the others. Reference in the fourth reporting standard to financial statements taken as a whole applies equally to a complete set of financial statements and to an individual financial statement.

95. (d) The auditor's inability to obtain sufficient competent evidential matter, such as being unable to obtain audited financial statements of a consolidated investee, is a scope limitation that, if material, may cause the auditor to qualify his opinion or to disclaim an opinion. Answers (a), (b) and (c) are situations that could result in a paragraph being added to the auditor's report, but would not result in a departure from an unqualified opinion. Specifically, the auditor can add a paragraph to an unqualified opinion that refers to a change in accounting principle, omitted quarterly data that are required by the SEC, or a matter that the auditor wants to emphasize such as a subsequent event.

96. (d) If the financial statements are affected by an uncertainty concerning future events, the outcome of which is not susceptible of reasonable estimation at the date of the auditor's report, the auditor could add an explanatory paragraph to the auditor's report to identify the uncertainty. The addition of an uncertainty paragraph does not cause a departure from an unqualified opinion. However, the auditor is not precluded from disclaiming an opinion in cases involving uncertainties. Answers (a) and (c) are incorrect because the auditor would consider expressing an adverse or qualified opinion due to a GAAP violation only if the auditor concludes that a matter involving an uncertainty is not adequately disclosed in the financial statements. Answer (b) is incorrect because a qualified opinion due to a scope limitation would only be expressed if the auditor has not obtained sufficient competent evidence to support management's assertions about the nature of a matter involving an uncertainty.

97. (c) If the financial statements, including footnotes, fail to disclose information that is required by GAAP, the auditor should express a qualified or adverse opinion. If the opinion is qualified, an additional paragraph would be added to the report describing the nature of the omitted disclosures, and the opinion paragraph of the report would include the phrase "except for the omission of the information discussed in the preceding paragraph." Answers (a) and (b) are incorrect because a qualified opinion should include the word "except" or "exception." The phrases "subject to" and "with the foregoing explanation" are not clear or forceful enough and should not be used. Answer (d) is incorrect because the phrase "does not present fairly" is used in an adverse opinion, not a qualified opinion.

98. (d) If the auditor concludes that there is substantial doubt about an entity's ability to continue as a going concern for a reasonable period of time, the audit report should include an explanatory paragraph following the opinion paragraph to reflect that conclusion. The auditor's conclusion should be expressed through use of the phrase "substantial doubt about its (the entity's) ability to continue as a going concern" (or similar wording that includes the terms "substantial doubt" and "going concern"). Answers (a), (b) and (c) are incorrect because the report is not required to include phrases such as "possible discontinuance of operations" or "reasonable period of time, not to exceed one year."

99. (a) If substantial doubt about the entity's ability to continue as a going concern existed at the date of prior period financial statements that are presented on a comparative basis, and that doubt has been removed in the current period, the explanatory paragraph included in the auditor's report on the financial statements of the prior period should not be repeated. Answers (b), (c) and (d) are incorrect because the explanatory paragraph is not repeated. nor is any other explanatory paragraph regarding the going concern issue of the prior period included.

100. (b) The auditor's standard report implies that the auditor is satisfied that the comparability of financial statements between periods has not been materially affected by changes in accounting principles and that such principles have been consistently applied between periods. Therefore. if the auditor is able to gather sufficient evidence about consistency in the first audit of a new client or in a recurring audit, no reference to consistency would be made in the report. Answer (a) is incorrect because the auditor can report on the income statement in this case. If the auditor were unable to obtain sufficient evidence about the consistent application of accounting principles as well as to the amounts of assets and liabilities at the beginning of the current period, then the auditor would be unable to express an opinion on the current year's income statement. Answer (c) is incorrect because the consistency standard of reporting, which states that the report shall identify those circumstances in which such principles have not been consistently observed in the current period in relation to the preceding period, applies to new and continuing audit clients. Answer (d) is incorrect because reference is not made to consistency when accounting principles have been consistently applied.

101. (a) If, during the current audit, an auditor becomes aware of circumstances or events that affect the financial statements of a prior period, the auditor should consider such matters when updating his or her report on the financial statements of the prior period. For example, if a qualified or adverse opinion had been expressed on financial statements of a prior period because of a departure from GAAP, and those financial statements are restated in the current period to conform with GAAP, the auditor's updated report should indicate that the financial statements have been restated and should express an unqualified opinion with respect to those restated financial statements. Answer (b) is incorrect because the predecessor auditor would not change a previously issued opinion if that auditor's report was still appropriate. Answer (c) is incorrect because a lack of consistency in the current period would not result in a change of an opinion on prior period financial statements. Answer (d) is incorrect because the auditor's opinion on prior period financial statements is not affected if those financial statements are properly restated for a pooling of interests, as required by GAAP.

102. (d) If the financial statements of a prior period have been audited by a predecessor auditor whose report is not presented, the successor auditor should indicate in the introductory paragraph of his report that the financial statements of the prior period were audited by another auditor, the date of his report, the type of report issued by the predecessor auditor, and if the report was other than a standard report, the substantive reasons therefor. Answers (a), (b) and (c) are incorrect because the successor auditor should not name the predecessor auditor, should indicate the type of report issued by the predecessor auditor, and should indicate the substantive reasons for the predecessor auditor's qualification.

103. (a) When a principal auditor decides not to assume responsibility for the work of an other auditor insofar as that work relates to the principal auditor's expression of an opinion on the financial statements as a whole, the principal auditor's report should make reference to the audit of the other auditor. In such a case, the introductory paragraph of the principal auditor's report should disclose the magnitude of the portion of the financial statements audited by the other auditor, as was done in this example. Answer (b) is incorrect because if the principal auditor decides to assume responsibility for the work of the other auditor, no reference would be made to the other auditor's work or report. Answer (c) is incorrect because reference to the fact that part of the audit was made by another auditor is not to be construed as a qualification of the opinion but rather as an indication of divided responsibility. Answer (d) is incorrect because reference to an other auditor is proper in certain circumstances.

104. (a) If an auditor is retained to audit the financial statements of a company that is not his client, the report is customarily addressed to the client and not to the directors or stockholders of the company whose financial statements are being audited. Answers (b), (c) and (d) are incorrect because, in this situation, the report would not be addressed to the entity being audited nor to users of the financial statements, but rather to Monday Corp., who is the client.

105. (c) Per S.A.S. #59, if there is substantial doubt about an entity's ability to continue as a going concern and the financial statements adequately disclose that fact, the auditor must add a fourth paragraph to his/her report referring to the footnote that discloses the problem. The additional paragraph must use the terms "Substantial doubt" and "going concern," but **nothing** about "reasonable period of time, not to exceed one year."

106. (a) The results of operations (income statement) and cash flows (statement of cash flows) of financial statements are for a period of time, usually for a year. If the auditor is unable to establish a starting point (beginning of year), an opinion cannot be formed because the opening balances cannot be verified. Therefore, the audit may be able to establish ending balance but if the opening balance cannot be established, it is impossible to conclude on what transpired during the year.

107. (a) Information that accompanies the basic financial statements is known as supplementary information. Under GAAS, the auditor must report on the responsibility he/she is taking with respect to such material.

Chapter Three - Solutions to Problems
Standards of Reporting

NUMBER 1

Circumstances	Type of Opinion	Report Modification
2. The scope of the auditor's examination is affected by conditions that preclude the application of a necessary auditing procedure.	2. The auditor should express an "except for" qualified opinion or a disclaimer of opinion.	2. The auditor should indicate the scope limitation in the scope paragraph, give the substantive reasons for the limitation in an explanatory paragraph, and modify the opinion paragraph.
3. The auditor decides to make reference to the report of another auditor as a basis, in part, for expressing an opinion.	3. The auditor should express an unqualified opinion.	3. The auditor should disclose this division of responsibility in the scope paragraph and refer to the other auditor's report in the opinion paragraph.
4. The financial statements are affected by an alternative accounting treatment that is a departure from an accounting principle promulgated by the body designated by the AICPA Council to establish such principles. The use of the promulgated principle would cause the financial statements to be misleading.	4. The auditor should express an unqualified opinion.	4. The auditor should give all of the substantive reasons why unusual circumstances justify the use of an alternative accounting treatment in an explanatory paragraph.
5. The generally accepted accounting principles have not been applied consistently.	5. The auditor should express an unqualified opinion as to consistency.	5. The auditor would add an additional paragraph to his report discussing the change.
6. The auditor wishes to emphasize a matter that is properly accounted for and adequately disclosed in the financial statements.	6. The auditor should express an unqualified opinion.	6. The auditor should describe the matter in an explanatory paragraph.

NUMBER 2

	Types of Opinions	Report Modifications
1.	F	L
2.	B	I
3.	B	Q
4.	A	J
5.	B	I
6.	B	H
7.	E	J

NUMBER 3

91. E,P   When the auditor expresses an unqualified opinion, the report should not refer to the work or findings of the specialist because it might be misunderstood to be a qualification of the auditor's opinion or a division of responsibility, neither of which is intended. If the specialist's findings which constitute sufficient competent evidential matter do not support the financial statements, the auditor can refer to them in an explanatory paragraph if the reference facilitates understanding for a possible qualified opinion. This is not the case and does not apply here.

92. A,I   This is a departure from generally accepted accounting principles, due to the failure to adjust for the decline of the note which results in either a qualified or adverse opinion due to its materiality. The introductory and scope paragraphs of the standard report are not modified. An explanatory paragraph is added and the *opinion paragraph is modified* to include a reference to the separate paragraph that discloses the basis for the qualified or adverse opinion.

93. B,J   This is a scope limitation which leads to either a qualified opinion or a disclaimer, depending on the materiality of the missing evidence. An explanatory paragraph describing the scope limitation should be added and *both the scope and opinion paragraphs* are modified to reflect the information contained in the explanatory paragraph.

94. E,H   The supplementary information which is not audited and not a required part for the fair presentation of the financial statements would not alter the unqualified opinion rendered by the auditor. However, since GASB requires for the information to be presented, an explanatory paragraph would have to be added to disclose the omission.

95. A,I   This is a departure from a generally accepted accounting principle due to inadequate disclosure, and depending on how pervasive and material the effect is, a qualified or adverse opinion should be rendered. The auditor should disclose in a separate explanatory paragraph, *preceding* the opinion, the substantive reasons that have led him/her to conclude that there has been a departure from GAAP. Furthermore, the opinion paragraph of the report should be modified to include appropriate language and a reference to the explanatory paragraph.

96. E,O   AU 543 states that if a principal auditor decides not to assume responsibility for the work of the other auditor insofar as that work relates to the principal auditor's expression of an opinion, the report should make reference to the audit of the other auditor and should indicate clearly the division of responsibility. When the principal auditor decides to make reference to the audit of the other auditor, the report should indicate clearly, in the *introductory, scope, and opinion paragraphs,* the division of responsibility between that portion of the financial statements covered by his or her own audit and that covered by the audit of the other auditor. The report should disclose the magnitude of the portion of the financial statements audited by the other auditor. This does not preclude the auditor from issuing an unqualified opinion.

97. E,H This is a consistency problem due to a change in accounting principles that has a material effect on the comparability of the company's financial statements. The auditor should refer to the change in an explanatory paragraph of the report following the opinion, identifying the nature of the change and refer the reader to the note in the financial statements that discusses the change in detail.

98. E,H AU 341 states that the auditor has a responsibility to evaluate whether there is substantial doubt about the entity's ability to continue as a going concern for a reasonable period of time, not to exceed one year beyond the date of the financial statements being audited. Depending on the magnitude, when going concern questions exist, the auditor may issue:

- A standard report with an unqualified opinion paragraph and an additional explanatory paragraph to direct attention to management's disclosures about the problem.
- A disclaimer of opinion, resulting from massive uncertainty about the ability of the business to continue. Both the introductory and scope paragraphs are modified, an explanatory paragraph is added, and no opinion is rendered.
- An adverse or qualified opinion for GAAP departure if the auditor believes the company's disclosures about financial difficulties and going concern problems are inadequate.
- A report qualified for a scope limitation if evidence that does exist or did exist is not made available to the auditor, leading to an "except for" type of qualified opinion.

NUMBER 4

91.	D
92.	I
93.	D
94.	C
95.	C
96.	D
97.	B
98.	A
99.	E
100.	C
101.	D
102.	G
103.	F
104.	J
105.	G

NUMBER 5

1. C
2. I
3. I
4. I
5. I
6. I
7. I
8. C
9. C
10. I
11. C
12. C
13. C
14. I
15. I

NUMBER 6

Land's criticism is Correct/Incorrect

61.	C	Correct
62.	I	Incorrect
63.	I	Incorrect
64.	I	Incorrect
65.	I	Incorrect
66.	I	Incorrect
67.	C	Correct
68.	C	Correct
69.	C	Correct
70.	I	Incorrect
71.	C.	Correct
72.	C	Correct
73.	C	Correct

Chapter Four
Attestation Standards, Government Auditing Standards, Quality Control Standards

Chapter Four
Attestation Standards, Government Auditing Standards, Quality Control Standards

ATTESTATION STANDARDS—SSAE No. 10, Section 101

I.   Applies to both public and non-public entities.

II. Attestation Engagement Defined—An engagement that must have the following three elements:
1. A practitioner is engaged to issue or does issue a written communication.
2. The written communication expresses a conclusion about the reliability of a written assertion made by a party on certain subject matter or directly on the presentation of the subject matter itself.
3. The practitioner's report and the written assertion is or is reasonably expected to be used by a third party.

III. Levels of attestation:
1. Positive Assurance—Reports that express conclusions on the basis of an "examination".
2. Negative Assurance—Reports that express conclusions on the basis of a **review.**
3. Reporting on the application of agreed-upon procedures.

IV. Examples of attestation engagements:
- Descriptions of the internal control structure.
- Descriptions of computer software.
- Compliance with statutory, regulatory and contractual requirements.
- Investment performance statistics.
- Information supplementary to financial statements.

V.   Types of engagements that are not considered to be attest engagements:
- Auditing, reviewing or compiling historical financial statements.
- Management consulting engagements in which the practitioner is engaged to provide advice or recommendations to a client.
- Engagements in which the practitioner is engaged to advocate a client's position (e.g., tax matters under review by the IRS).
- Tax preparation or tax advice engagements.
- Engagements in which the practitioner's role is solely to assist the client, for example:
  - Acting as the company accountant in preparing information other than financial statements.
  - Serving as an expert witness.
  - Providing an expert opinion on certain points of principle, such as the application of tax laws or accounting standards, based on facts provided by another party (so long as the expert opinion does not express a conclusion about the reliability of the facts provided by the other party).

VI. The Eleven Attestation Standards:

STANDARDS	EXPLANATION

GENERAL STANDARDS

1. The engagement shall be performed by a practitioner or practitioners having adequate technical training and proficiency in the attest function.

   Formal education and experience in gathering evidence as well as technical expertise in the field of public accounting.

2. The engagement shall be performed by a practitioner having adequate knowledge in the subject matter of the assertion.

   A practitioner may obtain adequate knowledge through formal or continuing education, or through the use of specialists.

3. The practitioner shall perform an engagement only if he or she has reason to believe that the following two conditions exist:

   - The assertion is capable of evaluation against reasonable criteria that either have been established by a recognized body or are stated in the presentation of the assertion in a sufficiently clear and comprehensive manner for a knowledgeable reader to be able to understand them.

     Examples include AICPA designated bodies (i.e., FASB), regulatory agencies, industry associations, etc.

   - The assertion is capable of reasonably consistent estimation or measurement using such criteria.

     Reasonable criteria are those which yield useful information. To be useful, the information must be both relevant and reliable. Thus, subjective criteria are not subject to attestation.

4. In all matters relating to the engagement, an independence in mental attitude shall be maintained by the practitioner or practitioners.

   The practitioner should maintain intellectual honesty and impartiality necessary to reach an unbiased conclusion. See the discussion of independence in Rule 101 of the Code of Conduct.

5. Due professional care shall be exercised in the performance of the engagement.

   Requires the critical review at every level of supervision of the work done and the judgment exercised by members participating in the engagement.

STANDARDS OF FIELD WORK

1. The work shall be adequately planned and assistants, if any, shall be properly supervised.

   Refer to Chapter 1 for guidance with respect to planning and supervision.

2. Sufficient evidence shall be obtained to provide a reasonable basis for the conclusion that is expressed in the report.

   The attestor should select and apply procedures that will accumulate evidence that is sufficient in the circumstances to afford a reasonable basis for the level of assurance to be expressed.

STANDARDS OF REPORTING

1. The report shall identify the assertion being reported on and state the character of the engagement.

   See report examples that follow.

2. The report shall state the practitioner's conclusion about whether the assertion is presented in conformity with the established or stated criteria against which it was measured.

   See report examples that follow.

3. The report shall state all of the practitioner's significant reservations about the engagement, subject matter, and, if applicable, the assertion related thereto.

   See report examples that follow.

4. The report on an engagement to evaluate an assertion that has been prepared in conformity with agreed-upon criteria or on an engagement to apply agreed-upon criteria should contain a statement limiting its use to the parties who have agreed upon such criteria or procedures.

   See report examples that follow.

VII. Description of Procedures and Nature of Report
   A. *Examination*

   An examination engagement is intended to provide the highest level of assurance on an assertion. The objective is to accumulate sufficient evidence to limit attestation risk to a level that is appropriately low for the high level of assurance to be given by the report. The auditor should perform whatever procedures are necessary to limit attestation risk to an appropriately low level. The report may express a positive opinion (or a qualified or modified opinion) on the presentation of assertions taken as a whole (positive assurance).

   B. *Review*

   A review engagement should be designed to accumulate sufficient evidence to limit attestation risk to a moderate level. Generally this is accomplished by performing inquiries and analytical procedures. The report should state whether any information came to our attention, on the basis of the work performed, that indicates that the assertions are not presented in all material respects in conformity with established or stated criteria (negative assurance).

   C. *Agreed-upon procedures or criteria*

   These engagements are designed **solely to meet the needs of specified users** who have participated in establishing the nature and scope of the engagement. Only those procedures that have been designed or agreed to by such users need be performed. Such procedures generally may be as limited or extensive as the users desire, except that the mere reading of the assertions ordinarily is not adequate for the auditor to report on the results of applying agreed-upon procedures.

VIII. Examples of Attestation Reports
   A. Examinations
      1. Highest level of assurance
      2. Expresses positive opinion on assertions
      3. Report may be unqualified or qualified or otherwise modified for some aspect of the presentation.
      4. Example of unqualified report:

I have examined the accompanying statistics and operating data included in the ABC brochure dated September 30, 19X1. My examination was conducted in accordance with the standards established by the AICPA and accordingly included such procedures as we considered necessary in the circumstances.

In my opinion, the statistics and operating data included in the ABC brochure dated September 30, 19X1, fairly present the information in conformity with the criteria explained in Note 1 to the data.

B. Review
1. Provides negative assurance
2. Disclaims an opinion (positive assurance)
3. Report may be modified if anything comes to the attestor's attention that the assertions are not presented in conformity with the established criteria.
4. Example of review report:

I have reviewed the accompanying statistics and operating data included in the ABC brochure dated September 30, 19X1. My review was conducted in accordance with the standards established by the AICPA.

A review is substantially less in scope than an examination, the objective of which is the expression of an opinion on the fairness of the statistics and operating data in the ABC brochure in conformity with the criteria explained in Note 1 accompanying the data. Accordingly, we do not express an opinion.

Based upon my review, nothing came to my attention that caused me to believe that the accompanying statistics and operating data included in the ABC brochure dated September 30, 19X1, are not presented in accordance with the criteria explained in Note 1 accompanying the data.

C. Agreed-Upon Procedures
1. Provides a summary of findings.
2. Disclaims an opinion and restricts use of report to named parties.
3. Example of attestor's report on agreed-upon procedures:

Independent Accountant's Report
on Applying Agreed-Upon Procedures

To the Audit Committees and Managements of ABC Inc. and XYZ Fund:

We have performed the procedures enumerated below, which were agreed to by the audit committees and managements of ABC Inc. and XYZ Fund, solely to assist you in evaluating the accompanying Statement of Investment Performance Statistics of XYZ Fund (prepared in accordance with the criteria specified therein) for the year ended December 31, 19X1. This agreed-upon procedures engagement was performed in accordance with standards established by the American Institute of Certified Public Accountants. The sufficiency of these procedures is solely the responsibility of the specified users of the report. Consequently, we make no representation regarding the sufficiency of the procedures described below either for the purpose for which this report has been requested or for any other purpose.

[Include paragraphs to enumerate procedures and findings.]

We were not engaged to, and did not, perform an examination, the objective of which would be the expression of an opinion on the accompanying Statement of Investment Performance Statistics of XYZ Fund. Accordingly, we do not express such an opinion. Had we performed additional procedures, other matters might have come to our attention that would have been reported to you.

This report in intended solely for the use of the audit committees and managements of ABC Inc. and XYZ Fund, and should not be used by those who have not agreed to the procedures and taken responsibility for the sufficiency of the procedures for their purposes.

REPORTING ON AN ENTITY'S INTERNAL CONTROL OVER FINANCIAL REPORTING — SSAE No. 10, Section 501

I. The standard applies to opinions on a client's internal control.

II. Under the SSAE, the client makes an assertion about the effectiveness of its internal control over financial reporting.

- The assertion can be explicit (that is, in a report) or implicit (that is, in a representation letter to the accountant).

- Management's assertion is as of a **point in time;** not for period of time.

III. The following **conditions have to exist** in order for an accountant to accept an engagement to examine and provide an opinion on internal control:

- Management presents its written assertion about the effectiveness of control either in a separate report or in a representation letter to the accountant. If management presents its assertion only in a representation letter, the accountant should limit the distribution of his or her report to management and specified regulatory agencies.

- Management accepts responsibility for the effectiveness of the internal control.

- Management evaluates internal control using reasonable criteria established by a recognized body.

- Sufficient competent evidential matter exists to support management's evaluation.

IV. In performing the examination, the accountant should:

- Obtain an understanding of the internal control components.

- Test and evaluate the effectiveness of the design and operation of internal control policies and procedures in the internal control components.

- These tests are similar to tests of controls done as part of an audit. They focus on: how the control policy or procedure was applied, who applied it, and how consistently it was applied.

- Although the report is as of a point in time, the accountant should perform the tests of control over a period of time that is adequate to determine, as of the date of management's assertion, whether the policies and procedures necessary for achieving the control objectives are operating effectively.

- If management's assertion about the control structure includes the effectiveness of controls over the preparation of **interim** financial statements, the accountant should test those controls as well.

- Obtain a representation letter in which management acknowledges its responsibility for the controls, states its assertion about their effectiveness, and discusses the existence of any reportable conditions, irregularities, or subsequent changes in the control structure. Refusal of management to supply a representation constitutes a scope limitation and the accountant is precluded from issuing an unqualified opinion.

V. Accountant's examination report:
- If the internal control structure over financial reporting is effective, the accountant renders an **unqualified** report.

- If the internal control structure contains **one or more material weaknesses,** it is not wholly effective. In that case, the accountant's report should be **modified** to discuss the weakness. The specific modification depends on whether management's report acknowledges the weakness and the pervasiveness of the effect on the control structure's effectiveness.

VI.

Report on Internal Control When Management's Assertion is Presented in a Separate Report -- Unqualified Opinion

Independent Accountant's Report

We have examined management's assertion (identify management's assertion - for example, that W Company maintained effective internal control over financial reporting as of December 31, 19XX) included in the accompanying (title of management's report).

Our examination was made in accordance with standards established by the American Institute of Certified Public Accountants and, accordingly, included obtaining an understanding of the internal controls over financial reporting, testing and evaluating the design and operating effectiveness of the internal control structure, and such other procedures as we considered necessary in the circumstances. We believe that our examination provides a reasonable basis for our opinion.

Because of the inherent limitations in internal control, errors or irregularities may occur and not be detected. Also, projections of any evaluation of internal control over financial reporting to future periods are subject to the risk that internal control may become inadequate because of changes in conditions, or that the degree of compliance with the policies or procedures may deteriorate.

In our opinion, management's assertion (identify management's assertion - for example, that W Company maintained an effective internal control structure over financial reporting as of December 31, 19XX) is fairly stated, in all material respects, based upon (identify established or stated criteria).

Material Weakness -- Qualified Opinion

Independent Accountant's Report

Opinion paragraph:

In our opinion, management's assertion that, except for the effect of the material weakness described in its report, (*identify management's assertion*) is fairly stated, in all material respects, based upon (*identify established or stated criteria*).

Explanatory paragraph:

As discussed in management's assertion, the following material weakness exists in the design or operation of the internal controls of W Company in effect at (*date*). *(Describe the material weakness and its effect on the achievement of the objectives of the control criteria.)* A material weakness is a condition that precludes the entity's internal control from providing reasonable assurance that material misstatements in the financial statements will be prevented or detected on a timely basis.

Material Weakness -- Adverse Opinion

Independent Accountant's Report

Explanatory paragraph (after introductory, scope, and inherent limitations paragraphs):

Our examination disclosed the following condition, which we believe is a material weakness in the design or operation of the internal controls of W Company in effect at (*date*). *(Describe the material weakness and its effect on the achievement of the objectives of the control criteria.)* A material weakness is a condition that precludes the entity's internal controls from providing reasonable assurance that material misstatements in the financial statements will be prevented or detected on a timely basis.

Opinion paragraph:

In our opinion, because of the effect of the material weakness described above on the achievement of the objectives of the control criteria, management's assertion (*identify management's assertion*) is not fairly stated based upon (*identify established or stated criteria*).

VII.

Report on Internal Control When Management's Assertion is Presented Only in the Representation Letter

Independent Accountant's Report

We have examined management's assertion, *included in its representation letter dated February 14, 19XY, that* (identify management's assertion - for example, that W Company maintained effective internal control over financial reporting as of December 31, 19XX).

Our examination was made in accordance with standards established by the American Institute of Certified Public Accountants and, accordingly, included obtaining an understanding of the internal control structure over financial reporting, testing and evaluating the design and operating effectiveness of the internal controls, and such other procedures as we considered necessary in the circumstances. We believe that our examination provides a reasonable basis for our opinion.

Because of the inherent limitations in internal control, errors or irregularities may occur and not be detected. Also, projections of any evaluation of internal control over financial reporting to future periods are subject to the risk that internal control may become inadequate because of changes in conditions, or that the degree of compliance with the policies or procedures may deteriorate.

In our opinion, management's assertion (identify management's assertion - for example, that W Company maintained effective internal control over financial reporting as of December 31, 19XX) is fairly stated, in all material respects, based upon (identify established or stated criteria).

This report is intended for the information and use of the board of directors and management of W Company (and, if applicable, a specified regulatory agency) and should not be used by third parties for any other purpose.

COMPLIANCE ATTESTATION — SSAE No. 10, Section 601

This SSAE provides general guidance to auditors who are engaged to perform services on management's written assertion about its compliance with specified requirements, such as laws and regulations.

I. Types of engagements are **examinations** of and application of **agreed-upon procedures** to:

-   An entity's compliance with requirements of specified laws, regulations, rules, contracts, or grants and/or

-   The effectiveness of an entity's internal control structure over compliance with such requirements.

The accountant is **prohibited** from performing a <u>review</u> of these matters.

II. The CPA should:

-   Plan the engagement

-   Obtain an understanding of the client's internal controls over compliance with specified requirements in an examination engagement.

-   Test the entity's compliance with the specified requirements.

-   Report on management's assertion.

III. Illustrative Report

Independent Accountant's Report
on Applying Agreed-Upon Procedures

We have performed the procedures enumerated below, which were agreed to by [*list specified users of report*], solely to assist the users in evaluating management's assertion about [*name of entity*]'s compliance with [*list specified requirements*] during the [*period*] ended [*date*], included in the accompanying [*title of management report*]. This agreed-upon procedures engagement was performed in accordance with standards established by the American Institute of Certified Public Accountants. The sufficiency of these procedures is solely the responsibility of the specified users of the report. Consequently, we make no representation regarding the sufficiency of the procedures described below either for the purpose for which this report has been requested or for any other purpose.

[Include paragraphs to enumerate procedures and findings.]

We were not engaged to, and did not, perform an examination, the objective of which would be the expression of an opinion on management's assertion. Accordingly, we do not express such an opinion. Had we performed additional procedures, other matters might have come to our attention that would have been reported to you.

This report is intended solely for the use of [*list or refer to specified users*] and should not be used by those who have not agreed to the procedures and taken responsibility for the sufficiency of the procedures for their purposes.

FINANCIAL FORECASTS AND PROJECTIONS (PROSPECTIVE FINANCIAL INFORMATION) – SSAE No. 10, Section 301

A. Standards for these engagements part of SSAE No. 1 referred to earlier.

B. These standards apply to financial statements for a future period that take the form of historical financial statements. These standards do not apply to cash budgets, sales forecasts, and the like.

C. Definitions:
1. Financial Forecast—Prospective financial statements that present to the best of the preparing party's knowledge and belief, an entity's expected financial position, results of operations, and cash flows. A forecast is based upon assumptions reflecting conditions the entity expects to exist and the course of action management expects to take.
2. Financial Projection—Prospective financial statements that present to the best of the responsible party's knowledge and belief, given one or more hypothetical assumptions, an entity's financial position, results of operations, and cash flows.
3. Hypothetical Assumption—Associated with financial projections only. Takes the form of a "what if" statement (i.e., what would happen if ...).
4   Responsible Party—The entity and the individuals within the entity responsible for the preparation of the Prospective Information.
5. General use -- Refers to the use of the prospective financial statements by users that the responsible party is not negotiating with directly. Users are not able to discuss the contents of the financial statements and possible outcomes directly with the responsible party. Only financial forecasts are appropriate for general use.
6. Limited use -- Refers to the use of prospective financial statements by the responsible party alone or by the responsible party and a third party that the responsible party is negotiating with directly. Third party users would then be able to ask questions of the responsible party. Any type of prospective financial statements (forecast or projection) would thus be appropriate.

D. Format for Prospective Financial Statements
1. The format is the same format used by the entity to prepare its historical financial statements including all footnotes.
2. Must include summary of significant assumptions.
3. The AICPA has separately issued guidelines for the preparation of prospective financial statements (refer subsequently herein as AICPA presentation guidelines).

E. Accountant's Services
1. Compilation
a. Involves an assembly to the extent necessary
b. Involves consideration of whether, in the accountant's judgment, the underlying assumptions appear to be obviously inappropriate with respect to the financial forecast
c. Involves reading the financial forecast and considering whether it appears to be presented in conformity with AICPA presentation guidelines.

2. Examination
   a. Evaluating the preparation of the prospective financial statements
   b. Evaluating the support underlying the significant assumptions
   c. Evaluating the presentation for conformity with AICPA presentation guidelines
   d. Issuing a report
3. Agreed-upon Procedures
   a. The service, applying agreed-upon procedures, may be performed only if:
      1) The specified users involved have participated in establishing the nature and scope of the engagement and take responsibility for the adequacy of the procedures.
      2) Distribution of the report is **restricted** to specified users.
      3) The prospective statements include a summary of significant assumptions.
      4) The accountant is independent.
   b. The accountant's procedures, in general, may be as limited or extensive as the specified users desire, as long as the specified users take responsibility for their adequacy. However, merely reading the statements does **not** constitute a procedure sufficient to permit an accountant to report on the results of applying agreed-upon procedures.

F. Report Examples
   1. Compilation—Standard Report - Forecast:

   We have compiled the accompanying forecasted balance sheet, statements of income, retained earnings, and cash flows of XYZ Company as of December 31, 19XX, and for the year then ending, in accordance with standards established by the American Institute of Certified Public Accountants.

   A compilation is limited to presenting in the form of a forecast information that is the representation of management and does not include evaluation of the support for the assumptions underlying the forecast. We have not examined the forecast and, accordingly, do not express an opinion or any other form of assurance on the accompanying statements or assumptions. Furthermore, there will usually be differences between the forecasted and actual results, because events and circumstances frequently do not occur as expected, and those differences may be material. We have no responsibility to update this report for events and circumstances occurring after the date of this report.

   - A compilation report on a financial projection would require the following paragraph restricting its distribution:

        The accompanying projection and this report were prepared for (state purpose, for example, "the DEF Bank for the purpose of negotiating a loan to expand XYZ Company's plant,") and should not be used for any other purpose.

   - Potential modifications to compilation reports on forecasts or projections:

     - Lack of independence - must be disclosed.
     - Presentation not in conformity with AICPA Presentation Guidelines.
     - Omission of disclosures other than significant assumptions.

2. Examinations
   a. Standard unqualified opinion:

   Projection

   We have examined the accompanying projected balance sheet, statements of income, retained earnings, and cash flows of XYZ Company as of December 31, 19XX, and for the year then ending. Our examination was made in accordance with standards for an examination of a projection established by the American Institute of Certified Public Accountants and, accordingly, included such procedures as we considered necessary to evaluate both the assumptions used by management and the preparation and presentation of the projection.

   The accompanying projection and this report were prepared for [state special purpose, for example, "the DEF National Bank for the purpose of negotiating a loan to expand XYZ Company's plant"], and should not be used for any other purpose. **

   In our opinion, the accompanying projection is presented in conformity with guidelines for presentation of a projection established by the American Institute of Certified Public Accountants, and the underlying assumptions provide a reasonable basis for management's projection [describe the hypothetical assumption, for example, "assuming the granting of the requested loan for the purpose of expanding XYZ Company's plant as described in the summary of significant assumptions"]. However, even if [describe hypothetical assumption, for example, "the loan is granted and the plant is expanded"], there will usually be differences between the projected and actual results, because events and circumstances frequently do not occur as expected, and those differences may be material. We have no responsibility to update this report for events and circumstances occurring after the date of this report.

   ** *In the report on Financial Forecast, this paragraph would not be needed.*

   b. Summary of Modifications to Accountants' Examination of a Financial Projection or Financial Forecast
      1) Departure from AICPA Presentation Guidelines
          — Qualified or Adverse
      2) Failure to Disclose Significant Assumptions
          — Adverse
      3) Assumptions Not Consistent with Forecast or Projection
          — Adverse
      4) Scope Limitations
          — Disclaim

   c. Example of an examination report resulting in an adverse opinion:

   We have examined the accompanying forecasted balance sheet, statements of income, retained earnings, and cash flows of XYZ Company as of December 31, 19XX, and for the year then ending. Our examination was made in accordance with standards for an examination of a financial forecast established by the American Institute of Certified Public Accountants and, accordingly, included such procedures as we considered necessary to evaluate both the assumptions used by management and the preparation and presentation of the forecast.

   As discussed under the caption "Sales" in the summary of significant forecast assumptions, the forecasted sales include, among other things, revenue from the Company's federal defense contracts continuing at the current level. The Company's present federal defense contracts will expire in March 19XX. No new contracts have been signed and no negotiations are under way for new federal defense contracts. Furthermore, the federal government has entered into contracts with another company to supply the items being manufactured under the Company's present contracts.

In our opinion, the accompanying forecast is not presented in conformity with guidelines for presentation of a financial forecast established by the American Institute of Certified Public Accountants because management's assumptions, as discussed in the preceding paragraph, do not provide a reasonable basis for management's forecast. We have no responsibility to update this report for events or circumstances occurring after the date of this report.

3. Agreed-Upon Procedures—Following is an example of a report resulting from applying agreed-upon procedures:

Independent Accountant's Report
on Applying Agreed-Upon Procedures

Board of Directors -- XYZ Corporation

Board of Directors -- ABC Company

At your request, we have performed certain agreed-upon procedures, as enumerated below, with respect to the forecasted balance sheet and the related forecasted statements of income, retained earnings, and cash flows of DEF Company, a subsidiary of ABC Company, as of December 31, 19XX, and for the year then ending. These procedures, which were agreed to by the Boards of Directors of XYZ Company and ABC Company, were performed solely to assist you in evaluating the forecast in connection with the proposed sale of DEF Company to XYZ Corporation. This agreed-upon procedures engagement was performed in accordance with standards established by the American Institute of Certified Public Accountants. The sufficiency of these procedures is solely the responsibility of the specified users of the report. Consequently, we make no representation regarding the sufficiency of the procedures described below either for the purpose for which this report has been requested or for any other purpose.

[Include paragraphs to enumerate procedures and findings.]

We were not engaged to, and did not, perform an examination, the objective of which would be the expression of an opinion on the accompanying prospective financial statements. Accordingly, we do not express an opinion on whether the prospective financial statements are presented in conformity with AICPA presentation guidelines or on whether the underlying assumptions provide a reasonable basis for the presentation. Had we performed additional procedures, other matters might have come to our attention that would have been reported to you. Furthermore, there will usually be differences between the forecasted and actual results, because events and circumstances frequently do not occur as expected, and those differences may be material. We have no responsibility to update this report for events and circumstances occurring after the date of this report.

This report is intended solely for the use of the Boards of Directors of ABC Company and XYZ Corporation and should not be used by those who have not agreed to the procedures and taken responsibility for the sufficiency of the procedures for their purposes.

REPORTING ON PRO FORMA FINANCIAL INFORMATION – SSAE No. 10, Section 401

I. APPLICABILITY
A. This standard provides guidance when an accountant is engaged to examine or review and report on pro forma financial information.
B. The accountant should comply with the general and field work standards set forth in the Statement on Standards for Attestation Engagement.

II. DESCRIPTION—PRO FORMA FINANCIAL INFORMATION
A. The objective of pro forma financial information is to show what the significant effects on historical financial information might have been had a **consummated or proposed transaction or event occurred at an earlier date.**

B. Examples—effect of:
   - Business combination
   - Disposition of part of business
   - Proposed sale of securities

III. CONDITIONS FOR REPORTING
A. The accountant may agree to report on pro forma information if the following conditions are met:
   1. The document that contains the pro forma financial information includes complete historical financial statements of the entity for the most recent year or interim period, if applicable.
   2. The historical financial statements on which the pro forma financial information is based have been audited or reviewed.
   3. The accountant who is reporting on the pro forma information should have an appropriate level of knowledge of the accounting and financial reporting practices of the reporting entity.

IV. ACCOUNTANT'S OBJECTIVES
A. The objective of the accountant's examination procedures applied to pro forma financial information is to provide reasonable assurance as to whether—
   - Management's assumptions provide a reasonable basis for presenting the significant effects directly attributable to the underlying transaction (or event).
   - The related pro forma adjustments give appropriate effect to those assumptions.
   - The pro forma column reflects the proper application of those adjustments to the historical financial statements.
B. The objective of the accountant's review procedures applied to pro forma financial information is to provide negative assurance as to whether any information came to the accountant's attention to cause him or her to believe that:
   - Management's assumptions do not provide a reasonable basis for presenting the significant effects directly attributable to the transaction (or event).
   - The related pro forma adjustments do not give appropriate effect to those assumptions.
   - The pro forma column does not reflect the proper application of those adjustments to the historical financial statements.

V. PROCEDURES
A. Obtain an understanding of the underlying transaction (or event), for example, by reading relevant contracts and minutes of meetings of the board of directors and by making inquiries of appropriate officials of the entity, and, in some cases, of the entity acquired or to be acquired.
B. Obtain a level of knowledge of each significant constituent part of the combined entity in a business combination that will enable the accountant to perform the required procedures. Procedures to obtain this knowledge may include communicating with other accountants who have audited or reviewed the historical financial information on which the pro forma financial information is based. Matters that may be considered include accounting principles and financial reporting practices followed, transactions between the entities, and material contingencies.

C. Discuss with management their assumptions regarding the effects of the transaction (or event).

D. Evaluate whether pro forma adjustments are included for all significant effects directly attributable to the transaction (or event).

E. Obtain sufficient evidence in support of such adjustments. The evidence required to support the level of assurance given is a matter of professional judgment. The accountant typically would obtain more evidence in an examination engagement than in a review engagement. Examples of evidence that the accountant might consider obtaining are purchase, merger or exchange agreements, appraisal reports, debt agreements, employment agreements, actions of the board of directors, and existing or proposed legislation or regulatory actions.

F. Evaluate whether management's assumptions that underlie the pro forma adjustments are presented in a sufficiently clear and comprehensive manner. Also, evaluate whether the pro forma adjustments are consistent with each other and with the data used to develop them.

G. Determine that computations of pro forma adjustments are mathematically correct and that the pro forma column reflects the proper application of those adjustments to the historical financial statements.

H. Obtain written representations from management concerning their—
- Responsibility for the assumptions used in determining the pro forma adjustments.
- Belief that the assumptions provide a reasonable basis for presenting all of the significant effects directly attributable to the transaction (or event), that the related pro forma adjustments give appropriate effect to those assumptions, and that the pro forma column reflects the proper application of those adjustments to the historical financial statements.
- Belief that the significant effects directly attributable to the transaction (or event) are appropriately disclosed in the pro forma financial information.

I. Read the pro forma financial information and evaluate whether—
- The underlying transaction (or event), the pro forma adjustments, the significant assumptions and the significant uncertainties, if any, about those assumptions have been appropriately described.
- The source of the historical financial information on which the pro forma financial information is based has been appropriately identified.

VI. REPORTING ON PRO FORMA FINANCIAL INFORMATION

A. The accountant's report on pro forma financial information should be dated as of the completion of the appropriate procedures. The accountant's report on pro forma financial information may be added to the accountant's report on historical financial information, or it may appear separately. If the reports are combined and the date of completion of the procedures for the examination or review of the pro forma financial information is after the date of completion of the fieldwork for the audit or review of the historical financial information, the combined report should be dual-dated. (For example, "February 15, 19X2, except for the paragraphs regarding pro forma financial information as to which the date is March 20, 19X2.")

B. An accountant's report on pro forma financial information should include—
1. An identification of the pro forma financial information.
2. A reference to the financial statements from which the historical financial information is derived and a statement as to whether such financial statements were audited or reviewed. The report on pro forma financial information should refer to any modification in the accountant's report on the historical financial statements.
3. A statement that the examination or review of the pro forma financial information was made in accordance with standards established by the American Institute of Certified Public Accountants. If a review is performed, the report should include the following statement:

   A review is substantially less in scope than an examination, the objective of which is the expression of an opinion on the pro forma financial information. Accordingly, we do not express such an opinion.

4. A separate paragraph explaining the objective of pro forma financial information and its limitations.
5. (a) If an examination of pro forma financial information has been performed, the accountant's opinion as to whether management's assumptions provide a reasonable basis for presenting the significant effects directly attributable to the transaction (or event), whether the related pro forma adjustments give appropriate effect to those assumptions, and whether the pro forma column reflects the proper application of those adjustments to the historical financial statements.

(b) If a review of pro forma financial information has been performed, the accountant's conclusion as to whether any information came to the accountant's attention to cause him or her to believe that management's assumptions do not provide a reasonable basis for presenting the significant effects directly attributable to the transaction (or event), or that the related pro forma adjustments do not give appropriate effect to those assumptions, or that the pro forma column does not reflect the proper application of those adjustments to the historical financial statements.

6. Restrictions on the scope of the engagement, significant uncertainties about the assumptions that could materially affect the transaction (or event), reservations about the propriety of the assumptions and the conformity of the presentation with those assumptions (including inadequate disclosure of significant matters), or other reservations may require the accountant to qualify the opinion, render an adverse opinion, disclaim an opinion or withdraw from the engagement. The accountant should disclose all substantive reasons for any report modifications. Uncertainty as to whether the transaction (or event) will be consummated would not ordinarily require a report modification.

VII. ILLUSTRATIVE EXAMINATION REPORT

Report of Independent Certified Public Accountants

Board of Directors
X Company

We have examined the pro forma adjustments reflecting the transaction (*or event*) described in Note 1 and the application of those adjustments to the historical amounts in (*the assembly of*) the accompanying pro forma condensed balance sheet of X Company as of December 31, 19X1, and the pro forma condensed statement of earnings for the year then ended. The historical condensed financial statements are derived from the historical financial statements of X Company, that were audited by us, and of Y Company, that were audited by other accountants appearing elsewhere herein (*or incorporated by reference*). Such pro forma adjustments are based upon management's assumptions described in Note 2. Our examination was made in accordance with standards established by the American Institute of Certified Public Accountants and, accordingly, included such procedures as we considered necessary in the circumstances.

The objective of this pro forma financial information is to show what the significant effects on the historical financial information might have been had the transaction (*or event*) occurred at an earlier date. However, the pro forma condensed financial statements are not necessarily indicative of the results of operations or related effects on financial position that would have been attained had the above mentioned transaction (*or event*) actually occurred earlier.

(*Additional paragraphs may be added to emphasize certain matters relating to the attest engagement.*)

In our opinion, management's assumptions provide a reasonable basis for presenting the significant effects directly attributable to the above mentioned transaction (*or event*) described in Note 1, the related pro forma adjustments give appropriate effect to those assumptions, and the pro forma column reflects the proper application of those adjustments to the historical financial statement amounts in the pro forma condensed balance sheet as of December 31, 19X1, and the pro forma condensed statement of earnings for the year then ended.

Report of Independent Certified Public Accountants

Board of Directors
X Company

We have audited the accompanying balance sheet of X Company, Inc. as of December 31, 19X2, and the related statements.... Our responsibility is to express an opinion on these financial statements based on our audit.

We conducted our audit in accordance with generally accepted auditing standards .... We believe our audit provides a reasonable basis for our opinion.

In our opinion, the financial statements referred to above present fairly, in all material respects, the financial position of X Company, Inc.... in conformity with generally accepted accounting principles.

We have also examined the pro forma adjustments reflecting the transaction described in Note 1 and the application of those adjustments to the historical amounts in the accompanying pro forma condensed balance sheet of X Company as of December 31, 19X2, and the pro forma condensed statement of earnings for the year then ended. The historical condensed financial statements are derived from the historical financial statements of X Company, that were audited by us, and of Y Company, that were audited by other accountants, appearing elsewhere herein. Such pro forma adjustments are based upon management's assumptions described in Note 2. Our examination was made in accordance with standards established by the American Institute of Certified Public Accountants and, accordingly, included such procedures as we considered necessary in the circumstances.

The objective of this pro forma financial information is to show what the significant effects on the historical financial information might have been had the transaction occurred at an earlier date. However, the pro forma condensed financial statements are not necessarily indicative of the results of operations or related effects on financial position that would have been attained had the above-mentioned transaction actually earlier.

(*Additional paragraphs may be added to emphasize certain matters relating to the attest engagement.*)

In our opinion, management's assumptions provide a reasonable basis for presenting the significant effects directly attributable to the above-mentioned transaction described in Note 1, the related pro forma adjustments give appropriate effect to those assumptions, and the pro forma column reflects the proper application of those adjustments to the historical financial amounts in the pro forma condensed balance sheet as of December 31, 19X2, and the pro forma condensed statement of earnings for the year then ended.

VIII. ILLUSTRATIVE REVIEW REPORT

Board of Directors
X Company

We have reviewed the pro forma adjustments reflecting the transaction (*or event*) described in Note 1 and the application of those adjustments to the historical amounts in (*the assembly of*) the accompanying pro forma condensed balance sheet of X Company as of March 31, 19X1, and the pro forma condensed statement of earnings for the three months then ended. These historical condensed financial statements are derived from the historical unaudited financial statements of X Company, that were reviewed by us, and of Y Company, that were reviewed by other accountants appearing elsewhere (*or incorporated by reference*). Such pro forma adjustments are based on management's assumptions as described in Note 2. Our review was conducted in accordance with standards established by the American Institute of Certified Public Accountants.

A review is substantially less in scope than an examination, the objective of which is the expression of an opinion on management's assumptions, the pro forma adjustments and the application of those adjustments to historical financial information. Accordingly, we do not express such an opinion.

The objective of this pro forma financial information is to show what the significant effects on the historical information might have been had the transaction (*or event*) occurred at an earlier date. However, the pro forma condensed financial statements are not necessarily indicative of the results of operations or related effects on financial position that would have been attained had the above mentioned transaction (*or event*) actually occurred earlier.

(*Additional paragraphs may be added to emphasize certain matters relating to the attest engagement.*)

Based on our review, nothing came to our attention that caused us to believe that management's assumptions do not provide a reasonable basis for presenting the significant effects directly attributable to the above-mentioned transaction (*or event*) described in Note 1, that the related pro forma adjustments do not give appropriate effect to those assumptions, or that the pro forma column does not reflect the proper application of those adjustments to the historical financial statement amounts in the pro forma condensed balance sheet as of March 31, 19X1, and the pro forma condensed statement of earnings for the three months then ended.

AGREED UPON PROCEDURES – SSAE No. 10, Section 201

A. **Definition** - An engagement to apply agreed-upon procedures is one in which an accountant is engaged by a client to issue a **report of findings** based on specific procedures performed on the specific subject matter of specified elements accounts, or items of a financial statement.

Specified elements, accounts, or items of a financial statement refers to accounting information that is part of, but significantly less than, a financial statement.
1. Such information may be directly identified in a financial statement or notes thereto; or they may be derived therefrom by analysis, aggregation, summarization, or mathematical computation.
2. Examples:
    a. Schedule of accounts receivable.
    b. The components under the caption on the financial statements identified as "property and equipment."

B. **Conditions for Engagement Performance**
1. The accountant is *independent.*
2. The accountant and the specified users agree upon the procedures performed or to be performed by the accountant.
3. The specified users take responsibility for the sufficiency of the agreed-upon procedures for their purposes.
4. The procedures to be performed are expected to result in reasonably consistent findings.
5. The basis of accounting of the specified elements, accounts, or items of a financial statement is clearly evident to the specified users and the accountant.
6. The specific subject matter to which the procedures are to be applied is subject to reasonably consistent estimation or measurement.
7. Evidential matter related to the specific subject matter to which the procedures are applied is expected to exist to provide a reasonable basis for expressing the findings in the accountant's report.
8. Where applicable, the accountant and the specified users agree on any materiality limits for reporting purposes.
9. Use of the report is restricted to the specified users.

C. **Agreement on and Sufficiency of Procedures**
1. Responsibility on the user of the accountant's report.
2. Normally the accountant should communicate directly with and obtain affirmative acknowledgment from each of the specific users (an engagement letter is encouraged but not required).
3. If the accountant is not able to communicate directly with all the specified users, this requirement can be satisfied by applying any one or more of the following:
   a. Compare the procedures to the written requirements of the users.
   b. Discuss the procedures with an appropriate representative of the users involved.
   c. Review relevant contracts with or correspondence from the specified users.
4. The accountant **should not** report unless the specified users agree among themselves as to the specific procedures.

D. **Nature, Timing, and Extent of Procedures**
1. Specified users are responsible for the sufficiency (nature, timing, and extent) of the agreed-upon procedures, because they best understand their needs.
2. The accountant is responsible for carrying out the procedures and reporting the finding in accordance with the applicable general, field work and reporting standards.
   a. The accountant assumes the risk that misapplication of the procedures may result in appropriate findings being reported.
   b. The accountant also assumes the risk that appropriate findings may not be reported or be reported inaccurately.
   c. The accountant should have adequate knowledge in the specific subject matter of the specified elements, accounts, or items, including the basis of accounting.
3. The procedures to be performed may be as limited or extensive as the specific users desire. The accountant should not agree to perform procedures that are overly subjective and open to varying interpretations.

Examples of appropriate procedures:
- Execution of a sampling application after agreeing on relevant parameters.
- Inspection of specified documents evidencing certain types of transactions or detailed attributes thereof.
- Confirmation of specific information with third parties.
- Comparison of documents, schedules, or analyses with certain specified attributes.
- Performance of mathematical computations.

Examples of inappropriate procedures:
- Mere reading of the work performed by others solely to describe their findings.
- Evaluating the competency or objectivity of another party.
- Obtaining an understanding about a particular subject.
- Interpreting documents outside the scope of the accountant's professional expertise.

4. The accountant should prepare and maintain workpaper that indicates that
   - The work was adequately planned and supervised.
   - Evidential matter was obtained to provide a reasonable basis for the findings expressed in the accountant's report.
5. Representation Letter
   a. The need for such a letter may depend on the nature of the engagement and users.
   b. The responsible party's refusal to furnish written representation determined to be appropriate for the engagement constitutes a limitation on the performance of the engagement and the accountant should do one of the following:
      - Disclose in his or her report the inability to obtain representations from the responsible party.
      - Withdraw from the engagement.
      - Change the engagement to another form of engagement.
6. Knowledge of matters outside agreed-upon procedures
   a. The accountant does not need to perform procedures outside those agreed to.
   b. If matters come to the accountant's attention by means other than those agreed to, that contradict the basis of accounting for the elements, account, or item referred to in the accountant's report, he or she should include the matter in the accountant's report.
7. When circumstances impose restrictions on the performance of the agreed-upon procedures, the accountant should attempt to obtain agreement from the specified users for such modification. Failing that, the accountant should describe any restrictions on the performance of procedures in his or her report or withdraw from the engagement.

E. **Change in Terms of Engagement**
   1. An accountant engaged to perform another form of engagement may be requested, before completion of the original engagement, to change the nature of the engagement to agreed-upon procedures.
   2. Before an accountant who was engaged to perform another form of engagement agrees to change the engagement to an engagement to apply agreed-upon procedures, he or she should consider the following:
      - The possibility that certain procedures performed as part of another type of engagement are not appropriate for inclusion in an engagement to apply agreed-upon procedures.
      - The reason given for the request, particularly the implications of a restriction on the scope of the original engagement or the matters to be reported.
      - The additional effort required to complete the original engagement.
      - If applicable, the reasons for changing from a general-distribution report to a restricted-use report.
   3. If the specified users acknowledge agreement to the procedures performed or to be performed and assume responsibility for the sufficiency of the procedures to be included in the agreed-upon procedures engagement, either of the following would be considered a reasonable basis for requesting a change in the engagement.
      - A change in circumstances that requires another form of engagement.
      - A misunderstanding concerning the nature of the original engagement or the available alternatives.
   4. If the accountant concludes that there is reasonable justification for the change, the accountant should issue the appropriate agreed-upon procedures report. The report should **not** make reference to the original engagement.

F. **Accountants' Reports**

The accountant's report should contain the following elements:

1. A title that includes the word *independent*.
2. Reference to the specified elements, accounts, or items of a financial statement of an identified entity and the character of the engagement.
3. Identification of specified users.
4. The basis of accounting of the specified elements, accounts, or items of a financial statement unless clearly evident.
5. A statement that the procedures performed were those agreed to by the specified users identified in the report.
6. Reference to standards established by the American Institute of Certified Public Accountants.
7. A statement that the sufficiency of the procedures is solely the responsibility of the specified users and a disclaimer of responsibility for the sufficiency of those procedures.
8. A list of the procedures performed (or reference thereto) and related findings (the accountant should not provide negative assurance).
9. Where applicable, a description of any agreed-upon materiality limits.
10. A statement that the accountant was not engaged to, and did not, perform an audit of the specified elements, accounts, or items; a disclaimer of opinion on the specified elements, accounts, or items; and a statement that if the accountant had performed additional procedures, other matters might have come to his or her attention that would have been reported.
11. A disclaimer of opinion on the effectiveness of the internal control structure over financial reporting or any part thereof when the accountant has performed procedures.
12. A statement of restrictions on the use of the report because it is intended to be used solely by the specified users. (However, if the report is a matter of public record, the accountant should include the following sentence: "However, this report is a matter of public record and its distribution is not limited.")
13. Where applicable, reservations or restrictions concerning procedures or findings.
14. Where applicable, a description of the nature of the assistance provided by a specialist.

Illustrative Report:

The following is an illustration of a report on applying agreed-upon procedures to specified elements, accounts, or items of a financial statement.

Independent Accountant's Report on Applying Agreed-Upon Procedures

We have performed the procedures enumerated below, which were agreed to by [*list specified users*], solely to assist you with respect to [*refer to the specified elements, accounts, or items of a financial statement for an identified entity and the character of the engagement*]. This engagement to apply agreed-upon procedures was performed in accordance with standards established by the American Institute of Certified Public Accountants. The sufficiency of the procedures is solely the responsibility of the specified users of the report. Consequently, we make no representation regarding the sufficiency of the procedures described below either for the purpose for which this report has been requested or for any other purpose.

[*Include paragraphs to enumerate procedures and findings.*]

We were not engaged to, and did not, perform an audit, the objective of which would be the expression of an opinion on the specified elements, accounts, or items. Accordingly, we do not express such an opinion. Had we performed additional procedures, other matters might have come to our attention that would have been reported to you.

This report is intended solely for the use of the specified users listed above and should not be used by those who have not agreed to the procedures and taken responsibility for the sufficiency of the procedures for their purposes.

STATEMENT ON GOVERNMENT AUDITING STANDARDS

I. INTRODUCTION
A. **Purpose**
1. These standards apply to audits of government organizations, programs, activities, and functions, and of government funds received by contractors, nonprofit organizations, and other nongovernment organizations.
2. The standards are to be followed by auditors and audit organizations when required by law, regulation, agreement or contract, or policy.

II. TYPES OF GOVERNMENT AUDITS
A. **Financial Audits**
1. **Financial statement audits** determine (a) whether the financial statements of an audited entity present fairly the financial position, results of operations, and cash flows or changes in financial position in accordance with generally accepted accounting principles, and (b) whether the entity has complied with laws and regulations for those transactions and events that may have a material effect on the financial statements.
2. **Financial related audits** include determining (a) whether financial reports and related items, such as elements, accounts, or funds are fairly presented, (b) whether financial information is presented in accordance with established or stated criteria, and (c) whether the entity has adhered to specific financial compliance requirements.
B. **Performance Audits**
1. **Economy and efficiency audits** include determining (a) whether the entity is acquiring, protecting, and using its resources (such as personnel, property, and space) economically and efficiently, (b) the causes of inefficiencies or uneconomical practices, and (c) whether the entity has complied with laws and regulations concerning matters of economy and efficiency.
2. **Program audits** include determining (a) the extent to which the desired results or benefits established by the legislature or other authorizing body are being achieved, (b) the effectiveness of organizations, programs, activities, or functions, and (c) whether the entity has complied with laws and regulations applicable to the program.

III. GENERAL STANDARDS FOR FINANCIAL AUDITS
A. **Qualifications:** The staff assigned to conduct the audit should collectively possess adequate professional proficiency for the tasks required.
B. **Independence:** In all matters relating to the audit work, the audit organization and the individual auditors, whether government or public, should be free from personal and external impairments to independence, should be organizationally independent, and should maintain an independent attitude and appearance.
C. **Due Professional Care:** Due professional care should be used in conducting the audit and in preparing related reports.
D. **Quality Control:** Audit organizations conducting government audits should have an appropriate internal quality control system in place and participate in an external quality control review program.

IV. FIELD WORK STANDARDS FOR FINANCIAL AUDITS
A. **Relationship to AICPA Standards**
1. The standards of field work for government financial audits **incorporate the AICPA standards of field work for financial audits**, and **prescribes supplemental standards** of field work needed to satisfy the unique needs of government financial audits.
2. The field work standards of the AICPA and the supplemental standards in this statement apply to both financial statement audits and financial related audits.

B. **Supplemental Field Work Standards**
   1. **Planning -- Follow-up:**
      - Auditors should follow up on known material findings and recommendations from previous audits.
   2. **Compliance with laws and regulations:**
   When laws, regulations, and other compliance requirements are significant to audit objectives, auditors should design the audit to provide reasonable assurance about compliance with them. In all performance audits, auditors should be alert to situations or transactions that could be indicative of illegal acts or abuse.
   3. **Management controls:**
   Auditors should obtain an understanding of management controls that are relevant to the audit. When management controls are significant to audit objectives, auditors should obtain sufficient evidence to support their judgments about those controls.
   4. **Evidence:**
   Sufficient, competent, and relevant evidence is to be obtained to afford a reasonable basis for the auditors' findings and conclusions. A record of the auditors' work should be retained in the form of working papers. Working papers should contain sufficient information to enable an experienced auditor having no previous connection with the audit to ascertain from them the evidence that supports the auditors' significant conclusions and judgments.

V. REPORTING STANDARDS FOR FINANCIAL AUDITS

A. **Relationship to AICPA Standards**
   1. The standards of reporting for government financial audits incorporate the AICPA standards of reporting for financial audits, and prescribes supplemental standards of reporting needed to satisfy the unique needs of government financial audits.
   2. The reporting standards of the AICPA and the supplemental standards in this statement apply to both financial statement audits and financial related audits.

B. **Supplemental reporting standards for government financial audits are:**
   1. **Form:**
   Auditors should prepare written audit reports communicating the results of each audit.
   2. **Timeliness:**
   Auditors should appropriately issue the reports to make the information available for timely use by management, legislative officials, and other interested parties.
   3. **Report contents:**
   Auditors should report the audit objectives and the audit scope and methodology.
   4. **Report presentation:**
   The report should be complete, accurate, objective, convincing, and as clear and concise as the subject permits.
   5. **Report distribution:**
   Written audit reports are to be submitted by the audit organization to the appropriate officials of the auditee and to the appropriate officials of the organizations requiring or arranging for the audits, including external funding organizations, unless legal restrictions prevent it. Copies of the reports should also be sent to other officials who have legal oversight authority or who may be responsible for acting on audit findings and recommendations and to others authorized to receive such reports. Unless restricted by law or regulation, copies should be made available for public inspection.

COMPLIANCE AUDITING APPLICABLE TO GOVERNMENTAL ENTITIES AND OTHER RECIPIENTS OF GOVERNMENTAL FINANCIAL ASSISTANCE, SAS No. 74

Introduction

1. This Statement establishes standards for testing and reporting on **compliance with laws and regulations** in the following engagements:
   - Audits under Generally Accepted Auditing Standards.
   - Audits under Government Auditing Standards.
   - Audits under OMB Circular A-133, *Audits of States, Local Governments and Other Nonprofit Institutions.*
2. The Statement also addresses reporting on internal control structure under Government Auditing Standards.

Compliance Auditing in Audits Conducted in Accordance with GAAS

1. In audits performed in accordance with GAAS, the auditor's responsibility for consideration of laws and regulations and how they affect the audit is described in SAS Nos. 53 and 54.
2. The auditor should design the audit to provide reasonable assurance that the financial statements are free of material misstatements resulting from violations of laws and regulations that have a **direct and material** effect on the determination of financial statement amounts.
3. It is important that the auditor understand the laws and regulations that are generally recognized to have a direct and material effect on the determination of amounts in a governmental entity's financial statements.
4. The auditor should consider audit risk in assessing compliance with laws and regulations.
5. Working paper documentation of procedures performed to evaluate compliance with laws and regulations is required along with a written representation letter from management that includes a statement on compliance with applicable laws and regulations.

Reporting Under Government Auditing Standards

1. In performing an audit in accordance with Governmental Auditing Standards (GAS), the auditor assumes responsibilities beyond those assumed in an audit conducted in accordance with GAAS to report on compliance with laws and regulations and on internal control structure.
2. GAS require that the audit be designed to provide reasonable assurance of detecting errors, irregularities, and illegal acts resulting from violations of laws and regulations that have a direct and material effect on the determination of financial statement amounts that are material to the financial statements.
3. The report issued under GAS on compliance with laws and regulations must indicate either there were no instances of noncompliance or list specific findings of noncompliance.
4. Material instances of noncompliance with laws and regulations will normally result in a **qualified** report. If the report is qualified, the following features should be included:
   - The definition of the material instances of noncompliance.
   - An identification of material instances of noncompliance noted in the audit.
   - A statement that the noncompliance noted was considered in forming an opinion on whether the entity's financial statements are presented fairly, in all material respects, in conformity with GAAP.
5. Material instances of noncompliance should be reported whether or not they have been corrected in the entity's financial statements.
6. Reporting on internal control structure under GAS differs from reporting under SAS No. 60. GAS requires a written report on the internal control structure in all audits; SAS No. 60 requires communication – oral or written – only when the auditor has noted **reportable conditions**.
7. In reporting on the internal control structure under GAS, the auditor is required to identify all reportable conditions noted and indicate which of the reportable conditions are considered to be material weaknesses.
8. When reporting on internal control structure in an audit under GAS, the following items must be communicated:
   - Identification of the categories of the internal control structure.
   - Description of the scope of the auditor's work in obtaining an understanding of the internal control structure and in assessing control risk.
   - Description of deficiencies in the internal control structure not considered significant enough to be reportable conditions.

REPORTING EXAMPLES—GOVERNMENTAL AUDITING STANDARDS

1. Report on Internal Control Structure	**Required Elements**

Addressee

We have audited the financial statements of *(name of entity)* as of and for the year ended June 30, 19X1, and have issued our report thereon dated August 15, 19X1.

1. Reference to Audit

We conducted our audit in accordance with generally accepted auditing standards and *Government Auditing Standards,* issued by the Comptroller General of the United States. Those standards require that we plan and perform the audit to obtain reasonable assurance about whether the financial statements are free of material misstatement.

2. Reference to Standards

In planning and performing our audit of the financial statement of *(name of entity)* for the year ended June 30, 19X1, we considered its internal control structure in order to determine our auditing procedures for the purpose of expressing our opinion on the financial statements and not to provide assurance on the internal control structure.

3. Reference to I.C.

The management of *(name of entity)* is responsible for establishing and maintaining an internal control structure. In fulfilling this responsibility, estimates and judgments by management are required to assess the expected benefits and related costs of internal control structure policies and procedures. The objectives of an internal control structure are to provide management with reasonable, but not absolute, assurance that assets are safeguarded against loss from unauthorized use or disposition and that transactions are executed in accordance with management's authorization and recorded properly to permit the preparation of financial statements in accordance with generally accepted accounting principles. Because of inherent limitations in any internal control structure, errors or irregularities may nevertheless occur and not be detected. Also, projection of any evaluation of the structure to future periods is subject to the risk that procedures may become inadequate because of changes in conditions or that the effectiveness of the design and operation of policies and procedures may deteriorate.

4. Management responsibility

5. Objective of I.C.

6. Limitations of I.C.

For the purpose of this report, we have classified the significant internal control structure policies and procedures in the following categories *(identify internal control structure categories).*

For all the internal control structure categories listed above, we obtained an understanding of the design of relevant policies and procedures and whether they have been placed in operation, and we assessed control risk.

7. Procedures followed

We noted certain matters involving the internal control structure and its operation that we consider to be reportable conditions under standards established by the American Institute of Certified Public Accountants. Reportable conditions involve matters coming to our attention relating to significant deficiencies in the design or operation of the internal control structure that, in our judgment, could adversely affect the entity's ability to record, process, summarize, and report financial data consistent with the assertions of management in the financial statements.

8. Reportable conditions

(Include paragraphs to describe the reportable conditions noted.)

A material weakness is a reportable condition in which the design or operation of one or more of the internal control structure elements does not reduce to a relatively low level the risk that errors or irregularities in amounts that would be material in relation to the financial statements being audited may occur and not be detected within a timely period by employees in the normal course of performing their assigned functions.

9. Material weaknesses

Our consideration of the internal control structure would not necessarily disclose all matters in the internal control structure that might be reportable conditions, and, accordingly, would not necessarily disclose all reportable conditions that are also considered to be material weaknesses as defined above. However, we believe none of the reportable conditions described above is a material weakness.

10. Limitations of procedures

We also noted other matters involving the internal control structure and its operation that we have reported to the management of *(name of entity)* in a separate letter dated August 15, 19X1.

This report is intended for the information of the audit committee, management and *(specify legislative or regulatory body).* However, this report is a matter of public record and its distribution is not limited.

11. Distribution of report

Signature, Date

2. Report on Compliance with Laws and Regulations

Required Elements

Addressee

We have audited the general-purpose financial statements of City X, Any State, as of and for the year ended June 30, 19X4, and have issued our report thereon dated August 15, 19X4.

Reference to the audited financial statements and audit report

We conducted our audit in accordance with generally accepted auditing standards and *Government Auditing Standards,* issued by the Comptroller General of the United States. Those standards require that we plan and perform the audit to obtain reasonable assurance about whether the financial statements are free of material misstatement.

Audit conducted in accordance with GAAS and Government Auditing Standards (GAS) What GAAS and GAS require

Compliance with laws, regulations, contracts, and grants applicable to City X is the responsibility of City X's management. As part of obtaining reasonable assurance about whether the financial statements are free of material misstatement, we performed tests of City X's compliance with certain provisions of laws, regulations, contracts, and grants. However, the objective of our audit of the general-purpose financial statements was not to provide an opinion on overall compliance with such provisions. Accordingly, we do not express such an opinion.

Management is responsible for compliance.

Tests of compliance were performed as part of audit, not to provide on opinion on compliance - disclaimer on compliance.

The results of our tests disclosed no instances of noncompliance that are required to be reported herein under *Government Auditing Standards*.

No reportable instances of noncompliance

This report is intended for the information of the audit committee, management, and city council. However, this report is a matter of public record and its distribution is not limited.

Intended use of report

Signature, date

SINGLE AUDIT ACT

I. Requirements of Single Audit Act
   A. Determine and report on whether the financial statements are presented fairly according to GAAP.
   B. Determine and report on whether the "schedule of expenditures of federal awards" is presented fairly in relation to the financial statements.
   C. Determine whether the entity has complied with laws, regulations and contracts with respect to programs or grants.
   D. Report on a schedule of findings and questioned costs.

II. Nonfederal entities that expend federal awards may be subject to a single audit or program specific audit
   A. Entities that expend $300,000 or more of federal awards are required to have a single audit.
   B. Entities that expend less than $300,000 of federal awards may have a program specific audit or elect a single audit.

III. With respect to I-C above, auditors should refer to OMB Circular A-133 "Audits of States, Local Governments, and Non-Profit Organizations" for guidance and the specific compliance requirements of various federal awards.
   A. Auditors are required to report on compliance with specific requirements of each federal program award received and expended.
   B. With respect to instances of non-compliance, the auditor must report on the frequency of non-compliance (referred to as questioned costs).

IV. Responsibilities Under OMB Circular A-133
   A. OMB Circular A-133, *Audits of States, Local Governments and Other Nonprofit Institutions*, prescribes audit requirements for entities receiving federal awards.
   B. If a nonprofit institution receives $300,000 or more per year in federal awards it is required to have an audit performed in accordance with Circular A-133.
   C. The auditor is to test and report on matters pertaining to:
   • Compliance with laws and regulations that may have a direct and material effect on the entity's financial statement amounts.
   • Compliance with general requirements applicable to the federal award programs.
   • Compliance with specific requirements that may have a direct and material effect on each major program, as defined in OMB Circular A-133.
   • Compliance with certain laws and regulations applicable to nonmajor federal financial assistance programs.

SYSTEM OF QUALITY CONTROL FOR A CPA FIRM'S ACCOUNTING AND AUDITING PRACTICE

I. **Introduction and Applicability**
A. This Statement provides that a CPA firm shall have a system of quality control for its accounting and auditing practice.

II. **System of Quality Control**
A. A firm has a responsibility to ensure its personnel comply with professional standards applicable to its accounting and auditing practice.

B. A *system of quality control* is broadly defined as a process to provide the firm with reasonable assurance that its personnel comply with applicable professional standards and the firm's standards of quality.

C. Any system of quality control has inherent limitations that can reduce its effectiveness.

D. The system of quality control should provide the firm with reasonable assurance that the segments of the firm's engagements performed by its foreign offices or by its domestic or foreign affiliates or correspondents are performed in accordance with professional standards in the United States when such standards are applicable.

III. **Quality Control Policies and Procedures**
A. Elements of Quality Control
1. Independence, Integrity, and Objectivity
a. Policies and procedures should be established to provide the firm with reasonable assurance that personnel maintain independence (in fact and in appearance) in all required circumstances, perform all professional responsibilities with integrity, and maintain objectivity in discharging professional responsibilities.
2. Personnel Management
a. A firm's quality control system depends heavily on the proficiency of its personnel. In making assignments, the nature and extent of supervision to be provided should be considered. Generally, the more able and experienced the personnel assigned to a particular engagement, the less direct supervision is needed.
3. Acceptance and Continuance of Clients and Engagements
a. Policies and procedures should be established for deciding whether to accept or continue a client relationship and whether to perform a specific engagement for that client. Such policies and procedures should provide the firm with reasonable assurance that the likelihood of association with a client whose management lacks integrity is minimized.
b. Such policies and procedures should also provide reasonable assurance that the firm ---
1). Undertakes only those engagements that the firm can reasonably expect to be completed with professional competence.
2). Appropriately considers the risks associated with providing professional services in the particular circumstances.
4. Engagement Performance
a. Policies and procedures should be established to provide the firm with reasonable assurance that the work performed by engagement personnel meets applicable professional standards, regulatory requirements, and the firm's standards of quality.
b. Policies and procedures should also be established to provide reasonable assurance that personnel refer to authoritative literature or other sources and consult, on a timely basis, with individuals within or outside the firm, when appropriate (for example, when dealing with complex, unusual, or unfamiliar issues). Individuals consulted should have appropriate levels of knowledge, competence, judgment, and authority.

5. Monitoring
   a. Policies and procedures should be established to provide the firm with reasonable assurance that the policies and procedures established by the firm for each of the other elements of quality control described are suitably designed and are being effectively applied.

IV. Administration of a Quality Control System

A. Assignment of Responsibilities
   1. Responsibility for the *design* and *maintenance* of the various quality control policies and procedures should be assigned to an appropriate individual or individuals in the firm.

B. Communication
   1. A firm should communicate its quality control policies and procedures to its personnel in a manner that provides reasonable assurance that those policies and procedures are understood and complied with.

C. Documentation of Quality Control Policies and Procedures
   1. The size, structure, and nature of the practice of the firm should be considered in determining whether documentation of established quality control policies and procedures is required for effective communication and, if so, the extent of such documentation.

D. Documentation of Compliance with Quality Control Policies and Procedures
   1. A firm should prepare appropriate documentation to demonstrate *compliance* with its policies and procedures for the quality control system discussed herein.
   2. The form and content of such documentation is a matter of judgment and depends on a number of factors, such as the size of a firm, the number of offices, the degree of authority allowed its personnel and its offices, the nature and complexity of the firm's practice, its organization, and appropriate cost-benefit considerations.

MONITORING A CPA FIRM'S ACCOUNTING AND AUDITING PRACTICE

I. Monitoring Procedures

A. Monitoring procedures taken as a whole should enable the firm to obtain reasonable assurance that its system of quality control is effective.

B. A firm's monitoring procedures may include ---
   1. Inspection procedures.
   2. Preissuance or postissuance review of selected engagements.
   3. Analysis and assessment of:
      - New professional pronouncements.
      - Results of independence confirmations.
      - Continuing professional education and other professional development activities undertaken by firm personnel.
      - Decisions related to acceptance and continuance of client relationships and engagements.
      - Interviews of firm personnel.
   4. Determination of any corrective actions to be taken and improvements to be made in the quality control system.
   5. Communication to appropriate firm personnel of any weaknesses identified in the quality control system or in the level of understanding or compliance therewith.
   6. Follow-up by appropriate firm personnel to ensure that any necessary modifications are made to the quality control policies and procedures on a timely basis.

II. Monitoring in Small Firms with a Limited Number of Management-Level Individuals

A. In small firms with a limited number of management-level individuals, monitoring procedures may need to be performed by some of the same individuals who are responsible for compliance with the firm's quality control policies and procedures.

B. To effectively monitor one's own compliance with the firm's policies and procedures, an individual must be able to critically review his or her own performance, assess his or her own strengths and weaknesses, and maintain an attitude of continual improvement.

C. A firm in this circumstance may find it beneficial to engage a qualified individual from outside the firm to perform inspection procedures.

D. A peer review does not substitute for monitoring procedures.

Chapter Four - Questions
Attestation Standards, Government Auditing Standards, Quality Control Standards

1. A CPA's report on a forecast should include all of the following **except**
a. A description of what the forecast information is intended to represent.
b. A caveat as to the ultimate attainment of the forecasted results.
c. A statement that the CPA assumes **no** responsibility to update the report for events occurring after the date of the report.
d. An opinion as to whether the forecast is fairly presented.

2. A CPA firm's personnel partner periodically studies the CPA firm's personnel advancement experience to ascertain whether individuals meeting stated criteria are assigned increased degrees of responsibility. This is evidence of the CPA firm's adherence to prescribed standards of
a. Quality control.
b. Due professional care.
c. Supervision and review.
d. Fieldwork.

3. In pursuing a CPA firm's quality control objectives, a CPA firm may maintain records indicating which partners or employees of the CPA firm were previously employed by the CPA firm's clients. Which quality control objective would this be **most** likely to satisfy?
a. Professional relationship.
b. Supervision.
c. Independence.
d. Advancement.

4. The party responsible for assumptions identified in the preparation of prospective financial statements is usually
a. A third-party lending institution.
b. The client's management.
c. The reporting accountant.
d. The client's independent auditor.

5. Which of the following is a prospective financial statement for general use upon which an accountant may appropriately report?
a. Financial projection.
b. Partial presentation.
c. Pro forma financial statement.
d. Financial forecast.

6. When third party use of prospective financial statements is expected, an accountant may **not** accept an engagement to
a. Perform a review.
b. Perform a compilation.
c. Perform an examination.
d. Apply agreed-upon procedures.

7. Which of the following bodies promulgates standards for audits of federal financial assistance recipients?
a. Governmental Accounting Standards Board.
b. Financial Accounting Standards Board.
c. General Accounting Office.
d. Governmental Auditing Standards Board.

8. A CPA firm's quality control procedures pertaining to the acceptance of a prospective audit client would most likely include
a. Inquiry of management as to whether disagreements between the predecessor auditor and the prospective client were resolved satisfactorily.
b. Consideration of whether sufficient competent evidential matter may be obtained to afford a reasonable basis for an opinion.
c. Inquiry of third parties, such as the prospective client's bankers and attorneys, about information regarding the prospective client and its management.
d. Consideration of whether the internal control structure is sufficiently effective to permit a reduction in the extent of required substantive tests.

9. An accountant's standard report on a compilation of a projection should **not** include
a. A separate paragraph that describes the limitations on the presentation's usefulness.
b. A statement that a compilation of a projection is limited in scope.
c. A disclaimer of responsibility to update the report for events occurring after the report's date.
d. A statement that the accountant expresses only limited assurance that the results may be achieved.

10. An examination of a financial forecast is a professional service that involves

a. Compiling or assembling a financial forecast that is based on management's assumptions.
b. Limiting the distribution of the accountant's report to management and the board of directors.
c. Assuming responsibility to update management on key events for one year after the report's date.
d. Evaluating the preparation of a financial forecast and the support underlying management's assumptions.

11. When an accountant compiles projected financial statements, the accountant's report should include a separate paragraph that
a. Describes the differences between a projection and a forecast.
b. Identifies the accounting principles used by management.
c. Expresses limited assurance that the actual results may be within the projection's range.
d. Describes the limitations on the projection's usefulness.

12. When an accountant examines a financial forecast that fails to disclose several significant assumptions used to prepare the forecast, the accountant should describe the assumptions in the accountant's report and issue a(an)
a. "Except for" qualified opinion.
b. "Subject to" qualified opinion.
c. Unqualified opinion with a separate explanatory paragraph.
d. Adverse opinion.

13. Which of the following statements concerning prospective financial statements is correct?
a. Only a financial forecast would normally be appropriate for limited use.
b. Only a financial projection would normally be appropriate for general use.
c. Any type of prospective financial statements would normally be appropriate for limited use.
d. Any type of prospective financial statements would normally be appropriate for general use.

14. An auditor most likely would be responsible for communicating significant deficiencies in the design of the internal control structure
a. To the Securities and Exchange Commission when the client is a publicly held entity.
b. To specific legislative and regulatory bodies when reporting under *Government Auditing Standards*.

c. To a court-appointed creditors' committee when the client is operating under Chapter 11 of the Federal Bankruptcy Code.
d. To shareholders with significant influence (more than 20% equity ownership) when the reportable conditions are deemed to be material weaknesses.

15. Which of the following professional services would be considered an attest engagement?
a. A management consulting engagement to provide EDP advice to a client.
b. An engagement to report on compliance with statutory requirements.
c. An income tax engagement to prepare federal and state tax returns.
d. The compilation of financial statements from a client's accounting records.

16. Accepting an engagement to compile a financial projection for a publicly held company most likely would be inappropriate if the projection were to be distributed to
a. A bank with which the entity is negotiating for a loan.
b. A labor union with which the entity is negotiating a contract.
c. The principal stockholder, to the exclusion of the other stockholders.
d. All stockholders of record as of the report date.

17. A CPA firm would be reasonably assured of meeting its responsibility to provide services that conform with professional standards by
a. Adhering to generally accepted auditing standards.
b. Having an appropriate system of quality control.
c. Joining professional societies that enforce ethical conduct.
d. Maintaining an attitude of independence in its engagements.

18. One of a CPA firm's basic objectives is to provide professional services that conform with professional standards. Reasonable assurance of achieving this basic objective is provided through
a. A system of quality control.
b. A system of peer review.
c. Continuing professional education.
d. Compliance with generally accepted reporting standards.

19. In reporting on an entity's internal control structure over financial reporting, a practitioner should include a paragraph that describes the

a. Documentary evidence regarding the control environment factors.
b. Changes in the internal control structure since the prior report.
c. Potential benefits from the practitioner's suggested improvements.
d. Inherent limitations of any internal control structure.

20. When reporting on an entity's internal control structure under *Government Auditing Standards,* an auditor should issue a written report that includes a
a. Statement of negative assurance that nothing came to the auditor's attention that caused the auditor to believe reportable conditions were present.
b. Statement of positive assurance that the results of tests indicate that the internal control structure either can, or cannot, be relied on to reduce control risk to an acceptable level.
c. Description of the weaknesses considered to be reportable conditions and the strengths that the auditor can rely on in reducing the extent of substantive testing.
d. Description of the scope of the auditor's work in obtaining an understanding of the internal control structure and in assessing control risk.

21. Hill, CPA, is auditing the financial statements of Helping Hand, a not-for-profit organization that receives financial assistance from governmental agencies. To detect misstatements in Helping Hand's financial statements resulting from violations of laws and regulations, Hill should focus on violations that
a. Could result in criminal prosecution against the organization.
b. Involve reportable conditions to be communicated to the organization's trustees and the funding agencies.
c. Have a direct and material effect on the amounts in the organization's financial statements.
d. Demonstrate the existence of material weaknesses in the organization's internal control structure.

22. Blue, CPA, has been asked to render an opinion on the application of accounting principles to a specific transaction by an entity that is audited by another CPA. Blue may accept this engagement, but should
a. Consult with the continuing CPA to obtain information relevant to the transaction.
b. Report the engagement's findings to the entity's audit committee, the continuing CPA, and management.

c. Disclaim any opinion that the hypothetical application of accounting principles conforms with generally accepted accounting principles.
d. Notify the entity that the report is for the restricted use of management and outside parties who are aware of all relevant facts.

23. Comfort letters ordinarily are signed by the client's
a. Independent auditor.
b. Underwriter of securities.
c. Audit committee.
d. Senior management.

24. Accepting an engagement to examine an entity's financial projection most likely would be appropriate if the projection were to be distributed to
a. All employees who work for the entity.
b. Potential stockholders who request a prospectus or a registration statement.
c. A bank with which the entity is negotiating for a loan.
d. All stockholders of record as of the report date.

25. Which of the following is an element of a CPA firm's quality control system that should be considered in establishing its quality control policies and procedures?
a. Complying with laws and regulations.
b. Using statistical sampling techniques.
c. Assigning personnel to engagements.
d. Considering audit risk and materiality.

26. In reporting on compliance with laws and regulations during a financial statement audit in accordance with *Government Auditing Standards,* an auditor should include in the auditor's report
a. A statement of assurance that all controls over fraud and illegal acts were tested.
b. Material instances of fraud and illegal acts that were discovered.
c. The materiality criteria used by the auditor in considering whether instances of noncompliance were significant.
d. An opinion on whether compliance with laws and regulations affected the entity's goals and objectives.

27. An accountant's report on a review of pro forma financial information should include a
a. Statement that the entity's internal control structure was **not** relied on in the review.

b. Disclaimer of opinion on the financial statements from which the pro forma financial information is derived.

c. Caveat that it is uncertain whether the transaction or event reflected in the pro forma financial information will ever occur.

d. Reference to the financial statements from which the historical financial information is derived.

28. Because of the pervasive effects of laws and regulations on the financial statements of governmental units, an auditor should obtain written management representations acknowledging that management has

a. Identified and disclosed all laws and regulations that have a direct and material effect on its financial statements.

b. Implemented internal control policies and procedures designed to detect all illegal acts.

c. Expressed both positive and negative assurance to the auditor that the entity complied with all laws and regulations.

d. Employed internal auditors who can report their findings, opinions, and conclusions objectively without fear of political repercussion.

29. An auditor notes reportable conditions in a financial statement audit conducted in accordance with *Government Auditing Standards*. In reporting on the internal control structure, the auditor should state that

a. Expressing an opinion on the entity's financial statements provides no assurance on the internal control structure.

b. The auditor obtained an understanding of the design of relevant policies and procedures, and determined whether they have been placed in operation.

c. The specified government funding or legislative body is responsible for reviewing the internal control structure as a condition of continued funding.

d. The auditor has not determined whether any of the reportable conditions described in the report are so severe as to be material weaknesses.

30. Which of the following conditions is necessary for a practitioner to accept an attest engagement to examine and report on an entity's internal control structure over financial reporting?

a. The practitioner anticipates relying on the entity's internal control structure in a financial statement audit.

b. Management presents its written assertion about the effectiveness of the internal control structure.

c. The practitioner is a continuing auditor who previously has audited the entity's financial statements.

d. Management agrees not to present the practitioner's report in a general-use document to stockholders.

31. The primary purpose of establishing quality control policies and procedures for deciding whether to accept a new client is to

a. Enable the CPA firm to attest to the reliability of the client.

b. Satisfy the CPA firm's duty to the public concerning the acceptance of new clients.

c. Minimize the likelihood of association with clients whose management lacks integrity.

d. Anticipate before performing any field work whether an unqualified opinion can be expressed.

32. Snow, CPA, was engaged by Master Co. to examine and report on management's written assertion about the effectiveness of Master's internal control structure over financial reporting. Snow's report should state that

a. Because of inherent limitations of any internal control structure, errors or irregularities may occur and not be detected.

b. Management's assertion is based on criteria established by the American Institute of Certified Public Accountants.

c. The results of Snow's tests will form the basis for Snow's opinion on the fairness of Master's financial statements in conformity with GAAP.

d. The purpose of the engagement is to enable Snow to plan an audit and determine the nature, timing, and extent of tests to be performed.

33. Wolf is auditing an entity's compliance with requirements governing a major federal financial assistance program in accordance with *Government Auditing Standards*. Wolf detected noncompliance with requirements that have a material effect on the program. Wolf's report on compliance should express

a. No assurance on the compliance tests.

b. Reasonable assurance on the compliance tests.

c. A qualified or adverse opinion.

d. An adverse or disclaimer of opinion.

34. Which of the following statements is a standard applicable to financial statement audits in accordance with *Government Auditing Standards?*
a. An auditor should assess whether the entity has reportable measures of economy and efficiency that are valid and reliable.
b. An auditor should report on the scope of the auditor's testing of internal controls.
c. An auditor should briefly describe in the auditor's report the method of statistical sampling used in performing tests of controls and substantive tests.
d. An auditor should determine the extent to which the entity's programs achieve the desired level of results.

35. The nature and extent of a CPA firm's quality control policies and procedures depend on

	The CPA firm's size	The nature of the CPA firm's practice	Cost-benefit considerations
a.	Yes	Yes	Yes
b.	Yes	Yes	No
c.	Yes	No	Yes
d.	No	Yes	Yes

36. Brown, CPA, has accepted an engagement to examine and report on Crow Company's written assertion about the effectiveness of Crow's internal control structure. In what form may Crow present its written assertion?

I. In a separate report that will accompany Brown's report.
II. In a representation letter to Brown.

a. I only.
b. II only.
c. Either I or II.
d. Neither I nor II.

37. When an accountant examines projected financial statements, the accountant's report should include a separate paragraph that
a. Describes the limitations on the usefulness of the presentation.
b. Provides an explanation of the differences between an examination and an audit.
c. States that the accountant is responsible for events and circumstances up to one year after the report's date.
d. Disclaims an opinion on whether the assumptions provide a reasonable basis for the projection.

38. In auditing a not-for-profit entity that receives governmental financial assistance, the auditor has a responsibility to
a. Issue a separate report that describes the expected benefits and related costs of the auditor's suggested changes to the entity's internal control structure.
b. Assess whether management has identified laws and regulations that have a direct and material effect on the entity's financial statements.
c. Notify the governmental agency providing the financial assistance that the audit is **not** designed to provide any assurance of detecting errors and irregularities.
d. Render an opinion concerning the entity's continued eligibility for the governmental financial assistance.

39. In auditing compliance with requirements governing major federal financial assistance programs under the Single Audit Act, the auditor's consideration of materiality differs from materiality under generally accepted auditing standards. Under the Single Audit Act, materiality is
a. Calculated in relation to the financial statements taken as a whole.
b. Determined separately for each major federal financial assistance program.
c. Decided in conjunction with the auditor's risk assessment.
d. Ignored, because all account balances, regardless of size, are fully tested.

40. Which of the following statements represents a quality control requirement under government auditing standards?
a. A CPA who conducts government audits is required to undergo an annual external quality control review when an appropriate internal quality control system is **not** in place.
b. A CPA seeking to enter into a contract to perform an audit should provide the CPA's most recent external quality control review report to the party contracting for the audit.
c. An external quality control review of a CPA's practice should include a review of the working papers of each government audit performed since the prior external quality control review.
d. A CPA who conducts government audits may **not** make the CPA's external quality control review report available to the public.

41. Although the scope of audits of recipients of federal financial assistance in accordance with federal audit regulations varies, these audits generally have which of the following elements in common?

a. The auditor is to determine whether the federal financial assistance has been administered in accordance with applicable laws and regulations.

b. The materiality levels are lower and are determined by the government entities that provided the federal financial assistance to the recipient.

c. The auditor should obtain written management representations that the recipient's internal auditors will report their findings objectively without fear of political repercussion.

d. The auditor is required to express both positive and negative assurance that illegal acts that could have a material effect on the recipient's financial statements are disclosed to the inspector general.

Chapter Four - Problems
Attestation Standards, Government Auditing
Standards, Quality Control Standards

NUMBER 1

An accountant is sometimes called on by clients to report on or assemble prospective financial statements for use by third parties.

Required:
a. 1. Identify the types of engagements that an accountant may perform under these circumstances.
    2. Explain the difference between "general use" of and "limited use" of prospective financial statements.
    3. Explain what types of prospective financial statements are appropriate for "general use" and what types are appropriate for "limited use".

b. Describe the contents of the accountant's standard report on a compilation of a financial projection.

NUMBER 2

Toxic Waste Disposal Co., Inc. (TWD) is a not-for-profit organization that receives grants and fees from various state and municipal governments as well as grants from several federal government agencies.

TWD engaged Hall & Hall, CPAs, to audit its financial statements for the year ended July 31, 1991, in accordance with *Government Auditing Standards.* Accordingly, the auditors' reports are to be submitted by TWD to the granting government agencies, which make the reports available for public inspection.

The auditors' separate report on compliance with laws and regulations that was drafted by a staff accountant of Hall & Hall at the completion of the engagement contained the statements below. It was submitted to the engagement partner who reviewed matters thoroughly and properly concluded that no material instances of noncompliance were identified.
1. A statement that the audit was conducted in accordance with generally accepted auditing standards and with *Government Auditing Standards* issued by the Comptroller General of the United States.
2. A statement that the auditors' procedures included tests of compliance.
3. A statement that the standards require the auditors to plan and to perform the audit to detect all instances of noncompliance with applicable laws and regulations.
4. A statement that management is responsible for compliance with laws, regulations, contracts, and grants.
5. A statement that the auditors' objective was to provide an opinion on compliance with the provisions of laws and regulations equivalent to that to be expressed on the financial statements.
6. A statement that the auditor's tests disclosed no instances of noncompliance.
7. A statement that the report is intended only for the information of the specific legislative or regulatory bodies, and that this restriction is intended to limit the distribution of the report.

Required:
For each of the above statements indicate whether each is an appropriate or inappropriate element within the report on compliance with laws and regulations. If a statement is **not** appropriate, explain why.

Chapter Four - Solutions to Questions
Attestation Standards, Government Auditing Standards, Quality Control Standards

1. (a) *Statements on Standards for Accountant's Services on Prospective Financial Information* states that forecasts take the form of historical financial statements. Thus, there is no need to explain what the information is since the forecast represents financial statements. Answers (b), (c) and (d) are part of the accountant's report (see examples in text).

2. (a) See Quality Control Standards.

3. (c) A record is kept of previous employees in order to ensure independence. Rule 101 of the Code of Conduct states that there is an independence problem when a CPA or member of his firm was employed by a client during the time period covered by the financial statements.

4. (b) As with all financial information, the client's management is responsible for the assertions in the information, not the user or the CPA reporting on the information.

5. (d) A financial forecast is defined by Statements on Standards for Accountants' Reports on Prospective Financial Information as a **general use** financial statement.

6. (a) Statements on Standards for Accountants' Reports on Prospective Financial Information do not permit the CPA performing reviews of such information.

7. (c) The General Accounting Office performs the audit function for Congress and has published Standards for Audits of Governmental Organizations, Programs, Activities, and Functions. The Governmental Accounting Standards Board (GASB) and the Financial Accounting Standards Board (FASB) establish accounting standards, not auditing standards. Answer (d) does not exist.

8. (c) The quality control element that is concerned with acceptance and continuance of clients suggests that a firm be selective in determining its professional relationships. Answer (a) would be done if there were a predecessor auditor and only if there were disagreements between the predecessor auditor and the client. Answers (b) and (d) relate primarily to field standards, not acceptance issues.

9. (d) The accountant's standard report on a compilation of prospective financial statements should include an identification of the financial statements, a statement that the accountant compiled the statements in accordance with AICPA standards, a statement that a compilation is limited in scope [answer (b)] and does not enable the accountant to express an opinion or any other form of assurance [answer (d)], a caveat that the results may not be achieved, a statement that the accountant assumes no responsibility to update the report for events and circumstances occurring after the date of the report [answer (c)]. When the presentation is a projection, the report should include a separate paragraph that describes the limitations on the usefulness of the presentation [answer (a)].

10. (d) An accountant may be engaged to examine, compile, or apply agreed-upon procedures to financial forecasts or other prospective financial statements. An examination of a financial forecast involves evaluating the preparation of the forecasted statements, evaluating the support underlying the assumptions used in preparing the statements, evaluating the presentation of the statements for conformity with AICPA guidelines, and issuing an examination report. Answer (a) is a compilation, not an examination. Answer (b) is incorrect because the accountant's report on the examination of a financial forecast can be distributed to parties outside of the reporting entity. Answer (c) is incorrect because the accountant's report specifically states that the accountant assumes no responsibility to update the report for events and circumstances occurring after the date of the report.

11. (d) Projected financial statements present to the best of the responsible party's knowledge, given one or more hypothetical assumptions, an entity's expected financial position, results of operations, and cash flows. These projected statements are for the limited use of parties with whom the responsible party is dealing directly. When compiling projected financial statements, the accountant's report should include a paragraph that describes these limitations on the usefulness of the presentation. The accountant's report does not include references to the items in answers (a), (b) and (c).

12. (d) An accountant should not examine a presentation that omits **all** disclosures of assumptions. If the presentation fails to disclose assumptions that appear to be significant, the accountant should describe the assumptions in his report and issue an adverse opinion. Answer (a) would be appropriate if, in the accountant's opinion, the prospective financial statements depart from AICPA presentation guidelines, other than a failure to disclose significant assumptions. Answers (b) and (c) are not examples of modified accountant's reports involving a financial forecast examination.

13. (c) According to the, "Statements on Standards for Prospective Financial Information," there are two types of prospective financial information: forecasts and projections. Forecasts are appropriate for "general use," meaning the CPA's report does not have to name a specific user. Projections are appropriate only for "limited use," meaning the CPA's report must specify a named user. Answer (c) is correct because both a forecast and a projection can be issued and specify a named user, thus "limited use."

14. (b) Significant deficiencies in the design or operation of the internal control structure that come to the auditor's attention are referred to as reportable conditions. Generally Accepted Auditing Standards require that these deficiencies be reported to the audit committee or others with equivalent authority and responsibility. Government Auditing Standards require that these deficiencies be reported to the auditee and to the appropriate officials of the organizations requiring or arranging for the audits, including legislative and regulatory bodies. Answers (a), (c) and (d) are incorrect because the auditor has no responsibility to communicate reportable conditions, including those that may be of such magnitude as to be considered a material weakness, to the SEC, court-appointed committees, or influential stockholders.

15. (b) An attestation engagement is an engagement that provides either positive or negative assurance concerning financial information. An engagement to report on compliance with a statutory requirement provides negative assurance that thus is an attestation engagement.

16. (d) A report on a financial projection is identified as a "limited use" report, which means that the report is not for general distribution. Such a report is restricted to be used only the parties *named* in the report. Since the stockholders could have changed from the report date it would be inappropriate to distribute a report on a financial projection to those individuals who are no longer stockholders.

17. (b) The objective of a system of quality controls within a CPA firm is to be reasonably assured of complying with the professional standards of the profession.

18. (a) A system of quality control for a CPA firm, which usually encompasses quality control policies and procedures, assignment of responsibilities, communication, and monitoring, can provide a CPA firm with reasonable assurance of conforming with professional standards. Answer (b) refers to peer review which, as an external study of a firm's quality controls, can help evaluate a firm's professional practice but is not done on a regular, ongoing basis. Answer (c) lists one example of an element of quality control. Answer (d) could be considered an example of a professional standard with which a firm should conform.

19. (d) A practitioner's report on an examination of management's assertion about the effectiveness of the entity's internal control structure should include a paragraph stating that, because of inherent limitations of any internal control structure, errors or irregularities may occur and not be detected. In addition, the report should include a title with the word independent, identify management's assertion, state that the examination was made in accordance with AICPA standards, and include the practitioner's opinion. The report would not include the statements presented in answers (a), (b) and (c).

20. (d) *Government Auditing Standards* requires a written report on the internal control structure in all audits. Those standards also require description of any reportable conditions noted, identification of the categories of the internal control structure, description of the scope of the auditor's work in obtaining an understanding of the internal control structure and in assessing control risk, and description of deficiencies in the internal control structure not considered significant enough to be reportable conditions. Regarding answer (a), if the auditor notes no reportable conditions during an audit he may so state, rather than give negative assurance. The report does not include the comments about reliable controls and strengths noted in answers (b) and (c).

21. (c) The auditor should design the audit to provide reasonable assurance that the financial statements are free of material misstatements resulting from violations of laws and regulations that have a direct and material effect on the determination of financial statement amounts. This responsibility exists for all audits conducted in accordance with generally accepted auditing standards. The auditor undertakes the same responsibility in an audit, in accordance with *Government Auditing Standards,* of financial statements of a not-for-profit organization that accepts financial assistance from a governmental entity.

22. (a) The reporting accountant Blue, CPA, should consult with the continuing accountant to ascertain all the available facts relevant to forming a professional judgment. This is a service which can be rendered and an opinion can be given, thus eliminating answer (c). Answers (b) and (d) include activities that are not required when undertaking this type of engagement.

23. (a) The services of independent auditors include audits of financial statements and schedules contained in registration statements filed with the Securities and Exchange Commission. In connection with this type of service, they are often called upon to perform other services, including the issuance of letters to underwriters, commonly called comfort letters.

24. (c) A financial projection is a prospective financial statement that presents, to the best of the knowledge of the party responsible for its preparation, given one or more hypothetical assumptions, an entity's financial position, results of operations, and changes in cash flows. As compared to a financial forecast, which is available for general use, a financial projection is a limited use report that is not appropriate for general distribution. Limited use refers to the use of prospective financial statements by the responsible party and third parties with whom the responsible party is dealing directly, such as a bank, that is able to question the responsible party directly about the information. Answers (a), (b) and (d) refer to general users of financial information who are typically not dealing directly with those responsible for preparing the prospective information.

25. (c) A CPA firm should consider nine elements of quality control, including the adoption of policies and procedures for assigning personnel to engagements to provide the firm with reasonable assurance that work will be performed by persons having the degree of technical training and proficiency required in the circumstances. The other eight elements of quality control are independence, consultation, supervision, hiring, professional development, advancement, acceptance and continuation of clients, and inspection. Answers (a), (b) and (d) affect audits, but are not quality control policies and procedures.

26. (b) Government Auditing Standards include additional reporting standards for financial statement audits. One of those standards requires that the report on the financial statements describe the scope of the auditors' testing of compliance with laws and regulations and internal controls and present the results of those tests. The standard goes on to state that in presenting the results of those tests, auditors should report irregularities, illegal acts, and other material noncompliance. Discoveries of fraud, which is a type of illegal act involving the obtaining of something of value through willful misrepresentation, would also be reported. Answer (a) is incorrect because the auditor does not test all controls. Answer (c) is incorrect because materiality criteria are not specified in the auditor's report. Answer (d) is incorrect because affects of compliance on an entity's goals and objectives, which relate more to performance audits than to financial audits, would not be included in the auditor's report.

27. (d) The objective of pro forma financial information is to show what the significant effects on historical financial information might have been had a consummated or proposed transaction occurred at an earlier date. An accountant can be engaged to examine or review pro forma financial information. In a review report, the accountant should identify the pro forma information, refer to the financial statements from which the historical information is derived

and state whether such financial statements were audited or reviewed, state that the review was in accordance with AICPA standards, explain the objective of pro forma information and its limitations, and provide negative assurance regarding the pro forma information. No reference is made to the internal control structure, as noted in answer (a). Answer (b) is incorrect because the historical information had to have been audited or reviewed. Answer (c) is incorrect because such a statement regarding achievability is included in reports on prospective financial statements, not on pro forma financial information.

28. (a) An auditor is required to obtain a client representation letter from management as part of every audit conducted in accordance with generally accepted auditing standards. Among the items covered in such a letter are violations or possible violations of laws and regulations whose effects should be considered for disclosure in the financial statements or as a basis for recording a loss contingency. In audits of governmental entities, auditors should consider obtaining additional representations from management acknowledging that management is responsible for the entity's compliance with laws and regulations applicable to it and that management has identified and disclosed to the auditor all laws and regulations that have a direct and material effect on the determination of financial statement amounts. Answer (b) is unrealistic in that it refers to detecting all illegal acts, which could include immaterial ones. Answer (c) is incorrect because the auditor would want positive assurance only; negative assurance from management would be inadequate in regard to compliance with laws and regulations. Answer (d) is desirable and at the discretion of management, but not typically included in a representation letter.

29. (b) When the auditor has noted reportable conditions in a financial statement audit conducted in accordance with Government Auditing Standards, the auditor's report on the internal control structure should contain a description of the scope of the auditor's work, stating that the auditor obtained an understanding of the design of relevant policies and procedures, determined whether these policies and procedures have been placed in operation, and assessed control risk. The auditor's report also includes a statement that the auditor considered the internal control structure in determining audit procedures for purposes of expressing an opinion on the financial statements and not to provide assurance on the internal control structure, rather that stating that no assurance on the internal control structure was provided, as indicated in answer (a). The auditor's report also contains a statement about whether the auditor believes any of the reportable conditions described in the report are material weaknesses, which is the opposite of what is stated in answer (d). No reference is made to responsibilities of funding or legislative bodies, as stated in answer (c).

30. (b) AT 400 states that a practitioner may examine and report on management's assertion about the effectiveness of an entity's internal control structure if the following conditions are met:
- Management accepts responsibility for the effectiveness of the entity's internal control structure.
- Management evaluates the effectiveness of the entity's internal control structure using reasonable "control criteria" for effective internal control structures established by a recognized body.
- Sufficient evidential matter exists or could be developed to support management's evaluation.
- Management presents its written assertion about the effectiveness of the entity's internal control structure based upon the control criteria referred to in its report.

Choice (a) is incorrect because the examination may be separate or in conjunction with an audit. Choice (c) is incorrect because no requirement for previous engagement exists in order to issue a report on the client's internal control. Choice (d) is incorrect because, if management's assertion is presented in a report that accompanies the practitioner's report, then it is considered appropriate for general distribution.

31. (c) QC 90 states that policies and procedures should be established for deciding whether to accept or continue a client in order to minimize the likelihood of association with a client whose management lacks integrity. Suggesting that there should be procedures for this purpose does not imply that a firm vouches for the integrity or reliability of a client, nor does it imply that a firm has a duty to anyone but itself with respect to the acceptance, rejection, or retention of clients.

32. (a) AT 400.50 states that when management presents its assertion in a separate report that will accompany the practitioner's report, the practitioner's report should include:

- A title that includes the word independent.
- An identification of management's assertion about the effectiveness of the entity's internal control structure over financial reporting.
- A statement that the examination was made in accordance with standards established by the AICPA and, accordingly, that it included obtaining an understanding of the internal control structure over financial reporting, testing and evaluating the design and operating effectiveness of the internal control structure, and performing other such procedures as the practitioner considered necessary in the circumstances. In addition, the report should include a statement that the practitioner believes the examination provides a reasonable basis for his or her opinion.
- A paragraph stating that because of inherent limitations of any internal control structure, errors or irregularities may occur and not be detected. In addition, the paragraph should state that projections of any evaluation of the internal control structure over financial reporting to future periods are subject to the risk that the internal control structure may become inadequate because of changes in conditions, or that the degree of compliance with the policies or procedures may deteriorate.
- The practitioner's opinion on whether management's assertion about the effectiveness of the entity's internal control structure over financial reporting as of the specified date is fairly stated, in all material respects, based on the control criteria.

33. (c) AU 801 states that when the audit of an entity's compliance with requirements governing a major federal financial assistance program detects noncompliance with those requirements which the auditor believes have a material effect on that program, the auditor should express a qualified or adverse opinion. The auditor should state the basis for such an opinion in the report.

34. (b) Government Auditing Standards include additional reporting standards for financial statement audits. One of those standards requires that the report on the financial statements describe the scope of the auditor's testing of compliance with laws and regulations and internal controls. Answers (a) and (d) relate to performance audits, which include economy and efficiency and program audits, rather than financial statement audits. Answer (c) is incorrect because specific descriptions of statistical testing methods are not included in an auditor's report.

35. (a) A system of quality control for a CPA firm encompasses the firm's organizational structure and the policies adopted and procedures established to provide the firm with reasonable assurance of conforming with professional standards. The nature and extent of a firm's quality control policies and procedures depend on a number of factors, such as its size, the degree of operating autonomy allowed its personnel and its practice offices, the nature of its practice, its organization, and appropriate cost-benefit considerations.

36. (c) A CPA may be engaged to examine and report on management's written assertion about the effectiveness of an entity's internal control structure. Management may present its written assertion in a separate report that will accompany the CPA's report or in a representation letter to the CPA. In the latter case, the CPA should restrict the use of his or her report to management and others within the entity and, if applicable, to specified regulatory agencies. Answers (a), (b) and (d) are incorrect because management's assertion can be presented in a separate report or in a representation letter.

37. (a) Financial projections are prospective financial statements that are based on one or more hypothetical assumptions. Projected financial statements should be distributed only to those who are negotiating directly with the party responsible for those financial statements because the negotiating parties are able to ask the responsible party directly about the presentation; specifically, the hypothetical assumptions. Thus, when an accountant examines a projection, his report should include a separate paragraph that describes the limitations on the usefulness of the presentation. That paragraph states that the projection and the accountant's report were prepared for a special purpose and should not be used for any other purpose. Answer (b) is incorrect because the accountant's report does explain that an examination was made in accordance with AICPA standards, but does not explain differences between an examination and an audit. Answer (c) is incorrect because the report includes a statement that the accountant assumes no responsibility to update the report. Answer (d) is incorrect because, in an examination, the

report does include the accountant's opinion that the underlying assumptions provide a reasonable basis for the projection given the hypothetical assumptions.

38. (b) When auditing recipients of governmental financial assistance, the auditor must design the audit to provide reasonable assurance that the financial statements are free of material misstatements resulting from violations of laws and regulations that have a direct and material effect on the determination of financial statement amounts. The auditor must understand the laws and regulations that are generally recognized to have a direct and material effect on the financial statements, and to assess whether management has identified such laws and regulations. Answer (a) is incorrect because although the auditor reports on internal control structure when auditing a recipient of governmental financial assistance, the auditor's report does not describe costs and benefits of control changes. Answer (c) is incorrect because the audit is designed to detect material errors and irregularities. Answer (d) is incorrect because the auditor's opinion does not address eligibility for financial assistance.

39. (b) In an audit of an entity's financial statements conducted in accordance with generally accepted auditing standards, the auditor considers materiality in relation to the financial statements. In auditing an entity's compliance with requirements governing each major federal financial assistance program in accordance with the Single Audit Act, the auditor considers materiality in relation to each such program. When reaching a conclusion as to whether the effect of noncompliance is material to a major federal financial assistance program, an auditor ordinarily should consider the nature of the noncompliance and the amount affected by the noncompliance in relation to the nature and amount of the major federal financial assistance program under audit. Answer (a) is incorrect because materiality is determined in relation to each major program, not in relation to the financial statements taken as a whole. Answer (c) is incorrect because materiality and risk, although related, are evaluated independently by the auditor. Answer (d) is incorrect because an auditor always considers materiality in an audit.

40. (b) Government auditing standards include a general standard stating that each audit organization conducting government audits should have an appropriate internal quality control system in place and participate in an external quality control review program. A CPA seeking to enter into a contract to perform an audit subject to government auditing standards should provide the CPA's most recent external quality review report to the party contracting for the audit. Answer (a) is incorrect because the external quality control review must take place at least every three years, not annually. Answer (c) is incorrect because an external quality control review involves reviewing working papers from a sample of audits, not reviewing working papers of each government audit. Answer (d) is incorrect because there is no restriction on making the external quality control review report available to the public.

41. (a) The audit of recipients of federal financial assistance is conducted under Generally Accepted Governmental Auditing Standards. Because the recipient has a legal obligation to spend monies in accordance with applicable laws and regulations, the auditor has the responsibility to audit and report on compliance.

Chapter Four - Solutions to Problems
Attestation Standards, Government Auditing Standards, Quality Control Standards

NUMBER 1

a. 1. An accountant who reports on or assembles prospective financial statements for use by third parties should perform any one of three engagements. The accountant may compile, examine, or apply agreed-upon procedures to the prospective financial statements.

2. "General use" of prospective financial statements refers to use of the statements by persons (creditors, stockholders, etc.) with whom the responsible party (management) is not negotiating directly. "Limited use" of prospective financial statements refers to the use of prospective financial statements by the responsible party alone or by the responsible party and third parties with whom the responsible party is negotiating directly.

3. Only a financial forecast is appropriate for general use, but any type of prospective financial statements (either a financial forecast or a financial projection) would normally be appropriate for limited use.

b. The accountant's standard report on a compilation of a financial projection should include

- An identification of the projection presented by the responsible party.
- A statement that the accountant has compiled the projection in accordance with standards established by the AICPA.
- A separate paragraph that describes the limitations on the use of the presentation.
- A statement that a compilation is limited in scope and does not enable the accountant to express an opinion or any other form of assurance on the projection or the assumptions.
- A caveat that the prospective results may not be achieved.
- A statement that the accountant assumes no responsibility to update the report for events and circumstances occurring after the date of the report.

NUMBER 2

1. Statement 1 is appropriate.
2. Statement 2 is appropriate.
3. Statement 3 is not appropriate because the auditors are required to plan and perform the audit to provide reasonable assurance of detecting instances of noncompliance having a direct and material effect on the financial statements, not all instances of noncompliance.
4. Statement 4 is appropriate.
5. Statement 5 is not appropriate because rendering an opinion is a higher level of reporting than the positive and negative assurance required by *Government Auditing Standards*.
6. Statement 6 is appropriate.
7. Statement 7 is not appropriate because *Government Auditing Standards* require that, unless restricted by law or regulation, copies of the reports should be made available for public inspection.

Chapter Five
Reviews, Compilations, Special Reports and Other Reports

Chapter Five
Reviews, Compilations, Special Reports and Other Reports

COMPILATION ENGAGEMENTS AND REVIEW ENGAGEMENTS,
Non-Public Companies (SSARS No. 1)

I. DEFINITIONS:

SSARS:
1. Statements on Standards for Accounting and Review Services.
2. Applies only to non-public entities.
3. Issued by the Accounting and Review Services Committee of the AICPA.

A **compilation** is the presentation in the form of financial statements, information that is the representation of management **without** undertaking to express any assurance on the statements.

A **review** involves inquiry and analytical procedures that provide the accountant with a reasonable basis for expressing **limited assurance** that there are no material modifications that should be made to the statements in order for them to be in conformity with generally accepted accounting principles or OCBOA.

A **nonpublic entity** is any entity **other than** one (a) whose securities trade publicly either locally, regionally, nationally, or in foreign markets, or (b) that makes a filing with a regulatory agency in preparation for the sale of any class of its securities in a public market.

II. FINANCIAL STATEMENTS DEFINED FOR PURPOSES OF THIS STATEMENT

A presentation of financial data, including accompanying notes, derived from accounting records and intended to communicate an entity's economic resources or obligations at a point in time, or the changes therein for a period of time, in accordance with GAAP or OCBOA.

Examples:

Balance sheet; Income statement-Statement of retained earnings; Statement of cash flows; Statement of changes in owners' equity; Statement of assets and liabilities; Statement of revenue and expenses; Summary of operations; Statement of operations by product lines; Statement of cash receipts and disbursements.

Financial statements may be that of a corporation, a consolidated group, a combined group of affiliated entities, a not-for-profit organization, a government unit, an estate or trust, a partnership, a proprietorship, a segment of any of these or an individual.

Excluded for purposes of this statement are financial forecasts, projections, and financial presentations included in tax returns.

III. COMPILATION OF FINANCIAL STATEMENTS

A. Statements compiled **without audit** or **review** should be accompanied by a report stating that:
   1. A compilation has been performed.
   2. It is limited to presenting, in the form of financial statements, information that is the representation of management.
   3. The statements have not been audited or reviewed and no opinion is expressed or any other form of assurance given.

No procedures performed by the accountant should be **described** in the report. The report should be dated as of the completion of the compilation. Each page of the statements should include a reference such as "See Accountant's Compilation Report".

> Addressee
>
> I (we) have compiled the accompanying balance sheet of XYZ Company as of December 31, 20XX, and the related statements of income, retained earnings, and cash flows for the year then ended, in accordance with Statements on Standards for Accounting and Review Services issued by the American Institute of Certified Public Accountants.
>
> A compilation is limited to presenting in the form of financial statements, information that is the representation of management (owners). I (we) have not audited or reviewed the accompanying financial statements and, accordingly, do not express an opinion or any other form of assurance on them.
>
> Signature, date

Reporting on a Compilation When Substantially All Disclosures are Omitted

Statements may be prepared omitting substantially all disclosures provided the omission is clearly indicated in the accountant's report. When the entity wishes to disclose only a few matters in the form of notes, such disclosures should be labeled, "Selected Information—Substantially All Disclosures Required by Generally Accepted Accounting Principles Are Not Included."

If the statements are prepared on a comprehensive basis of accounting other than GAAP, the basis should be disclosed in the accountant's report.

The following form of report should be used when substantially all disclosures have been omitted.

> Addressee
>
> I (we) have compiled the accompanying balance sheet of XYZ Company as of December 31, 20XX, and the related statements of income, retained earnings, and cash flows for the year then ended, in accordance with Statements on Standards for Accounting and Review Services issued by the American Institute of Certified Public Accountants.
>
> A compilation is limited to presenting in the form of financial statements information that is the representation of management (owners). I (we) have not audited or reviewed the accompanying financial statements and, accordingly, do not express an opinion or any other form of assurance on them.
>
> Management has elected to omit substantially all of the disclosures (and the statement of cash flows) required by generally accepted accounting principles. If the omitted disclosures were included in the financial statements, they might influence the user's conclusions about the company's financial position, results of operations, and cash flows. Accordingly, these financial statements are not designed for those who are not informed about such matters.
>
> Signature, date

B. **Procedures to be Followed—Compilation**
   1. The accountant should possess a level of knowledge of the accounting principles and practices of the industry in which the entity operates. This will allow him to compile financial statements that are appropriate in turn with the industry.
   2. Through a continuing relationship with the client or inquiry of client personnel, the accountant should obtain an understanding of the nature of the entity's business transactions, the form of accounting records, the qualifications of accounting personnel, and the form and content of the financial statements. On the basis of this understanding, the accountant may decide to provide other accounting services such as assistance in adjusting the accounting records.
   3. The accountant is not required to make inquiries or perform other procedures. However, the accountant may have done so, and as such, it may come to the accountant's attention that the information supplied by the entity is in error, incomplete, or otherwise unsatisfactory. Under such circumstances, the accountant should obtain additional or revised information. If the entity refuses to cooperate, the accountant should withdraw from the engagement.

Reporting on a Compilation That Has Departures from GAAP

If the accountant concludes that modification of his standard report is appropriate, the departure should be disclosed in a separate paragraph of his report, including disclosure of the effects of the departure on the financial statements if such effects have been determined by management or are known as the result of the accountant's procedures.

Example:

Addressee

I (we) have compiled the accompanying balance sheet of XYZ Company as of December 31, 20XX, and the related statements of income, retained earnings, and cash flows for the year then ended, in accordance with Statements on Standards for Accounting and Review Services issued by the American Institute of Certified Public Accountants.

A compilation is limited to presenting in the form of financial statements information that is the representation of management (owners). I (we) have not audited or reviewed the accompanying financial statements and, accordingly, do not express an opinion or any other form of assurance on them. However, I (we) did become aware of a departure (certain departures) from generally accepted accounting principles that is (are) described in the following paragraph(s).

(Separate paragraph)
As disclosed in note X to the financial statements, generally accepted accounting principles require that land be stated at cost. Management has informed me (us) that the company has stated its land at appraised value and that, if generally accepted accounting principles had been followed, the land account and stockholders' equity would have been decreased by $500,000.

C. **Compilation Engagements – Issuance of Management Use Only Financial Statements (SSARS No. 8)**
   1. Management use only engagements are compilations and thus follow all the standards for <u>performing</u> (performance standards) a compilation. The difference is that **no** compilation report is issued by the accountant.
   2. Conditions necessary to conduct the engagement:
      a. A written understanding must be reached with management regarding the services to be performed and the limitations on the use of the financial statements.
      b. Each page of the financial statements must include a reference such as:
         "Restricted for Management Use Only."

IV. REVIEW OF FINANCIAL STATEMENTS

A. **Requirements for a Review**
   1. The accountant should obtain a level of knowledge of both the industry and entity's accounting principles and practices. Such an understanding will serve as a basis for the performance of inquiry and analytical procedures which lead to the accountant's limited assurance that there are no material modifications that should be made to the financial statements.
   2. The accountant should have a thorough understanding of the entity's operation characteristics, the nature of its assets, liabilities, revenue and expenses, and the entity's production and distribution patterns. Such an understanding is usually obtained through experience with the entity or inquiry of the entity's personnel.
   3. The accountant's inquiry and analytical procedures should ordinarily consist of the following:
      - Inquiry concerning the entity's accounting principles.
      - Inquiry concerning the entity's procedures for recording, classifying, and summarizing transactions.
      - Analytical procedures designed to identify relationships and individual items that appear to be unusual.
      - Inquiry concerning meetings of stockholders, directors, or committees of the board of directors.
      - Reading the financial statements, with the information the accountant has gathered to date, to determine whether the statements appear to conform with GAAP.
      - Obtaining reports from other accountants, if any, who have been engaged to audit or review the financial statements of significant subsidiaries.
      - Inquiry of persons having responsibility for financial and accounting matters concerning (1) whether the financial statements are in conformity with GAAP, (2) changes in the entity's business activities or accounting principles, (3) matters as to which questions have arisen in the course of the review, and (4) events subsequent to the date of the financial statements that would have a material effect on the statements.
   4. Knowledge acquired in the performance of audits of the entity's financial statements, compilation of the financial statements, or other accounting services may require modification of the aforementioned procedures.
   5. A review is not as complete an examination of financial statements as an audit. Thus, a review does not provide assurance that the accountant will become aware of all significant matters that would be disclosed in an audit.
   6. The accountant **must obtain a representation letter signed by the manager, owner, or chief executive officer.** Failure to obtain such a letter renders the review incomplete and the accountant is prohibited from issuing a review report. Also the accountant may not step down the service and issue a compilation report.

B. **Report on Review of Financial Statements**
   1. A report on a review of financial statements should include information that:
      a. A review was performed in accordance with the standards for such engagements established by the AICPA.
      b. The financial statements are representations of management.
      c. The review consists principally of inquiries and analytical procedures.
      d. The review is less in scope than an audit and, as such, no opinion expressed on the financial statements.
      e. The accountant is not aware of any material modifications that should be made to the financial statements.

   Example
   Addressee

   I (we) have reviewed the accompanying balance sheet of XYZ Company as of December 31, 20XX, and the related statements of income, retained earnings, and cash flows for the year then ended, in accordance with Statements on Standards for Accounting and Review Services issued by the American Institute of Certified Public Accountants. All information included in these financial statements is the representation of the management (owners) of XYZ Company.

A review consists principally of inquiries of company personnel and analytical procedures applied to financial data. It is substantially less in scope than an examination in accordance with generally accepted auditing standards, the objective of which is the expression of an opinion regarding the financial statements taken as a whole. Accordingly, I (we) do not express such an opinion.

Based on my (our) review, I am (we are) not aware of any material modifications that should be made to the accompanying financial statements in order for them to be in conformity with generally accepted accounting principles.

Signature, date

C. **Reporting on a Review That Has Departures from GAAP**
When the accountant determines that the statements are not in accordance with GAAP, the accountant should revise his report on the financial statements. Such a report should disclose the effects of the departure, if determined by management or known to the accountant as the result of his procedures.

Example:

Addressee

I (we) have reviewed the accompanying balance sheet of XYZ Company as of December 31, 20XX, and the related statements of income, retained earnings, and cash flows for the year then ended, in accordance with Statements on Standards for Accounting and Review Services issued by the American Institute of Certified Public Accountants. All information included in these financial statements is the representation of the management (owners) of XYZ Company.

A review consists principally of inquiries of company personnel and analytical procedures applied to financial data. It is substantially less in scope than an examination in accordance with generally accepted auditing standards, the objective of which is the expression of an opinion regarding the financial statements taken as a whole. Accordingly, I (we) do not express such an opinion.

Based on my (our) review, with the exception of the matter(s) described in the following paragraph(s), I am (we are) not aware of any material modifications that should be made to the accompanying financial statements in order for them to be in conformity with generally accepted accounting principles.

As disclosed in note X to the financial statements, generally accepted accounting principles require that inventory cost consist of material, labor, and overhead. Management has informed me (us) that the inventory of finished goods and work in process is stated in the accompanying financial statements at material and labor cost only, and that the effects of this departure from generally accepted accounting principles on financial position, results of operations, and cash flows have not been determined.

or

As disclosed in note X to the financial statements, the company has adopted (description of newly adopted method), whereas it previously used (description of previous method). Although the (description of newly adopted method) is in conformity with generally accepted accounting principles, the company does not appear to have reasonable justification for making a change as required by Opinion No. 20 of the Accounting Principles Board.

V. OTHER MATTERS—COMPILATION AND REVIEW ENGAGEMENTS

A. **Change in the nature of engagement**

An accountant who has been engaged to examine the financial statements of a nonpublic entity in accordance with GAAS, may, before completion of his engagement, be requested to change the scope of his engagement to a review or compilation.

Such a request, if it results from the entity's requirement for an audit or a misunderstanding concerning the nature of an audit, would ordinarily be considered a reasonable basis for a change in the scope of examination.

If a request was a result of a restriction on the scope of an audit examination, the accountant should evaluate the possibility that information affected by the scope restriction may be incorrect or incomplete. If, however, the accountant was prohibited from corresponding with the client's legal counsel, or when management refuses to sign a client representation letter, the accountant ordinarily would be precluded from issuing a review or compilation report.

B. **Engagement letters**

In all cases the accountant should (although not required to) prepare an engagement letter. Such a letter would outline the degree of responsibility the accountant is taking for the financial statements.

SUMMARY OF
COMPILATION AND REVIEW
ENGAGEMENTS

FACTOR	COMPILATION	REVIEW
Level of Assurance	None	Limited (Negative Assurance)
Type of Entity	Non-Public	Non-Public
Type of Evidence Obtained	None Required	1. Inquiry 2. Analytical procedures
Knowledge of client's industry and business	Yes	Yes
Responsibility for information in financial statements	Client	Client
Required Reasons to modify standard report	1. Known GAAP or disclosure departures 2. Election by client to omit all disclosures and/or statements of cash flows 3. Accountant not independent	1. Known GAAP or disclosure departures
Representation Letter required	No	Yes
Account needs to be independent	No	Yes
Engagement Letter required	No, but should reach understanding with client*	No, but should reach understanding with client

*If engaged to prepare "management use only financial statements," must document terms of engagement in a written form with the entity.

I. This section establishes standards for reporting on comparative financial statements of a nonpublic entity when financial statements of one or more periods presented have been compiled or reviewed in accordance with SSARS No. 1.

II. An example of a continuing accountant's standard report on comparative financial statements for two periods when the financial statements of the current period have been reviewed and those of the prior period have been compiled is presented below:

Addressee

I (we) have reviewed the accompanying balance sheet of XYZ Company as of December 31, 20XX, and the related statements of income, retained earnings, and cash flows for the year then ended, in accordance with Statements on Standards for Accounting and Review Services issued by the American Institute of Certified Public Accountants. All information included in these financial statements is the representation of the management (owners) of XYZ Company.

A review consists principally of inquiries of company personnel and analytical procedures applied to financial data. It is substantially less in scope than an examination in accordance with generally accepted auditing standards, the objective of which is the expression of an opinion regarding the financial statements taken as a whole. Accordingly, I (we) do not express such an opinion.

Based on my (our) review, I am (we are) not aware of any material modifications that should be made to the 20XX financial statements in order for them to be in conformity with generally accepted accounting principles.

The accompanying 20X0 financial statements of XYZ Company were compiled by me (us). A compilation is limited to presenting in the form of financial statements information that is the representation of management (owners). I (we) have not audited or reviewed the 20X0 financial statements and, accordingly, do not express an opinion or any other form of assurance on them.

Signature
Date

III. A continuing accountant who performs a compilation of the current-period financial statements and has previously reviewed one or more prior-period financial statements should report as indicated in either (a) or (b) below:
   a. Issue a compilation report on the current-period financial statements that includes a description of the responsibility assumed for the financial statements of the prior period. The description should include the original date of the accountant's report and should also state that he has not performed any procedures in connection with that review engagement after that date.
   b. Combine his compilation report on the financial statements of the current period with his reissued review report on the financial statements of the prior period or present them separately. The combined report should state that the accountant has not performed any procedures in connection with that review engagement after the date of his review report.

   An example of a paragraph that may be added to a compilation report on the current-period financial statements describing the responsibilities assumed when prior-period financial statements were reviewed follows:

The accompanying 20X0 financial statements of XYZ Company were previously reviewed by me (us) and my (our) report dated March 1, 20XX, stated that I was (we were) not aware of any material modifications that should be made to those statement in order for them to be in conformity with generally accepted accounting principles. I (we) have not performed any procedures in connection with that review engagement after the date of my (our) report on the 20X0 financial statements.

IV. Continuing Accountant's Changed Reference to a Departure from Generally Accepted Accounting Principles

    A. During his current engagement, the accountant should be aware that circumstances or events may affect the prior-period financial statements presented, including the adequacy of informative disclosures. The accountant should consider the effects on his report on the prior-period financial statements of circumstances or events coming to his attention.

    B. When the accountant's report on the financial statements of the prior period contains a changed reference to a departure from generally accepted accounting principles, his report should include a separate explanatory paragraph indicating—
      1. The date of the accountant's previous report.
      2. The circumstances or events that caused the reference to be changed.
      3. When applicable, that the financial statements of the prior period have been changed.

The following is an example of an explanatory paragraph appropriate when an accountant's report contains a changed reference to a departure from generally accepted accounting principles:

In my (our) previous (compilation) (review) report dated March 1, 19X2, on the 19X1 financial statements, I (we) referred to a departure from generally accepted accounting principles because the company carried its land at appraised values. However, as disclosed in note X, the company has restated its 19X1 financial statements to reflect its land at cost in accordance with generally accepted accounting principles.

V. Predecessor's Compilation or Review Report

A predecessor may reissue his report at the client's request if he is able to make satisfactory arrangements with his former client and performs additional procedures outlined below. However, a predecessor is not required to reissue his compilation or review report on the financial statements of a prior period. If he does not reissue his compilation or review report on the financial statements of a prior period, a successor should either (a) make reference to the report of the predecessor, or (b) perform a compilation, review, or audit of the financial statements of the prior period and report on them accordingly.

    A. Predecessor's Compilation or Review Report Not Presented

When the financial statements of a prior period have been compiled or reviewed by a predecessor whose report is not presented and the successor has not compiled or reviewed those financial statements, the successor should make reference in an additional paragraph(s) of his report on the current-period financial statements to the predecessor's report on the prior-period financial statements. This reference should include the following matters:
      1. A statement that the financial statements of the prior period were compiled or reviewed by another accountant (other accountants).
      2. The date of his (their) report.
      3. A description of the standard form of disclaimer or limited assurance, as applicable, included in the report.
      4. A description or a quotation of any modifications of the standard report and of any paragraphs emphasizing a matter regarding the financial statements.

When the predecessor reviewed the financial statements of the prior period, an example of the last paragraph of the successor's report is as follows:

The 20X0 financial statements of XYZ Company were reviewed by other accountants whose report dated March 1, 20XX, stated that they were not aware of any material modifications that should be made to those statements in order for them to be in conformity with generally accepted accounting principles.

When the predecessor compiled the financial statements of the prior period, an example of the last paragraph of the successor's report is as follows:

The 20X0 financial statements of XYZ Company were compiled by other accountants whose report dated February 1, 20XX, stated that they did not express an opinion or any other form of assurance on those statements.

B. Predecessor's Compilation or Review Report Reissued

Before reissuing a compilation or review report on the financial statements of a prior period, a predecessor should consider whether his report is still appropriate. In making this determination, the predecessor should consider (a) the current form and manner of presentation of the prior-period financial statements, (b) subsequent events not previously known, and (c) changes in the financial statements that require the addition or deletion of modifications to the standard report.

A predecessor should perform the following procedures before reissuing his compilation or review report on the financial statements of a prior period:
1. Read the financial statements of the current period and the successor's report.
2. Compare the prior-period financial statements with those previously issued and with those of the current period.
3. Obtain a letter from the successor that indicates whether he is aware of any matter that, in his opinion, might have a material effect on the financial statements, including disclosures, reported on by the predecessor. The predecessor should not refer in his reissued report to this letter or to the report of the successor.

If a predecessor becomes aware of information, including information about events or transactions occurring subsequent to the date of his previous report, that he believes may affect the prior-period financial statements or his report on them, he should (a) make inquiries or perform analytical procedures similar to those he would have performed if he had been aware of such information at the date of his report on the prior-period financial statements and (b) perform any other procedures he considers necessary in the circumstances.

A predecessor's knowledge of the current affairs of his former client is obviously limited in the absence of a continuing relationship. Consequently, when reissuing his report on the prior-period financial statements, a predecessor should use the date of his previous report to avoid any implication that he has performed procedures after that date. If the predecessor revises his report or if the financial statements are restated, he should dual-date his report (for example, "March 1, 20XX, except for note X, as to which the date is March 15, 20XX"). The predecessor's responsibility for events occurring subsequent to the completion of his engagement is limited to the specific event referred to in the note or otherwise disclosed. He should also obtain a written statement from the former client setting forth the information currently acquired and its effect on the prior-period financial statements and, if applicable, expressing an understanding to its effect on the predecessor's reissued report.

If a predecessor is unable to complete the procedures described, he should not reissue his report and may wish to consult with his attorney regarding the appropriate course of action.

VI. Changed Prior-Period Financial Statements

When the financial statements of the prior period have been changed, either the predecessor or the successor should report on them as restated. If a successor reports on the restated financial statements, he should not refer in his report to the predecessor's previously issued report.

If the restatement does not involve a change in accounting principles or their application (for example, the correction of an error), the accountant may wish to include an explanatory paragraph in his report with respect to the restatement, but he should not otherwise modify his standard report provided the financial statements appropriately disclose such matters.

VII. Reporting When One Period is Audited

The accountant should follow the guidance in statement on auditing standards, which provide guidance on reporting on comparative financial statements when the current-period financial statements have been audited and those for one or more prior periods have been compiled or reviewed.

When the current-period financial statements of a nonpublic entity have been compiled or reviewed and those of the prior period have been audited, the accountant should issue an appropriate compilation or review report on the current-period financial statements and either (a) the report on the prior period should be reissued or (b) the report on the current period should include as a separate paragraph an appropriate description of the responsibility assumed for the financial statements of the prior period. In the latter case, the separate paragraph should indicate (a) that the financial statements of the prior period were examined previously, (b) the date of the previous report, (c) the type of opinion expressed previously, (d) if the opinion was other than unqualified, the substantive reasons therefor, and (e) that no auditing procedures were performed after the date of the previous report. An example of such a separate paragraph is the following:

> The financial statements for the year ended December 31, 20X0, were examined by us (other accountants) and we (they) expressed an unqualified opinion on them in our (their) report dated March 1, 20XX, but we (they) have not performed any auditing procedures since that date.

VIII. Reporting on Financial Statement That Previously Did Not Omit Substantially All Disclosures

An accountant who has compiled, reviewed, or audited financial statements that did not omit substantially all of the disclosures required by generally accepted accounting principles may subsequently be requested to compile statements for the same period that do omit substantially all of those disclosures when they are to be presented in comparative financial statements. In these circumstances the accountant may report on comparative financial statements that omit such disclosures if he includes in his report an additional paragraph indicating the nature of the previous service rendered with respect to those financial statements and the date of his previous report.

An example of a report appropriate when prior-period financial statements that omit substantially all disclosures have been compiled from previous reviewed financial statements for the same period follows:

> Addressee
>
> I (we) have compiled the accompanying balance sheet of XYZ Company as of December 31, 20XX, and the related statements of income, retained earnings, and cash flows for the year then ended, in accordance with Statements on Standards for Accounting and Review Services issued by the American Institute of Certified Public Accountants.
>
> A compilation is limited to presenting in the form of financial statements information that is the representation of management (owners). I (we) have not audited or reviewed the accompanying

financial statements and, accordingly, do not express an opinion or any other form of assurance on them.

Management has elected to omit substantially all of the disclosures required by generally accepted accounting principles. If the omitted disclosures were included in the financial statements, they might influence the user's conclusions about the company's financial position, results of operations, and cash flows. Accordingly, these financial statements are not designed for those who are not informed about such matters.

The accompanying 20X0 financial statements were compiled by me (us) from financial statements that did not omit substantially all of the disclosures required by generally accepted accounting principles and that I (we) previously reviewed as indicated in my (our) report dated March 1, 20X0.

Signature
Date

IX.   Change of Status—Public/Nonpublic Entity

When reporting on comparative financial statements for either interim or annual periods, the current status of the entity should govern whether the accountant is guided by statements on auditing standards or statements on standards for accounting and review services. A previously issued report that is not appropriate for the current status of the entity should not be reissued or referred to in the report on the financial statements of the current period.

For example, if the entity is a public entity in the current period and was a nonpublic entity in the prior period, a compilation or review report previously issued on the financial statements of the prior period should not be reissued or referred to in the report on the financial statements of the current and one or more prior periods. If an entity is a nonpublic entity in the current period and was a public entity in the prior period, the annual financial statements of the prior period may have been audited. In these circumstances, the accountant should refer to the prior section, "Reporting When One Period is Audited."

COMPILATION REPORTS ON FINANCIAL STATEMENTS INCLUDED IN CERTAIN PRESCRIBED FORMS, NON-PUBLIC COMPANIES (SSARS No. 3)

A _**prescribed form**_ is any standard preprinted form designed or adopted by the body to which it is to be submitted.

There is a presumption that the information required by a prescribed form is sufficient to meet the needs of the body that designed or adopted the form and that there is no need for that body to be advised of departures from generally accepted accounting principles required by the prescribed form or related instructions. Therefore, in the absence of a requirement or a request for a review report on the financial statements included in a prescribed form, the following form of standard compilation report may be used when the unaudited financial statements of a nonpublic entity are included in a prescribed form that calls for departure from generally accepted accounting principles.

If the accountant becomes aware of a departure from the requirements of the prescribed form or related instructions, he should consider that departure as the equivalent of a departure from generally accepted accounting principles in determining its effect on his report.

COMMUNICATIONS BETWEEN PREDECESSOR AND SUCCESSOR ACCOUNTANTS, NON-PUBLIC COMPANIES (SSARS No. 4)

I. The following definitions apply:

Successor accountant. An accountant who has been invited to make a proposal for an engagement to compile or review financial statements or who has accepted such an engagement.

Predecessor accountant. An accountant who has resigned or who has been notified that his services have been terminated and who, at a minimum, was engaged to compile the financial statements of the entity for the prior year or for a period ended within twelve months of the date of the financial statements to be compiled or reviewed by the successor.

II. Inquiries Regarding Acceptance of an Engagement

A successor accountant is not required to communicate with a predecessor accountant in connection with acceptance of a compilation or review engagement, but he may decide to do so, for example, when circumstances such as the following exist:
1. The information obtained about the prospective client and its management and principals is limited or appears to require special attention.
2. The change in accountants takes place substantially after the end of the accounting period for which financial statements are to be compiled or reviewed.
3. There have been frequent changes in accountants.

When the successor accountant decides to communicate with the predecessor, he should request the client (a) to permit him to make inquiries of the predecessor accountant and (b) to authorize the predecessor accountant to respond fully to those inquiries. If the client refuses to comply fully with this request, the successor accountant should consider the reasons for, and implications of, that refusal in connection with acceptance of the engagement.

When the successor accountant decides to communicate with the predecessor, his inquiries may be oral or written and ordinarily would include inquiries concerning (a) information that might bear on the integrity of management (owners), (b) disagreements with management (owners) about accounting principles or the necessity for the performance of certain procedures, (c) the cooperation of management (owners) in providing additional or revised information, if necessary, and (d) the predecessor's understanding of the reason for the change of accountants.

III. Other Inquiries

The successor accountant may wish to make other inquiries of the predecessor to facilitate the conduct of his compilation or review engagement. Examples of such inquiries, which may be made either before or after acceptance of the engagement, might include questions about prior periods regarding (a) inadequacies noted in the entity's underlying financial data, (b) the necessity to perform other accounting services, and (c) areas that have required inordinate time in prior periods.

A successor accountant also may wish to obtain access to the predecessor's working papers. In these circumstances, the successor should request the client to authorize the predecessor to allow such access. Ordinarily, the predecessor should provide the successor access to working papers relating to matters of continuing accounting significance and those relating to contingencies. Valid business reasons (including but not limited to unpaid fees), however, may lead the predecessor to decide not to allow access to his working papers.

REVIEW OF INTERIM FINANCIAL INFORMATION—**Public Companies**
(SAS No. 71)

I. OBJECTIVE OF A REVIEW OF INTERIM FINANCIAL INFORMATION

The objective of a review of interim financial information differs from an audit of financial statements in accordance with GAAS. The examination of financial statements provides a reasonable basis for the expression of an opinion on the financial statements taken as a whole. A review of interim financial information does not provide a basis for the expression of an opinion because the review does not contemplate a study and evaluation of internal control, tests of accounting records, and obtaining corroborating evidence to support responses to auditor inquiries.

Timely reporting is essential when performing a review of interim financial data. At an interim period most accounting data is estimated, especially deferrals, accruals and estimates. The accountant should be aware of this and plan the conduct of the review to account for such factors.

II. PROCEDURES FOR A REVIEW OF INTERIM FINANCIAL INFORMATION

The accountant should be concerned with (a) the nature of procedures, (b) timing of procedures, and (c) extent of procedures.

A. **Nature of procedures**
1. Inquiry concerning (a) the accounting system in order to obtain an understanding of how transactions are recorded, classified, and summarized for the preparation on interim financial information, (b) any significant changes in the system of internal accounting control and how such changes could affect the generation of interim financial information.
2. Application of analytical review procedures such as comparison with prior periods, anticipated results, and adherence to a predictable pattern of results based upon the entity's experience. These procedures provide a basis for inquiry about relationships or results that seem unusual.
3. Reading the minutes of committees of the entity such as stockholders, board of directors, and related subcommittees.
4. Reading the interim information to consider whether such information is in accordance with GAAP. In applying this procedure the accountant would use all information that has come to his attention from applying the aforementioned procedures.
5. Obtaining and reading the reports of other accountants who have been engaged to make interim reviews of significant components of the reporting entity.
6. Inquire of officers and other executives who have responsibility for financial and accounting matters concerning:
    a. Whether the financial information is in accordance with GAAP.
    b. Changes in the entity's business activity or accounting practices.
    c. Questions concerning items that have arisen in applying the foregoing procedures.
    d. Subsequent events that would have effect on the presentation of such interim financial information.
7. Obtaining written representations from management concerning its responsibility for the financial information, completeness of minutes, availability of accounting data, subsequent events, and other matters the accountant believes appropriate.

B. **Timing of Procedures**
Adequate planning by the accountant is contemplated so that the review can be completed in an expeditious manner. As such, the accountant should consider performing some procedures prior to the ending of the interim period.

C. **Extent of Procedures**

The extent of procedures referred to under "Nature of Procedures" would be determined by:

1. The accountant's knowledge of the client's accounting and reporting practices.
2. The accountant's knowledge of weakness in internal control—If the system of internal control appears to contain weaknesses that do not permit the preparation of interim financial information, the accountant should consider whether the weakness represents a restriction of the scope of his engagement sufficient to preclude completion of such a review. In this case the accountant should also advise senior management and the board of directors.
3. The accountant's knowledge of changes in nature or volume of activity or accounting changes— Unusual or infrequent transactions require inquiry of management in order to determine the effects and disclosure requirements to be reported in the interim financial information.
4. Issuance of accounting pronouncements—The accountant should be aware of any new pronouncements on financial accounting standards and consider their potential effect on the interim financial information.
5. Accounting records maintained at multiple locations—A client who maintains records at multiple locations must be treated in a manner similar to the manner used in the examination of audited financial statements. Usually this involves applying procedures both at corporate headquarters and other locations selected by the accountant.
6. Questions raised in performing other procedures—If the auditor questions whether the interim information is in conformity with GAAP, he should employ procedures he considers appropriate to permit him to report on the interim financial information.
7. Modification of review procedures—The procedures for a review of interim financial information may be modified to take into consideration the results of auditing procedures applied in performing an examination in accordance with GAAP.

D. **Communication with Audit Committees**

The following matters should be reported to the Audit Committee:

1. Any material irregularities
2. Any material illegal acts

If, in the accountant's opinion, the audit committee does not respond appropriately to the accountant's communication within a reasonable period of time, the accountant should evaluate:

1. Whether to resign from the engagement, and
2. Whether to remain as the entity's auditor.

III. REPORTING ON INTERIM FINANCIAL INFORMATION PRESENTED OTHER THAN IN A NOTE TO AUDITED FINANCIAL STATEMENTS

A. **No modification necessary**

Form of Report —

Address: Board of Directors, Company or Stockholders

We have made a review of (describe the information or statements reviewed) of ABC Company and consolidated subsidiaries as of September 30, 20X0, and for the three-month and nine-month periods then ended, in accordance with standards established by the American Institute of Certified Public Accountants.

A review of interim financial information consists principally of obtaining an understanding of the system for the preparation of interim financial information, applying analytical review procedures to financial data, and making inquiries of persons responsible for financial and accounting matters. It is substantially less in scope than an examination in accordance with generally accepted auditing standards, the objective of which is the expression of an opinion regarding the financial statements taken as a whole. Accordingly, we do not express such an opinion. These financial (information or statements) is(are) the responsibility of the company's management.

Based on our review, we are not aware of any material modifications that should be made to the accompanying financial (information or statements) for them to be in conformity with generally accepted accounting principles.

Date: Completion of review
Signature

B. **Departures from GAAP**

Report example:

(Explanatory third paragraph)
Based on information furnished us by management, we believe that the Company has excluded from property and debt in the accompanying balance sheet certain lease obligations that should be capitalized in order to conform with generally accepted accounting principles. This information indicates that if these lease obligations were capitalized at September 30, 20XX, property would be increased by $........, and long-term debt by $........, and net income and earnings per share would be increased (decreased) by $........, $........, $........, and $........, respectively, for the three-month and nine-month periods then ended.

(Concluding paragraph)
Based on our review, with the exception of the matter(s) described in the preceding paragraph(s), we are not aware of any material modifications that should be made to the accompanying financial (information or statements) for them to be in conformity with generally accepted accounting principles.

C. **Inadequate Disclosure**

Report example:

(Explanatory third paragraph)
Management has informed us that the Company is presently contesting deficiencies in federal income taxes proposed by the Internal Revenue Service for the years 20X0 through 20XX in the aggregate amount of approximately $......., and that the extent of the Company's liability, if any, and the effect on the accompanying (information or statements) are not determinable at this time. The (information or statements) fail to disclose these matters, which we believe are required to be disclosed in conformity with generally accepted accounting principles.

(Concluding paragraph)
Based on our review, with the exception of the matter(s) described in the preceding paragraph(s), we are not aware of any material modifications that should be made to the accompanying financial (information or statements) for them to be in conformity with generally accepted accounting principles.

D. Normally, neither an uncertainty nor lack of consistency in the application of accounting principles affecting interim financial information would cause the accountant to modify his report, provided that the interim financial information or statements appropriately describe such matters.

IV. REPORTING ON INTERIM FINANCIAL INFORMATION PRESENTED IN A NOTE TO AUDITED FINANCIAL STATEMENTS

A. The procedures set forth previously are appropriate for the accountant's review of the interim financial information designated as unaudited and presented in a note to audited financial statements.

B. There is no requirement to perform these procedures at other than the time of examination of the financial statements under audit.

C. The auditor ordinarily need not modify his report for unaudited interim financial information. Such information is not needed for a fair presentation of financial statements.

D. The auditors' report on the audited financial statements should be expanded if the scope of his review of the interim financial information was restricted or if the interim financial information does not appear to be presented in conformity with GAAP. The auditor should also expand his report if the interim financial information was not reviewed unless that fact is stated in the footnote.

Example of modification:

Note X, "Unaudited Interim Financial Information," contains information that we did not audit and, accordingly, we do not express an opinion on the information. We attempted but were unable to make a review of such interim information in accordance with standards established by the American Institute of Certified Public Accountants because we believe that the Company's system for preparing interim financial information does not provide an adequate basis to enable us to complete such a review.

E. The auditor's report should also be modified if the unaudited financial information is not clearly marked unaudited, or the footnote does not contain a clear statement that a review of interim financial information is substantially less in scope than an audit is in accordance with GAAP.

SPECIAL REPORTS (SAS No. 62)

I. AUDITING STANDARDS PROVIDE GUIDANCE ON REPORTS (KNOWN AS SPECIAL REPORTS) ISSUED IN CONNECTION WITH THE FOLLOWING TYPES OF SERVICE:

A. Financial statements prepared in conformity with a comprehensive basis of accounting other than generally accepted accounting principles.
B. Specified elements, accounts or items of a financial statement.
C. Compliance with aspects of contractual agreements or regulatory requirements related to audited financial statements.
D. Financial presentations to comply with contractual agreements or regulatory provisions.
E. Other matters, including financial information presented in prescribed forms or schedules that require a prescribed form of auditor's report.

II. FINANCIAL STATEMENTS PRESENTED IN CONFORMITY WITH COMPREHENSIVE BASIS OF ACCOUNTING OTHER THAN GAAP (OCBOA)

Generally accepted auditing standards are applicable when an auditor conducts an audit of and reports on any financial statement. The term "financial statement" refers to a presentation of financial data, including accompanying notes, derived from accounting records and intended to communicate an entity's economic resources or obligations at a point in time, or the changes therein for a period of time, in accordance with a comprehensive basis of accounting.

Normally, the auditor's judgment concerning the overall presentation of financial statements is in relation to generally accepted accounting principles. However, a comprehensive basis of accounting other than GAAP may be used. OCBOA statements include the following:
* A basis of accounting that the reporting entity uses to comply with the requirements or financial reporting provisions of a governmental regulatory agency.
* A basis of accounting that the reporting entity uses or expects to use to file its income tax return.
* The cash receipts and disbursements basis of accounting, and modifications of the cash basis having substantial support.
* A definite set of criteria having substantial support that is applied to all material items appearing in financial statements, such as the price-level basis of accounting.

A. **Reporting Requirements**
   When reporting on OCBOA financial statements, the report should include:
   1. A title that includes the word "independent".
   2. Introductory and scope paragraphs which include the same elements as the standard auditor's report.
   3. A paragraph that (1) states the basis of presentation and refers to the note to the financial statements that describes such basis; (2) states that the basis of presentation is a comprehensive basis of accounting other than generally accepted accounting principles.
   4. An opinion paragraph that expresses the auditor's opinion (or disclaims an opinion) on whether the financial statements are presented fairly, in all material respects, in conformity with the basis of accounting described. If the auditor concludes that the financial statements are not presented fairly on the basis of accounting described, or if there has been a limitation on the scope of the audit, all the substantive reasons for that conclusion should be disclosed in an explanatory paragraph(s), preceding the opinion paragraph, and the opinion paragraph should be appropriately modified and include a reference to such explanatory paragraph(s).
   5. If the financial statements are prepared in accordance with the requirements or financial reporting provisions of a governmental regulatory agency, a paragraph that restricts the distribution of the report solely to those within the entity and for filing with the regulatory agency. Such a restrictive paragraph is appropriate, even though by law or regulation, the auditor's report may be made a matter of public record. Such restrictions may also be used if any additional distribution of the financial statements is recognized as appropriate by an AICPA accounting or audit guide or auditing interpretation.
   6. The signature of the Firm.
   7. The date.

If the financial statements do not meet the criteria for OCBOA presentation, the standard form auditor's report should be used with appropriate modifications because of the departures from GAAP.

An illustrative report on income-tax basis statements follows:

<u>*Report of Independent Certified Public Accountants*</u>

The Partners
ABC Partnership

We have audited the accompanying statements of assets, liabilities and capital—income tax basis of ABC Partnership as of December 31, 20XX and 20X0, and the related statements of revenue and expenses—income tax basis and changes in partners' capital accounts—income tax basis for the years then ended. These financial statements are the responsibility of the Partnership's management. Our responsibility is to express an opinion on these financial statements based on our audits.

We conducted our audits in accordance with generally accepted auditing standards. Those standards require that we plan and perform the audit to obtain reasonable assurance about whether the financial statements are free of material misstatement. An audit includes examining, on a test basis, evidence supporting the amounts and disclosures in the financial statements. An audit also includes assessing the accounting principles used and significant estimates made by management, as well as evaluating the overall financial statement presentation. We believe that our audits provide a reasonable basis for our opinion.

As described in Note _____, these financial statements were prepared on the same basis of accounting the Partnership uses for income tax purposes, which is a comprehensive basis of accounting other than generally accepted accounting principles.

In our opinion, the financial statements referred to above present fairly, in all material respects, the assets, liabilities, and capital of ABC Partnership as of December 31, 20XX and 20X0, and its revenue and expenses and changes in partners' capital accounts for the years then ended, on the basis of accounting described in Note_____.

Signature
Date

B. **Statement Titles and Disclosures**
The auditor should consider whether the financial statements are suitably titled. **Titles such as** *balance sheet, statement of income, statement of cash flows,* etc., are generally understood to be applicable only to financial statements that are intended to present financial position, results of operations or cash flows in conformity with generally accepted accounting principles. Accordingly, titles of OCBOA statements should be appropriately modified; if they are not, the auditor should disclose his or her reservations in an explanatory paragraph and qualify the opinion.

The auditor should consider whether the financial statements (including the accompanying notes) include all informative disclosures that are appropriate for the basis of accounting used. The auditor should apply essentially the same criteria to OCBOA financial statements as for GAAP statements.

Notes to OCBOA financial statements should include a summary of significant accounting policies that discusses the basis of presentation and describes how that basis differs from GAAP. However, the effects of the differences between GAAP and OCBOA need not be quantified. *When the statements presented contain items that are the same or similar to GAAP financial statements, similar disclosures are appropriate.* For example, income tax basis statements usually reflect depreciation, long-term debt and owners' equity; disclosures about such items should be comparable to those for GAAP financial statements. The auditor should also consider the adequacy of disclosures about matters not specifically identified on the face of the statements, such as related party transactions, restrictions on assets and owners' equity, subsequent events and uncertainties.

SUMMARY OF ENGAGEMENTS ON OCBOA FINANCIAL STATEMENTS

	AUDIT	REVIEW	COMPILATION
Level of Assurance	Positive	Negative	None
Standards Followed	GAAS	SSARS	SSARS
Procedures Followed	Same as for GAAP Presentations	← As stated	← As stated
Statements Usually Presented	1. Statements of Assets, Liabilities and Equity		
	2. Statement of Revenues Earned and Expenses Paid	← As stated	← As stated
	3. Statement of Equity		
Report	1. Essentially standard audit report for GAAP but modified for statement titles and basis of presentation	← As stated	← As stated
	2. Reference in report (separate paragraph) that discusses the basis of accounting in statements	Not needed	Not needed except need to include information on basis of accounting in compiling without disclosures
	3. Must be modified for a) departures from Basis of Accounting, b) inadequate disclosures, or c) improper statement titles	← As stated	← As stated

III. SPECIFIED ELEMENTS, ACCOUNTS, OR ITEMS OF A FINANCIAL STATEMENT

A. Audit Engagements in Accordance with GAAS

An auditor may be requested to express an opinion on one or more specified elements, accounts or items (referred to hereinafter as "item(s)") of a financial statement, such as rentals, royalties, profit participation, provision for income taxes, etc. The specified item may be presented in the auditor's report or in a document accompanying such report.

Generally accepted auditing standards are applicable to such an engagement, except that the auditor's report should indicate whether the presentation is in conformity with GAAP only when the item being reported on is intended to be in conformity with GAAP.

An engagement to express an opinion on one or more items may be undertaken as a separate engagement or in conjunction with an audit of financial statements. However, materiality must be measured in relation to each individual item being reported on rather than the aggregate of all items or the financial statements taken as a whole. Accordingly, an audit of a specified item(s) is usually more extensive than if the same information were being considered in conjunction with an audit of financial statements taken as a whole. The auditor should also be satisfied that other items that are interrelated with the item being reported on have also been considered (e.g., sales and receivables; inventory and accounts payable; buildings and equipment and depreciation).

If the auditor has expressed an adverse opinion or disclaimed an opinion on the financial statements taken as a whole, an opinion should not be expressed on specified items within those statements if such reporting would be tantamount to expressing a piecemeal opinion on the financial statements. However, the auditor may be able to express an opinion on specified items if they do not constitute a major portion of the financial statements. For example, it may be appropriate to express an opinion on accounts receivable when the auditor has disclaimed an opinion on the financial statements due to an uncertainty regarding legal action against the entity. In such cases, the report on the specified item should be presented separately from the report on the financial statements.

Reporting Requirements

When reporting on one or more specified elements, accounts or items of a financial statement, the report should include:

1. A title that includes the word "independent".
2. A paragraph that:
    *   States that the specified elements, accounts or items identified in the report were audited. If applicable, the paragraph should also state that the audit was made in conjunction with an audit of the company's financial statements and indicate the date of the auditor's report on those financial statements. Furthermore, any departure from the standard report on those statements should also be disclosed if considered relevant to the presentation of the specified element, account or item.
    *   States the specified elements, accounts or items are the responsibility of the company's management and that the auditor is responsible for expressing an opinion on the specified elements, accounts or items based on the audit.
3. A scope paragraph which includes the same elements as the standard auditor's report.
4. A paragraph that (1) states the basis on which the specified elements, accounts or items are presented and, when applicable, any agreements specifying such basis (if the presentation is not prepared in conformity with GAAP); and (2) if considered necessary, includes a description and source of significant interpretations, if any, made by the company's management relating to the provisions of a relevant agreement.
5. An opinion paragraph that expresses the auditor's opinion (or disclaims an opinion) on whether the specified elements, accounts or items are presented fairly, in all material respects, in conformity with the basis of accounting described. If the auditor concludes that the specified elements, accounts or

items are not presented fairly on the basis of accounting described, or if there has been a limitation on the scope of the audit, all the substantive reasons for that conclusion should be disclosed in an explanatory paragraph(s), preceding the opinion paragraph, and the opinion paragraph should be appropriately modified and include a reference to such explanatory paragraph(s).

6. If the specified element, account or item is prepared to comply with the requirements or financial reporting provisions of a contract or agreement that results in a presentation that is not in conformity with GAAP or OCBOA, a paragraph that restricts the distribution of the report solely to those within the entity and the parties to the contract or agreement. (Such a restriction is necessary because the basis of presentation is determined by reference to a document that would not generally be available to other third parties.)

7. Signature of the Firm.

8. The date.

Illustrative Reports:

Example of an audit report when auditing an item in accordance with GAAP:

Report of Independent Certified Public Accountants

Board of Directors
ABC Company

We have audited the accompanying schedule of accounts receivable of ABC Company as of December 31, 19X2. This schedule is the responsibility of the Company's management. Our responsibility is to express an opinion on this schedule based on our audit.

We conducted our audit in accordance with generally accepted auditing standards. Those standards require that we plan and perform the audit to obtain reasonable assurance about whether the schedule of accounts receivable is free of material misstatement. An audit includes examining, on a test basis, evidence supporting the amounts and disclosures in the schedule. An audit also includes assessing the accounting principles used and significant estimates made by management, as well as evaluating the overall schedule presentation. We believe that our audit provides a reasonable basis for our opinion.

In our opinion, the schedule of accounts receivable referred to above presents fairly, in all material respects, the accounts receivable of ABC Company as of December 31, 19X2, in conformity with generally accepted accounting principles.

Signature
Date

Example of an audit report when auditing an item in accordance with the terms of a contract:

Report of Independent Certified Public Accountants

Board of Directors
ABC Company

We have audited, in accordance with generally accepted auditing standards, the financial statements of ABC Company for the year ended December 31, 19X2, and have issued our report thereon dated March 10, 19X3. We have also audited ABC Company's schedule of profit-sharing contribution for the year ended December 31, 19X2. This schedule is the responsibility of the Company's management. Our responsibility is to express an opinion on this schedule based on our audit.

We conducted our audit of the schedule in accordance with generally accepted auditing standards. Those standards require that we plan and perform the audit to obtain reasonable assurance about whether the schedule of profit-sharing contribution is free of material misstatement. An audit includes examining, on a test basis, evidence supporting the amounts and disclosures in the schedule. An audit also includes assessing the accounting principles used and significant estimates made by management, as well as evaluating the overall schedule presentation. We believe that our audit provides a reasonable basis for our opinion.

Management has informed us that the document that governs the determination of the Company's profit-sharing documentation is the ABC Company Employees' Profit-Sharing Plan, dated January 10, 19XX, as amended February 12, 19XX.

In our opinion, the schedule of profit-sharing contribution referred to above presents fairly, in all material respects, ABC Company's profit-sharing contribution for the year ended December 31, 19X2, in accordance with the provisions of the Plan referred to above.

This report is intended solely for the information and use of the board of directors and management of ABC Company and the trustees (members) of ABC Company Employees' Profit-Sharing Plan.

Signature
Date

IV. COMPLIANCE WITH ASPECTS OF CONTRACTUAL AGREEMENTS OR REGULATORY REQUIREMENTS RELATED TO AUDITED FINANCIAL STATEMENTS

An auditor may be requested to provide a compliance report, in conjunction with an audit of financial statements, as required by a bond indenture, loan agreement or regulatory agencies to give assurance about compliance with loan covenants, payments into sinking funds, dividend restrictions, etc. The auditor normally satisfies this request by giving negative assurance relative to the applicable covenants, either in a separate report or in one or more paragraphs of the auditor's report on the financial statements. Such assurance should not be given unless the auditor has audited the financial statements related to the contractual agreements or regulatory requirements and should not extend to covenants that relate to matters not subjected to audit procedures. Assurances should not be given if the auditor has expressed an adverse opinion or disclaimed an opinion on the related financial statements.

A. **Reporting Requirements**

When reporting on compliance with contractual agreements or regulatory provisions in a separate report, the report should include:

1. A title that includes the word "independent".
2. A paragraph that states that the financial statements were audited in accordance with generally accepted auditing standards and includes the date of that auditor's report on those financial statements. Any departure from the standard report on those financial statements should be disclosed.
3. A paragraph that includes a reference to the specific covenants or paragraphs of the agreement, provides negative assurance relative to compliance with the applicable covenants of the agreement insofar as they relate to accounting matters, and specifies that the negative assurance is being given in connection with an audit of financial statements. The report should ordinarily state that the audit was not directed primarily toward obtaining knowledge regarding compliance.
4. A paragraph that includes a description and source of significant interpretations, if any, made by the company's management in the course of the engagement relating to the provisions of a relevant agreement.
5. A paragraph that restricts the distribution of the report solely to those within the entity and the parties to the contract or for filing with the regulatory agency (since the matters on which the auditor is reporting are set forth in a document that is generally not available to other third parties).
6. Signature of the Firm.
7. The date.

When a report on compliance is included in the report on the financial statements, the auditor should include a paragraph, after the opinion paragraph, that *provides negative assurance relative to compliance* with the applicable covenants of the agreement, insofar as they relate to accounting matters, and specifies that it is being given in connection with the audit of financial statements. The auditor should also ordinarily state that the audit was not directed primarily toward obtaining knowledge regarding compliance. In addition, the report should include a paragraph that describes any significant interpretations made by management as well as a paragraph that restricts its distribution.

An illustrative separate negative assurance report follows:

Report of Independent Certified Public Accountants

Board of Directors
ABC Company

We have audited, in accordance with generally accepted auditing standards, the balance sheet of ABC Company as of December 31, 20XX, and the related statements of earnings, retained earnings and cash flows for the year then ended, and have issued our report thereon dated February 16, 2XXX.

In connection with our audit, nothing came to our attention that caused us to believe that the Company failed to comply with the terms, covenants, provisions or conditions of sections ____ to ____, inclusive, of the Indenture dated July 21, 20X0, with XYZ Bank insofar as they relate to accounting matters. However, our audit was not directed primarily toward obtaining knowledge of such noncompliance.

This report is intended solely for the information and use of the boards of directors and managements of ABC Company and XYZ Bank and should not be used for any other purpose.

Signature
February 16, 2XXX

V. SPECIAL-PURPOSE FINANCIAL PRESENTATIONS TO COMPLY WITH CONTRACTUAL AGREEMENTS OR REGULATORY PROVISIONS

An auditor may be asked to report on special-purpose financial statements prepared to comply with a contractual agreement or regulatory provisions, including:
- A special-purpose financial presentation prepared in compliance with a contractual agreement or regulatory provision that does not constitute a complete presentation of the entity's assets, liabilities, revenues and expenses, but is otherwise prepared in conformity with GAAP or OCBOA.
- A special-purpose financial presentation (may be a complete presentation of financial statements or a single financial statement) prepared on a basis of accounting prescribed in an agreement that does not result in a presentation in conformity with GAAP or OCBOA.

A. Incomplete Presentations
A contractual agreement or regulatory provision may prescribe the form for financial statements which are in conformity, except for the omission of certain items, with GAAP or OCBOA.

Examples of such financial statements include:
- A governmental agency may require a schedule of gross income and certain expenses of an entity's real estate operation in which income and expenses are measured in conformity with GAAP, but expenses are defined to exclude certain items such as interest, depreciation and income taxes.
- A buy-sell agreement may specify a schedule of gross assets and liabilities of the entity measured in conformity with GAAP, but limited to the assets to be sold and liabilities to be transferred pursuant to the agreement.

Such presentations, which differ from complete financial statements only to the extent necessary to meet the special purpose for which they were prepared, should be considered financial statements as defined by this Statement. Accordingly, the measurement of materiality should be related to the presentation taken as a whole. The statements should include appropriate disclosures and be suitably titled.

B. **Reports on incomplete presentations should include:**
1. A title that includes the word "independent".
2. Introductory and scope paragraphs which include the same elements as for the standard auditor's report.
3. A paragraph that: (1) explains what the presentation is intended to present and refers to the note that describes the basis of presentation; (2) if the presentation is in conformity with GAAP, states that the presentation is not intended to be a complete presentation of the entity's assets, liabilities, revenues and expenses. (If the presentation is prepared on a basis of accounting prescribed in an agreement that results in an incomplete OCBOA presentation, the paragraph should state that the presentation is in conformity with a comprehensive basis of accounting other than GAAP and is not intended to be a complete presentation on such basis.)
4. An opinion paragraph that expresses the auditor's opinion related to the fair presentation, in all material respects, of the information in conformity with GAAP or OCBOA. If the auditor concludes that the information intended to be presented is not presented fairly on the basis of accounting described, or if there has been a limitation on the scope of the audit, the auditor should disclose all the substantive reasons for that conclusion in an explanatory paragraph(s), preceding the opinion paragraph. The opinion paragraph should include appropriate modifying language and a reference to such explanatory paragraph(s).
5. A paragraph that restricts the distribution of the report solely to those within the entity; to parties to the contract or agreement; for filing with a regulatory agency; or to those with whom the entity is negotiating directly. However, a restrictive paragraph is not appropriate when the report and related financial presentation are to be filed with a regulatory agency (e.g., the SEC) and are to be included in a document (e.g., a prospectus) which is distributed to the general public.
6. Signature of the Firm.
7. The date.

___Report of Independent Certified Public Accountants___

Board of Directors
ABC Company

We have audited the accompanying statement of net assets sold of ABC Company as of June 30, 20XX. This statement of net assets sold is the responsibility of ABC Company's management. Our responsibility is to express an opinion on the statement of net assets sold based on our audit.

We conducted our audit in accordance with generally accepted auditing standards. Those standards require that we plan and perform the audit to obtain reasonable assurance about whether the statement of net assets sold is free of material misstatement. An audit includes examining, on a test basis, evidence supporting the amounts and disclosures in the statement. An audit also includes assessing the accounting principles used and significant estimates made by management, as well as evaluating the overall presentation of the statement of net assets sold. We believe that our audit provides a reasonable basis of our opinion.

The accompanying statement was prepared to present the net assets of ABC Company sold to XYZ Corporation pursuant to the purchase agreement described in Note _____, and is not intended to be a complete presentation of ABC Company's assets and liabilities.

In our opinion, the accompanying statement of net assets sold presents fairly, in all material respects, the net assets of ABC Company, as of June 30, 20XX, sold pursuant to the purchase agreement referred to in Note _____, in conformity with generally accepted accounting principles.

This report is intended solely for the information and use of the boards of directors and managements of ABC Company and XYZ Corporation and should not be used for any other purpose.

Signature
Date

C. **Presentation Not in Conformity with GAAP or OCBOA**

An auditor may be asked to report on special-purpose financial statements prepared in conformity with a basis of accounting that departs from GAAP or OCBOA. For example, an acquisition agreement may require financial statements of an entity being acquired to be prepared in conformity with GAAP principles except for certain assets which are to be valued in accordance with the terms of the acquisition agreement. These are not considered to be OCBOA financial statements because they do not conform to "criteria having substantial support."

When reporting on such financial presentations, the auditor's report should include:
1. A title that includes the word "independent".
2. Introductory and scope paragraphs which include the same elements as for the standard auditor's report.
3. A paragraph that: (1) explains what the presentation is intended to present and refers to the note that describes the basis of presentation; (2) states that the presentation is not intended to be a presentation in conformity with GAAP.
4. A paragraph that includes a description and source of significant interpretations, if any, made by the Company's management relating to the provisions of a relevant agreement.
5. An opinion paragraph that expresses the auditor's opinion related to the fair presentation, in all material respects, of the information the presentation is intended to present on the basis of accounting specified. If the auditor concludes that the information intended to be presented is not presented fairly on the basis of accounting described, or if there has been a limitation on the scope of the audit, all the substantive reasons for that conclusion should be described in an explanatory paragraph(s), preceding the opinion paragraph. The opinion paragraph should include appropriate modifying language and a reference to such explanatory paragraph(s).
6. A paragraph that restricts the distribution of the report solely to those within the entity; to the parties to the contracts or agreement; for filing with a regulatory agency; or to those with whom the entity is negotiating directly.
7. Signature of the Firm.
8. The date.

Report of Independent Certified Public Accountants

Board of Directors
ABC Company

We have audited the accompanying special-purpose statement of assets and liabilities of ABC Company as of December 31, 20XX and 20X0, and the related special-purpose statements of revenues and expenses and cash flows for the years then ended. These statements are the responsibility of the Company's management. Our responsibility is to express an opinion on these financial statements based on our audits.

We conducted our audits in accordance with generally accepted auditing standards. Those standards require that we plan and perform the audit to obtain reasonable assurance about whether the financial statements are free of material misstatement. An audit includes examining, on a test basis, evidence supporting the amounts and disclosures in the financial statements. An audit also includes assessing the basis of accounting used and significant estimates made by management, as well as evaluating the overall financial statement presentation. We believe that our audits provide a reasonable basis for our opinion.

The accompanying special-purpose financial statements were prepared for the purpose of complying with Section 4 of a loan agreement between DEF Bank and the Company, as discussed in Note X, and are not intended to be a presentation in conformity with generally accepted accounting principles.

In our opinion, the special-purpose financial statements referred to above present fairly, in all material respects, the assets and liabilities of ABC Company at December 31, 20XX and 20X0, and the revenues, expenses and cash flows for the years then ended, on the basis of accounting described in Note X.

This report is intended solely for the information and use of the boards of directors and managements of ABC Company and DEF Bank and should not be used for any other purpose.

Signature
Date

SUMMARY OF ENGAGEMENTS
TO REPORT ON SPECIAL
PURPOSE FINANCIAL PRESENTATIONS
IN COMPLIANCE WITH CONTRACTUAL
OR REGULATORY AGREEMENTS

	Type of Service	
	Incomplete presentation of assets, liabilities, equities, revenues and expenses, but otherwise prepared in conformity with GAAP or OCBOA.	Special Purpose Financial Statements prepared in accordance with a contractual or regulatory requirement that does not result in a GAAP or OCBOA presentation.
Standards Followed	GAAS	GAAS
Report	Basic Audit report modified as appropriate for: 1) reference to the financial presentation 2) reference to the document that specifies the basis of presentation 3) a restriction on the distribution of the report	Basic Audit report modified as needed for: 1) reference to the titles of the financial statements as named in the contract or regulatory provision 2) reference to the document that specifies the basis of presentation 3) a reference that the financial statements are not intended to be GAAP presentations 4) a reference that the financial statements are "special purpose" 5) a restriction on the distribution of the report

VI. OTHER MATTERS

Prescribed Forms or Schedules

Printed forms or schedules adopted or designed by the bodies with which they are to be filed often prescribe wording for an auditor's report. If such wording does not conform to professional reporting standards, the auditor should reword the form or attach a separate report.

REPORTS ON THE APPLICATION OF ACCOUNTING PRINCIPLES (SAS No. 50)

CPAs are often called upon to report to a client on the application of an accounting principle. Such a report may result in:

a. Preparing a written report on the application of accounting principles to specified transactions, either completed or proposed.

b. A written report on the type of opinion that may be rendered on a specific entity's financial statements.

c. Preparing a written report to intermediaries on the application of accounting principles not involving facts or circumstances of a particular principal.

d. Oral advice on the application of accounting principles to a specific transaction, or the type of opinion that may be rendered on an entity's financial statements, when the reporting accountant concludes the advice is intended to be used by a principal to the transaction as an important factor considered in reaching a decision.

I. PROCEDURES

To aid in forming a judgment, the reporting accountant should perform the following procedures:

A. Obtain an understanding of the form and substance of the transaction(s);

B. Review applicable generally accepted accounting principles;

C. If appropriate, consult with other professionals or experts; and

D. If appropriate, perform research or other procedures to ascertain and consider the existence of creditable precedents or analogies.

II. REPORTING STANDARDS

The accountant's written report should be addressed to the principal to the transaction or to the intermediary, and should ordinarily include the following:

A. A brief description of the nature of the engagement and a statement that the engagement was performed in accordance with applicable AICPA standards.

B. A description of the transaction(s), a statement of the relevant facts, circumstances, and assumptions, and a statement about the source of the information. Principals to specific transactions should be identified, and hypothetical transactions should be described as involving nonspecific principals (for example, Company A, Company B).

C. A statement describing the appropriate accounting principle(s) to be applied or type of opinion that may be rendered on the entity's financial statements, and, if appropriate, a description of the reasons for the reporting accountant's conclusion.

D. A statement that the responsibility for the proper accounting treatment rests with the preparers of the financial statements, who should consult with their continuing accountants.

E. A statement that any difference in the facts, circumstances, or assumptions presented may change the report.

The following is an illustration of sections of the report described above.

Introduction

We have been engaged to report on the appropriate application of generally accepted accounting principles to the specific (hypothetical) transaction described below. This report is being issued to the

ABC Company (XYZ Intermediaries) for assistance in evaluating accounting principles for the described specific (hypothetical) transaction. Our engagement has been conducted in accordance with standards established by the American Institute of Certified Public Accountants.

Description of Transaction
The facts, circumstances, and assumptions relevant to the specific (hypothetical) transaction as provided to us by the management of the ABC Company (XYZ Intermediaries) are as follows:

Appropriate Accounting Principles
(Text discussing principles)

Concluding Comments
The ultimate responsibility for the decision on the appropriate application of generally accepted accounting principles for an actual transaction rests with the preparers of financial statements, who should consult with their continuing accountants. Our judgment on the appropriate application of generally accepted accounting principles for the described specific (hypothetical) transaction is based solely on the facts provided to us as described above; should these facts and circumstances differ, our conclusion may change.

REPORTING ON FINANCIAL STATEMENTS PREPARED FOR USE IN OTHER COUNTRIES (SAS No. 51)

A U.S. entity ordinarily prepares financial statements for use in the United States in conformity with accounting principles generally accepted in the United States, but it may also prepare financial statements that are intended for use outside the United States and are prepared in conformity with accounting principles generally accepted in another country.

I. GENERAL AND FIELDWORK STANDARDS

When examining the financial statements of a U.S. entity prepared in conformity with accounting principles generally accepted in another country, the auditor should perform the procedures that are necessary to comply with the general and fieldwork standards of U.S. generally accepted auditing standards (GAAS).

In those circumstances in which the auditor is requested to apply the auditing standards of another country when reporting on financial statements prepared in conformity with accounting principles generally accepted in that country, the auditor should comply with the general and fieldwork standards of that country as well as with those standards in the U.S. GAAS.

II. REPORTING STANDARDS

If financial statements prepared in conformity with accounting principles generally accepted in another country are prepared for use only outside the United States, the auditor may report using either (a) a U.S.-style report modified to report on the accounting principles of another country, or (b) if appropriate, the report form of the other country.

Financial statements prepared in conformity with accounting principles generally accepted in another country ordinarily are not useful to U.S. users. Therefore, if financial statements are needed for use both in another country and within the United States, the auditor may report on two sets of financial statements for the entity— one prepared in conformity with accounting principles generally accepted in another country for use outside the United States, and the other prepared in accordance with accounting principles generally accepted in the United States.

III. USE ONLY OUTSIDE THE UNITED STATES

A U.S.-style report modified to report on financial statements prepared in conformity with accounting principles generally accepted in another country that are intended for use only outside the United States should:

A. Identify the financial statements examined.
B. Refer to the note to the financial statements that describes the basis of presentation of the financial statements on which the auditor is reporting, including identification of the nationality of the accounting principles.
C. State that the examination was made in accordance with auditing standards generally accepted in the United States (and, if appropriate, with the auditing standards of the other country).
D. Include a paragraph that expresses the auditor's opinion (or disclaims an opinion) on the following:
    (1) Whether the financial statements are presented fairly in conformity with the basis of accounting described. If the auditor concludes that the financial statements are not presented fairly on the basis of accounting described, all of the substantive reasons for that conclusion should be disclosed in an additional explanatory paragraph(s) of the report, and the opinion paragraph should include appropriate modifying language as well as a reference to the explanatory paragraph(s).
    (2) Whether the disclosed basis of accounting used has been applied in a consistent manner.

The following is an illustration of such a report.

Addressee

We have examined the balance sheet of the International Company as of December 31, 20XX, and the related statements of income, retained earnings, and cash flows for the year then ended, which, as described in Note X, have been prepared on the basis of accounting principles generally accepted in (name of country). Our examination was made in accordance with the auditing standards generally accepted in the United States (and in [name of country]) and, accordingly, included such tests of the accounting records and such other auditing procedures as we considered necessary in the circumstances.

In our opinion, the financial statements referred to above present fairly the financial position of the International Company at December 31, 20XX, and the results of its operations and cash flows for the year then ended, in conformity with accounting principles generally accepted in (name of country) applied on a basis consistent with that of the preceding year.

Signature, date

The independent auditor may also use the auditor's standard report of another country, provided that:
a. Such a report would be used by auditors in the other country in similar circumstances.
b. The auditor understands, and is in a position to make, the attestations contained in such a report.

Use in the United States

If the auditor is requested to report on the fair presentation of financial statements, prepared in conformity with the accounting principles generally accepted in another country, that will have more than limited distribution in the United States, he should use the U.S. standard form of report, modified as appropriate, because of departures from accounting principles generally accepted in the United States. The auditor may also, in a separate paragraph to the report, express an opinion on whether the financial statements are presented in conformity with accounting principles generally accepted in another country.

REPORTING ON INFORMATION ACCOMPANYING THE BASIC FINANCIAL STATEMENTS IN AUDITOR-SUBMITTED DOCUMENTS (SAS No. 29)

Applicability

This section describes the form and content of the audit report when a CPA submits to his client or to others a document that contains information in addition to the client's basic financial statements and the auditor's standard report thereon.

The following presentations are considered part of the basic financial statements: descriptions of accounting policies, notes to financial statements, and schedules and explanatory material that are identified as being part of the basic financial statements.

The information covered by this Statement is presented outside the basic financial statements and is not considered necessary for presentation of financial position, results of operations, or cash flows in conformity with generally accepted accounting principles. Such information includes additional details or explanations of items in or related to the basic financial statements.

Reporting Responsibility

An auditor's report on information accompanying the basic financial statements in an auditor-submitted document has the same objective as an auditor's report on the basic financial statements: to describe clearly the character of the auditor's examination and the degree of responsibility, if any, he is taking.

The following guidelines apply to an auditor's report on information accompanying the basic financial statements in an auditor-submitted document:
a. The report should state that the examination has been made for the purpose of forming an opinion on the basic financial statements taken as a whole.
b. The report should identify the accompanying information. (Identification may be by descriptive title or page number of the document.)
c. The report should state that the accompanying information is presented for purposes of additional analysis and is not a required part of the basic financial statements.
d. The report should include either an opinion on whether the accompanying information is fairly stated in all material respects in relation to the basic financial statements taken as a whole or a disclaimer of opinion, depending on whether the information has been subjected to the auditing procedures applied in the examination of the basic financial statements. The auditor may express an opinion on a portion of the accompanying information and disclaim an opinion on the remainder.
e. The report on the accompanying information may be added to the auditor's standard report on the basic financial statements or may appear separately in the auditor-submitted document.

If the auditor concludes, on the basis of facts known to him, that any accompanying information is materially misstated in relation to the basic financial statements taken as a whole, he should discuss the matter with the client and propose appropriate revision of the accompanying information. If the client will not agree to revision of the accompanying information, the auditor should either modify his report on the accompanying information and describe the misstatement or refuse to include the information in the document.

The auditor should consider the effect of any modifications in his standard report when reporting on accompanying information. When the auditor expresses a qualified opinion on the basic financial statements, he should make clear the effects upon any accompanying information as well. When the auditor expresses an adverse opinion, or disclaims an opinion, on the basic financial statements, he should not express an opinion.

A client may request that nonaccounting information and certain accounting information not directly related to the basic financial statements be included in an auditor-submitted document. Ordinarily, such information would not have been subjected to the auditing procedures applied in the examination of the financial statements, and, accordingly, the auditor would disclaim an opinion on it.

Reporting Examples
Unqualified
Our audit was made for the purpose of forming an opinion on the basic financial statements taken as a whole. The (identify accompanying information) is presented for purposes of additional analysis and is not a required part of the basic financial statements. Such information has been subjected to the auditing procedures applied in the audit of the basic financial statements and, in our opinion, is fairly stated in all material respects in relation to the basic financial statements taken as a whole.

Disclaimer on All of the Information
Our audit was made for the purpose of forming an opinion on the basic financial statements taken as a whole. The (identify the accompanying information) is presented for purposes of additional analysis and is not a required part of the basic financial statements. Such information has not been subjected to the auditing procedures applied in the audit of the basic financial statements, and, accordingly, we express no opinion on it.

Disclaimer on Part of the Information
Our audit was made for the purpose of forming an opinion on the basic financial statements taken as a whole. The information on pages XX-YY is presented for purposes of additional analysis and is not a required part of the basic financial statements. Such information, except for that portion marked "unaudited," on which we express no opinion, has been subjected to the auditing procedures applied in the audit of the basic financial statements; and, in our opinion, the information is fairly stated in all material respects in relation to the basic financial statements taken as a whole.

Qualification
Our audit was made for the purpose of forming an opinion on the basic financial statements taken as a whole. The schedules of investments (page 7), property (page 8), and other assets (page 9) as of December 31, 19XX, are presented for purposes of additional analysis and are not a required part of the basic financial statements. The information in such schedules has been subjected to the auditing procedures applied in the audit of the basic financial statements; and, in our opinion, except for the effects on the schedule of investments of not accounting for the investments in certain companies by the equity method as explained in the second preceding paragraph [second paragraph of our report on page 1], such information is fairly stated in all material respects in relation to the basic financial statements taken as a whole.

LETTERS FOR UNDERWRITERS AND CERTAIN OTHER REQUESTING PARTIES
(SAS No. 76 as amended)

The services of independent certified public accountants include examination of financial statements and schedules contained in registration statements filed with the Securities and Exchange Commission (the SEC) under the Securities Act of 1933 (the Act). In connection with this type of service, accountants often are called upon to confer with clients, underwriters, and their respective counsel concerning the accounting and auditing requirements of the Act and of the SEC, as well as to perform other services. One of these other services is the issuance of letters for underwriters, commonly called *comfort letters*.

Comfort letters are not required under the Act, and copies are not filed with the SEC. It is nonetheless a common condition of an underwriting agreement in connection with the offering for sale of securities registered with the SEC under the Act that the accountants are to furnish a comfort letter.

Because the underwriter will expect the accountants to furnish a comfort letter of a scope to be specified in the underwriting agreement, the client and the underwriter, when they have tentatively agreed upon a draft of the agreement, are well advised to furnish a copy of it to the accountants so that the latter can indicate whether they will be able to furnish a letter in acceptable form. A desirable practice is for the accountants, promptly after they have received the draft of the agreement (or have been informed that a letter covering specified matters, although not a condition of the agreement, will nonetheless be requested), to prepare a draft of the form of letter that they expect to furnish. The draft letter should be identified as a draft in order to avoid giving the impression that the procedures described therein have been performed. Unless otherwise indicated by the underwriter, the accountants may reasonably assume that the underwriter, by indicating his acceptance of the draft comfort letter, and subsequently, by his acceptance of the letter in final form, considers the procedures described sufficient for his purposes.

The letter ordinarily is dated at or shortly before the *closing date* (the date on which the issuer or selling security holder delivers the securities to the underwriter in exchange for the proceeds of the offering). The underwriting agreement ordinarily specifies the date, often referred to as the *cutoff date*, to which the letter is to relate (for example, a date five business days before the date of the letter); the accountants should see that the cutoff date will not place an unreasonable burden on them. The letter should state that the inquiries and other procedures carried out in connection with the letter did not cover the period from the cutoff date to the date of the letter.

Because the letter is a result of the underwriter's request, many accountants address the letter only to the underwriter, with a copy furnished to the client.

Underwriters occasionally request the accountants to repeat in the comfort letter their opinion on the audited financial statements included in the registration statement. Because of the special significance of the date of an accountants' report, the accountants should not repeat their opinion.

The matters covered in a typical comfort letter are described below:

1. A statement regarding the independence of the accountants.
2. An opinion regarding whether the audited financial statements and schedules included in the registration statement comply in form in all material respects with the applicable accounting requirements of the Securities Act of 1933 and the published rules and regulation thereunder.
3. A description of the procedures requested and performed.
4. A disclaimer of an opinion on the financial information covered by the comfort letter.
5. A statement of specific findings as a result of applying the procedures in part (c) above.
6. A statement that restricts distribution of the report.
7. A statement that the CPA has no responsibility to update report for events after a specified cutoff date.

Chapter Five - Questions
Reviews, Compilations, Special Reports and Other Reports

1. An auditor's report would be designated as a special report when it is issued in connection with which of the following?
a.   Financial statements for an interim period which are subjected to limited review.
b.   Financial statements which are prepared in accordance with a comprehensive basis of accounting other than generally accepted accounting principles.
c.   Financial statements which purport to be in accordance with generally accepted accounting principles but do not include a presentation of the statement of cash flows.
d.   Financial statements which are unaudited and are prepared from a client's accounting records.

2. When making a review of interim financial information the auditor's work consists primarily of
a.   Studying and evaluating limited amounts of documentation supporting the interim financial information.
b.   Scanning and reviewing client-prepared, internal financial statements.
c.   Making inquiries and performing analytical procedures concerning significant accounting matters.
d.   Confirming and verifying significant account balances at the interim date.

3. One example of a "special report," as defined by Statements on Auditing Standards, is a report issued in connection with
a.   A feasibility study.
b.   A limited review of interim financial information.
c.   Price-level basis financial statements.
d.   Compliance with a contractual agreement **not** related to the financial statements.

4. Whenever special reports, filed on a printed form designed by authorities, call upon the independent auditor to make an assertion that the auditor believes is **not** justified, the auditor should
a.   Submit a short-form report with explanations.
b.   Reword the form or attach a separate report.
c.   Submit the form with questionable items clearly omitted.
d.   Withdraw from the engagement.

5. Which of the following procedures is **not** included in a review engagement of a nonpublic entity?
a.   Inquiries of management.
b.   Inquiries regarding events subsequent to the balance sheet date.
c.   Any procedures designed to identify relationships among data that appear to be unusual.
d.   A study and evaluation of internal control.

6. An auditor is reporting on cash-basis financial statements. These statements are **best** referred to in his opinion by which one of the following descriptions?
a.   Financial position and results of operations arising from cash transactions.
b.   Assets and liabilities arising from cash transactions, and revenue collected and expenses paid.
c.   Balance sheet and income statement resulting from cash transactions.
d.   Cash balance sheet and the source and application of funds.

7. When an independent CPA is associated with the financial statements of a publicly held entity, but has **not** audited or reviewed such statements, the appropriate form of report to be issued must include a (an)
a.   Negative assurance.
b.   Compilation opinion.
c.   Disclaimer of opinion.
d.   Explanatory paragraph.

8. The objective of a review of the interim financial information of a publicly held company is to
a.   Provide the accountant with a basis for the expression of an opinion.
b.   Estimate the accuracy of financial statements based upon limited tests of accounting records.
c.   Provide the accountant with a basis for reporting to the board of directors or stockholders.
d.   Obtain corroborating evidential matter through inspection, observation and confirmation.

9. A CPA who is associated with the financial statements of a public entity, but has **not** audited or reviewed such statements, should
a. Insist that they be audited or reviewed before publication.
b. Read them to determine whether there are obvious material errors.
c. State these facts in the accompanying notes to the financial statements.
d. Issue a compilation report.

10. In performing a compilation of financial statements of a nonpublic entity, the accountant decides that modification of the standard report is not adequate to indicate deficiencies in the financial statements taken as a whole, and the client is not willing to correct the deficiencies. The accountant should therefore
a. Perform a review of the financial statements.
b. Issue a special report.
c. Withdraw from the engagement.
d. Express an adverse audit opinion.

11. An auditor who was engaged to perform an examination of the financial statements of a nonpublic entity has been asked by the client to refrain from performing various audit procedures and change the nature of the engagement to a review of the financial statements in accordance with standards established by the AICPA. The client's request was made because the cost to complete the examination was significant. Under the circumstances the auditor would most likely
a. Qualify the auditor's report and refer to the scope limitation.
b. View the request as an indication of a possible irregularity.
c. Complete the examination which was in progress.
d. Honor the client's request.

12. During a review of the financial statements of a nonpublic entity, the CPA finds that the financial statements contain a material departure from generally accepted accounting principles. If management refuses to correct the financial statement presentations, the CPA should
a. Disclose the departure in a separate paragraph of the report.
b. Issue an adverse opinion.
c. Attach a footnote explaining the effects of the departure.
d. Issue a compilation report.

13. Each page of the financial statements compiled by an accountant should include a reference such as
a. See accompanying accountant's footnotes.
b. Unaudited, see accountant's disclaimer.
c. See accountant's compilation report.
d. Subject to compilation restrictions.

14. A CPA who is **not** independent may issue
a. A review report.
b. A comfort letter.
c. A qualified opinion.
d. A compilation report.

15. When an auditor performs a review of interim financial statements, which of the following steps would **not** be a part of the review?
a. Review of computer controls.
b. Inquiry of management.
c. Review of ratios and trends.
d. Reading the minutes of the stockholders' meetings.

16. Baker, CPA, was engaged to review the financial statements of Hall Company, a nonpublic entity. Evidence came to Baker's attention that indicated substantial doubt as to Hall's ability to continue as a going concern. The principal conditions and events that caused the substantial doubt have been fully disclosed in the notes to Hall's financial statements. Which of the following statements best describes Baker's reporting responsibility concerning this matter?
a. Baker is **not** required to modify the accountant's review report.
b. Baker is **not** permitted to modify the accountant's review report.
c. Baker should issue an accountant's compilation report instead of a review report.
d. Baker should express a qualified opinion in the accountant's review report.

17. An auditor's report on financial statements prepared in accordance with another comprehensive basis of accounting should include all of the following **except**
a. An opinion as to whether the basis of accounting used is appropriate under the circumstances.
b. An opinion as to whether the financial statements are presented fairly in conformity with the other comprehensive basis of accounting.
c. Reference to the note to the financial statements that describes the basis of presentation.
d. A statement that the basis of presentation is a comprehensive basis of accounting other than generally accepted accounting principles.

18. An accountant who is **not** independent of a client is precluded from issuing a
a. Report on management advisory services.
b. Compilation report on historical financial statements.
c. Compilation report on prospective financial statements.
d. Special report on compliance with contractual agreements.

19. The authoritative body designated to promulgate standards concerning an accountant's association with unaudited financial statements of an entity that is **not** required to file financial statements with an agency regulating the issuance of the entity's securities is the
a. Financial Accounting Standards Board.
b. General Accounting Office.
c. Accounting and Review Services Committee.
d. Auditing Standards Board.

20. If requested to perform a review engagement for a nonpublic entity in which an accountant has an immaterial direct financial interest, the accountant is
a. Not independent and, therefore, may issue a review report, but may **not** issue an auditor's opinion.
b. Not independent and, therefore, may **not** issue a review report.
c. Not independent and, therefore, may **not** be associated with the financial statements.
d. Independent because the financial interest is immaterial and, therefore, may issue a review report.

21. An accountant has been asked to issue a review report on the balance sheet of a nonpublic company but not to report on the other basic financial statements. The accountant may **not** do so
a. Because compliance with this request would result in an incomplete review.
b. Because compliance with this request would result in a violation of the ethical standards of the profession.
c. If the scope of the inquiry and analytical procedures has been restricted.
d. If the review of the balance sheet discloses material departures from generally accepted accounting principles.

22. Inquiry and analytical procedures ordinarily performed during a review of a nonpublic entity's financial statements include
a. Analytical procedures designed to identify material weaknesses in internal accounting control.
b. Inquiries concerning actions taken at meetings of the stockholders and the board of directors.
c. Analytical procedures designed to test the accounting records by obtaining corroborating evidential matter.
d. Inquiries of knowledgeable outside parties such as the client's attorneys and bankers.

23. A CPA should **not** submit unaudited financial statements of a nonpublic company to a client or others unless, as a minimum, the CPA complies with the provisions applicable to
a. Compilation engagements.
b. Review engagements.
c. Statements on auditing standards.
d. Attestation standards.

24. When providing limited assurance that the financial statements of a nonpublic entity require **no** material modifications to be in accordance with generally accepted accounting principles, the accountant should
a. Understand the system of internal accounting control that the entity uses.
b. Test the accounting records that identify inconsistencies with the prior year's financial statements.
c. Understand the accounting principles of the industry in which the entity operates.
d. Develop audit programs to determine whether the entity's financial statements are fairly presented.

25. Which of the following procedures is **not** usually performed by the accountant in a review engagement of a nonpublic entity?
a. Communicating any material weaknesses discovered during the study and evaluation of internal accounting control.
b. Reading the financial statements to consider whether they conform with generally accepted accounting principles.
c. Writing an engagement letter to establish an understanding regarding the services to be performed.
d. Issuing a report stating that the review was performed in accordance with standards established by the AICPA.

26. Performing inquiry and analytical procedures is the primary basis for an accountant to issue a (an)
a. Compilation report on financial statements for a nonpublic entity in its first year of operations.
b. Review report on comparative financial statements for a nonpublic entity in its second year of operations.
c. Management advisory report prepared at the request of a client's audit committee.
d. Internal accounting control report for a governmental agency in accordance with GAO standards.

27. Which of the following circumstances requires modification of the accountant's report on a review of interim financial information of a publicly held entity?

	An uncertainty	Inadequate disclosure
a.	Yes	Yes
b.	No	No
c.	Yes	No
d.	No	Yes

28. If compiled financial statements presented in conformity with the cash receipts and disbursements basis of accounting do **not** disclose the basis of accounting used, the accountant should
a. Disclose the basis in the notes to the financial statements.
b. Clearly label each page, "Unaudited".
c. Disclose the basis of accounting in the accountant's report.
d. Recompile the financial statements using generally accepted accounting principles.

29. The objective of a review of interim financial information of a public entity is to provide an accountant with a basis for reporting whether
a. Material modifications should be made to conform with generally accepted accounting principles.
b. A reasonable basis exists for expressing an updated opinion regarding the financial statements that were previously audited.
c. Condensed financial statements or pro forma financial information should be included in a registration statement.
d. The financial statements are presented fairly in accordance with generally accepted accounting principles.

30. One of the conditions required for an accountant to submit a written personal financial plan containing unaudited financial statements to a client without complying with the requirements of SSARS 1 (Compilation and Review of Financial Statements) is that the
a. Client agrees that the financial statements will **not** be used to obtain credit.
b. Accountant compiled or reviewed. the client's financial statements for the immediate prior year.
c. Engagement letter acknowledges that the financial statements will contain departures from generally accepted accounting principles.
d. Accountant expresses limited assurance that the financial statements are free of any material misstatements.

31. An accountant has been asked to compile the financial statements of a nonpublic company on a prescribed form that omits substantially all the disclosures required by generally accepted accounting principles. If the prescribed form is a standard preprinted form adopted by the company's industry trade association, and is to be transmitted only to such association, the accountant
a. Need **not** advise the industry trade association of the omission of all disclosures.
b. Should disclose the details of the omissions in separate paragraphs of the compilation report.
c. Is precluded from issuing a compilation report when all disclosures are omitted.
d. Should express limited assurance that the financial statements are free of material misstatements.

32. An auditor who conducts an examination in accordance with generally accepted auditing standards and concludes that the financial statements are fairly presented in accordance with a comprehensive basis of accounting other than generally accepted accounting principles, such as the cash basis of accounting, should issue a
a. Special report.
b. Disclaimer of opinion.
c. Review report.
d. Qualified opinion.

33. Comfort letters ordinarily are addressed to
a. The Securities and Exchange Commission.
b. Underwriters of securities.
c. Creditor financial institutions.
d. The client's audit committee.

34. An accountant who reviews the financial statements of a nonpublic entity should issue a report stating that a review
a. Is substantially less in scope than an audit.
b. Provides negative assurance that the internal control structure is functioning as designed.
c. Provides only limited assurance that the financial statements are fairly presented.
d. Is substantially more in scope than a compilation.

35. When an accountant compiles a nonpublic entity's financial statements that omit substantially all disclosures required by generally accepted accounting principles, the accountant should indicate in the compilation report that the financial statements are
a. Restricted for internal use only by the entity's management.
b. Not to be given to financial institutions for the purpose of obtaining credit.
c. Compiled in conformity with a comprehensive basis of accounting other than generally accepted accounting principles.
d. Not designed for those who are uninformed about the omitted disclosures.

36. The objective of a review of interim financial information is to provide an accountant with a basis for reporting whether
a. The financial statements are presented fairly in accordance with generally accepted accounting principles.
b. A reasonable basis exists for expressing an updated opinion regarding the financial statements that were previously audited.
c. Material modifications should be made to conform with generally accepted accounting principles.
d. The financial statements are presented fairly in accordance with standards of interim reporting.

37. When an auditor is requested to express an opinion on the rental and royalty income of an entity, the auditor may
a. Not accept the engagement because to do so would be tantamount to agreeing to issue a piecemeal opinion.
b. Not accept the engagement unless also engaged to audit the full financial statements of the entity.
c. Accept the engagement provided the auditor's opinion is expressed in a special report.
d. Accept the engagement provided distribution of the auditor's report is limited to the entity's management.

38. If information accompanying the basic financial statements in an auditor-submitted document has been subjected to auditing procedures, the auditor may include in the auditor's report on the financial statements an opinion that the accompanying information is fairly stated in
a. Accordance with generally accepted auditing standards.
b. Conformity with generally accepted accounting principles.
c. All material respects in relation to the basic financial statements taken as a whole.
d. Accordance with attestation standards expressing a conclusion about management's assertions.

39. If information accompanying the basic financial statements in an auditor-submitted document has been subjected to auditing procedures, the auditor may express an opinion that the accompanying information is fairly stated in
a. Conformity with generally accepted accounting principles.
b. All material respects in relation to the basic financial statements taken as a whole.
c. Conformity with standards established by the AICPA.
d. Accordance with generally accepted auditing standards.

40. Before performing a review of a nonpublic entity's financial statements, an accountant should
a. Complete a series of inquiries concerning the entity's procedures for recording, classifying, and summarizing transactions.
b. Apply analytical procedures to provide limited assurance that **no** material modifications should be made to the financial statements.
c. Obtain a sufficient level of knowledge of the accounting principles and practices of the industry in which the entity operates.
d. Inquire whether management has omitted substantially all of the disclosures required by generally accepted accounting principles.

41. If requested to perform a review engagement for a nonpublic entity in which an accountant has an immaterial direct financial interest, the accountant is
a.   Independent because the financial interest is immaterial and, therefore, may issue a review report.
b.   Not independent and, therefore, may **not** be associated with the financial statements.
c.   Not independent, and therefore, may **not** issue a review report.
d.   Not independent and, therefore, may issue a review report, but may **not** issue an auditor's opinion.

42. When reporting on financial statements prepared on the same basis of accounting used for income tax purposes, the auditor should include in the report a paragraph that
a.   Emphasizes that the financial statements are **not** intended to have been examined in accordance with generally accepted auditing standards.
b.   Refers to the authoritative pronouncements that explain the income tax basis of accounting being used.
c.   States that the income tax basis of accounting is a comprehensive basis of accounting other than generally accepted accounting principles.
d.   Justifies the use of the income tax basis of accounting.

43. During a review of the financial statements of a nonpublic entity, an accountant becomes aware of a lack of adequate disclosure that is material to the financial statements. If management refuses to correct the financial statement presentations, the accountant should
a.   Issue an adverse opinion.
b.   Issue an "except for" qualified opinion.
c.   Disclose this departure from generally accepted accounting principles in a separate paragraph of the report.
d.   Express only limited assurance on the financial statement presentations.

44. If compiled financial statements presented in conformity with the cash receipts and disbursements basis of accounting do **not** disclose the basis of accounting used, the accountant should
a.   Recompile the financial statements using generally accepted accounting principles.
b.   Disclose the basis in the notes to the financial statements.
c.   Clearly label each page, "Unaudited."
d.   Disclose the basis of accounting in the accountant's report.

45. An auditor's report would be designated a special report when it is issued in conjunction with
a.   Interim financial information of a publicly held company that is subject to a limited review.
b.   Compliance with aspects of regulatory requirements related to audited financial statements.
c.   Application of accounting principles to specified transactions.
d.   Limited use prospective financial statements such as a financial projection.

46. Which of the following procedures would most likely be included in a review engagement of a nonpublic entity?
a.   Preparing a bank transfer schedule.
b.   Inquiring about related party transactions.
c.   Assessing the internal control structure.
d.   Performing cutoff tests on sales and purchases transactions.

47. When compiling a nonpublic entity's financial statements, an accountant would be **least** likely to
a.   Perform analytical procedures designed to identify relationships that appear to be unusual.
b.   Read the compiled financial statements and consider whether they appear to include adequate disclosure.
c.   Omit substantially all of the disclosures required by generally accepted accounting principles.
d.   Issue a compilation report on one or more, but **not** all, of the basic financial statements.

48. The objective of a review of interim financial information of a public entity is to provide the accountant with a basis for
a.   Determining whether the prospective financial information is based on reasonable assumptions.
b.   Expressing a limited opinion that the financial information is presented in conformity with generally accepted accounting principles.
c.   Deciding whether to perform substantive audit procedures prior to the balance sheet date.
d.   Reporting whether material modifications should be made for such information to conform with generally accepted accounting principles.

49. Financial statements of a nonpublic entity that have been reviewed by an accountant should be accompanied by a report stating that

a. The scope of the inquiry and analytical procedures performed by the accountant has **not** been restricted.
b. All information included in the financial statements is the representation of the management of the entity.
c. A review includes examining, on a test basis, evidence supporting the amounts and disclosures in the financial statements.
d. A review is greater in scope than a compilation, the objective of which is to present financial statements that are free of material misstatements.

50. Which of the following accounting services may an accountant perform **without** being required to issue a compilation or review report under the Statements on Standards for Accounting and Review Services?

I. Preparing a working trial balance.
II. Preparing standard monthly journal entries.

a. I only.
b. II only.
c. Both I and II.
d. Neither I nor II.

51. Which of the following inquiry or analytical procedures ordinarily is performed in an engagement to review a nonpublic entity's financial statements?

a. Analytical procedures designed to test the accounting records by obtaining corroborating evidential matter.
b. Inquiries concerning the entity's procedures for recording and summarizing transactions.
c. Analytical procedures designed to test management's assertions regarding continued existence.
d. Inquiries of the entity's attorney concerning contingent liabilities.

52. When compiling the financial statements of a nonpublic entity, an accountant should

a. Review agreements with financial institutions for restrictions on cash balances.
b. Understand the accounting principles and practices of the entity's industry.
c. Inquiry of key personnel concerning related parties and subsequent events.
d. Perform ratio analyses of the financial data of comparable prior periods.

53. Which of the following procedures is **not** usually performed by the accountant during a review engagement of a nonpublic entity?

a. Inquiring about actions taken at meetings of the board of directors that may affect the financial statements.
b. Issuing a report stating that the review was performed in accordance with standards established by the AICPA.
c. Reading the financial statements to consider whether they conform with generally accepted accounting principles.
d. Communicating any material weaknesses discovered during the consideration of the internal control structure.

54. Which of the following procedures ordinarily should be applied when an independent accountant conducts a review of interim financial information of a publicly held entity?

a. Verify changes in key account balances.
b. Read the minutes of the board of directors' meetings.
c. Inspect the open purchase order file.
d. Perform cut-off tests for cash receipts and disbursements.

55. Jones Retailing, a nonpublic entity, has asked Winters, CPA, to compile financial statements that omit substantially all disclosures required by generally accepted accounting principles. Winters may compile such financial statements provided the

a. Reason for omitting the disclosures is explained in the engagement letter and acknowledged in the management representation letter.
b. Financial statements are prepared on a comprehensive basis of accounting other than generally accepted accounting principles.
c. Distribution of the financial statements is restricted to internal use only.
d. Omission is **not** undertaken to mislead the users of the financial statements and is properly disclosed in the accountant's report.

56. The standard report issued by an accountant after reviewing the financial statements of a nonpublic entity states that
a. A review includes assessing the accounting principles used and significant estimates made by management.
b. A review includes examining, on a test basis, evidence supporting the amounts and disclosures in the financial statements.
c. The accountant is **not** aware of any material modifications that should be made to the financial statements.
d. The accountant does **not** express an opinion or any other form of assurance on the financial statements.

57. An auditor's special report on financial statements prepared in conformity with the cash basis of accounting should include a separate explanatory paragraph before the opinion paragraph that
a. Justifies the reasons for departing from generally accepted accounting principles.
b. States whether the financial statements are fairly presented in conformity with another comprehensive basis of accounting.
c. Refers to the note to the financial statements that describes the basis of accounting.
d. Explains how the results of operations differ from financial statements prepared in conformity with generally accepted accounting principles.

58. Davis, CPA, accepted an engagement to audit the financial statements of Tech Resources, a nonpublic entity. Before the completion of the audit, Tech requested Davis to change the engagement to a compilation of financial statements. Before Davis agrees to change the engagement, Davis is required to consider the

	Additional audit effort necessary to complete the audit	Reason given for Tech's request
a.	No	No
b.	Yes	Yes
c.	Yes	No
d.	No	Yes

59. Smith, CPA, has been asked to issue a review report on the balance sheet of Cone Company, a nonpublic entity, and not on the other related financial statements. Smith may do so only if
a. Smith compiles and reports on the related statements of income, retained earnings, and cash flows.
b. Smith is not aware of any material modifications needed for the balance sheet to conform with GAAP.
c. The scope of Smith's inquiry and analytical procedures is not restricted.
d. Cone is a new client and Smith accepts the engagement after the end of Cone's fiscal year.

60. May an accountant accept an engagement to compile or review the financial statements of a not-for-profit entity if the accountant is unfamiliar with the specialized industry accounting principles, but plans to obtain the required level of knowledge before compiling or reviewing the financial statements?

	Compilation	Review
a.	No	No
b.	Yes	No
c.	No	Yes
d.	Yes	Yes

61. An accountant should perform analytical procedures during an engagement to

	Compile a nonpublic entity's financial statements	Review a nonpublic's entity's financial statements
a.	No	No
b.	Yes	Yes
c.	Yes	No
d.	No	Yes

62. Which of the following procedures most likely would not be included in a review engagement of a nonpublic entity?
a. Obtaining a management representation letter.
b. Considering whether the financial statements conform with GAAP.
c. Assessing control risk.
d. Inquiring about subsequent events.

63. Investment and property schedules are presented for purposes of additional analysis in an auditor-submitted document. The schedules are not required parts of the basic financial statements, but accompany the basic financial statements. When reporting on such additional information, the measurement of materiality is the

a. Same as that used in forming an opinion on the basic financial statements taken as a whole.
b. Lesser of the individual schedule of investments or schedule of property taken by itself.
c. Greater of the individual schedule of investments or schedule of property taken by itself.
d. Combined total of both the individual schedules of investments and property taken as a whole.

64. In connection with a proposal to obtain a new client, an accountant in public practice is asked to prepare a written report on the application of accounting principles to a specific transaction. The accountant's report should include a statement that

a. Any difference in the facts, circumstances, or assumptions presented may change the report.
b. The engagement was performed in accordance with Statements on Standards for Consulting Services.
c. The guidance provided is for management use only and may not be communicated to the prior or continuing auditors.
d. Nothing came to the accountant's attention that caused the accountant to believe that the accounting principles violated GAAP.

65. Compiled financial statements should be accompanied by a report stating that

a. A compilation is substantially less in scope than a review or an audit in accordance with generally accepted auditing standards.
b. The accountant does not express an opinion but expresses only limited assurance on the compiled financial statements.
c. A compilation is limited to presenting in the form of financial statements information that is the representation of management.
d. The accountant has compiled the financial statements in accordance with standards established by the Auditing Standards Board.

66. An accountant may compile a nonpublic entity's financial statements that omit all of the disclosures required by GAAP only if the omission is

I.   Clearly indicated in the accountant's report.

II. Not undertaken with the intention of misleading the financial statement users.

a. I only.
b. II only.
c. Both I and II.
d. Either I or II.

67. An accountant's standard report on a review of the financial statements of a nonpublic entity should state that the accountant

a. Does not express an opinion or any form of limited assurance on the financial statements.
b. Is not aware of any material modifications that should be made to the financial statements for them to conform with GAAP.
c. Obtained reasonable assurance about whether the financial statements are free of material misstatement.
d. Examined evidence, on a test basis, supporting the amounts and disclosures in the financial statements.

68. An accountant has been asked to issue a review report on the balance sheet of a nonpublic company but not to report on the other basic financial statements. The accountant may not do so

a. Because compliance with this request would result in a violation of the ethical standards of the profession.
b. Because compliance with this request would result in an incomplete review.
c. If the review of the balance sheet discloses material departures from GAAP.
d. If the scope of the inquiry and analytical procedures has been restricted.

69. Which of the following statements is correct concerning an auditor's responsibilities regarding financial statements?

a. Making suggestions that are adopted about the form and content of an entity's financial statements impairs an auditor's independence.
b. An auditor may draft an entity's financial statements based on information from management's accounting system.
c. The fair presentation of audited financial statements in conformity with GAAP is an implicit part of the auditor's responsibilities.
d. An auditor's responsibilities for audited financial statements are not confined to the expression of the auditor's opinion.

70. An accountant has been engaged to review a nonpublic entity's financial statements that contain several departures from GAAP. If the financial statements are not revised and modification of the standard review report is not adequate to indicate the deficiencies, the accountant should
a. Withdraw from the engagement and provide no further services concerning these financial statements.
b. Inform management that the engagement can proceed only if distribution of the accountant's report is restricted to internal use.
c. Determine the effects of the departures from GAAP and issue a special report on the financial statements.
d. Issue a modified review report provided the entity agrees that the financial statements will not be used to obtain credit.

71. Statements on Standards for Accounting and Review Services (SSARS) require an accountant to report when the accountant has
a. Typed client-prepared financial statements, without modification, as an accommodation to the client.
b. Provided a client with a financial statement format that does not include dollar amounts, to be used by the client in preparing financial statements.
c. Proposed correcting journal entries to be recorded by the client that change client-prepared financial statements.
d. Generated, through the use of computer software, financial statements prepared in accordance with a comprehensive basis of accounting other than GAAP.

72. An accountant may accept an engagement to apply agreed-upon procedures to prospective financial statements provided that
a. Distribution of the report is restricted to the specified users.
b. The prospective financial statements are also examined.
c. Responsibility for the adequacy of the procedures performed is taken by the accountant.
d. Negative assurance is expressed on the prospective financial statements taken as a whole.

73. Which of the following procedures would an accountant least likely perform during an engagement to review the financial statements of a nonpublic entity?
a. Observing the safeguards over access to and use of assets and records.
b. Comparing the financial statements with anticipated results in budgets and forecasts.
c. Inquiring of management about actions taken at the board of directors' meetings.
d. Studying the relationships of financial statement elements expected to conform to predictable patterns.

74. Which of the following procedures should an accountant perform during an engagement to review the financial statements of a nonpublic entity?
a. Communicating reportable conditions discovered during the assessment of control risk.
b. Obtaining a client representation letter from members of management.
c. Sending bank confirmation letters to the entity's financial institutions.
d. Examining cash disbursements in the subsequent period for unrecorded liabilities.

75. When an independent CPA is associated with the financial statements of a publicly held entity but has not audited or reviewed such statements, the appropriate form of report to be issued must include a(an)
a. Regulation S-X exemption.
b. Report on pro forma financial statements.
c. Unaudited association report.
d. Disclaimer of opinion.

76. An accountant who had begun an audit of the financial statements of a nonpublic entity was asked to change the engagement to a review because of a restriction on the scope of the audit. If there is reasonable justification for the change, the accountant's review report should include reference to the

	Scope limitation that caused the changed engagement	Original engagement that was agreed to
a.	Yes	No
b.	No	Yes
c.	No	No
d.	Yes	Yes

77. Gole, CPA, is engaged to review the 1994 financial statements of North Co., a nonpublic entity. Previously, Gole audited North's 1993 financial statements and expressed an unqualified opinion. Gole decides to include a separate paragraph in the 1994 review report because North plans to present comparative financial statements for 1994 and 1993. This separate paragraph should indicate that

a. The 1994 review report is intended solely for the information of management and the board of directors.
b. The 1993 auditor's report may no longer be relied on.
c. No auditing procedures were performed after the date of the 1993 auditor's report.
d. There are justifiable reasons for changing the level of service from an audit to a review.

78. Which of the following statements should be included in an accountant's standard report based on the compilation of a nonpublic entity's financial statements?

a. A compilation consists principally of inquiries of company personnel and analytical procedures applied to financial data.
b. A compilation is limited to presenting in the form of financial statements information that is the representation of management.
c. A compilation is not designed to detect material modifications that should be made to the financial statements.
d. A compilation is substantially less in scope than an audit in accordance with generally accepted auditing standards.

79. Miller, CPA, is engaged to compile the financial statements of Web Co., a nonpublic entity, in conformity with the income tax basis of accounting. If Web's financial statements do not disclose the basis of accounting used, Miller should

a. Disclose the basis of accounting in the accountant's compilation report.
b. Clearly label each page "Distribution Restricted-Material Modifications Required."
c. Issue a special report describing the effect of the incomplete presentation.
d. Withdraw from the engagement and provide no further services to Web.

80. When an accountant is engaged to compile a nonpublic entity's financial statements that omit substantially all disclosures required by GAAP, the accountant should indicate in the compilation report that the financial statements are

a. Not designed for those who are uninformed about the omitted disclosures.
b. Prepared in conformity with a comprehensive basis of accounting other than GAAP.
c. Not compiled in accordance with Statements on Standards for Accounting and Review Services.
d. Special-purpose financial statements that are not comparable to those of prior periods.

81. An accountant's compilation report on a financial forecast should include a statement that

a. The forecast should be read only in conjunction with the audited historical financial statements.
b. The accountant expresses only limited assurance on the forecasted statements and their assumptions.
c. There will usually be differences between the forecasted and actual results.
d. The hypothetical assumptions used in the forecast are reasonable in the circumstances.

82. In the standard report on condensed financial statements that are derived from a public entity's audited financial statements, a CPA should indicate that the

a. Condensed financial statements are prepared in conformity with another comprehensive basis of accounting.
b. CPA has audited and expressed an opinion on the complete financial statements.
c. Condensed financial statements are not fairly presented in all material respects.
d. CPA expresses limited assurance that the financial statements conform with GAAP.

83. Before reporting on the financial statements of a U.S. entity that have been prepared in conformity with another country's accounting principles, an auditor practicing in the U.S. should

a. Understand the accounting principles generally accepted in the other country.
b. Be certified by the appropriate auditing or accountancy board of the other country.
c. Notify management that the auditor is required to disclaim an opinion on the financial statements.
d. Receive a waiver from the auditor's state board of accountancy to perform the engagement.

84. If requested to perform a review engagement for a nonpublic entity in which an accountant has an immaterial direct financial interest, the accountant is
a. Not independent and, therefore, may **not** be associated with the financial statements.
b. Not independent and, therefore, may **not** issue a review report.
c. Not independent and, therefore, may issue a review report, but may **not** issue an auditor's opinion.
d. Independent because the financial interest is immaterial and, therefore, may issue a review report.

85. Kell engaged March, CPA, to submit to Kell a written personal financial plan containing unaudited personal financial statements. March anticipates omitting certain disclosures required by GAAP because the engagement's sole purpose is to assist Kell in developing a personal financial plan. For March to be exempt from complying with the requirements of SSARS 1, *Compilation and Review of Financial Statements,* Kell is required to agree that the
a. Financial statements will **not** be presented in comparative form with those of the prior period.
b. Omitted disclosures required by GAAP are **not** material.
c. Financial statements will **not** be disclosed to a non-CPA financial planner.
d. Financial statements will **not** be used to obtain credit.

86. When providing limited assurance that the financial statements of a nonpublic entity require **no** material modifications to be in accordance with generally accepted accounting principles, the accountant should
a. Assess the risk that a material misstatement could occur in a financial statement assertion.
b. Confirm with the entity's lawyer that material loss contingencies are disclosed.
c. Understand the accounting principles of the industry in which the entity operates.
d. Develop audit programs to determine whether the entity's financial statements are fairly presented.

87. Which of the following procedures is ordinarily performed by an accountant in a compilation engagement of a nonpublic entity?
a. Reading the financial statements to consider whether they are free of obvious mistakes in the application of accounting principles.
b. Obtaining written representations from management indicating that the compiled financial statements will **not** be used to obtain credit.

c. Making inquiries of management concerning actions taken at meetings of the stockholders and the board of directors.
d. Applying analytical procedures designed to corroborate management's assertions that are embodied in the financial statement components.

88. Compiled financial statements should be accompanied by an accountant's report stating that
a. A compilation includes assessing the accounting principles used and significant management estimates, as well as evaluating the overall financial statement presentation.
b. The accountant compiled the financial statements in accordance with Statements on Standards for Accounting and Review Services.
c. A compilation is substantially less in scope than an audit in accordance with GAAS, the objective of which is the expression of an opinion.
d. The accountant is **not** aware of any material modifications that should be made to the financial statements to conform with GAAP.

89. Moore, CPA, has been asked to issue a review report on the balance sheet of Dover Co., a nonpublic entity. Moore will not be reporting on Dover's statements of income, retained earnings, and cash flows. Moore may issue the review report provided the
a. Balance sheet is presented in a prescribed form of an industry trade association.
b. Scope of the inquiry and analytical procedures has **not** been restricted.
c. Balance sheet is **not** to be used to obtain credit or distributed to creditors.
d. Specialized accounting principles and practices of Dover's industry are disclosed.

90. Baker, CPA, was engaged to review the financial statements of Hall Co., a nonpublic entity. During the engagement Baker uncovered a complex scheme involving client illegal acts and irregularities that materially affect Hall's financial statements. If Baker believes that modification of the standard review report is **not** adequate to indicate the deficiencies in the financial statements, Baker should
a. Disclaim an opinion.
b. Issue an adverse opinion.
c. Withdraw from the engagement.
d. Issue a qualified opinion.

91. Each page of a nonpublic entity's financial statements reviewed by an accountant should include the following reference:

a. See Accompanying Accountant's Footnotes.
b. Reviewed, **No** Material Modifications Required.
c. See Accountant's Review Report.
d. Reviewed, **No** Accountant's Assurance Expressed.

92. An auditor's report on financial statements prepared on the cash receipts and disbursements basis of accounting should include all of the following **except**
a. A reference to the note to the financial statements that describes the cash receipts and disbursements basis of accounting.
b. A statement that the cash receipts and disbursements basis of accounting is **not** a comprehensive basis of accounting.
c. An opinion as to whether the financial statements are presented fairly in conformity with the cash receipts and disbursements basis of accounting.
d. A statement that the audit was conducted in accordance with generally accepted auditing standards.

93. Financial statements of a nonpublic entity that have been reviewed by an accountant should be accompanied by a report stating that a review
a. Provides only limited assurance that the financial statements are fairly presented.
b. Includes examining, on a test basis, information that is the representation of management.
c. Consists principally of inquiries of company personnel and analytical procedures applied to financial data.
d. Does **not** contemplate obtaining corroborating evidential matter or applying certain other procedures ordinarily performed during an audit.

94. Financial statements of a nonpublic entity compiled without audit or review by an accountant should be accompanied by a report stating that
a. The scope of the accountant's procedures has **not** been restricted in testing the financial information that is the representation of management.
b. The accountant assessed the accounting principles used and significant estimates made by management.
c. The accountant does **not** express an opinion or any other form of assurance on the financial statements.
d. A compilation consists principally of inquiries of entity personnel and analytical procedures applied to financial data.

95. Field is an employee of Gold Enterprises. Hardy, CPA, is asked to express an opinion on Field's profit participation in Gold's net income. Hardy may accept this engagement only if

a. Hardy also audits Gold's complete financial statements.
b. Gold's financial statements are prepared in conformity with GAAP.
c. Hardy's report is available for distribution to Gold's other employees.
d. Field owns controlling interest in Gold.

96. An auditor is engaged to report on selected financial data that are included in a client-prepared document containing audited financial statements. Under these circumstances, the report on the selected data should
a. Be limited to data derived from the audited financial statements.
b. Be distributed only to senior management and the board of directors.
c. State that the presentation is a comprehensive basis of accounting other than GAAP.
d. Indicate that the data are **not** fairly stated in all material respects.

97. A registration statement filed with the SEC contains the reports of two independent auditors on their audits of financial statements for different periods. The predecessor auditor who audited the prior-period financial statements generally should obtain a letter of representation from the
a. Successor independent auditor
b. Client's audit committee.
c. Principal underwriter.
d. Securities and Exchange Commission.

Chapter Five - Problems
Reviews, Compilations, Special Reports and Other Reports

NUMBER 1

Rose & Co., CPAs, has satisfactorily completed the examination of the financial statements of Bale & Booster, a partnership, for the year ended December 31, 1985. The financial statements which were prepared on the entity's income tax (cash) basis include footnotes which indicate that the partnership was involved in continuing litigation of material amounts relating to alleged infringement of a competitor's patent. The amount of damages, if any, resulting from this litigation could not be determined at the time of completion of the engagement. The prior years' financial statements were not presented.

Required:
Based upon the information presented, prepare an auditor's report which includes appropriate explanatory disclosure of significant facts.

NUMBER 2

The auditor's report below was drafted by a staff accountant of Baker and Baker, CPAs, at the completion of the audit of the comparative financial statements of Ocean Shore Partnership for the years ended December 31, 1990 and 1989. Ocean Shore prepares its financial statements on the income tax basis of accounting. The report was submitted to the engagement partner who reviewed matters thoroughly and properly concluded that an unqualified opinion should be expressed.

Auditor's Report

We have audited the accompanying statements of assets, liabilities, and capital-income tax basis of Ocean Shore Partnership as of December 31, 1990 and 1989, and the related statements of revenue and expenses-income tax basis and changes in partners' capital accounts-income tax basis for the years then ended.

We conducted our audits in accordance with standards established by the American Institute of Certified Public Accountants. Those standards require that we plan and perform the audit to obtain reasonable assurance about whether the financial statements are free of material misstatement. An audit includes examining, on a test basis, evidence supporting the amounts and disclosures in the financial statements. An audit also includes assessing the accounting principles used as well as evaluating the overall financial statement presentation.

As described in Note A, these financial statements were prepared on the basis of accounting the Partnership uses for income tax purposes. Accordingly, these financial statements are not designed for those who do not have access to the Partnership's tax returns.

In our opinion, the financial statements referred to above present fairly, in all material respects, the assets, liabilities, and capital of Ocean Shore Partnership as of December 31, 1990 and 1989, and its revenue and expenses and changes in partners' capital accounts for the years then ended, in conformity with generally accepted accounting principles applied on a consistent basis.

Baker and Baker, CPAs
April 3, 1991

Required:

Identify the deficiencies contained in the auditors' report as drafted by the staff accountant. Group the deficiencies by paragraph, where applicable. Do **not** redraft the report.

NUMBER 3

Number 3 consists of 15 items. Select the **best** answer for each item.

Required:
Items 106 through 120 represent a series of unrelated procedures that an accountant may consider performing in separate engagements to review the financial statements of a nonpublic entity (a review) and to compile the financial statements of a nonpublic entity (a compilation). Select, as the best answer for each item, whether the procedure is required (R) or not required (N) for both review and compilation engagements. Make two selections for each item.

Procedures
106. The accountant should establish an understanding with the entity regarding the nature and limitations of the services to be performed.

107. The accountant should make inquiries concerning actions taken at the board of directors' meetings.

108. The accountant, as the entity's successor accountant, should communicate with the predecessor accountant to obtain access to the predecessor's working papers.

109. The accountant should obtain a level of knowledge of the accounting principles and practices of the entity's industry.

110. The accountant should obtain an understanding of the entity's internal control.

111. The accountant should perform analytical procedures designed to identify relationships that appear to be unusual.

112. The accountant should make an assessment of control risk.

113. The accountant should send a letter of inquiry to the entity's attorney to corroborate the information furnished by management concerning litigation.

114. The accountant should obtain a management representation letter from the entity.

115. The accountant should study the relationships of the financial statement elements that would be expected to conform to a predictable pattern.

116. The accountant should communicate to the entity's senior management illegal employee acts discovered by the accountant that are clearly inconsequential.

117. The accountant should make inquiries about events subsequent to the date of the financial statements that would have a material effect on the financial statements.

118. The accountant should modify the accountant's report if there is a change in accounting principles that is adequately disclosed.

119. The accountant should submit a hard copy of the financial statements and accountant's report when the financial statements and accountant's report are submitted on a computer disk.

120. The accountant should perform specific procedures to evaluate whether there is substantial doubt about the entity's ability to continue as a going concern.

NUMBER 4

Number 4 consists of 17 items pertaining to possible deficiencies in an accountant's report on comparative financial statements.

Wallace & Wallace, CPAs, audited the financial statements of West Co., a nonpublic entity, for the year ended September 30, 1995, and expressed an unqualified opinion. For the year ended September 30, 1996, West issued comparative financial statements. Wallace & Wallace reviewed West's 1996 financial statements and Gordon, an assistant on the engagement, drafted the accountant's review report below. Martin, the engagement supervisor, decided not to reissue the prior year's auditor's report, but instructed Gordon to include a separate paragraph in the current year's review report describing the responsibility assumed for the prior year's audited financial statements.

Martin reviewed Gordon's draft and indicated in *Martin's Review Notes* that there were many deficiencies in Gordon's draft.

Accountant's Review Report

We have reviewed the accompanying balance sheet of West Company as of September 30, 1996, and the related statements of income and cash flows for the year then ended, in accordance with standards issued by the American Institute of Certified Public Accountants. All information included in these financial statements is the representation of the management of West Company. Our responsibility is to express limited assurance on these financial statements based on our review.

A review consists principally of inquiries of company personnel and analytical procedures applied to financial data. A review also includes assessing the accounting principles used and significant estimates made by management, as well as evaluating the overall financial statement presentation.

Based on our review, we are not aware of any material modifications that should be made to the accompanying financial statements. Accordingly, the accompanying financial statements have been prepared assuming that the company will continue as a going concern. Furthermore, we have no responsibility to update this report for events and circumstances occurring after the date of this report.

The financial statements for the year ended September 30, 1995, were audited by us and we expressed an unqualified opinion on them in our report dated November 7, 1995, but we have not performed any auditing procedures since that date. In our opinion, the financial statements referred to above are presented fairly, in all material respects, for the year then ended in conformity with generally accepted accounting principles.

Wallace & Wallace, CPAs
November 6, 1996

Required:
Items 1 through 17 represent the deficiencies noted by Martin. For each deficiency, indicate whether Martin is correct and Gordon is incorrect (M); Gordon is correct and Martin is incorrect (G); or both Martin and Gordon are incorrect (B).

**Martin's Review Notes**

1. There should be a reference to the prior year's audited financial statements in the first (introductory) paragraph.

2. All of the current year's basic financial statements are **not** properly identified in the first (introductory) paragraph.

3. The standards referred to in the first (introductory) paragraph should **not** be standards issued by the American Institute of Certified Public Accountants, but should be standards for the compilation and review of financial statements.

4. The accountant's responsibility to express limited assurance on the financial statements, mentioned in the first (introductory) paragraph, should be in the second (scope) paragraph.

5. There should be a reference to the prior year's audited financial statements in the second (scope) paragraph.

6. There should be a comparison of the scope of a review to an audit in the second (scope) paragraph.

7. There should be **no** reference to "assessing the accounting principles used," "significant estimates made by management," and "evaluating the overall financial statement presentation" in the second (scope) paragraph.

8. There should be a statement that **no** opinion is expressed on the current year's financial statements in the second (scope) paragraph.

9. There should be a reference to "conformity with generally accepted accounting principles" in the third paragraph.

10. There should be a reference to consistency in the third paragraph.

11. There should be a restriction on the distribution of the accountant's review report in the third paragraph.

12. The reference to "going concern" in the third paragraph should be in the second (scope) paragraph.

13. The accountant's lack of responsibility to update the report in the third paragraph should be in the second (scope) paragraph.

14. There should be **no** mention of the type of opinion expressed on the prior year's audited financial statements in the fourth (separate) paragraph.

15. All of the prior year's basic financial statements are **not** properly identified in the fourth (separate) paragraph.

16. The reference in the fourth (separate) paragraph to the fair presentation of the prior year's audited financial statements in accordance with generally accepted accounting principles should be omitted.

17. The report should be dual dated to indicate the date of the prior year's auditor's report.

NUMBER 5

The auditors' report below was drafted by a staff accountant of Baker & Baker, CPAs, at the completion of the audit of the comparative financial statements of Ocean Shore Partnership for the years ended December 31, 1998 and 1999. Ocean Shore prepares its financial statements on the income tax basis of accounting. The report was submitted to the engagement partner who reviewed matters thoroughly and properly concluded that an unqualified opinion should be expressed.

Auditor's Report

To: The Board of Directors

We have audited the accompanying statements of assets, liabilities, and capital – income tax basis of Ocean Shore Partnership as of December 31, 1999 and 1998, and the related statements of revenue and expenses – income tax basis and changes in partners' capital accounts – income tax basis for the years then ended.

We conducted our audits in accordance with standards established by the American Institute of Certified Public Accountants. Those standards require that we plan and perform the audit to obtain reasonable assurance about whether the financial statements are free of material misstatement. An audit includes examining, on a test basis, evidence supporting the amounts and disclosures in the financial statements. An audit also includes assessing the accounting principles used as well as evaluating the overall financial statement presentation.

As described in Note A, these financial statements were prepared on the basis of accounting the Partnership uses for income tax purposes. Accordingly, these financial statements are not designed for those who do not have access to the Partnership's tax returns.

In our opinion, the financial statements referred to above present fairly, in all material respects, the assets, liabilities, and capital of Ocean Shore Partnership as of December 31, 1999 and 1998, and its revenue and expenses and changes in partners' capital accounts for the years then ended, in conformity with generally accepted accounting principles applied on a consistent basis.

Baker & Baker, CPAs
April 3, 2000

Required:
This report contains deficiencies. For the following statements, indicate (Y for Yes, N for No) whether the noted correction should be made to correct the deficiencies in the report.

1. "External" should be added to the title of the report.

2. Management's responsibility for the financial statements should be referred to in the introductory paragraph.

3. The auditors' responsibility to express an opinion on the financial statements should be referred to in the introductory paragraph.

4. A reference to assessing "significant estimates made by the auditor" should be included in the scope paragraph.

5. Reference to the income tax basis of accounting as "a comprehensive basis of accounting other than generally accepted accounting principles" should be included in the explanatory paragraph.

6. The statement that the auditors' "audits provide a reasonable basis for our opinion" should be included in the scope paragraph.

7. "Generally accepted accounting standards" should be referred to in the scope paragraph, not standards established by the AICPA.

8. The income tax basis of accounting "described in Note A" should be referred to in the opinion paragraph, not "generally accepted accounting principles."

9. The statement that the financial statements are "not designed for those who do not have access to the Partnership tax returns" is inappropriate in the explanatory paragraph.

10. There should be no reference to consistency in the opinion paragraph.

NUMBER 6

Lambers & Lambers, CPAs, audited the financial statements of East Co., a nonpublic entity, for the year ended September 30, 1998 and expressed an unqualified opinion. For the year ended September 30, 1999, East issued comparative financial statements. Lambers & Lambers reviewed East's 1999 financial statements, and Del, an assistant on the engagement, drafted the accountant's review report below. Cutler, the engagement supervisor, decided not to reissue the prior year's auditor's report but instructed Del to include a separate paragraph in the current year's review report describing the responsibility assumed for the prior year's audited financial statements.

Cutler reviewed Del's draft and indicated in *Cutler's Review Notes* that there were many deficiencies in Del's draft.

Accountant's Review Report

We have reviewed the accompanying balance sheet of East Company as of September 30, 1999 and the related statements of income and cash flows for the year then ended, in accordance with standards issued by the American Institute of Certified Public Accountants. All information included in these financial statements is the representation of the management of East Company. Our responsibility is to express limited assurance on these financial statements based on our review.

A review consists principally of inquiries of company personnel and analytical procedures applied to financial data. A review also includes assessing the accounting principles used and significant estimates made by management, as well as evaluating the overall financial statement presentation.

Based on our review, we are not aware of any material modifications that should be made to the accompanying financial statements. Accordingly, the accompanying financial statements have been prepared assuming that the company will continue as a going concern. Furthermore, we have no responsibility to update this report for events and circumstances occurring after the date of this report.

The financial statements for the year ended September 30, 1998 were audited by us, and we expressed an unqualified opinion on them in our report dated November 7, 1998, but we have not performed any auditing procedures since that date. In our opinion, the financial statements referred to above are presented fairly, in all material respects, for the year then ended in conformity with generally accepted accounting principles.

Lambers & Lambers, CPAs
November 6, 1999

Required:

Items 1 through 17 represent the deficiencies noted by Cutler. For each deficiency, indicate whether Cutler is correct and Del is incorrect (**C**), Del is correct and Cutler is incorrect (**D**), or both Cutler and Del are incorrect (**B**).

Cutler's Review Notes

1. The first (introductory) paragraph should refer to the prior year's audited financial statements.

2. All of the current year's basic financial statements are not properly identified in the first (introductory) paragraph.

3. The standards referred to in the first (introductory) paragraph should not be standards issued by the American Institute of Certified Public Accountants but should be standards for the compilation and review of financial statements.

4. The accountant's responsibility to express limited assurance on the financial statements, mentioned in the first (introductory) paragraph, should be in the second (scope) paragraph.

5. The second (scope) paragraph should refer to the prior year's audited financial statements.

6. The second (scope) paragraph should compare the scope of a review with that of an audit.

7. References to "assessing the accounting principles used," "significant estimates made by management," and "evaluating the overall financial statement presentation" should not be in the second (scope) paragraph.

8. A statement that no opinion is expressed on the current year's financial statements should be in the second (scope) paragraph.

9. A reference to "conformity with generally accepted accounting principles" should be in the third paragraph.

10. A reference to consistency should be in the third paragraph.

11. A restriction on the distribution of the accountant's review report should be in the third paragraph.

12. The reference to "going concern" in the third paragraph should be in the second (scope) paragraph.

13. The accountant's lack of responsibility to update the report in the third paragraph should be in the second (scope) paragraph.

14. The type of opinion expressed on the prior year's audited financial statements should not be mentioned in the fourth (separate) paragraph.

15. All of the prior year's basic financial statements are not properly identified in the fourth (separate) paragraph.

16. The reference in the fourth (separate) paragraph to the fair presentation of the prior year's audited financial statements in accordance with generally accepted accounting principles should be omitted.

17. The report should be dual dated to indicate the date of the prior year's auditor's report.

Chapter Five - Solutions to Questions
Reviews, Compilations, Special Reports and Other Reports

1. (b) Special Reports are reports issued in connection with (a) financial statements that are prepared in accordance with a comprehensive basis of accounting other than generally accepted accounting principles, (b) specified elements, accounts, or items of a financial statement, (c) compliance with aspects of contractual agreements or regulatory requirements related to audited financial statements, (d) financial information presented in prescribed forms or schedules that require a prescribed form of auditor's report. Reports that meet the foregoing criteria are special reports or special purpose reports.

2. (c) Review engagements, whether for a public or non-public company, include, among other procedures, an analytical review and inquiries of company personnel.

3. (c) There are four types of special reports, one of which in a definite set of criteria having substantial support that is applied to all material items appearing in financial statements. Price-level financial statements qualify as a basis of accounting having substantial authoritative support.

4. (b) Reports on preprinted forms is a type of special report. GAAS specifically states that if the auditor is not satisfied with the wording of the form, it should be reworded.

5. (d) A study and evaluation of internal control is associated with audit engagements, not review engagements.

6. (b) Statements upon which the CPA reports that are not GAAP representations but rather "special reports" should not use the terms "Balance Sheet," "Income Statement," etc. Such terms are associated with GAAP and should not be used with statements that are not GAAP.

7. (c) If the CPA has not audited he must disclaim an opinion.

8. (c) Answer (a) is incorrect because the CPA has not audited. Answer (b) is incorrect because the CPA does not report on accuracy. Answer (d) is incorrect because it implies an audit. (c) is correct because a limited review provides a basis for reporting to the Board of Directors.

9. (b) For a non-public entity the type of service described would be a compilation. The only work the accountant must do for this service is described by the answer.

10. (c) Should the client refuse to make changes and the modifications in the accountant's report are not sufficient, the CPA should withdraw from the engagement.

11. (d) The client has changed the type of service that it wishes the CPA to perform. Before honoring the request, the CPA should determine whether the client has a sound business reason for the change. In this case, the cost of the audit was excessive and could be honored by the CPA.

12. (a) If the financial statements contain a departure from GAAP that the client refuses to change, the CPA should disclose this fact in a separate paragraph of his Review Report.

13. (c) Each page of the accountant's compilation report should contain a reference to the Compilation Report.

14. (d) A CPA may issue a compilation report even though he is not independent, but his report must clearly state that he is not independent.

15. (a) During a review of a client's financial statements, a CPA will:

1. Discuss with management the nature of the accounting system used to generate the financial statements (answer b)
2. Perform an analytical review (answer c)
3. Read the minutes of meetings in order to determine if disclosure is adequate (answer d)

The CPA will not review any controls since this is associated with an audit.

16. (a) An accountant's review report **must** be modified for departures from GAAP and/or inadequate disclosure only. The going concern problem is adequately disclosed in the financial statements, therefore no modification of the accountant's review report is necessary. The accountant **may** modify his review report but again it is **not** necessary to do so.

17. (a) Answers (b), (c) and (d) include information that would be included in the auditor's report on financial statements prepared in accordance with another comprehensive basis of accounting other than GAAP. It would be inappropriate to justify the basis of accounting used in the auditor's report. Therefore, answer (a) is the correct answer to the question because the method of accounting does not have to be justified in the auditor's report.

18. (d) Answers (b) and (c) do not require the accountant to render any assurance on the fairness of presentation of the information contained in the financial statements (historical or prospective). Answer (a) (report on management advisory services) does not require that an accountant to be independent. However, when issuing a report on compliance with a contractual agreement the CPA must be independent before a negative assurance is issued.

19. (c) The FASB promulgates GAAP. The GAO promulgated Governmental Auditing Standards. There is no such body designated as the Auditing Standards Board. The Accounting and Review Services Committee promulgates standards for nonpublic companies (entities not subject to SEC reporting) called Statements on Standards for Accounting and Review Services (SSARS).

20. (b) The magnitude of the financial interest has no bearing. Any financial interest makes the CPA not independent. Answer (b) is correct because the CPA may not issue a review report. Answer (c) is not correct because the CPA may be associated in a compilation even though he is not independent.

21. (c) An accountant may report (audit or review) on only one basic financial statement as long as he has access to all evidence and the scope of his procedures are not restricted.

22. (b) Answer (a) is incorrect because there is no testing of internal control in a review. Answer (c) is incorrect because corroborating evidence is sought only in an audit; (d) is incorrect because these procedures imply confirmations and that is an audit procedure.

23. (a) Since the CPA is associated with the financial statements (he is submitting them), he must indicate the degree of responsibility he is taking with respect to the statements. Since the statements are unaudited and the company is nonpublic, the appropriate standards are compilation standards.

24. (c) Answers (a), (b) and (d) are normally performed in an audit engagement. Answer (c) is performed in a review engagement.

25. (a) There is no requirement to study and evaluate internal controls in a review engagement.

26. (b) Inquiry and analytical review procedures are the basis for a review engagement.

27. (d) There are only two reasons an auditor would modify a review report, and they are (1) departures from GAAP and (2) inadequate disclosure. Uncertainties would not require modification of a review report.

28. (c) If not disclosed in the footnotes to the financial statements, the CPA would disclose the basis of accounting in his report.

29. (a) The objective of a review is to provide the accountant, based on applying his or her knowledge of financial reporting practices to significant accounting matters of which he or she becomes aware through inquiries and analytical procedures, with a basis for reporting whether material modifications should be made for such information to conform with generally accepted accounting principles. Answers (b) and (d) are incorrect because a review, which does not provide assurance that the accountant will become aware of all significant matters that would be disclosed in audit, does not provide the basis for expressing or updating an audit opinion. Answer (c) is incorrect because a review does not provide a basis for reporting on whether certain information should or should not be included in a registration statement under the Securities Act of 1933.

30. (a) An accountant may submit a written personal financial plan containing unaudited personal financial statements to a client without complying with the requirements of SSARS 1 when all of the following conditions exist: the accountant establishes an understanding with the client that the financial statements will be used solely to assist the client and the client's advisors to develop the client's personal goals and objectives, and will not be used to obtain credit or for any purposes other than developing these goals and objectives; nothing comes to the accountant's attention during the engagement that would cause the accountant to believe that the financial statements will be used to obtain credit or for any other purposes other than developing the client's financial goals and objectives. Answer (a) is one of the above conditions.

31. (a) There is a presumption that the information required by a prescribed form is sufficient to meet the needs of the body that designed or adopted the form and that there is no need for that body to be advised of departures from generally accepted accounting principles required by the prescribed form or related instructions.

32. (a) Special reports, or special purpose reports, include reports issued in connection with: financial statements that are prepared in accordance with a comprehensive basis of accounting other than generally accepted accounting principles; specified elements, accounts, or items of a financial statement; compliance with aspects of contractual agreements or regulatory requirements related to audited financial statements; financial information presented in prescribed forms or schedules that require a prescribed form of auditor's report. A comprehensive basis of accounting other than GAAP, which is the first type of report listed above, includes the cash basis of accounting.

33. (b) The services of CPAs include examination of financial statements and schedules contained in registration statements filed with the Securities and Exchange Commission under the Securities Act of 1933. In connection with this type of service, accountants are often called upon to issue letters to underwriters, commonly called comfort letters.

34. (a) Financial statements of a nonpublic entity that are reviewed by an accountant should be accompanied by a report stating that a review is substantially less in scope than an audit. Answers (c) and (d) are true regarding reviews of financial statements of a nonpublic entity, but they are not referred to in the accountant's report. Answer (b) does not apply to a review of financial statements.

35. (d) When a nonpublic entity's financial statements that an accountant has compiled omit substantially all disclosures, a paragraph is added to the compilation report indicating that the financial statements are not designed for those who are not informed about the omitted disclosures. The accountant may compile such financial statements provided the omissions are not undertaken with the intention of misleading users of those statements. There is no requirement that these statements be restricted for internal use [answer (a)] and no prohibition on giving them to financial institutions [answer (b)]. Answer (c) has nothing to do with omitting disclosures.

36. (c) The objective of a review of interim financial information is to provide the accountant, based on objectively applying his knowledge of financial reporting practices to significant accounting matters of which he becomes aware through inquiries and analytical procedures, with a basis for reporting whether material modifications should be made for such information to conform with GAAP. A review does not provide a basis for the expression of an opinion regarding the financial statements. Answer (a) is the objective of an audit. Answer (b) also refers to audits. Answer (d) involves expressing an opinion.

37. (c) An independent auditor may be requested to express an opinion on one or more specified elements, accounts, or items of a financial statement. Examples include rentals and royalties. The auditor's opinion should be expressed in a special report presented separately from the report on the financial statements of the entity. The auditor should not express an opinion on specified elements, accounts, or items included in financial statements on which he has expressed an adverse opinion or disclaimed an opinion based on an audit, if such reporting would be tantamount to expressing a piecemeal opinion on the financial statements. An opinion on rental and royalty income would not typically be equivalent to issuing a piecemeal opinion [answer (a)]. An engagement to express an opinion on specified elements, accounts, or items of a financial statement may be undertaken as a separate engagement [answer (b)] or in conjunction with an audit of financial statements. There are no limitations on the distribution of the special report [answer (d)].

38. (c) When an auditor submits a document containing audited financial statements to his client, he has a responsibility to report on all the information included in the document. If accompanying information is included, the auditor's report should describe clearly the degree of responsibility the auditor is taking, which is to evaluate the accompanying information in relation to the audited financial statements. The report, therefore, should include either an opinion on whether the accompanying information is fairly stated in all material respects in relation to the basic financial statements taken as a whole or a disclaimer of opinion. Answer (a) is incorrect because generally accepted auditing standards deal with how an audit is performed, not with the fairness of information presented. Answer (b) is incorrect because the accompanying information, some of which may come from sources outside the accounting system and therefore not be subject to accounting principles, is presented outside the financial statements and is not considered necessary for those statements to conform with generally accepted accounting principles. Answer (d) is incorrect because the auditor's responsibility regarding information that has been subjected to auditing procedures is addressed in the auditing standards, not the attestation standards.

39. (b) An auditor's report on information accompanying the basic financial statements in an auditor-submitted document has the same objective as an auditor's report on the basic financial statements: to describe clearly the character of the auditor's work and the degree of responsibility the auditor is taking. The report should include either an opinion on whether the accompanying information is fairly stated in all material respects in relation to the basic financial statements taken as a whole or a disclaimer of opinion.

40. (c) The accountant should possess a level of knowledge of the accounting principles and practices of the industry in which the entity operates and an understanding of the entity's business that will provide him, through the performance of inquiry and analytical procedures, with a reasonable basis for expressing limited assurance that there are no material modifications that should be made to the financial statements in order for the statements to be in conformity with GAAP. This level of knowledge should be obtained **before** performing a review of a nonpublic entity's financial statements. The procedures in answers (a), (b) and (d) would be performed as part of the review.

41. (c) The CPA must be independent when performing a review service. Independence is considered impaired if the accountant had or was committed to acquire any direct or material indirect financial interest in the client. Answer (a) is incorrect because materiality is not a factor when the accountant has a **direct** interest. Answer (b) ignores the compilation level of association with a client's financial statements, which is permitted when the accountant is not independent. Answer (d) is incorrect in stating that a review report can be issued when the accountant is not independent.

42. (c) Financial statements prepared on the income tax basis of accounting are a type of special report as defined by auditing standards. Those standards state that the income tax basis of accounting is, "a comprehensive basis of accounting other than GAAP." In writing a report on such a basis, the auditor must expand the standard report to include a separate paragraph that states the income tax basis of accounting is a comprehensive basis of accounting other than GAAP.

43. (c) Answers (a) and (b) only apply to audit reports, not review reports. Answer (d) is true about review reports. A review does express limited assurance, but (d) does not answer the question posed. Answer (c) is correct because the accountant (CPA) must disclose the departure from GAAP in the review report.

44. (d) The accountant may compile financial statements that omit all footnote disclosures. Normally, the footnotes to the financial statements would disclose the basis of accounting in preparing the financial statements. If all disclosures are omitted, then the CPA must disclose the basis of accounting followed in the compilation report.

45. (b) There are five types of reports designated as special reports by auditing standards. These are:

1. Financial statements prepared on a comprehensive basis of accounting other than GAAP.
2. Reports on specified elements, accounts, or items of a financial statement.
3. Compliance with aspects of a contractual agreement or regulatory requirements related to audited financial statements.
4. Financial presentations to comply with contractual agreements.
5. Financial information presented in prescribed forms.

Answer (b) is the third type of special report enumerated above.

46. (b) A review consists *primarily* of analytical review procedures and inquiry of the client personnel. Answer (a), (c) and (d) are usually performed in an audit, not a review.

47. (a) Analytical procedures are performed in a review, not a compilation.

48. (d) Answer (a) is incorrect because interim financial information is a historical financial presentation and has nothing to do with prospective financial information. Answer (c) is incorrect because substantive procedures are used in an audit, not a review. Answer (b) is incorrect because a review does not express an opinion. Only an audit expresses an opinion. Answer (d) is correct because a review report provides limited assurance and refers to whether or not material modifications should be made to the information.

49. (b) Answer (a) is incorrect because no reference is made in a review report about the scope of procedures. Answer (c) is incorrect because this statement would appear in an audit report. Answer (d) is incorrect due to the fact that a review is greater in scope than a compilation.

50. (c) An accountant is required to issue a report whenever he compiles or reviews financial statements in accordance with Statements on Standards for Accounting and Review Services (SSARS). SSARS does not establish procedures for other accounting and bookkeeping services such as preparing a working trial balance and standard monthly journal entries.

51. (b) A review consists principally of inquiries of company personnel and analytical procedures applied to financial data. The review should ordinarily include inquiries concerning the entity's procedures for recording and summarizing transactions. A review does not contemplate tests of records and assertions, as illustrated in answers (a) and (c), and inquiries of non-company personnel, such as the entity's attorney in answer (d).

52. (b) In order to compile financial statements that are appropriate in form, the accountant should possess a level of knowledge of the accounting principles and practices of the industry in which the client operates. The accountant is not required to make inquiries or perform other procedures to verify, corroborate, or review information supplied by the entity unless the accountant becomes aware that information supplied by the client may be unsatisfactory.

53. (d) A review does not contemplate obtaining an understanding of the internal control structure or assessing control risk. Accordingly, in a review engagement of a nonpublic entity, the accountant will not typically communicate material weaknesses discovered during the consideration of the internal control structure. Answers (a), (b) and (c) are examples of review procedures that should ordinarily be performed.

54. (b) Procedures for conducting a review of interim financial information are generally limited to inquiries and analytical procedures. Included in these procedures is reading the minutes of meetings of stockholders, the board of directors, and committees of the board of directors. A review does not typically include tests of balances and transactions such as those reflected in answers (a), (c) and (d).

55. (d) Even though the accountant gives no opinion or other explicit assurances on compiled financial statements, if he becomes aware that information is incorrect, incomplete, or otherwise unsatisfactory, he should obtain additional or revised information. The accountant may, however, compile financial statements that omit substantially all of the disclosures required by generally accepted accounting principles, provided the omission is clearly indicated in the accountant's report and is not, to his knowledge, undertaken with the intention of misleading those who might reasonably be expected to use such financial statements.

56. (c) Statements on Standards for Accounting and Review Services require the accountant's review report for a nonpublic entity to state that a review is less in scope than an audit and that the accountant is not aware of any material modifications that should be made to the financial statements. Thus, a review does not typically include assessing accounting principles and examining evidence, as presented in answers (a) and (b) and a review report does not include an opinion, as noted in answer (d), but does provide negative assurance.

57. (c) When reporting on financial statements prepared in conformity with a comprehensive basis of accounting other than generally accepted accounting principles (GAAP), an independent auditor's report should include a paragraph that states the basis of presentation and refers to the note in the financial statements that discusses the basis of presentation and describes how that basis differs from GAAP. The separate paragraph in the auditor's report does not include any justification, opinion, or explanation as presented in answers (a), (b) and (d).

58. (b) A CPA who has been engaged to audit the financial statements of a nonpublic entity may, before the completion of the engagement, be requested to change the engagement to a compilation. Such a request may result from a change in circumstances affecting the client's requirement for an audit, a misunderstanding regarding the nature of an audit, or a restriction on the scope of the audit. Before agreeing to the change to a compilation, the CPA should consider the reason for the client's request, the additional audit effort required to complete the audit, and the estimated cost to complete the audit. Answers (a) and (d) are incorrect because the CPA is required to consider the additional audit effort necessary to complete the audit. Answer (c) is incorrect because the CPA is required to consider the reason given for the client's request, particularly the implications of a restriction on the scope of the audit, whether imposed by the client or by circumstances.

59. (c) A CPA may be asked to issue a review report on one financial statement, such as a balance sheet, and not on related financial statements such as statements of income, retained earnings, and cash flows. The CPA may do so if the scope of his or her inquiry and analytical procedures has not been restricted. Answer (a) is incorrect because the CPA can issue a review report on a balance sheet without reporting on other related financial statements. Answer (b) is incorrect because the CPA can issue a review report on a balance sheet that is modified to disclose a departure from GAAP. Answer (d) is incorrect because whether the client is a new or continuing client, and whether the engagement is accepted before or after the end of the client's fiscal year are irrelevant. The CPA can issue a review report on a balance sheet for new or continuing clients, and for engagements accepted before or after fiscal year end.

60. (d) When accepting an engagement to compile or review the financial statements of a nonpublic entity, the accountant should possess a level of knowledge of the accounting principles and practices of the industry in which the entity operates. This requirement does not preclude the accountant from accepting an engagement for an entity in an industry with which the accountant has no previous experience, if the accountant plans to obtain the required level of knowledge before compiling or reviewing the financial statements. In this context, the term industry includes not-for-profit activities and the requirement to obtain the necessary knowledge applies to not-for-profit entities. Answers (a), (b) and (c) are incorrect because the accountant can accept a compilation or review engagement if the accountant has or plans to obtain the required knowledge.

61. (d) A compilation is defined as presenting in the form of financial statements information that is the representation of management without undertaking to express any assurance on the statements. In a compilation, the accountant is not required to make inquiries or to perform other procedures to verify, corroborate, or review information supplied by the entity. A review is defined as performing inquiry and analytical procedures that provide the accountant with a reasonable basis for expressing limited assurance that there are no material modifications that should be made to the financial statements in order for them to be in conformity with GAAP, or, if applicable, with another comprehensive basis of accounting. Answers (a) and (c) are incorrect because analytical procedures are

required in a review engagement. Answer (b) is incorrect because analytical procedures are not required in a compilation engagement.

62. (c) A review engagement for a nonpublic entity does not include obtaining an understanding of the internal control structure or assessing control risk, testing accounting records and responses to inquiries by obtain corroborating evidential matter, and certain other procedures ordinarily performed during an audit. The accountant is required to obtain a representation letter from management, as indicated in answer (a). The accountant also must consider whether the financial statements conform with GAAP, as indicated in answer (b), in order for the accountant to state in his or her report that the accountant is not aware of any material modifications that should be made to the financial statements in order for them to be in conformity with GAAP. Additionally, as part of the inquiry and analytical procedures that are performed in a review, the accountant would inquire about events subsequent to the date of the financial statements that would have a material affect on the financial statements, as indicated in answer (d).

63. (a) When an auditor submits a document containing financial statements to a client or others, the auditor has a responsibility to report on all the information included in the document. If the auditor-submitted document contains information that is presented outside the basic financial statements that is not required for those financial statements to be presented in accordance with GAAP, such as investment and property schedules presented for purposes of additional analysis, the auditor must express an opinion on that accompanying information. When reporting on this information, the measurement of materiality is the same as that used in forming an opinion on the basic financial statements taken as a whole. Answers (b), (c) and (d) are incorrect because the auditor is not expressing an opinion on the additional information taken by itself. Instead, the auditor is expressing an opinion on whether the accompanying information is fairly stated in relation to the basic financial statements taken as whole.

64. (a) Accountants in public practice are sometimes engaged to report on the application of accounting principles to specific transactions and financial products. When providing such a service, in connection with a proposal to obtain a new client or otherwise, the accountant should follow AICPA guidance, which includes reporting guidelines. The written report should include a description of the nature of the engagement; a description of the transaction; a statement describing the appropriate accounting treatment; a statement that the responsibility for proper accounting rests with the financial statement preparers; and a statement that any difference in the facts, circumstances, or assumptions presented may change the report. Answer (b) is incorrect because an engagement to report on the application of accounting principles is performed in accordance with AICPA standards, not with Statements on Standards for Consulting Services. Answer (c) is incorrect because there is generally no restriction on distribution of the report. Answer (d) is incorrect because the accountant's report includes a statement that describes the appropriate accounting principles to be applied instead of negative assurance.

65. (c) Compiled financial statements should be accompanied by a report stating that: a compilation has been performed in accordance with Statements on Standards for Accounting and Review Services (SSARS) issued by the AICPA; a compilation is limited to presenting in the form of financial statements information that is the representation of management; and the financial statements have not been audited or reviewed and, accordingly, the accountant does not express an opinion or any other form of assurance on them. Answer (a) is incorrect because, although it is true that a compilation is substantially less in scope than a review or audit in accordance with GAAS, the compilation report does not include such a statement. Answer (b) is incorrect because the accountant expresses no assurance on the compiled financial statements. Answer (d) is incorrect because the accountant follows SSARS issued by the AICPA Accounting and Review Services Committee, not Statements on Auditing Standards (SAS) or any other standards issued by the Auditing Standards Board.

66. (c) An entity may request an accountant to compile financial statements that omit substantially all of the disclosures required by GAAP, including disclosures that might appear in the body of the financial statements. The accountant may compile such financial statements provided the omission is clearly indicated in the accountant's report and is not, to his or her knowledge, undertaken with the intention of misleading those who might reasonably be expected to use such financial statements. Answer (a), (b) and (d) are incorrect because both statements are correct.

67. (b) Financial statements of a nonpublic entity reviewed by an accountant should be accompanied by a report stating that: a review was performed in accordance with Statements on Standards for Accounting and Review Services issued by the AICPA; all information presented in the financial statements is the representation of management; a review consists principally of inquiries and analytical procedures; a review is substantially less in scope than an audit; and the accountant is not aware of any material modifications that should be made to the financial statements in order for them to be in conformity with GAAP. Answer (a) is incorrect because the accountant expresses limited negative assurance when the accountant states that he or she is not aware of any material modifications that should be made to the financial statements in order for them to be in conformity with GAAP. Answers (c) and (d) are incorrect because in an audit, the auditor obtains reasonable assurance about whether the financial statements are free of material misstatement by examining evidence. Whereas, in a review, the accountant performs inquiry and analytical procedures and expresses limited assurance on the financial statements.

68. (d) An accountant may be asked to issue a review report on one financial statement of a nonpublic entity, such as a balance sheet, and not on other related financial statements, such as the statements of income, retained earnings, and cash flows. He or she may do so if the scope of the accountant's inquiry and analytical procedures has not been restricted. Answer (a) is incorrect because the accountant is allowed to accept an engagement to review just the balance sheet and, therefore, would not violate any ethical standards by doing so. Answer (b) is incorrect because this type of engagement would be considered a complete review of the balance sheet. Answer (c) is incorrect because if the review of the balance sheet discloses material departures from GAAP and the financial statements are not revised, the accountant's review report on the balance sheet would be modified to reflect the GAAP departure.

69. (b) AU 110 states that the financial statements are management's responsibility. Management is responsible for adopting sound accounting policies and for establishing and maintaining an internal control structure that will record, process, summarize, and report financial data that is consistent with management's assertions embodied in the financial statements. The internal control structure should include an accounting system to identify, assemble, analyze, classify, record, and report an entity's transactions and to maintain accountability for the related assets and liabilities, the entity's transactions and the related assets and liabilities which are within the direct knowledge and control of management. The auditor's knowledge of these matters is limited to that acquired through the audit. Thus, the fair presentation of financial position, results of operations, and cash flows in conformity with generally accepted accounting principles is an implicit and integral part of management's responsibility. The auditor's responsibility for the financial statements is confined to the expression of an opinion on them.

70. (a) AR 100 states that if the accountant believes that modification of the standard report is not adequate to indicate the deficiencies in the financial statements taken as a whole, he should withdraw from the compilation or review engagement and provide no further services with respect to those financial statements. The accountant may wish to consult with legal counsel in those circumstances. Choices (b), (c), and (d) are incorrect because in the stated facts, the auditor has no alternatives but to withdraw from the engagement.

71. (d) AR 100 states that the accountant should not submit unaudited financial statements of a nonpublic entity to his or her client or others unless, as a minimum, he or she complies with the provisions of this statement applicable to a compilation engagement. Submission of financial statements is defined as presenting to a client or others financial statements that the accountant has:

- Generated, either manually or through the use of computer software, or
- Modified by materially changing account classification, amounts, disclosures directly on client-prepared F/S.

The following services do not constitute a submission of financial statements:

- Reading client-prepared financial statements.
- Typing or reproducing client-prepared financial statements, without modification, as a service to a client.
- Proposing correcting journal entries or disclosures to the financial statements, either orally or in written form, that materially change client-prepared financial statements, as long as the accountant does not directly modify the client-prepared financial statements.

- Preparing standard monthly journal entries such as entries for depreciation and expiration of prepaid expenses.
- Providing a client with a financial statement format that does not include dollar amounts, to be used by the client to prepare financial statements.
- Advising a client about the selection or use of computer software that the client will use to generate statements.
- Providing the client with the use of, or access to, computer hardware or software that the client will use to generate statements.

72. (a) AT 200.49 states that an accountant may accept an engagement to apply agreed-upon procedures to prospective financial statements provided that:

- the specified users involved have participated in establishing the nature and scope of the engagement and take responsibility for the adequacy of the procedures,
- distribution of the report is to be restricted to the specified users involved, and
- the prospective financial statements include a summary of significant assumptions.

Choice (b) is incorrect because the work performed was less in scope than an examination. Choice (c) is incorrect because responsibility is assumed by the specific users and not the accountant. Choice (d) is incorrect because negative assurance is not expressed.

73. (a) AR 100 states that the review of financial statements involves performing inquiry and analytical procedures that provide the accountant with a reasonable basis for expressing limited assurance that there are no material modifications that should be made to the statements in order for them to be in conformity with generally accepted accounting principles or, if applicable, with another comprehensive basis of accounting. The objective of a review differs significantly from the objective of a compilation. The inquiry and analytical procedures performed in a review should provide the accountant with a reasonable basis for expressing limited assurance that there are no material modifications that should be made to the financial statements. No expression of assurance is contemplated in a compilation. The objective of a review also differs significantly from the objective of an audit of financial statements in accordance with generally accepted auditing standards. The objective of an audit is to provide a reasonable basis for expressing an opinion regarding the financial statements taken as a whole. A review does not provide a basis for the expression of such an opinion because a review does not contemplate obtaining an understanding of the internal control structure or assessing control risk, tests of accounting records and of responses to inquiries by obtaining corroborating evidential matter through inspection, observation or confirmation, and certain other procedures ordinarily performed during an audit. A review may bring to the accountant's attention significant matters affecting the financial statements, but it does not provide assurance that the accountant will become aware of all significant matters that would be disclosed in an audit.

74. (b) AR 100 states that in an engagement to review the financial statements of a nonpublic entity, the accountant *is required* to obtain a representation letter from members of management whom the accountant believes are responsible for and knowledgeable, directly or through others in the organization, about the matters covered in the representation letter. Normally, the chief executive officer and chief financial officer should sign the representation letter. Choices (a), (c), and (d) are incorrect because they are not performed during a review.

75. (d) AU 504 states that when an accountant is associated with financial statements of a public entity, but has not audited or reviewed such statements, the report to be issued is as follows:

- The accompanying balance sheet of X Company as of December 31, 19X1, and the related statements of income, retained earnings, and cash flows for the year then ended were not audited by us and, accordingly, we do not express an opinion on them. (Signature and date)
- This disclaimer of opinion is the means by which the accountant complies with the fourth standard of reporting when associated with unaudited financial statements in these circumstances. The disclaimer may accompany the unaudited financial statements or it may be placed directly on them. In addition, each page of the statements should be clearly and conspicuously marked as unaudited.

76. (c) AR 100 states that if the accountant concludes that there is reasonable justification to change the engagement and if he or she complies with the standards applicable to the changed engagement, the accountant should issue an appropriate review or compilation report. The report should not include reference to:

- the original engagement,
- any auditing or review procedures that may have been performed, or
- scope limitations that resulted in the changed engagement.

77. (c) AR 200 states that when the current-period financial statements of a nonpublic entity have been compiled or reviewed and those of the prior period have been audited, the accountant should issue an appropriate compilation or review report on the current-period financial statements and either:

- the report on the prior period should be reissued or
- the report on the current period should include, as a separate paragraph, an appropriate description of the responsibility assumed for the financial statements of the prior period.

In the latter case, the separate paragraph should indicate:

- that the financial statements of the prior period were audited previously,
- the date of the previous report,
- the type of opinion expressed previously,
- if the opinion was other than unqualified, the substantive reasons therefore, and
- that no auditing procedures were performed after the date of the previous report.

An example of such a separate paragraph is the following:

> The financial statements for the year ended December 31, 19X1, were audited by us (other accountants) and we (they) expressed an unqualified opinion on them in our (their) report dated March 1, 19X2, but we (they) have not performed any auditing procedures since that date.

Choice (a) is incorrect because there is no limitation on the distribution. Choice (b) is incorrect because the previous year's audit can still be relied upon. Choice (d) is incorrect because there is no mention of the changing of services.

78. (b) AR 100 states that the following form of standard report is appropriate for a compilation:

> We have compiled the accompanying balance sheet of XYZ Company as of December 31, 19XX, and the related statements of income, retained earnings, and cash flows for the year then ended, in accordance with Statements on Standards for Accounting and Review Services issued by the American Institute of Certified Public Accountants.

> A compilation is limited to presenting in the form of financial statements information that is the representation of management (owners). I (we) have not audited or reviewed the accompanying financial statements and, accordingly, do not express an opinion or any other form of assurance on them.

79. (a) AR 100 states that if financial statements compiled in conformity with a comprehensive basis of accounting other than generally accepted accounting principles do not include disclosure of the basis of accounting used, the basis should be disclosed in the accountant's report.

80. (a) AR 100 states that when financial statements that the accountant has compiled omit substantially all disclosures, the following form of standard report is appropriate:

> We have compiled the accompanying balance sheet of XYZ Company as of December 31, 19XX, and the related statements of income, retained earnings, and cash flows for the year then ended, in accordance with Statements on Standards for Accounting and Review Services issued by the American Institute of Certified Public Accountants.
>
> A compilation is limited to presenting in the form of financial statements information that is the representation of management (owners). I (we) have not audited or reviewed the accompanying financial statements and, accordingly, do not express an opinion or any other form of assurance on them.
>
> Management has elected to omit substantially all of the disclosures (and the statement of cash flows) required by generally accepted accounting principles. If the omitted disclosures were included in the financial statements, they might influence the user's conclusions about the company's financial position, results of operations, and cash flows. Accordingly, these financial statements are not designed for those who are not informed about such matters.

Choice (b) is incorrect because a compilation is prepared in conformity with SSARS issued by the AICPA and not a comprehensive basis of accounting. Choice (c) is incorrect because a compilation is prepared in conformity with SSARS issued by the AICPA. Choice (d) is incorrect because this disclosure is not appropriate for a compilation.

81. (c) AT 200 states that the following is the form of the accountant's standard report on the compilation of a forecast that does not contain a range:

> "We have compiled the accompanying forecasted balance sheet, statements of income, retained earnings, and changes in financial position of XYZ Company as of December 31, 19XX, and for the year then ending, in accordance with standards established by the American Institute of Certified Public Accountants.
>
> A compilation is limited to presenting in the form of a forecast information that is the representation of management and does not include evaluation of the support for the assumptions underlying the forecast. We have not examined the forecast and, accordingly, do not express an opinion or any other form of assurance on the accompanying statements or assumptions. *Furthermore, there will usually be differences between the forecasted and actual results,* because events and circumstances frequently do not occur as expected, and those differences may be material. We have no responsibility to update this report for events and circumstances occurring after the date of this report."

82. (b) AU 552 states that the following is an example of wording that an auditor may use to report on condensed financial statements that are derived from financial statements that he has audited and on which he has issued a standard report:

Independent Auditor's Report

> We have audited, in accordance with generally accepted auditing standards, the consolidated balance sheet of X Company and subsidiaries as of December 31, 19X0, and the related consolidated statements of income, retained earnings, and cash flows for the year then ended (not presented herein); and in our report dated February 15, 19X1, we expressed an unqualified opinion on those consolidated financial statements.
>
> In our opinion, the information set forth in the *accompanying condensed consolidated financial statements* is fairly stated, in all material respects, in relation to the consolidated financial statements from which it has been derived.

83. (a) AU 534 states that when auditing the financial statements of a US entity prepared in conformity with accounting principles generally accepted in another country, the auditor should perform the procedures that are necessary to comply with the general and fieldwork standards of US Generally Accepted Auditing Standards. The auditor should understand the accounting principles generally accepted in the other country. Such knowledge may be obtained by reading the statutes or professional literature that establish or describe the accounting principles generally accepted in the other country. Choice (b) is incorrect because the standard report of another country may also require that the auditor provide explicit or implicit assurance of statutory compliance or otherwise require understanding of the local law. The requirement of the other country may vary significantly. Choice (c) is incorrect because the auditor need not disclaim opinion on the financial statements prepared in conformity with another country's principles. Choice (d) is incorrect because a waiver is not necessary.

84. (b) Since a CPA, when performing a review, provides negative assurance about the financial statements, he must be independent of the client. If the accountant has a direct financial interest in the client, even if immaterial, the accountant is not considered independent according to the Code of Professional Conduct. Answer (a) is incorrect because an accountant who is not independent can compile financial statements. Answers (c) and (d) are incorrect because the accountant is not independent if he holds any direct financial interest, and if not independent, he cannot issue a review report or give any assurances about the financial statements.

85. (d) An accountant may submit a written personal financial plan containing unaudited financial statements to a client without complying with SSARS 1 when the client agrees that the financial statements will be used solely to assist the client and the client's advisers to develop the client's personal financial goals and objectives, and will not be used to obtain credit or for any purposes other than developing these goals and objectives. Answer (a) is incorrect because there is no prohibition against presenting these financial statements in comparative form. Answer (b) is incorrect because such financial statements frequently contain departures from GAAP and omit material disclosures required by GAAP. Answer (c) is incorrect because these financial statements can be used by the client's advisers, which includes non-CPA financial planners.

86. (c) A review of a nonpublic entity's financial statements provides limited assurance that there are no material modifications that should be made to the statements in order for them to be in conformity with generally accepted accounting principles. The accountant, in order to perform the inquiry and analytical procedures required in a review engagement, should possess a level of knowledge of the accounting principles and practices of the industry in which the entity operates and an understanding of the entity's business. Answers (a), (b) and (d) are incorrect because a review does not contemplate procedures that are typically performed in an audit to understand the internal control structure and obtain corroborating evidence, such as assessing risks, sending confirmations, and developing audit programs.

87. (a) A compilation is the presentation in the form of financial statements information that is the representation of management without undertaking to express any assurance on the statements. Before issuing his or her compilation report, the accountant should read the compiled financial statements and consider whether such financial statements appear to be appropriate in form and free from obvious material errors, including mistakes in the application of accounting principles. Answer (b) is incorrect because a written representation letter is not typically obtained in a compilation engagement and compiled financial statements can be used to obtain credit. Answers (c) and (d) are incorrect because although in a review engagement the accountant is required to make inquires and perform analytical procedures, in a compilation the accountant has no such requirement.

88. (b) Financial statements compiled by an accountant should be accompanied by a report stating that a compilation has been performed in accordance with Statements on Standards for Accounting and Review Services issued by the AICPA, a compilation is limited to presenting in the form of financial statements information that is the representation of management, and the financial statements have not been audited or reviewed and no opinion is expressed or any other form of assurance given. Answer (a) is found in reports on audited financial statements. Answers (c) and (d) include statements that are properly included in reports on reviewed financial statements.

89. (b) An accountant may be asked to issue a review report on one financial statement, such as a balance sheet, and not on related financial statements. He may do so if the scope of his inquiry and analytical procedures has not been restricted. Answer (a) is incorrect because an accountant may be asked to compile, rather than review, financial statements included in prescribed forms, such as forms used by industry trade associations. Answers (c) and (d) are incorrect because a reviewed balance sheet, whether issued alone or with other financial statements, can be used to obtain credit and distributed to creditors, and should contain necessary disclosures.

90. (c) If the accountant believes that modification of his standard report is not adequate to indicate the deficiencies in the financial statements taken as a whole, he or she should withdraw from the review engagement and provide no further services with respect to those financial statements. Answer (a) is incorrect because the standard review report states that no opinion is expressed. Answers (b) and (d) are incorrect because a review does not provide the basis for the expression of an opinion.

91. (c) Statements on Standards for Accounting and Review Services (SSARS), which provide guidance for reviews of nonpublic entities, specifically require that each page of the nonpublic entity's financial statements include the phrase "see Accountant's Review Report." SSARS do not require the references listed in answers (a), (b) and (d).

92. (b) Generally accepted auditing standards are applicable when an auditor conducts an audit of and reports on any financial statements, including those prepared in conformity with an Other Comprehensive Basis Of Accounting (OCBOA). The cash receipts and disbursements basis is an OCBOA, and the auditor's report would include a statement to that effect. The report should also include a reference to the note that describes the OCBOA, answer (a); an opinion on whether the financial statements are fairly presented in conformity with the OCBOA, answer (c); and a standard scope paragraph that refers to generally accepted auditing standards, answer (d).

93. (c) Financial statements of a nonpublic entity reviewed by an accountant should be accompanied by a report stating that a review consists principally of inquiries of company personnel and analytical procedures applied to financial data. Answer (a) is incorrect because the report does not state that a review provides only limited assurance; rather, the report states that the accountant is not aware of any material modifications that should be made to the financial statements in order for them to be in conformity with GAAP. Answer (b) is incorrect because a review does not involve examining information that is the representation of management, as is done in an audit. Answer (d) is incorrect because although a review does not contemplate obtaining corroborating evidence or applying certain other procedures ordinarily performed during an audit, the review report does not include a statement to that effect.

94. (c) Financial statements of a nonpublic entity compiled without audit or review by an accountant should be accompanied by a report stating that the financial statements have not been audited or reviewed, and, accordingly, the accountant does not express an opinion or any other form of assurance on them. Answer (a) is incorrect because the accountant, when compiling financial statements, is not required to make inquiries or perform other procedures to test the financial information. Answer (b) is incorrect because assessing accounting principles and estimates, which is done in an audit and is stated in an auditor's report, is not part of a compilation. Answer (d) is incorrect because a review, rather than a compilation, consists of inquiries and analytical procedures.

95. (a) An auditor may be requested to express an opinion on a specified element, account, or item of a financial statement, such as rentals, royalties, a profit participation, or a provision for income taxes. If the specified item is based on an entity's net income, as is the case with profit participation, the auditor should have audited the complete financial statements to express an opinion on the specified item. Answer (b) is incorrect because the financial statements could be prepared in conformity with GAAP or an other comprehensive basis of accounting (OCBOA). Answer (c) is incorrect because distribution of the report on profit participation could be limited to Field, the individual who hired the auditor. Answer (d) is incorrect because whether or not Field owns a controlling interest has nothing to do with the decision to accept the engagement.

96. (a) When an auditor is engaged to report on selected financial data that are included in a client-prepared document that contains audited financial statements, the auditor's report should be limited to the data that are derived from the audited financial statements. If the selected financial data that management presents include both data derived from audited financial statements and from other information, the auditor's report should specifically identify the data on which he is reporting. Answer (b) is incorrect because there is no necessary restriction on the distribution of an auditor's report on selected financial data. Answer (c) is incorrect because the selected data are derived from the audited financial statements, which would have been prepared in accordance with GAAP or an other comprehensive basis of accounting (OCBOA). Answer (d) is incorrect because the auditor's report on selected financial data should indicate whether, in the auditor's opinion, the information set forth in the selected financial data is fairly stated in all material respects in relation to the complete financial statements from which it has been derived.

97. (a) An auditor who has audited the financial statements for prior periods but has not audited the financial statements for the most recent audited period included in a registration statement filed with the SEC has a responsibility relating to events subsequent to the date of the prior-period financial statements, and extending to the effective date of the registration statement, that bear materially on the prior-period financial statements on which he reported. Generally, the predecessor auditor should read pertinent portions of the registration statement and obtain a letter of representation from the successor independent auditor regarding whether his audit revealed any matters that might have a material effect on the financial statements reported on by the predecessor auditor. Answers (b), (c) and (d) are incorrect because the necessary letter of representation is from the successor auditor, not from the client's audit committee, the underwriter, or the SEC.

Chapter Five - Solutions to Problems
Reviews, Compilations, Special Reports and Other Reports

NUMBER 1

Addressee:

We have audited the statement of assets, liabilities, and capital (income tax basis) of Bale & Booster, a partnership, as of December 31, 1985, and the related statement of revenue and expenses (income tax basis) and the related statement of changes in partners' capital accounts for the year then ended. These financial statements are the responsibility of the partnership's management. Our responsibility is to express an opinion on the financial statements based upon our audit.

We conducted our audit in accordance with generally accepted auditing standards. Those standards require that we plan and perform the audit to obtain reasonable assurance about whether the financial statements are free of material misstatement. An audit includes examining, on a test basis, evidence supporting the amounts and disclosures in the financial statements. An audit also includes assessing the accounting principles used and significant estimates made by management, as well as evaluating the overall financial statement presentation. We believe that our audits provide a reasonable basis for our opinion.

As described in note X, the partnership's policy is to prepare its financial statements on the accounting basis used for income tax purposes; which is a comprehensive basis of accounting other than generally accepted accounting principles.

In addition, the company is involved in continuing litigation relating to patent infringement. The amount of damages, if any, resulting from this litigation cannot be determined at this time.

In our opinion, the financial statements referred to above present fairly the assets, liabilities, and capital of the Bale & Booster partnership as of December 31, 1985, and its revenue and expenses and changes in its partners' capital accounts for the year then ended, on the income tax (cash) basis of accounting as described in note X.

    Date   ***Firm Name***

NUMBER 2

The auditors' report contains the following deficiencies:

1. "Independent" is omitted from the title of the auditor's report.

Introductory paragraph
2. Management's responsibility for the financial statements is omitted.

3. The auditor's responsibility to express an opinion on the financial statements is omitted.

Scope paragraph
4. "Generally accepted auditing standards" should be referred to, not standards established by the AICPA.

5. Reference to assessing "significant estimates made by management" is omitted.

6. The concluding statement that the auditors "believe that our audits provide a reasonable basis for our opinion" is omitted.

Explanatory paragraph
7. Reference to the income tax basis of accounting as "a comprehensive basis of accounting other than generally accepted accounting principles" is omitted.

8. The statement that the financial statements are "not designed for those who do not have access to the Partnership tax returns" is inappropriate.

Opinion paragraph
9. The income tax basis of accounting "described in Note A" should be referred to, not "generally accepted accounting principles."

10. There should be no reference to consistency unless the accounting principles have not been applied consistently.

NUMBER 3

	Review		**Compilation**	
106.	R	Required	R	Required
107.	R	Required	N	Not required
108.	N	Not required	N	Not required
109.	R	Required	R	Required
110.	N	Not required	N	Not required
111.	R	Required	N	Not required
112.	N	Not required	N	Not required
113.	N	Not required	N	Not required
114.	R	Required	N	Not required
115.	R	Required	N	Not required
116.	N	Not required	N	Not required
117.	R	Required	N	Not required
118.	N	Not required	N	Not required
119.	N	Not required	N	Not required
120.	N	Not required	N	Not required

NUMBER 4

1.   G   Gordon is correct and Martin is incorrect.

2.   M   Martin is correct and Gordon is incorrect.

3.   B   Both Martin and Gordon are incorrect.

4.   B   Both Martin and Gordon are incorrect.

5.   G   Gordon is correct and Martin is incorrect.

6.   M   Martin is correct and Gordon is incorrect.

7.   M   Martin is correct and Gordon is incorrect.

8.   M   Martin is correct and Gordon is incorrect.

9.   M   Martin is correct and Gordon is incorrect.

10.   G   Gordon is correct and Martin is incorrect.

11.   G   Gordon is correct and Martin is incorrect.

12.   B   Both Martin and Gordon are incorrect.

13.   B   Both Martin and Gordon are incorrect.

14.   G   Gordon is correct and Martin is incorrect.

15.   G   Gordon is correct and Martin is incorrect.

16.   M   Martin is correct and Gordon is incorrect.

17.   G   Gordon is correct and Martin is incorrect.

NUMBER 5

1.   N   No
2.   Y   Yes
3.   Y   Yes
4.   N   No
5.   Y   Yes
6.   Y   Yes
7.   N   No
8.   Y   Yes
9.   Y   Yes
10.   Y   Yes

NUMBER 6

1.	D	Del is correct and Cutler is incorrect.
2.	C	Cutler is correct and Del is incorrect.
3.	B	Both Cutler and Del are incorrect.
4.	B	Both Cutler and Del are incorrect.
5.	D	Del is correct and Cutler is incorrect.
6.	C	Cutler is correct and Del is incorrect.
7.	C	Cutler is correct and Del is incorrect.
8.	C	Cutler is correct and Del is incorrect.
9.	C	Cutler is correct and Del is incorrect.
10.	D	Del is correct and Cutler is incorrect.
11.	D	Del is correct and Cutler is incorrect.
12.	B	Both Cutler and Del are incorrect.
13.	B	Both Cutler and Del are incorrect.
14.	D	Del is correct and Cutler is incorrect.
15.	D	Del is correct and Cutler is incorrect.
16.	C	Cutler is correct and Del is incorrect.
17.	D	Del is correct and Cutler is incorrect.

Chapter Six
The Audit Sampling Process

Chapter Six
The Audit Sampling Process

AUDIT SAMPLING DEFINED: Application of an audit procedure to less than 100% of the items within an account balance or class of transactions for the purpose of evaluating some characteristic of the balance or class.

The following questions apply to planning any audit sampling procedure, whether statistical or nonstatistical:

1. What is the objective of the test? What do you want to learn or be able to infer about the population?
2. What is to be sampled? Define what the population is under study.
3. What is the auditor looking for in the sample? Define what constitutes an error.
4. How is the population to be sampled? What is the sampling method and how are items selected in the sample?
5. How much is to be sampled (size of sample)?
6. What do the results mean? (Interpret results.)

TYPES OF SAMPLING

1. **Nonstatistical Sampling**—Involves the selection of items on a judgment basis. This method is sometimes referred to as judgment sampling.

2. **Statistical Sampling**—(a) Involves the selection of items according to a systematic, unbiased process; (b) statistical sampling helps the auditor design an efficient sample, measure the sufficiency of the evidence obtained and evaluate the sample results; (c) statistical sampling measures the sampling risks associated with the sampling procedure. This process is not employed with nonstatistical sampling.

GLOSSARY OF SAMPLING TERMS

Allowance for sampling risk (precision, sampling error)—A measure of the difference between a sample estimate and the corresponding population characteristic at a specified sampling risk.

Alpha risk—*See* risk of incorrect rejection and risk of underreliance on the internal control structure.

Attribute—Any characteristic that is either present or absent. In tests of controls the presence or absence of evidence of the application of a specified internal control structure procedure is sometimes referred to as an attribute.

Attributes sampling—Statistical sampling that reaches a conclusion about a population in terms of a rate of occurrence.

Audit risk—*See* ultimate risk.

Audit sampling—The application of an audit procedure to less than 100 percent of the items within an account balance or class of transactions for the purpose of evaluating some characteristic of the balance or class.

Beta risk—*See* risk of incorrect acceptance and risk of overreliance on the internal control structure.

Block sample (cluster sample)—A sample consisting of contiguous transactions.

Classical variables sampling—A sampling approach that measures sampling risk using the variation of the underlying characteristic of interest. This approach includes methods such as mean-per-unit, ratio estimation, and difference estimation.

CMA sampling—*See* probability-proportional-to-size sampling.

Confidence level (reliability level)—The complement of the applicable sampling risk (*see* risk of incorrect acceptance, risk of overreliance on the internal control structure, risk of incorrect rejection, risk of underreliance on the internal control structure).

Control risk—The auditor's assessment of the risk that error exceeding tolerable error that may occur will not be prevented or detected on a timely basis by the system of the internal control structure.

Detection risk—The auditor's assessment of the risk that his procedures will lead him to conclude the error exceeding tolerable error does not exist when in fact it does exist.

Difference estimation—A classical variables sampling technique that uses the average difference between audited amounts and individual recorded amounts to estimate the total audited amount of a population and an allowance for sampling risk.

Discovery sampling—A procedure for determining the sample size required to have a stipulated probability of observing at least one occurrence when the expected population occurrence rate is at a designated level.

Dollar-unit sampling—*See* probability-proportional-to-size sampling.

Dollar-value estimation—A decision model to estimate the dollar amount of the population.

Expansion factor—A factor used in the calculation of sample size in a probability-proportional-to-size sampling application if errors are expected.

Expected population deviation rate—An anticipation of the deviation rate in the entire population. It is used in determining an appropriate sample size for an attributes sample.

Field—*See* population.

Haphazard sample—A sample consisting of sampling units selected without any conscious bias, that is, without any special reason for including or omitting items from the sample. It does not consist of sampling units selected in a careless manner, and is selected in a manner that can be expected to be representative of the population.

Hypothesis testing—A decision model to test the reasonableness of an amount.

Inherent risk—The auditor's assessment of the susceptibility of an account balance or class of transactions to errors exceeding tolerable error before considering the operation of related internal control structure.

Logical unit—The balance or transaction that includes the selected dollar in a probability-proportional-to-size sample.

Mean-per-unit approach—A classical variables sampling technique that projects the sample average to the total population by multiplying the sample average by the total number of items in the population.

Nonsampling risk—All aspects of ultimate risk not due to sampling.

Nonstatistical sampling—A sampling technique for which the auditor considers sampling risk in evaluating an audit sample without using statistical theory to measure that risk.

Population (field, universe)—The items constituting the account balance or class of transactions of interest. The population excludes individually significant items that the auditor has decided to examine 100 percent or other items that will be tested separately.

Precision—*See* allowance for sampling risk.

Probability-proportional-to-size (PPS) sampling (dollar-unit sampling, CMA sampling)—A variables sampling procedure that uses attributes theory to express a conclusion in dollar amounts.

Random sample—A sample selected so that every combination of the same number of items in the population has an equal probability of selection.

Ratio estimation—A classical variables sampling technique that uses the ratio of audited amounts to recorded amounts in the sample to estimate the total dollar amount of the population and an allowance for sampling risk.

Reliability level—*See* confidence level.

Risk of incorrect acceptance (beta risk, Type II error)—The risk that the sample supports the conclusion that the recorded account balance is not materially misstated when it is materially misstated.

Risk of incorrect rejection (alpha risk, Type I error)—The risk that the sample supports the conclusion that the recorded account balance is materially misstated when it is not.

Risk of overreliance on the internal control structure (beta risk, Type II error)—The risk that the sample supports the auditor's planned degree of reliance on the control when the true compliance rate does not justify such reliance.

Risk of underreliance on the internal control structure (alpha risk, Type I error)—The risk that the sample does not support the auditor's planned degree of reliance on the control when the true compliance rate supports the reliance.

Sample—Items selected from a population to reach a conclusion about the population.

Sampling error—*See* allowance for sampling risk.

Sampling risk—The risk that the auditor's conclusion based on a sample might be different from the conclusion he would reach if the test were applied in the same way to the entire population. For tests of controls, sampling risk is the risk of overreliance on the internal control structure or the risk of underreliance on the internal control structure. For substantive testing, sampling risk is the risk of incorrect acceptance or the risk of incorrect rejection.

Sampling unit—Any of the individual elements, as defined by the auditor, that constitute the population.

Sequential sampling (stop-or-go sampling)—A sampling plan for which the sample is selected in several steps, with each step conditional on the results of the previous steps.

Standard deviation—A measure of the dispersion among the respective amounts of a particular characteristic as measured for all items in the population for which a sample estimate is developed.

Statistical sampling—Audit sampling that uses the laws of probability for selecting and evaluating a sample from a population for the purpose of reaching a conclusion about the population.

Stop-or-go sampling—*See* sequential sampling.

Stratification—Division of the population into relatively homogeneous groups.

Systematic sampling —- A method of selecting a sample in which every *n*th item is selected.

Tainting—In a probability-proportional-to-size sample, the proportion of error present in a logical unit. It is usually expressed as the ratio of the amount of error in the item to the item's recorded amount.

Tolerable error—An estimate of the maximum monetary error that may exist in an account balance or class of transactions, when combined with error in other accounts, without causing the financial statements to be materially misstated.

Tolerable rate—The maximum population rate of deviations from a prescribed control procedure that the auditor will tolerate without modifying the planned reliance on the internal control structure.

Type I error—*See* risk of incorrect rejection and risk of underreliance on the internal control structure.

Type II error—*See* risk of incorrect acceptance and risk of overreliance on the internal control structure.

Ultimate risk (audit risk)—A combination of the risk that material errors will occur in the accounting process used to develop the financial statements and the risk that any material errors that occur will not be detected by the auditor.

Universe—*See* population.

Variables sampling—Statistical sampling that reaches a conclusion on the monetary amounts of a population.

SAMPLING IN TESTS OF THE INTERNAL CONTROL STRUCTURE

Audit sampling for tests of controls (might also be referred to as compliance testing) generally involves the following eight considerations, and they apply equally to statistical and nonstatistical sampling plans.

1. **Consideration One**—Determining the objectives of the test.
    a. The objective of tests of controls is to provide reasonable assurance that internal control structure procedures are being applied as prescribed.
    b. Tests of controls are concerned with three questions:
        1) Where were the necessary procedures performed?
        2) How were they performed?
        3) By whom were they performed?
    c. The auditor tests controls he plans to rely on in determining the nature, timing and extent of substantive tests.

2. **Consideration Two**—Defining the deviation conditions.
    a. For tests of controls, a deviation is a departure from the prescribed internal control structure procedure.
    b. Based upon the auditor's knowledge of the internal control structure, the auditor should identify the characteristics that would indicate compliance with a control procedure on which he plans to rely. The auditor then defines the possible deviation conditions.

3. **Consideration Three**—Defining the population.
    a. Consists of the items constituting the account balance or class of transactions of interest.
    b. The auditor should determine that the population from which the sample is drawn is appropriate for the specific audit objective (i.e., if the auditor wishes to test that all shipments are billed, it would be inappropriate to test items that have been billed, because some items might have been shipped but not billed).

c. Once the population is defined, the auditor should then define the period covered by the test.

    1) Per GAAS, "Tests of controls ... ideally should be applied to transactions executed throughout the period under audit because of the general sampling concept that the items to be examined should be selected from the entire set of data to which the resulting conclusions are to be applied."

    2) In some cases it might be more efficient to test transactions for the period from the beginning of the year to an interim date. This procedure is sufficient as long as the auditor is aware that conditions may change during the interim period and he should design procedures to detect such changes (i.e., inquiry of client personnel, results of substantive tests, etc.).

d. Within the population the auditor must define the sampling unit.

    1) A sampling unit is any of the individual elements constituting the population (i.e., a document, an entry, or a line item in a report).

    2) The sampling unit should be defined in terms of the control procedure being tested. For example, if the objective of the test is to determine whether disbursements have been authorized, the sampling unit may be defined as the authorized voucher.

e. It is also necessary for the auditor to consider the completeness of the population.

    1) The auditor will actually select items (sampling units) from a physical representation of the population (i.e., a printout of customer accounts receivable).

    2) It is important that the physical representation includes the entire population because any conclusions based upon the sample related only to the physical representation. Thus, if the physical representation and the population differ, the auditor may make erroneous conclusions about the population.

4. **Consideration Four**—Determining the method of selecting the sample.

a. Sample items should be selected in a way that the sample can be expected to be representative of the population. Thus, all items in the population must have the same opportunity to be selected.

b. The various selection methods are:

    1) **Random-number sampling**—A method where every sampling unit has the same probability of being selected as every other sampling unit in the population. This approach is appropriate for both statistical and nonstatistical sampling.

    2) **Systematic sampling**—In this method the auditor determines a uniform interval by dividing the number of physical units by the sample size. A starting point is selected in the first interval and one item is selected from the population at each of the uniform intervals from the starting point. This method can be used in both statistical and nonstatistical sampling.

    3) **Block sampling**—This method consists of contiguous transactions. For example, for invoices numbered 1 through 1000, the auditor may select five blocks of ten consecutive invoice numbers. Generally used with nonstatistical sampling.

    4) **Haphazard sampling**—Selection of sampling units without any conscious bias, thus there is no special reason for including or excluding items from the sample. Used with nonstatistical sampling.

5. **Consideration Five**—Determining the sample size.

The following five factors must be considered by the auditor when determining the sample size:

a. Consider the acceptable risk of overreliance on the internal control structure.

    1) The risk of **overreliance** on the internal control structure is the risk that the sample supports the auditor's planned degree of reliance on internal control when the true compliance rate for the population does not. As opposed to overreliance, the risk of **underreliance** on the internal control structure is the risk that the sample does **not** support the auditor's planned degree of reliance on the control when the true compliance rate of the population does.

    2) The risk of underreliance causes the auditor to do **more** substantive testing than he ordinarily would.

    3) Because the test of controls is the primary source of evidence of whether a control procedure is being applied as prescribed, the auditor generally wishes to obtain a high degree of assurance that the conclusions reached on the basis of a sample would not differ from the conclusions that would be reached if the test were applied to the population. Therefore, the auditor should allow for a low level of risk for **overreliance**.

    4) There is an inverse relationship between the risk of overreliance on the internal control structure and sample size.

b. Consider the tolerable rate.
1) The tolerable rate is the maximum rate of deviation from a prescribed control that an auditor is willing to accept without altering the planned reliance on internal control.
2) There is an inverse relationship between the tolerable rate and the sample size.
c. Consider the expected population deviation rate.
1) The auditor may control the risk of underreliance on internal control by adjusting the sample size for his assessment of the deviation rate he expects to find in the population.
2) The expected population deviation rate should not equal or exceed the tolerable rate. If so, the auditor would omit tests of controls and perform substantive tests of 100% on the account.
3) There is a direct relationship between the expected deviation rate and sample size.
d. Consider the effect of population size.
The size of the population has very little effect on the determination of sample size (i.e., it is generally appropriate to treat any population over 5,000 sampling units as if it were infinite).
e. Consider a sequential or a fixed sample size approach.
1) **Fixed sample size plan**—The auditor examines a single sample of a specified size.
2) **Sequential sampling plan**—The auditor samples in steps; each step is conditional on the results of the previous step.

6. **Consideration Six**—Performing the sampling plan.
a. After the sampling plan has been designed, the auditor selects the sample and examines the selected items to determine if they contain deviations from the prescribed control procedure.
b. The auditor may decide to stop the testing before completion if a large number of deviations are identified during the initial phase of the test. The auditor may conclude that even if he were to complete the test and no additional deviations are found, the sample would not support the planned reliance on the internal control structure.

7. **Consideration Seven**—Evaluating sample results.
Whether the sample is statistical or nonstatistical, the auditor would compile the sample results and apply judgment in evaluating the results and reach an overall conclusion on reliability. The steps involved in this process are as follows:
a. Calculate the Deviation Rate.
1) Computed as follows:

$$\frac{\text{Deviations}}{\text{Sample Size}} = \text{Deviation Rate}$$

2) The deviation rate is the auditor's best estimate of the deviation rate in the population.
b. Consider sampling risk.
1) Sampling risk is the risk that the estimate of the population deviation rate is less than the tolerable rate for the population and **that conclusion is incorrect**!
2) If an auditor is using statistical sampling, he can estimate the sampling risk inherent in the sampling process.
3) If an auditor is using nonstatistical sampling, sampling risk cannot be measured directly, and the auditor must use professional judgment in evaluating sampling risk.
c. Consider the qualitative aspects of the deviations.
In addition to evaluating the quantitative aspects of the deviations, the auditor should also consider the qualitative (nature of deviation) aspects of the deviations. As such, an irregularity (intentional) deviation would be viewed as qualitatively more serious than an error (unintentional) deviation.

8. **Consideration Eight**—Documenting the sampling procedure.
   a) The auditor must document the work performed during any phase of the audit and the documentation of tests of controls is no exception.
   b) Some items that may be included in the workpaper documentation include:
      1) A description of the control being tested
      2) A definition of the population and the sampling unit
      3) A definition of what would constitute a deviation
      4) The method of sample size determination
      5) The method of sample selection
      6) Overall evaluation of the test and conclusions reached.

SAMPLING IN SUBSTANTIVE TESTS OF DETAILS

The objective of substantive tests is to obtain evidence to support an opinion that the balances of all accounts "presents fairly in accordance with GAAP." Depending upon the conclusions reached in the auditor's study and evaluation of the internal control structure, the auditor may decide to apply audit sampling to test less than 100% of the monetary value of an account. The following eight considerations are applicable to the use of sampling in substantive tests of details. The considerations apply equally to statistical as well as nonstatistical sampling.

1. **Consideration One**—Determining the audit objective of the test.
   a. A sampling plan for substantive testing may be designed to do either of the following:
      1) Test the reasonableness of an amount (referred to as hypothesis testing). An example of this might be to test the balance of accounts receivable.
      2) To make an independent estimate of same amount (referred to as dollar-value estimation). The objective of dollar-value estimation is to develop an original estimate of an amount, for example, estimating LIFO inventory values when the client has been employing FIFO valuation.
      3) Hypothesis testing is primarily used by an auditor when examining financial statements, since the balances of accounts are known.

2. **Consideration Two**—Defining the population.
   a. The population consists of the items constituting the account balance or class of transactions.
   b. The auditor should determine that the population that the sample is drawn from is appropriate for the specific audit objective.
   c. The auditor would then define the sampling unit.
      1) A sampling unit is any of the individual elements that constitute the population.
      2) The definition of a sampling unit depends on the nature of the audit procedures being applied and may be a customer account balance, an individual transaction or part of a transaction, etc.
   d. The auditor then determines the completeness of the population.
      1) The auditor selects a sample from a physical representation of the population, for example, an aged trial balance of accounts receivable.
      2) Before selecting the sample, the auditor should conduct tests to determine that the physical representation actually represents the entire population. For example, in the case of accounts receivable, the auditor would reconcile the aged trial balance to the general ledger.

3. **Consideration Three**—Choosing an audit sampling technique.
   a) The auditor would choose between nonstatistical and statistical sampling techniques.
   b) The most common statistical approaches are classical variables sampling and probability-proportion-to-size (PPS) sampling. These techniques are discussed beginning on page 6-10.

4. **Consideration Four**—Determining the sample size.
   a. An important consideration in determining the sample size is the variation of the items in a population.
      1) A measure of variation in the population is called the standard deviation.
      2) Generally speaking, the larger the variation of items in the population, the larger the sample size.
   b. The auditor is concerned with two aspects of sampling risk when performing substantive tests of details.
      1) The risk of incorrect acceptance:
         a) Risk that the sample supports a conclusion that the recorded account balance is not materially misstated when it is misstated.
         b) In assessing this risk the auditor considers (1) the level of **audit risk** that he is willing to accept, and (2) the level of reliance to be placed on internal control.
      2) The risk of incorrect rejection:
         a) The risk of incorrect rejection is related to the efficiency of the audit.
         b) The risk of concluding that a balance is incorrect when it is in fact correct. This would lead to the auditor performing more work than was necessary.
         c) There is an inverse relationship between the sample size and the amount of risk of incorrect rejection the auditor is willing to accept.
   c. The auditor must consider, in planning a sample, the amount of monetary error (tolerable risk) that could exist in the population without the amount being materially misstated.
   d. In determining sample size, the auditor considers the rate and amount of error expected in the population. As the estimate approaches the tolerable error, the auditor would consider increasing the sample size because more information is needed from the sample.

5. **Consideration Five**—Determine the method for selecting the sample.
   a. The auditor should select the sample in a way that the sample will be representative of the population.
   b. See pages 6-9 through 6-11 for methods of selection that involve statistical sampling techniques.

6. **Consideration Six**—Performing the sampling plan.
   a. Appropriate audit procedure should be applied to each item in the sample.
   b. The selection of a particular audit procedure is based upon the audit objective under review. For example, in auditing for proper value in accounts receivable, the auditor would use confirmation.

7. **Consideration Seven**—Evaluating the sample results.
   a. The auditor must project the error results in the sample to the population from which the sample was drawn.
   b. The auditor should also consider the qualitative aspects of the errors in reaching an overall conclusion about the population. These would include:
      1) the nature and cause of the misstatements, and
      2) the possible relationship of the misstatements to other phases of the audit.

8. **Consideration Eight**—Documenting the sample procedure.
   a. The auditor should appropriately document the sampling procedures and results obtained.
   b. Generally this would involve documenting the first seven considerations discussed above.

APPLICATION OF STATISTICAL SAMPLING IN THE AUDIT PROCESS

I. Types of Statistical Sampling Plans

A. Attributes Sampling
   1. Used to reach a conclusion about a population in terms of rate of occurrence.
   2. Used most commonly in auditing to test the rate of deviation from a prescribed internal control.
   3. The dollar amount of the transaction is not important, but rather the rate of occurrence of, or deviation from, a prescribed control.

B. Variables Sampling
   1. Used to reach conclusions about a population in terms of dollar amount.
   2. Used to answer either of the following questions:
      a) How much? (i.e., dollar value estimation).
      b) Is the account materially misstated? (i.e., by hypothesis testing).
   3. Principally used in substantive testing.

II. Statistical Sampling Basics

A. Sample results may not be indicative of the true population (sampling risk) whether the auditor is using attribute or variables sampling, in order to measure and control sampling error by calculating precision and confidence levels.
   1. **Precision**—Range within which the true value of the population characteristic being measured is likely to lie. The range is set by plus and minus limits. For example, in attribute sampling, an auditor determines that there is a 3% error rate in his sample, +/- 1%. Thus, the auditor concludes that the true error rate of the population is between 2% and 4%. In variables sampling, the precision limits would be set in terms of dollars and become the limits of the tolerable error that the auditor will accept. Less precision means a wider interval. More precision means a narrower interval.
   2. **Confidence level**—Indicates the percentage of time the true population characteristics lie with the specified precision interval. Confidence level is the **reliability** (synonymous with confidence level) of the sample. The inverse of the confidence level (reliability) is risk. Thus, if we are 95% confident, then we are accepting a 5% risk. There is an inverse relationship between precision and reliability.

AS PRECISION <u>DECREASES</u>, CONFIDENCE LEVEL <u>INCREASES</u>.

   3. **Sample size**—Sample size has a direct effect upon precision and confidence level. As the sample size approaches the total population, confidence level and degree of precision are increased.

B. Statistical approach to tests of controls
   1. Precision and confidence level
      a) The auditor is usually concerned with the upper precision limit, since the concern is that deviations do not exceed an acceptable level. This level is considered to be the **maximum tolerable deviation rate.**
      b) The risk of overreliance on a control procedure is controlled through the specified confidence level. The risk of overreliance is the complement of the confidence level.
      c) Tables have been developed with which the auditor can easily determine the sample size given the expected population deviation rate and desired precision and confidence levels. The following table is an example of such for a 95% confidence level (5% risk of overreliance):

TABLE 1

Statistical Sample Sizes for Compliance Testing
Five-Percent Risk of Overreliance
(with number of expected errors in parentheses)

Expected Population Deviation Rate	Tolerable Rate										
	2%	3%	4%	5%	6%	7%	8%	9%	10%	15%	20%
0.00%	149(0)	99(0)	74(0)	59(0)	49(0)	42(0)	36(0)	32(0)	29(0)	19(0)	14(0)
.25	236(1)	157(1)	117(1)	93(1)	78(1)	66(1)	58(1)	51(1)	46(1)	30(1)	22(1)
.50	*	157(1)	117(1)	93(1)	78(1)	66(1)	58(1)	51(1)	46(1)	30(1)	22(1)
.75	*	208(2)	117(1)	93(1)	78(1)	66(1)	58(1)	51(1)	46(1)	30(1)	22(1)
1.00	*	*	156(2)	93(1)	78(1)	66(1)	58(1)	51(1)	46(1)	30(1)	22(1)
1.25	*	*	156(2)	124(2)	78(1)	66(1)	58(1)	51(1)	46(1)	30(1)	22(1)
1.50	*	*	192(3)	124(2)	103(2)	66(1)	58(1)	51(1)	46(1)	30(1)	22(1)
1.75	*	*	227(4)	153(3)	103(2)	88(2)	77(2)	51(1)	46(1)	30(1)	22(1)
2.00	*	*	*	181(4)	127(3)	88(2)	77(2)	68(2)	46(1)	30(1)	22(1)
2.25	*	*	*	208(5)	127(3)	88(2)	77(2)	68(2)	61(2)	30(1)	22(1)
2.50	*	*	*	*	150(4)	109(3)	77(2)	68(2)	61(2)	30(1)	22(1)
2.75	*	*	*	*	173(5)	109(3)	95(3)	68(2)	61(2)	30(1)	22(1)
3.00	*	*	*	*	195(6)	129(4)	95(3)	84(3)	61(2)	30(1)	22(1)
3.25	*	*	*	*	*	148(5)	112(4)	84(3)	61(2)	30(1)	22(1)
3.50	*	*	*	*	*	167(6)	112(4)	84(3)	76(3)	40(2)	22(1)
3.75	*	*	*	*	*	185(7)	129(5)	100(4)	76(3)	40(2)	22(1)
4.00	*	*	*	*	*	*	146(6)	100(4)	89(4)	40(2)	22(1)
5.00	*	*	*	*	*	*	*	158(8)	116(6)	40(2)	30(2)
6.00	*	*	*	*	*	*	*	*	179(11)	50(3)	30(2)
7.00	*	*	*	*	*	*	*	*	*	68(5)	37(3)

*Sample size is too large to be cost-effective for most audit applications.

NOTE: This table assumes a large population. For a discussion of the effect of population size on sample size, see chapter 2.

Using this table for an expected population deviation rate of .5% and a maximum tolerable deviation rate of 6%, the auditor would use a sample size of 78 and would expect one deviation in the sample.

C. Discovery sampling
   1. Used when the auditor expects a low error rate. Thus, it is used for testing for irregularities (intentional errors).
   2. In applying this method, the auditor can determine, given a specific level of confidence, say 95%, that a sample will include at least one error. If the error rate in the sample is less than one, then the auditor has at least 95% confidence that the error rate in the population is within tolerable limits.
   3. To illustrate, assume an auditor is concerned about fraudulent transactions involving writeoffs of accounts receivable. By reference to the table above for 95% confidence level, the auditor would use an expected deviation rate of 0% and assume some population deviation rate, say 2%. Based upon this, the auditor would select a sample size of 149 items. If the auditor does not find a fraudulent transaction in the sample, then he is 95% sure there are not more than 2% errors in the population.

D. Nonstatistical sampling—The use of nonstatistical sampling involves the use of judgment in applying the factors discussed on pages 6-8 through 6-10. The following table summarizes the effect of various factors on the determination of sample size in judgment sampling:

Factor	Effect on sample size
Tolerable rate	
Increases	Smaller
Decreases	Larger
Risk of overreliance on Internal Control	
Increase	Smaller
Decrease	Larger
Expected population deviation rate	
Increase	Larger
Decrease	Smaller
Population size	No effect

III. Substantive Tests of Details

A. Classical variables sampling
   1. Statistical sampling that reaches a conclusion on the monetary amounts of a population.
   2. Types:
      a) *Mean-per-unit approach*—Use of this method involves the auditor making estimates of the population value by using the audited sample amount to project the population value. For example, if an auditor selects a sample of 200 items from a population of 1,000 items and determines that, on the average, the cost of each item in the sample is $100, then the value of the population is estimated to be $100,000 ($100 × 1,000).
      b) *Difference estimation approach*—The use of this method involves the auditor calculating the difference between audited amounts and book amounts and projecting that amount to the population. For example, if the average difference between book amounts and audited amounts for a sample of 100 items is $10, then the auditor infers that the difference in the population of 10,000 items to be $100,000 ($10 × 10,000). The amount so calculated is compared to previous estimates of materiality (tolerable error) to determine if the account is fairly stated or not.
      c) *Ratio approach*—Use of this method involves the auditor calculating the ratio between the sum of the audited amounts and the sum of the recorded amounts and projecting this ratio to the population. For example, should the auditor determine that the ratio of audited value to book value of a sample to be 1.10 (audit $110,000; book $100,000) and the book value of the population to be $500,000, then the auditor would infer that the audited value of the population would be $550,000 (1.10 × $500,000). Again the auditor would consider materiality.

B. Probability-proportional-to-size sampling
   1. Use of this method gives each individual dollar in the population an equal chance of selection.
   2. Helps the auditor to direct audit effort toward large balances or transactions because every dollar has an equal chance of being selected; items having more dollars have a greater chance of being selected. Each balance or transaction in the population has a probability of selection proportional to its recorded dollar amount.
   3. Selecting a sample:
      a) Divide the population into equal groups of dollars (sampling interval).
      b) Select a random number between one and the sampling interval.
      c) The auditor then selects the first sampling unit (random number in b) above) and then adds the sampling interval to the random start to obtain each successive sampling unit.
      d) *Example:*
      Sampling interval $5,000
      Random start 2,000 dollars
      Sample then becomes 2000th, 7000th, 12000th dollars in the population.

AUDIT SAMPLING (SAS No. 39)

Audit sampling is the application of an audit procedure to less than 100 percent of the items within an account balance or class of transactions for the purpose of evaluating some characteristic of the balance or class. This Statement provides guidance for planning, performing, and evaluating audit samples.

There are two general approaches to audit sampling: nonstatistical and statistical. Both approaches require that the auditor use professional judgment in planning, performing, and evaluating a sample and in relating the evidential matter produced by the sample to other evidential matter when forming a conclusion about the related account balance or class of transactions.

The third standard of field work states, "Sufficient competent evidential matter is to be obtained through inspection, observation, inquiries, and confirmations to afford a reasonable basis for an opinion regarding the financial statements under examination." Either approach to audit sampling, when properly applied, can provide sufficient evidential matter.

Some degree of uncertainty is implicit in the concept of "a reasonable basis for an opinion." The justification for accepting some uncertainty arises from the relationship between such factors as the cost and time required to examine all of the data and the adverse consequences of possible erroneous decisions based on the conclusions resulting from examining only a sample of the data.

For purposes of this Statement, the uncertainty inherent in applying auditing procedures will be referred to as **audit risk**. Audit risk is a combination of the risk that material errors will occur in the accounting process used to develop the financial statements and the risk that any material errors that occur will not be detected by the auditor. The risk of these adverse events occurring jointly can be viewed as the product of the respective individual risks. The auditor may rely on the internal control structure to reduce the first risk and on substantive tests (tests of details of transactions and balances and analytical review procedures) to reduce the second risk.

Audit risk includes both uncertainties due to sampling and uncertainties due to factors other than sampling. These aspects of ultimate risk are sampling risk and nonsampling risk, respectively.

Sampling risk arises from the possibility that, when a test of controls or a substantive test is restricted to a sample, the auditor's conclusions may be different from the conclusions he would reach if the test were applied in the same way to all items in the account balance or class of transactions.

Nonsampling risk includes all the aspects of ultimate risk that are not due to sampling. Nonsampling risk includes the possibility of selecting audit procedures that are not appropriate to achieve the specific objective.

The auditor should apply professional judgment in assessing sampling risk. In performing substantive tests of details the auditor is concerned with two aspects of sampling risk:
- *The risk of incorrect acceptance* is the risk that the sample supports the conclusion that the recorded account balance is not materially misstated when it is materially misstated.
- *The risk of incorrect rejection* is the risk that the sample supports the conclusion that the recorded account balance is materially misstated when it is not materially misstated.

The auditor is also concerned with two aspects of sampling risk in performing tests of controls of the internal control structure:
- *The risk of overreliance* on the internal control structure is the risk that the sample supports the auditor's planned degree of reliance on the control when the true compliance rate does not justify such reliance.
- *The risk of underreliance* on the internal control structure is the risk that the sample does not support the auditor's planned degree of reliance on the control when the true compliance rate supports such reliance.

Sampling in Substantive Tests of Details

Planning Samples

Planning involves developing a strategy for conducting an audit of financial statements. For general guidance on planning.

When planning a particular sample for a substantive test of details, the auditor should consider
- The relationship of the sample to the relevant audit objective.
- Preliminary estimates of materiality levels.
- The auditor's allowable risk of incorrect acceptance.
- Characteristics of the population; that is, the items comprising the account balance or class of transactions of interest.

When planning a particular sample, the auditor should consider the specific audit objective to be achieved and should determine that the audit procedure, or combination of procedures, to be applied will achieve that objective. The auditor should determine that the population from which he draws the sample is appropriate for the specific audit objective.

When planning a sample for a substantive test of details, the auditor should consider how much monetary error in the related account balance or class of transactions may exist without causing the financial statements to be materially misstated. This maximum monetary error for the balance or class is called *tolerable error* for the sample. Tolerable error is a planning concept and is related to the auditor's preliminary estimates of materiality levels in such a way that tolerable error, combined for the entire audit plan, does not exceed those estimates.

The second standard of field work states, "The auditor should obtain a sufficient understanding of the internal control structure to plan the audit and to determine the nature, timing, and extent of tests to be performed." The second standard of field work recognizes that the extent of substantive tests required to obtain sufficient evidential matter under the third standard should vary inversely with the auditor's reliance on the internal control structure. These standards taken together imply that the combination of the auditor's reliance on the internal control structure and his reliance on his substantive tests should provide a reasonable basis for his opinion, although the portion of reliance derived from the respective sources may vary.

To determine the number of items to be selected in a sample for a particular substantive test of details, the auditor should consider the tolerable error, the allowable risk of incorrect acceptance, and the characteristics of the population.

The auditor should project the error results of the sample to the items from which the sample was selected. There are several acceptable ways to project errors from a sample. For example, an auditor may have selected a sample of every twentieth item (50 items) from a population containing one thousand items. If he discovered overstatement errors of $3,000 in that sample, the auditor could project a $60,000 overstatement by dividing the amount of error in the sample by the fraction of total items from the population included in the sample. The auditor should add that projection to the errors discovered in any items examined 100 percent. This total projected error should be compared with the tolerable error for the account balance or class of transactions, and appropriate consideration should be given to sampling risk. If the total projected error is less than tolerable error for the account balance or class of transactions, the auditor should consider the risk that such a result might be obtained even though the true monetary error for the population exceeds tolerable error.

In addition to the evaluation of the frequency and amounts of monetary misstatements, consideration should be given to the qualitative aspects of the errors. These include (a) the nature and cause of misstatements, such as whether they are differences in principle or in application, are errors or irregularities, or are due to misunderstanding of instructions or to carelessness, and (b) the possible relationship of the misstatements to other phases of the audit. The discovery of an irregularity ordinarily requires a broader consideration of possible implications than does the discovery of an error.

Sampling in Tests of Controls of the Internal Control Structure

Planning Samples

When planning a particular audit sample for a control testing, the auditor should consider

- The relationship of the sample to the objective of the test of controls.
- The maximum rate of deviations from prescribed control procedures that would support his planned reliance.
- The auditor's allowable risk of overreliance.
- Characteristics of the population; that is, the items comprising the account balance or class of transactions of interest.

When designing samples for the purpose of tests of controls with internal control structure procedures that leave an audit trail of documentary evidence, the auditor ordinarily should plan to evaluate compliance in terms of deviations from (or compliance with) pertinent control procedures, as to either the rate of such deviations or the monetary amount of the related transactions. In this context, pertinent control procedures are ones that, had they not been included in the design of the internal control structure, would have adversely affected the auditor's preliminary evaluation of the system.

The auditor should assess the maximum rate of deviations from a prescribed control procedure that he would be willing to accept without altering his planned reliance on the control. This is the *tolerable rate*. In assessing the tolerable rate, the auditor should consider the relationship of procedural deviations to (a) the accounting records being tested, (b) any related internal control structure procedures, and (c) the purpose of the auditor's evaluation.

Samples taken for tests if controls are intended to provide a basis for the auditor to conclude whether internal control structure procedures are being applied as prescribed. Because the test of controls is the primary source of evidence of whether the procedure is being applied as prescribed, the auditor should allow for a low level of risk of overreliance.

To determine the number of items to be selected for a particular sample for a control test, the auditor should consider the tolerable rate of deviation from the control(s) being tested, based on the planned degree of reliance; the likely rate of deviations; and the allowable risk of overreliance on the internal control structure. An auditor applies professional judgment to relate these factors in determining the appropriate sample size.

Auditing procedures that are appropriate to achieve the objective of the tests of controls should be applied to each sample item. If the auditor is not able to apply the planned audit procedures or appropriate alternative procedures to selected items, he should consider the reasons for this limitation and he should ordinarily consider those selected items to be deviations from the procedures for the purpose of evaluating the sample.

The deviation rate in the sample is the auditor's best estimate of the deviation rate in the population from which it was selected. If the estimated deviation rate is less than the tolerable rate for the population, the auditor should consider the risk that such a result might be obtained even though the true deviation rate for the population exceeds the tolerable rate for the population.

In addition to the evaluation of the frequency of deviations from pertinent procedures, consideration should be given to the qualitative aspects of the deviations. These include (a) the nature and cause of the deviations, such as whether they are errors or irregularities or are due to misunderstanding of instructions or to carelessness, and (b) the possible relationship of the deviations to other phases of the audit. The discovery of an irregularity ordinarily requires a broader consideration of possible implications than does the discovery of an error.

Dual-Purpose Samples

In some circumstances the auditor may design a sample that will be used for dual purposes: testing compliance with a control procedure that provides documentary evidence of performance, and testing whether the recorded monetary amount of transactions is correct. In general, an auditor planning to use a dual-purpose sample would have made a preliminary assessment that there is an acceptably low risk that the rate of compliance deviations in the population exceeds the tolerable rate. The size of a sample designed for dual purposes should be the larger of the samples that would otherwise have been designed for the two separate purposes. In evaluating such tests, deviations from pertinent procedures and monetary errors should be evaluated separately using the risk levels applicable for the respective purposes.

Selecting a Sampling Approach

Either a nonstatistical or statistical approach to audit sampling, when properly applied, can provide sufficient evidential matter.

Statistical sampling helps the auditor (a) to design an efficient sample, (b) to measure the sufficiency of the evidential matter obtained, and (c) to evaluate the sample results. By using statistical theory, the auditor can quantify sampling risk to assist himself in limiting it to a level he considers acceptable. However, statistical sampling involves additional costs of training auditors, designing individual samples to meet the statistical requirements, and selecting the items to be examined. Because either nonstatistical or statistical sampling can provide sufficient evidential matter, the auditor chooses between them after considering their relative cost and effectiveness in the circumstances.

Table 2

Factors Influencing Sample Sizes for a Substantive Test of Details in Sample Planning

Factor	Conditions Leading to Smaller sample size	Conditions Leading to Larger Sample Size	Related factor for substantive sample planning
a. Reliance on internal accounting controls.	Greater reliance on internal accounting controls.	Lesser reliance on internal accounting controls.	Allowable risk of incorrect acceptance.
b. Reliance on other substantive tests related to same account balance or class of transactions (including analytical review procedures and other relevant substantive tests).	Substantial reliance to be placed on other relevant substantive tests.	Little or no reliance to be placed on other relevant substantive tests.	Allowance risk of incorrect acceptance.
c. Measure of tolerable error for a specific account.	Larger measure of tolerable error.	Smaller measure of tolerable error.	Tolerable error.
d. Expected size and frequency of errors.	Smaller errors or lower frequency.	Larger errors or higher frequency.	Assessment of population characteristics.
e. Number of items in population.	Virtually no effect on sample size unless population is very small.	Virtually no effect on sample size unless population is very small.	

AUDIT RISK AND MATERIALITY IN CONDUCTING AN AUDIT (SAS No. 47)

Audit Risk Model

$$AR = IR \times CR \times DR$$

where:

AR	=	Audit Risk
IR	=	Inherent Risk
CR	=	Control Risk
DR	=	Detection Risk

Audit Risk

1. The risk that the auditor may unknowingly fail to modify his opinion on a set of financial statements that are materially misstated.
2. The auditor's opinion that states "the financial statements present fairly in conformity with GAAP" implicitly means that the statements taken as a whole do not contain material errors or irregularities.
   a. errors—unintentional mistakes
   b. fraud—intentional misrepresentations
3. An auditor's consideration of materiality is a matter of professional judgment. The auditor should consider audit risk and materiality in both (a) planning the audit and (b) evaluating whether the financial statements taken as a whole are presented fairly.

Planning the Audit

1. The auditor should consider audit risk and materiality in (a) planning the audit and designing audit procedures and (b) evaluating whether the financial statements taken as a whole are presented fairly in accordance with GAAP.
2. Considerations at the Financial Statement Level
   a. At the financial statement level the auditor should establish an overall materiality level for each statement giving appropriate consideration to the interrelationship of the statements.
   b. The auditor plans for the lowest aggregate level of errors that could be material to any one of the statements. For example, if the auditor concludes that $100,000 is material to the income statement, and that $200,000 is material to the balance sheet, the auditor should plan to detect errors or irregularities of $100,000.
   c. Generally the auditor looks for quantitative errors; however, he should also be aware that qualitative factors are also important (i.e., the type of error and its potential effect even though not material in dollar value).
3. Considerations at the Individual Account Balance or Class-of-Transaction-Level
   a. There is an inverse relationship between audit risk and materiality.
   b. As it relates to account balances, or classes of transactions, audit risk is a combination of three component risks.
      1. **Inherent Risk**—the susceptibility of an account balance or class-of-transactions to an error that could be material.
      2. **Control Risk**—the risk that an error that could occur in an account balance or class of transactions will not be prevented or detected on a timely basis by the client's system of internal control.
      3. **Detection Risk**—the risk that an auditor's procedures will lead him to conclude that an error in an account balance does not exist, when in fact such an error does exist.
         - Detection risk is a function of the effectiveness of an auditing procedure and its application by the auditor.
         - Detection risk arises partly from uncertainties that exist when an auditor does not examine 100% of an account balance, and partly because of uncertainties that exist even if the auditor were to examine every item. These risks are referred to as:
         a) **Sampling risk**—relates to selection of items in a sample that are not representative of the population.

b) **Nonsampling risk**—related to the misinterpretation of facts and is controlled through proper audit planning, supervision, and firm quality control review.
- Detection risk bears an inverse relationship to inherent and control risk.

Evaluating Audit Findings

1. The auditor should aggregate errors that the entity has not corrected in a way that enables him to consider whether in relation to individual amounts, subtotals, or totals in the statements, they materially misstate the financial statements taken as a whole.

   a. An aggregating procedure generally used is an "adjustment passed (not made) schedule". This schedule allows the auditor to determine the aggregate effect of seemingly immaterial adjustments on the financial statements by aggregating them.

   b. In evaluating the effect of errors on the financial statements, the auditor should consider
   - **Likely errors** - best estimate of errors in an account balance, and
   - **Known errors** - the actual errors discovered in account balances
   - When an auditor uses Audit Sampling to test an account balance or class of transactions, the auditor projects the amount of **known errors** identified in the sample to the population balance (projected error). The projected error contributes to the auditors assessment of the **likely error** in the account balance.

   c. The risk of material misstatements in the financial statements is generally greater when account balances include accounting estimates rather than factual data.

2. If the auditor concludes, based upon his accumulation of sufficient evidential matter, that the aggregation of likely errors causes the financial statements to be materially misstated, he should request management to eliminate the material misstatement.

   a. If the material misstatement is not eliminated, he should issue a qualified or adverse opinion.

   b. If the aggregate of likely errors does not cause the statements to be materially misstated, the risk (audit risk) that the financial statements are in fact misstated increases. If the auditor believes that this causes the risk to be unacceptably high, he should perform additional auditing procedures to reduce audit risk to an acceptable level.

Chapter Six - Questions
The Audit Sampling Process

Items 1 through 5 apply to an examination by Robert Lambert, CPA, of the financial statements of Rainbow Manufacturing Corporation for the year ended December 31, 19X3. Rainbow manufactures two products: Product A and Product B. Product A requires raw materials which have a very low per-item cost, and Product B requires raw materials which have a very high per-item cost. Raw materials for both products are stored in a single warehouse. In 19X2, Rainbow established the total value of raw materials stored in the warehouse by physically inventorying an unrestricted random sample of items selected without replacement.

Mr. Lambert is evaluating the statistical validity of alternative sampling plans Rainbow is considering for 19X3. Lambert knows the size of the 19X2 sample and that Rainbow did **not** use stratified sampling in 19X2. Assumptions about the population, variability, specified precision (confidence interval), and specified reliability (confidence level) for a possible 19X3 sample are given in each of the following five items. You are to indicate in each case the effect upon the size of the 19X3 sample as compared to the 19X2 sample. Each of the five cases is independent of the other four and is to be considered separately.

1. Rainbow wants to use stratified sampling in 19X3 (the total population will be divided into two strata, one each for the raw materials for Product A and Product B). Compared to 19X2, the population size of the raw materials inventory is approximately the same, and the variability of the items in the inventory is approximately the same. The specified precision and specified reliability are to remain the same. Under these assumptions, the required sample size for 19X3 should be
a. Larger than the 19X2 sample size.
b. Equal to the 19X2 sample size.
c. Smaller than the 19X2 sample size.
d. Of a size that is indeterminate based upon the information given.

2. Rainbow wants to use stratified sampling in 19X3. Compared to 19X2, the population size of the raw materials inventory is approximately the same, and the variability of the items in the inventory is approximately the same. Rainbow specified the same precision but desires to change the specified reliability from 90% to 95%. Under these assumptions, the required sample size for 19X3 should be

a. Larger than the 19X2 sample size.
b. Equal to the 19X2 sample size.
c. Smaller than the 19X2 sample size.
d. Of a size that is indeterminate based upon the information given.

3. Rainbow wants to use unrestricted random sampling without replacement in 19X3. Compared to 19X2, the population size of the raw-materials inventory is approximately the same, and the variability of the items in the inventory is approximately the same. Rainbow specifies the same precision but desires to change the specified reliability from 90% to 95%. Under these assumptions, the required sample size for 19X3 should be
a. Larger than the 19X2 sample size.
b. Equal to the 19X2 sample size.
c. Smaller than the 19X2 sample size.
d. Of a size that is indeterminate based upon the information given.

4. Rainbow wants to use unrestricted random sampling without replacement in 19X3. Compared to 19X2, the population size of the raw-materials inventory has increased, and the variability of the item in the inventory has increased. The specified precision and specified reliability are to remain the same. Under these assumptions, the required sample size for 19X3 should be
a. Larger than the 19X2 sample size.
b. Equal to the 19X2 sample size.
c. Smaller than the 19X2 sample size.
d. Of a size that is indeterminate based upon the information given.

5. Rainbow wants to use unrestricted random sampling without replacement in 19X3. Compared to 19X2, the population size of the raw-materials inventory has increased, but the variability of the items in the inventory has decreased. The specified precision and specified reliability are to remain the same. Under these assumptions, the required sample size for 19X3 should be
a. Larger than the 19X2 sample size.
b. Equal to the 19X2 sample size.
c. Smaller than the 19X2 sample size.
d. Of a size that is indeterminate based upon the information given.

6. As the specified reliability is increased in a discovery sampling plan for any given population and maximum occurrence rate, the required sample size
a. Increases.
b. Decreases.
c. Remains the same.
d. **Cannot** be determined.

7. A CPA who believes the occurrence rate of a certain characteristic in a population being examined is 3% and who has established a maximum acceptable occurrence rate at 5% should use a (an)
a. Attribute sampling plan.
b. Discovery sampling plan.
c. Stratified sampling plan.
d. Variable sampling plan.

8. The auditor's failure to recognize an error in an amount or an error in an internal-control data-processing procedure is described as a
a. Statistical error.
b. Sampling error.
c. Standard error of the mean.
d. Nonsampling error.

9. Precision is a statistical measure of the maximum likely difference between the sample estimate and the true but unknown population total, and is directly related to
a. Reliability of evidence.
b. Relative risk.
c. Materiality.
d. Cost benefit analysis.

10. Which of the following is an advantage of systematic sampling over random number sampling?
a. It provides a stronger basis for statistical conclusions.
b. It enables the auditor to use the more efficient "sampling with replacement" tables.
c. There may be correlation between the location of items in the population, the feature of sampling interest, and the sampling interval.
d. It does not require establishment of correspondence between random numbers and items in the population.

11. For a large population of cash disbursement transactions, Smith, CPA, is testing compliance with internal control by using attribute sampling techniques. Anticipating an occurrence rate of 3% Smith found from a table that the required sample size is 400 with a desired upper precision limit of 5% and reliability of 95%. If Smith anticipated an occurrence rate of only 2% but wanted to maintain the same desired upper precision limit and reliability the sample size would be closest to
a. 200.
b. 400.
c. 533.
d. 800.

12. An auditor makes separate compliance and substantive tests in the accounts payable area which has good internal control. If the auditor uses statistical sampling for both of these tests, the confidence level established for the substantive tests is normally
a. The same as that for tests of compliance.
b. Greater than that for tests of compliance.
c. Less than that for tests of compliance.
d. Totally independent of that for tests of compliance.

13. An example of sampling for attributes would be estimating the
a. Quantity of specific inventory items.
b. Probability of losing a patent infringement case.
c. Percentage of overdue accounts receivable.
d. Dollar value of accounts receivable.

14. The purpose of tests of controls is to provide reasonable assurance that the accounting control procedures are being applied as prescribed. The sampling method that is **most** useful when testing for compliance is
a. Judgment sampling.
b. Attribute sampling.
c. Unrestricted random sampling with replacement.
d. Stratified random sampling.

15. In performing a review of his client's cash disbursements, a CPA uses systematic sampling with a random start. The primary **disadvantage** of systematic sampling is that population items

a. Must be reordered in a systematic pattern before the sample can be drawn.
b. May occur in a systematic pattern, thus negating the randomness of the sample.
c. May occur twice in the sample.
d. Must be replaced in the population after sampling to permit valid statistical inference.

16. From prior experience, a CPA is aware of the fact that cash disbursements contain a few unusually large disbursements. In using statistical sampling, the CPA's best course of action is to

a. Eliminate any unusually large disbursements which appear in the sample.
b. Continue to draw new samples until no unusually large disbursements appear in the sample.
c. Stratify the cash-disbursements population so that the unusually large disbursements are reviewed separately.
d. Increase the sample size to lessen the effect of the unusually large disbursements.

17. In connection with his test of the accuracy of inventory counts, a CPA decides to use discovery sampling. Discovery sampling may be considered a special case of

a. Judgmental sampling.
b. Sampling for variables.
c. Stratified sampling.
d. Sampling for attributes.

18. A CPA's test of the accuracy of inventory counts involves two storehouses. Storehouse A contains 10,000 inventory items and Storehouse B contains 5,000 items. The CPA plans to use sampling without replacement to test for an estimated 5% error rate. If the CPA's sampling plan calls for a specified reliability of 95% and a maximum tolerable error occurrence rate of 7.5% for both storehouses, the ratio of the size of the CPA's sample from Storehouse A to the size of the sample from Storehouse B should be

a. More than 1:1 but less than 2:1.
b. 2:1.
c. 1:1.
d. More than .5:1 but less than 1:1.

19. Approximately 5% of the 10,000 homogeneous items included in Barletta's finished-goods inventory are believed to be defective. The CPA examining Barletta's financial statements decides to test this estimated 5% defective rate. He learns that by sampling without replacement that a sample of 284 items from the inventory will permit specified reliability (confidence level) of 95% and specified precision (confidence interval) of -.025. If specified precision is changed to -.05, and specified reliability remains 95%, the required sample size is

a. 72.
b. 335.
c. 436.
d. 1,543.

20. The "reliability" (confidence level) of an estimate made from sample data is a mathematically determined figure that expresses the expected proportion of possible samples of a specified size from a given population

a. That will yield an interval estimate that will encompass the true population value.
b. That will yield an interval estimate that will not encompass the true population value.
c. For which the sample value and the population value are identical.
d. For which the sample elements will not exceed the population elements by more than a stated amount.

21. In an examination of financial statements, a CPA generally will find stratified-sampling techniques to be **least** appropriate to

a. Examining charges to the maintenance account during the audit year.
b. Tests of transactions for compliance with internal control.
c. The recomputation of a sample of factory workers' net pay.
d. Year-end confirmation of bank balances.

22. A CPA's client wishes to determine inventory shrinkage by weighing a sample of inventory items. If a stratified random sample is to be drawn, the strata should be identified in such a way that

a. The overall population is divided into subpopulations of equal size so that each subpopulation can be given equal weight when estimates are made.

b. Each stratum differs as much as possible with respect to expected shrinkage but the shrinkages expected for items within each stratum are as close as possible.

c. The sample mean and standard deviation of each individual stratum will be equal to the means and standard deviation of all other strata.

d. The items in each stratum will follow a normal distribution so that probability theory can be used in making inferences from the sample data.

23. In estimating the total value of supplies on repair trucks, Baker Company draws random samples from two equal-sized strata of trucks. The mean value of the inventory stored on the larger trucks (stratum 1) was computed at $1,500 with a standard deviation of $250. On the smaller trucks (stratum 2), the mean value of inventory was computed as $500, with a standard deviation of $45. If Baker had drawn an unstratified sample from the entire population of trucks, the expected mean value of inventory per truck would be $1,000, and the expected standard deviation would be

a. Exactly $147.50.

b. Greater than $250.

c. Less than $45.

d. Between $45 and $250, but not $147.50.

24. Omaha Sales Company asked a CPA's assistance in planning the use of multiple regression analysis to predict district sales. An equation has been estimated based upon historical data, and a standard error has been computed. When regression analysis based upon past periods is used to predict for a future period, the standard error associated with the predicted value, in relation to the standard error for the base equation, will be

a. Smaller.

b. Larger.

c. The same.

d. Larger or smaller, depending upon the circumstances.

25. A CPA's client maintains perpetual inventory records. In the past, all inventory items have been counted on a cycle basis at least once during the year.

Physical count and perpetual record differences have been minor. Now, the client wishes to minimize the cost of physically counting the inventory by changing to a sampling method in which many inventory items will not be counted during a given year. For purposes of expressing an opinion on his client's financial statements, the CPA will accept the sampling method only if

a. The sampling method has statistical validity.

b. A stratified sampling plan is used.

c. The client is willing to accept an opinion qualification in the auditor's report.

d. The client is willing to accept a scope qualification in the auditor's report.

———————

Items 26 to 30 apply to an examination by Lee Melinda, CPA, of the financial statements of Summit Appliance Repair Co. for the year ended June 30, 19X2. Summit has a large fleet of identically stocked repair trucks. It establishes the total quantities of materials and supplies stored on the delivery trucks at year-end by physically inventorying a random sample of trucks.

Mr. Melinda is evaluating the statistical validity of Summit's 19X2 sample. He knows that there were 74 trucks in the 19X1 required sample. Assumptions about the size, variability, specified precision (confidence interval), and specified reliability (confidence level) for he 19X2 sample are given in each of the following five items. You are to indicate in each case the effect upon the size of the 19X2 sample as compared to the 19X1 sample. Each of the five cases is independent of the other four and is to be considered separately.

26. Summit has the same number of trucks in 19X2, but supplies are replenished more often, meaning that there is less variability in the quantity of supplies stored on each truck. The specified precision and specified reliability remain the same. Under these assumptions the required sample size for 19X2 should be

a. Larger than the 19X1 sample size.

b. Equal to the 19X1 sample size.

c. Smaller than the 19X1 sample size.

d. Of a size that is indeterminate based upon the assumptions as given.

27. Summit has the same number of trucks; supplies are replenished less often (greater variability); Summit specifies the same precision but decides to change the specified reliability from 95% to 90%. Under these assumptions, the required sample size for 19X2 should be

a. Larger than the 19X1 sample size.

b. Equal to the 19X1 sample size.
c. Smaller than the 19X1 sample size.
d. Of a size that is indeterminate based upon the assumptions as given.

28. Summit has more trucks in 19X2. Variability and specified reliability remain the same, but with Melinda's concurrence Summit decides upon a wider specified precision. Under these assumptions the required sample size for 19X2 should be
a. Larger than the 19X1 sample size.
b. Equal to the 19X1 sample size.
c. Smaller than the 19X1 sample size.
d. Of a size that is indeterminate based upon the assumptions as given.

29. The number of trucks and variability remain the same, but with Melinda's concurrence Summit decides upon a wider specified precision and a specified reliability of 90% rather than 95%. Under these assumptions the required sample size for 19X2 should be
a. Larger than the 19X1 sample size.
b. Equal to the 19X1 sample size.
c. Smaller than the 19X1 sample size.
d. Of a size that is indeterminate based upon the assumptions as given.

30. The number of trucks increases, as does the variability of quantities stored on each truck. The specified reliability remains the same, but the specified precision is narrowed. Under these assumptions the required sample size for 19X2 should be
a. Larger than the 19X1 sample size.
b. Equal to the 19X1 sample size.
c. Smaller than the 19X1 sample size.
d. Of a size that is indeterminate based upon the assumptions as given.

---

31. What is the primary objective of using stratification as a sampling method in auditing?
a. To increase the confidence level at which a decision will be reached from the results of the sample selected.
b. To determine the occurrence rate for a given characteristic in the population being studied.
c. To decrease the effect of variance in the total population.
d. To determine the precision range of the sample selected.

32. To satisfy the auditing standard to make a proper study and evaluation of internal control, Harvey Jones, CPA, uses statistical sampling to test compliance with internal control procedures. Why does Jones use this statistical-sampling technique?
a. It provides a means of measuring mathematically the degree of reliability that results from examining only a part of the data.
b. It reduces the use of judgment required of Jones because the AICPA has established numerical criteria for this type of testing.
c. It increases Jones' knowledge of the client's prescribed procedures and their limitations.
d. It is specified by generally accepted auditing standards.

33. There are many kinds of statistical estimates that an auditor may find useful, but basically every accounting estimate is either of a quantity or of an error rate. The statistical terms that roughly correspond to "quantities" and "error rate," respectively, are
a. Attributes and variables.
b. Variables and attributes.
c. Constants and attributes.
d. Constants and variables.

The following items apply to random sampling for attributes, a sampling technique often employed in transaction testing. Assume that all samples are to be drawn from large populations.

34. Which of the following is an application of sampling for attributes?
a. Estimating the total dollar value of accounts receivable.
b. Estimating the reliability of a sample estimate.
c. Estimating the precision of a sample estimate.
d. Estimating the percentage of sales invoices with totals of less than $10.

35. In a random sample of 1,000 records, a CPA determines that the rate of occurrence of errors is 2%. He can state that the error rate in the population is
a. Not more than 3%.
b. Not less than 2%.
c. Probably about 2%.
d. Not less than 1%.

36. From a random sample of items listed from a client's inventory count, a CPA estimates with 90% confidence that the error occurrence rate is between 4% and 6%. The CPA's major concern is that there is one chance in twenty that the true error rate in the population is
a. More than 6%.
b. Less than 6%.
c. More than 4%.
d. Less than 4%.

37. If from a particular random sample, a CPA can state with 90% confidence that the occurrence rate in the population does not exceed 20%, he can state that the occurrence rate does not exceed 25% with
a. 95% confidence.
b. Greater reliability on his sample.
c. The same reliability on his sample.
d. Less reliability on his sample.

38. If a CPA wishes to select a random sample which must have a 90% confidence level and an upper precision limit of 10%, the size of the sample he must select will decrease as his estimate of the
a. Occurrence rate increases.
b. Occurrence rate decreases.
c. Population size increases.
d. Reliability of the sample decreases.

39. If a CPA selects a random sample for which he specified a confidence level of 99% and upper precision limit of 5% and subsequently changes the confidence level to 90%, the sample will produce an estimate which is
a. More reliable and more precise.
b. More reliable and less precise.
c. Less reliable and more precise.
d. Less reliable and less precise.

40. If the result obtained from a particular sample will be critical, e.g., the CPA would not be able to render an unqualified opinion (unless every item in the population were examined), which of the following is the most important to the CPA?
a. Size of the population.
b. Estimated occurrence rate.
c. Specified upper precision limit.
d. Specified confidence level.

41. An advantage of statistical sampling over nonstatistical sampling is that statistical sampling helps an auditor to
a. Eliminate the risk of nonsampling errors.
b. Reduce the level of audit risk and materiality to a relatively low amount.
c. Measure the sufficiency of the evidential matter obtained.
d. Minimize the failure to detect errors and irregularities.

Items 42 through 46 are based on the following information:

An audit partner is developing an office training program to familiarize his professional staff with statistical decision models applicable to the audit of dollar-value balances. He wishes to demonstrate the relationship of sample sizes to population size and variability and the auditor's specifications as to precision and confidence level. The partner prepared the following table to show comparative population characteristics and audit specifications of two populations.

	Characteristics of Population 1 Relative to Population 2		Audit Specifications as to a Sample from Population 1 Relative to a Sample from Population 2	
	Size	Variability	Specified Precision	Specified Confidence Level
Case 1	Equal	Equal	Equal	Higher
Case 2	Equal	Larger	Wider	Equal
Case 3	Larger	Equal	Tighter	Lower
Case 4	Smaller	Smaller	Equal	Lower
Case 5	Larger	Equal	Equal	Higher

In each item 42 through 46 you are to indicate for the specified case from the above table the required sample size to be selected from population 1 relative to the sample from population 2.

42. In case 1 the required sample size from population 1 is
a. Larger than the required sample size from population 2.
b. Equal to the required sample size from population 2.
c. Smaller than the required sample size from population 2.
d. Indeterminate relative to the required sample size from population 2.

43. In case 2 the required sample size from population 1 is
a. Larger than the required sample size from population 2.
b. Equal to the required sample size from population 2.
c. Smaller than the required sample size from population 2.
d. Indeterminate relative to the required sample size from population 2.

44. In case 3 the required sample size from population 1 is
a. Larger than the required sample size from population 2.
b. Equal to the required sample size from population 2.
c. Smaller than the required sample size from population 2.
d. Indeterminate relative to the required sample size from population 2.

45. In case 4 the required sample size from population 1 is
a. Larger than the required sample size from population 2.
b. Equal to the required sample size from population 2.
c. Smaller than the required sample size from population 2.
d. Indeterminate relative to the required sample size from population 2.

46. In case 5 the required sample size from population 1 is
a. Larger than the required sample size from population 2.
b. Equal to the required sample size from population 2.
c. Smaller than the required sample size from population 2.
d. Indeterminate relative to the required sample size from population 2.

_____

47. While performing a substantive test of details during an audit, the auditor determined that the sample results supported the conclusion that the recorded account balance was materially misstated. It was, in fact, not materially misstated. This situation illustrates the risk of

a. Incorrect rejection.
b. Incorrect acceptance.
c. Overreliance.
d. Underreliance.

48. Which of the following would be designed to estimate a numerical measurement of a population, such as a dollar value?
a. Sampling for variables.
b. Sampling for attributes.
c. Discovery sampling.
d. Numerical sampling.

49. Which of the following combinations results in a decrease in sample size in a sample for attributes?

	Risk of overreliance	Tolerable rate	Expected population deviation rate
a.	Increase	Decrease	Increase
b.	Decrease	Increase	Decrease
c.	Increase	Increase	Decrease
d.	Increase	Increase	Increase

50. What is an auditor's evaluation of a statistical sample for attributes when a test of 100 documents results in 4 deviations if tolerable rate is 5%, the expected population deviation rate is 3%, and the allowance for sampling risk is 2%?
a. Accept the sample results as support for planned reliance on the control because the tolerable rate less the allowance for sampling risk equals the expected population deviation rate.
b. Modify planned reliance on the control because the sample deviation rate plus the allowance for sampling risk exceeds the tolerable rate.
c. Modify planned reliance on the control because the tolerable rate plus the allowance for sampling risk exceeds the expected population deviation rate.
d. Accept the sample results as support for planned reliance on the control because the sample deviation rate plus the allowance for sampling risk exceeds the tolerable rate.

51. A principal advantage of statistical methods of attribute sampling over nonstatistical methods is that they provide a scientific basis for planning the
a. Risk of overreliance.
b. Tolerable rate.
c. Expected population deviation rate.
d. Sample size.

52. As the acceptable level of detection risk decreases, an auditor may change the
a. Timing of substantive tests by performing them at an interim date rather than at year end.
b. Nature of substantive tests from a less effective to a more effective procedure.
c. Timing of tests of controls by performing them at several dates rather than at one time.
d. Assessed level of inherent risk to a higher amount.

53. If all other factors specified in a sampling plan remain constant, changing the specified reliability from 90% to 95% would cause the required sample size to
a. Increase.
b. Remain the same.
c. Decrease.
d. Become indeterminate.

54. If all other factors specified in a sampling plan remain constant, changing the specified precision from 8% to 12% would cause the required sample size to
a. Increase.
b. Remain the same.
c. Decrease.
d. Become indeterminate.

55. If all other factors specified in a sampling plan remain constant, changing the estimated occurrence rate from 2% to 4% would cause the required sample size to
a. Increase.
b. Remain the same.
c. Decrease.
d. Become indeterminate.

56. In the evaluation of the results of a sample of a specified reliability and precision, the fact that the occurrence rate in the sample was 2% rather than the estimated occurrence rate of 4% would cause the required sample size to
a. Increase.
b. Remain the same.
c. Decrease.
d. Become indeterminate.

57. In the evaluation of the results of a sample of a specified reliability and precision, the fact that the occurrence rate in the sample was the same as the estimated occurrence rate would cause the reliability of the sample estimate to
a. Increase.
b. Remain the same.

c. Decrease.
d. Become indeterminate.

58. Statistical sampling generally may be applied to test compliance with internal accounting control when the client's internal accounting control procedures
a. Depend primarily on appropriate segregation of duties.
b. Are carefully reduced to writing and are included in client accounting manuals.
c. Leave an audit trail in the form of documentary evidence of compliance.
d. Enable the detection of material irregularities in the accounting records.

59. Which of the following **best** describes what the auditor means by the rate of occurrence in an attribute sampling plan?
a. The number of errors that can reasonably be expected to be found in a population.
b. The frequency with which a certain characteristic occurs within a population.
c. The degree of confidence that the sample is representative of the population.
d. The dollar range within which the true population total can be expected to fall.

60. An auditor selects a preliminary sample of 100 items out of a population of 1,000 items. The sample statistics generate an arithmetic mean of $120, a standard deviation of $12 and a standard error of the mean of $1.20. If the sample was adequate for the auditor's purposes and the auditor's desired precision was plus or minus $2,000, the minimum acceptable dollar value of the population would be
a. $122,000.
b. $120,000.
c. $118,000.
d. $117,600.

61. In estimation sampling for variables, which of the following must be known in order to estimate the appropriate sample size required to meet the auditor's needs in a given situation?
a. The total amount of the population.
b. The desired standard deviation.
c. The desired confidence level.
d. The estimated rate of error in the population.

62. Which of the following sampling plans would be designed to estimate a numerical measurement of a population, such as a dollar value?
a. Numerical sampling.
b. Discovery sampling.
c. Sampling for attributes.
d. Sampling for variables.

63. Auditors who prefer statistical to judgmental sampling believe that the **principal** advantage of statistical sampling flows from its unique ability to
a. Define the precision required to provide audit satisfaction.
b. Provide a mathematical measurement of uncertainty.
c. Establish conclusive audit evidence with decreased audit effort.
d. Promote a more legally defensible procedural approach.

64. Failure to detect material dollar errors in the financial statements is a risk which the auditor primarily mitigates by
a. Performing substantive tests.
b. Performing compliance tests.
c. Evaluating internal control.
d. Obtaining a client representation letter.

65. An auditor selects a preliminary sample of 100 items out of a population of 1,000 items. The sample statistics generate an arithmetic mean of $60, a standard deviation of $6 and a standard error of the mean of $.60. If the sample was adequate for the auditor's purposes and the auditor's desired precision was plus or minus $1,000, the **minimum** acceptable dollar value of the population would be
a. $61,000.
b. $60,000.
c. $59,000.
d. $58,800.

66. In the application of statistical techniques to the estimation of dollar amounts, a preliminary sample is usually taken primarily for the purpose of estimating the population.
a. Variability.
b. Mode.
c. Range.
d. Median.

67. In which of the following cases would the auditor be most likely to conclude that all of the items in an account under consideration should be examined rather than tested on a sample basis?

	The measure of tolerable error is	*Error frequency is expected to be*
a.	Large	Low
b.	Small	High
c.	Large	High
d.	Small	Low

68. The risk of incorrect acceptance and the risk of overreliance on internal accounting control relate to the
a. Preliminary estimates of materiality levels.
b. Allowable risk of tolerable error.
c. Efficiency of the audit.
d. Effectiveness of the audit.

69. When assessing the tolerable rate, the auditor should consider that, while deviations from control procedures increase the risk of material errors, such deviations do not necessarily result in errors. This explains why
a. A recorded disbursement that does **not** show evidence of required approval may nevertheless be a transaction that is properly authorized and recorded.
b. Deviations would result in errors in the accounting records only if the deviations and the errors occurred on different transactions.
c. Deviations from pertinent control procedures at a given rate ordinarily would be expected to result in errors at a higher rate.
d. A recorded disbursement that is properly authorized may nevertheless be a transaction that contains a material error.

70. As lower acceptable levels of both audit risk and materiality are established, the auditor should plan more work on individual accounts to
a. Find smaller errors.
b. Find larger errors.
c. Increase the tolerable error in the accounts.
d. Decrease the risk of overreliance.

71. A number of factors influences the sample size for a substantive test of details of an account balance. All other factors being equal, which of the following would lead to a larger sample size?
a. Greater reliance on internal accounting controls.
b. Greater reliance on analytical review procedures.
c. Smaller expected frequency of errors.
d. Smaller measure of tolerable error.

72. Which of the following audit risk components may be assessed in nonquantitative terms?

	Inherent risk	Control risk	Detection risk
a.	Yes	Yes	No
b.	Yes	No	Yes
c.	No	Yes	Yes
d.	Yes	Yes	Yes

73. As a result of tests of controls, an auditor overrelied on internal control and decreased substantive testing. This overreliance occurred because the true deviation rate in the population was
a. Less than the risk of overreliance on the auditor's sample.
b. Less than the deviation rate in the auditor's sample.
c. More than the risk of overreliance on the auditor's sample.
d. More than the deviation rate in the auditor's sample.

74. An auditor who uses statistical sampling for attributes in testing internal controls should reduce the planned reliance on a prescribed control when the
a. Sample rate of deviation is less than the expected rate of deviation used in planning the sample.
b. Tolerable rate less the allowance for sampling risk exceeds the sample rate of deviation.
c. Sample rate of deviation plus the allowance for sampling risk exceeds the tolerable rate.
d. Sample rate of deviation plus the allowance for sampling risk equals the tolerable rate.

75. Which of the following factors is generally **not** considered in determining the sample size for a test of controls?
a. Population size.
b. Tolerable rate.
c. Risk of overreliance.
d. Expected population deviation rate.

76. An advantage of using statistical over nonstatistical sampling methods in tests of controls is that the statistical methods
a. Afford greater assurance than a nonstatistical sample of equal size.
b. Provide an objective basis for quantitatively evaluating sample risks.
c. Can more easily convert the sample into a dual-purpose test useful for substantive testing.
d. Eliminate the need to use judgment in deter-mining appropriate sample sizes.

77. In a probability-proportional-to-size sample with a sampling interval of $10,000, an auditor discovered that a selected account receivable with a recorded amount of $5,000 had an audit amount of $2,000. The projected error of this sample was
a. $3,000
b. $4,000
c. $6,000
d. $8,000

78. An auditor is performing substantive tests of pricing and extensions of perpetual inventory balances consisting of a large number of items. Past experience indicates numerous pricing and extension errors. Which of the following statistical sampling approaches is most appropriate?
a. Unstratified mean-per-unit.
b. Probability-proportional-to-size.
c. Stop or go.
d. Ratio estimation.

79. As the acceptable level of detection risk increases, an auditor may change the
a. Assessed level of control risk from below the maximum to the maximum level.
b. Assurance provided by tests of controls by using a larger sample size than planned.
c. Timing of substantive tests from year end to an interim date.
d. Nature of substantive tests from a less effective to a more effective procedure.

80. In planning a statistical sample for a test of controls, an auditor increased the expected population deviation rate from the prior year's rate because of the results of the prior year's test of controls and the overall control environment. The auditor most likely would then increase the planned
a. Tolerable rate.
b. Allowance for sampling risk.
c. Risk of assessing control risk too low.
d. Sample size.

81. An auditor may decide to increase the risk of incorrect rejection when
a. Increased reliability from the sample is desired.
b. Many differences (audit value minus recorded value) are expected.
c. Initial sample results do **not** support the planned level of control risk.
d. The cost and effort of selecting additional sample items is low.

82. Which of the following courses of action would an auditor most likely follow in planning a sample of cash disbursements if the auditor is aware of several unusually large cash disbursements?
a. Increase the sample size to reduce the effect of the unusually large disbursements.
b. Continue to draw new samples until all the unusually large disbursements appear in the sample.
c. Set the tolerable rate of deviation at a lower level than originally planned.
d. Stratify the cash disbursements population so that the unusually large disbursements are selected.

83. For which of the following audit tests would an auditor most likely use attribute sampling?
a. Making an independent estimate of the amount of a LIFO inventory.
b. Examining invoices in support of the valuation of fixed asset additions.
c. Selecting accounts receivable for confirmation of account balances.
d. Inspecting employee time cards for proper approval by supervisors.

84. When an auditor increases the assessed level of control risk because certain control procedures were determined to be ineffective, the auditor would most likely increase the
a. Extent of tests of controls.
b. Level of detection risk.

c. Extent of tests of details.
d. Level of inherent risk.

85. An auditor uses the assessed level of control risk to
a. Evaluate the effectiveness of the entity's internal control policies and procedures.
b. Identify transactions and account balances where inherent risk is at the maximum.
c. Indicate whether materiality thresholds for planning and evaluation purposes are sufficiently high.
d. Determine the acceptable level of detection risk for financial statement assertions.

86. While performing a test of details during an audit, an auditor determined that the sample results supported the conclusion that the recorded account balance was materially misstated. It was, in fact, not materially misstated. This situation illustrates the risk of
a. Assessing control risk too high.
b. Assessing control risk too low.
c. Incorrect rejection.
d. Incorrect acceptance.

87. The sample size of a test of controls varies inversely with

	Expected population deviation rate	Tolerable rate
a.	Yes	Yes
b.	No	No
c.	Yes	No
d.	No	Yes

88. Inherent risk and control risk differ from detection risk in that they
a. Arise from the misapplication of auditing procedures.
b. May be assessed in either quantitative or nonquantitative terms.
c. Exist independently of the financial statement audit.
d. Can be changed at the auditor's discretion.

89. The existence of audit risk is recognized by the statement in the auditor's standard report that the

a. Auditor is responsible for expressing an opinion on the financial statements, which are the responsibility of management.
b. Financial statements are presented fairly, in all material respects, in conformity with GAAP.
c. Audit includes examining, on a test basis, evidence supporting the amounts and disclosures in the financial statements.
d. Auditor obtains reasonable assurance about whether the financial statements are free of material misstatement.

90. Which of the following statements is correct concerning statistical sampling in tests of controls?

a. As the population size increases, the sample size should increase proportionately.
b. Deviations from specific internal control procedures at a given rate ordinarily result in misstatements at a lower rate.
c. There is an inverse relationship between the expected population deviation rate and the sample size.
d. In determining tolerable rate, an auditor considers detection risk and the sample size.

91. Which of the following sampling methods would be used to estimate a numerical measurement of a population, such as a dollar value?

a. Attributes sampling.
b. Stop-or-go sampling.
c. Variables sampling.
d. Random-number sampling.

92. Which of the following courses of action would an auditor most likely follow in planning a sample of cash disbursements if the auditor is aware of several unusually large cash disbursements?

a. Set the tolerable rate of deviation at a lower level than originally planned.
b. Stratify the cash disbursements population so that the unusually large disbursements are selected.
c. Increase the sample size to reduce the effect of the unusually large disbursements.
d. Continue to draw new samples until all the unusually large disbursements appear in the sample.

93. Which of the following sample planning factors would influence the sample size for a substantive test of details for a specific account?

	Expected amount of misstatements	Measure of tolerable misstatement
a.	No	No
b.	Yes	Yes
c.	No	Yes
d.	Yes	No

94. Which of the following audit risk components may be assessed in nonquantitative terms?

	Control risk	Detection risk	Inherent risk
a.	Yes	Yes	No
b.	Yes	No	Yes
c.	Yes	Yes	Yes
d.	No	Yes	Yes

95. As a result of tests of controls, an auditor assessed control risk too low and decreased substantive testing. This assessment occurred because the true deviation rate in the population was

a. Less than the risk of assessing control risk too low, based on the auditor's sample.
b. Less than the deviation rate in the auditor's sample.
c. More than the risk of assessing control risk too low, based on the auditor's sample.
d. More than the deviation rate in the auditor's sample.

96. In determining the sample size for a test of controls, an auditor should consider the likely rate of deviations, the allowable risk of assessing control risk too low, and the

a. Tolerable deviation rate.
b. Risk of incorrect acceptance.
c. Nature and cause of deviations.
d. Population size.

97. An advantage of using statistical over nonstatistical sampling methods in tests of controls is that the statistical methods
a. Can more easily convert the sample into a dual-purpose test useful for substantive testing.
b. Eliminate the need to use judgment in determining appropriate sample sizes.
c. Afford greater assurance than a nonstatistical sample of equal size.
d. Provide an objective basis for quantitatively evaluating sample risk.

98. In confirming a client's accounts receivable in prior years, an auditor found that there were many differences between the recorded account balances and the confirmation replies. These differences, which were not misstatements, required substantial time to resolve. In defining the sampling unit for the current year's audit, the auditor most likely would choose
a. Individual overdue balances.
b. Individual invoices.
c. Small account balances.
d. Large account balances.

99. In statistical sampling methods used in substantive testing, an auditor most likely would stratify a population into meaningful groups if
a. Probability proportional to size (PPS) sampling is used.
b. The population has highly variable recorded amounts.
c. The auditor's estimated tolerable misstatement is extremely small.
d. The standard deviation of recorded amounts is relatively small.

100. The use of the ratio estimation sampling technique is most effective when
a. The calculated audit amounts are approximately proportional to the client's book amounts.
b. A relatively small number of differences exist in the population.
c. Estimating populations whose records consist of quantities, but **not** book values.
d. Large overstatement differences and large understatement differences exist in the population.

101. The diagram below depicts an auditor's estimated maximum deviation rate compared with the tolerable rate, and also depicts the true population deviation rate compared with the tolerable rate.

Auditor's estimate based on sample results	True state of population	
	Deviation rate is less than tolerable rate	Deviation rate exceeds tolerable rate
Maximum deviation rate is less than tolerable rate	I.	III.
Maximum deviation rate exceeds tolerable rate	II.	IV.

As a result of tests of controls, the auditor assesses control risk too low and thereby decreases substantive testing. This is illustrated by situation
a. I.
b. II.
c. III.
d. IV.

102. The risk of incorrect acceptance and the likelihood of assessing control risk too low relate to the
a. Allowable risk of tolerable misstatement.
b. Preliminary estimates of materiality levels.
c. Efficiency of the audit.
d. Effectiveness of the audit.

103. An auditor who uses statistical sampling for attributes in testing internal controls should reduce the planned reliance on a prescribed control when the
a. Sample rate of deviation plus the allowance for sampling risk equals the tolerable rate.
b. Sample rate of deviation is less than the expected rate of deviation used in planning the sample.
c. Tolerable rate less the allowance for sampling risk exceeds the sample rate of deviation.
d. Sample rate of deviation plus the allowance for sampling risk exceeds the tolerable rate.

104. In addition to evaluating the frequency of deviations in tests of controls, an auditor should also consider certain qualitative aspects of the deviations. The auditor most likely would give broader consideration to the implications of a deviation if it was

a. The only deviation discovered in the sample.
b. Identical to a deviation discovered during the prior year's audit.
c. Caused by an employee's misunderstanding of instructions.
d. Initially concealed by a forged document.

105. Which of the following factors is(are) considered in determining the sample size for a test of controls?

	Expected deviation rate	*Tolerable deviation rate*
a.	Yes	Yes
b.	No	No
c.	No	Yes
d.	Yes	No

106. How would increases in tolerable misstatement and assessed level of control risk affect the sample size in a substantive test of details?

	Increase in tolerable misstatement	*Increase in assessed level of control risk*
a.	Increase sample size	Increase sample size
b.	Increase sample size	Decrease sample size
c.	Decrease sample size	Increase sample size
d.	Decrease sample size	Decrease sample size

107. An advantage of statistical sampling over nonstatistical sampling is that statistical sampling helps an auditor to

a. Eliminate the risk of nonsampling errors.
b. Reduce the level of audit risk and materiality to a relatively low amount.
c. Measure the sufficiency of the evidential matter obtained.
d. Minimize the failure to detect errors and irregularities.

Chapter Six - Problems
The Audit Sampling Process

NUMBER 1

One of the generally accepted auditing standards states that sufficient competent evidential matter is to be obtained through inspections, observation, inquiries, and confirmation to afford a reasonable basis for an opinion regarding the financial statements under examination. Some degree of uncertainty is implicit in the concept of "a reasonable basis for an opinion," because the concept of sampling is well established in auditing practice.

Required:
a. Explain the auditor's justification for accepting the uncertainties that are inherent in the sampling process.
b. Discuss the uncertainties which collectively embody the concept of ultimate audit risk.
c. Discuss the nature of the sampling risk and nonsampling risk. Include the effect of sampling risk on substantive tests of details and on compliance tests of internal accounting control.

NUMBER 2

Edwards has decided to use Probability Proportional to Size (PPS) sampling, sometimes called dollar-unit sampling, in the audit of a client's accounts receivable balance. Few, if any, errors of account balance overstatement are expected.

Edwards plans to use the following PPS sampling table:

TABLE
Reliability Factors for Errors of Overstatement

Number of Overstatement Errors	Risk of Incorrect Acceptance				
	1%	*5%*	*10%*	*15%*	*20%*
0	4.61	3.00	2.31	1.90	1.61
1	6.64	4.75	3.89	3.38	3.00
2	8.41	6.30	5.33	4.72	4.28
3	10.05	7.76	6.69	6.02	5.52
4	11.61	9.16	8.00	7.27	6.73

Required:
a. Identify the advantages of using PPS sampling over classical variables sampling.

Note: Requirements b and c are **not** related.

b. Calculate the sampling interval and the sample size Edwards should use given the following information:

Tolerable error $15,000
Risk of incorrect acceptance 5%
Number of errors allowed 0
Recorded amount of accounts receivable.....................................$300,000

Note: Requirements b and c are **not** related.

c. Calculate the total projected error if the following three errors were discovered in a PSS sample:

	Recorded Amount	Audit Amount	Sampling Interval
1st error	$ 400	$ 320	$1,000
2nd error	500	0	1,000
3rd error	3,000	2,500	1,000

NUMBER 3

During the course of an audit engagement, a CPA attempts to obtain satisfaction that there are no material misstatements in the accounts receivable of a client. Statistical sampling is a tool that the auditor often uses to obtain representative evidence to achieve the desired satisfaction. On a particular engagement, an auditor determined that a material misstatement in a population of accounts would be $35,000. To obtain satisfaction the auditor had to be 95% confident that the population of accounts was not in error by $35,000. The auditor decided to use unrestricted random sampling with replacement and took a preliminary random sample of 100 items (n) from a population of 1,000 items (N). The sample produced the following data:

Arithmetic mean of sample items (x)	$4,000
Standard deviation of sample items (SD)	$ 200

The auditor also has available the following information:

Standard error of the mean (SE) = SD $\div \sqrt{n}$

Population precision (P) = N $\times$ R $\times$ SE

Partial List of Reliability Coefficients

If Reliability Coefficient (R) is	Then Reliability is
1.70	91.086%
1.75	91.988
1.80	92.814
1.85	93.568
1.90	94.256
1.95	94.882
1.96	95.000
2.00	95.450
2.05	95.964
2.10	96.428
2.15	96.844

Required:

a. Define the statistical terms "reliability" and "precision" as applied to auditing.

b. If all necessary audit work is performed on the preliminary sample items and no errors are detected,
   1. What can the auditor say about the total amount of accounts receivable at the 95% reliability level?
   2. At what confidence level can the auditor say that the population is not in error by $35,000?

c. Assume that the preliminary sample was sufficient,
   1. Compute the auditor's estimate of the population total.
   2. Indicate how the auditor should relate this estimate to the client's recorded amount.

NUMBER 4

Jiblum, CPA, is planning to use attribute sampling in order to determine the degree of reliance to be placed on an audit client's system of internal accounting control over sales. Jiblum has begun to develop an outline of the main steps in the sampling plan as follows:
1. State the objective(s) of the audit test (e.g. to test the reliability of internal accounting controls over sales).
2. Define the population (define the period covered by the test; define the sampling unit, define the completeness of the population).
3. Define the sampling unit (e.g. client copies of sales invoices).

Required:

a. What are the remaining steps in the above outline which Jiblum should include in the statistical test of sales invoices? **Do not present a detailed analysis of tasks which must be performed to carry out the objectives of each step. Parenthetical examples need not be provided.**

b. How does statistical methodology help the auditor to develop a satisfactory sampling plan?

NUMBER 5

Smith, CPA, has decided to rely on an audit client's internal accounting controls affecting receivables. Smith plans to use sampling to obtain substantive evidence concerning the reasonableness of the client's accounts receivable balances. Smith has identified the first few steps in an outline of the sampling plan as follows:
   1. Determine the audit objectives of the test.
   2. Define the population.
   3. Define the sampling unit.
   4. Consider the completeness of the population.
   5. Identify individually significant items.

Required:

Identify the remaining steps which Smith should include in the outline of the sampling plan. Illustrations and examples need **not** be provided.

NUMBER 6

Audit risk and materiality should be considered when planning and performing an examination of financial statements in accordance with generally accepted auditing standards. Audit risk and materiality should also be considered together in determining the nature, timing, and extent of auditing procedures and in evaluating the results of those procedures.

Required:

a.   1. Define audit risk.
     2. Describe its components of inherent risk, control risk, and detection risk.
     3. Explain how these components are interrelated.

b.   1. Define materiality.
     2. Discuss the factors affecting its determination.
     3. Describe the relationship between materiality for planning purposes and materiality for evaluation purposes.

NUMBER 7

Sampling for attributes is often used to allow an auditor to reach a conclusion concerning a rate of occurrence in a population. A common use in auditing is to test the rate of deviation from a prescribed internal accounting control procedure to determine whether planned reliance on that control is appropriate.

Required:

a.   When an auditor samples for attributes, identify the factors that should influence the auditor's judgment concerning the determination of
     1.   Acceptable level of risk of overreliance,
     2.   Tolerable deviation rate, and
     3.   Expected population deviation rate.

b.   State the effect on sample size of an increase in each of the following factors, assuming all other factors are held constant:
     1.   Acceptable level of risk of overreliance,
     2.   Tolerable deviation rate, and
     3.   Expected population deviation rate.

c.   Evaluate the sample results of a test for attributes if authorizations are found to be missing on 7 check requests out of a sample of 100 tested. The population consists of 2500 check requests, the tolerable deviation rate is 8%, and the acceptable level of risk of overreliance is low.

d.   How may the use of statistical sampling assist the auditor in evaluating the sample results described in (c) above?

NUMBER 8

Baker, CPA, was engaged to audit Mill Company's financial statements for the year ended September 30, 1991. After obtaining an understanding of Mill's internal control structure, Baker decided to obtain evidential matter about the effectiveness of both the design and operation of the policies and procedures that may support a low assessed level of control risk concerning Mill's shipping and billing functions. During the prior years' audits Baker used nonstatistical sampling, but for the current year Baker used a statistical sample in the tests of controls to eliminate the need for judgment.

Baker wanted to assess control risk at a low level, so a tolerable rate of deviation or acceptable upper precision limit (UPL) of 20% was established. To estimate the population deviation rate and the achieved UPL, Baker decided to apply a discovery sampling technique of attribute sampling that would use a population expected error rate of 3% for the 8,000 shipping documents, and decided to defer consideration of allowable risk of assessing control risk too low (risk of overreliance) until evaluating the sample results. Baker used the tolerable rate, the population size, and the expected population error rate to determine that a sample size of 80 would be sufficient. When it was subsequently determined that the actual population was about 10,000 shipping documents, Baker increased the sample size to 100.

Baker's objective was to ascertain whether Mill's shipments had been properly billed. Baker took a sample of 100 invoices by selecting the first 25 invoices from the first month of each quarter. Baker then compared the invoices to the corresponding prenumbered shipping documents.

When Baker tested the sample, eight errors were discovered. Additionally, one shipment that should have been billed at $10,443 was actually billed at $10,434. Baker considered this $9 to be immaterial and did not count it as an error.

In evaluating the sample results Baker made the initial determination that a reliability level of 95% (risk of assessing control risk too low 5%) was desired and, using the appropriate statistical sampling table, determined that for eight observed deviations from a sample size of 100, the achieved UPL was 14%. Baker then calculated the allowance for sampling risk to be 5%, the difference between the actual sample deviation rate (8%) and the expected error rate (3%). Baker reasoned that the actual sample deviation rate (8%) plus the allowance for sampling risk (5%) was less than the achieved UPL (14%); therefore, the sample supported a low level of control risk.

Required:
Describe each incorrect assumption, statement, and inappropriate application of attribute sampling in Baker's procedures.

Chapter Six - Solutions to Questions
The Audit Sampling Process

Sampling for Variables
Many of the questions on Statistical Sampling are concerned with the effect of increases and decreases on the size of a sample. This is caused by increases and decreases in the following four elements: standard deviation, reliability, precision and population. The following are the formulas expressed in the AICPA statistical notation and also on a mnemonic basis.

$$\sqrt{n} = \frac{S_{X_j} \cdot U_R \cdot N}{A} \quad \text{or} \quad \sqrt{\text{sample}} = \frac{SD \cdot REL. \cdot POP.}{PREC.}$$

Any element in the numerator that increases will cause a corresponding increase in the size of the sample. In the denominator (precision interval), as the amount gets smaller or narrower the sample size will increase, while as the precision increases or gets wider the sample will be smaller. When any two elements are given in a question which causes an increase and a decrease in sample sizes, the answer is of necessity indeterminate, unless the actual figures are given.

The addition of the finite population correction factor $\left(\cdot \sqrt{1 - n / N} \right)$ is always required when sampling without replacement is mentioned in a problem. While this would complicate the mathematics, the effect is always a decrease in sample size or precision.

Sampling for Attributes
The formulas for attribute sampling are complex and the determination of sample size is generally taken from a table. The subject is quite abstract so the following memory aides are recommended:

$$\frac{\text{Sample}}{\text{Size}} = \frac{*E.O.R. \cdot REL.}{PREC. \%}$$

Add population as an additional factor to the numerator when "sampling without replacement" is indicated.

*Estimated Occurrence Rate

1. (c) (Smaller). Stratification will cause the standard deviation to decrease; as this is the only element affected, the sample will be smaller.

2. (d) (Indeterminate). Stratification reduces the standard deviation and the sample size; however, the increase in reliability from 90% to 95% will increase the sample size, and, accordingly, the answer is indeterminate.

3. (a) (Larger). Sampling without replacement was in use for the two years compared and the finite population correction factor will not have any effect. An increase in the reliability from 90 to 95% will cause an increase in the sample size.

4. (a) (Larger). The standard deviation (variability) and population are larger in 1973 and, therefore, the sample will be larger.

5. (d) (Indeterminate). The standard deviation (variability) decreases while the population increases and the effect on the sample size is, therefore, indeterminate.

6. (a) Increasing reliability in any kind of a sampling plan, including discovery, while the other elements stay the same, will always cause the required sample size to increase.

7. (a) Occurrence rates and maximum acceptable occurrence rates are always an indication of an attribute sampling plan. There is no maximum acceptable occurrence rate applicable to discovery sampling plans. Stratified sampling and variable sampling apply to the estimation of some dollar amount.

8. (d) Failing to recognize an error in an amount, or error in an internal control data processing procedure, is not related to statistical sampling and therefore would be characterized as a nonsampling error.

9. (c) Precision or confidence interval represents the range of values within which the true but unknown population total will fall and this is directly related to materiality.

10. (d) Systematic sampling is a method of using every nth item in a population as a sample. Its advantage, of course, is that it does not require the use of a random number system and the establishing of correspondence with the population.

11. (a) In this problem, the occurrence rate of 3% and the other factors indicated call for a sample of 400. If the occurrence rate is made smaller, then the sample would decrease and the only possible answer would be 200.

12. (c) A confidence level of 95% indicates that a good system of internal control has been determined by means of a sample. Having met that test, the auditor could place much less reliance on the substantive tests.

13. (c) Attribute sampling always deals with the rate of occurrence, and, accordingly, the percentage of overdue accounts receivable would be one type of application. Items (a) and (d) are examples of variable sampling. (b), of course, is not related to sampling.

14. (b) Testing for compliance is always related to attribute sampling.

15. (b) Systematic sampling is one in which every nth item in a population is selected as a sample. Its disadvantage, however, is that the items selected may occur in a systematic pattern which would negate the randomness of the sample.

16. (c) The inclusion of large amounts in accounting populations will cause a larger standard deviation with a resulting increase in sample size. By separating the population into two or more strata, and reviewing the large amounts as a separate stratum, the standard deviation or variability of the remaining items will be less with the result that the sample size will be smaller.

17. (d) Discovery sampling is a type of attribute sampling. However, the objective is not one of estimation of a specific occurrence rate. Rather, the basic objective of discovery sampling is to provide a sample size large enough that we will have a prescribed change of seeing at least one example of some designated attribute.

18. (a) The AICPA attribute sampling tables do not provide for differences in population. If the CPA had used sampling with replacement, the sample size from Storehouse A and Storehouse B would have been equal and (c) would have been the correct answer. By using sampling without replacement, smaller samples would result and there would be a slight difference in the sample size as between Storehouse A and Storehouse B because of the finite population correction factor. Therefore, (a) is the best answer.

19. (a) This is an example of an attribute sampling plan. A sample of 284 items was determined based on a reliability of 95% and a specified precision of plus or minus .025. If the specified precision is made wider to plus or minus .05 and the reliability stays the same, the required sample size will be smaller and item (a) would be the only possible answer.

20. (a) The reliability of an estimate made from sample data is a mathematically determined figure that expresses the expected proportion of possible samples of a specified size from a given population that will yield an interval estimate that will encompass the true population value.

21. (d) Stratified sampling techniques would be least appropriate in the confirmation of the year-end bank balances. Confirmation of bank balances would always be done at 100% and sampling would not be involved.

22. (b) A stratified sample used to determine inventory shrinkage would identify the strata in such a way that each stratum differs as much as possible with respect to expected shrinkage, but the shrinkages expected for items within each stratum are as close as possible.

23. (b) The problem states that the standard deviation of stratum 1 is 250, and the standard deviation of stratum 2 is $45. If the sample was not based on stratification and all the amounts were combined into one sample, it is obvious that the standard deviation would have to be greater than 250.

24. (b) The standard error associated with the predicted value, in relation to the standard error for the base equation will always be larger. The calculation of the standard error of the base equation is based on a regression line which makes it smaller.

25. (a) For purposes of expressing an opinion on the client's financial statements, the CPA will accept the sampling method only if it has statistical validity.

26. (c) (Smaller). The only element in this problem that is changed is the standard deviation (variability) which is decreasing and this would cause the sample size to be smaller.

27. (d) (Indeterminate). The problem states that there will be greater variability which would increase the sample while the reliability will be decreased from 95% to 90%. Accordingly, the effect on sample size would be indeterminate.

28. (d) (Indeterminate). The population has increased in 19X2, which would cause an increase in sample size, while the precision is being made wider, which would cause a decrease in sample size. Accordingly, the increases and decreases would make this indeterminate.

29. (c) (Smaller). A wider precision and a smaller reliability would cause the sample in 19X2 to be smaller than 19X1.

30. (a) (Larger). The number of trucks or population increases as does the variability, and, in addition, the precision is made smaller. All of these items would cause an increase in the sample size, and, therefore, the sample in 19X2 would be larger than that in 19X1.

31. (c) The primary objective of using stratification as a sampling method in auditing is to decrease the effect of the standard deviation (variability) in the total population.

32. (a) Testing compliance by the use of statistical sampling provides a means of measuring mathematically the degree of reliability that results from the examination of only part of the data.

33. (b) The statistical terms that roughly correspond to "quantities" and "error rate," respectively, are variables and attributes.

34. (d) Estimating the percentage of sales invoices with totals of less than $10 would be an application of sampling for attributes. Item (a) would be a case of sampling for variables. Items (b) and (c) are items used in the determination of sample size in both sampling for attributes and variables.

35. (c) Sampling generally deals with ranges within which error rates will fall, and (c) would be the best answer.

36. (a) The precision interval in this case is 90%; however, the upper precision would be 95% or one chance in 20 that the rate exceeds 6%.

37. (b) When precision ranges are widened, the reliability is increased.

38. (b) An increase in sample size varies directly with an increase in the estimated occurrence rate, all other factors remaining the same.

39. (c) Decreasing the confidence level (reliability) will make the estimate less reliable but more precise.

40. (d) If the results of a sample estimate are critical, then the highest possible confidence level would be selected.

41. (c) Statistical sampling provides a mathematical model for determining sample size. Because of this the auditor is able to quantify the selection of sample size rather than rely on judgment.

42. (a) (Larger). In case number one, the specified confidence level (reliability) increases; therefore, the sample size will increase.

43. (d) (Indeterminate). In case two, the variability is larger while the precision is wider. The former increases the sample size and the latter decreases the sample size; therefore, the result is indeterminate.

44. (d) (Indeterminate). In case three, the increase in population and the tighter precision will cause the sample size to increase, while decreasing the confidence level will cause it to decrease. Therefore, in the facts given, the answer is indeterminate.

45. (c) (Smaller). The decrease in population, variability and confidence level all will tend to decrease the sample size.

46. (a) (Larger). In case five, the population is larger as well as the specified confidence level; therefore, both will cause an increase in the sample.

47. (a) Incorrect rejection occurs when the auditor concludes, based on a sample, that a recorded account balance is materially misstated when it is not materially misstated. The auditor rejects an acceptable balance. Answer (b) refers to incorrect acceptance, which occurs when the auditor concludes, based on a sample, that a recorded account balance is not materially misstated when it is. Answers (c) and (d) are risks associated with tests of controls, not substantive tests.

48. (a) Variables sampling, which is typically associated with substantive testing, is a type of sampling that reaches a conclusion on the monetary amounts of a population. Answers (b) and (c) refer to measurement of the presence or absence of control deviations. They are typically associated with tests of controls.

49. (c) There is an inverse relationship between acceptable level of risk of overreliance on the internal control structure and sample size (as risk of overreliance increases, sample size decreases). There is also an inverse relationship between the tolerable deviation rate and sample size (as tolerable rate increases, sample size decreases). There is a direct relationship between expected population deviation rate and sample size (as expected rate decreases, sample size decreases).

50. (b) The tolerable rate is the maximum population rate of deviation from a prescribed control procedure that the auditor will tolerate without modifying the planned reliance on the control procedure. The sample deviation rate is the rate of deviation found in the sample. The allowance for sampling risk is a measure of the difference between a sample result and the corresponding population characteristic. The auditor adds the allowance for sampling risk to the sample deviation rate to estimate the population deviation rate. Since the rate of deviation found in this sample (4 deviations in a test of 100 documents = 4%) plus an allowance for sampling risk (2%) results in a population rate (6%) which exceeds the tolerable rate (5%), the auditor would modify planned reliance on the control.

51. (d) In attribute sampling, the auditor considers factors which determine sample size. These factors include the risk of overreliance [answer (a)], the tolerable rate [answer (b)], and the expected population deviation rate [answer (c)]. Based on these factors, statistical methods of sampling, which use the laws of probability, can provide a scientific basis for planning the sample size.

52. (a) Detection risk is defined as the risk that the auditor's procedures will not detect an error or irregularity when one exists in the account being audited. As detection risk is decreased the auditor will select (1) a greater sample size of items to be tested, and (2) change audit tests (substantive procedures) to more effective procedures. In this way the auditor is minimizing the risk of not detecting an error when one in fact exists.

53. (a) Increasing reliability while the factors remain the same will increase the sample size.

54. (c) Widening the precision range from 8% to 12% will cause a decrease in sample size.

55. (a) Increasing the estimated occurrence rate will directly increase the sample size, all other factors remaining the same.

56. (b) Evaluation of sample results in attribute sampling does not use the estimated occurrence rate, and, accordingly, there is no effect on sample size.

57. (b) Evaluation of sample results in attribute sampling would use the table at the same reliability level, and, accordingly, it would remain the same.

58. (c) Compliance testing using attribute sampling techniques requires the analysis of some sort of document such as an invoice, ledger card, etc.

59. (b) Attribute sampling is designed to test the frequency of specified characteristics that occur within a given population.

60. (c) The best estimate of the population total and the associated precision is as follows:

Population	*Mean of the Sample*	*Point Estimate*
$1,000	$120	$120,000

With a desired precision of plus or minus $2,000 the range around the point estimate would be from $118,000 to $122,000. The minimum acceptable value of the population would be $118,000.

61. (c) Confidence level measures the reliability of the sample and the probability that the true population characteristic value lies within the precision interval of the sample.

62. (d) This plan enables auditors to estimate numerical quantities such as the dollar value of a population, with prescribed precision and reliability.

63. (b) Statistical sampling is preferable to judgmental sampling in that it provides a mathematical measurement of uncertainty.

64. (a) Material dollar errors in the financial statements are best detected by adequate substantive testing.

65. (c) The best estimate of the population total and the associated precision is as follows:

Population	Sample Mean	Point Estimate
$1,000	$60	$60,000

With a desired precision of plus or minus $1,000, the range around the point estimate would be from $59,000 to $61,000. The minimum acceptable value of the population would be $59,000.

66. (a) A preliminary sample suggests that the auditor is trying to determine an overall characteristic of the population. Answers (b), (c) and (d) are specific characteristics developed during the audit.

67. (b) The tolerable error is what the CPA will accept as a material exception. The smaller the tolerable error, then the higher the likelihood of occurrence. For example, if the auditor considers a tolerable error to be $1,000 in an audited amount rather than $10,000, the more likely the frequency of deviation.

68. (d) The risk of incorrect acceptance is accepting a transaction as being correct when in fact it is incorrect. Overreliance on internal control will lead the auditor to reduce the scope of the audit. These two affect the effectiveness of the audit since they bear directly on the auditor's opinion.

69. (a) The question states that a deviation from a control procedure does not necessarily mean that there will be an error in the account balance. Thus, answer (a) is correct because this answer fits the requirements of the question.

70. (a) As the level of audit risk (risk of an incorrect opinion) and materiality are decreased, the auditor would have to plan to find smaller errors. This is based upon the fact that with a lower materiality level the risk of an incorrect opinion is increased because of the probability that the number of smaller errors is greater.

71. (d) There is an inverse relationship between sample size and tolerable error. As the tolerable error is decreased the sample size would increase because of the need to examine more items to discover smaller errors if they exist.

72. (d) Audit risk may be assessed in quantitative (i.e., 5%, 10%) or nonquantitative (i.e., high, low, moderate) terms. At the account-balance or class-of-transactions level, audit risk consists of inherent risk, control risk and detection risk. GAAS does not differentiate among these components of audit risk in terms of assessing the risks quantitatively or nonquantitatively. Each of these components of audit risk can, therefore, be assessed nonquantitatively.

73. (d) The purpose of a test of controls is to determine if the client is adequately following the prescribed controls. The auditor assesses the maximum rate of deviations from a prescribed control that he would be willing to accept and still rely on the control (tolerable deviation rate). The auditor then tests a sample, computes a sample deviation rate and projects that sample result to the population. If he decides to rely on the control, he runs the risk that the true deviation rate in the population is more than the deviation rate in the sample. In such a case, the auditor will have overrelied on the control.

74. (c) In a test of controls, the auditor takes a sample, determines the sample deviation rate, compares this rate to the maximum rate he can tolerate and still rely on the control, and decides whether to rely on the control or not. When sampling, the auditor runs the risk that the sample is not representative of the population. Statistical sampling, which in a test of controls is termed statistical sampling for attributes, can measure that risk by computing an allowance for sampling risk. This allowance is added to the sample deviation rate to give a statistically-sound estimate of the true population rate. If this population deviation rate exceeds the tolerable deviation rate for the control, the auditor should not rely on the control.

75. (a) Population size has little or no effect on sample size except for very small populations. Tolerable rate and risk of overreliance are inversely related to sample size, resulting in larger samples when these factors are set low. The expected population deviation rate has a direct relationship with sample size, resulting in a larger sample when this factor is set high.

76. (b) When sampling, the auditor runs sampling risk, which is the risk that the sample is not representative of the population. If the sample is not representative, the auditor may reach incorrect conclusions about the population. Statistical sampling, which is based on the laws of probability, can quantitatively measure this sampling risk. This allowance for sampling risk can then provide the auditor with an objective basis for evaluating sample results.

77. (c) The projected error is computed by determining the relationship between the error ($5,000 – $2,000) and the recorded amount ($5,000), and applying that percentage to the sampling interval. The projected error is $6,000, with is 60% ($3,000 ÷ $5,000) of $10,000.

78. (d) Ratio estimation is used to measure the total estimated error amount in a population. This sampling method is most appropriate when the size of the errors are proportionate to the recorded amounts. Since the auditor is performing tests of pricing and extensions of inventory and the auditor expects numerous errors, the auditor is most interested in estimating the total dollar error and the ratio estimation approach would be the best choice of those listed. The mean-per-unit method is used when the auditor wants to estimate the audited value, rather than the error amount. An unstratified approach means that the population has not been divided into groups. Stop or go sampling is an approach in which the sample is selected in several steps, with each step conditional on the results of the previous steps. Probability-proportional-to-size is used when the auditor believes that there are not many errors in the population.

79. (c) In determining the nature, timing, and extent of substantive tests, the auditor considers how much detection risk, which is the risk that he will not detect a material misstatement that exists in an assertion, he is willing to accept. As the level of acceptable detection risk increases, which it does when the auditor's assessment of inherent risk and control risk decreases, the auditor may perform substantive tests that are less effective (nature), are performed at other than year end (timing) and/or use smaller samples (extent). Answer (a) is incorrect because control risk affects acceptable detection risk, not vice versa.

80. (d) There is a direct relationship between expected population deviation rate and sample size. If the auditor expects to find more deviations from a control, he must test a larger sample. Answers (a) and (b) are factors affecting sample size and are not affected by the expected population deviation rate. Answer (c) is an aspect of sampling risk and has nothing to do with the expected deviation rate.

81. (d) When an auditor uses a sample to substantively test a balance, the auditor runs the risk of incorrectly rejecting the balance. If the sample result causes the auditor to reject the balance, the auditor may perform additional substantive tests which, if the balance was incorrectly rejected, will lead to the conclusion that the balance should be accepted as fairly stated. The auditor performed additional, unnecessary testing because he incorrectly rejected the balance. If the cost and effort of these extra tests is low, the auditor may be more willing to increase the risk of incorrect rejection and possibly end up performing the extra tests. Answers (a) and (b) are incorrect because in those situations the auditor would want to minimize sampling risk, including the risk of incorrect rejection. Answer (c) relates to tests of controls whereas the risk of incorrect rejection relates to substantive testing.

82. (d) If an auditor wants to test the large items in a population, he may want to stratify, or divide, that population into relatively homogeneous groups. When stratifying a population of cash disbursements, one group could be all the balances over a certain amount (e.g., over $10,000), another group could be a range of disbursement amounts ($1,000 – $10,000), and a third group could be all the disbursements below a certain amount (under $1,000). With this stratification, the auditor could test all the disbursements in the first group and samples selected from the other groups. Answers (a) and (b) result in larger sample sizes that may or may not include the large disbursements which the auditor wants to test. Answer (b) would be very inefficient.

83. (d) Attribute sampling is audit sampling in which auditors look for the presence or absence of a control condition. It is a type of sampling that reaches a conclusion about a population in terms of a rate of occurrence. Inspecting time cards for proper approval is an example of attribute sampling because it is a test of controls designed to determine how frequently an approval control is complied with. Answers (a), (b) and (c) are incorrect because they are examples of variables sampling, not attribute sampling. Variables sampling is audit sampling in which auditors are testing monetary amounts of inventory, fixed assets, accounts receivable, etc.

84. (c) Control risk is the risk that a material misstatement that could occur in an assertion will not be prevented or detected on a timely basis by an entity's internal control structure policies or procedures. The auditor assesses the level of control risk to determine the acceptable level of detection risk for financial statement assertions. Detection risk is defined as the risk that the auditor will not detect a material misstatement that exists in an assertion. The auditor uses the acceptable level of detection risk to determine the nature, timing and extent of the auditing procedures to be used to detect material misstatements in the financial statement assertions. Auditing procedures designed to detect such misstatements are referred to as substantive tests, which include tests of details and analytical procedures. If certain control procedures are ineffective, the auditor will increase the assessed level of control risk, decrease the acceptable detection risk, and increase substantive tests of details. Answer (a) is incorrect because if a control is found to be ineffective, the auditor would increase substantive tests, not tests of controls. Answer (b) is incorrect because the level of acceptable detection risk would decrease, not increase. Answer (d) is incorrect because inherent risk, which is defined as the susceptibility of an assertion to a material misstatement assuming there are no related internal control structure policies or procedures, is independent of control risk and would not change with a change in assessed control risk.

85. (d) According to the audit risk model, acceptable detection risk is a function of allowable audit risk, inherent risk, and control risk. This question is concerned with control risk, which is defined as the risk that a material misstatement that could occur in an assertion will not be prevented or detected on a timely basis by an entity's internal control structure policies or procedures, and detection risk, which is defined as the risk that the auditor will not detect a material misstatement that exists in an assertion. The auditor uses the assessed level of control risk to determine the acceptable level of detection risk for financial statement assertions. Answer (a) is incorrect because the auditor's assessment of control risk reflects his or her evaluation of the effectiveness of the entity's internal control structure policies and procedures. Answer (b) is incorrect because inherent risk assessment is independent from control risk assessment. Answer (c) is incorrect because materiality levels are based on factors other than assessed control risk.

86. (c) Incorrect rejection occurs when the auditor concludes, based on a sample, that a recorded account balance is materially misstated when it is not materially misstated. As a result, the auditor rejects an acceptable balance. Answers (a) and (b) refer to risks associated with tests of controls, not substantive tests of details. Answer (d) refers to incorrect acceptance, which occurs when the auditor concludes, based on a sample, that a recorded account balance is not materially misstated when it is, resulting in the auditor accepting an incorrect balance.

87. (d) In determining sample size for a test of controls, the auditor will consider the expected population deviation rate and tolerable rate. If, based on prior experience with the client or a preliminary sample, the auditor expects to find few deviations from a control, the expected population deviation rate would be low and sample size would be small. Thus, there is a direct relationship between the expected population deviation rate and sample size, not an inverse relationship. The tolerable rate is the maximum rate of deviation from a prescribed control that an auditor is willing to accept without altering the planned reliance on internal control. If the auditor can tolerate a higher rate, he or she will test a smaller sample. Thus, tolerable rate varies inversely with sample size. Answers (a) and (c) are incorrect because sample size does not vary inversely with the expected population deviation rate. Answer (b) is incorrect because sample size does vary inversely with tolerable rate.

88. (c) AU 312 states that inherent risk and control risk differ from detection risk in that they exist independently of the audit, whereas detection risk relates to the auditor's procedures and can be changed at his or her discretion. Detection risk should have an inverse relationship to inherent and control risk. The less the inherent and control risk the auditor believes exists, the greater the acceptable level of detection risk. Conversely, when the inherent and control risk increase, the auditor must decrease the detection risk. These components of audit risk may be assessed in quantitative terms such as percentages or in non-quantitative terms such as a minimum to a maximum.

89. (d) AU 312 states that the existence of audit risk is recognized by the statement in the auditor's standard report that the auditor obtained *reasonable assurance* about whether the financial statements are free of material misstatement. Audit risk is the risk that the auditor may *unknowingly* fail to appropriately modify the opinion on financial statements that are materially misstated. Choice (a) is incorrect because the sentence in the opinion is a division of responsibilities between management and auditor. Choice (b) is incorrect because that portion of the

report is supporting the opinion rendered. Choice (c) is incorrect because the statement explains that due to timing and cost constraints the auditor has to audit *less than all* evidence available through the use of statistical sampling.

90. (b) AU 350 states that in assessing the tolerable rate of deviations, the auditor should consider that, while deviations from pertinent control structure policies or procedures increase the risk of material misstatements in the accounting records, such deviations do not necessarily result in misstatements. For example, a recorded disbursement that does not show evidence of required approval may nevertheless be a transaction that is properly authorized and recorded. Deviations would result in misstatements in the accounting records only if the deviations and the misstatements occurred on the same transactions. Deviations from pertinent control procedures at a given rate ordinarily would be expected to result in misstatements at a lower rate. Choice (a) is incorrect because population size has no effect on sample size when testing for compliance, unless the population is really small. Choice (c) is incorrect because there is a direct relationship between expected population and sample size. Choice (d) is incorrect because the tolerable rate is the maximum rate of deviation the auditor is willing to accept without changing his level of risk.

91. (c) Variables sampling estimates numerical measures of a population, such as the quantity of units or a dollar value. Choice (a) is incorrect because attributes sampling is used when testing internal control and estimates the percentage of items in the population that possess a desired attribute, not a dollar value. Choice (b) is incorrect because stop-or-go sampling continues to select additional sample items until a desired level of assurance has been obtained. Choice (d) is incorrect because random-number sampling is a technique used to select items and assure that each population item has an equal chance of being selected for the sample.

92. (b) An auditor would normally select 100% of unusually large cash disbursements and a lower percentage of smaller cash disbursements because the larger disbursements are more material to the financial statements. Stratified sampling divides the population into strata, or groups of transactions that possess the same characteristics. The auditor would select 100% of the items in the category that includes the unusually large disbursements and a smaller percentage of the other categories. Choice (a) is incorrect because rate of deviation relates to tests of controls and not substantive tests. Choice (c) is incorrect because the auditor selects the sample so that 100 % of the larger disbursements are selected. You can't increase more than 100%. Choice (d) is incorrect because you don't continue to draw new samples since you already have 100%.

93. (b) AU 350 states that when planning a particular sample for a substantive test of details, the auditor should consider how much monetary misstatement in the account may exist without causing the financial statements to be materially misstated, as well as the expected size and frequency of misstatements. The factors influencing sample sizes for a substantive test of details in sample planning include:

Factor:	*Conditions leading to Smaller Sample Size*	*Conditions leading to Larger Sample Size*
Measure of tolerable misstatement for an account	Larger measure of tolerable misstatement	Smaller measure of. tolerable misstatement
Expected size and frequency of misstatements	Smaller misstatements or lower frequency	Larger misstatements or higher frequency

94. (c) Audit risk may be assessed in quantitative (i.e., 5%, 10%) or nonquantitative (i.e., high, low, moderate) terms. At the account-balance or class-of-transactions level, audit risk consists of control risk, detection risk, and inherent risk. GAAS does not differentiate among these components of audit risk in terms of assessing the risks quantitatively or nonquantitatively. Each of these components of audit risk can, therefore, be assessed nonquantitatively.

95. (d) The purpose of a test of controls is to determine if the client is adequately following the prescribed controls. Before testing the controls, the auditor determines the tolerable deviation rate, which is the maximum rate of deviations from a prescribed control that he or she would be willing to accept and still rely on the control. The auditor then tests a sample, computes a sample deviation rate and projects that result to the population. If the auditor decides to rely on the control, he or she runs the risk that the true deviation rate in the population is more than the deviation rate in the sample. When this happens, the auditor will overrely on the control, assess control risk too low, and decrease substantive testing. Answers (a) and (c) are incorrect because deviation rates are independent of and not compared to the risk of assessing control risk too low. Answer (b) is the incorrect, opposite conclusion.

96. (a) To determine the number of items to be selected for a particular sample for a test of controls, the auditor should consider the tolerable rate of deviation from the control structure policies or procedures being tested, the likely rate of deviations, and the allowable risk of assessing control risk too low. An auditor applies professional judgment to relate these factors in determining the appropriate sample size. Answer (b) relates to substantive tests, not to tests of controls. Answer (c) is considered by the auditor in evaluating the sample results, not in determining the sample size. Answer (d) has very little effect on the determination of sample size.

97. (d) When sampling, the auditor runs sampling risk, which is the risk that the sample is not representative of the population. If the sample is not representative, the auditor may reach incorrect conclusions about the population. Statistical sampling, which is based on the laws of probability, can quantitatively measure the sampling risk. This allowance for sampling risk can then provide the auditor with an objective basis for evaluating sample results. Answer (a) is incorrect because samples used for the dual purposes of assessing control risk and substantiating monetary amounts can be statistically or nonstatistically based. Answer (b) is incorrect because factors that affect sample size, such as the tolerable deviation rate and acceptable risk of assessing control risk too low, involve judgment. Answer (c) is incorrect because although statistical sampling helps the auditor evaluate sample results, the extent of assurance provided by a sample does not differ if done statistically or nonstatistically.

98. (b) A sampling unit is any of the individual elements, as defined by the auditor, that constitute the population. In the case of accounts receivable, each customer's account balance could be defined as the sampling unit. If confirming these balances is inefficient because of the time needed to resolve differences, the auditor could decide to define the sampling unit as a smaller part of the population, such as individual invoices. The auditor can then confirm and test invoices rather than balances. Because answers (a), (c) and (d) are account balances, choosing any of them as the sampling unit would not eliminate the difficulties that were encountered.

99. (b) If a population is highly variable or spread out, such as would be the case when individual accounts receivable balances range from $10 to $1,000,000, the auditor would have to select many items to get a representative sample. To reduce the total sample size and thus be more efficient, the auditor may decide to stratify a population that has highly variable recorded amounts by dividing it into subpopulations, such as $1 to $1,000, $1,001 to $10,000, and over $10,000. Answer (a) is incorrect because PPS sampling automatically stratifies the population by selecting all amounts greater than the sampling interval. Answer (c) is incorrect because estimated tolerable misstatement has nothing to do with sample selection techniques. Answer (d) is incorrect because a population with a small standard deviation, which occurs when the population is not highly variable, does not need to be stratified.

100. (a) Ratio estimation is a sampling technique that is appropriate when auditors want to estimate a population value based on the ratio of audited amounts and recorded amounts. Therefore, the technique can be used most effectively when the calculated audit amounts are approximately proportional to the client-furnished book amounts. Answer (b) is incorrect because if a small number of differences exist in the population a larger sample may be needed to ensure that the sample is representative of the population, thereby erasing the benefits of ratio estimation. Answer (c) is incorrect because ratio estimation is used to estimate book values. Answer (d) is incorrect because when using ratio estimation, the amount and direction of the differences can vary as long as the ratios of audited to book amounts are fairly consistent.

101. (c) The purpose of a test of controls is to determine if the client is adequately following the prescribed controls. Before testing the controls, the auditor determines the tolerable deviation rate, which is the maximum rate of deviation from a prescribed control that the auditor is willing to accept at a given level of control risk. For example, if the auditor plans to assess control risk as low, the auditor would only tolerate a low rate of deviation from that control. After setting the tolerable deviation rate, the auditor then tests a sample, computes a sample deviation rate and projects that rate to the population. In projecting the sample result to the population, the auditor is concerned with the maximum deviation rate that could exist in the population. If the maximum deviation rate is less than the tolerable deviation rate, the auditor will assess control risk at the level that was originally planned. If the true population deviation rate (which is unknown since the auditor only tests a sample) is greater than the tolerable deviation rate, as depicted in situations III and IV, the auditor should assess control risk higher than originally planned. In situation III, based on the sample, which was not representative of the population, the auditor assessed control risk lower than he should have. As a result of assessing control risk too low, the auditor will perform less substantive testing. Answers (a) and (d) are incorrect because in situations I and IV the auditor's estimate based on the sample results was the same as the result that would have been obtained by testing the entire population. Answer (b) is incorrect because in situation II the auditor would assess control risk too high, not too low.

102. (d) When sampling, the auditor runs the risk that the sample is unrepresentative of the population. As a result, the auditor may reach the wrong conclusion. When the auditor performs substantive tests, he runs the risk of incorrect acceptance, which is the risk of accepting a balance as fairly stated when, in fact, the balance is not fairly stated. When the auditor performs tests of controls, he runs the risk of assessing control risk too low, which is the risk of deciding, based on the sample, that the controls are operating effectively when, in fact, they are not. These risks relate to the effectiveness of the audit because these erroneous conclusions, based on sampling, could cause the auditor to issue the wrong audit opinion and therefore be ineffective. Answers (a) and (b) are incorrect because allowable risk of tolerable misstatement and estimated materiality levels, which relate to the auditor's judgments about how much risk he is willing to take that the financial statements are materially misstated, are judgments the auditor makes in planning a sample. The risk of incorrect acceptance and the risk of assessing control risk too low are related to evaluating the results of a sample. Answer (c) is incorrect because it refers to efficiency of the audit, which is related to the sampling risk of incorrect rejection, which occurs when the sample results cause the auditor to reject a balance when it is fairly stated, and the risk of assessing control risk too high, which occurs when the auditor's sample results cause the auditor to assess control risk higher than it really is. As a result, the auditor is inefficient because he performs additional unnecessary testing.

103. (d) In a test of controls, the auditor takes a sample, determines the sample deviation rate, compares this rate to the maximum rate he can tolerate and still rely on the control, and decides whether to rely on the control as planned or not. When sampling, the auditor runs the risk that the sample is not representative of the population. Statistical sampling, which in a test of controls is termed statistical sampling for attributes, can measure that risk by computing an allowance for sampling risk. This allowance is added to the sample deviation rate to compute a statistical estimate of the maximum population deviation rate, based on that sample result. If this population deviation rate exceeds the tolerable deviation rate for the control, the auditor should reduce the planned reliance on the control. Answers (a) and (c) are incorrect because if the sample deviation rate plus the allowance for sampling risk is less than or equal to the tolerable deviation rate, the test results support the auditor's planned reliance on the control. Answer (b) is incorrect because the expected rate of deviation is used to determine sample size, not to evaluate the results of a sample.

104. (d) When evaluating the qualitative aspects of deviations discovered in tests of controls, the auditor should consider the nature and cause of the deviations and the possible relationship of the deviations to other phases of the audit. The discovery of an irregularity, such as a forged document, ordinarily requires a broader consideration of possible implications than does the discovery of an error. Answer (a) is incorrect because the discovery of only one error would not typically give rise to additional concern. Answer (b) is incorrect because an error recurring in a subsequent year would not be uncommon. Answer (c) is an unintentional error that would cause less concern than an intentional irregularity.

105. (a) To determine the number of items to be selected for a particular sample for a test of controls, the auditor should consider the tolerable rate of deviation from the control structure policies or procedures being tested, the expected rate of deviations, and the allowable risk of assessing control risk too low. An auditor uses professional judgment to relate these factors in determining the appropriate sample size. Answers (b), (c) and (d) are incorrect because the expected deviation rate and the tolerable deviation rate are considered in determining sample size.

106. (c) If the auditor can tolerate a larger misstatement in an account, the auditor would need less assurance from a sample that the account is fairly stated in all material respects; thus, sample size would decrease. If the auditor assesses a higher control risk, there is a greater likelihood that accounts are misstated. As a result, the extent of substantive testing, and thus sample sizes in substantive tests, will increase. Answers (a), (b) and (d) are incorrect because an increase in tolerable misstatement results in a decrease in sample size, and an increase in assessed level of control risk results in an increase in sample size.

107. (c) When sampling, the auditor runs sampling risk, which is the risk that the sample is not representative of the population. If the sample is not representative, the auditor may reach incorrect conclusions about the population. By using statistical theory, which is based on the laws of probability, the auditor can quantify sampling risk to assist himself in limiting it to a level he considers acceptable. Statistical sampling thus helps the auditor to design an efficient sample, to measure the sufficiency of the evidential matter obtained, and to evaluate the sample results. Answer (a) is incorrect because the risk of nonsampling errors exists in all sampling plans, whether statistical or not. Answer (b) is incorrect because the level of audit risk and materiality are auditor judgments that are made whether or not the sampling is statistical. Answer (d) is incorrect because the failure to detect errors and irregularities, which is referred to as detection risk, exists in statistical and nonstatistical sampling.

Chapter Six - Solutions to Problems
The Audit Sampling Process

NUMBER 1

a. The auditor's justification for accepting the uncertainties that are inherent in the sampling process, are based upon the premise that the
  - Cost of examining all of the financial data would usually outweigh the benefit of the added reliability of a complete (100%) examination.
  - Time required to examine all of the financial data would usually preclude issuance of a timely auditor's report.

b. The uncertainties inherent in applying auditing procedures are collectively referred to as ultimate audit risk. Ultimate audit risk, with respect to a particular account balance or class of transactions, is the risk that there is a monetary error greater than tolerable error in the balance or class that the auditor fails to detect. Ultimate audit risk is a combination of three types of risks as follows:
  - *Inherent risk* is the risk that errors will occur in the accounting system.
  - *Control risk* is the risk that material errors will not be detected by the client's system of internal accounting control.
  - *Detection risk* is the risk that any material errors that occur will not be detected by the auditor.

Ultimate audit risk includes both uncertainties due to sampling and uncertainties due to factors other than sampling. These aspects of ultimate audit risk are referred to as sampling risk and nonsampling risk, respectively.

c. Sampling risk arises from the possibility that, when a compliance or a substantive test is restricted to a sample, the auditor's conclusions may be different from the conclusions that might be reached if the test were applied in the same way to all items in the account balance or class of transactions. That is, a particular sample may contain proportionately more or less monetary errors or compliance deviations than exist in the balance or class as a whole.

Nonsampling risk includes all the aspects of ultimate audit risk that are not due to sampling. An auditor may apply a procedure to all transactions or balances and still fail to detect a material misstatement or a material internal accounting control weakness. Nonsampling risk includes the possibility of selecting audit procedures that are not appropriate to achieve the specific objective, or failing to recognize errors in documents examined, which would render the procedure ineffective even if all items were examined. The auditor should apply professional judgment in assessing sampling risk. In performing substantive tests of details the auditor is concerned with two aspects of sampling risk:
  - *The risk of incorrect acceptance* is the risk that the sample supports the conclusion that the recorded account balance is not materially misstated when it is materially misstated.
  - *The risk of incorrect rejection* is the risk that the sample supports the conclusion that the recorded account balance is not materially misstated when it is materially misstated.

The auditor is also concerned with two aspects of sampling risk in performing compliance tests of internal accounting control:
  - *The risk of overreliance* of internal accounting control is the risk that the sample supports the auditor's planned degree of reliance on the control when the true compliance rate does not justify such reliance.
  - *The risk of underreliance* on internal accounting control is the risk that the sample does not support the auditor's planned degree of reliance on the control when the true compliance rate supports such reliance.

The risk of incorrect acceptance and the risk of overreliance on internal accounting control relate to the effectiveness of an audit in detecting an existing material misstatement. The risk of incorrect rejection and the risk of underreliance on internal accounting control relate to the efficiency of the audit.

NUMBER 2

a. The advantages of PPS sampling over classical variables sampling are as follows:
   - PPS sampling is generally easier to use than classical variables sampling.
   - Size of a PPS sample is not based on the estimated variation of audited amounts.
   - PPS sampling automatically results in a stratified sample.
   - Individually significant items are automatically identified.
   - If no errors are expected, PPS sampling will usually result in a smaller sample size than classical variables sampling.
   - A PPS sample can be easily designed and sample selection can begin before the complete population is available.

b.

$$\text{Sampling Interval} = \frac{\text{Tolerable Error}}{\text{Reliability Factor for Errors of Overstatement}}$$

$$= \frac{\$15,000}{\$3.00}$$

$$= \underline{\$5,000}$$

$$\text{Sample Size} = \frac{\text{Recorded Amount}}{\text{Sampling Interval}}$$

$$= \frac{\$300,000}{\$5,000}$$

$$= \underline{60}$$

c.

	Recorded Amount	Audit Amount	Tainting	Sampling Interval	Projected Error
1st error	$ 400	$ 320	20%	$1,000	$ 200
2nd error	500	0	100%	1,000	1,000
3rd error	3,000	2,500	*	1,000	500
Total Projected Error					$1,700

*The recorded amount is greater than the sampling interval; therefore, the projected error equals the actual error.

NUMBER 3

a. Reliability and precision are statistical terms that are interdependent and inseparable. Precision is expressed as a range of values, plus or minus, around the sample result, and "reliability," or confidence, is expressed as the proportion of such ranges from all possible similar samples of the same size that would include the actual population value. Stated in another way, precision expresses the range or limits within which the sample result is expected to be accurate, while reliability expresses the mathematical probability of achieving that degree of accuracy.

The terms are usefully adapted to the auditor's purposes by relating precision to materiality and reliability to the reasonableness of the basis for the auditor's opinion.

b.

(1) At the 95% confidence level the auditor can be assured that the estimated population total is not in error by more than or less than $39,200.

$$P = N \times R \times SE$$
$$P = 1,000 \times 1.96 \times \left(\frac{200}{\sqrt{100}}\right) = 1,000 \times 1.96 \times \left(\frac{200}{10}\right) = 1,000 \times 1.96 \times 20 = \$39,200$$

(2) The auditor can be 91.988% confident that the estimated population total is not in error by more or less than $35,000.

$$P = N \times R \times SE$$
$$R = \left(\frac{P}{N \times E}\right) = \left(\frac{\$35,000}{1,000 \times 20}\right) = 1.75$$

$$R = 91.988\%$$

c.

(1) The estimated population total, or point estimate, based on the preliminary sample data would be equal to the arithmetic mean multiplied by the number of items in the population or $4,000 \times 1,000 = \$4,000,000$.

(2) If the original sample is sufficient, the auditor would be willing to accept an accounts receivable balance that is within plus or minus $35,000 from this amount. The auditor would be willing to accept an accounts receivable balance anywhere between $3,965,000 ($4,000,000 − $35,000) and $4,035,000 ($4,000,000 + $35,000). If the client's accounts receivable balance is not within this range, the auditor could not accept the client's balance based on the work performed on the preliminary sample items. The auditor would likely extend the sample by selecting additional items until the recorded amount fell within the precision limits. The additional sample items would have to change the sample mean by an amount sufficient enough to make the point estimate acceptable.

NUMBER 4

a. The remaining steps are as follows:

4. Define the attributes (characteristics) of interest to be tested (including the criteria for establishing the existence of errors or deviant conditions).
5. Set the maximum rate of deviations from a prescribed control procedure that would support the planned reliance on the control (tolerable rate).
6. Select a confidence level (quantify the risk of over-reliance).
7. Estimate the population error rate (deviation rate).
8. Determine the sample size.
9. Choose a method for randomly selecting a sample.
10. Perform the compliance audit procedures.
11. Perform error analysis (calculate the deviation rate and consider the qualitative aspects of the deviations).
12. Interpret sample results (calculate a population deviation rate).
13. Decide on the acceptability of the results of the sample.

b. Statistical sampling methodology helps the auditor (1) to design an efficient sample, (2) to measure the sufficiency of the evidential matter obtained, and (3) to evaluate the sample results. By using a statistical sampling methodology, the auditor can quantify sampling risk to assist in limiting it to an acceptable level.

NUMBER 5

The remaining steps are as follows:

6. Treat the individually significant items as a separate population.
7. Choose an audit sampling technique.
8. Determine the sample size, giving consideration for --
    a. Variations within the population.
    b. Acceptable level of risk.
    c. Tolerable error.
    d. Expected amount of error.
    e. Population size.
9. Determine the method of selecting a representative sample.
10. Select the sample items.
11. Apply appropriate audit procedures to the sample items.
12. Evaluate the sample results.
    a. Project the error to the population and consider sampling risk.
    b. Consider the qualitative aspects of errors and reach an overall conclusion.
13. Document the sampling procedure.

NUMBER 6

a. 1. Audit risk is the risk that the auditor may unknowingly fail to appropriately modify the auditor's opinion on financial statements that are materially misstated.

2. Inherent risk is the susceptibility of an account balance or class of transactions to error that could be material, when aggregated with error in other balances or classes, assuming that there were no related internal accounting controls.

   Control risk is the risk that error that could occur in an account balance or class of transactions and that could be material, when aggregated with error in other balances or classes, will not be prevented or detected on a timely basis by the system of internal accounting control.

   Detection risk is the risk that an auditor's procedures will lead the auditor to conclude that error in an account balance or class of transactions that could be material, when aggregated with error in other balances or classes, does not exist when in fact such error does exist.

3. Inherent risk and control risk differ from detection risk in that they exist independently of the audit of financial statements, whereas detection risk relates to the auditor's procedures and can be changed at the auditor's discretion. Detection risk should bear an inverse relationship to inherent and control risk. The less the inherent and control risk the auditor believes exists, the greater the acceptable detection risk. Conversely, the greater the inherent and control risk the auditor believes exists, the less the acceptable detection risk.

b. 1. Materiality is the magnitude of an omission or misstatement of accounting information that, in the light of surrounding circumstances, makes it probable that the judgment of a reasonable person relying on the information would have been changed or influenced by the omission or misstatement. This concept recognizes that some matters, either individually or in the aggregate, are important for the fair presentation of financial statements in conformity with generally accepted accounting principles, while other matters are not important.

2. Materiality is affected by the nature and amount of an item in relation to the nature and amount of items in the financial statements under examination, and the auditor's judgment as influenced by the auditor's perception of the needs of a reasonable person who will rely on the financial statements.

3. The auditor's judgment about materiality for planning purposes is ordinarily different from materiality for evaluation purposes because the auditor, when planning an audit, cannot anticipate all of the circumstances that may ultimately influence judgment about materiality in evaluating the audit findings at the completion of the audit. If significantly lower materiality levels become appropriate in evaluating the audit findings, the auditor should reevaluate the sufficiency of the audit procedures already performed.

NUMBER 7

a. 1. In determining an acceptable level of risk of overreliance, an auditor should consider the importance of the control to be tested in determining the extent to which substantive tests will be restricted and the planned degree of reliance on that control.
2. In determining the tolerable deviation rate, an auditor should consider the planned degree of reliance on the control to be tested and how materially the financial statements would be affected if the control does not function properly. For example, how likely is the control to prevent or detect material errors.
3. In determining the expected population deviation rate, an auditor should consider the results of prior years' tests, the overall control environment, or utilize a preliminary sample.

b. 1. There is a decrease in sample size if the acceptable level of risk of overreliance is increased.
   2. There is a decrease in sample size if the tolerable deviation rate is increased.
   3. There is an increase in sample size if the population deviation rate is increased.

c. For a low risk of overreliance it is generally appropriate to reconsider the planned reliance as the calculated estimate of the population deviation rate identified in the sample (7%) approaches the tolerable deviation rate (8%). This is because there may be an unacceptably high sampling risk that these sample results could have occurred with an actual population deviation rate higher than the tolerable deviation rate.

d. If statistical sampling is used, an allowance for sampling risk can be calculated. If the calculated estimate of the population deviation rate plus the allowance for sampling risk is greater than the tolerable deviation rate, the sample results should be interpreted as not supporting the planned reliance on the control.

NUMBER 8

1. Statistical sampling does not eliminate the need for professional judgment.
2. The tolerable rate of deviation or acceptable upper precision limit (UPL) is too high (20%) if Baker plans to assess control risk at a low level (substantial reliance).
3. Discovery sampling is not an appropriate sampling technique in this attribute sampling application.
4. The sampling technique employed is not discovery sampling.
5. The increase in the population size has little or no effect on determining sample size.
6. Baker failed to consider the allowable risk of assessing control risk too low (risk of overreliance) in determining the sample size.
7. The population from which the sample was chosen (invoices) was an incorrect population.
8. The sample selected was not randomly selected.
9. Baker failed to consider the difference of an immaterial amount to be an error.
10. The allowance for sampling risk was incorrectly calculated.
11. Baker's reasoning concerning the decision that the sample supported a low assessed level of control risk was erroneous.

Chapter Seven
Auditing with Technology

Chapter Seven
Auditing with Technology

AUDITOR RESPONSIBILITIES / METHODOLOGY
INTERNAL CONTROLS

I. RESPONSIBILITIES
A. Gain sufficient understanding of the Internal Control Elements (refer to Chapter 1 for a complete discussion of this responsibility) to plan the audit and determine the nature, timing, and extent of tests to be performed.
B. Assess Control Risk.
C. Communicate reportable conditions and internal control weaknesses to appropriate level of management.

II. METHODOLOGY

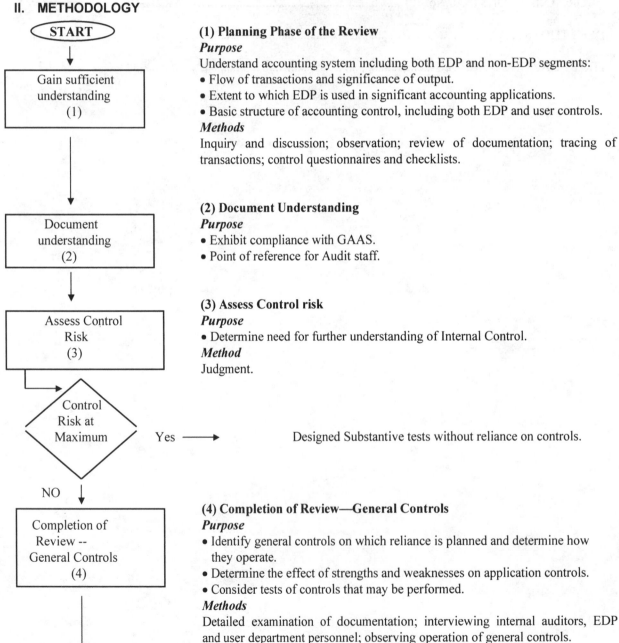

(1) Planning Phase of the Review
Purpose
Understand accounting system including both EDP and non-EDP segments:
• Flow of transactions and significance of output.
• Extent to which EDP is used in significant accounting applications.
• Basic structure of accounting control, including both EDP and user controls.
Methods
Inquiry and discussion; observation; review of documentation; tracing of transactions; control questionnaires and checklists.

(2) Document Understanding
Purpose
• Exhibit compliance with GAAS.
• Point of reference for Audit staff.

(3) Assess Control risk
Purpose
• Determine need for further understanding of Internal Control.
Method
Judgment.

Designed Substantive tests without reliance on controls.

(4) Completion of Review—General Controls
Purpose
• Identify general controls on which reliance is planned and determine how they operate.
• Determine the effect of strengths and weaknesses on application controls.
• Consider tests of controls that may be performed.
Methods
Detailed examination of documentation; interviewing internal auditors, EDP and user department personnel; observing operation of general controls.

(Continued Next Page)

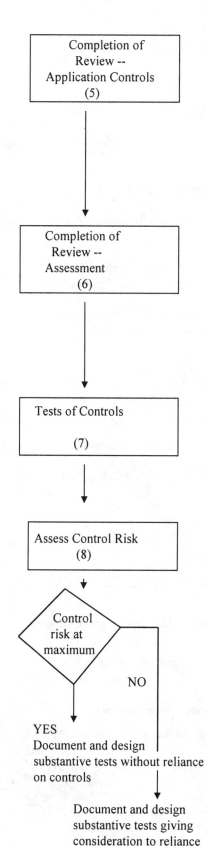

(5) Completion of Review—Application Controls

Purpose

Identify application controls on which reliance is planned, and determine how the controls operate.

Consider tests of controls that may be performed.

Consider the potential effect of identified strengths and weaknesses on tests of controls.

Methods

Detailed examination of documentation; interviewing internal auditors, EDP, and user department personnel; observing operation of application controls.

(6) Completion of Review—Preliminary Evaluation
Purpose

For each significant accounting application

Consider the types of errors or irregularities that could occur.

Determine the accounting control procedures that prevent or detect such errors and irregularities.

Assess effectiveness of EDP and non-EDP accounting controls.

Method

Judgment.

(7) Tests of Controls
Purpose

Determine whether the necessary control procedures are prescribed and followed satisfactorily.

Provide reasonable assurance that controls are functioning properly.

Consider and, to the extent appropriate, document when, how, and by whom controls are provided.

Methods

Examination of records; test of control procedures; inquiry; observation.

(8) Assess Control Risk
Purpose

For each significant accounting application

Consider the types of errors or irregularities that could occur.

Determine the accounting control procedures that prevent or detect such errors and irregularities.

Determine whether the necessary control procedures are prescribed and followed satisfactorily.

Evaluate weaknesses and assess their effect on the nature, timing, and extent of auditing procedures to be applied.

Method

Judgment.

ELECTRONIC COMMERCE

I. In general, electronic commerce includes individuals, businesses and other organizations involved in various transactions involving communication via computers.

II. Risks
   A. Confidentiality of information.
   B. Transaction Integrity – Proper controls must be in place to ensure that transactions cannot be changed, altered, duplicated or incorrectly processed.

III. Types of Transactions
   A. Electronic funds transfers (i.e., online banking)
   B. Electronic Data Interchange
      1. Business transactions accomplished between one entity and another through electronic communications networks.
      2. Traditional paper transactions are replaced by electronic transactions, thereby obscuring audit trails.
      3. Communication Methods
         • Point to Point: Direct privately managed system linking two or more computers. The major advantages of such a network include access control and no reliance on third parties for communication.
         • Public Networks (i.e., internet): The major advantages include cost of developing dedicated networks and widespread use. The major disadvantages are risks associated with confidentiality, hackers, and viruses.

IV. Benefits and Risks of Using EDI
   A. Benefits
      1. Speed
      2. Cost savings
      3. Reduced paperwork
      4. Ability to remain competitive
      5. Efficient communication
   B. Risks
      1. Security of information
      2. Concentration of control
      3. Loss of flexibility

Computer-Assisted Audit Techniques (CAAT)

The use of computer audit programs is probably advisable when the auditor needs an efficient means of analyzing large masses of machine-readable data and of selecting those items which require review.

Three different methods for using computer programs for the evaluation of client machine-readable records are as follows:

1. Client programs tested by the auditor and run under his/her control to produce the analysis needed.

2. Generalized computer audit routines.

3. Special audit routines prepared under the supervision of the auditor and run under his/her control.

The use of these computer audit routines must be considered in the context of the economic advisability of a computer approach versus that of alternative methods. The use of generalized computer audit routines is probably the least expensive of the computer alternatives; the use of a tested, controlled client program is more expensive and the use of a routine written especially for an audit is the most expensive.

Substantive
Audit Techniques
Using Computer

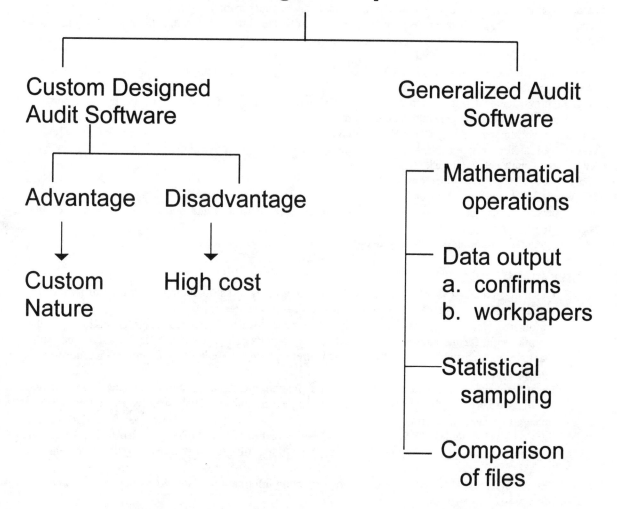

Custom Designed Audit Software

Advantage → Custom Nature

Disadvantage → High cost

Generalized Audit Software

— Mathematical operations

— Data output
a. confirms
b. workpapers

— Statistical sampling

— Comparison of files

Using the Computer as an Audit Tool

The auditor may use the computer as a "tool" in the audit process. The computer may be used to:

1. Select data for testing.
2. Compare source document data to data recorded in computer files.
3. Recompute or compute data.
4. Prepare confirmations.
5. Select accounts to be confirmed from a population based upon the auditor's predetermined criteria.
6. Test account distributions.
7. Analyze accounts and print out schedules.
8. Examine populations to extract items exceeding certain limits.

Using Microcomputers in Audits

The potential benefits to an auditor of using microcomputer software in an audit as compared to performing an audit without the use of a computer include the following:

1. Time may be saved by eliminating manual footing, cross-footing, and other routine calculations.
2. Calculations, comparison, and other data manipulations are more accurately performed.
3. Analytical procedures calculations may be more efficiently performed.
4. The scope of analytical procedures may be broadened.
5. Audit sampling may be facilitated.
6. Potential conditions in a client's internal control system may be more readily identified.
7. Preparation and revision of flowcharts depicting the flow of financial transactions in a client's system may be facilitated.
8. Working papers may be easily stored and accessed.
9. Graphics capabilities may allow the auditor to generate, display, and evaluate various financial and nonfinancial relationships graphically.
10. Engagement-management information such as time budgets and the monitoring of actual time vs. budgeted amounts may be more easily generated and analyzed.
11. Customized working papers may be developed with greater ease.
12. Standardized audit correspondence such as engagement letters, client representation letters, and attorney leters may be stored and easily modified.
13. Supervisory-review time may be reduced.
14. Staff morale and productivity may be improved by reducing the time spent on clerical tasks.
15. Client's personnel may not need to manually prepare as many schedules and otherwise spend as much time assisting the auditor.
16. Computer-generated working papers are generally more legible and consistent.

Computer Audit Tools

- Generalized audit software – Developed to perform many tasks, including the testing of transactions and controls, sampling, data selection, and analytical procedures.
- Automated workpaper software – Designed to generate a trial balance, lead schedules, and other reports useful for the auditor. The schedules and reports can be created once the auditor has either manually entered or electronically imported through using the client's account balance information into the system.
- Database management systems – Manages the creation, maintenance, and processing of information. The data are organized in the form of predefined records, and the database software is used to select, update, sort, display, or print the records.
- Text retrieval systems – Allow the user to view any text that is available in an electronic format. The software programs allow the user to browse through text files much as a user would browse through books.
- Public databases – May be used to obtain accounting information related to particular companies and industries.
- Word processing software – Considered an audit-assist function.
- Electronic spreadsheets – Contain a variety of predefined mathematical operations and functions that can be applied to data entered into the cells of a spreadsheet.

AUDITING A COMPUTER SYSTEM WITHOUT USING THE COMPUTER

This audit approach to a computer-based system is as follows:

1. Evaluation of internal control, involving (a) review of the system to ascertain how it is purported to work and what controls should be operable, and (b) tests of systems to accumulate evidence of how system actually does work.
2. Evaluation of computer-prepared records.

A system which performs relatively uncomplicated processing and produces detailed output can be audited without examination or direct testing of the computer program. The computer processing system is tested indirectly by tracing transactions and examining error and control lists. The auditor views the computer program as a black box; that is, an unknown which can be understood by inferring what must take place in order for a known input to result in a known output. (See diagram below.) The records produced by the computer are evaluated by comparison with source documents, by outside confirmations, or by similar tests which do not depend on the program. All computer records to be used must be available in printout form (or at least capable of being printed out at the auditor's request). The tests also furnish additional evidence on the processing which has taken place.

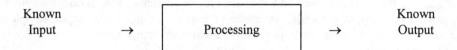

| Known | | | | Known |
| Input | $\rightarrow$ | Processing | $\rightarrow$ | Output |

The computer program as a black box.

Auditing by testing the input and output instead of the program itself does not detect program errors which do not show up in the output sampled. An erroneous input transaction rejected by the program (as shown by the error listing) is evidence that a control to detect such an error is present in the program, but missing controls are not revealed. However, the auditor can rely upon procedural and output controls to detect many errors even if some program controls are missing. Batch totals or ledger controls are examples.

An audit which does not use the computer is implemented by the following general steps:

AUDIT APPROACH	IMPLEMENTATION
Review of system	Interviews with personnel in data processing.
	Use of questionnaire.
	Examination of general system description.
	General review of major controls.
	Review of controls for each application vital to the audit.
Tests of systems	Examination of evidence for controls (error listings, batch control records, authorizations, etc.).
	Use of printouts to trace items in output to source documents, source documents to reports, report totals to controls, etc.
	Checking of transaction sample for correct processing.
	Other typical tests.
Evaluation of records	Tests to check correctness of summary accounts (foot, crossfoot, etc.).
	Tests of samples of detail items by confirmation, reasonableness tests, etc.

The system review is not limited to the electronic data processing portion. The work steps and procedures for an application are traced through the entire processing system—manual, electromechanical and computer—and through all departments involved. Thus, the specific controls for an application are considered within the framework of general controls imposed by the organization and management of the business.

In the area of computer data processing, an application is reviewed for:

1. Adequacy of control over input and output.
2. Adequacy of control over processing.
3. Adequacy of control over programs and files.
4. Adequacy of audit trail.

These data processing controls are evaluated within the framework of controls established by the organization and management of the data processing department.

When to Audit Without Using the Computer

The data processing systems which may be audited without the use of the computer are usually batch-processed or batch-controlled systems having detailed audit trails. This type of system is characterized by:

1. The collection of transactions in batches, to be sorted and processed sequentially against a master file (this process normally involves the development of batch totals to control the movement of data within the system).
2. The recording of transactions manually, followed by conversion to machine-readable form.
3. The production of numerous printouts (often at each processing run).

The feasibility of auditing the processing without testing the program directly depends on the auditor's being able to obtain evidence about the quality of processing by means of tests on the input and output, sample computations, tests of the controls, etc. Complicating conditions which obscure or impair the auditor's ability to obtain such evidence may include the following:

1. Processing may result in a summarized end-product output, so that individual items are not identifiable by manual means. A knowledge of the computer program is then necessary for tracing items from source to output or from output to source.
2. There may be so many transactions and transaction types that the tracing of processing becomes difficult without the use of the computer.
3. The system may be integrated so that a transaction is posted to several files at the same time without intermediate printout. It may also trigger a variety of systems responses. Tracing transactions and testing the system without an understanding of the computer program may be difficult. The number of printouts is reduced and the feasibility of using printouts for understanding system performance is usually lessened in comparison to simpler non-integrated systems.

REPORTS ON THE PROCESSING OF TRANSACTIONS BY SERVICE ORGANIZATIONS (SAS No. 70) AS AMENDED BY SAS NO. 88

For purposes of this Statement, the following definitions apply:

- *Client organization*. The entity whose financial statements are being examined.
- *User auditor*. The auditor who reports on the financial statements of the client organization.
- *Service organization*. The entity (or a segment of that entity) that provides services to the client organization.
- *Service auditor*. The auditor who reports on certain aspects of the system of internal accounting control of the service organization.

The guidance in this Statement is applicable to the examination of the financial statements of a client organization that obtains the following services from another organization:

- Executing transactions and maintaining the related accountability
- Recording transactions and processing related data
- Various combinations of these services

Examples of service organizations include:

- bank trust departments that invest and hold assets for employee benefit plans or others.
- EDP service centers that process transactions and related data for others.
- mortgage bankers that service mortgages for others.
- organizations that develop, provide, and maintain the software being used by client organizations.

SAS No. 70 provides guidance on:

- the user auditor's consideration of the effect of the service organization on the internal control structure of the user and the availability of sufficient evidence for the audit of the user organization.
- considerations in using a service auditor's report.
- responsibilities of service auditors, such as due care, independence, and performance in accordance with standards.

The User Auditor's Consideration

When the audit client uses a service organization, part of the accounting system and "internal control structure" are not internal. The processing of the transactions is physically and operationally separate from the client.

SAS No. 55 on internal control structure requires the auditor to—

- obtain the necessary understanding of the user organization's internal control structure to plan the audit of the financial statements.
- assess control risk.
- perform substantive procedures.

The most important factors to be considered in deciding whether additional information, such as a service auditor's report, is needed are:

- the degree of interaction between the policies and procedures at the service organization and those at the user organization.
- the nature of the transactions processed.
- the materiality of the transactions processed.

The auditor of the user organization decides whether he or she has sufficient information. If the user organization is relying on the service organization's accurate processing or their control procedures, the auditor needs information about the processing and control procedures. Additional information from the service center or a service auditor's report may not be necessary if the auditor has already obtained a sufficient understanding to:

- identify types of potential misstatements,
- consider factors that affect the risk of material misstatement, and
- design substantive tests.

If the user auditor is unable to obtain sufficient evidence to achieve his or her audit objectives, the user auditor should qualify the audit opinion or disclaim an opinion on the financial statements because of a scope limitation.

Considerations in Using a Service Auditor Report

- The service auditor's professional reputation.
- Whether the service auditor's report (in both scope and results) is sufficient to meet the user auditor's objectives.
- Assessment of policies and procedures in conjunction with the user's internal control structure policies and procedures.

Reports

Two types of reports are defined:

- opinion on a description of policies and procedures placed in operation at a service organization
- opinion on a description of policies and procedures placed in operation and tests of operating effectiveness.

Report on Policies and Procedures Placed in Operation

Purpose: This type of report helps the user auditor obtain an understanding of the entity's internal control structure sufficient to plan the audit. This report has two aspects:

- The service auditor's report on whether the service organization's description of its policies and procedures presents fairly the policies and procedures placed in operation as of a specified date.
- The service auditor's opinion on whether the policies and procedures are suitably designed to provide reasonable assurance that stated control objectives would be achieved if the control policies and procedures were complied with satisfactorily.

Report on Policies and Procedures Placed in Operation and Tests of Operating Effectiveness

This report covers both aspects of a "placed in operation" report and provides an additional element. It lists tests performed by the service auditor, and states the service auditor's opinion that the tested policies and procedures were operating with sufficient effectiveness to provide reasonable, but not absolute, assurance that the specified control objectives were achieved during the period covered by the tests.

The user auditor decides what evidential matter is needed to reduce the assessed level of control risk for his or her client. In some cases, the tests of operating effectiveness performed by the service auditor may provide this evidence.

SERVICE AUDITOR'S REPORT ON POLICIES AND PROCEDURES PLACED IN OPERATION—No Exceptions Noted

To XYZ Service Organization:

We have examined the accompanying description of the _____ application of XYZ Service Organization. Our examination included procedures to obtain reasonable assurance about whether (1) the accompanying description presents fairly, in all material respects, the aspects of XYZ Service Organization's policies and procedures that may be relevant to a user organization's internal control structure, (2) the control structure policies and procedures included in the description were suitably designed to achieve the control objectives specified in the description, if those policies and procedures were complied with satisfactorily [and user organizations applied the internal control structure policies and procedures contemplated in the design of XYZ Service Organization's policies and procedures], and (3) such policies and procedures had been placed in operation as of [*date*]. The control objectives were specified by [*the service organization, regulatory authorities, a user group or others*]. Our examination was performed in accordance with standards established by the American Institute of Certified Public Accountants and included those procedures we considered necessary in the circumstances to obtain a reasonable basis for rendering our opinion.

We did not perform procedures to determine the operating effectiveness of policies and procedures for any period. Accordingly, we express no opinion on the operating effectiveness of any aspects of XYZ Service Organization's policies and procedures, individually or in the aggregate.

In our opinion, the accompanying description of the aforementioned application presents fairly, in all material respects, the relevant aspects of XYZ Service Organization's policies and procedures that had been placed in operation as of [*date*]. Also, in our opinion, the policies and procedures, as described, are suitably designed to provide reasonable assurance that the specified control objectives would be achieved if the described policies and procedures were complied with satisfactorily [and user organizations applied the internal control structure policies and procedures contemplated in the design of XYZ Service Organization's policies and procedures].

The description of policies and procedures at XYZ Service Organization is as of [*date*] and any projection of such information to the future is subject to the risk that, because of change, the description may no longer portray the system in existence. The potential effectiveness of specific policies and procedures at the Service Organization is subject to inherent limitations and, accordingly, errors or irregularities may occur and not be detected. Furthermore, the projection of any conclusions, based on our findings, to future periods is subject to the risk that changes may alter the validity of such conclusions.

This report is intended solely for use by the management of XYZ Service Organization, its customers, and the independent auditors of its customers.

SERVICE AUDITOR'S REPORT ON POLICIES AND PROCEDURES PLACED IN OPERATION AND TESTS OF OPERATING EFFECTIVENESS— No Exceptions Noted

To XYZ Service Organization:

We have examined the accompanying description of the _____ application of XYZ Service Organization. Our examination included procedures to obtain reasonable assurance about whether (1) the accompanying description presents fairly, in all material respects, the aspects of XYZ Service Organization's policies and procedures that may be relevant to a user organization's internal control structure, (2) the control structure policies and procedures included in the description were suitably designed to achieve the control objectives specified in the description, if those policies and procedures were complied with satisfactorily [and user organizations applied the internal control structure policies and procedures contemplated in the design of XYZ Service Organization's policies and procedures], and (3) such policies and procedures had been placed in operation as of [*date*]. The control objectives were specified by [*the service organization, regulatory authorities, a user group or others*]. Our examination was performed in accordance with standards established by the American Institute of Certified Public Accountants and included those procedures we considered necessary in the circumstances to obtain a reasonable basis for rendering our opinion.

In our opinion, the accompanying description of the aforementioned application presents fairly, in all material respects, the relevant aspects of XYZ Service Organization's policies and procedures that had been placed in operation as of [*date*]. Also, in our opinion, the policies and procedures, as described, are suitably designed to provide reasonable assurance that the specified control objectives would be achieved if the described policies and procedures were complied with satisfactorily [and user organizations applied the internal control structure policies and procedures contemplated in the design of XYZ Service Organization's policies and procedures].

In addition to the procedures we considered necessary to render our opinion as expressed in the previous paragraph, we applied tests to specific policies and procedures, listed in Schedule X, to obtain evidence about their effectiveness in meeting the control objectives, described in Schedule X, during the period from [*date*] to [*date*]. The specific policies and procedures and the nature, timing, and extent, and results of the tests are listed in Schedule X. This information has been provided to user organizations of XYZ Service Organization and to their auditors to be taken into consideration, along with information about the internal control structure at user organizations, when making assessments of control risk for user organizations. In our opinion the policies and procedures that were tested, as described in Schedule X, were operating with sufficient effectiveness to provide reasonable, but not absolute, assurance that the control objectives specified in Schedule X were achieved during the period from [*date*] to [*date*]. [However, the scope of our engagement did not include tests to determine whether control objectives not listed in Schedule X were achieved; accordingly we express no opinion on the achievement of control objectives not included in Schedule X.]

The relative effectiveness and significance of specific policies and procedures at XYZ Service Organization and their effect on assessments of control risk at user organizations are dependent on their interaction with the policies, procedures, and other factors present at individual user organizations. We have performed no procedures to evaluate the effectiveness of policies and procedures at individual user organizations.

The description of policies and procedures at XYZ Service Organization is as of [*date*], and information about tests of the operating effectiveness of specified policies and procedures covers the period from [*date*] to [*date*]. Any projection of such information to the future is subject to the risk that, because of change, the description may no longer portray the system in existence. The potential effectiveness of specific policies and procedures at the Service Organization is subject to inherent limitations and, accordingly, errors or irregularities may occur and not be detected. Furthermore, the projection of any conclusions, based on our findings, to future periods is subject to the risk that changes may alter the validity of such conclusions.

This report is intended solely for use by the management of XYZ Service Organization, its customers, and the independent auditors of its customers.

DEFINITIONS

APPLICATION CONTROLS: Internal controls relating to a specific computer operation such as the processing of customer invoices.

BATCH PROCESSING: A technique in which items to be processed are collected into groups (batched) to permit convenient and efficient processing. Note: The records of all transactions affecting a particular master file are accumulated over a period of time (one day, for example), then arranged in sequence and processed against the master file; most business applications are of the batch processing type.

BATCH TOTAL: A sum of a set of items which is used to check the accuracy of operations on a particular batch of records.

BUG: A mistake in the design of a program or computer system, or an equipment fault.

CHANGE REQUEST LOG: A log of suggested changes to existing programs requested by users experiencing difficulties with employing programs.

CHECK BIT: A binary check digit. Note: A parity check usually involves the appending of a check bit of appropriate value to an array of bits.

CHECK DIGIT: A digit associated with a word or part of a word for the purpose of checking for the absence of certain classes of errors.

CODING: (1) An ordered list or lists of the successive instructions which direct a computer to perform a particular process; (2) the act of preparing a coding.

CONTROL CLERK: A person having responsibility for performing duties associated with the control over data processing operations. Note: Such duties usually include the checking of control totals, the checking of run-to-run controls, the checking of output before distribution, etc.

DATA BASE SYSTEM: A system whereby data is stored for multiple computer applications in an integrated data base. Eliminates the need to duplicate data storage for two or more computer routines.

DOCUMENTATION: Preparation of documents during programming that describe the program and document its preparation, its approval, and any subsequent changes; usually assembled in a run manual.

DUAL READ: The use of two separate reading stations to read the same record; results of the two operations are compared to detect reading errors.

DUMP: (1) To copy the contents of a set of storage locations, usually from an internal storage device (such as core storage) to an external storage medium (such as magnetic tape) and usually for diagnostic or rerun purposes; (2) Data that results from the process as defined in (1).

ECHO CHECK: A check upon the accuracy of a data transfer operation in which data received (usually by an output device) is transmitted back to its source (usually a control unit) and compared with the original data; for example, an echo check on a output operation usually can verify that the proper print hammers or punch pins were actuated at the proper moments, though it cannot ensure that the proper marks were actually recorded on the output medium.

EDIT: To modify the form or format of data; may involve the rearrangement, addition (for example, insertion of dollar signs and decimal points) and deletion (for example, suppression of leading zeros) of data, code translation and the control of layouts for printing (for example, provision for headings and page numbers).

FIELD: (1) In a punched card, a group of columns whose punchings represent one item; (2) a subdivision of a computer word or instruction (for example, a group of bit positions within an instruction that hold an address); (3) a subdivision of a record; that is, an item.

FILE: A collection of related information. For example, a payroll file.

FILE LABEL: A label identifying a file. Note: An internal label is recorded as the first or last record of a file and is machine-readable; an external label is attached to the outside of the file holder and is not machine-readable.

FILE PROTECTION RING: A removable plastic or metal ring, the presence or absence (depending on the computer manufacturer) of which prevents an employee from writing on a magnetic tape and thereby prevents the accidental destruction of a magnetic tape file. Note: The most common method involves the insertion of the ring to allow writing and the removal of the ring to prevent writing.

FLOWCHART: A diagram showing by means of symbols and interconnecting lines, (1) the structure and general sequence of operations of a program (program flowchart), or (2) a system of processing (system flowchart).

GENERAL CONTROLS: Control procedures applicable to all computer systems in an organization.

GENERALIZED AUDIT SOFTWARE: Auditor used computer software used to perform various routine audit procedures such as comparing records, selecting samples or making calculations.

HARD COPY: Documentation containing data printed by data processing equipment in a form suitable for permanent retention (printed reports, listings and logs). Note: Volatile output, by contrast, is data such as that displayed on the screen of a cathode ray tube.

HASH TOTAL: A sum of numbers in a specified field of a record, or of a batch of records, used for checking and control purposes. For example, the number of hours worked by everyone in a department.

HEADER LABEL: A machine-readable record at the beginning of a file containing data identifying the file and data used in file control.

INTEGRATED TEST FACILITY: A set of auditor-generated dummy transactions that is processed with valid client transactions. The objective is to test the effectiveness of the client's processing system.

INTERBLOCK GAP: The distance on a magnetic tape between the end of one block and the beginning of the next. Note: Within this distance the tape can be stopped and brought up to normal speed again; since, therefore, the tape speed may be changing, no reading or writing is permitted in the gap.

LIMIT TEST: A programmed check for errors in input data or processing. Note: For this test, a data item is compared with a test amount larger (or smaller) than the data item should be if it is correct; if the checked item is larger (or smaller) than the test amount, an error is indicated.

LOCAL AREA NETWORK (LAN): A communication facility that interconnects computers with a specific area.

LOG: A record of the operations of data processing equipment; each job or run, the time it required, operator actions, and other pertinent data are listed.

MANUAL INPUT: (1) The entry of data into a device by manual means at the time of processing; (2) data entered into a device by manual means at the time of processing; for example, data entered by means of a keyboard, or by setting switches, dials or levers.

MASTER FILE: A file containing relatively permanent information which is used as a source of reference and is generally updated periodically.

NETWORKING SYSTEM: A method of interconnecting computers in different locations.

OFF-LINE (OR OFFLINE): Pertaining to equipment or devices that are not in direct communication with the central processor of a computer system. Note: Off-line devices cannot be controlled by a computer except through human intervention. Contrast with "on-line".

ON-LINE (OR ONLINE): Pertaining to equipment or devices that are in direct communication with the central processor of a computer system. Note: On-line devices are usually under the direct control of the computer with which they are in communication.

PARALLEL SIMULATION: A testing process used by the auditor where actual client data are processed on the auditor's EDP equipment. The output is then compared with information processed on the client's equipment.

PARITY BIT: A bit (binary digit) appended to an array of bits to make the sum of all the "1" bits in the array either always even (even parity) or always odd (odd parity); for example:

	Even Parity			Odd Parity		
	0	1	1	0	1	1
	0	1	0	0	1	0
Data bits	0	1	0	0	1	0
	0	1	1	0	1	1
	0	1	1	0	1	1
	1	1	0	1	1	0
Parity bit	1	0	1	0	1	0

PROGRAM FLOWCHART: A flowchart diagramming the processing steps and logic of a computer program; contrast with "system flowchart."

RANDOM ACCESS: Pertaining to a storage device whose access time is not significantly affected by the location of the data to be accessed. Note: Any item of data stored on-line can be accessed within a relatively short time (usually less than one second).

REAL-TIME (OR REALTIME): (1) Pertaining to the time during which a physical process actually takes place; (2) pertaining to a mode of operation in which the moments of occurrence of certain events in a system must satisfy restrictions determined by the moments of occurrence of events in some other independent system; for example, realtime operation is essential in computers associated with process control systems, message switching and reservation systems.

RECORD COUNT: A count of the number of records in a file or the number of records processed by a program. Note: Such a count is used in error control to detect the nonprocessing of records.

RECORD MARK: A special character used in some computers either to limit the number of characters in a data transfer operation or to separate blocked records on tape.

RUN MANUAL: A manual documenting the processing system, program logic, controls, program changes and operating instructions associated with a computer run.

SELF-CHECKING NUMBER: A numeral that contains redundant information (such as an appended check digit) permitting it to be checked for accuracy after it has been transferred from one medium or device to another (for example, by means of a residue check); see "check digit."

SOURCE DOCUMENT: A document from which data is extracted; for example, a document that contains typed or handwritten data to be keypunched.

SYSTEM FLOWCHART: A flowchart diagramming the flow of work, documents and operations in a data processing application.

TEST DATA: A set of transactions developed by the auditor with a known output result. Some of the transactions may include errors. The transactions are processed on the client's system. The objective is to test the effectiveness of the client's system by comparing the processed information with the known output.

TRANSACTION CODE: One or more characters that form a part of a record and signify the type of transaction represented by that record; in inventory control, for example, a transaction code may signify deliveries to stock, disbursements from stock, orders, etc.

VALIDITY CHECK: A hardware check that determines whether or not a particular character is a legitimate member of the permissible character set.

PROGRAM FLOWCHARTING

The major symbols used in **program** flowcharting are shown below:

Terminal
Any start or stop point in the program

Input/Output
Any function of an Input or Output Device

Processing
Operation or operations to be performed

Decision
A choice is to be made from two or more options
(yes/no; greater than; less than/equal)

Onpage Connector
An entry to or exit from a point on the same page

Offpage Connector
An entry to or exit from different page

Flowline
The rule for direction of flow is always down and to the right unless an arrow indicates otherwise.

SYSTEM FLOWCHARTING

The major symbols used in **system** flowcharting refer to tapes, hardcopy printouts, paper handling, and the like. The system flowchart represents an entire accounting system, while a program flowchart will be the specific computer activity in just one part of the system. Major system symbols are shown below:

Document or Hardcopy printouts

Manual Operation

Any non-machine operations in the system

Magnetic Tape

Appears where magnetic tape is used or produced

Online Storage

Offline Storage

Display or Video Devices

Flowlines

Chapter Seven - Questions
Auditing with Technology

1. When an accounting application is processed by computer, an auditor cannot verify the reliable operation of programmed control procedures by
a. Manually comparing detail transaction files used by an edit program to the program's generated error listings to determine that errors were properly identified by the edit program.
b. Constructing a processing system for accounting applications and processing actual data from throughout the period through both the client's program and the auditor's program.
c. Manually reperforming, as of a point in time, the processing of input data and comparing the simulated results to the actual results.
d. Periodically submitting auditor-prepared test data to the same computer process and evaluating the results.

2. To obtain evidence that user identification and password controls are functioning as designed, an auditor would most likely
a. Attempt to sign-on to the system using invalid user identifications and passwords.
b. Write a computer program that simulates the logic of the client's access control software.
c. Extract a random sample of processed transactions and ensure that the transactions were appropriately authorized.
d. Examine statements signed by employees stating that they have **not** divulged their user identifications and passwords to any other person.

3. Computer systems are typically supported by a variety of utility software packages that are important to an auditor because they
a. May enable unauthorized changes to data files if **not** properly controlled.
b. Are very versatile programs that can be used on hardware of many manufacturers.
c. May be significant components of a client's application programs.
d. Are written specifically to enable auditors to extract and sort data.

4. Which of the following computer documentation would an auditor most likely utilize in obtaining an understanding of the internal control structure?
a. Systems flowcharts.
b. Record counts.
c. Program listings.
d. Record layouts.

5. When an auditor tests a computerized accounting system, which of the following is true of the test data approach?
a. Test data must consist of all possible valid and invalid conditions.
b. The program tested is different from the program used throughout the year by the client.
c. Several transactions of each type must be tested.
d. Test data are processed by the client's computer programs under the auditor's control.

6. Data Corporation has just completely computerized its billing and accounts receivable recordkeeping. You want to make maximum use of the new computer in your audit of Data Corporation. Which of the following audit techniques could not be performed through a computer program?
a. Tracing audited cash receipts to accounts receivable credits.
b. Selecting on a random number basis accounts to be confirmed.
c. Examining sales invoices for completeness, consistency between different items, valid conditions and reasonable amounts.
d. Resolving differences reported by customers on confirmation requests.

7. Which of the following best describes the principal advantage of the use of flowcharts in reviewing internal control?
a. Standard flowcharts are available and can be effectively used for describing most company internal operations.
b. Flowcharts aid in the understanding of the sequence and relationships of activities and documents.
c. Working papers are not complete unless they include flowcharts as well as memoranda on internal control.
d. Flowcharting is the most efficient means available for summarizing internal control.

8. Daylight Corporation's organization chart provides for a controller and an EDP manager, both of whom report to the financial vice-president. Internal control would not be strengthened by

a. Assigning the programming and operating of the computer to an independent control group which reports to the controller.
b. Providing for maintenance of input data controls by an independent control group which reports to the controller.
c. Rotating periodically among machine operators the assignments of individual application runs.
d. Providing for review and distribution of computer output by an independent control group which reports to the controller.

9. The primary purpose of a generalized computer audit program is to allow the auditor to

a. Use the client's employees to perform routine audit checks of the electronic data processing records that otherwise would be done by the auditor's staff accountants.
b. Test the logic of computer programs used in the client's electronic data processing systems.
c. Select larger samples from the client's electronic data processing records than would otherwise be selected without the generalized program.
d. Independently process client electronic data processing records.

10. An auditor can use a generalized computer audit program to verify the accuracy of

a. Data processing controls.
b. Accounting estimates.
c. Totals and sub-totals.
d. Account classifications.

11. Which of the following client electronic data processing (EDP) systems generally can be audited without examining or directly testing the EDP computer programs of the system?

a. A system that performs relatively uncomplicated processes and produces detailed output.
b. A system that affects a number of essential master files and produces a limited output.
c. A system that updates a few essential master files and produces no printed output other than final balances.
d. A system that performs relatively complicated processing and produces very little detailed output.

12. An auditor who is testing EDP controls in a payroll system would most likely use test data that contain conditions such as

a. Deductions not authorized by employees.
b. Overtime not approved by supervisors.
c. Time tickets with invalid job numbers.
d. Payroll checks with unauthorized signatures.

13. Which of the following is not a major reason why an accounting audit trail should be maintained for a computer system?

a. Monitoring purposes.
b. Analytical procedures.
c. Query answering.
d. Deterrent to irregularities.

14. Which of the following computer-assisted auditing techniques allows fictitious and real transactions to be processed together without client operating personnel being aware of the testing process?

a. Parallel simulation.
b. Generalized audit software programming.
c. Integrated test facility.
d. Test data approach.

15. In a computerized payroll system environment, an auditor would be least likely to use test data to test controls related to

a. Missing employee numbers.
b. Proper approval of overtime by supervisors.
c. Time tickets with invalid job numbers.
d. Agreement of hours per clock cards with hours on time tickets.

16. An auditor using audit software probably would be least interested in which of the following fields in a computerized perpetual inventory file?

a. Economic order quantity.
b. Warehouse location.
c. Date of last purchase.
d. Quantity sold.

17. Processing data through the use of simulated files provides an auditor with information about the operating effectiveness of control policies and procedures. One of the techniques involved in this approach makes use of

a. Controlled reprocessing.
b. An integrated test facility.
c. Input validation.
d. Program code checking.

18. An auditor most likely would test for the presence of unauthorized EDP program changes by running a
a. Program with test data.
b. Check digit verification program.
c. Source code comparison program.
d. Program that computes control totals.

19. An auditor most likely would introduce test data into a computerized payroll system to test internal controls related to the
a. Existence of unclaimed payroll checks held by supervisors.
b. Early cashing of payroll checks by employees.
c. Discovery of invalid employee I.D. numbers.
d. Proper approval of overtime by supervisors.

20. Lake, CPA, is auditing the financial statements of Gill Co. Gill uses the EDP Service Center, Inc. to process its payroll transactions. EDP's financial statements are audited by Cope, CPA, who recently issued a report on EDP's internal control structure. Lake is considering Cope's report on EDP's internal control structure in assessing control risk on the Gill engagement. What is Lake's responsibility concerning making reference to Cope as a basis, in part, for Lake's own opinion?
a. Lake may refer to Cope only if Lake is satisfied as to Cope's professional reputation and independence.
b. Lake may refer to Cope only if Lake relies on Cope's report in restricting the extent of substantive tests.
c. Lake may refer to Cope only if Lake's report indicates the division of responsibility.
d. Lake may not refer to Cope under the circumstances above.

21. Using microcomputers in auditing may affect the methods used to review the work of staff assistants because
a. The audit field work standards for supervision may differ.
b. Documenting the supervisory review may require assistance of consulting services personnel.
c. Supervisory personnel may not have an understanding of the capabilities and limitations of microcomputers.
d. Working paper documentation may not contain readily observable details of calculations.

22. Which of the following computer-assisted auditing techniques allows fictitious and real transactions to be processed together without client operating personnel being aware of the testing process?
a. Integrated test facility.
b. Input controls matrix.
c. Parallel simulation.
d. Data entry monitor.

23. When an auditor tests a computerized accounting system, which of the following is true of the test data approach?
a. Several transactions of each type must be tested.
b. Test data are processed by the client's computer programs under the auditor's control.
c. Test data must consist of all possible valid and invalid conditions.
d. The program tested is different from the program used throughout the year by the client.

24. Able Co. uses an online sales order processing system to process its sales transactions. Able's sales data are electronically sorted and subjected to edit checks. A direct output of the edit checks most likely would be a
a. Report of all missing sales invoices.
b. File of all rejected sales transactions.
c. Printout of all user code numbers and passwords.
d. List of all voided shipping documents.

25. Which of the following types of evidence would an auditor most likely examine to determine whether internal control structure policies and procedures are operating as designed?
a. Gross margin information regarding the client's industry.
b. Confirmations of receivables verifying account balances.
c. Client records documenting the use of EDP programs.
d. Anticipated results documented in budgets or forecasts.

26. Computer Services Company (CSC) processes payroll transactions for schools. Drake, CPA, is engaged to report on CSC's policies and procedures placed in operation as of a specific date. These policies and procedures are relevant to the schools' internal control structure, so Drake's report will be useful in providing the schools' independent auditors with information necessary to plan their audits. Drake's report expressing an opinion on CSC's policies and procedures placed in operation as of a specific date should contain a(an)

a. Description of the scope and nature of Drake's procedures.
b. Statement that CSC's management has disclosed to Drake all design deficiencies of which it is aware.
c. Opinion on the operating effectiveness of CSC's policies and procedures.
d. Paragraph indicating the basis for Drake's assessment of control risk.

27. A primary advantage of using generalized audit software packages to audit the financial statements of a client that uses an EDP system is that the auditor may

a. Access information stored on computer files while having a limited understanding of the client's hardware and software features.
b. Consider increasing the use of substantive tests of transactions in place of analytical procedures.
c. Substantiate the accuracy of data through self-checking digits and hash totals.
d. Reduce the level of required tests of controls to a relatively small amount.

Chapter Seven - Problems
Auditing with Technology

NUMBER 1

A CPA's client, Boos and Baumkirchner, Inc., is a medium-sized manufacturer of products for the leisure-time activities market (camping equipment, scuba gear, bows and arrows, etc.). During the past year, a computer system was installed, and inventory records of finished goods and parts were converted to computer processing. The inventory master file is maintained on a disk. Each record of the file contains the following information:

Item or part number	Total value of inventory on hand at cost
Description	Date of last sale or usage
Size	Quantity used or sold this year
Unit of measure code	Economic order quantity
Quantity on hand	Code number of major vendor
Cost per unit	Code number of secondary vendor

In preparation for year-end inventory the client has two identical sets of preprinted inventory count cards. One set is for the client's inventory counts, and the other is for the CPA's use to make audit test counts. The following information has been keypunched into the cards and interpreted on their face:
- Item or part number
- Description
- Size
- Unit of measure code

In taking the year-end inventory, the client's personnel will write the actual counted quantity on the face of each card. When all counts are complete, the counted quantity will be keypunched into the cards. The cards will be processed against the disk file, and quantity-on-hand figures will be adjusted to reflect the actual count. A computer listing will be prepared to show any missing inventory count cards and all quantity adjustments of more than $100 in value. These items will be investigated by client personnel, and all required adjustments will be made. When adjustments have been completed, the final year-end balances will be computed and posted to the general ledger.

The CPA has available a general purpose computer audit software package that will run on the client's computer and can process both card and disk files.

Required:
a. In general and without regard to the facts above, discuss the nature of general purpose computer audit software packages and list the various types and uses of such packages.
b. List and describe at least five ways a general purpose computer audit software package can be used to assist in all aspects of the audit of the inventory of Boos and Baumkirchner, Inc. (For example, the package can be used to read the disk inventory master file and list items and parts with a high unit cost or total value. Such items can be included in the test counts to increase the dollar coverage of the audit verification.)

NUMBER 2

The following five topics are part of the relevant body of knowledge for CPAs having field work or immediate supervisory responsibility in audits involving a computer:

1. Electronic data processing (EDP) equipment and its capabilities.
2. Organization and management of the data processing function.
3. Characteristics of computer based systems.
4. Fundamentals of computer programming.
5. Computer center operations.

CPAs who are responsible for computer audits should possess certain general knowledge with respect to each of these five topics. For example, on the subject of EDP equipment and its capabilities, the auditor should have a general understanding of computer equipment and should be familiar with the uses and capabilities of the central processor and the peripheral equipment.

Required:
For each of the topics numbered 2 through 5 above, describe the general knowledge that should be possessed by those CPAs who are responsible for computer audits.

NUMBER 3

An auditor is conducting an examination of the financial statements of a wholesale cosmetics distributor with an inventory consisting of thousands of individual items. The distributor keeps its inventory in its own distribution center and in two public warehouses. An inventory computer file is maintained on a computer disc and at the end of each business day the file is updated. Each record of the inventory file contains the following data:
- Item number
- Location of item
- Description of item
- Quantity on hand
- Cost per item
- Date of last purchase
- Date of last sale
- Quantity sold during year

The auditor is planning to observe the distributor's physical count of inventories as of a given date. The auditor will have available a computer tape of the data on the inventory file on the date of the physical count and a general purpose computer software package.

Required: The auditor is planning to perform basic inventory auditing procedures. Identify the basic inventory auditing procedures and describe how the use of the general purpose software package and the tape of the inventory file data might be helpful to the auditor in performing such auditing procedures.

Organize your answer as follows:

Basic inventory auditing procedure	How general purpose computer software package and tape of the inventory file data might be helpful
1 Observe the physical count, making and recording test counts where applicable.	Determining which items are to be test counted by selecting a random sample of a representative number of items from the inventory file as of the date of the physical count.

NUMBER 4

In the past, the records to be evaluated in an audit have been printed reports, listings, documents and written papers, all of which are visible output. However, in fully computerized systems which employ daily updating of transaction files, output and files are frequently in machine-readable forms such as cards, tapes, or disks. Thus, they often present the auditor with an opportunity to use the computer in performing an audit.

Required:
Discuss how the computer can be used to aid the auditor in examining accounts receivable in such a fully computerized system.

NUMBER 5

After determining that computer controls are valid, Hastings is reviewing the sales system of Rosco Corporation in order to determine how a computerized audit program may be used to assist in performing tests of Rosco's sales records.

Rosco sells crude oil from one central location. All orders are received by mail and indicate the preassigned customer identification number, desired quantity, proposed delivery date, method of payment and shipping terms. Since price fluctuates daily, orders do not indicate a price. Price sheets are printed daily and details are stored in a permanent disc file. The details of orders are also maintained in a permanent disc file.

Each morning the shipping clerk receives a computer printout which indicates details of customers' orders to be shipped that day. After the orders have been shipped, the shipping details are inputted in the computer which simultaneously updates the sales journal, perpetual inventory records, accounts receivable, and sales accounts.

The details of all transactions, as well as daily updates, are maintained on discs which are available for use by Hastings in the performance of the audit.

Required:
a. How may a computerized audit program be used by Hastings to perform substantive tests of Rosco's sales records in their machine readable form? **Do not discuss accounts receivable and inventory.**
b. After having performed these tests with the assistance of the computer, what other auditing procedures should Hastings perform in order to complete the examination of Rosco's sales records?

Chapter Seven - Solutions to Questions
Auditing with Technology

1. (c) An auditor can verify the reliable operation of programmed control procedures by auditing around the computer, comparing the results from manually reperforming the processing of input data with the actual results; however, doing this as of a **point** in time will not determine if the controls are operating reliably over the period of time affected by the programmed control procedures. Answers (a), (b) and (d) go beyond one point in time, involving tests of several listings, data from throughout the period, and periodic submissions of test data.

2. (a) This will provide the auditor with the most competent evidence that the user identification and password controls are functioning as designed. The other answers do not relate directly to actual system access; they refer to programming, authorization and written statements.

3. (a) Utility programs perform common data processing tasks such as copying, sorting, merging, reorganizing data in a file, and printing. They can also be used to enter and change data. Utility software packages are important to the auditor because if not properly controlled, unauthorized changes to data files may occur. Answers (b) and (c) may be true regarding utility software packages but are less important to the auditor. Answer (d) is an incorrect statement since these packages are not specifically written for the auditor.

4. (a) A systems flowchart is a pictorial representation of the processing steps in moving an item through processing. The question deals with understanding the internal control structure. Therefore, a flowchart would aid the auditor in understanding the flow of the system.

5. (d) The purpose of a test data approach is to validate the processing of accounting data by the client's EDP equipment. The test data has a known outcome and this known outcome is compared with the processing outcome to validate the processing of data.

6. (d) The computer could be used to perform items (a), (b) and (c). However, resolving differences reported by customers on confirmation request would have to be done manually.

7. (b) A flow chart is a diagram showing by means of symbols and interconnecting lines (1) the structure and general sequence of operations of a program (program flow chart) or (2) a system of processing (system flow chart). Accordingly, a system flow chart would be the best means in the understanding of the sequence and relationships of activities and documents.

8. (a) The assignment of programmers and the operation of a computer are the prime responsibilities of an EDP manager. An independent control group should function between the user department and the EDP department. Items (b), (c) and (d) are good examples of internal control within an EDP system.

9. (d) The primary use of a generalized computer audit program is to allow the auditor to independently process and verify client electronic data processing records.

10. (c) A generalized computer program provides an independent means of checking totals and subtotals using the client's data processing records.

11. (a) A system that, for instance, debits, credits and computes the balances of customer accounts receivable subsidiary ledger, but also printed out all the entries made plus the beginning and ending balances could be audited without directly testing it because external documentation is provided as evidence of each transaction.

12. (c) EDP controls can be tested by processing test data using the client's program. The auditor's test data must include valid and invalid transactions in order to determine if the programs will react correctly to the different kinds of data. In a test of the payroll system, the auditor would want to determine that the programs are processing time tickets and other data correctly and would, therefore, include in his test data time tickets with invalid job numbers. The other answers refer primarily to authorizations, not to data processing.

13. (b) Analytical procedures are substantive audit tests, not a reason why an accounting audit trail should be maintained for a computer system. An audit trail is a change of evidence connecting account balances and other summary results with original transaction data. The trail is used by management to monitor the system, to respond to inquiries, and to deter misuse. Auditors use the accounting audit trail to vouch and trace transactions.

14. (c) An integrated test facility is a method of testing programmed controls by creating a small subsystem within the regular EDP system. Dummy files and records are appended to existing client files and fictitious test transactions, specifically coded to correspond with the dummy files and records, are introduced into a system together with actual real transactions. Answer (a) is an approach which involves reprocessing actual company data using auditor-controlled programs. Answer (d) is an approach which involves dummy transactions prepared and processed by the auditor using the client's computer program.

15. (b) A department supervisor would indicate approval of overtime by signing the employee's time card. Visual inspection of the time card by the auditor would determine whether or not total hours worked were properly approved.

16. (a) Answer (b) is incorrect because the auditor would be interested in the warehouse location of inventory because he(she) would be concerned with the existence of the inventory. Answer (c) is incorrect because the auditor could use the date of the last purchase to test for obsolete inventory. Answer (d) is incorrect because the auditor could use this information to test for slow moving inventory. Answer (a) is correct because the auditor would be *least* concerned with the quantities purchased (E.O.Q.).

17. (b) An integrated test facility is a method of testing the effectiveness of programmed controls by creating a small subsystem within the regular EDP system. Simulated files and records are appended to existing client files and fictitious test transactions, specifically coded to correspond with the simulated files and records, are introduced into a system together with actual real transactions. Answer (a) involves reprocessing actual data, not simulated files. Answer (c) is a client control procedure. Answer (d) may be something an auditor does, but it does not involve processing data and does not use simulated files.

18. (c) If the auditor wants to discover unauthorized changes to an EDP program, he could compare the authorized program's source code with the unauthorized program's source code. Answers (a), (b) and (d) are programs that are designed primarily to test a client's application programs and programmed controls, not controls over unauthorized program changes.

19. (c) Auditors may run test data, which simulate actual transactions, on a client's computerized system to determine if the controls related to processing those transactions are operating effectively. The types of controls that can be tested in this manner are control procedures that can be programmed, such as discovering invalid employee I.D. numbers. The auditor could introduce simulated payroll data that have invalid I.D. numbers to determine if the computerized payroll system detects the error. Answers (a), (b) and (d) are not programmable controls, which exist in a computerized payroll system, that can be tested using test data. Control over the existence of unclaimed payroll checks held by supervisors, answer (a), is outside of the computer system and could be tested through inquiry and observation. Control over early cashing of payroll checks, answer (b), is outside the computer system and could be tested by inquiry, observation and examination of canceled checks. Control over approval of overtime by supervisors, answer (d), is typically outside the computer system and can be tested by examining timecards or other documentation for authorization.

20. (d) When an entity uses a service organization to process certain transactions, part of its accounting system and internal control structure are not internal. Such an entity is referred to as a user organization and its auditor is referred to as the user auditor. In this situation, the user auditor may consider work done by the service auditor, which is the term used to describe the auditor of the service organization, in evaluating the internal control structure and assessing control risk. If a report by the service auditor on the service organization's internal control structure is considered, the user auditor should not make reference to the report of the service auditor as a basis for his or her opinion on the user organization's financial statements. Since the service auditor is not responsible for examining any portion of the user organization's financial statements, there cannot be a division of responsibility for the audit of the user organization's financial statements. Answer (a) is incorrect because the user auditor, Lake, would not consider the report of the service auditor, Cope, if the service auditor were not reputable and independent. Answers (b) and (c) are incorrect because the user auditor cannot refer to the service auditor in his or her report.

21. (d) Work performed by assistants should be reviewed to determine whether it was adequately performed and to evaluate whether the results are consistent with the conclusions to be presented in the auditor's report. Working papers, which may be in the form of data stored on tapes or other media, are used to document procedures applied, tests performed, information obtained, and conclusions reached by the audit staff. Examples of working papers are audit programs, analyses, memoranda, letters, abstracts of documents, and schedules or commentaries. When prepared manually, working paper documentation would typically contain readily observable details of calculations. This may not be true when using microcomputers since working paper documentation may be in the form of computer files. Answer (a) is incorrect because the field work standard for planning and supervision is the same whether or not microcomputers are used in the audit. Answers (b) and (c) are incorrect because audit supervisors should be able to document their review of staff assistants' work and should understand the capabilities and limitations of microcomputers.

22. (a) AU 8016 states that test data techniques are used in conducting audit procedures by entering data into an entity's computer system, and comparing the results obtained with predetermined results. Examples are:

- Test data used to test specific controls in computer programs, such as password and data access controls.
- Test transactions selected from previously processed transactions or created by the auditor to test specific processing characteristics of an entity's computer system. Such transactions are generally processed separately from the entity's normal processing.
- Test transactions used in an integrated test facility where a "dummy" unit is established, and to which test transactions are posted during the normal processing cycle.

Choices (b) and (d) are incorrect because they are an input control. Choice (c) is incorrect because a parallel simulation involves rewriting a program with the client's data and comparing the output to test the program's logic.

23. (b) The test data approach tests computer controls by processing the auditor's test data, which consist of valid and invalid transactions, using the client's program. Answer (a) is incorrect because the basic concept of test data is that a computer program will handle every transaction exactly the same way, therefore only one transaction of each type has to be tested. Answer (c) is incorrect because the auditor needs only to prepare a limited number of simulated transactions to determine whether controls are operating. Answer (d) is incorrect because the test data are processed with the client program that is supposed to have been used during the period under audit.

24. (b) Edit checks are computer-programmed routines that are designed to detect data entry errors. Accordingly, a direct output of the edit checks of sales data being entered into a system would be a file or list of all sales transactions rejected by the edit checks. Answers (a) and (d) are incorrect because missing sales invoices and voided shipping documents would not be reflected on output generated from edit checks on data entry because sales invoices and shipping documents are generated after sales data are entered into the system. Answer (c) is incorrect because a printout of user codes and passwords would relate to general controls over access rather than application controls over data entry.

25. (c) In a computerized environment, there are general controls that are pervasive in their effect and relate to all computerized accounting activities. Control over access to electronic data processing (EDP) programs is an example of a general control. In order to test control over access, the auditor would most likely examine client records documenting the use of EDP programs. Answers (a), (b) and (d) are incorrect because they are examples of substantive tests, not tests of controls. The examples in (a) and (d) that refer to analysis and comparisons of gross margins and budgeted results are examples of analytical procedures that can be performed as part of substantive testing. Example (b) refers to confirmation of receivables, which is a substantive test of balances.

26. (a) A service auditor's report expressing an opinion on a description of policies and procedures placed in operation at a service organization should contain a description of the scope and nature of the service auditor's procedures. The report should also contain a reference to applications, services, products, or other aspects of the service organization covered; identification of the party specifying the control objectives; an indication of the purpose of the service auditor's engagement; a disclaimer of opinion on the operating effectiveness of the policies and procedures; the service auditor's opinion on whether the policies and procedures are suitably designed to provide reasonable assurance that stated control objectives would be achieved if the control policies and procedures were complied with satisfactorily; a statement of inherent limitations; and identification of the parties for whom the report is intended. Answers (b), (c) and (d) are incorrect because the service auditor's report expressing an opinion on a description of policies and procedures placed in operation at a service organization does not indicate that management of the user service organization disclosed design deficiencies to the service auditor; does not give an opinion on operating effectiveness, which is a different type of report that a service auditor can provide; and does not indicate the basis for the service auditor's assessment of control risk.

27. (a) Generalized audit software packages can be used to access client data, perform tests on those data, and produce audit workpapers. Because generalized audit software contains preprogrammed routines, limited additional programming is required. Accordingly, the auditor does not need an in-depth understanding of the client's hardware and software features in order to use generalized audit software packages. Answer (b) is incorrect because the choice between tests of transactions and analytical procedures is based on which substantive test is more effective and efficient, not on the use of audit software. Answer (c) is incorrect because self-checking digits and hash totals are input controls that the client uses, which are unrelated to audit procedures performed with audit software. Answer (d) is incorrect because the extent of tests of controls depends on planned assessment of control risk and other related factors, not the use of audit software.

Chapter Seven - Solutions to Problems
Auditing with Technology

NUMBER 1

a.

The nature of a general purpose computer audit software package is to provide computer programs that can process a variety of file media and record formats to perform a number of functions.

There are several types of general purpose computer audit software packages. A package may contain programs that create or generate other programs, programs that modify themselves to perform requested functions, or skeletal frameworks of programs that must be completed by the user.

A package can be used to perform or verify mathematical calculations; to include, exclude, or summarize items having specified characteristics; to provide subtotals and final totals; to compute, select, and evaluate statistical samples for audit tests; to print results in a form specified by the auditor; to arrange detailed items in a format or sequence that will facilitate an audit step; to compare, merge, or match the contents of two or more files, and to produce machine-readable files in a format specified by the auditor.

b.

Ways in which a general purpose computer audit software package can be used to assist in the audit of inventory of Boos & Baumkirchner, Inc., include the following:

1. Compare data on the CPA's set of prepunched inventory count cards to data on the disc inventory master file and list all differences. This will assure that the set of count cards furnished to the CPA is complete.
2. Determine which items and parts are to be test-counted by making a random selection of a sample from the audit deck of count cards or the disc inventory master file. Exclude from the population items with a high unit cost or total value that have already been selected for test counting.
3. Read the client's disc inventory master file and list all items or parts for which the date of last sale or usage indicates a lack of recent transactions. This list provides basic data for determining possible obsolescence.
4. Read the client's disc inventory master file and list all items or parts of which the quantity on hand seems excessive in relation to quantity used or sold during the year. This list provides basic data for determining over-stocked or slow-moving items or parts.
5. Read the client's disc inventory master file and list all items or parts of which the quantity on hand seems excessive in relation to economic order quantity. This list should be reviewed for possible slow-moving or obsolete items.
6. Keypunch the audit test-count quantities into the cards. Match these cards against the client's adjusted disc inventory master file comparing the quantities on the cards to the quantities on the disc file and list any differences. This will indicate whether the client's year-end inventory counts and the master file are substantially in agreement.
7. Use the adjusted disc inventory master file and independently extend and total the year-end inventory and print the grand total on an output report. When compared to the balance determined by the client, this will verify the calculations performed by the client.
8. Use the client's disc inventory master file and list all items with a significant cost per unit. The list should show cost per unit and both major and secondary vendor codes. This list can be used to verify the cost per unit.
9. Use the costs per unit on the client's disc inventory master file, and extend and total the dollar value of the counts on the audit text count cards. When compared to the total dollar value of the inventory, this will permit evaluation of audit coverage.

2. **Organization and management of the data processing function**

   The auditor should understand the typical duties and different structural arrangements of organization, supervision, and division of EDP duties. The auditor should understand the application of management principles to the data processing function.

3. **Characteristics of computer based systems.**

   The auditor should have a broad knowledge of file organization, process flow, and system design and should also understand the various methods for safeguarding computer files and the problems of including audit trails. The auditor should have the ability to analyze and design an information system of modest complexity. The auditor should be familiar with accounting control procedures that relate to all EDP activities (general controls) and those that relate to specific accounting tasks (application controls).

4. **Fundamentals of computer programming**

   The auditor should understand what programming entails and should have the ability to prepare specifications for and supervise preparation of a computer program.

5. **Computer center operations**

   The auditor should understand the use of software in the operation of the computer. The auditor should understand the role of the computer operator and should be able to supervise the running of the computer audit programs.

NUMBER 3

Basic Inventory Auditing Procedures	How General Purpose Computer Software Package and Tape of Inventory File Data Might Be Helpful
1. Observe the physical count, making and recording test counts where applicable.	Determining which items are to be test counted by making a random sample of a representative number of items from the inventory file as of the date of the physical count.
2. Test the mathematical accuracy of the inventory compilation (summary).	Mathematically computing the dollar value of each inventory item counted by multiplying the quantity on hand by the cost per unit and verifying the addition of the extended dollar values.
3. Compare the auditor's test counts to the inventory records.	Arranging test counts in a tape-format identical to the inventory file and matching the tapes.
4. Compare physical count data to inventory records.	Comparing the total extended values of all inventory items counted and the extended values of each inventory item counted to the inventory records.
5. Test the pricing of the inventory by obtaining a list of costs per item from buyers, vendors, or other sources.	Preparing a tape in a format identical to the tape of the inventory file and matching the tapes.
6. Examine purchase and sale cutoff.	Listing a sample of items on the inventory file for which the date of last purchase and date of the last sale are on or immediately prior to the date of the physical count.
7. Ascertain the propriety of items of inventory located in public warehouses.	Listing items located in public warehouses.
8. Analyze inventory for evidence of possible obsolescence.	Listing items on the inventory file for which the date of last sale indicates a lack of recent transactions.
9. Analyze inventory for evidence of possible overstocking or slow-moving items.	Listing items on the inventory file for which the quantity on hand is excessive in relation to the quantity sold during the year.
10. Perform overall test for accuracy of inventory master file.	Listing items, if any, with negative quantities or costs.

NUMBER 4

1. Testing Extensions and Footings: The computer can be used to perform simple summations and other computations to test the correctness of extensions and footings. The auditor may choose to perform tests on all records instead of just on samples, since the speed and low cost per computation of the computer enable this at only a small extra amount of time and expense.

2. Selecting and Printing Confirmation Requests: The computer can select and print out confirmation requests on the basis of quantifiable selection criteria. The program can be written to select the accounts according to any set of criteria desired and using any sampling plan.

3. Examining Records for Quality (Completeness, Consistency, Valid Conditions, etc.): The quality of visible records is readily apparent to the auditor. Sloppy recordkeeping, lack of completeness, and so on, are observed by the auditor in the normal course of the audit. If machine-readable records, however, are evaluated manually, a complete printout is needed to examine their quality. The auditor may choose to use the computer for examining these records for quality. If the computer is to be used for the examination, a program is written which examines the record for completeness, consistency between different items, valid conditions, reasonable amounts, etc. For instance, customer file records might be examined to determine those for which no credit limit is specified, those for which account balances exceed credit limit and those for which credit limits exceed a stipulated amount.

4. Summarizing Data and Performing Analyses Useful to the Auditor: The auditor frequently needs to have the client's data analyzed and/or summarized. Such procedures as aging accounts receivable or listing all credit balances in accounts receivable can be accomplished with a computer program.

5. Selecting and Printing Audit Samples: The computer may be programmed to select audit samples by the use of random numbers or by systematic selection techniques. The sample selection procedure may be programmed to use multiple criteria, such as the selection of a random sample of items under a certain dollar amount plus the selection of all items over a certain dollar amount. Other considerations can be included, such as unusual transactions, dormant accounts, etc.

6. Comparing Duplicate Data (Maintained in Separate Files) for Correctness and Consistency: Where there are two or more separate records having identical data fields, the computer can be used in testing for consistency; for instance, comparing catalogue prices with invoice prices.

7. Comparing confirmation information with company records. For example, the computer can be used to compare payment dates per customer confirmations with client cash receipts records.

8. The computer may be programmed to print a workpaper listing of each account selected, with relevant data inserted in applicable columns.

9. The computer may be programmed to compare the customer's account balance with the customer's history of purchases or to determine whether credit limits have been exceeded.

NUMBER 5

a. Based upon the information given, the computer may be used by Hastings to do the following:

- Test extensions and footings of computerized sales records that serve as a basis for the preparation of the invoices and sales journal.
- Verify the mathematical accuracy of postings from the sales journal to appropriate ledger accounts.
- Determine that all sales invoices and other related documents have been accounted for (for example, by accounting for the integrity of the numerical sequence).
- Select sales transactions for review (based upon predetermined criteria) through a review of the sales journal or the accounts receivable subsidiary ledger.
- Print a workpaper that lists each item selected, with relevant data inserted in applicable columns.
- Select all debits posted to the sales account and all postings to the sales account from a source other than the sales journal.
- Analytically review recorded sales by use of predetermined criteria (percentage relationships, gross margin, trends, and so forth, on a periodic or annual basis).
- Compare duplicate data maintained in separate files for correctness. For example, the computer may be used to compare the client's records of quantities sold with the client's record of quantities shipped.
- Examine records for quality (completeness, consistency, and so forth). [The quality of visible records is readily apparent to the auditor. Sloppy recordkeeping, lack of completeness, and so on, are observed by the auditor in the normal course of the audit. If machine-readable records are evaluated manually, a complete printout is needed to examine their quality. Hastings may choose to use the computer to examine these records for quality.]

b. In addition to the procedures outlined above, Hastings should do the following:

- Trace postings from the sales journal to invoice copies.
- Trace data from sales invoices to the sales journal.
- Compare dates of recorded sales transactions with dates on shipping records.
- Determine that all shipping documents have been accounted for (for example, by accounting for the integrity of the numerical sequence).
- Examine documents for appropriate approval (for example, grant of credit, shipment of goods, and determination of price and billing).
- Determine the extent and nature of business transactions with major customers (for indications of previously undisclosed relationships—related parties—and for determination of applicability of disclosure requirements required by generally accepted accounting principles).
- Verify the sales cutoff at the beginning and end of the period to determine whether the recorded sales represent revenues of the period.
- Test pricing by comparing invoices to daily price list.